Praise for Best

"Best Places *are the best regiona.* ───── ─────── ─────── ──── *in America.*
—THE SEATTLE TIMES

"Best Places *covers must-see portions of the West Coast with style and authority. In-the-know locals offer thorough info on restaurants, lodgings, and the sights.*"
—NATIONAL GEOGRAPHIC TRAVELER

". . . *travelers swear by the recommendations in the* Best Places *guidebooks . . .*"
—SUNSET MAGAZINE

"*For travel collections covering the Northwest, the* Best Places *series takes precedence over all similar guides.*"
—BOOKLIST

"Best Places Northwest *is the bible of discriminating travelers to BC, Washington, and Oregon. It promises, and delivers, the best of everything in the region.*"
—THE VANCOUVER SUN

"*Not only the best travel guide in the region, but maybe one of the most definitive guides in the country, which many look forward to with the anticipation usually sparked by a best-selling novel. A browser's delight,* Best Places Northwest *should be chained to dashboards throughout the Northwest.*"
—THE OREGONIAN

"*Still the region's undisputed heavyweight champ of guidebooks.*"
—SEATTLE POST-INTELLIGENCER

"*Trusting the natives is usually good advice, so visitors to Washington, Oregon, and British Columbia would do well to pick up* Best Places Northwest *for an exhaustive review of food and lodging in the region. . . . An indispensable glove-compartment companion.*"
—TRAVEL AND LEISURE

"Best Places Southern California *is just about all the inspiration you need to start planning your next road trip or summer vacation with the kids.*"
—THE FRESNO BEE

"Best Places Alaska *is the one guide to recommend to anyone visiting Alaska for the first or one-hundredth time.*"
—KETCHIKAN DAILY NEWS

"Best Places Northern California *is great fun to read even if you're not going anywhere.*"
—SAN FRANCISCO CHRONICLE

TRUST THE LOCALS

The original insider's guides, written by local experts

EVERY PLACE STAR-RATED & RECOMMENDED

★★★★ The very best in the city

★★★ Distinguished; many outstanding features

★★ Excellent; some wonderful qualities

★ A good place

HELPFUL ICONS

Watch for these quick-reference symbols throughout the book:

 FAMILY FUN

 GOOD VALUE

 ROMANTIC

 EDITORS' CHOICE

BEST PLACES®

NORTHWEST

**The Locals' Guide to the Best Restaurants,
Lodgings, Sights, Shopping, and More!**

Edited by
SALLY FARHAT

EDITION **16**

SASQUATCH BOOKS
SEATTLE

Printed in the United States of America
Published by Sasquatch Books
Distributed by Publishers Group West

Sixteenth edition
15 14 13 12 11 10 09 08 07   10 9 8 7 6 5 4 3 2

ISBN 1-57061-503-9
ISSN 1041-2484

Project editor: Kurt Stephan
Assistant editor: Rachelle Longé
Cover design: Bob Suh
Interior composition/design: Scott Taylor/FILTER/Talent
Interior maps: GreenEye Design

SPECIAL SALES

Best Places guidebooks are available at special discounts on bulk purchases for
corporate, club, or organization sales promotions, premiums, and gifts. For more
information, contact your local bookseller or Special Sales, Best Places Guidebooks,
119 South Main Street, Suite 400, Seattle, Washington 98104, 800/775-0817.

SASQUATCH BOOKS

119 South Main Street, Suite 400
Seattle, Washington 98104
(206) 467-4300
www.sasquatchbooks.com
custserv@sasquatchbooks.com

CONTENTS

British Columbia

Contributors and Acknowledgments

This book is the result of many months of hard work, a true collaboration. I'd first like to thank the contributors, whose bios follow.

Born in Oregon and raised in five foreign countries (with travel to 30 more), **ANNISSA ANDERSON** has lived in the Northwest for the past 20 years. A culinary school graduate, Annissa is now settled in Central Oregon where she writes about food, living, and travel.

A technical editor by day, **SHELLEY ARENAS** co-authored *The Lobster Kids' Guide to Exploring Seattle* and has contributed to numerous Northwest guidebooks. She also designs and manages Web sites, including *Seattle Woman* and *Seattle's Child*.

AUDREY D. BRASHICH has been an intern, editor, freelancer, and writer for *Sassy, YM, Seventeen, Shape, Ms., Health*, and many others. She is the author of *All Made Up: A Girl's Guide to Seeing Through Celebrity Hype and Celebrating Real Beauty*. Audrey lives in Vancouver, B.C., and New York City (where she was born and raised).

Native Kansan **BEAU EASTES** moved to Oregon in 2001, immediately falling in love with the local bicycle lanes, micro-brews, and land-use laws. He worked at the *East Oregonian* and now resides in Cedar City, Utah, with his boxer Addie.

Dividing her time between Portland and Cannon Beach, writer-speaker **LISA EVANS** has been in Oregon for 30 years. Lisa writes a monthly newsletter called "Lighten Up" about living with less stress and more play. To learn more, visit www. playful-spirit.com.

KRISTIN HARRISON is the former editor of *Where Seattle* and has worked for *National Geographic* and *Consumer's Union*. She is currently the managing editor of *Her Sports + Fitness* magazine.

Since relocating to Vancouver in 2003, **CAROLYN B. HELLER** has been discovering the charms of her adopted city. She's the co-editor of the 2006 *Zagat Survey Vancouver Restaurants Pocket Guide* and her travel articles have appeared in everything from *The Boston Globe* to the *Los Angeles Times*. Carolyn has also contributed to more than 30 other travel and restaurant guides.

ERIC P. LUCAS is the author of *Hidden British Columbia, Seattle Survival Guide*, and *Michelin Must See Vancouver*. He's also been published in *Alaska Airlines Magazine, GoWorldTravel.com, Los Angeles Times, National Geographic Traveler*, and *Western Journey*.

IVY MANNING is a freelance writer who has been published in *Food & Wine Magazine*, the *Willamette Week*, and *The Oregonian*. She pursues her love of food as a personal chef and cooking instructor in Portland.

DREW MYRON lives on the central Oregon coast. A former editor of two Columbia River Gorge newspapers, she has worked in marketing and media relations for both the nonprofit and corporate sectors, and covered arts, entertainment, and travel for America Online's CityGuide. Her Web site is www.drewmyron.com.

JEANNE LOUISE PYLE is a transplanted Marylander who has lived in the Northwest for 30 years. She has worked in the publishing industry for nearly that long.

She lives in Bellingham, where she writes, edits, and looks forward to "retirement" at the tender age 85.

ALETA RAPHAEL-BROCK is a freelance writer in Bend, Oregon. In her free time she explores different corners of her state, constantly re-discovering the unique characters of the Northwest.

Seattle native **RITZY RYCIAK** appreciates hiking as much as an after-hours steely martini. Exploring the Olympic Peninsula provided opportunities for both. Ritzy contributes to *Conscious Choice* magazine, *The Seattle Times*, the *Seattle Post-Intelligencer*, and *Seattle Weekly*.

LAUREN SANCKEN is an adventurous Seattle native and Harvard graduate who has written for the Let's Go USA series and lived in Nicaragua.

LEAH SOTTILE is a former staff writer for *The Pacific Northwest Inlander* and has written for the *Willamette Week* and *Boise Weekly*. She is currently a board member for the Portland homeless newspaper, *Street Roots*.

KATHY SCHULTZ re-discovered Port Townsend after a friend moved there and makes frequent excuses to visit and sample the best restaurants on the Olympic Peninsula. Schultz is a regular contributor to *Lucky*, and has written for *Sunset*, *Virtuoso Life*, *Seattle Magazine*, *Seattle Metropolitan*, and *Best Places Seattle*.

Washington native and current Yakima resident **RICK STEDMAN** has written travel articles for *Northwest Travel Magazine*, *Visit Los Cabos*, *The Oregonian*, and *The News Tribune*. He writes a monthly golf column for *RV Life* magazine.

JANET THOMAS wrote a book about West Coast hostels and was the editor of *Spa Magazine*. Her most recent book is *The Battle in Seattle: The Story Behind and Beyond the WTO Demonstrations*.

KATE VAN GELDER has been writing about Western Washington for 20 years. She is a contributor to *The News Tribune* and other Northwest publications.

Seattle native **SALLY FARHAT** is the editor of this book. A journalist, she's worked at publications ranging from the *Detroit Free Press* to *Parents* magazine. She also teaches a 300-level media writing course at the University of Washington, her alma mater. Learn more at www.sallyfarhat.com.

I would like to thank the other wonderful people who made this project possible:

First, David Brewster, who started this legacy. To Giselle Smith and her crews over the last decade—I respect your hard work.

To my friends and colleagues who helped, whether through their advice or support: Jim Kershner, Ann Kuo, Wendi Parriera, Cassie Martin, Rachel Crocker, Kelly Stanmore, Adam Anderson, Sarah Jio, Michael Bradbury, Molly Lori, Talin Bahadarian, Georges Dib, Valerie Farris, George and Marcelle Faddoul, Fr. Tom and Pres. Pat Tsagalakis, Wema Slyter, Annie Goodwin, Paul and Susie Hamidi, Stefanie Durbin, Thomas Kohnstamm, Heidi Schuessler, and Viv of the fabulous Bon Vivant blog who so graciously shared her input with us.

To Gerry Baldasty, David Domke, and David Sherman at UW, who gave me my first shot.

To Gary Luke and Kurt Stephan at Sasquatch Books for being the best people in the world to work with. Thanks also to the other members of the Sasquatch team:

assistant editor Rachelle Longé, copy editor Kris Fulsaas, proofreader Karen Parkin, indexer Michael Ferreira, and compositor/designer Scott Taylor of FILTER/Talent.

Katherine Koberg and Rachel Hart, for making Seattle shine and for believing in me.

Kathleen Krems and Linda Fears, for giving me my first chance. To Chandra Czape Turner, for creating ed2010, which started this path.

To my dad Bill, sister Nina, brother Andrew, and sister-in-law Daisy. I love you. To Paul, the love of my life.

And to my mom, Ferial, the top chef in the universe: for your undying patience, love, encouragement, expert advice, and support. I could not have done this without you.

—Sally Farhat

About Best Places® Guidebooks

People trust us. Best Places guidebooks, which have been published continuously since 1975, represent one of the most respected regional travel series in the country. Our reviewers know their territory, and seek out the very best a city or region has to offer. We provide tough, candid reports about places that have rested too long on their laurels, and delight in new places that deserve recognition. We describe the true strengths, foibles, and unique characteristics of each establishment listed.

Best Places Northwest is written by and for locals, and is therefore coveted by travelers. It's written for people who live here and who enjoy exploring the region's bounty and its out-of-the-way places of high character and individualism. It's these very characteristics that make *Best Places Northwest* ideal for tourists, too. The best places in and around the region are the ones that denizens favor: independently owned establishments of good value, touched with local history, run by lively individuals, and graced with natural beauty. With this sixteenth edition of *Best Places Northwest*, travelers will find the information they need: where to go and when, what to order, which rooms to request (and which to avoid), where the best skiing, hiking, wilderness getaways, and local attractions are, and how to find the region's hidden secrets.

NOTE: *The reviews in this edition are based on information available at press time and are subject to change. Readers are advised that places listed in previous editions may have closed or changed management or may no longer be recommended by this series. The editors welcome information conveyed by users of this book. A report form is provided at the end of the book, and feedback is also welcome via email: bestplaces@sasquatchbooks.com.*

BEST PLACES® STAR RATINGS

Any travel guide that rates establishments is inherently subjective—and Best Places is no exception. We rely on our professional experience, yes, but also on a gut feeling. And, occasionally, we even give in to soft spot for a favorite neighborhood hangout. Our star-rating system is not simply a checklist; it's judgmental, critical, sometimes fickle, and highly personal.

For each new edition, we send local food and travel experts out to review restaurants and lodgings, and then to rate them on a scale of one to four, based on uniqueness, loyalty of local clientele, performance measured against the establishment's goals, excellence of cooking, cleanliness, value, and professionalism or service. That doesn't mean a one-star establishment isn't worth dining or sleeping at. Far from it! When we say that all the places listed in our books are recommended, we mean it. That one-star pizza joint may be just the ticket for the end of a whirlwind day of shopping with the kids. But if you're planning something more special, the star ratings can help you choose an eatery or hotel that will wow

---

How to Use This Book

This book is divided into 20 regional chapters covering a wide range of establishments, destinations, and activities. All evaluations are based on numerous reports from local and traveling inspectors. Final judgments are made by Sasquatch editors. Every place featured in this book is recommended.

STAR RATINGS (*for restaurants and lodgings only*) Restaurants and lodgings are rated on a scale of one to four stars (with half stars in between), based on uniqueness, loyalty of local clientele, performance measured against the establishment's goals, excellence of cooking, cleanliness, value, and professionalism of service. Reviews are listed alphabetically by region, and every place is recommended.

★★★★   The very best in the region

★★★   Distinguished; many outstanding features

★★   Excellent; some wonderful qualities

★   A good place

(For more on how we rate places, see the Best Places Star Ratings box above.)

PRICE RANGE (*for restaurants and lodgings only*) Prices for restaurants are based primarily on dinner for two, including dessert and tip, but not alcohol. Prices for lodgings are based on peak season rates for one night's lodging for two people (i.e., double occupancy). Peak season is typically Memorial Day to Labor Day for summer destinations, or November through March for winter

your new clients or be a stunning, romantic place to celebrate an anniversary or impress a first date.

We award four-star ratings sparingly, reserving them for what we consider truly the best. And once an establishment has earned our highest rating, everyone's expectations seem to rise. Readers often write us specifically to point out the faults in four-star establishments. With changes in chefs, management, styles, and trends, it's always easier to get knocked off the pedestal than to ascend it. Three-star establishments, on the other hand, seem to generate healthy praise. They exhibit outstanding qualities, and we get lots of love letters about them. The difference between two and three stars can sometimes be a very fine line. Two-star establishments are doing a good, solid job and are gaining attention, while one-star places are often dependable spots that have been around forever.

The restaurants and lodgings described in *Best Places Northwest* have earned their stars from hard work and good service (and good food). They're proud to be included in this book: look for our Best Places sticker in their windows. And we're proud to honor them in this, the sixteenth edition of *Best Places Northwest*.

destinations; off-season rates vary but often can be significantly less. Call ahead to verify, as all prices are subject to change. *Note:* Prices in British Columbia chapters are given in Canadian dollars.

$$$$	Very expensive (more than $100 for dinner for two; more than $200 for one night's lodging for two)
$$$	Expensive (between $65 and $100 for dinner for two; between $120 and $200 for one night's lodging for two)
$$	Moderate (between $35 and $65 for dinner for two; between $80 and $120 for one night's lodging for two)
$	Inexpensive (less than $35 for dinner for two; less than $80 for one night's lodging for two)

RESERVATIONS (*for restaurants only*) For each dining establishment listed in the book, we used one of the following terms for its reservations policy: reservations required, reservations recommended, or no reservations.

ADDRESSES AND PHONE NUMBERS Every attempt has been made to provide accurate information on an establishment's location and phone number, but it's always a good idea to call ahead and confirm.

WEB SITE/E-MAIL ADDRESSES Web site or e-mail addresses have been included where available. Please note that the Web is a fluid and evolving medium, and that Web pages are often "under construction" or, as with all time-sensitive information, may no longer be valid.

CHECKS AND CREDIT CARDS Many establishments that accept checks also require a major credit card for identification. Note that some accept only local checks. Credit cards are abbreviated in this book as follows: American Express (AE), Carte Blanche (CB), Diners Club (DC), Discover (DIS), Enroute (E), Japanese credit card (JCB), MasterCard (MC), Visa (V).

ACCESS AND INFORMATION At the beginning of each chapter, you'll find general guidelines about how to get to a particular region and what types of transportation are available, as well as basic sources for any additional tourist information. Also check individual town listings for specifics about visiting those places.

MAPS AND DIRECTIONS Each chapter in the book begins with a regional map that shows the general area being covered. Throughout the book, basic directions are provided with each entry. Whenever possible, call ahead to confirm hours and location.

THREE-DAY TOURS In every chapter, we've included a quick-reference, three-day itinerary designed for travelers with a short amount of time. Perfect for weekend getaways, these tours outline the highlights of a region or town; each of the establishments or attractions that appear in boldface within the tour are discussed in greater detail elsewhere in the chapter.

THE DETAILS Most bed and breakfasts don't allow children, or have age limits. Most don't allow pets, either. Some places require two-night stays during weekends or busy seasons. Ask about these topics when you make reservations.

HELPFUL ICONS Watch for these quick-reference symbols throughout the book:

 FAMILY FUN Places that are fun, easy, and great for kids.

 GOOD VALUE While not necessarily cheap, these places offer a good deal within the context of the region.

 ROMANTIC These spots offer candlelight, atmosphere, intimacy, or other romantic qualities—kisses and proposals are encouraged!

 EDITORS' CHOICE These are places we especially love.

 Appears after listings for establishments that have wheelchair-accessible facilities.

INDEXES All restaurants, lodgings, town names, and major tourist attractions are listed alphabetically at the back of the book.

READER REPORTS At the end of the book is a report form. We receive hundreds of reports from readers suggesting new places or agreeing or disagreeing with our assessments. They greatly help in our evaluations, and we encourage you to respond.

PORTLAND AND ENVIRONS

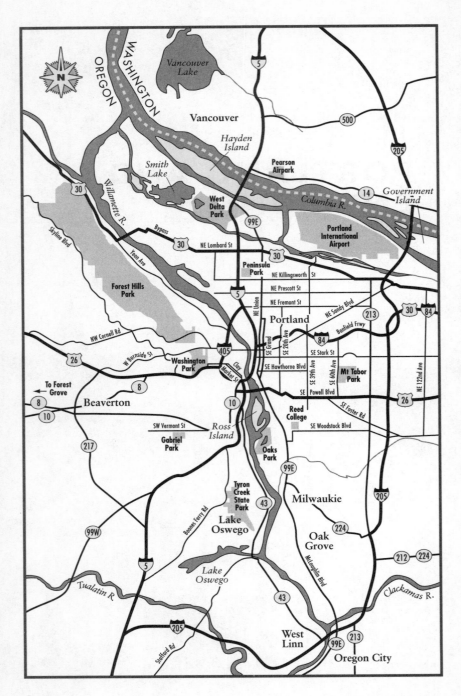

PORTLAND AND ENVIRONS

Ask any Portlander about their city, and they'll tell you it's the best of all worlds. Its location on the Willamette and Columbia rivers and proximity to both the Pacific Coast and Mount Hood (each about an hour and a half away) make it ideal for natural beauty. Portland's size provides many of the same amenities as those found in other large cities, but it still feels small enough to be safe, friendly, and easy to get around in.

Dubbed "the city that works," thanks to progressive civic planning, Portland is a model for other cities. A state-of-the-art public transportation system, a large system of well-maintained parks, excellent museums, and a year-long calendar of events like the Portland Rose Festival and the Oregon Brewers Festival bring proud residents and travelers together year-round.

Like the rest of the Northwest, the City of Roses is at its best in midsummer to early fall (mid-June–early October), when the frequent rain abates to reveal a vividly green city bustling with festivals and outdoor events. Other times of the year, frequent but gentle showers set a laid-back feel to the city—perfect cappuccino- or microbrew-sipping weather.

ACCESS AND INFORMATION

PORTLAND INTERNATIONAL AIRPORT, or PDX (7000 NE Airport Way; 503/460-4040; www.flypdx.com), is served by most major airlines. Allow plenty of time to get from the airport to downtown—at least 30 minutes. All major **CAR RENTAL** companies operate from the airport. Taxis and shuttles are readily available; expect to pay at least $26–$30 for the trip downtown. The most economical ride ($1.95) is via the airport **METROPOLITAN AREA EXPRESS**, aka **MAX**. Catch the sleek MAX light-rail train just outside the baggage claim area; the ride to the center of downtown at Pioneer Courthouse Square takes approximately 38 minutes. Another mode of transportation is the **GRAYLINE OF PORTLAND AIRPORT EXPRESS** (503/285-9845) for $12; buses leave every 45 minutes. Many hotels provide free pickup service; check the reservation board in the baggage claim area to see if yours does.

Most drivers reach Portland via either **INTERSTATE 5**, which runs north-south, or **INTERSTATE 84**, running east-west. **US HIGHWAY 26**, "the Sunset Highway," runs west to Beaverton and the coast; **INTERSTATE 205** loops east off Interstate 5 from Vancouver, Washington, to Lake Oswego and points south.

AMTRAK (503/273-4866 or 800/USA-RAIL; www.amtrak.com) operates out of the historic **UNION STATION** (800 NW 6th Ave) just 12 blocks north of downtown. This romantic red-brick structure stands in memory to the bygone era of the great railways. The nearby **GREYHOUND** station (550 NW 6th Ave; 503/238-7433 or 800/231-2222; www.greyhound.com) has a complete daily schedule.

TRI-MET (503/238-7433; www.trimet.org) operates the city bus and MAX systems; tickets for the two are interchangeable. Almost all bus lines run through the **PORTLAND TRANSIT MALL** (SW 5th and 6th aves, Portland);

PORTLAND THREE-DAY TOUR

DAY ONE: Spend your first day exploring downtown. Wake up to an eclectic breakfast at **MOTHER'S BISTRO AND BAR**, then stroll down the beautiful **SOUTH PARK BLOCKS** to either the **PORTLAND ART MUSEUM** or the **OREGON HISTORY CENTER**. Shoppers should head to the multilevel **PIONEER PLACE MALL**. For lunch, stop at the **PEARL BAKERY** (102 NW 9th Ave; 503/827-0910) for a European-style sandwich before wandering the stacks at **POWELL'S CITY OF BOOKS** and posh shopping in the **PEARL DISTRICT**. Check in to the **5TH AVENUE SUITES HOTEL** and rest up for a lovely dinner at **HIGGINS** or **CLARKLEWIS**.

DAY TWO: Head to the northwest section of town and start with a homespun breakfast at **MERIWETHER'S**, then explore some of Portland's best parks. Stop to smell the roses and see sweeping views at the **WASHINGTON PARK INTERNATIONAL ROSE TEST GARDEN**; gain serenity at the **JAPANESE GARDEN**; or visit the critters at the **OREGON ZOO**. When your stomach starts rumbling, head down the hill to trendy NW 23rd and NW 21st avenues and refuel with a bowl

---

MAX lines also pass through downtown. Ride free downtown in the "Fareless Square," which extends from points downtown to the Convention Center. To ride to the most outlying neighborhoods, you'll need a two-zone ticket ($1.65), which you can purchase from the bus driver (exact change only) or at MAX stops. Another popular option is the **PORTLAND STREETCAR** (www.portlandstreetcar.org), which travels from the South Park Blocks through the Pearl District to NW 23rd Avenue.

Portland

Though Portland is a manageable size with or without a car, it's helpful to keep in mind that the city is divided into four segments: Interstate 5 divides the city into an east side and a west side, while Burnside Street divides the city into north and south sections. Downtown addresses generally begin with the prefix "SW," while the streets of the northwest quadrant, including the **PEARL DISTRICT**, have the NW prefix and run alphabetically starting at Burnside, moving north to NW Couch Street, NW Davis Street, and so on. The southeast area is a densely populated collection of neighborhoods, including laid-back **SE HAWTHORNE BOULEVARD**. The northeast section of the city, bordered by the Columbia River on the north side, includes up-and-coming areas like the **NE ALBERTA STREET ARTS DISTRICT**. Alberta was urban blight just a decade ago, but has blossomed with shops, restaurants, and galleries.

of pasta at **BALVO**. Spend the rest of the day browsing the boutiques of **NW 23RD AVENUE** and make reservations for **PALEY'S PLACE** for a romantic dinner before returning to your room at the **5TH AVENUE SUITES HOTEL**.

DAY THREE: Begin the day by grabbing a pastry and a cup of Portland's best coffee at **STUMPTOWN COFFEE ROASTERS** (2271 NW Johnson St; 503/221-1469). If it's a weekend, head over to the outdoor crafts shopping extravaganza of the **SATURDAY MARKET**; if it's a weekday, stroll **TOM MCCALL WATER-FRONT PARK** instead. Cross the river and shop in the laid-back **HAWTHORNE DISTRICT**. For lunch, tip back a sampling of famous Portland microbrews and a burger at **BRIDGEPORT ALE HOUSE** (3632 SE Hawthorne Blvd; 503/233-6540), or catch a weekend matinee and some pizza at the beautifully refurbished **BAGDAD THEATER AND PUB** (3702 SE Hawthorne Blvd; movie line: 503/249-7474). Afterward, stretch your legs with a hike on an extinct volcano at nearby **MOUNT TABOR PARK** (SE 60th Ave at SE Salmon St, 503/823-2223), and then conclude your tour by enjoying a fine Italian dinner at the charming **THREE DOORS DOWN**.

The cultural district downtown is home to the performing arts center complex, a first-class art museum, and a historical center, all located along a several-blocks-long greenbelt called the **SOUTH PARK BLOCKS**, which begin at **PORTLAND STATE UNIVERSITY** to the south and extend to Salmon Street to the north. At the very heart of the downtown core, **PIONEER COURTHOUSE SQUARE** (SW Broadway and SW Yamhill sts) has been called Portland's living room, featuring the public art *Weather Machine*, which predicts the weather at noon, plus food carts and places to sit and enjoy the weekday lunchtime concerts and events.

MAJOR ATTRACTIONS

While visiting Pioneer Courthouse Square, stop in at the **VISITOR CENTER** (503/275-8355; www.travelportland.com). The friendly folks here supply excellent maps and will help you navigate the city, make dinner reservations, and buy event tickets.

The **OREGON MUSEUM OF SCIENCE AND INDUSTRY**, or OMSI (1945 SE Water Ave; 503/797-4000; www.omsi.edu), is just across the river from downtown. It's anything but your typical museum; pick from planetarium shows, tours of an authentic U.S. Navy submarine, and movies at the IMAX theater. The **OREGON HISTORY CENTER** (1200 SW Park Ave; 503/222-1741) pays tribute to the Native Americans, pioneers, and others who have lived on the banks of the Willamette. Reachable by the MAX train, the **OREGON ZOO** (4001 SW Canyon Rd; 503/226-1561; www.oregonzoo.org) includes exhibits of Pacific Northwest creatures and a train ride for the little ones. **CM2,**

MOBILE ART SHOWS

There are fine museums in Portland, but one of the best ways to see what the artistic community has to offer is to go walking—gallery walking, that is. On the **FIRST THURSDAY** of every month, all the **PEARL DISTRICT** galleries (between NE Broadway and NW 14th Ave, and NW Burnside and NW Northrup sts) open their doors from 6 to 9pm to host opening receptions for their new art shows. The event is not only for art buyers; this see-and-be seen evening is one of the rare times you may see Portlanders dressed up. Well, a little.

Not to be outdone by their predecessors, **NE ALBERTA STREET** galleries (between 12th and 31st sts) host a more grassroots gallery walk the **LAST THURSDAY** of every month, which includes street performers and live music.

—Ivy Manning

the Children's Museum 2nd Generation (503/223-6500; www.portlandcm2. org), is just across the parking lot.

In June, the city's roses and its **ROSE FESTIVAL** (www.rosefestival.org) are in full bloom. This month-long extravaganza includes three parades, a riverfront carnival, and—what else?—a rose show.

Portlanders flock to the banks of the **TOM MCCALL WATERFRONT PARK**, on the west side of the Willamette River, for a run or stroll or just to enjoy one of the city's many waterfront festivals. **THE PORTLAND SPIRIT** riverboat (503/226-2517; www.portlandspirit.com) docks here.

The gentrified warehouse district known as the **PEARL DISTRICT** (between NW 9th and NW 15th aves, and NW Burnside and NW Lovejoy sts) is the home of art galleries, hip restaurants, and lots of shopping.

GALLERIES AND MUSEUMS

The **PORTLAND ART MUSEUM** (1219 SW Park Ave; 503/226-2811; www. portlandartmuseum.org) is the place to go for art exhibits with national acclaim. Other artsy options include picking up the "Public Art: Walking Tour" brochure at the visitor center at Pioneer Courthouse Square, visiting the Pacific Northwest College of Arts' **FELDMAN GALLERY** in the Pearl District (1241 NW Johnson St; 503/226-4391) or the campy **3-D CENTER OF ART AND PHOTOGRAPHY** (1928 NW Lovejoy St; 503/227-6667; www.3dcenter. us), or taking part in the First Thursday or Last Thursday gallery walks (see "Mobile Art Shows").

PARKS AND GARDENS

Besides the semiwilderness of **FOREST PARK** (see Sports and Recreation), the West Hills are also home to **WASHINGTON PARK**, which includes the **HOYT ARBORETUM** (4000 SW Fairview Blvd; 503/228-8733; www.hoyt

POOCH-FRIENDLY PORTLAND

Portlanders are keenly fond of taking their dogs with them almost everywhere, so don't hesitate in bringing Fido for a visit. Dogs are welcome at the **5TH AVENUE SUITES HOTEL, HOTEL VINTAGE PLAZA**, and the **MARK SPENCER HOTEL** downtown, as well as at other lodgings in the city.

Microbrews and dogs seem to go paw in hand at the **LUCKY LAB** brew pub (915 SE Hawthorne Blvd; 503/236-3555), the **OLD LOMPOC** (1616 NW 23rd Ave; 503/225-1855), and the **BLUE MOON TAVERN** (432 NW 21st Ave; 503/223-3184), where you can sit outdoors with your dog, dig into pub food, and sip suds all at the same time.

There's an abundance of hiking trails in **FOREST PARK** to walk your dog on leash, and the **PORTLAND PARKS** Web site (www.portlandonline.com/parks) has a list of off-leash park areas. Take the off-leash area boundaries in parks seriously; there are random patrols, and tickets can be hefty.

Specialty doggie boutiques are seemingly everywhere here: Check out **FUREVER PETS** (1902 NE Broadway; 503/282-4225) for toys, treats, and gourmet dog food, or **URBAN FAUNA** (235 NW Park Ave; 503/223-4602) in the North Park blocks for a sweet outfit for your teacup poodle.

—Ivy Manning

arboretum.org). The arboretum visitor center offers maps of their native and exotic flora and pleasant hikes. Also in the park is the comprehensive collection of rose bushes and excellent views of the city at the **INTERNATIONAL ROSE TEST GARDEN** (www.rosegardenstore.org/thegardens.cfm). Don't miss the serene **JAPANESE GARDEN** (503/823-3640; www.japanesegarden.com) across the street. Five formal garden styles are laid out on 5½ acres of photogenic serenity. The garden is especially beautiful in the fall, when the maple leaves turn brilliant red. A short drive up the hill is the **VIETNAM VETERANS' LIVING MEMORIAL**, an inspiring monument with an introspective garden featuring a wall engraved with the names of fallen Oregon soldiers.

Downtown you'll find the **CLASSICAL CHINESE GARDEN—THE GARDEN OF THE AWAKENING ORCHIDS** (NW Everett St and NW 3rd Ave; 503/228-8131, www.portlandchinesegarden.org), which offers insight into the world of urban Chinese flora. Guided tours are at noon and 1pm. Stop at the Tao of Tea within the garden; the upper level has the best views.

SHOPPING

There is a plethora of unique Portland shops downtown. Nike Headquarters is here, including their flagship **NIKETOWN** (SW 6th and Salmon sts; 503/221-6453). Bargain hunters will appreciate the **NIKE FACTORY STORE** across

CITY WITH A VIEW

Portland offers stunning views, and with a bit of cloud cover, it's common to spot rainbows. The city skyline and Mount Hood are visible from the **WASHINGTON PARK INTERNATIONAL ROSE TEST GARDEN**, and a short walk on the Oak Trail at nearby **HOYT ARBORETUM** rewards hikers with a view of three mountain peaks on a clear day. Portlanders flock to the **PORTLAND CITY GRILL** (111 SW 5th Ave; 503/450-0030) to take in the panorama from 30 floors up; the bar's excellent happy-hour menu draws a lively crowd.

For all the water surrounding Portland, there are only a few places to dine on the riverfront. **THREE DEGREES** (1510 SW Harbor Way; 503/295-6166), part of the **RIVERPLACE HOTEL**, has patio seating with views of the Willamette marina accompanying standard Pacific Northwest fare. The **HARBORSIDE AT THE MARINA** (0309 SW Montgomery; 503/220-1865) features a multitiered dining room, so every table has a view of the river. For a look at the Columbia, try the seafood or champagne brunch at **SALTY'S** (3839 NE Marine Dr; 503/288-4444).

—Ivy Manning

the river (2650 NE Martin Luther King Blvd; 503/281-5901). The **PIONEER PLACE MALL** (700 SW 5th Ave) houses three square blocks of retail therapy, a better-than-average food court, and a movie theater. Crafts, live music, and food carts are found at **SATURDAY MARKET** under the Burnside Bridge on the west side of the Willamette River (10am–5pm Sat–Sun, closed Jan–Feb). While in the **PEARL DISTRICT**, don't miss **POWELL'S CITY OF BOOKS** (1005 W Burnside Ave; 503/228-4651; www.powells.com), all 77,000 square feet of it. Gourmet cooks will love **SUR LA TABLE** (1120 NW Couch St; 503/295-9679) and **IN GOOD TASTE** (231 NW 11th Ave; 503/248-2015). Stop at **CARGO** (380 NW 13th Ave; 503/209-8349), a warehouse full of artifacts imported from Asia and beyond. If you really want to unwind, treat yourself to one of the region's most distinctive Ayurvedic spas at **AEQUIS** (419 SW 11th Ave, Penthouse Ste; 503/223-7847). The trendy **NW 23RD STREET** neighborhood, reachable by streetcar, is a shopper's paradise with major upscale chains like **POTTERY BARN** (310 NW 23rd; 503/525-0280), locally made **MOONSTRUCK CHOCOLATES** (526 NW 23rd; 503/542-3400), gifts for Italophiles at **URBINO HOME** (638 NW 23rd; 503/220-0053), and oodles of charming clothing boutiques like the **ENGLISH DEPARTMENT** (724 NW 23rd St; 503/224-0724).

SE HAWTHORNE BOULEVARD has a laid-back, San Francisco–bohemian feel and hosts some of the most distinctive shopping in Portland. Jewelry and antiques are sold at the **GOLD DOOR** (1434 SE 37th Ave; 503/232-6069), while cookbook buffs will love **POWELL'S BOOKS FOR HOME AND GARDEN** (3747 SE Hawthorne Blvd; 503/235-3802). Shoe lovers will find heaven at **IMELDA'S SHOES** (3426 SE Hawthorne Blvd; 503/233-7476), and kids will love the fascinating **KIDS AT HEART** (3445 SE Hawthorne Blvd; 503/231-2954) toy store. Check out **LOCAL 35** (3556 SE Hawthorne Blvd; 503/963-8200) for men's and women's designer garb and monthly art openings.

PERFORMING ARTS

Portlanders come to the **ARLENE SCHNITZER CONCERT HALL** (1000 SW Broadway) 52 weeks a year for concerts, lectures, and comedy performances; tickets are across the street at the **PORTLAND CENTER FOR THE PERFORMING ARTS** (PCPA, 1111 SW Broadway) or from **TICKETSWEST** (503/224-8499; www.ticketswest.com). The **OREGON SYMPHONY ORCHESTRA** (503/228-1353; www.orsymphony.org) performs regularly at "the Schnitz." Classical music fans will appreciate the events put on by **CHAMBER MUSIC NORTHWEST** (503/294-6400; www.cmnw.org) at various venues.

The PCPA also has a resident theater company, **PORTLAND CENTER STAGE** (503/274-6588; www.pcs.org), which offers excellent productions. The **ARTISTS REPERTORY THEATER** (1516 SW Alder St; 503/241-1278; www.artistsrep.org) garners lavish critical praise for their intimate "theater on the edge."

The **KELLER AUDITORIUM** (222 SW Clay St) hosts the **OREGON BALLET THEATER** (503/222-5538; www.obt.org) and musicals throughout the year. Contemporary arts fans are energetically served by the performances and exhibitions of **PICA**, the Portland Institute of Contemporary Art (503/242-1419; www.pica.org), including its 10-day Time-Based Arts Festival.

SPORTS AND RECREATION

Catch the NBA's **PORTLAND TRAIL BLAZERS** (503/797-9600; www.nba.com/blazers) and the Western Hockey League's youthful **PORTLAND WINTER HAWKS** hockey team (Ticketmaster: 503/224-4400; www.winterhawks.com) at the huge, domed **ROSE GARDEN ARENA**. Baseball fans are still waiting for the major league to come, but for now they content themselves with the triple-A **PORTLAND BEAVERS** games at **PGE PARK** (1844 SW Morrison St; 503/553-5400; www.pgepark.com). The United Soccer League's **PORTLAND TIMBERS** (503/553-5500) also play here to energetic, loyal crowds.

Individual sports also thrive in Portland: runners, hikers, and mountain bikers have access to more than 50 miles of trails in the 4,800 acres of **FOREST PARK** (www.portlandonline.com/parks/), with trailheads easily accessed at points throughout the West Hills. Birders and naturalists appreciate the **AUDUBON SOCIETY OF PORTLAND** (5151 NW Cornell Rd; 503/292-9453; www.audubonportland.org), while rowers are guaranteed miles of flat water on the Willamette. The bike paths in Portland are a national model, including the loop along the **TOM MCCALL WATERFRONT TO THE EASTBANK ESPLANADE** along the Willamette River.

NIGHTLIFE

Check the calendar listings in Portland's two free weekly papers, the *Willamette Week* and the *Portland Mercury*, for club and music goings-on. National acts play the **ALADDIN THEATER** (3017 SE Milwaukie Ave; 503/233-1994), **MCMENAMIN'S CRYSTAL BALLROOM** (1332 W Burnside St; 503/225-0047), and the **ROSELAND THEATER** (8 NW 6th Ave; 503/224-2038).

The minimalist-chic club **HOLOCENE** (1001 SE Morrison St; 503/239-7639) hosts electronica DJs and theme dance parties. Indie rockers flock to the retro–ski lodge interior of **DOUG FIR** (830 E Burnside St; 503/231-9663) for live music and a happening lounge scene; discounted rooms are offered after midnight at the adjacent Jupiter Hotel if you party too hard. **MISSISSIPPI STUDIOS** (3939 N Mississippi Ave; 503/288-3895) hosts grassroots performances by folk and rock acts in an intimate theater setting, while **DANTE'S INFERNO** (1 SW 3rd Ave; 503/226-6630) downtown features small touring acts and pizza by the slice late into the night.

The locally produced *BarFly* is a free listing of Portland's bars; you can find it online (503/813-9999; www.barflymag.com) and at local watering holes. The organization hosts monthly bar-crawl bus tours.

RESTAURANTS

Andina / ★★★

1314 NW GLISAN ST, PORTLAND; 503/228-9535

Walk into this Pearl District "hot spot," and you'll swear you've landed in South America. The warm terra-cotta color scheme, *nueva* Peruvian menu, and lively Latin music in the bar create an energy that's hot, hot, hot. The long menu of small-plate appetizers like citrus-marinated seafood *cebiche* and potato-smoked trout *causa* are your best bets. Entrées like lamb shank with *salsa criolla* and quinoa-crusted scallops with passion-fruit reduction are creative, sometimes to a fault. Don't leave without indulging in the Peruvian national drink, the tart and lovely Pisco Sour. *$$–$$$; AE, DIS, MS,V; local checks only; lunch Mon–Sat, dinner every day; full bar; reservations recommended; www.andinarestaurant.com; at NW 13th.* ⅙

Balvo / ★

529 NW 23RD AVE, PORTLAND; 503/445-7400

Chef Kenny Giambalvo has been cooking luxurious dishes for five years at Bluehour. His new enterprise, Balvo, is a more casual, modern trattoria—a tribute to the simple Italian-American food he grew up on. Authentic plates like fresh mushroom salad with shaved Parmesan, daily risottos, and rigatoni with his grandmother's meat-sauce recipe are refined without being fussy. This new spot is the place to be, so avoid the crush of folks and slow service during peak times and take advantage of their long hours for more peaceful dining. *$–$$; AE, MC, V; no checks; breakfast, lunch, dinner every day; full bar; reservations recommended; www.balvo.com; at NW Hoyt St.* ⅙

Bluehour / ★★★☆

250 NW 13TH AVE, PORTLAND; 503/226-3394

This modern restaurant has maintained iconic status among foodies for years, while the bar is still the high court for Portland's beautiful and moneyed crowd. The pricey, upscale Mediterranean menu changes frequently, blending decadent dishes like Sonoma foie gras with quince paste or caviar sampling plates with more familiar dishes such as hearty double-cut veal chops with whipped potatoes or feather-light gnocchi. The desserts, including the 10-layer chocolate cake, are sublime, but the decadent international cheese cart steals the show. *$$$–$$$$; AE, DIS, MC, V; checks OK; lunch, dinner every day; full bar; reservations recommended; www.bluehouronline.com; at NW Everett St.* ♿

Caffé Mingo / ★★

807 NW 21ST AVE, PORTLAND; 503/226-4646

This small trattoria doesn't take reservations, but that doesn't keep the crowds away from this charming Italian eatery. Once you're seated, there's a decidedly convivial feel here. You're likely to share a large, rustic table with locals digging into huge plates of bread-and-tomato *panzanella* salad, homemade pastas tossed with rich Chianti-braised beef ragù, or halibut with roasted local mushrooms. The tiramisu here is the dreamiest version in town. *$$; AE, DIS, MC, V; no checks; dinner every day; full bar; no reservations; between NW Johnson and Kearny sts.* ♿

Caprial's Bistro / ★

7015 SE MILWAUKIE AVE, PORTLAND; 503/236-6457

Fans of Caprial Pence's PBS cooking show and cookbooks swear by the fusion cooking here; others claim the food and service have faded in recent years. Four or five dishes are offered nightly and include interpretations of international cuisine, like Northwest clams in kaffir lime and coconut broth or pork loin perched atop blue posole stew. The low-backed booths can be uncomfortable; opt instead for a table or kitchen-counter seating. *$$$; AE, MC, V; checks OK; lunch, dinner Tues–Sat; full bar; reservations recommended; www.caprial.com; in Westmoreland.* ♿

Carafe / ★★★

200 SW MARKET ST, PORTLAND; 503/248-0004

This Parisian-style bistro is a favorite with theater goers and politicos alike (there's little chance of getting a table on nights there's a show across the street at the Keller Auditorium). The small dining room with tin ceiling and red leather booths is absolutely charming, despite its location in the ground floor of an office building. Paris native chef Pascal Sauton makes authentic French food accessible, with delicious versions of classics like foie gras terrine, cassoulet, and excellent steak *frites*. The wine list is extensive, and—as the restaurant's name implies—some options are available by the carafe and half carafe. *$$; AE, DIS, MC, V; no checks; lunch Mon–Fri, dinner Mon–Sat; full bar; reservations recommended; at SW 2nd Ave.* ♿

CHEAP EATS

If you've come to Portland with little pocket change, never fear! There's a wide range of inexpensive dining options if you know where to find them. Downtown, go for smoky sausages with all the fixings at **GOOD DOG/BAD DOG** (708 SW Alder St; 503/222-3410); a wide range of **ETHNIC FOOD CARTS** (SW 5th Ave and Oak St) feed nine-to-fivers at lunchtime; or hit Chinatown for authentic, no-frills Chinese at **GOLDEN HORSE** (238 NW 4th Ave; 503/228-1688). Just over the Burnside Bridge on the east side, locals pack into **NICHOLAS' RESTAURANT** (318 SE Grand Ave; 503/235-5123) and feast on falafel, while great Vietnamese food can be found on **SANDY BOULEVARD** at mainstays like **MI WA** (6852 NE Sandy Blvd; 503/493-7460).

The artsy **ALBERTA STREET** neighborhood in Northeast Portland features a funky vibe with inexpensive dining options, from authentic Cajun at **LAGNIAPPE** (1934 NE Alberta St; 503/493-4094) to spicy organic Thai at **THAI NOON** (2635 NE Alberta St; 503/282-2021). The N Mississippi Avenue neighborhood, just minutes from downtown, has great low-dough options like **LORENZO'S TAVOLA CALDA** (3807 N Mississippi Ave; 503/284-6200), where you can get a grown-up meal of Italian pasta and gelato for very few lira.

—Ivy Manning

Carlyle / ★★★

1632 NW THURMAN ST, PORTLAND; 503/595-1782

You'll feel like an insider when you finally find this luxe place, tucked beneath the Fremont Bridge in the unlikely industrial Northwest Portland neighborhood. The dark furniture, muted overhead lighting, and polished waitstaff contribute to the exclusive feel. Chef Daniel Mondok (formerly of Napa's French Laundry) beguiles patrons with creativity anchored by formidable cooking skills—double-cut pork chops countered by lemongrass apple compote, or seared salmon on feather-light crab gnocchi. The bar menu has half-price offerings Tuesday and Wednesday. $$$–$$$$; AE, DIS, V; checks OK; lunch Mon–Fri, dinner Mon–Sat; full bar; reservations recommended; www. carlylerestaurant.com; at 16th Ave. ﾑ

Castagna / ★★
Castagna Café / ★

1752 SE HAWTHORNE BLVD, PORTLAND; 503/231-7373
1758 SE HAWTHORNE BLVD, PORTLAND; 503/231-9959

The ultra-minimalist white dining room showcases a menu of ever-changing seasonal dishes, with nods to Mediterranean cooking like fresh pasta with Dungeness crab and Meyer lemon or semolina gnocchi with artichokes and chanterelles. The livelier Castagna Café next door is less austere in ambience and features comforting dishes like penne with four cheeses or seasonal pizzas. *$$–$$$; $$; AE, DIS, MC, V; checks OK; dinner Wed–Sat (Castagna), dinner every day (Castagna Café); full bar; reservations recommended; www.castagnarestaurant.com; at SE 17th Ave.* ♿

clarklewis / ★★★½

1001 SE WATER AVE, PORTLAND; 503/235-2294

Foodies crowd into this dark (christened "dark lewis" by locals), industrial space for exceptional Italian-inspired small plates, handmade pastas, and spit-roasted meats. Most menu items are available in "small," "large," and "family" portions, so roll up your sleeves, bring some friends, and eat family style, but beware: Small-plate dining can get spendy. *$$–$$$; AE, MC, V; dinner Mon–Sat; full bar; reservations recommended; www.ripepdx.com; at SE Yamhill St.* ♿

El Gaucho / ★★

319 SW BROADWAY, PORTLAND; 503/227-8794

The luxurious, dim dining room here is the very picture of an elegant steak house, with huge velveteen chairs, tableside preparations of caesar salad, and expense-account prices. No surprises here; just American classics like oysters Rockefeller, meaty crab cakes, and dry-aged grain-fed steaks. The signature Gaucho Steak, an 8-ounce sirloin with a lobster tail and béarnaise sauce, is the ultimate in artery-clogging luxury. A great bar menu, live jazz, and a cigar room draw the suit-and-tie crowd to the bar. *$$$; AE, DC, MC, V; checks OK; dinner every day; full bar; reservations recommended; www.elgaucho.com; in Benson Hotel at SW Washington St.* ♿

Fife / ★★

4440 NE FREMONT ST, PORTLAND; 971/222-3433

The open dining room awash in woodsy neutral colors and warm lighting lends a convivial feel to this neighborhood eatery, though its popularity means the decibel level is frequently high. The cooking is straightforward, modern American fare. The menu changes daily, with exceptional dishes like heirloom-carrot bisque, crisp-skinned free-range chicken cooked in a cast-iron skillet, and grilled hanger steak. Vegetable lovers may want to order side dishes—the entrées are often devoid of extras. Don't miss the desserts; the Chocolate Four Ways dessert plate is among one of the many sweet ways to indulge. *$$–$$$; DIS, MC, V; no checks; dinner Tues–Sat; full bar; reservations recommended; www.fiferestaurant.com; at NE 44th Ave.* ♿

Giorgio's / ★★

1131 NW HOYT ST, PORTLAND; 503/221-1888

The warm amber glow of art deco fixtures and huge mirrors provide this small, elegant trattoria with an inviting stage for eclectic food that's rooted in the traditions of Northern Italy. New chef Peter Schuh (formerly of Thomas

Keller's Per Se in New York City) has upped the ante at what was already an excellent restaurant with sublime dishes like warm figs with goat-cheese fonduta and wisps of prosciutto, succulent lamb dishes, and delicate handmade pastas. *$$$–$$$$; AE, MC, V; no checks; lunch Tues–Sat, dinner Tues–Sun; full bar; reservations recommended; at 12th Ave.* &

The Heathman Restaurant and Bar / ★★★

1001 SW BROADWAY, PORTLAND; 503/241-4100
The formal dining room, decorated with cream-colored marble and opulent fabrics, has been the center of Portland power lunches and presymphony suppers for decades. The menu is an expression of Pacific Northwest bounty— roasted halibut with wild mushrooms—and French cuisine like foie gras with rhubarb compote or coq au vin. The voluminous wine list should keep even the snobbiest wine lover busy for hours. Call ahead for availability of their seasonal high teas, including a kid-friendly "Tea for Little Sippers," in the gorgeous Tea Court. *$$$–$$$$; AE, DC, DIS, MC, V; checks OK; breakfast, lunch, dinner every day; full bar; reservations recommended; www.heathman hotel.com; at SW Salmon St.* &

Higgins / ★★★★

1239 SW BROADWAY, PORTLAND; 503/222-1244
Pioneering chef Greg Higgins has been an outspoken advocate for organic and sustainable food production since the opening of his upscale restaurant in 1994. He continues to garner a loyal following for cooking that is the very picture of Pacific Northwest cuisine. The menu, which changes weekly, may include a generous house-made charcuterie plate, local mussels in garlic broth, local albacore tuna with Meyer-lemon marmalade, and thoughtful vegetarian dishes. The casual bar features excellent burgers and a legendary beer menu. *$$$; AE, DC, DIS, MC, V; local checks only; lunch Mon–Fri, dinner every day; full bar; reservations recommended; www.higgins.citysearch. com; at SE Jefferson St.* &

Meriwether's / ★★

2601 NW VAUGHN ST, PORTLAND; 503/228-1250
History buffs will dig the lodgelike restaurant decorated with mural-sized photographs of the exposition of 1905 that took place on the Meriwether's site, two fieldstone fireplaces, and the homespun feel of the menu. Brunches include Swedish pancakes, homemade sausage and jam, and smoked-salmon Benedict. Pacific Northwest cooking is blended with international touches in dinner entrées like braised lamb with Medjool date butter or fried razor clams with nori-scented quinoa. The verdant back patio is prime seating in warmer months. *$$–$$$; AE, DC, DIS, MC, V; no checks; breakfast, lunch, dinner every day, brunch Sat–Sun; full bar; reservations recommended; www. meriwethersnw.com; at NW 26th Ave.* &

Mother's Bistro and Bar / ★★

212 SW STARK ST, PORTLAND; 503/464-1122

Chef-owner Lisa Schroeder hit upon a great idea some years back: Make a restaurant that features food just like *everyone's* mom used to make—hence, the food here is homey and familiar yet ethnically diverse. Families crowd into the dining room decorated with distressed white furniture and chandeliers for excellent brunch items like *migas* (a Mexican egg dish) and wild-salmon hash, lunches like matzo-ball soup and chopped liver, and satisfying dinners of chicken and dumplings or meatloaf and mashers. *$$; AE, MC, V; no checks; breakfast, lunch Tues–Sun, dinner Tues–Sat; full bar; reservations recommended; www.mothersbistro.com; at 2nd Ave.* &

Restaurant Murata / ★

200 SW MARKET ST, PORTLAND; 503/227-0080

This unassuming Japanese restaurant in an office building across from the Keller Auditorium may look like a run-of-the-mill sushi spot, but once you're greeted by the kimono-wearing staff and get a glimpse of the vast menu, you'll hardly be tempted by basic California rolls. Sushi chef Makunonchi Murata has been making traditional fare like meltingly fresh sushi, crisp tempura, and the rarely seen multicourse *kaiseki* meals for longer than most of us have been able to pick up a chopstick. The tables are tightly spaced; call ahead and ask for a private tatami room for some breathing space. *$$$; AE, DC, JCB, MC, V; no checks; lunch Mon–Fri, dinner Mon–Sat; beer and wine; reservations recommended; at SW 2nd Ave.* &

Noble Rot / ★★

2724 SE ANKENY ST, PORTLAND; 503/233-1999

The odd name refers to *Botrytis cinerea*, the fungus that facilitates the honeyed sweetness of dessert wines, tipping you off to how serious they are here about wine. The casual bar and brick-lined dining room are the perfect setting for quaffing one of their wine flights—from boutique Spanish Tempranillos to local pinot gris or a bottle from the extensive wine list. Plates of imported cheeses and well-prepared entrées like seared duck breast with cherry are here to complement the all-important vino. *$$; AE, MC, V; no checks; dinner Mon–Sat; beer and wine; reservations recommended; www.noblerotpdx.com; between SE 27th and SE 28th aves.* &

¡Oba! / ★★

555 NW 12TH AVE, PORTLAND; 503/228-6161

This pan-Latin restaurant in the Pearl District is always buzzing. Come during happy hour, and you'll find the colorful bar full of pretty people sipping exotic cocktails and nibbling on spicy appetizers. Come for dinner, and you'll find intimate booths, a welcoming fireplace, and upscale, creative cuisine with just the right spice. The chef has a gift for pairing mesquite-grilled seafood with spicy fruit salsas and rotisserie-roasted meats with piquant sides like poblano mashed potatoes. *$$–$$$; AE, DC, MC, V; no checks; dinner every day; full bar; reservations recommended; www.obarestaurant.com; at NW Hoyt St.* &

Olea / ★★★

1338 NW HOYT ST, PORTLAND; 503/275-0800
The modern interior with soaring ceilings and chic neutral color palette sets the scene for the daring, Mediterranean-informed cuisine. The menu is large, and indulgence is the word of the day here, so plan on multiple courses. Start with a seafood course like the inventive paella-stuffed mussels; continue with a pasta dish liked veal breast and fontina ravioli, or try the duck prepared three ways; and finish with a sinful dessert like the trio of ice-cream profiteroles. *$$$; AE, CB, DC, MC, V; no checks; dinner every day; full bar; reservations recommended; www.olearestaurant.com; at 14th Ave.* &

Paley's Place / ★★★★

1204 NW 21ST AVE, PORTLAND; 503/243-2403
Chef Vitaly Paley was named best chef of the Pacific Northwest by the James Beard Foundation in 2005, for good reason: He and his wife, Kimberly, run their intimate 50-seat restaurant with passion and refined talent. The French-influenced cuisine presents delicacies like grilled diver scallops with leek fondue and caviar butter, crispy veal sweetbreads with mushroom-chestnut relish, and grilled Kobe beef with seared foie gras. Their chocolate soufflé cake with honey-vanilla ice cream is the most sensuous dessert in town. *$$$; AE, MC, V; no checks; dinner every day; full bar; reservations recommended; www.paleysplace.citysearch.com; at NW Northrup St.* &

Park Kitchen / ★★★☆

422 NW 8TH AVE, PORTLAND; 503/223-7275
This tiny bistro and bar is so popular that in warm weather they raise the garage-door wall and seat people at sidewalk tables looking out over the North Park blocks. Don't miss the excellent lunches, which include homey, creative fare like homemade hot dogs and duck confit Reubens. The dinner menu offers small plates like salt-cod fritters and green-bean tempura, alongside creative entrées like Berkshire pork with pickled watermelon or duck with root-beer spices and cornbread pudding. Desserts are especially good during berry season. *$$–$$$; AE, MC, V; no checks; lunch Mon–Fri, dinner Mon–Sat; full bar; reservations recommended; www.parkkitchen.com; at NW Glisan St.* &

Pho Van / ★

1919 SE 82ND AVE, PORTLAND; 503/788-5244
3420 SE HAWTHORNE BLVD, PORTLAND; 503/230-1474
Pho Van is one of the best-loved cheap-eats options in Portland. Something about the steaming-hot beef noodle soup with heaps of herbs seems to warm even the rainiest of days. It's not all Vietnamese noodles and broth at these two cheap-and-chic outposts, though; the giant bowls overflowing with rice

HOME OF THE MICROBREW

If the 50,000 people who flock annually to the Oregon Brew Fest the last weekend in July are any indication, this town loves its craft beers. The kings of the brew scene are Mike and Brian **MCMENAMIN**, who serve Portland faves like Terminator Stout and Ruby Ale in their many historically refurbished pubs around Portland; check their Web site (www.mcmenamins.com) for locations. **WIDMER BROTHERS BREWING** also serves up excellent brews, including their famous Hefeweizen wheat beer at their cozy **GASTHAUS** (955 N Russell Ave; 503/281-3333). The oldest craft brewery, **BRIDGEPORT BREWING COMPANY**, wins international accolades for their IPA and local raves for their pizza at their loading dock–turned–public house (1313 NW Marshall St; 503/241-7179). The **MACTARNAHAN'S TAPROOM AT PORTLAND BREWING** (2730 NW 31st Ave; 503/228-5269) in industrial Northwest Portland features beers made on-site and homey food made with their beer. In addition, there are dozens of small breweries; for more brew-pub listings, check out www.realbeer.com.

—Ivy Manning

vermicelli noodles and grilled chicken, herb-packed salad rolls with spicy peanut sauce, and the multicourse beef lunch are excellent options too. *$; DIS, MC, V; no checks; lunch, dinner Mon–Sat; beer and wine; reservations recommended; www.phovan.com; between SE Division and SE Mill sts.* &

Roux / ★★★☆

1700 N KILLINGSWORTH ST, PORTLAND; 503/285-1200
Roux is always packed with folks willing to wait for excellent nouveau Creole-Cajun cuisine. The space may be noisy, but that's just the buzz of delighted diners tucking into satisfying starters like crawfish stew in a buttery piecrust or deep-fried soft-shell crab. Soulful entrées like smoked short ribs or rabbit stuffed with andouille-cornbread dressing are so good, they're moan-inducing. Save room for funky desserts like the chocolate doughnuts with chicory-coffee ice cream. *$$–$$$; AE, DC, DIS, MC, V; checks OK; dinner every day; full bar; reservations recommended; www.rouxrestaurant.us; 1 block west of N Interstate Ave.* &

Saucebox / ★

214 SW BROADWAY, PORTLAND; 503/241-3393
The chic modern interior, hip DJs, and inventive cocktail list (litchi martini, anyone?) draw a 20-something crowd to the boisterous bar; the new dining room offers a slightly calmer setting to explore the pan-Asian menu, but be warned: No matter where you sit, it's a see and be seen crowd. Founding chef Chris Israel has returned and is cooking up favorites like his signature Javanese roasted salmon with a sweet spicy glaze and a fun appetizer pupu platter

that lets you sample everything from shrimp dumplings to baby back ribs. *$$–$$$; AE, DC, MC, V; local checks only; dinner Tues–Sat; full bar; reservations recommended; www.saucebox.com; at SW Ankeny St.* &

Syun Izakaya / ★★

209 NE LINCOLN ST, HILLSBORO; 503/640-3131
Rice-paper-screen windows, giant sake bottles lining the walls, and an exhaustive menu of Japanese soul food make this small subterranean spot feel like a quaint Asian inn rather than a slick sushi bar. The sushi menu draws raw lovers all the way out to these suburbs for unusual offerings like baby yellowtail and pen shell, while the homey cooked items like the *nasu miso*—buttery eggplant pieces stir-fried in miso—and lighter-than-air shrimp and vegetable tempura keeps droves of expatriate Japanese clients returning. *$$; AE, DC, DIS, MC, V; local checks only; lunch Mon–Fri, dinner every day; full bar; reservations recommended; downtown Hillsboro, off Hwy 26.* &

Tabla / ★★★

200 NE 28TH AVE, PORTLAND; 503/238-3777
The appeal of this Mediterranean bistro is immediate. The chic retro-modern decor lends a big-city feel; the wine list, full of undiscovered gems, includes a wine sampling for $15; and the sophisticated menu won't put a serious dent in your wallet. A three-course meal with offerings like chilled melon soup, hand-cut angel hair pasta with truffle butter, and crisp duck confit with an orange slice cooked in port for $24 is the best deal in town. Desserts aren't show stopping, so if you're in the mood for something sweet, try Staccato Gelato just a few doors down. *$$; AE, MC, V; no checks; dinner Tues–Sat; full bar; reservations recommended; www.tabla–restaurant.com; at NE Davis St.* &

Taqueria Nueve / ★★

28 NE 28TH AVE, PORTLAND; 503/236-6195
This small hot spot, decorated with rustic blond-wood tables, modish magenta walls, and a cool tiled bar, is every inch a modern Mexican taqueria. The menu takes traditional regional Mexican cuisine and gives it a twist with organic, upscale ingredients. There's everything from tacos featuring grilled fish or wild boar to complex moles adorning unusual meats like buffalo or goose. Don't ask for chips and salsa here; the chef disdains the lowbrow appetizer in favor of more authentic ceviche with crisp tortillas on the side. *$$; AE, MC, V; no checks; dinner every day; full bar; reservations recommended; at Burnside St.* &

Three Doors Down / ★★

1429 SE 37TH AVE, PORTLAND; 503/236-6886
Just off bustling, hippie-spirited Hawthorne Boulevard you'll find this Italian eatery always packed with regulars; be prepared to wait for a table. The recent expansion has added a large bar and much-needed waiting area. The food is classic Italian trattoria fare; most notable is their penne in a creamy

tomato-vodka sauce with spicy sausage, as well as the ethereal scallop preparations. The terra-cotta-pink dining room with thick wooden shades and flickering votives is almost as romantic as the rich tiramisu dessert. *$$$; AE, DC, DIS, MC, V; no checks; dinner Tues–Sat; full bar; reservations recommended; at Hawthorne Blvd.* &

Typhoon! / ★★

2310 NW EVERETT ST, PORTLAND; 503/243-7557
400 SW BROADWAY (HOTEL LUCIA), PORTLAND; 503/224-8385
Typhoon! is a mini-empire, with six locations in Oregon and one in Seattle; they set themselves apart by chic interior design, quality ingredients, and authentic dishes rarely found in the cheap phad thai joints. The *miang kum* (spinach leaves folded with a half-dozen ingredients), *larb* (sweet and salty minced chicken salad), and curries are mainstays, with seasonal specials added. The service is perfunctory, especially as the chain grows. *$$; AE, DC, MC, V; no checks; lunch Mon–Sat, dinner every day (NW Everett St), breakfast, lunch, dinner every day (Broadway); full bar; reservations recommended; www. typhoonrestaurants.com; at NW 23rd Ave (NW Everett St), between SW Stark and Washington sts (Broadway).* &

Wildwood / ★★★

1221 NW 21ST AVE, PORTLAND; 503/248-9663
Native son Cory Schrieber is one of the pioneers of the Pacific Northwest's culinary movement, and his elegant yet woodsy dining room has been the anchor of Portland's dining scene for more than a decade. The kitchen's tandoori oven roasts local lamb loin, pork, and beef to smoky perfection, while the brick oven turns out stellar skillets of mussels in saffron broth as well as creative pizzas. The menu changes weekly, always using local organic ingredients to great effect. The chalkboard bar menu is a great option for those on a budget; there's a family-style supper on Sundays. *$$$; AE, MC, V; checks OK; lunch Mon–Sat, dinner every day; full bar; reservations recommended; www. wildwoodrestaurant.com; at Overton St.* &

Wong's King Seafood / ★

8733 SE DIVISION ST, PORTLAND; 503/788-8883
Wong's King Seafood is a grand, chaotic palace of Chinese eating. Chinese-American families and dim sum lovers come in droves to this squeaky-clean, expansive dining room to feast off lazy Susans laden with dishes like Sichuan shrimp and Peking duck from the 150-item menu or dumplings and chicken feet plucked off the retinue of rattling dim sum carts that make the rounds at lunchtime. The service is crisp at best, short at worst. *$–$$; AE, DIS, MC, V; no checks; lunch, dinner every day; beer and wine; no reservations; www. wongsking.com; between 87th and 88th aves.* &

IN WITH THE "IN" CROWD

With a high per-capita hipster ratio, Portland's young, creative types are at the heart of the city's entrepreneurial spirit. Witness this artistic energy in the up-and-coming **MISSISSIPPI AVENUE**–area at indie shops like **PIN ME** (3705 N Mississippi St; 503/281-1572), which has locally made clothes, then stop in at the **MISSISSIPPI PIZZA PUB** (3552 N Mississippi St; 503/288-3231) to get a slice and hear live local bands.

The "LoBu," or Lower Burnside, neighborhood is indie-rock central with the **DOUG FIR LOUNGE** (see Nightlife); organic, vegetarian-friendly dining at the **FARM CAFÉ** (10 SE 7th Ave; 503/736-3276); and chic clothing shops.

Late at night when you're downtown, you'll find those in the know stuffing down creative doughnuts like the Coco Puff–topped Triple Chocolate Penetration at **VOODOO DONUTS** (22 SW 3rd Ave; 503/241-4704) or around the corner noshing hefty sandwiches on artisan bread at **VALENTINE'S** (232 SW Ankeny St; 503/248-1600).

—Ivy Manning

Ya Hala / ★★☆

8005 SE STARK ST, PORTLAND; 503/256-4484

This is our favorite Lebanese restaurant in the city. Its large dining room is always busy, and you'll find fresh meats on the rotisserie. Owners Mirna and John Attar are friendly, and Mirna's food is truly authentic. Hot, puffy pita bread that's popped out of the stone oven is perfect for dipping into her creamy hummus. Try her vegetarian kibbee or the other familiar dishes: baba gannoujh, tabbouleh, and falafel. A Middle Eastern grocery store is attached. *$; AE, DIS, M, V; checks OK; breakfast, lunch, dinner Mon–Sat; no reservations; www.yahalarestaurant.com; Stark St exit off I-84—parking 2 blocks west of 82nd St.*

LODGINGS

Avalon Hotel and Spa / ★★

0455 SW HAMILTON CT, PORTLAND; 503/802-5800 OR 888/556-4402

Overlooking the Willamette River in the South Waterfront District off Macadam Avenue, this serene boutique hotel is a short hop from the bustle of downtown, with complimentary town-car service available for transportation into the city. Seventy-eight of the 99 rooms, including all 18 fireplace suites, have peaceful river-view balconies. All rooms feature a calming neutral color scheme with Asian art, marble bathrooms, and CD players. The popular Avalon Spa and Fitness Club features treatments, personal trainer–guided river walks, and soaking pools. *$$$; AE, DC, DIS, MC, V; checks OK; www.avalonhotelandspa.com; exit 299A off I-5.* ♿

The Benson Hotel / ★★★

309 SW BROADWAY, PORTLAND; 503/228-2000 OR 888/523-6766
The grande dame of luxury hotels in Portland, the Benson has been operating since 1913. The palatial lobby features a stamped-tin ceiling, sparkling chandeliers, stately columns, and a huge fireplace. The service is impeccable, if sometimes a bit impersonally formal. The rooms are done up in conservative colonial style and heavenly memory foam beds. The suites, with beds longer than usual, are a favorite among NBA players. *$$$–$$$$; AE, CB, DC, DIS, JCB, MC, V; checks OK, www.bensonhotel.com; exit 299A off I-5.* &

Embassy Suites Portland–Downtown / ★★⯪

319 SW PINE ST, PORTLAND; 503/279-9000
The Embassy Suites chain bought the languishing, once-grand, historic Multnomah Hotel in 1997 and brought it back to its former glory. The massive lobby boasts a soaring two-story ceiling with gilded columns, luxurious furniture, and a fountain. All rooms are suites, done up in a somewhat stuffy contemporary style, with living rooms, refrigerators, and microwaves. The indoor pool, free hot breakfasts, and game room with pool table and video games makes this a good bet when traveling with kids. The Portland Steak and Chophouse offers a fresh seafood menu that changes daily and average American fare at steeper-than-average prices. *$$$; AE, DC, DIS, MC, V; no checks; www.embassysuites.com; between 2nd and 3rd aves.* &

5th Avenue Suites Hotel / ★★★

506 SW WASHINGTON ST, PORTLAND; 503/222-0001 OR 888/207-2201
This elegant 10-story hotel is part of the Pacific Northwest–owned Kimpton Boutique Hotels chain. The 5th Avenue features a cozy lobby with a large corner fireplace, complimentary Starbucks coffee, and evening wine tastings. Nearly two-thirds of the 221 rooms are spacious suites with contemporary lemon-yellow striped walls, sofas, cushy animal-print bathrobes, hip magazines, and Aveda bath products. The corner rooms are smaller; if you're looking for space, request another room in advance. The fitness room is open all hours. The staff is attentive and gracious, especially to your four-legged companions, who get their name entered on a lobby chalkboard. *$$$; AE, DC, DIS, JCB, MC, V; checks OK; www.5thavenuesuites.com; at 5th Ave.* &

The Governor Hotel / ★★

611 SW 10TH AVE, PORTLAND; 503/224-3400 OR 800/554-3456
Opened in 1909, in the heady days following the centennial 1905 Lewis and Clark Exposition, this hotel lives and breathes Pacific Northwest history. Arts and Crafts–style furnishings, murals depicting local Native American tribes, and a wood-burning fireplace give the lobby a clubby feel. The adjoining Jake's Grill, with its cigar-friendly bar and great happy-hour menu, is a popular watering hole for locals. Rooms are decorated in rather bland earth tones; suites feature jetted tubs, and some have sky-lit rooms. Take a peek at

the meeting rooms and ballrooms—modeled after palatial Italian villas. Maid and room service are available 24 hours a day. *$$$; AE, DC, DIS, JCB, MC, V; checks OK; www.govhotel.com; at SW Alder St.* &

The Heathman Hotel / ★★★

1001 SW BROADWAY, PORTLAND; 503/241-4100; 800/551-0011

Exceptional service has helped this intimate boutique hotel rise to the top of Portand's downtown lodgings. A personal concierge is assigned to you upon check-in; there's a mattress and pillow menu to choose from; and original art is displayed on the mezzanine level and in rooms like the Andy Warhol suite. The lobby is art deco in style, with an opulent tearoom for lounging and nightly jazz performances. Bathrooms tend to be characteristically small for a building of this era. The Heathman Restaurant and Bar features top-notch cuisine and an excellent cocktail menu. *$$$–$$$$; AE, DC, DIS, JCB, MC, V; checks OK; www.heathmanhotel.com; at SW Salmon St.* &

Heron Haus Bed and Breakfast / ★★☆

2545 NW WESTOVER RD, PORTLAND; 503/274-1846

This spacious 1904 English Tudor set at the foot of the West Hills in the quiet Nob Hill neighborhood is in walking distance from the fashionable shops of NW "Trendy"-Third Street. The six guest rooms have king- or queen-sized beds, somewhat dated but tasteful decor without all the frilliness one finds in other B and Bs, private baths, gas fireplaces, air-conditioning, cable TV, and data ports. The deluxe Kulia Room boasts a cloverleaf spa tub and a city view. Creative breakfasts are served fireside. *$$$; MC, V; checks OK; www. heronhaus.com; near NW 25th Ave and Johnson St.*

Hotel deLuxe / ★★★

729 SW 15TH AVE, PORTLAND; 866/895-2094

Formerly the Hotel Mallory, this 1912 hotel saw an $8 million renovation in 2006. The air of 1940s Hollywood glamour prevails, with each floor dedicated to a film director or movie genre, with film stills on the walls. Each of the 130 rooms are decorated in bright blues and greens, with marble-floored bathrooms, flat-screen TVs, and MP3 listening docks. The rooms ending in "03" have sweeping northern views of the city. There's also a fitness center, the brat pack–style Driftwood Room lounge, and Gracie's Restaurant, which offers worldly cuisine and 24-hour room service. *$$$–$$$$; AE, CB, DC, DIS, JCB, MC, V; no checks; www.hotel deluxeportland.com; between SW Morrison and SW Yamhill sts.* &

Hotel Lucia / ★★☆

400 SW BROADWAY, PORTLAND; 503/225-1717 OR 877/225-1717

This is one of the most stylish of all of Portland's boutique hotels, rivaling anything the W chain might offer in larger cities, for much less money. The white and black minimalism of the lobby is softened by splashy modern art, unusual fresh flowers, and a seating area warmed by a fireplace. The hip staff are good guides to what's hot in the city. The pet-friendly rooms, while not exactly spacious, do offer amenities like a pillow menu, feather-top beds, and 24-hour room service from Typhoon! restaurant (see review) next door. *$$$; AE, DC, DIS, MC, V; checks OK; www.hotellucia.com; at Stark St.* &

Hotel Vintage Plaza / ★★☆

422 SW BROADWAY, PORTLAND; 503/228-1212 OR 800/263-2305
This intimate 107-room boutique hotel of the Kimpton group is both playful and elegant. The 10-story hotel resides in an 1894 restored building, with upscale antique furnishings in the lobby and wine tastings in the evenings. The rooms vary from double-bed rooms with intense jewel-toned bedding and curtains to the more modern top-floor "Starlight" rooms with conservatory windows and star-themed decor. The best suites are the three "Garden Spa" rooms with balconies equipped with two-person spa tubs. Pets are welcomed upon check-in and are treated to gourmet treats and springwater. *$$–$$$; AE, DC, DIS, JCB, MC, V; checks OK; www.vintageplaza.com; at SW Washington St.* &

The Jupiter Hotel / ★

800 E BURNSIDE ST, PORTLAND; 503/230-9200, 877/800-0004
This once-seedy motor lodge just over the Burnside Bridge from downtown has been transformed into an island of indie hipness. Rooms are done up with sleek Blu Dot furnishings, wireless Internet access, retro '70s lighting, and photographic wall murals. The hotel offers an after-midnight "get a room" rate, catering to the partying concertgoers from the Doug Fir lounge next door. Though they're full of smart design details, these are budget accommodations—linens and bathrooms aren't luxurious, and the clientele is young and noisy. Ask for a room on the "quiet side" if you're not up for all-hours partying. *$–$$; AE, DIS, MC, V; no checks; www.jupiterhotel.com; between SE 8th and 9th aves.* &

The Kennedy School / ★★

5736 NE 33RD AVE, PORTLAND;
503/249-3983 OR 888/249-3983
Located 10 minutes from downtown in a residential neighborhood, this former public schoolhouse built in 1915 offers one of the most unusual stays in Portland. Owned by the McMenamin brothers' empire, this 35-room hotel includes two restaurants, a courtyard with fireplace, a tiled soaking pool, a movie theater, and four bars. Don't miss a cocktail in the Detention Room—a cozy janitor's closet turned bar, complete with potbellied stove. Rooms include queen-sized beds, private baths, Asian antiques, and, in some cases, old chalkboards. Because the complex is popular with non–hotel guests, the hallways on weekends can be noisy. *$$; AE, DIS, MC, V; checks OK; www. mcmenamins.com; 1 one block north of NE Killingsworth St.* &

The Lion and the Rose / ★★★

1810 NW 15TH AVE, PORTLAND; 503/287-9245 OR 800/955-1647
This Queen Anne mansion built in 1906 is set in the historic Irvington District, just blocks from the bustling Lloyd Center Mall. It may be close

to the modern world outside, but once you're inside, you're surrounded by the romance of another era. This stately house features six guest rooms done in Victorian-Edwardian style with floral prints and massive antiques, augmented with convenient amenities like data ports and modern marble bathrooms. The lavish two-course breakfasts are excellent. The friendly innkeepers also serve snacks in the late afternoon in the parlor. *$$$; AE, DC, DIS, MC, V; checks OK; www.lionrose.com; north of NE Broadway.*

The Paramount Hotel / ★★☆

808 SW TAYLOR ST, PORTLAND; 503/223-9900
This 15-story luxury hotel opened in 2000, just one block from the Arlene Schnitzer Concert Hall downtown, to much acclaim. Each of the 154 rooms is decorated with restrained elegance in beige fabrics, Biedermeier furniture, and granite-topped bathroom counters. The executive rooms include either jetted tubs or private balconies with views of peaceful Park Street. All guest rooms include large desks equipped with two phone lines and data ports. The elegant marble lobby is flanked by Dragonfish, a Japanese restaurant, on one side and their lively bar on the other. Try their excellent sushi deals at happy hour. *$$$–$$$$; AE, CB, DC, DIS, JCB, MC, V; checks OK; www.portland paramount.com; at Park Ave.* &

Portland's White House / ★★★

1914 NE 22ND AVE, PORTLAND; 503/287-7131
On the outside, this 1911 Greek Revival mansion with circular driveway, carriage house, and fountain is almost as grand as its namesake in Washington, DC. Inside this six-room B and B, you'll find rooms with tasteful antiques, heavenly feather beds, wireless Internet access, and updated bathrooms. Every room boasts either a jetted tub, an original claw-foot bathtub, or a six-head steam shower. A full gourmet breakfast with local hormone-free meats and espresso is served daily. Weddings are frequently held in the beautiful garden. *$$$–$$$$; AE, DIS, MC, V; no checks; www.portlandswhitehouse. com; 2 blocks north of NE Broadway.*

RiverPlace Hotel / ★★★

1510 SW HARBOR WAY, PORTLAND; 503/228-3233 OR 800/227-1333
Located directly on the busy Willamette River downtown, this casually elegant hotel is known for its optimal river views and warm service. The best rooms among the 74 kings, doubles, and suites face the water. Decor echoes the river, with Cape Cod–style beige and powder blues and Craftsman-style furniture. Plush furnishings include feather beds and CD players in every room. The concierge service is among the best in the city; complimentary continental breakfast, as well as 24-hour room service from 3 Degrees Restaurant, can be brought to your room. *$$$–$$$$; AE, DC, DIS, JCB, MC, V; checks OK; www.riverplacehotel.com; south end of Tom McCall Waterfront Park.* &

COLUMBIA RIVER RIVER GORGE AND MOUNT HOOD

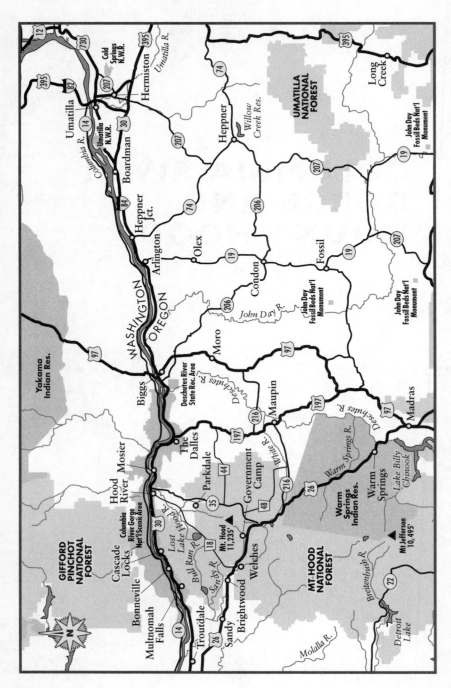

COLUMBIA RIVER GORGE AND MOUNT HOOD

Carved out by the catastrophic floodwaters of the last Ice Age, the Columbia River Gorge has the natural drama of the Grand Canyon, minus the busloads of tourists and Disneyland atmosphere. Eighty miles long and 4,200 feet deep, this river canyon winds at sea level through the Cascade Range. Hood River and The Dalles, the two largest cities in the area, have become home to outdoor enthusiasts and adventure seekers.

ACCESS AND INFORMATION

The Columbia River Gorge and Mount Hood are most commonly approached from Portland on **INTERSTATE 84**, the main highway through the gorge. I-84 connects to both **INTERSTATE 5** and **INTERSTATE 205**. For the scenic route, exit at Troutdale to the **HISTORIC COLUMBIA RIVER HIGHWAY**. Keep in mind, however, that most of the narrow and winding road isn't suitable for RVs. **HIGHWAY 26** is the main road from Portland to Mount Hood.

In the winter, tracti on devices are often necessary on Mount Hood. The **OREGON DEPARTMENT OF TRANSPORTATION** (503/588-2941 outside Oregon, or 800/977-6368; www.tripcheck.com) has reports. Winter sports on the mountain require an ODOT **WINTER SNO-PARK PERMIT** ($3 per day, $7 for 3 days, $15 per year); these are sold at resorts, state Department of Motor Vehicle offices, service stations, and retailers.

GREYHOUND (503/243-2357 or 800/221-222; www.greyhound.com) has daily service to Hood River and The Dalles. The **AMTRAK EMPIRE BUILDER** (800/872-7245; www.amtrak.com) has a daily train to Bingen, Washington, just across the Columbia River from Hood River, and to Wishram, Washington, 15 miles east of The Dalles.

Local tourist information is available from the **HOOD RIVER COUNTY CHAMBER OF COMMERCE** (405 Portway Ave; 541/386-2000 or 800/366-3530; www.hoodriver.org), **THE DALLES AREA CHAMBER OF COMMERCE** (404 W 2nd St; 541/296-2231 or 800/255-3385; www.thedalleschamber. com), and **MOUNT HOOD INFORMATION CENTER** (65000 E US Hwy 26, Welches; 503/622-3017; www.mthood.org).

Columbia River Gorge National Scenic Area

To protect the gorge's 292,500 acres of natural beauty from the perils of development, Congress established it as the Columbia River Gorge National Scenic Area in 1986. It begins near the mouth of the Sandy River near Troutdale in the west at ends at the Deschutes River near The Dalles in the east.

COLUMBIA RIVER GORGE THREE-DAY TOUR

DAY ONE: Start with breakfast at the Black Rabbit Restaurant at **MCME-NAMIN'S EDGEFIELD**, then head east on I-84. Turn off the freeway at Corbett and follow the **HISTORIC COLUMBIA RIVER HIGHWAY** east to **CROWN POINT**; stop for a hike and lunch at **MULTNOMAH FALLS LODGE**. Back on the old highway, pull off in a few miles to tour **BONNEVILLE DAM** and **CASCADE LOCKS**; pause at Cascade Locks for a ride on the **STERNWHEELER COLUMBIA GORGE** if you have time. Continue east to Hood River, then check in to and freshen up at the **HOOD RIVER BnB** before taking a leisurely drive through the "**FRUIT LOOP**," a 35-mile drive through the valley's orchards. Head back to Hood River for dinner at **BRIAN'S POURHOUSE**.

DAY TWO: Enjoy a full breakfast at your B and B, then choose between trains, scenery, and shopping or recreation on the river for your morning itinerary: Take a ride on the **MOUNT HOOD RAILROAD**, then walk around the shops on **OAK STREET** in downtown Hood River, or visit **BIG WINDS** to take a windsurfing lesson on the Columbia River. Fuel the day's activities with lunch at the **NEW YORK**

Troutdale

From the highway, Troutdale's looks can be deceiving. The glowing, neon strip-mall feel of I-84 masks the true character of a town whose main street is contrastingly quaint, with galleries, antique shops, and cafés. Tourist information is available at **WEST COLUMBIA GORGE CHAMBER OF COMMERCE** (107 E Historic Columbia River Hwy, Troutdale; 503/669-7473; www.westcolumbiagorge chamber.com).

Follow Troutdale's main street east across the narrow Sandy River bridge, bear right, and you will be on the **HISTORIC COLUMBIA RIVER HIGHWAY**, an intact 22-mile stretch of nearly century-old highway. It winds past numerous waterfalls—77 on the Oregon side of the gorge—and its ornate railings are the work of Italian stonemasons. At the spectacular viewpoint of **CROWN POINT**, the newly restored 1918 **VISTA HOUSE** (40700 E Historic Columbia River Hwy, Troutdale; 503/695-2230; www.vistahouse.com; May–Oct) overlooks a 733-foot-high cliff and boasts marble floors, ornate carvings, and historic displays. Some 2 million visitors a year visit **MULTNOMAH FALLS**, the second-highest year-round waterfall in the United States. The 620-foot waterfall can bring overwhelming crowds in summer, but just as stunning are the less-crowded winter views of the frozen falls. The U.S. Forest Service staffs an interpretive center on the ground floor of the **MULTNOMAH FALLS LODGE** (see review).

CITY SUB SHOP or **PANZANELLA ARTISAN BAKERY AND ITALIAN DELI.** In the afternoon, take in the area's history with a visit the **HOOD RIVER COUNTY HISTORICAL MUSEUM**, then head east to The Dalles to see the **COLUMBIA GORGE DISCOVERY CENTER** and the **WASCO COUNTY HISTORICAL MUSEUM.** Return to Hood River for dinner at **CORNERSTONE CUISINE** before turning in at your B and B.

DAY THREE: Get up early and drive the interstate to Mosier for a leisurely breakfast at the **WILDFLOWER CAFÉ**, then continue east on the **HISTORIC COLUMBIA RIVER HIGHWAY** to views at **ROWENA CREST** and a hike at the **TOM MCCALL PRESERVE.** Take the interstate west again to State Route 35 south, then spend the rest of the day exploring **MOUNT HOOD**'s hiking trails, ski runs, and historic sites. Depending on where your explorations take you, grab lunch at the **BREW PUB AT MOUNT HOOD BREWING COMPANY** in Government Camp or at **RENDEZVOUS GRILL & TAP ROOM** in Welches. Finally, check in at the **TIMBERLINE LODGE**, where you can swim in the outdoor pool or read in front of the fireplace before enjoying dinner in the **CASCADE DINING ROOM**, with snowy Mount Hood peeking in at every window.

RESTAURANTS

Multnomah Falls Lodge

53000 HISTORIC COLUMBIA RIVER HWY (US HWY 30 E), BRIDAL VEIL; 503/695-2376

Portland architect A. E. Doyle used every type of stone in the gorge while building this place. The stonework, combined with the setting—the lodge sits at the base of 620-foot Multnomah Falls—gives the restaurant great ambience. The main dining room has floor-to-ceiling windows, and a new annex even has glass walls and ceiling for maximum waterfall viewing. The menu is basic and seafood-inspired, with salmon and oyster omelets, fish-and-chips for lunch, and a more formal dinner selection. The spectacular view from every table, not the food, is the draw here. *$$; AE, DIS, MC, V; no checks; breakfast, lunch, dinner every day, brunch Sun; full bar; reservations recommended; www.multnomahfallslodge.com; exit 31 from I-84.* &

Tad's Chicken 'n Dumplings

1325 E HISTORIC COLUMBIA RIVER HWY (US HWY 30 E), TROUTDALE; 503/666-5337

Tad's, the lone survivor of the many roadhouses along the Columbia River Highway in the 1920s and 1930s, has a full menu of comfort food and a side of nostalgia for its loyal fans. Opened by local fisherman Tad Johnson, this former roadhouse evolved into a classier establishment without losing its roots. Decorated with knotty pine paneling and red-and-white checked curtains, the building is perched in the woods on the banks of the Sandy River. The menu is home-style comfort food—a true meat-and-potatoes kind of place. Tad's is so popular that the benches outside are usually filled with waiting customers. *$; AE, MC, V; checks OK; dinner every day; full bar; reservations recommended; www.tadschicdump.com; just southeast of Sandy River Bridge, exit 18 off I-84.*

LODGINGS

Bridal Veil Lodge / ★

**46650 E HISTORIC COLUMBIA RIVER HWY (US HWY 30 E),
BRIDAL VEIL; 503/695-2333**

Named after nearby Bridal Veil Falls, the lodge dates back to 1927 and the beginnings of the American automobile heyday. At this lodge and auto camp, travelers could pull off the Columbia River Highway for a hot meal and a place to sleep (when rooms were full, it was common to see clusters of tents perched next to Model Ts). Laurel Brown Macdonald, whose great-grandfather was responsible for the lodge, reopened her former home as a bed-and-breakfast in 1987. The two rooms are in a cottage near the main lodge, decorated with family antiques, matchboard walls, and original furnishings. Breakfast is still served around the pine-plank table built by Laurel's father. *$$; no credit cards; checks OK; www.bridalveillodge.com; about 4 miles west of Multnomah Falls.*

McMenamin's Edgefield / ★

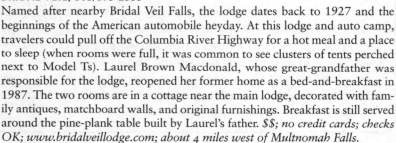

2127 SW HALSEY ST, TROUTDALE; 503/669-8610 OR 800/669-8610

Edgefield was built in 1911 as the Multnomah County Poor Farm. By 1962 it had morphed into a nursing home before it was shuttered in 1982. Brothers and microbrewery specialists Brian and Mike McMenamin bought the 38-acre complex in 1990 and transformed it into their vision of a European-style village, with a winery, a brewery, gardens, a pub, and restaurants. The main building is a 100-room hotel with 1930s furnishings, wall murals, and door art. Most rooms are basic, turn-of-the century European style with vintage furniture and porcelain sinks. Most have shared baths and no TVs, and for the very low budget, there are hostel bunk-bed lodgings. Find plenty of activity right on the premises, with an 18-hole golf course and a movie theater. Complimentary breakfast is served at the Black Rabbit Restaurant. *$–$$; AE, MC, V; checks OK; www.mcmenamins.com; Wood Village exit off I-84, south to Halsey St, turn left, drive ¼ mile to Edgefield sign on right.* &

Cascade Locks

Early travelers were in for a challenge when crossing the fierce cascades (rapids) of the Columbia River, and most boats had to be portaged. In fact, the first steam locomotive in the Pacific Northwest, the Oregon Pony, pulled cars on a portage railroad next to the river starting in 1864. Navigational locks built in 1896 let boaters breathe a sigh of relief, and the echoes of stern-wheelers on the river were heard through the mountains. Unfortunately, when Bonneville Dam was built in 1937 and the water behind it rose 60 feet, the locks were submerged and not rebuilt again until 1993.

Just upriver from the old locks, the Port of Cascade Locks' 600-passenger **STERNWHEELER COLUMBIA GORGE** (Cascade Locks Marina Park, 355 Wa-Na-Pa St; 541/374-8427 or 800/643-1354; www.sternwheeler.com) is moored. The 140-foot replica makes daily excursions on the Columbia summer through autumn, with weekend brunch and dinner cruises year-round.

BONNEVILLE DAM, just a couple miles downstream (exit 40 off I-84; 541-374-8820; www.nwp.usace.army.mil/op/b/), was a New Deal project started in 1934, along with Grand Coulee Dam on the upper Columbia. Bonneville's three years of construction employed some 3,000 workers at the height of the Depression. The dam has fish ladders and a visitor center on Bradford Island. Since the terrorist attacks of September 11, 2001, access is occasionally limited. The **BONNEVILLE FISH HATCHERY** (541/374-8393) features tree-shaded ponds that hold large trout and giant, prehistoric-looking sturgeon.

The **BRIDGE OF THE GODS**, a 1926 cantilever toll bridge linking Oregon and Washington near the Pacific Crest Trail, is named after a mysterious geologic event that left a land bridge elevated above the Columbia rapids. Ancient legend and modern science hold different versions of the story. More information can be found at the **CASCADE LOCKS VISITOR CENTER** (Cascade Locks Marina Park; 541/374-8619 or 800-643-1354; www.cascade-locks.or.us).

Hood River

In days past, Hood River was a quiet riverside town with a bucolic orchard backdrop. But the howling winds in the gorge have now given it an impressive reputation as the windsurfing capital of the world. If you don't windsurf, don't worry: Pretty much any outdoor sport can be found here. The town's increasing popularity has meant a string of new developments, rising real estate prices, and a lively buzz of restaurants, breweries, and gear shops.

Windsurfing lessons and rental gear are available at **BIG WINDS** (207 Front St; 541/386-6086 or 888-509-4210; www.bigwinds.com/lessons). Kiteboarding lessons are offered by the **NEW WIND KITE SCHOOL** (13 Oak St; 541/387-2440; www.newwindkiteboarding.com); **GORGE PADDLING** (2070 Freedom Loop; 541-386-9343; www.gorgepaddling.com) offers kayaking.

It's not just the outdoors crowd that's flocking to Hood River. **OAK STREET**, the town's main drag, is filled with specialty shops. Downtown also includes the painted ponies of the **INTERNATIONAL MUSEUM OF CAROUSEL ART** (304 Oak St; 541/387-4622) and tours of the **FULL SAIL BREWERY AND PUB** (506 Columbia St; 541/386-2247).

Agriculture still plays a vital role here. The valley's fruit industry is celebrated with two festivals: the **HOOD RIVER VALLEY BLOSSOM FESTIVAL** in April and the **HOOD RIVER VALLEY HARVEST FESTIVAL** in October. And don't miss the wineries. **COLUMBIA GORGE WINEGROWERS ASSOCIATION** (www.columbia gorgewine.com) has tours and tastings. Check out the **MOUNT HOOD WINERY** (3189 SR 35; 541/386-8333).

The **MOUNT HOOD RAILROAD** (110 Railroad Ave; 541/386-3556 or 800/872-4661; www.mthoodrr.com), which marked its centennial in 2006, hauls freight and passengers in historic railcars from Hood River south to Parkdale regularly from March through mid-December. The company offers a **FRUIT BLOSSOM SPECIAL**, which tours through spring orchards, as well as scenic brunch and dinner trains. The railroad's headquarters are in the former Union Pacific depot, built in 1911.

April through December, local artists exhibit downtown on the **FIRST FRIDAY** of each month (Hood River Downtown Business Association; 541/308-6738; www.downtownhoodriver.com). At the **HOOD RIVER SATURDAY MARKET** (5th and Columbia sts; 9am–3pm May–mid-Oct), there's often live music as well as the usual produce.

Hood River history is on display at the **HOOD RIVER COUNTY HISTORICAL MUSEUM** (300 E Port Marina Dr; 541/386-6772; open every day summer–early fall). The **HOOD RIVER COUNTY CHAMBER OF COMMERCE** (405 Portway Ave; 541/386-2000 or 800/366-3530; www.hoodriver.org) is a good resource.

RESTAURANTS

Abruzzo Italian Grill / ★★

1810 W CASCADE ST, HOOD RIVER; 541/386-7779
The smell of fresh pasta and the sound of happy chatter waft down the street from this small, olive-green building a few blocks from downtown. Abruzzo is a local favorite featuring generous dishes from the Abruzzo region of Italy. It's not unusual to wait for a table; the homemade gnocchi, rich pancetta sauces, and fresh berry panna cotta often draw a crowd. The cement floors and wood tabletops lend an informal note, and the atmosphere can be noisy. Opt for the outdoor seating in summer. *$; MC, V; local checks only; dinner Tues–Sat; full bar; no reservations; west of downtown on north side of Cascade St.* &

Brian's Pourhouse / ★★

606 OAK ST, HOOD RIVER; 541/387-4344
This one-story white-clapboard house feels like a beach vacation home. The setting, like the menu, has something for everyone. The front-room bar is often packed with a louder singles crowd, but the back dining room is family friendly, complete with crayons. More casual fare includes pizzas, fish tacos, and gourmet burgers, but Brian's true culinary specialties are innovative fish dishes, such as jerk salmon, sesame ahi tuna, and crispy oyster starters. *$$; MC, V; local checks only; lunch Sat–Sun, dinner every day; full bar; reservations recommended; www.brianspourhouse.com; between 6th and 7th sts.* &

Cornerstone Cuisine / ★★☆

102 OAK ST, HOOD RIVER; 541/386-1900

Few restaurants can boast an upscale "seafood station" without sounding like a highwayside buffet, but the Cornerstone, formerly Pasquale's Ristorante, has reinvented the idea. Chef Mark Whitehead has managed to fuse the restaurant's Italian roots with more modern Northwest fare. Breakfast rivals the lunch and dinner menus for creative spins on old favorites, like the fried egg sandwich on challah bread with roasted-pepper ketchup, vanilla french toast, and orange ricotta blintzes. For lunch and dinner, try the chicken Parmesan sandwich or the sea scallop linguine. *$$; AE, DIS, MC, V; local checks only; breakfast, lunch, dinner every day; full bar; reservations recommended; www. hoodriverhotel.com/cornerstone.html; at 1st Ave.* &

New York City Sub Shop

1020-B WASCO ST, HOOD RIVER; 541/386-5144

In an area awash with chain sub sandwich shops, NYCSS is a refreshing change, an opportunity to savor a sub sandwich as it's meant to be: good honest bread with East Coast fillings, like fried onions and sweet banana peppers. Cheese steak and hot pastrami are among the favorites. Colorful murals decorate the walls, poking fun at the idiosyncrasies in Hood River. *$; MC, V; local checks only; lunch every day; no alcohol; no reservations; exit 62 off I-84, from Westcliff Dr turn right onto Cascade Dr and left onto Wasco St.* &

Panzanella Artisan Bakery and Italian Deli / ★

102 5TH ST, HOOD RIVER; 541/386-2048

Providing Hood River with the staff of life, Panzanella sells artisan breads, sandwiches, and picnic-ready goodies. Grab a stool at the high counter and enjoy the paintings by local artists, or take out your lunch, which most folks do. Breakfasts are light, such as toast with preserves. *$; MC, V; checks OK; breakfast, lunch Mon–Sat; no alcohol; no reservations; 5th St at Cascade Ave.* &

Stonehedge Gardens / ★★

3405 CASCADE DR, HOOD RIVER; 541-386-3940

The winding road to Stonehedge Gardens is mined with potholes, but the century-old clapboard house—originally a summer cottage—sits in the midst of trees and gardens, making it a winner for romantic outdoor dining. The fire-warmed interior has walls and ceilings paneled with age-darkened Douglas fir. The bistro-styled menu could be better, but it's the charming setting that makes this place worth visiting. In winter, try the bargain $10 entrées like portobello mushroom ravioli or spicy Thai chicken in peanut sauce. *$$; AE, DC, DIS, MC, V; checks OK; dinner every day; full bar; reservations recommended; www.stonehedgegardens.com; exit 62 off I-84, look for sign on south side of Cascade Dr, follow gravel road for ⅓ mile.*

LODGING

Columbia Gorge Hotel / ★★☆

4000 WESTCLIFF DR, HOOD RIVER; 541/386-5566 OR 800/345-1921
Opened in 1921 as a destination on the then-new Columbia River Highway, the Columbia Gorge Hotel scores big for history and setting—stucco, red tile edifice with green shutters, surrounding gardens that overlook the Columbia River and Wah Gwin Gwin Falls. Once a favorite of Rudolph Valentino, the hotel offers spacious, view-filled common areas. Most bedrooms are unfortunately tiny, and the salmon-pink woodwork needs updating. Rooms facing the gorge are the quietest and have the best views. The room rate includes turndown service and the trademarked, titanic-sized "World Famous Farm Breakfast." *$$$; AE, DIS, MC, V; checks OK; www.columbiagorgehotel.com; exit 62 off I-84.* &

Hood River BnB / ★

918 OAK ST, HOOD RIVER; 541/387-2997
Hardwood floors and cozy, light-filled rooms make Hood River BnB a relaxing respite with a river view. Built in 1909, the sunny house sits just a few blocks from downtown; each of its four guest rooms has wi-fi Internet access and a gear storage area. Well-behaved dogs are allowed in the Sun room, and children are welcome in the Sky room and Sun room, both with en suite bathrooms and futon couches. The upstairs River and Mountain rooms share a bath; Sky has a spectacular tiled bathroom, Sun gets a claw-foot tub, and River has, by far, the best view of Mount Adams. *$$; MC, V; checks OK; www.hoodriverbnb.com; between 8th and 9th sts.*

Hood River Hotel / ★

102 OAK ST, HOOD RIVER; 541/386-1900 OR 800/386-1859
This sweet old downtown hotel was built in 1912 as the annex to the long-gone Mount Hood Hotel. The rooms, all with private baths, are small and not overly fancy. The nicer river view rooms feature lace canopy– and four poster–queen beds; other rooms have basic wood frames, hardwood floors, and minimal decor. There's a bit of noise from night trains and highway traffic, but it's a charming hotel in a prime downtown location. Room rates include a $10 voucher for breakfast in the hotel restaurant. *$$–$$$; AE, DIS, MC, V; local checks only; www.hoodriverhotel.com; 1st and Oak sts.* &

Hood River Inn / ★

1108 E MARINA WAY, HOOD RIVER; 541/386-2200 OR 800-828-7873
The Best Western–affiliated Hood River Inn boasts something no other Hood River lodging can offer: It's right on the Columbia River. Opt for a riverside room, and you'll have spectacular sunset views. The heated outdoor pool is a family hangout. The Riverside Grill, with a deck that overlooks the river, is great in summer. The Cebu Lounge has a thriving happy hour. *$$–$$$; AE, DC, DIS, MC, V; no checks; www.hoodriverinn.com; exit 64 off I-84.* &

Lakecliff B&B ★★

3820 WESTCLIFF DR, HOOD RIVER; 541/386-7000
A. E. Doyle, the respected Portland architect whose work includes Reed College and Multnomah Falls Lodge, designed Lakecliff as a getaway cottage for a Portland lumber magnate in 1908. Some cottage! The 3-acre, two-story estate sits cliff-side above the Columbia River, surrounded by secluding woods and pristine lawns. Nonetheless, a country-house atmosphere prevails, with five stone fireplaces and four inviting flower-themed guest rooms. For good reason, Lakecliff has become a popular place for weddings and is booked nearly every summer weekend, but it is generally available as a B and B Sunday through Thursday. *$$$; MC, V; no checks; www.lakecliffbnb.com; exit 62 off I-84, east on Westcliff Dr.*

Vagabond Lodge

**4070 WESTCLIFF DR, HOOD RIVER; 541/386-2992
OR 877/386-2992**
Parts of Vagabond Lodge hark back to the auto courts of the 1950s—and that's not a compliment. However, for the informed traveler on a budget, this place can be a money-saving gem. The rooms in the hackneyed front part of the motel are Spartan and nondescript. Avoid those rooms, and grab one in the new three-story riverside building. These rooms have an almost identical view to those at the Columbia Gorge Hotel, and most are twice the size at half the price. Some have balconies overlooking the Columbia River, some have fireplaces, and a few have kitchens. Families love the hide-away sleeper sofas, which fit six to a room. *$$; AE, DC, DIS, MC, V; no checks; www. vagabondlodge.com; exit 62 off I-84, go west on Westcliff Dr past Columbia Gorge Hotel.*

Mosier

Mosier doesn't look like much from the highway, but drive in closer and you'll see that this small charmer boasts a mix of historic buildings, new homes, and just 400 residents. It's set between two stretches of the Historic Columbia River Highway; the one to the west, about a half mile up Rock Creek Drive, is open only to hikers and bicyclists. Called the **HISTORIC COLUMBIA RIVER HIGHWAY STATE TRAIL**, its 4½-mile length goes through the historic **MOSIER TWIN TUNNELS**, affords stunning views of the river and the gorge, and ends just east of Hood River. Take the old highway to the east, and you'll eventually end up in The Dalles. About midway, the road climbs to the scenic viewpoint at **ROWENA CREST**, which overlooks the **TOM MCCALL PRESERVE** and stunning wildflower fields.

RESTAURANTS

Wildflower Café / ★

902 2ND AVE, MOSIER; 541/478-0111

Salvaged, century-old wood warms the outside of this popular café, and a screened-in porch lets in sun-soaked views of the Columbia River. The simple, wholesome menu draws locals looking to fuel up with marionberry-hazelnut pancakes or a bowl of Hungarian mushroom soup. The café is for sale, but the current owners promise the same quality and service will continue. *$$; AE, DIS, MC, V; checks OK; breakfast, lunch, dinner Wed–Sat, hours change seasonally; beer and wine; no reservations; www.cafewildflower.com; just east of "downtown."* &

LODGINGS

Mosier House Bed & Breakfast

703 3RD AVE, MOSIER; 541/478-3640

The town's founder, Jefferson Newton Mosier, built this Queen Anne Victorian house in 1904, overlooking the Columbia River, and it's now on the National Register of Historic Places; present owner Matt Koerner tenderly restored it over several years. The house features period furnishing throughout, four guest rooms with shared baths upstairs, and a master guest room with a claw-foot tub, private entrance, and porch. The full breakfast sometimes includes crepes. *$$; MC, V; checks OK; www.mosierhouse.com; turn up Washington St and go left on 3rd Ave.*

The Dalles

Approaching The Dalles from the west, it's easy to focus on the sprawling, closed aluminum smelters and follow the urge to take Interstate 84 straight past town.

Don't do it. The Dalles, one of Oregon's oldest cities, is chockablock with history. Methodist missionaries built an outpost here in the late 1830s, and when the Great Migration began, it was at The Dalles that pioneers had to decide whether to take their wagons around Mount Hood by the Barlow Trail—a steep and treacherous route—or lash wagon and belongings onto crude rafts and brave the Columbia's rapids.

French voyageurs traveling through this narrow stretch of the Columbia River called it *le dalle*, meaning "the trough," to describe the basalt rock outcroppings in the narrow stretch of river. Explorers **LEWIS AND CLARK** and their **CORPS OF DISCOVERY** camped at **ROCK FORT** (northeast of 2nd and Webber sts; for directions call 541/296-2231) in The Dalles in October 1805 and again in April 1806 on their way home from a cold winter on the Pacific Coast.

A few of the wonderful old buildings include the **FORT DALLES MUSEUM** (15th and Garrison sts; 541/296-4547) in the 1857 surgeon's quarters of the former fort and **ST. PETER'S LANDMARK** (3rd and Lincoln sts; 541/296-5686), built in 1898 as a Roman Catholic church and saved by preservationists when the parish moved to a modern building. The **WASCO COUNTY COURTHOUSE** (5th and Court sts), resplendent in golden oak and marble, dates from the early 1900s. It was the third courthouse built for a county that, in 1854, was the largest in the nation. Its 130,000 square miles included all of Eastern Oregon and parts of Idaho, Montana, and Wyoming. All three courthouses still exist.

A large area of The Dalles was leveled by fire in 1891, and there's a mark from the 1894 flood well up the front of **KLINDT'S BOOKSELLERS** (315 E 2nd St; 541/296-3355). Klindt's, the oldest continually operating bookstore in Oregon, was founded in 1870 and moved to the store on Second Street in 1893, the year before the flood. The **COLUMBIA GORGE DISCOVERY CENTER AND WASCO COUNTY HISTORICAL MUSEUM** complex about 3 miles west of town (5000 Discovery Dr; 541/296-8600; www.gorgediscovery.org) chronicles much of the area's natural and man-made history.

The Dalles is a market center for the region's cherry growing, wheat farming, and cattle ranching. It's also a lively parade town, with **THE DALLES CHERRY FESTIVAL** parade in late April and the **FORT DALLES RODEO PARADE** (lots of cowboys and horses!) in mid-July. Visitor information is available from **THE DALLES AREA CHAMBER OF COMMERCE** (404 W 2nd St; 541/296-2231; www. thedalleschamber.com).

RESTAURANTS

Baldwin Saloon / ★

205 COURT ST, THE DALLES; 541/296-5666
The 1876 Baldwin Saloon has seen a bit of everything between its brick walls. In the span of a century it's been a steamboat navigational office, a coffin storage site, an employment office, and a saddlery before finally returning to its origins as a bar and restaurant. The most recent restoration added an impressive collection of early 20th-century Northwest oil paintings. The American food is consistently good, with noteworthy oysters Rockefeller and rich desserts (the walnut tart, in particular). *$$; MC, V; checks OK; lunch, dinner Mon–Sat; full bar; reservations recommended; www.baldwinsaloon. com; at 1st St.* &

Columbia Gorge Doughnut Company / ★

216 COURT ST, THE DALLES; 541/296-1800
When former restaurateur and museum director Cal McDermid opened the Columbia Gorge Doughnut Company, he indulged the sweet tooth of salivating locals and visitors with his fresh-baked, gooey, sprinkled (and everything else that makes a doughnut grand) hole-filled goodies. There's nothing but coffee and doughnuts here, but the shiny little storefront bakery is a trendy place for a quick, sugary boost. *$; no credit cards; checks OK; breakfast, lunch Mon–Sat; no alcohol; no reservations; 2nd and Courts sts.*

BURGERVILLE USA

A fast-food restaurant that *Fast Food Nation* author Eric Schlosser likes? Yup—and it's here in The Dalles.

BURGERVILLE restaurant (118 W 3rd St; 541/298-5753) has no ordinary fast food. The Vancouver, Washington–based chain has 39 restaurants in Oregon and southwest Washington—and unusually ardent fans. The chain has earned praise from gourmet magazines as well as Schlosser for its socially responsible practices. Burgerville focuses on environmental sustainability and slow (regional) fast food. Restaurants use electricity generated by renewable wind energy, and used frying oil is recycled into biodiesel. Employees even get health insurance.

The menu changes seasonally: strawberry shakes in the spring, for example; Walla Walla onion rings in the summer; sweet-potato fries in the fall. Burgerville buys all its beef from Oregon Country Natural Beef, a cooperative of ranchers who raise their cattle without additives or hormones. Particularly in The Dalles, you're more than likely to spot a rancher in boots and cowboy hat enjoying a socially conscious meal at Burgerville.

Romul's / ★★☆

312 COURT ST, THE DALLES; 541/296-9771
With Mediterranean fusion cuisine, Romul's incorporates Greek and Bulgarian ideas into an Italian-focused menu. *Surmi* (stuffed grape leaves) is served alongside more traditional Italian dishes of bruschetta and veal saltimbocca. Exotic murals, paintings, and scattered Romanesque statues enliven the space. The restaurant is a special-occasion hit in this town. *$$; MC, V; checks OK; lunch, dinner Mon–Sat; full bar; reservations recommended; www.romuls. com; just off 3rd St (US Hwy 30).* &

Mount Hood

Perpetually snowcapped, 11,245-foot Mount Hood is the highest place in Oregon and one of the most climbed glaciated mountains in the world. With a chair lift and ski slope at 10,000 feet, **PALMER SNOWFIELD** makes skiing possible almost year-round. Aspiring young Olympians, including the U.S. Ski Team, come from all over the world for summer training.

Encompassing more than 1 million acres, the **MOUNT HOOD NATIONAL FOREST** (www.fs.fed.us/r6/mthood/) is beautiful. Information is at the **HOOD RIVER RANGER STATION** (6780 SR 35, Parkdale; 541/352-6002) or at the **ZIGZAG RANGER STATION** (70220 E US Hwy 26, Zigzag; 503/622-319).

Mount Hood has five main ski areas. **COOPER SPUR**, 27 miles south of Hood River on State Route 35 (11000 Cloud Cap Rd; 541/352-7803; www.cooper

spur.com), is an affordable day-ski area at 4,500 feet, with 10 runs, a chair lift, three rope tows, and a T-bar. The biggest one, **MOUNT HOOD MEADOWS** (2 miles north of SR 35 on Forest Rd 3555; 503/337-2222; www.skihood.com), is at 7,300 feet elevation. It has a day lodge, 87 runs, four high-speed quads, six double chair lifts, and a Nordic center. Meadows, as it's known, teams with many lodgings in the Mount Hood–Hood River area to offer bargain lift tickets.

GOVERNMENT CAMP, 53 miles east of Portland on US Highway 26, is the village center of the inexpensive and popular **SUMMIT SKI AREA** (near the Rest Area at the east end of Government Camp; 503/272-3206; www.summitskiarea.com), founded in 1927 and the oldest ski area on Mount Hood. Ski and tube rentals are available. The **MOUNT HOOD CULTURAL CENTER AND MUSEUM** (88900 E US Hwy 26; 503/272-3301; www.mthoodmuseum.org) displays a photo collection and exhibits of Mount Hood winter sports history.

MOUNT HOOD SKIBOWL (87000 E US Hwy 26; 503/272-3206; www.skibowl. com), at 5,026 feet, bills itself as America's largest night-ski area, with 34 lighted runs, four double chairlifts, and a tubing hill. In the summer, it's transformed into the **MOUNT HOOD SKIBOWL SUMMER ACTION PARK**, with 25-plus activities including a dual alpine slide, Indy Karts, miniature golf, bungee jumping, batting cages, croquet, and a 40-mile mountain bike park.

At the top of the hill is **TIMBERLINE** (4 miles north of US Hwy 26, just east of Government Camp; 503/622-7979; www.timberlinelodge.com), with six lifts; four are high-speed quads, including the Palmer Lift, which takes skiers up to the Palmer Snowfield. In the summer, the **MAGIC MILE SUPER EXPRESS** lift carries riders 1,000 feet to Palmer Junction, where the Magic Mile Interpretive Trail leads to Timberline Lodge.

Climbers who want to scale Mount Hood must register and obtain a free but mandatory wilderness permit in the 24-hour climbing room at Timberline's Wy'east Day Lodge. **TIMBERLINE MOUNTAIN GUIDES** (541/312-9242) does guided climbs. The easiest route up the mountain is on the south side, but the glacier near the summit may still require technical rope work. Check with the Zigzag Ranger Station for conditions.

RESTAURANTS

Cascade Dining Room / ★★★★

TIMBERLINE LODGE, TIMBERLINE; 503/622-0700
The rustic, carved wood of the main lodge provides a warm, casual setting for some of the most sophisticated food in the region. Executive chef Leif Eric Benson has presided here for almost three decades, winning a steady stream of awards for his deftly prepared Cascadian cuisine, which samples liberally from fresh Northwest-grown, -gathered, and -caught ingredients. Sweeping views of the mountain have made this a special-occasion favorite. Diners can tour the downstairs wine vault. *$$$; AE, MC, V; checks OK; breakfast, lunch, dinner every day; full bar; reservations recommended; www.timberlinelodge. com; 60 miles east of Portland off US Hwy 26.* &

The Brew Pub at Mount Hood Brewing Company

87304 E GOVERNMENT CAMP LOOP HWY,
GOVERNMENT CAMP; 503/622-0724
Watch the brewing activities and grab a cold one—beer aficionados speak highly of the Ice Axe IPA and the Hogsback Oatmeal Stout—at this family-friendly pub. Hearty, Tuscan-style pizzas, burgers, beer-battered vegetables, and kid cuisine match nicely with a variety of ales—and Snowbargers Old-Fashioned Root Beer, also on tap. *$; AE, DIS, MC, V; checks OK; lunch, dinner every day; beer and wine; no reservations; www.mthoodbrewing.com; west end of Government Camp business loop, on south side.* ৬

Rendezvous Grill & Tap Room / ★★

67149 E US HWY 26, WELCHES; 503/622-6837
In Welches, the 'Vous serves up "serious food," including Dungeness crab and Willapa Bay oysters, in a "not-so-serious place." (Chef Kathryn Bliss has been known to host a harvest-moon belly-dance festival.) The Tap Room, open from early afternoon to evening, has a more informal menu. *$–$$; AE, DIS, MC, V; lunch, dinner every day June–Sept, Wed–Sun Oct–May; beer and wine; reservations recommended; www.rendezvousgrill.net; north side of hwy, 20 minutes west of Government Camp.* ৬

LODGINGS

Mount Hood Hamlet Bed & Breakfast / ★★

6741 SR 35, MOUNT HOOD; 541/352-3574 OR 800/407-0570
Retired teachers Paul and Diane Romans built this colonial-style house—inspired by an ancestral home in Rhode Island—on the farmland where Paul was raised. Decorating is tasteful early American, and the bed-and-breakfast has a spectacular, up-close view of Mount Hood. All guest rooms have private baths, fireplaces, Jacuzzis, and TVs. Families should ask for the larger Orchard Room. The outdoor hot tub, with a great view, is heated year-round. *$$$; AE, DIS, MC, V; checks OK; www.mthoodhamlet.com; 20 miles north of Mount Hood Meadows.* ৬

Timberline Lodge / ★★★✫

TIMBERLINE SKI AREA, TIMBERLINE;
503/622-7979 OR 800/547-1406
Timberline Lodge was the brilliant product of one of President Franklin D. Roosevelt's New Deal initiatives. Filled with handcrafted furniture and original art, it's like staying in an art museum. The building belongs to the U.S. government and Forest Service, which mandates that a few less-expensive rooms are available to guests. Thus, European-style Chalet rooms sleep up to 10 people in bunk beds with shared baths, while the most expensive rooms have stone fireplaces and views. It's best to ask about rooms, as deep snow can disappointingly obscure some views. *$–$$$; AE, MC, V; checks OK; www. timberlinelodge.com; 60 miles east of Portland, off US Hwy 26.* ৬

WILLAMETTE VALLEY

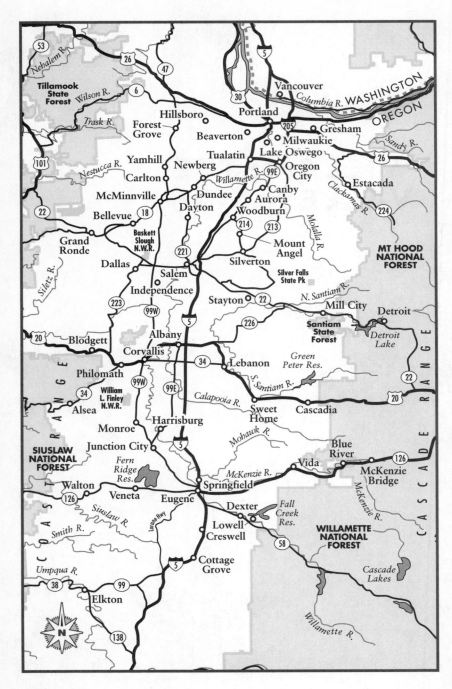

WILLAMETTE VALLEY

Carved by the wide Willamette River, the Willamette Valley is quintessential Oregon: green and lush.

Wine from the Willamette Valley has quickly risen to the top tiers of the world. The cool climate supports sensitive grapes such as pinot noir, the region's star. Touring the valley's wineries (see sidebar) is a treat for your palate and a perfect opportunity for sightseeing.

Although most of Oregon is covered by high desert or mountains, 9 out of 10 Oregonians live in the Willamette Valley.

ACCESS AND INFORMATION

Commuter airlines serve the **PORTLAND INTERNATIONAL AIRPORT** (Northeast Portland, off I-84; 503/460-4040; www.flypdx.com) and the **EUGENE AIRPORT** (northwest of Eugene, off Route 99W; 541/682-5430; www.eugeneairport.com). **CAR RENTALS** are available at both airports and in Eugene and Portland.

Most travelers arrive via **INTERSTATE 5**, which parallels the Willamette River from Portland to Eugene. This is the express route through the Willamette Valley. It may take about two hours to drive from Portland to Eugene. **ROUTE 99W** parallels Interstate 5 west of the Willamette and makes for a more leisurely north-south commute through agricultural fields, small country towns, and the wine country of Yamhill County. Contact the **OREGON DEPARTMENT OF TRANSPORTATION** (503/588-2941 or 800/977-6368) for road conditions. **TRAVEL ADVISOR** (www.tripcheck.com) also has helpful information.

AMTRAK (800/USA-RAIL; www.amtrak.com) commutes from Portland to Eugene and stops in Salem, Albany, and Eugene. The **WILLAMETTE VALLEY VISITOR'S ASSOCIATION** (866/548-5018; www.willamettevalley.org) is a good source.

Newberg

Located in the Northwest part of the valley, Newberg, along with its neighbors, is most often visited by wine seekers. The expansion of vineyards and the popularity of area wineries brought a collection of great restaurants and places to stay.

LODGINGS

Springbrook Hazelnut Farm / ★★

30295 N ROUTE 99W, NEWBERG; 503/538-4606 OR 800/793-8528
In the heart of Oregon wine country, this landmark farmhouse is not only an exquisitely decorated B and B but a working hazelnut farm as well. Two upstairs rooms are decorated with wicker furnishings and share a bathroom; downstairs two others are furnished with antiques and have half

WILLAMETTE VALLEY THREE-DAY TOUR

DAY ONE: Starting in Eugene, enjoy eggs Benedict or thick french toast at **STUDIO ONE CAFÉ**, then take Interstate 5 to exit 182 at Creswell and visit **KING ESTATE** (80854 Territorial Rd, Eugene; 541/942-9874 or 800/884-4441; www. kingestate.com; noon–5pm every day) for a tour of the winery, a walk in the garden, and small-plate wine pairings on the patio. Take the winding back roads about 20 miles to Eugene, following the Lorane Highway north. For the afternoon, if the weather permits, stop at **SPENCER'S BUTTE** on South Willamette Street for a steep 1½-mile hike to a viewpoint, or walk the **PREFONTAINE TRAIL** along the Willamette River. For an indoor option, check out crafts and shopping at the **FIFTH AVENUE PUBLIC MARKET**, or visit the **JORDAN SCHNITZER MUSEUM OF ART** at the University of Oregon campus. Check in to the **CAMPBELL HOUSE** near the public market, then dine at **CAFÉ SORIAH** for Mediterranean-inspired specialties.

DAY TWO: Enjoy your breakfast at the Campbell House before taking a two-hour drive north to Silverton. Stop to explore landscaped acres at the **OREGON**

baths, sharing a full one down the hall. Behind the main house are the Rose Cottage and the Carriage House, each with a kitchen. The old barn is now a small winery, and the hazelnut stand is open in the fall. Visitors can explore the orchards, swim in the pool, play tennis, and explore wine country. *$$–$$$; DIS, MC, V; checks OK; www.nutfarm.com; just off Route 99 W north of Newberg.*

Dundee

Dundee has quickly become the culinary center of northern Oregon wine country. You'll find several restaurants lining Route 99W.

RESTAURANTS

Dundee Bistro / ★★★

100-A SE 7TH ST, DUNDEE; 503/554-1650

This bustling bistro-pizzeria-bar on Dundee's restaurant row was built by the Ponzi family, respected winemakers. The courtyard and large windows, with walls and floor in tones of sage and pumpkin, lend it a Tuscan air, but the food is inventively Northwestern. A fall dinner might start with garnet-yam flan with smoked salmon or a sweet beet-root salad. The half-dozen entrée choices may include mesquite-roasted chicken or Oregon petrale sole. Pizza is topped with unique but delicious combinations. Next door is the Ponzi wine bar. *$$;*

GARDEN before checking in to the **WATER STREET INN BED AND BREAK-FAST** in downtown Silverton. Walk a block to **O'BRIAN'S CAFE** for lunch featuring the best country cooking, and sit on the patio overlooking **SILVER CREEK**. Either tour the wineries around Silverton (see sidebar) or drive to **SILVER FALLS STATE PARK** for a hike or to view the falls. Dine at either **MAURICE'S BISTRO** in Sublimity or at **SILVER GRILLE CAFÉ & WINES** in downtown Silverton.

DAY THREE: Take breakfast at the inn and then drive west to Mount Angel to tour the **MOUNT ANGEL ABBEY**. Then continue northwest to **NEWBERG**, the heart of the Willamette's wine country. Begin your tour by driving south on Route 99W, stopping for tastes at **ANNE AMIE WINERY** and **ARGYLE WINERY** (see sidebar). For lunch, either pack a picnic to enjoy at a winery or drive to McMinnville and partake of fine French cuisine at **BISTRO MAISON**. Continue visiting wineries as you drive north to Carlton. Stop at the **CARLTON WINE-MAKER STUDIO AND TASTING ROOM**. Enjoy the shops along Main Street in Carlton. For dinner, take the short drive to Dayton to enjoy a meal at the **JOEL PALMER HOUSE** to conclude your tour.

AE, MC, V; local checks only; lunch, dinner every day; full bar; reservations recommended; www.dundeebistro.com; on Route 99 W at 7th St. &

Red Hills Provincial Dining / ★★★

276 ROUTE 99W, DUNDEE; 503/538-8224

You'll be warmly received in this 1912 Craftsman-style house-turned-restaurant. The simple European-country dinner menu changes often, and the choices are all intriguing: veal osso buco with creamy polenta, perhaps, or fricasee of game hen with chanterelles. All the details are just right, whether it's bread dusted with fresh rosemary or poached pears with caramel sauce. The huge wine list is from all over the world. A private dining room seats up to 12. *$$; AE, MC, V; checks OK; dinner every day; full bar; reservations recommended; www.redhillsdining.com; north edge of town.*

Tina's / ★★★

760 ROUTE 99W, DUNDEE; 503/538-8880

This local gathering place resides in a small, unassuming house on the side of the highway. Inside, it's stylish, with bright white walls and a fireplace. The cuisine is contemporary French. The sea scallops and their thyme-infused sauce is great, as is the purée of corn soup, creamy without cream. Surprises include salmon spring rolls served with hazelnut sauce. The list of house-made desserts is short, and the wine list is long: the right proportion in these parts. *$$; AE, DIS, MC, V; checks OK; lunch Tues–Fri, dinner every day; full bar; reservations recommended; center of town, across from fire station.* &

Dayton

RESTAURANTS

Joel Palmer House / ★★★

600 FERRY ST, DAYTON; 503/864-2995

A trip to Oregon wine country is not complete without a stop at the Joel Palmer House. Chef Jack Czarnecki is an authority on cooking with mushrooms, and rare is the dish here that emerges without some variety of them. Appetizers might include a three-mushroom tart, escargot with black chanterelles, or corn chowder. The rack of lamb comes with rich pinot noir–hazelnut sauce, while wild mushrooms duxelles and a Creole–pinot gris sauce accompany tender sautéed scallops. Or consider Jack's Mushroom Madness, a prix-fixe multicourse dinner emphasizing—what else?—wild mushrooms. Positioned in a white Southern Revival home built in the 1850s by town cofounder General Joel Palmer, the restaurant has a sense of romance and formality. *$$–$$$; AE, DIS, MC, V; local checks only; dinner Tues–Sat; full bar; reservations required; www.joelpalmerhouse.com; downtown.* &

LODGINGS

Wine Country Farm / ★

6855 BREYMAN ORCHARDS RD, DAYTON; 503/864-3446 OR 800/261-3446

The Wine Country Farm is nestled into the "red hills of Dundee," where the soil really is red and the expansive vineyards are spectacular. The six colorful and vibrant guest rooms in the white stucco 1910 house have private bathrooms; two have fireplaces. A hot tub, sauna, and on-site massage are available. There's a large wine-tasting room next door. Owners of the 13-acre farm also own Arabian horses and offer guided trail rides as well as buggy rides to wineries. Enjoy the farm breakfast on a sun-washed deck with a spectacular view. *$$–$$$; MC, V; checks OK; www.winecountryfarm.com; right onto McDugal Rd just past Sokol Blosser Winery, then right to Breyman Orchards Rd.*

Carlton

Carlton's 19th-century brick and stone storefronts make for a pleasant stroll through downtown. Small quilting, gardening, and art shops provide local small-town ambience, and there are several tasting rooms and wine cellars. **CUNEO CELLARS** (750 W Lincoln St; 503/852-0002; www.cuenocellars.com) is at the north end of town and **THE TASTING ROOM** (105 W Main St; 503/852-6733) features wines from several local wineries, which are often closed to the public. **CARLTON WINEMAKER STUDIO AND TASTING ROOM** (801 N Scott St; 503/852-6100) is where resident winemakers showcase and sell their wines.

The **FLYING M RANCH** (23029 NW Flying M Rd; 503/662-3222; www.flying-m-ranch.com) is 10 miles west of nearby Yamhill and offers horseback riding, Spartan overnighting, an airstrip for private pilots, and meat-and-potatoes fare in a big log lodge. Follow W Main Street west to Fairdale Road to find the ranch.

McMinnville

This country burg with historic buildings and a shaded town center has been nudged into the high life with the thriving wine and agriculture industries, so now it's pulsing with a collection of wine shops, cafés, and boutiques inhabiting the buildings from the early 1900s. McMinnville's central location makes it good headquarters for wine touring. The area is especially bustling around Memorial Day, Thanksgiving, and late July or early August during the **INTERNATIONAL PINOT NOIR CELEBRATION** (503/472-8964 or 800/775-4762; www.inpc.org) at Linfield College. Purchase tickets in advance; it's very popular. Pick up information at the **MCMINNVILLE CHAMBER OF COMMERCE** (417 N Adams St; 503/472-6196; www.mcminnville.org).

A **FARMERS MARKET** (S Cowles St between 2nd and 3rd sts) is held on Thursday afternoons from June to September. **THE EVERGREEN AVIATION MUSEUM** (3685 NE Cumulus Ave, off SR 18; 503/434-4180; www.sprucegoose.org) features Howard Hughes' Flying Boat.

RESTAURANTS

Bistro Maison / ★★

729 E 3RD ST, MCMINNVILLE; 503/474-1888
This inviting French café, owned by chef Jean-Jacques and his wife, Deborah, is found on the ground floor of a historic bungalow decorated with cheery French wallpaper and leather-backed booths. There is a wine tasting bar at the front. A good place to start is the *moules*, mussels cooked in three different styles. Entrées include classic coq au vin in a rich pinot noir sauce and Confit de Canard, braised duck crisped with orange cognac. Dessert includes puff pastries filled with vanilla ice cream. Outdoor seating in the courtyard is pleasant. *$$; DIS, MC, V; local checks only; lunch Wed–Fri, dinner Wed–Sun, late brunch Sun; full bar; reservations recommended; www.bistromaison.com; on 3rd St next to train station.*

Golden Valley Brewery / ★

980 E 4TH ST, MCMINNVILLE; 503/472-2739
This spacious, traditional brew pub with wooden-backed booths and a long bar serves local brews such as Muddy Valley Oatmeal Stout and Red Thistle Ale, as well as hearty pub fare. Owners Peter and Celia Kircher raise their beef at the nearby Angus Springs Ranch, so you can be assured that your steak is free of hormones. Friday and Saturday are slow-roasted prime rib

nights. Vegetarian options are slim but available. *$–$$$; AE, DIS, MC, V; local checks only; lunch, dinner every day, brunch Sun; full bar; no reservations; www.goldenvalleybrewery.com; 1 mile off SR 18.* &

La Rambla / ★★☆

238 NE 3RD ST, MCMINNVILLE; 503/435-2126

As a relatively new addition to McMinnville's family of restaurants, La Rambla is a warm beacon, offering Northwest-inspired Spanish cuisine, including small-plate tapas and full entrées. Found in an 1898 building that was originally a bar, La Rambla has returned to those roots and has won awards for restoration and beautification. Entrées include traditional paella and *lomode cerdo*, slow-roaster pork loin. Tapas take the starring role, with good reason: they're inexpensive ($6–$14) and delicious. *$$–$$$; AE, DIS, MC, V; checks OK; lunch, dinner Wed–Mon; full bar; reservations recommended; www.larambla.com; between Cowels and Baker sts.* &

Nick's Italian Café / ★★

521 E 3RD ST, MCMINNVILLE; 503/434-4471

Nick Peirano's restaurant in McMinnville is the original culinary headquarters of Oregon's wine country; Nick's was famous for spectacular cuisine long before other restaurants came here. Peirano offers Northern Italian cooking and a five-course, fixed-price menu. Start with an appetizer, perhaps fresh melon and pears with prosciutto. Follow with garlic minestrone. The pasta course may include fresh Dungeness crab and pine nut lasagne. Entrées include a salt-grilled salmon steak or rabbit. Desserts may include a chocolate brandy hazelnut torte. *$$$; AE, MC, V; checks OK; dinner Tues–Sun; beer and wine; reservations recommended; www.nicksitaliancafe.com; next door to Hotel Oregon.* &

LODGINGS

Hotel Oregon / ★★

310 NE EVANS ST, MCMINNVILLE; 503/472-8427 OR 888/472-8427

The microbrew brothers of the Northwest, Mike and Brian McMenamin, have revitalized a 1905 hotel in the center of town. Though rarely full, the hotel is a popular place to stay during wine festivals. Most rooms are small with colorful decor; only a few of the 42 rooms have private baths. There is a pub and restaurant downstairs, which can contribute to the street noise. The Rooftop Bar is spectacular during good weather, when yon can relax at the top of the town while enjoying McMenamin's famous ales. *$$; AE, DIS, MC, V; checks OK; www.hoteloregon.com; at 3rd St.* &

Steiger Haus Inn / ★

360 SE WILSON ST, MCMINNVILLE; 503/472-0821

Tucked in a neighborhood of older homes, Steiger Haus is a peaceful oasis. The contemporary cedar-shingled house has a comfortable Northwest feel, with a lot of light. The two downstairs suites are large and comfortable, and two of the three rooms have private decks extending into the woodsy backyard. All five rooms and suites have private baths; one downstairs has a fireplace, another, a jetted tub; the upstairs suite has a soaking tub and bay window. Breakfast might include poached pears, raisin muffins, and German pancakes. *$$; DIS, MC, V; checks OK; www.steigerhaus.com; ¼ mile east of Linfield College entrance.*

Youngberg Hill Vineyards & Inn / ★★★

10660 YOUNGBERG HILL RD, MCMINNVILLE;
503/472-2727 OR 888/657-8668
Set on the crest of a 700-foot hill, this quiet inn is set apart from the rest by its views of the Willamette Valley. A large wraparound porch beckons, even on cold days, for gazing at the rolling hills. Owners Wayne and Nicolette Bailey plan to extend the 12-acre vineyard and add a spa. The seven spacious rooms and suites have private baths; three have fireplaces. There's a cozy music room, living room, and gift shop. Breakfast might include guava juice and muffins, baked apples, and eggs Florentine with grilled salmon. *$$$; MC, V; checks OK; www.youngberghill.com; 12 miles southwest of McMinnville off Youngberg Hill Rd.* ♿

Bellevue

This small intersection 8 miles southwest of McMinnville on Route 18 is home to Oregon's largest art gallery: **LAWRENCE GALLERY** (19700 SW Route 18; 503/843-3633), complete with a water and sculpture garden outside. The attached **OREGON WINE TASTING ROOM** (19690 SW SR 18; 503/843-3787; www.winesnw.com/oregonwinetastingroom.htm) has samplings from about two-dozen wineries.

RESTAURANTS

Fresh Palate Café / ★

19706 SW ROUTE 18, BELLEVUE; 503/843-4400
Lunch at this appropriately named atelier café overlooking the Lawrence Gallery features fresh produce, homemade breads and dressings, and scrumptious desserts. The airy, informal space is decorated with original artwork. Sandwiches and entrées such as acclaimed crab cakes or pasta are available for lunch, while dinner includes grilled honey-mustard filet mignon and Northwest cioppino. While the dinner menu is small, the wine list is huge. *$$; AE, MC, V; checks OK; lunch every day, dinner Fri–Sat; full bar; reservations recommended; www.freshpalatecafe.com; 7 miles southwest of McMinnville.*

Woodburn

As you're driving along Interstate 5, you may associate Woodburn with only the huge outlet mall that has taken the town's name. While it's true that the shopping there is great, Woodburn has much more than clothing and furnishings for unbelievable prices. From Interstate 5, heading east for about 1½ miles, follow signs to the city center and you'll find clusters of Latino-owned businesses reminiscent of their Mexican and Central American roots.

Your first stop should be **SALVATOR'S BAKERY** (405 N 1st St; 503/982-4513) for traditional Mexican deli items such as *carnitas* or *queso cotija*. **LUPITA'S RESTAURANT** (311 N Front St; 503/982-0483) is a good choice for a sit-down meal with an English-Spanish menu. Several inexpensive taquerias with fast service are spread throughout downtown; **TAQUERIA EL REY** (966 N Pacific Hwy; 503/982-1303) offers traditional versions of tacos, made with beef *cabeza* (head), *tripa* (tripe), and *lengua* (tongue).

Mount Angel

This memorable country town was definitely founded by Germans. Most well known for its **OKTOBERFEST** (503/845-9440) in mid-September, the town is a treat. Visit the **MOUNT ANGEL ABBEY** (1 Abbey Dr, St. Benedict; 503/845-3030; www.mtangel.edu), a century-old Benedictine seminary with a library constructed by celebrated Finnish architect Alvar Aalto. Go for a brew and hearty fare at **MOUNT ANGEL BREWING COMPANY** (210 Monroe St; 503/845-9624; www.mountangelbrewing.com).

RESTAURANTS

Angel's Table / ☆

415 S MAIN ST, MOUNT ANGEL; 503/845-9289

Angel's Table offers a comfortable collaboration of fine dining and German-style home cooking. While the spacious dining room and light-filled front café don't offer the same contemporary elegance as other area fine-dining establishments, the service is attentive and the food is above average. For lunch, try the wiener schnitzel, breaded pork scallops, or Willapa Bay oyster stew. The dinner menu pairs local seafood and pasta dishes with traditional German fare. Enjoy the sausage sampler for a starter. German entrées include *pfefferpotthast* (short ribs) and thick, juicy *zwischenrippenstuck* (tenderloin). $$; AE, DIS, MC, V; local checks only; lunch, dinner Tues–Sun; beer and wine; no reservations; downtown off N Main St. &

Silverton

This artistic and historical town with shops and great cafés and restaurants is the perfect place to stay if you're visiting the east valley vineyards or **SILVER FALLS STATE PARK** southeast of town (off SR 214, 26 miles east of Salem; 503/873-8681; www.oregonstateparks.org/park_211). A 5-mile moderately difficult hiking trail circles several spectacular waterfalls ranging from 10 to 200 feet. Several of the falls are accessible by car or a short walk.

The **OREGON GARDEN** (on SR 213, 2 miles southwest of Silverton; 503/874-8100; www.oregongarden.org) has 240 landscaped acres of lush foliage, making it a world-class attraction, especially during the late-spring bloom. Iris farmers cultivate acres of fields around town, creating a brilliant palette in April and May.

RESTAURANTS

O'Brian's Cafe / ★★

105 N WATER ST, SILVERTON; 503/873-7554

At O'Brian's Cafe, you'll feel like you're staring into your mother's pantry and she's offered to cook you whatever your heart desires. So which would you prefer with your grilled turkey and bacon melt: homemade slaw, potato salad, green salad, macaroni salad, fries, or sliced tomatoes? O'Brian's is the local favorite for home-style cooking because of its huge, all-day lunch and breakfast menu, the thick slices of bacon, and service with a sincere smile. Enjoy casual patio seating next to Silver Creek. *$; AE, DIS, MC, V; checks OK; breakfast, lunch every day; no alcohol; no reservations; between E Main and Oak sts.*

Silver Grille Café & Wines / ★★★

206 E MAIN ST, SILVERTON; 503/873-4035

Chef Jeff Nizlek runs this well-known contemporary bistro and wine shop in downtown Silverton. The interior is elegant: dimly lit, with dark wood wainscoting below dark red grass-paper walls. Entrées may include Oregon chinook salmon with a garden dill sauce and wild rice pilaf or locally raised rib-eye with garlic mashed potatoes. Start with Oregon buffalo served with basil sauce and tomatoes. Finish with a dome of Scharffenberger chocolate mousse with cassis made from local black currants, swimming in local berry sauce and crème anglaise. *$$; AE, MC, V; checks OK; dinner Wed–Sun; full bar; reservations recommended; www.silvergrille.com; at 1st St.* &

LODGINGS

Water Street Inn Bed and Breakfast / ★★

421 WATER ST, SILVERTON; 503/873-3344 OR 866/873-3344

This beautifully appointed B and B reflects the efforts of a mother and daughter-in-law team. Recently renovated, this spacious historic home, originally built in 1890 as the Wolfard Hotel, boasts five immensely comfortable, unique—

though not huge—guest rooms, all with private baths, several with double whirlpool tubs, and one with a double shower. The attention to detail is evident, from the added period crown sconces to the exquisite decor and linens in the rooms. Breakfast might include Grand Marnier french toast or eggs Benedict. *$$–$$$; AE, MC, V; checks OK; www.thewaterstreetinn.com; downtown, 1 block off Silver Creek.*

Stayton and Sublimity

These small communities are close enough to Salem to enjoy the hustle of town, yet full of country ambience. If you want to explore east valley wineries and the foothills of the Cascades, this area makes for a great jumping-off point.

Stayton's historic downtown is quaint. **SANTIAM HISTORICAL MUSEUM** (260 N 2nd Ave; 503/769-1406) has artifacts from the valley. The covered **STAYTON-JORDAN BRIDGE** and short walking trails are at **PIONEER PARK** (7th and Pioneer sts). **MAURICE'S BISTRO** (390 Church St, off Cascades Hwy, Sublimity; 503/769-8303; www.mauricesbistro.com) at Marion Estates is a nice place for fine dining.

LODGINGS

Bird & Hat Inn / ★

717 N 3RD ST, STAYTON; 503/769-7817
Bird & Hat Inn is a delightful B and B on a quiet block near downtown where you're sure to receive a warm welcome. The Brewer House, built in 1907, was first opened as a B and B in 1986. The current owner has recently restored the Sunken Garden, a charming addition. The three rooms located on the second floor are spacious and filled with light. Two have private patios and all have private baths, with one off the hallway. Accommodation choices in the area are slim, so be sure to make reservations well in advance. *$; AE, MC, V; checks OK; 2 blocks north of downtown.*

Salem

The handsome parks of the state capital invite a long stroll. Historic homes and buildings highlight a visit to Salem, along with good shopping and restaurants. The 1938 **CAPITOL BUILDING** (900 Court St NE; 503/986-1388; www.leg.state. or.us/capinfo) is topped by a tall statue of a pioneer sheathed in gold. Tours of the building are free.

The **SALEM VISITOR INFORMATION CENTER** (503/581-4325 or 800/874-7012; www.scva.org) is located at the **HISTORIC MISSION MILL VILLAGE** (1313 Mill St SE; 503/585-7012; www.missionmill.org), a large cluster of restored buildings from the 1800s that includes several homes, a Presbyterian church, and a woolen mill. The Northwest's oldest remaining frame house is here: the

JASON LEE HOUSE, dating from 1841. The **SALEM CHAMBER OF COMMERCE** (1110 Commercial St NE; 503/581-1466; www.salemchamber.org) has useful information.

BUSH HOUSE (600 Mission St SE; 503/363-4714; www.oregonlink.com/bush_house; tours Tues–Sun, noon–5pm May–Sept, 2–5pm Oct–April) is an 1877 Victorian home built by Aashal Bush, a pioneer newspaper publisher. The house is situated in **BUSH'S PASTURE PARK,** complete with rose gardens, hiking trails, a conservatory, and an art gallery.

The oldest university in the West, **WILLAMETTE UNIVERSITY** (900 State St; 503/370-6300; www.willamette.edu), is a pleasant place to stroll. Stop at the botanical gardens and the **HALLIE FORD MUSEUM OF ART** (700 State St; 503/370-6855; www.willamette.edu/museum_of_art), the second-largest museum in the state, with 3,000 pieces.

Children will have fun at **AC GILBERT'S DISCOVERY VILLAGE** (116 Marion St NE; 503/371-3631; www.acgilbert.org) at Riverfront Park. They'll also love **ENCHANTED FOREST** (8462 Enchanted Way SE, Turner; 503/363-3060), a wooded storybook amusement park just off Interstate 5.

Summer brings the **WORLD BEAT FESTIVAL** (503/581-2004; www.worldbeatfestival.org), held in late June. Around Labor Day, the **OREGON STATE FAIR** (503/947-3247; www.oregonstatefair.org) runs for 10 days and is the largest in the state.

RESTAURANTS

Alessandro's 120 / ★★

120 COMMERCIAL ST NE, SALEM; 503/370-9951
Simple, elegant pasta and seafood are the strong suits at this longtime favorite. The menu isn't particularly original, but the classics are mostly done well, starting with fresh ingredients: perfectly cooked veal piccata, meat-stuffed tortellini in light cream sauce. There's also a multicourse dinner; the staff asks if there's a particular dish you don't like, and they surprise you with the rest. There's live jazz on Friday and Saturday evenings. *$$; AE, DIS, MC, V; no checks; lunch Mon–Fri, dinner every day; full bar; reservations recommended; downtown near Court St.* &

Bentley's Grill / ★★☆

291 LIBERTY ST SE (PHOENIX GRAND HOTEL), SALEM; 503/779-1660
This high-class grill was voted best new restaurant by the *Salem Monthly*. It serves small plates from a rotisserie chicken quesadilla to an Italian deli platter. Entrées include traditional grill fare: grilled Angus New York strip loin with garlic mashed potatoes and vegetables, smoked prime rib, seared halibut. Sandwiches and pizza are available all day. *$–$$$; AE, DIS, MC, V; checks OK; lunch, dinner every day, brunch Sun; full bar; reservations recommended; downtown between Trade and Ferry Sts.* &

j. james restaurant / ★★

325 HIGH ST SE, SALEM; 503/362-0888

Chef-owner Jeff James's eponymous restaurant is a bright light in the Salem dining scene. An Oregon native, James makes simple but creative dishes, including starters such as figs with cheese. There are entrées like grilled pork loin or salmon. The kitchen occasionally missteps—overdone fish in one daily special and a mustard vinaigrette that overwhelmed the salad—but the chef's experience often prevails. The space by a parking garage is softened by white linens and big windows. *$$; AE, MC, V; checks OK; lunch Mon–Fri seasonally; dinner Mon–Sat; full bar; reservations recommended; www.jjamesrestaurant. com; downtown, in Pringle Park Plaza.* &

Morton's Bistro Northwest / ★★★

1128 EDGEWATER ST NW, SALEM; 503/585-1113

A clever design puts the diner below roadway level, looking out on an attractive courtyard backed by an ivy-covered wall. The interior is intimate, with dark wood beams and soft lighting. Hints of international influences can be seen in the solidly Northwestern menu. A salmon fillet might be accompanied by a potato-pumpkin mash; vegetarian lasagne is great. Consider the mixed grill or the cioppino. *$$; MC, V; checks OK; dinner Tues–Sat; full bar; reservations recommended; mortonsbistronw.com; between Gerth and McNary aves in West Salem.* &

Wild Pear Restaurant & Catering / ★★★

3635 RIVER RD S, SALEM; 503/589-4532
372 STATE ST, SALEM; 503/378-7515

Sisters Cecilia and Jessica Ritter's charming country restaurant on River Road has recently been formalized from a casual café and catering business to a unique dining experience with an attached country gift shop and spectacular menu. The café in front is a bit crowded, while the dining room is spacious. On the far side of the pleasant outdoor patio is Carl's Place, a log-constructed bar where occasional dinners and wine-tastings are held. Seared sea scallops with pearl couscous or the rockfish on pesto linguine are both house favorites. The downtown café serves homemade soups and delicious deli fare with a counter-service setting. *$$–$$$, $; AE, DIS, MC, V; checks OK; lunch, dinner Mon–Sat (River Rd), lunch Mon–Sat (downtown); beer and wine (River Rd), no alcohol (downtown); reservations recommended (River Rd); from downtown, take Commercial St south, right on Owens St, becomes River Rd; downtown between Liberty and Commercial sts.*

LODGINGS

Phoenix Grand Hotel / ★★★

201 LIBERTY ST SE, SALEM; 503/540-7800 OR 877/540-7800

This modern hotel attached to the Salem Conference Center opened its doors in March 2005. The lobby is spacious and inviting, and the 193 rooms and suites are as well. All rooms have kitchenettes, separate living and sleeping areas, and some suites have Jacuzzis. The hotel has a pool, spa, and fitness room, and its central location makes for an easy walk to the capitol building, downtown shops, and parks. *$$$–$$$$; AE, DIS, MC, V; checks OK; www. phoenixgrandhotel.com; downtown between Trade and Ferry sts.* ⅙

Independence

This riverside town may appear to be untouched by modern time, but its proximity to Salem has made it popular for commuters. Still, its old-fashioned charm lives on, with places like **TAYLOR'S FOUNTAIN AND GIFT** (296 S Main St; 503/838-1124). The **RIVER GALLERY** (184 S Main St; 503/838-6171; www.oregonlink. com/rivergallery) exhibits work of local artists. Southeast of town is the four-car **BUENA VISTA FERRY** (503/588-7979; Wed–Sun, April–Oct), which will take you and your car across the Willamette.

RESTAURANTS

Buena Vista House Café and Lodging

11265 RIVERVIEW ST, INDEPENDENCE; 503/838-6364
This lively house is "out of the way, but worth it," says proprietor Claudia Prevost of her well-known inn and café. She bakes scones and serves items like smoked sausages, salmon croquettes, or wild-mushroom quiche. A wood-fired pizza oven is lighted Fridays for dinner, accompanied by live music. Three rooms are appointed with antiques in a refreshingly spare country style; all share a bath. *$–$$; no credit cards; checks OK; breakfast, lunch, dinner Wed–Sat, brunch Sun; reservations required (lunch, dinner, Sun brunch); beer and wine; south of town on ferry access road.*

Albany

Although Albany was bypassed during the construction of Interstate 5, it was once an important transportation hub of the Willamette Valley. With an unequaled selection of historic homes and buildings in the Monteith Historic District, you can see 13 architectural styles here. A free guide is at the **ALBANY CONVENTION AND VISITORS CENTER** (300 SW 2nd Ave; 800/526-2256; www.albanyvisitors. com). The **MONTEITH RIVERPARK** (Water Ave and Washington St) features the **RIVER RHYTHMS** concert series (541/917-772; www.riverrhythms.org).

Most of the remaining **COVERED BRIDGES** characteristic of the mid-1900s Willamette Valley—there were once about 300 throughout Oregon, and today there are fewer than 50—are in Linn and Lane counties. Six are in the vicinity of Scio, northeast of Albany, and several cross the rivers around Eugene and Cottage Grove. For maps, contact the Albany Convention and Visitors Center or the **COVERED BRIDGE SOCIETY OF OREGON** (PO Box 1804, Newport, OR 97365; 541/265-2934; coveredbridges.stateoforegon.com).

WINE TASTING IN THE WILLAMETTE VALLEY

The Willamette Valley's mild climate—with warm summers; wet, mild winters; and rainy springs—provides optimum conditions for growing cool-climate grapes. Most of the area's wineries are open year-round, but summer weekends, Memorial Day, and Thanksgiving are especially busy times. Arm yourself with a map from **WILLAMETTE VALLEY WINERIES ASSOCIATION** (503/646-2985; www. willamettewines.com).

The **NORTH VALLEY** of Yamhill County has more than 175 wineries, mostly between Newberg and McMinnville on Route 99W, which is accessible from Interstate 5 south of Portland. The wineries are worth visiting despite the traffic and congestion in this area. Try **ARGYL WINERY** (691 Route 99W, south of Newberg; 503/538-8520 or 888/4ARGYLE), where Rollin Soles creates renowned sparkling wines. At **ANNE AMIE WINERY** (6580 NE Mineral Springs Rd, Carlton; 503/864-2991), enjoy some of the best pinot noirs, with a view of the Coast Range. Don't miss the **CARLTON WINEMAKER STUDIO & TASTING ROOM** (801 N Scott St, Carlton; 503/852-6100; www.winemakersstudio.com), which has a lively tasting room (take Lincoln St from SR 47 just north of Carlton).

The **EAST VALLEY** wineries east of Interstate 5 are more spread out than

RESTAURANTS

Sybaris / ★★★

442 SW 1ST AVE, ALBANY; 541/928-8157

Along historic First Avenue in downtown Salem is this elegant and eclectic restaurant. With exposed brick walls, large windows, and high ceilings, it might feel cold if it weren't for the fireplace. The menu changes monthly; you might have steamed halibut with a spicy lemon-wasabi sauce on a sushi-rice "puck" (think hockey) or a roasted venison loin with vegetables and a huckleberry-port sauce. The entrées are generous, but save room for the chocolate hazelnut cake. *$$; AE, MC, V; checks OK; dinner Tues–Sat; full bar; reservations recommended; www.sybarisbistro.com; downtown between Washington and Ferry sts.* &

Corvallis

Some might call this town surrounded by fields sleepy, but the influx of youth from **OREGON STATE UNIVERSITY** (15th and Jefferson sts; 541/737-0123; www. orst.edu) enlivens the place. Interesting shops and stores are downtown, including **NEW MORNING BAKERY** (219 SW 2nd St; 541/754-0181). The renovated **RIVERFRONT PARK** (1st and Madison sts) has a paved esplanade along the Willamette

those west of the freeway, but you'll enjoy country roads and unique wineries. This tour route may be paired with a stop at the **OREGON GARDEN** or **SILVER FALLS STATE PARK**. Most of these wineries are open at least on weekends, 11am–5pm. Try **SILVER FALLS VINEYARD** (4972 SE Cascades Hwy, 2 miles north of Sublimity; 503/769-5056; www.silverfallsvineyard.com). **MARQUAM HILL VINEYARD** (35803 S SR 213, just north of Marquam; 503/829-6677) is in a tranquil setting.

The **SOUTH VALLEY** wineries, though sparsely located and off the beaten path south of Salem, are tucked in dense, rolling foothills, with winding roads and memorable views. Just outside of Corvallis off Route 99W, you'll find **TYEE WINE CELLARS** (26335 Greenberry Rd, Corvallis; 541/753-8754; www.tyeewine.com). Tyee features handcrafted wines, as well as a picnic area, an outdoor stage, and a trail. To arrive at **KING ESTATE** (80854 Territorial Rd, Eugene; 541/942-9874 or 800/884-4441; www.kingestate.com), you'll maneuver steep, curvy roads. The estate has quickly become the standard for the region. In downtown Eugene, you'll find the **OREGON WINE WAREHOUSE** (943 Olive St; 541/342-8598; www.oregonww.com), with a huge selection.

—Aleta Raphael-Brock

River where you'll find a fountain, stone benches, picnic tables, and artistry. The **SATURDAY FARMERS MARKET** runs May through October; get information at **CORVALLIS TOURISM** (553 NW Harrison Blvd; 541/757-1544 or 800/334-8118; www.visitcorvallis.com).

Trails are easily accessible at **MCDONALD STATE FOREST** (off Route 99W, 6 miles north of Corvallis). Here you'll find **PEAVY ARBORETUM**. **MARY'S PEAK** (on SR 34, west of Corvallis) is the tallest point in the Coast Range, at 4,097 feet.

RESTAURANTS

Big River / ★★★

101 NW JACKSON ST, CORVALLIS; 541/757-0694

Arty, jazzy, noisy—Big River is a big hit in Corvallis. Food is bold as well, and solidly Northwest. The menu changes daily, making it a treat even for regulars. You might try the rolled polenta with spinach, provolone, and portobellos or the buffalo short ribs. Pizzas are baked in the wood-fired oven. The glass dessert case's contents are tantalizing. In the bar, cozy into a lounge chair and enjoy live jazz. *$$; AE, DC, MC, V; checks OK; lunch Mon–Fri, dinner Mon–Sat; full bar; reservations recommended for 8 or more; www. bigriverrest.com; at 1st St.* &

Bombs Away Café / ★

2527 NW MONROE AVE, CORVALLIS; 541/757-7221
This wholesome taqueria serves Tex-Mex favorites with a wholesome twist. We're talking flautas stuffed with duck confit, chimichangas loaded with tofu. The ambience is typical of a college campus scene, with speedy counter service. Live music often graces the front of the house, while a bar in back offers tons of tequilas. *$; MC, V; checks OK; lunch Mon–Fri, dinner every day; full bar; reservations recommended; www.bombsawaycafe.com; at NW 25th St.* &

Iovino's / ★★★

126 SW 1ST ST, CORVALLIS; 541/738-9015
Located in a former garage, Iovino's industrial feel is similar to that of a converted New York loft: stylish sophistication, which you don't expect in Corvallis. They serve nouvelle Italian, with pleasant surprises such as caramelized onions and capers on bruschetta or sweet marsala sauce over turkey scallops and mashed ricotta potatoes. Basil dressing marries the plate of tiger prawns to the breaded eggplant underneath. *$$; AE, MC, V; checks OK; lunch Mon–Fri, dinner every day; full bar; reservations recommended; at Monroe Ave.* &

Magenta / ★★

1425 NW MONROE AVE, STE A, CORVALLIS; 541/758-3494
"European style with Asian flair" is how chef-owner Kim Hoang, a former Nike executive, describes her elegant little bistro. She's created the feel of a genteel establishment in French colonial Vietnam—antiques and tropical plants—and her eclectic menu follows suit. You'll find seafood and fowl, but Hoang specializes in unusual meats, from buffalo steak to emu. A menu of small dishes is available in the bar all evening and in the dining room after 8:30pm. *$$; AE, DIS, MC, V; lunch Mon–Fri, dinner every day; full bar; reservations recommended; next to Oregon State University.* &

LODGINGS

Hanson Country Inn / ★★

795 SW HANSON ST, CORVALLIS; 541/752-2919
You'll feel like you're in the country, yet you'll be just minutes from town. A former poultry ranch, the inn has expansive grounds. The 1928 wood-and-brick farmhouse is a registered historic home with a trove of antiques. Each of the two suites have a private bath, cable TV, telephone, Internet access, and private deck. The cottage, with two bedrooms and a kitchen, is perfect for families. Breakfasts include crepes with blackberries or a frittata. After breakfast, explore the formal garden and the original egg house. *$$–$$$; AE, DIS, MC, V; checks OK; www.hcinn.com; 5 minutes west of town.*

Harrison House Bed and Breakfast / ★

2310 NW HARRISON BLVD, CORVALLIS; 541/752-6248 OR 800/233-6248
Just a few blocks from campus, this B and B has simply decorated guest rooms—nothing innovative—and pleasant lounging space. Owners Maria and Charlie Tomlinson, who moved from New York, are gracious. Talk local politics with Charlie; he's on the city council. All four rooms have private baths. The English Garden Cottage has a kitchenette and sitting area, yet is available only when the hosts' sons are out of town. Enjoy a microbrew or a glass of wine when you arrive and let Maria know your preferences for the next morning: fruit with muffins, eggs Benedict, or stuffed crepes. *$$; AE, DC, DIS, JCB, MC, V; checks OK; www.corvallis-lodging.com; at 23rd St.*

Eugene and Springfield

The laid-back, overgrown town of Eugene nestles in the narrowest part of the Willamette Valley, where the round buttes of the Cascade foothills collide with sprawling agricultural fields. The Willamette River slices the city line of Springfield, Eugene's neighbor to the east.

Eugene has a thriving arts scene with a respected symphony, ballet, opera, and small theater companies. The **HULT CENTER FOR THE PERFORMING ARTS** (7th Ave and Willamette St; 541/342-5746; www.hultcenter.org) is the city's world-class concert facility.

The **UNIVERSITY OF OREGON** (13th Ave and University St; 541/346-3111; www.uoregon.edu) is the state's flagship institution, featuring a natural history museum and the **JORDAN SCHNITZER MUSEUM OF ART** (on UO campus; 541/346-3027; www.uoma.uoregon.edu), with Japanese, Chinese, and European exhibits.

There are several trendy coffeehouses, bakeries, and brew pubs. **SWEET LIFE PATISSERIE** (755 Monroe St; 541/683-5676) is a local favorite. For microbrews, **MCMENAMIN'S HIGH STREET BREWERY & CAFE** (1243 High St; 541/345-4905) is near the university, or try **STEELHEAD BREWERY** (199 E 5th Ave; 541/686-2739) in the railroad district. **STUDIO ONE CAFÉ** (1473 E 19th St; 541/342-8596) offers an original breakfast and lunch menu, complete with old favorites and reflecting the alternative style of Eugene with vegan and vegetarian options. If you prefer wine, **OREGON WINE WAREHOUSE** (943 Olive St; 541/342-8598) is worth a visit. Also, several local wineries, such as **TERRITORIAL VINEYARDS & WINE COMPANY** (907 W 3rd Ave; 541/684-9463; www.territorialvineyards.com), have opened tasting rooms.

At the **FIFTH AVENUE PUBLIC MARKET** (5th Ave and High St) you can peruse boutiques, outlet stores, and import shops. The **SATURDAY MARKET** (Oak St at 8th Ave; 541/686-8885; April–fall) is the state's oldest outdoor fair and farmers market. In September, the **EUGENE CELEBRATION** (www.eugenecelebration.com) takes over the railroad district at Fifth Avenue with music, food booths, and crafts.

HENDRICKS PARK (follow signs from Fairmount Blvd east of UO) is a great place to walk or run; it also features a 10-acre rhododendron garden that blooms in

---

CYCLING THE WILLAMETTE VALLEY

The Willamette Valley is perfect for bicycling. There are plenty of options, whether you want to spend a few days on the road or just enjoy an afternoon ride.

The **WILLAMETTE VALLEY SCENIC BIKEWAY ROUTE** spans 130 miles from Champoeg State Park just south of Newberg to Alton Baker Park in Eugene; the route follows country roads along the Willamette River. You'll find yourself amid the region's agricultural ambience for most of the trek. Contact **CYCLE OREGON** (503/287-0405 or 800/292-5367; www.cycleoregon.com) for details.

There is an abundance of paths along the Willamette River in Salem, Corvallis, and Eugene. In Corvallis, head west along the river toward Philomath; information is at the **CORVALLIS PARKS AND RECREATION DEPARTMENT** (1310 SW Avery Park Dr; 541/766-6918). In Salem, there are many miles of paths in parks; the largest is Minto-Brown Island. Contact the **CITY OF SALEM** for maps (1460 20th St SE; 503/588-6336; www.cityofsalem.com). In Eugene, visit Alton Baker Park and ride the loop trail, crossing the Willamette River at one of two large bridges. **CITY OF EUGENE PARKS AND OPEN SPACE** (777 Pearl St; 541/682-5010; www.eugene-or.gov) has maps.

Bike rentals are available at **SOUTH SALEM CYCLEWORKS** (4071 Liberty Road S, Salem; 503/399-9848) and at **PAUL'S BICYCLE WAY OF LIFE** (152 W 5th Ave, Eugene; 541/344-4105).

—Aleta Raphael-Brock

May and June. The **PREFONTAINE TRAIL** along the Willamette River is accessible from several locations, including **ALTON BAKER PARK** (off Centennial Blvd).

Springfield is the gateway to the McKenzie River, one of the coldest rivers in Oregon that flows out of the Cascades. A guided fishing and rafting trip is worthwhile; try **ADVENTURE RIVER CENTER** (49701 McKenzie Hwy/SR 126, Blue River; 541/549-1336 or 800/423-8868; www.adventurerivercenter.com).

Springfield's old downtown isn't much to look at, but secondhand collectibles and antique shops often yield a gem. Wander riverside paths and old orchards at the **DORIS RANCH LIVING HISTORY FARM** (2nd St S and Dorris St; 541/747-5552), birthplace of Oregon's thriving filbert (hazelnut) industry.

RESTAURANTS

Adam's Place / ★★★

30 E BROADWAY, EUGENE; 541/344-6948

Adam Bernstein, a third-generation restaurateur, has tastefully decorated this intimate downtown spot by adding arches, pillars, sconces, and a lovely fireplace. The result is quietly sophisticated, unpretentious yet classy. For an entrée, consider salmon topped with a sweet, tangy orange glaze. Vegetarian options are always interesting, and desserts are yummy, especially the crème brûlée. Attached is Luna, featuring Spanish tapas—it's the spot to hear live jazz. *$$–$$$; AE, MC, V; checks OK; dinner Tues–Sat; full bar; reservations recommended; www.adamsplacerestaurant.com; on downtown mall.* &

Ambrosia / ★★☆

174 E BROADWAY, EUGENE; 541/342-4141

Ambrosia is much more than a designer pizzeria. There's the ravioli San Remo, handmade and stuffed with veal, chicken, and ricotta; or the crepes filled with smoked salmon, spinach, and ricotta. Low lighting creates an intimate atmosphere, and tables are tucked into "rooms" or scattered in an airy mezzanine; sit at the wooden bar to take in the chefs' action. End the evening with homemade gelato. *$$; MC, V; local checks only; lunch Mon–Fri, dinner every day; full bar; reservations recommended for 6 or more; www.ambrosiarestaurant.com; at Pearl St.* &

Beppe and Gianni's Trattoria / ★★

1646 E 19TH AVE, EUGENE; 541/683-6661

This neighborhood trattoria, created by John Barofsky and Beppe Macchi, reflects the spirit and flavor of Beppe's homeland, Italy. Located in an old house, the restaurant is often jam-packed. The menu is small but covers the bases. Antipasto choices include roasted garlic and warm cheese. *Primi* dishes—mostly pasta—are generous enough to serve as a main course. *Secondi* entrées include sautéed chicken with wild mushrooms or marsala- and rosemary-perfumed lamb chops. *$$; MC, V; checks OK; dinner every day; beer and wine; reservations recommended for 8 or more; east of Agate St.* &

Café Soriah / ★★★

384 W 13TH AVE, EUGENE; 541/342-4410

In this smart and sophisticated restaurant, chef-owner Ibrahim Hamide has created an exciting and irresistible Mediterranean and Middle Eastern menu. It's comfortable enough for casual dining, but the flavors are deserving of a special occasion. The tiny bar in the front is a work of art in wood. A leafy, walled terrace offers comfortable outdoor seating. Stellar appetizer options include hummus and *baba gannoujh*. The menu, which changes monthly, might include roasted salmon with saffron rice and herbed yogurt. Count on favorites such as lamb *tagine*, moussaka, and marinated steak kebabs. Desserts may include spiced rice pudding or baklava. *$$; AE, MC, V; checks OK; lunch Mon–Fri, dinner every day; full bar; reservations recommended; www.soriah.com; at Lawrence St.* &

Chanterelle / ★★

207 E 5TH ST, EUGENE; 541/484-4065

Chef Ralf Schmidt's intimate restaurant is sophisticated and understated, with a small menu that reflects his classical French culinary sensibilities and hints at his Austrian roots. You'll find escargots and oysters Rockefeller among a handful of appetizers; the traditional baked French onion soup is deeply satisfying. A dozen entrée choices range from delicate coquilles St. Jacques to richly sauced tournedos of beef and a classic *zwiebel* steak. *$$$; AE, DC, MC, V; checks OK; dinner Tues–Sat; full bar; reservations recommended; across from public market.* &

Koho Bistro / ★★★

2101 BAILEY HILL RD, EUGENE; 541/681-9335
Koho Bistro is Eugene's neighborhood gem for relaxed fine dining. Its location about 10 minutes from downtown deters crowds; if you drive by the Churchill Shopping Center, you wouldn't even know Koho Bistro was there. Voted Best Northwest Vegetarian Restaurant by the *Eugene Weekly*, Koho Bistro serves an original Northwest menu with unrivaled variety. On the first page of the menu you'll find a note of appreciation to the local farmers who provide the ingredients. To start, try the Italian sausage-stuffed calamari appetizer. For an entrée try the rich seafood cannelloni or the locally raised fried chicken. The restaurant is well appointed and cozy, but can feel crowded when busy. *$$; AE, DIS, MC, V; local checks only; lunch Mon–Fri, dinner Mon–Sat; reservations recommended; www.kohobistro.com; south on Bailey Hill Rd from W 11th Ave, across from athletic field.* &

Marché / ★★★

296 E 5TH AVE, EUGENE; 541/342-3612
This elegant restaurant on the ground floor of the Fifth Avenue Public Market is influenced by French sensibility. The dinner menu features pork chops and sage-infused roasted leg of venison. Lunch is just as good: Consider a portobello mushroom sandwich with sun-dried tomato relish and mozzarella. The ambience is hip and stylish, with an open kitchen and oven. Service can be scattered on busy evenings. In a hurry? Try Cafe Marché upstairs. *$$–$$$; AE, DC, DIS, MC, V; checks OK; lunch, dinner every day, brunch Sun; full bar; reservations recommended; www.marcherestaurant.com; in public market.* &

Misako / ★

5 E 8TH AVE, EUGENE; 541/686-3464
In the mood for fantastic Japanese? Misako, a small, well-decorated, and friendly restaurant, is a longtime local favorite. If the extensive sake list doesn't persuade you, the appetizers, selection of sushi rolls, and sashimi menu will. Most meals start with smooth, tasty miso soup and *kobachi*, marinated bean sprouts. Don't miss the tempura cheesecake. Service is friendly but occasionally inconsistent. *$–$$; MC, V; checks OK; lunch Mon–Fri, dinner every day; beer and wine; reservations recommended for 5 or more; at Willamette St.* &

Mookie's Place / ★

1507 CENTENNIAL BLVD, SPRINGFIELD; 541/744-4148 OR 541/746-8298
Housed in a former drive-in, Mookie's is a local favorite for come-as-you-are casual dining or takeout. Try the spicy Cajun chicken Alfredo or honey-marinated grilled salmon. For an appetizer, the artichoke dip with garbanzo beans is a good bet. Slow-roasted prime rib is offered Friday and Saturday. Portions are generous, and there is a large kids' menu. *$–$$; AE, MC, V; checks OK; lunch Tues–Fri, dinner Tues–Sat; beer and wine; no reservations; at Mohawk Blvd.* &

Ring of Fire / ★★

1099 CHAMBERS ST, EUGENE; 541/344-6475
The exotic fragrances and elegant decor will transport you far, far away from the sprawling strip malls of W 11th Avenue. Thai, Indonesian, and Korean cuisines are featured, with reliable favorites such as phad thai and vegetable tempura. Try one of the specialties like crispy ginger red snapper or Thai coconut curry. For dessert, don't miss the tempura bananas with cool coconut ice cream. Portions are generous; takeout is available late. *$$; MC, V; no checks; lunch, dinner every day; full bar; reservations recommended; www. ringoffirerestaurant.com; off W 11th Ave.*

Zenon Café / ★★

898 PEARL ST, EUGENE; 541/343-3005
This noisy, crowded urban restaurant offers an ever-changing international menu featuring, on any given night, Italian, Greek, Middle Eastern, Cajun, Caribbean, Thai, or Northwest cuisine. Nothing disappoints, from Chinese "Hot as Hell" skewered pork tenderloin to sautéed duck breast, shiitake mushrooms, and wild rice. The atmosphere is friendly and casual, and the display of cakes and pies will have the whole family eager for dessert. *$$; MC, V; checks OK; breakfast, lunch, dinner every day; beer and wine; no reservations; corner of E Broadway.* &

LODGINGS

Campbell House / ★★★

252 PEARL ST, EUGENE; 541/343-1119
This city inn was built in 1892 and was restored as a huge and luxurious bed-and-breakfast inn. Each of the 18 rooms shine with old-world charm (four-poster beds, high ceilings, dormer windows) and include private baths and modern amenities. For a special occasion, reserve the Dr. Eva Johnson Suite, with a bathroom alcove and a two-person jetted tub. The Celeste Cottage is a house next door. If you like the personalized service of a B and B but don't like to feel hovered over, this inn is for you. *$$–$$$$; AE, DC, DIS, MC, V; no checks; www.campbellhouse.com; 2 blocks north of public market.* &

Excelsior Inn / ★★

754 E 13TH AVE, EUGENE; 541/342-6963 OR 800/321-6963
This European-style inn sits two blocks from the university. Each of the 14 rooms is named for a composer and features hardwood floors, arched windows, and a marble-and-tile bath with fluffy towels. There are rooms for a range of budgets. Two rooms have Jacuzzi tubs; most are small without views, and the reception at the alley entrance can be uncertain; you may have to chase down an innkeeper at the attached restaurant. *$–$$$$; AE, DC, DIS, MC, V; no checks; www.excelsiorinn.com; across from Sacred Heart Medical Center.* ♿

Hilton Eugene and Conference Center / ★

66 E 6TH AVE, EUGENE; 541/342-2000 OR 800/937-6660
The Hilton works well as a convenient home base for exploring Eugene. Most rooms have views of either the city or Skinner Butte. There's a small indoor pool and sauna, Jacuzzi, fitness room, bike rentals, and on-site Hertz rental car office. The lobby, bar, and attached Big River Grille, which specializes in seafood, have tastefully playful art and decor. *$$–$$$; AE, DC, DIS, MC, V; checks OK; www.eugene.hilton.com; exit 194B off I-5, next to Hult Center.* ♿

Secret Garden / ★★

1910 UNIVERSITY ST, EUGENE; 541/484-6755 OR 888/484-6755
This 1910 farmhouse is now an airy, enchanting 10-room inn with art and antiques that brings to mind the Edwardian era from which the novel of the same name sprung. Each room takes cues from the garden, from the rusticity of the Barn Owl room to the refinement of the Scented Garden room. Fix a cup of tea in the sitting room, or lounge in the great room, where you may meet the house dog or a guest playing the piano. Depending on the university's schedule, the neighborhood can get a little rowdy. *$$–$$$$; AE, DIS, MC, V; checks OK; www.secretgardenbbinn.com; 1 block south of UO campus.* ♿

Valley River Inn

1000 VALLEY RIVER WY, EUGENE; 541/687-0123 OR 800/543-8266
While this low-profile hotel sounds as though it may be a retreat, it is actually next to a large shopping mall. However, the hotel itself faces the Willamette River. With a pretty inner courtyard, lovely plantings, and an inviting pool, this sprawling complex creates a world of its own. All 257 large rooms were recently renovated, with the best ones facing the river. The inn's restaurant, Sweetwaters, has a nice outdoor dining area overlooking the river and frequently hosts live music. *$$$–$$$$; AE, DC, DIS, MC, V; checks OK; www.valleyriverinn.com; exit 194B off I-5.* ♿

NORTHERN
OREGON COAST

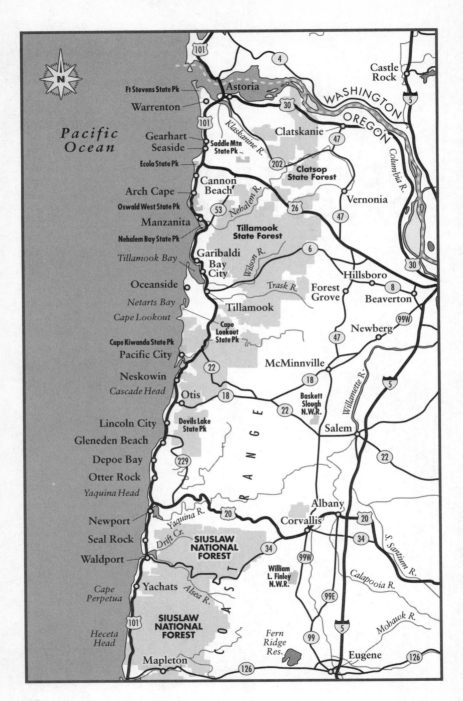

NORTHERN OREGON COAST

From Astoria to Yachats—the mouth of the Columbia to Cape Perpetua—the Northern Oregon Coast is marked with a spectacular diversity of awe-inspiring landscapes.

Thanks to Oregon's unique "beach bill," public access to the shoreline is guaranteed. And that pristine coastline beauty—from the tiny towns of Gearhart and Manzanita to bustling areas of Newport and Lincoln City—is evident throughout the North Coast. It is that very beauty that attracts visitors by the droves. Though everyone comes to escape urban evils, fast-food franchises, big-box retailers, and corporate chains are numerous here. Summer traffic through Seaside, or between Lincoln City and Newport, can be a real challenge.

ACCESS AND INFORMATION

Driving is your best bet to and from the Northern Oregon Coast. From Portland, take US Highway 26 west to its intersection with **US HIGHWAY 101** at the Cannon Beach junction. US Highway 101 is the only route along Oregon's coast. The **STATE WELCOME CENTER** (111 W Marine Dr, Astoria; 503/325-6311 or 800/875-6807) is a good starting point.

Bus and air service is limited. Check with **GREYHOUND** (800/231-2222; www.greyhound.com) or the **GREATER NEWPORT CHAMBER OF COMMERCE** (555 SW Coast Hwy, Newport; 541/265-8801 or 800/262-7844).

North Coast weather is rainy in winter and mostly dry in summer (July–Sept) but rarely hot. Tourist season runs from spring break in late March to the onset of the wet season, usually mid- to late October.

Astoria

Surrounded by water—the Columbia River to the north, Youngs Bay to the south, and just a few miles from the Pacific Ocean—Astoria is the oldest American settlement west of the Rockies, a town steeped in history. It boasts more buildings per square foot on the National Historic Register than anywhere else in Oregon. Two hundred years ago, Lewis and Clark spent a winter just southwest of modern-day Astoria. Several years later, in 1811 John Jacob Astor's Pacific Fur Company made Fort Astoria its primary fur-trading post in the Northwest and established American claims on the land. By the late 1800s, salmon canneries, forestry, and shipping turned Astoria into a boomtown.

Boasting a genuine sense of time and place, Astoria has several worthy historical attractions, including **FORT CLATSOP NATIONAL MEMORIAL** (92343 Fort Clatsop Rd; 503/861-2471), where Lewis and Clark built their winter encampment; the **COLUMBIA RIVER MARITIME MUSEUM** (1792 Marine Dr; 503/325-2323), a first-rate museum depicting the maritime history of the area known as the "Graveyard of the Pacific"; the **CAPTAIN GEORGE FLAVEL HOUSE** (8th and Duane St; 503/325-2563), which showcases the city's ornate Queen Anne architecture; the **ASTORIA COLUMN** (follow signs to top of 16th St), which stands 125

NORTHERN OREGON COAST THREE-DAY TOUR

DAY ONE: After breakfast at the **SCHOONER TWELFTH STREET BISTRO**, spend the day exploring history in **ASTORIA**. Drive to the **ASTORIA COLUMN** to see the lay of the land, then tour several of the restored Victorian homes, such as **CAPTAIN GEORGE FLAVEL HOUSE**. Grab lunch at **T. PAUL'S URBAN CAFÉ**, then head to the **COLUMBIA RIVER MARITIME MUSEUM**. Check in at the **CANNERY PIER HOTEL** and clean up before dinner at the **SILVER SALMON GRILLE**.

DAY TWO: Hit the road south for **CANNON BEACH** and breakfast at the **LAZY SUSAN CAFE** (126 N Hemlock St; 503/436-2816), a homey locals' hangout with robust meals. Browse the **SHOPS AND GALLERIES** along Hemlock Street. Next, drive a few miles south to **MANZANITA** for lunch-to-go from **BREAD**

---

feet tall and has 164 steps, offering the city's best views; and the **ASTORIA RIVERFRONT TROLLEY** (503/325-6311), a refurbished 1913 streetcar—for only $1, passengers can ride from the Port of Astoria to the East Mooring Basin.

But for all its noteworthy past, this town isn't just for history buffs. A city of 10,000 residents, Astoria is undergoing a renaissance. New restaurants, hotels, and boutiques line the historic 1920s-era downtown, while the steep wooded hillsides are peppered with renovated Victorian homes. The once-lagging Commercial Street boasts renovated spaces, including the **LIBERTY THEATRE** (1203 Commercial St; 503/325-592), an Italian Renaissance–style structure back in business after a $8.5 million restoration.

Though Astoria has a storied past, its present is equally alluring. Local events include the beloved and busy **ASTORIA SUNDAY MARKET** (on 12th St waterfront; May–Oct) and the **FISHER POETS GATHERING**, (Feb), which celebrates the fishing life.

RESTAURANTS

Schooner Twelfth Street Bistro / ★★

360 12TH ST, ASTORIA; 503/325-7882
Husband-and-wife entrepreneurs Chris and Jennifer Holen made their mark with two highly regarded Astoria restaurants. Baked Alaska, a popular waterfront spot, was doing so well that in 2004 they opened the Schooner, a casually cosmo restaurant-lounge. Serving as restaurant for the Hotel Elliott (see review) across the street, Schooner attracts a blend of tourists and locals. Warm red hues and mahogany wood play nicely against a bank of windows. Fish tacos, buffalo burgers, and crab cakes—all generously portioned—are notable, but it's the martinis that earn the real buzz. *$$–$$$; AE, MC, V;*

OCEAN. Enjoy a picnic on the beach before heading south toward Newport, marveling at the views on the **THREE CAPES SCENIC DRIVE**. In **NEWPORT**, have dinner at **LOCAL OCEAN SEAFOODS** before retiring to **TYEE LODGE**.

DAY THREE: After your candlelit breakfast at Tyee, take a hike around the **YAQUINA HEAD OUTSTANDING AREA** (north of Agate Beach, off Hwy 101; 541/574-3100), home to Oregon's tallest lighthouse. The area boasts paved hiking trails, stunning ocean vistas, and an interpretive center. Cross town to the **HISTORIC BAY FRONT** and stroll through the shops before enjoying lunch at **LA MAISON BAKERY AND CAFE**. Afterward, drive south to **YACHATS** to relish the views at **CAPE PERPETUA SCENIC AREA**, then tour the **SEA LION CAVES**. Head back to Yachats to catch sunset cocktails at the oceanfront lounge at the **ADOBE RESORT** (1555 Hwy 101; 541/547-3141), followed by dinner and music at the **DRIFT INN**. Call it a day in a cabin at the **SHAMROCK LODGETTES**.

checks OK; breakfast Sat–Sun, lunch, dinner every day; full bar; reservations recommended; www.schoonerbistro.com; downtown. &

Silver Salmon Grille / ★★

1105 COMMERCIAL ST, ASTORIA; 503/338-6640
Visionaries Jeff and Laurie Martin remodeled the historic Fisher Building and created an upscale destination downtown. With an intimate white tablecloth–and–candles elegance, the grill is a top-tier choice garnering consistent accolades. As the name implies, salmon takes center stage, including the popular Silver Salmon Supreme, an over-the-top meal of salmon stuffed with Dungeness crab, bay shrimp, and smoked Gouda. Want more? Head next door to Silver Salmon Cellars, a wine bar. $$–$$$; AE, MC, V; checks OK; lunch, dinner every day; full bar; reservations recommended; www.silversalmongrille. com; downtown at 11th St. &

T. Paul's Urban Café / ★★

1119 COMMERCIAL ST, ASTORIA; 503/338-5133
On the sleepy Oregon coast, "urban" is relative. But T. Paul's delivers a hip and urbane vibe to counter the predictability lulling the coast. Both eclectic and original, this comfy bistro-coffeehouse blend has a loyal, if not diverse, following of artsy locals and buttoned-down professionals. Meals range from routine salads, soups, and chowder to more adventurous dishes such as crab-stuffed ravioli and chipotle pesto pasta. It's worth the risk. Linger over coffee and dessert (caramel-apple pie, creamy cheesecake). On weekends, sink into a music groove and people-peeping as local bands take the stage. $–$$; MC, V; checks OK; lunch, dinner Mon–Sat; beer and wine; no reservations; downtown at 11th St.

LODGINGS

Cannery Pier Hotel / ★★★☆

NO. 10 BASIN ST, ASTORIA; 503/325-4996 OR 800/325-4996
Astoria's newest and most ambitious hotel is built on the site of the former Union Fish Cannery. The hotel is literally on the Columbia River, at the end of a 600-foot pier directly below the soaring Astoria-Megler Bridge. The hotel deftly juxtaposes grit with luxe: exposed steel beams and wooden trusses blend seamlessly with contemporary furnishings and plush linens. All 46 rooms boast fireplaces, balconies, hardwood floors, and eye-popping river views. Book one of the deluxe rooms; these spacious studios surpass the boxy feel—and higher rates—of the one-bedroom suites. *$$$–$$$$; AE, DIS, MC, V; checks OK; www.cannerypierhotel.com; Basin St beneath Astoria-Megler Bridge.* &

Fisherman's Suites / ★★

PIER 39, 100 39TH ST, ASTORIA; 503/325-2502
In 2005, Astoria native Floyd Holcom transformed the historic Bumble Bee Cannery into an upscale but unpretentious respite. Trading a gritty past for new waterfront luxury, Fisherman's Suites occupies a small corner of a vast warehouse. With no concierge or hype and an intentionally bland exterior, the place is popular among celebrities. All three spacious suites feature commanding views of the Columbia River, but it's the Captain's digs that puts the luxe in luxury. Rich wood beams, mahogany accents, and stone finishes—combined with 270-degree views—call for riverfront cocktails and dinner parties. *$$$$; AE, DIS, MC, V; no checks; www.pier39-astoria.com; foot of 39th St.*

Hotel Elliott / ★★★

357 12TH ST, ASTORIA; 503/325-2222 OR 877/378-1924
A massive $4 million renovation transformed downtown's historic Hotel Elliott into a 32-room jewel. The recent restoration of the 1924 hotel retained the warm mahogany details and original lobby desk but vamped up the old girl with an underground wine bar, a cigar lounge, and a rooftop garden providing panoramic views of the Columbia River and the manicured Victorians peppering the hillside. Typical of early 1900s hotels, the rooms are snug but made cozy with plump duvets and heated bathroom floors. *$$–$$$$; AE, DIS, MC, V; checks OK; www.hotelelliott.com; between Commercial and Duane sts.*

Gearhart

In lovely Gearhart, old money mixes with well-heeled living in an elite enclave of elegant vacation homes. Unlike other coastal towns, Gearhart is mostly residential, and it showcases some of the best Oregon Coast architecture. The stately homes, pristine beaches, and grassy dunes are reminiscent of Cape Cod in its early days.

"Downtown" Gearhart is an overstatement: The main street features just a sprinkling of tidy businesses, most notably gourmet market **GEARHART GROCERY** (599 Pacific Way; 503/738-7312); a café (see review), and garden shop **FITZGER-ALD'S HOME & GARDEN** (738 Pacific Way; 503/717-9748). Lodgings are limited, and the one restaurant is, not surprisingly, always busy. **GEARHART GOLF LINKS** (503/738-3538), the oldest golf course in the Northwest, is an 18-hole public adventure carefully placed among the coastal dunes.

RESTAURANTS

Pacific Way Bakery & Café / ★★

> **601 PACIFIC WY, GEARHART; 503/738-0245**
> The line snaking out the door and down the block is a harbinger of gourmet treats inside this Gearhart gem. Windows wrap the corner restaurant, and friendly service creates a comfy café with the best bread, pastries, and desserts on the North Coast. As the only restaurant in downtown Gearhart (admittedly, a single intersection), the café does a brisk business. Fortunately, the food is worth the wait. Top picks include grilled halibut with mango-ginger chutney, portobello burger with roasted-red-pepper mayo, and top-notch pizzas with inspired toppings. *$$; MC, V; checks OK; lunch, dinner Thurs–Mon; beer and wine; reservations recommended; corner of Cottage Ave.*

Seaside

Seaside is the quintessential beach town serving as an affordable, family-friendly vacation destination. Long considered the rowdy cousin of its classy, quiet Gearhart neighbor, Seaside is slowly gaining respect with its revitalized downtown. New condos and luxury timeshares are bookending the increasingly enlivened historic core.

To be sure, Seaside still sports plenty of reminders of its Coney Island–like past, but it also sports wonderful landmarks. The early 1900s boardwalk, known as the **PROM**, is a 2-mile pedestrian walkway that parallels the beach. At its center is the automobile roundabout known as the Turnaround. In addition, downtown's historic Gilbert District is experiencing an overhaul.

For proof of the place's grand and unfettered past, look to the forest. Seaside is home to the **LARGEST SITKA SPRUCE** tree in the United States (3 miles east of US Hwy 101 and US Hwy 26 junction). Estimated at 750 years old, the tree is 56 feet in diameter and stands 216 feet tall.

Other outdoor attractions include the **NECANICUM RIVER**, which flows through town, where steelhead and salmon can be caught, and the nearby **QUATAT MARINE PARK** (downtown, along Necanicum River) for picnicking and free summer concerts. **SURFERS** are often spotted at "the Point" at the south edge of town. And, best of all, there's always a stretch of wide, sandy, **WALKABLE BEACH**.

RESTAURANTS

Lil' Bayou and Magnolia Lounge / ★

20 N HOLLADAY DR, SEASIDE; 503/717-0624
Crawfish, gumbo, jambalaya? This sunny Cajun-Creole restaurant seems a bit misplaced in the rain-drenched Northwest, but it's a culinary risk worth taking. In a town lacking significant dining choices, this small spot in Seaside's increasingly hip downtown really shines. A hearty menu features ample doses of authentic Louisiana-style dishes, including chowder, catfish, alligator, and muffaletta, New Orleans' signature sandwich. Leave room for dessert—sweet potato pecan pie or chocolate bourbon pie—then slide over to the restaurant's Magnolia Lounge, a bluesy setting, for live music. *$$; AE, MC, V; local checks only; lunch Fri–Sun, dinner every day; full bar; reservations recommended; www.lilbayou.com; at Broadway.* &

Seaside Coffee Roasting Company / ★

5 N HOLLADAY DR, SEASIDE; 503/717-8300
A sign on the wall says it all: "Any day is too short to drink bad coffee." You get only the good stuff at this coffeehouse with special on-site roasting. Owners Stephanie and Richard Homer offer more than 40 flavors at this warm and comfy counter-service spot in downtown's emerging Gilbert Historic District. Caffeine insiders know to skip the line at the counter and head straight to the "honesty box," an honor system that lets you pour your own cup. The fare, pastries and panini, is simple but good. Cushy upholstered chairs, stacks of magazines, and soft jazz create a relax-and-unwind vibe. *$; MC, V; local checks only; breakfast, lunch every day (closed Sun in winter); no alcohol; no reservations; www.seasidecoffee.com; at Broadway.*

LODGINGS

Inn of the Four Winds / ★★

820 N PROMENADE, SEASIDE; 503/738-9524 OR 800/818-9524
Amid the clatter of kitschy Seaside, Inn of the Four Winds is a quiet, understated find. A major renovation of this stately 1940s-era home created a fresh-scrubbed, two-story, 14-room hotel. All rooms have typical hotel amenities, along with ocean-view decks. Deluxe rooms sport bay windows but are just a bit larger than the standard rooms. For families, the first-floor suites sleep up to five and feature grassy patios for seaside lazing. But it's the location—oceanfront, on the Prom, on the sedate north end of town—that seals the deal. *$$–$$$; AE, MC, V; no checks; www. innofthefourwinds.com; 8th Ave and Downing St.*

Cannon Beach

In Oregon's hipped-up seaside town—flush with upscale restaurants, trendy boutiques, and high-end lodging—the question is not where should you go and what should you do, but how much time do you have? This tony town is packed with world-class art galleries, specialty shops, cozy cafés, and top-shelf dining.

Still, the wide, white-sand beach is the main draw. **HAYSTACK ROCK**, one of the world's largest coastal monoliths, is the town's most prominent natural wonder. Rising 235 feet out of the sea, Haystack Rock is a protected marine garden.

ECOLA STATE PARK (on town's north end; www.oregonstateparks.org) offers views, picnic areas, and hiking trails. A mile offshore rests the **TILLAMOOK ROCK LIGHTHOUSE**, built more than a century ago and decommissioned in 1957. Today the lighthouse stores cremated remains.

Galleries are too many to mention, but highlights include: **DRAGONFIRE GALLERY** (123 S Hemlock St; 503/436-1533), showing contemporary art, and **NORTHWEST BY NORTHWEST GALLERY** (232 N Spruce St; 503/436-0741), exhibiting fine art and crafts. For indulgence, don't miss **BRUCE'S CANDY KITCHEN** (256 S Hemlock St; 503/436-2641) for coastal sweet treats.

RESTAURANTS

Evoo—Cannon Beach Cooking School / ★★★☆

188 S HEMLOCK ST, CANNON BEACH; 503/436-8555
OR 877-436-EVOO

Evoo is an insider nod to extra virgin olive oil, the critical ingredient and epicurean start to this innovative find. A unique blend of cooking school and retail shop, Evoo provides top-shelf food entertainment. Owners-teachers Bob Neroni and Lenore Emery opened the upscale exhibition kitchen in 2004, turning their accomplished culinary skills into hands-on classes and demos during which diners enjoy up-close lessons and accomplished meals. Evoo welcomes both seasoned foodies and novice cooks. The Small Plates dinner, for example, pairs fresh, local ingredients with Oregon wines for inspirational, I-can-do-that! meals. Limited seatings of just 18 guarantee fun food adventures. *$$–$$$$; MC, V; checks OK; meals, days vary with event; wine only; reservations required; www.evoo.biz.com; corner of Taft and Hemlock sts.*

Lumberyard Rotisserie & Grill / ★★

264 3RD ST, CANNON BEACH; 503/436-0285

In a city bursting with romantic meals at heart-attack prices, this affordable, family-friendly restaurant is a welcome addition. Formerly the Cannon Beach Lumber Company, the Lumberyard retains its woodsy roots with giant timbers, hefty wood booths, and a river-rock fireplace. You'll find high-volume dining on busy weekends, so in warm weather, the patio offers a more serene option. Casual fare leads the menu, with an assorted lineup of—you guessed it—rotisserie meats, most notably organic chicken. Start with the Tillamook mac and cheese, a decadent appetizer of entrée proportions. *$$; AE, MC, V; no checks; lunch, dinner every day; full bar; no reservations; www.thelumber yardgrill.com; 3rd and Antler sts.* &

Newmans at 988 / ★★★☆

988 S HEMLOCK ST, CANNON BEACH; 503/436-1151
For nearly a decade, Cannon Beach regulars enjoyed the culinary feats of John Newman when he was executive chef at the famed Stephanie Inn. In 2006, the Culinary Institute of America grad—with wife Sandy—opened his own namesake. Housed in a small 1920s farmhouse, the restaurant's flashy yellow exterior betrays the intimate old-world ambience that glows inside. White linens, dark wood, and candlelight set the scene for standout dishes showcasing French-Italian preparations of lamb, fish, and pork. Three- and four-course prix-fixe meals are pricey—but worthy—best bets. *$$$–$$$$; MC, V; local checks only; dinner Thurs–Tues; beer and wine; reservations recommended; www.newmansat988.com; midtown at Hemlock and Harrison sts.*

LODGINGS

Ocean Lodge / ★★★

2864 S PACIFIC ST, CANNON BEACH; 503/436-2241
OR 888/777-4047
It's difficult to attract and satisfy both snuggling couples and active families, but the Ocean Lodge meets the challenge. Located at the south end of town—overlooking Haystack Rock on a primo strip of wide, sandy beach—the 37-room lodge is both a romantic retreat and kid equipped (as well as pet friendly). True to its name, the fresh and ultraclean two-story resort is lodge-cozy with floors of recycled old-growth wood, massive timbers, and comfy common spaces. Here, pampering is standard issue; every guest enjoys an in-room fireplace, Jacuzzi tub, sundeck, and light breakfast in the library. *$$$–$$$$; AE, DC, DIS, MC, V; checks OK; www.theoceanlodge.com; oceanfront, between Nelchena and Chisana sts.*

Stephanie Inn / ★★★

2740 S PACIFIC ST, CANNON BEACH; 503/436-2221
OR 800/633-3466
Named after the owner's young daughter, this 50-room hotel manages to feel intimate and cozy despite its size. Flower boxes, manicured grounds, and a spectacular on-the-beach location create a romantic, upscale splurge. Guests enjoy all the feel-good luxuries, including oversize whirlpool tubs, fireplaces, complimentary wine tasting, and an elegant, four-course dinner (for an additional charge). A chief complaint is that the inn is well aware of its stature, often resulting in unnecessary pretension. Many rooms do not offer ocean views. *$$$$; AE, DC, DIS, MC, V; checks OK; www.stephanie-inn.com; oceanfront at Matanuska St.*

Arch Cape

An enclave of manicured vacation homes 4 miles south of Cannon Beach, Arch Cape is a pocket community tucked between **HUG POINT STATE PARK** (along US Hwy 101; 800/551-6949) and **OSWALD WEST STATE PARK** (along US Hwy 101; 800/551-6949). This hideaway is nestled against an uncrowded coastline. At low tide, a stony beach turns into a soft, sandy shore with dark and dramatic monoliths in the distance.

Arch Cape has just a deli, a post office, and two choice lodgings: the ornate **ARCH CAPE HOUSE** (see review) and the **INN AT ARCH CAPE** (800/352-8034; www.innatarchcape.com), a recently renovated six-room spot less than a block from the beach.

LODGINGS

Arch Cape House / ★★

31970 E OCEAN LANE, ARCH CAPE; 503/436-2800 OR 800/436-2848
Combine an English country manor with French provincial decor, and you've got Arch Cape House, a seaside castle within a sleepy wayside town. Previously known as St. Bernards, the name was changed by owners Bob Shaw and Barbara Dau, but they retained the upscale charm of this pampered bed-and-breakfast. Each of the eight rooms—with forgivably restrained theme names such as Gauguin, Parisian, Provence—are warmly adorned with antiques. Breakfast is a three-course affair served in the sunny dining room. It's located on the east side of US Highway 101, so beach walks require a short jaunt across the highway. $$$–$$$$; AE, MC, V; checks OK; www.archcapehouse. com; across from post office.

Manzanita, Nehalem, and Wheeler

This trio of waterfront towns are referred to as Manzanita on the beach, Nehalem on the river, and Wheeler on the bay. Sleepy but sophisticated Manzanita boasts 7 miles of sandy beach. In recent years, tranquil Manzanita has begun to stir, with new restaurants and shops.

Just a few miles south of Manzanita, the quiet towns of Nehalem and Wheeler sit tucked against the beautiful Nehalem River and Bay. Both cities are experiencing fits and starts of rejuvenation.

The area is rich with outdoor opportunities. Get your bearings at **NEAHKAHNIE MOUNTAIN WAYSIDE** (1 mile north of Manzanita, along US Hwy 101) and take in majestic vistas of the area's graceful and dramatic curving shoreline. The **NEHALEM RIVER** is a calm, serene place to kayak. Rent equipment at **WHEELER ON THE BAY LODGE** (580 Marine Dr, Wheeler; 503/368-5858). **NEHALEM BAY** is a great fishing spot. Rent boats and tackle at the **WHEELER MARINA** (278 Marine Dr, Wheeler; 503-368-5780). **NEHALEM BAY STATE PARK** (off US Hwy 101, south of Manzanita; 503/368-5154) is an unusual site, offering an airstrip, a horse camp with corrals and campsites, and yurt rentals. Entry to the park is off US Highway 101 at the Bayshore junction south of Manzanita. **MANZANITA BEACH** (in Manzanita, on Ocean Rd; www.iwindsurf.com) is a popular windsurfing site, known for its reliable 18 to 24mph summer winds. Golfing is available at **MANZANITA GOLF COURSE** (Lakeview Dr; 503/368-5744), a public nine-hole course.

RESTAURANTS

Bread and Ocean / ★★

387 LANEDA AVE, MANZANITA; 503/368-5823
When owner Julie Barker closed the door on the uber-popular Blue Sky Cafe, loyal patrons wore heavy disappointment. Thankfully, Barker didn't leave the kitchen for long, launching this small but mighty artisan bakery in the heart of town. The counter-service spot was an immediate hit. And no wonder. This postage stamp–sized gem creates a variety of craft breads daily, including inspired cinnamon rolls, delicate scones, and savory rolls and baguettes. Keeping it simple and delish, Bread and Ocean has no seating but offers takeout for a picnic on the beach. *$; no credit cards; checks OK; breakfast, lunch, Wed–Sun; no alcohol; no reservations; center of town.*

Wanda's Cafe & Bakery / ★★

12870 US HWY 101, NEHALEM; 503/368-8100
Wanda's Cafe is all wink and kitsch. Decorated with a wacky collection of Americana—formica tables, dozens of old toasters, and a fish tank dressed as a television and labeled "telefishin," for example—this diner-bakery is an entertaining spot at the Nehalem bend. But it's not all show; the eats are consistently good. Breakfast and lunch feature fresh and bountiful omelets, quiches, salads, homemade soups, and an assortment of fresh baked goods. With its good value, great sense of humor, and relaxed vibe, Wanda's won't be a locals-only haunt for long. *$; no credit cards; checks OK; breakfast, lunch every day; no alcohol; no reservations; center of town.*

LODGINGS

Coast Cabins / ★★

635 LANEDA AVE, MANZANITA; 503/368-7113 OR 800/435-1269
Elegantly casual defines this set of five modern cabins set back from the beach. Combining the warmth of cedar exteriors with the stylish, clean lines of Scandinavian design, this place is a romantic retreat. Think solitude without isolation, high-end without the homogeny. Cabins have original artwork and colorful, terraced gardens. For a real splurge, the Spa Cabin is a 700-square-foot, two-level love nest complete with private sauna, spa, and sandstone patio. The downside? The cabins are six blocks from the beach and not far from the highway. *$$$–$$$$; AE, MC, V; checks OK; www.coastcabins.com; at Division St.*

The Inn at Manzanita / ★★

67 LANEDA AVE, MANZANITA; 503/368-6754
Infused with light and ocean views, this getaway located just 200 feet from the ocean and in the heart of downtown is tranquility itself. Here, the soothing sounds of surf lull and satisfy, proving that location really does matter. A mix of shingled, multilevel structures provides 13 guest rooms, each complete with spa tub, fireplace, and deck (as well as standard amenities such as robes, coffee, and wet bar). Securing a reservation at this popular spot lauded by several national publications requires long-range planning. *$$$–$$$$; MC, V; checks OK; www.oceaninnatmanzanita.com; at the beach.*

Old Wheeler Hotel / ★★

495 US HWY 101, WHEELER; 503/368-6000 OR 877/653-4683
Housed on the second floor of a storefront in the center of undiscovered Wheeler, this historic jewel experienced massive restoration in 2004. The owners took great pains to turn the 1920s structure into a charming but comfy bayfront bed-and-breakfast. All five guest rooms overlook Nehalem Bay and offer free access to a collection of American Film Institute's top 10 movies (in a nod to Winston's father, who was a Hollywood screenwriter). With its hardwood floors, claw-foot tubs, and ornate chandeliers, the hotel's mood is Victorian vacation—without the steep rates. *$–$$; AE, DIS, MC, V; no checks; www.oldwheelerhotel.com; across from bay and train depot.*

Rockaway–Twin Rocks

A seaside escape for Portlanders in the 1920s, Rockaway has lost its allure over the years to trendier beach spots. Still, what Rockaway doesn't offer in upscale boutiques or fine dining, it makes up for with 7 miles of wide, sandy beach. Several old school–style big-box motels line the shore, and dozens of oceanfront homes serve as vacation rentals. Untapped and mostly undeveloped, Rockaway is still—but likely not for long—an uncrowded and affordable beach retreat.

LODGINGS

Twin Rocks Motel / ★

7925 MINNEHAHA, ROCKAWAY BEACH; 877-355-2391
Although billed as a motel, this oceanfront lodging is really a set of five fresh-scrubbed cottages. Each individual cottage has two bedrooms and a kitchen. All but Cottage 4 have fireplaces. Best of all, this low-fuss spot is on the beach, with the sun and surf lapping at the door. Fronting a 7-mile stretch of sandy beach, this place was made for the family vacation. The downside? Area dining is a risky adventure. Stock up on groceries and fire up the barbie. *$$–$$$; no credit cards; checks OK; 1 mile south of Rockaway, on beach.*

Garibaldi, Bay City, and Tillamook

The Tillamook, Trask, Wilson, and Kilchis rivers and Dougherty Slough all pass through or near the town of Tillamook—part of a network of more than 20 rivers and streams that feed into Tillamook Bay and out to the Pacific Ocean. Garibaldi and Bay City, small towns nestled on the bay, are peppered with proof of underwater industry: fishing boats and oyster-shell mounds. To get a taste of local flavor, stop at **PACIFIC OYSTER COMPANY** (5150 Oyster Dr, Bay City; 503/377-2323) for oysters and a view.

Tillamook, with its broad expanse of green pastures, is best known as dairy land. It is home to the world-famous **TILLAMOOK COUNTY CREAMERY ASSOCIATION** plant and visitor center (4175 US Hwy 101, Tillamook; 503/842-4481 or 800/542-7290; www.tillamookcheese.com), which offers self-guided tours and tastes. Across town, check out the **TILLAMOOK AIR MUSEUM** (6030 Hangar Rd, Tillamook; 503/842-1130) a former blimp hangar showcasing restored aircrafts.

Oceanside

A quaint town carved from a cliff, Oceanside lies 8 miles west of Tillamook along **THREE CAPES SCENIC DRIVE**, a gorgeous 34-mile loop traversing a changing landscape of ocean vistas, green pastures, rolling dunes, and thickets of alder, birch, and spruce.

On the route, **CAPE MEARES STATE PARK** (just north of Oceanside) offers hiking and scenic views of Tillamook Bay and the Pacific. Walk up to and inside **CAPE MEARES LIGHTHOUSE** (503/842-2244). At only 38 feet tall, it's the shortest lighthouse in Oregon, though it stands more than 200 feet above the ocean. The Three Capes route winds along Netarts Bay before reaching **CAPE LOOKOUT STATE PARK** (13000 Whiskey Creek Rd, 11 miles southwest of Tillamook; 503/842-4981), with 212 campsites and a huge expanse of beach.

Oceanside itself is a quiet residential town crisscrossed with vacation homes. Plan ahead to secure a rental. With scant restaurants, shops, or lodging, this town is all about the ocean.

RESTAURANTS

Roseanna's Oceanside Café / ★

1490 PACIFIC ST, OCEANSIDE; 503/842-7351

Everyone loves Roseanna's, as evidenced by long lines and the number of locals lining the bar. The secret to success? Stunning tableside views of the Pacific and a long list of homemade desserts. But the real answer is the most obvious: It's the only place in town. For those willing to fork over $10 for grilled cheese sandwiches and much more for dinner entrées, this small and cheery eatery is the top choice. *$$–$$$; MC, V; checks OK; breakfast Sun, lunch, dinner Thurs–Tues; full bar; no reservations; on main street.* &

Pacific City

Just off the main drag of US Highway 101, Pacific City is a secret spot gaining momentum. With the Big Nestucca River running through it, the small town is experiencing a rush of residential development.

Pacific City has three beach accesses: **ROBERT STRAUB PARK** (800/551-6949) to the south; **PACIFIC AVENUE** in the center of town; and the most popular, **CAPE KIWANDA**—a dramatic sandstone headland—at the north end of town. The dory fleets (classic fishing boats) launch here, and surfers ride the waves.

Open to the public only for special events, the **NESTUCCA BAY NATIONAL WILDLIFE REFUGE** (south of Pacific City just off US Hwy 101; 541/867-4550) is habitat for rare wildlife, including the world's small population of Semidi Islands Aleutian cackling geese, and is the only coastal wintering population of dusky Canada geese.

In the center of town you'll find boutiques including **VILLAGE MERCHANTS** (at River Pl, 34950 Brooten Rd; 503/965-6911) for clothing and gifts, **PACIFIC CITY GALLERY** (35350 Brooten Rd; 503/965-7181) for art, and **BEACH DOG SUPPLY** (at River Pl, 34950 Brooten Rd; 503/965-6455) for canine apparel.

Go gourmet at **HARVEST FRESH RIVER PLACE DELI** (at River Pl, 34950 Brooten Rd; 503/965-0090), or settle into the **VILLAGE COFFEE SHOPPE** (34910 Brooten Rd; 503/965-7635), a homey café serving budget breakfasts.

RESTAURANTS

Grateful Bread Bakery & Restaurant / ★

34805 BROOTEN RD, PACIFIC CITY; 503/965-7337
Locals sing praises for this bright and cheery bakery-restaurant consistently dishing up good, affordable meals. Though unassuming, Grateful Bread turns out innovative fare. Breakfast standouts include challah french toast, gingerbread pancakes, and a hearty scramble of oysters, eggs, and veggies. Robust sandwiches on fresh bread highlight the lunch menu, while dinner is dominated by pizzas, pastas, and vegetarian options. The Tillamook cheddar cheese and corn chowder is a must-have. Eat in, linger on the deck, or pack a picnic for the beach. *$-$$; MC, V; checks OK; breakfast, lunch, dinner Thurs–Mon; no alcohol; no reservations; north end of Brooten Rd.*

Pelican Pub & Brewery / ★

33180 CAPE KIWANDA DR, PACIFIC CITY; 503/965-7007
Surfboards hanging from wood beams, a young laid-back staff, and the smell of hops give this brew pub a chill-on-the-beach vibe. The fare is basic sports-bar grub, but it's the brews and views that make this spot stop-worthy. Named "Small Brewpub of the Year" by the prestigious Great American Beer Festival, Pelican consistently earns top honors for its Kiwanda Cream Ale, MacPelican Scottish Style Ale, and Doryman's Dark Ale. Beer is serious fun

here; even the dessert menu suggests beer pairings. Perched on the windswept beach, it's the perfect spot to kick back and watch surfers and dory fleets. *$–$$; AE, MC, V; breakfast, lunch, dinner every day; full bar; no reservations; www.pelicanbrewery.com; on Brooten Rd.*

LODGINGS

Inn at Cape Kiwanda / ★★

33105 CAPE KIWANDA DR, PACIFIC CITY; 503/965-7001 OR 888/965-7001
Earth tones and fireplaces create a Northwestern feel throughout this 35-room hotel. Though not exactly oceanfront, every room boasts Pacific views, with the commanding Haystack Rock at the forefront. The Haystack Suite offers a romantic tub with an ocean view, two private balconies, and all the goods to entertain: espresso machine, wine chiller, and full sets of dish and glassware. Despite the nice decor and attention to detail, the inn still feels more like a homogenized hotel than a homey inn. *$$$–$$$$; AE, DIS, MC, V; no checks; www.innatcapekiwanda.com; across street from Pelican Pub.*

Neskowin

Boasting just 300 full-time residents (the population swells to 2,000 in summer), Neskowin is a small town with a concentration of tidy cottages in the center village and motels-turned-condos on its south edge. Signs of growth are evident, especially north of town on the east side of US Highway 101, where large homes spread across the hillside. Still, the diminutive town boasts just a few hotels, vacation rentals, and one restaurant.

In the center village, colorful homemade yard signs plead drivers to "slow down." And that sentiment best sums this slow and sleepy coastal town with an unspoiled coastline.

A white-sandy beach, though narrow, is walkable, and **PROPOSAL ROCK** stands as a sentinel just offshore. **CASCADE HEAD** (trailhead 2 miles south of US Hwy 101) is a temperate rain forest with miles of trails through old-growth forest. And the nearby **SITKA CENTER FOR ART AND ECOLOGY** (503/994-5485), at the southern base of Cascade Head, offers workshops.

RESTAURANTS

Hawk Creek Café / ★★

4505 SALEM AVE, NESKOWIN; 503/392-3838
Though it doesn't look like much from the outside, this bustling café reigns as the town's culinary epicenter. A cozy interior of warm wood, windows, and a woodstove brighten this pint-size place. As Neskowin's only restaurant, it's a good thing the food here shines. Along with an ambitious beer selection, top picks include wood-fired pizzas, homemade soups, hefty burgers, and generous salads. In the summer, prepare for a long wait. Even with a wraparound

deck, seating is at a premium. *$$–$$$; MC, V; checks OK; breakfast, lunch, dinner every day; beer and wine; no reservations; adjacent to Neskowin Beach Wayside.*

Lincoln City

In this city congested with visitor traffic, tourism dominates, and small businesses have all but evaporated in the wake of corporate chains. Unlike many Oregon coast destinations, Lincoln City demands car travel. Spread along both sides of bustling US Highway 101, Lincoln City is actually several towns (Cutler City, Taft, Nelscott, Delake, and Oceanlake) joined in one long sprawl.

With a mix of dated and new big-box motels, lodging is plentiful. Upscale digs, however, are rare. And it is the beach that redeems this bustle. Seven miles of wide, sandy, walkable shore stretch from Road's End (north end of town) to the peaceful shores of Siletz Bay.

Lincoln City has some real treasures. It's just that the quality spots can get lost in the din of development. **BIJOU THEATRE** (1624 NE US Hwy 101; 541/994-8255) is a historic theater showing art-house films; **BOB'S BEACH BOOKS** (1747 NW US Hwy 101; 541/994-4467) is an independent bookshop in the Oceanlake district; **CATCH THE WIND KITES** (240 NE US Hwy 101; 541/994-9500) sells hundreds of varieties for breezy shores.

Art galleries are plentiful: **FREED GALLERY** (6119 SW US Hwy 101; 541/994-5600) and **MOSSY CREEK POTTERY** (483 Immonen Rd, Gleneden Beach; 541/996-2415) among them. The **JENNIFER SEARS GLASS ART STUDIO** (4821 SW US Hwy 101; 541/996-2569) offers free glassblowing demos.

Lincoln City has a lot to digest. Stop by the **LINCOLN CITY VISITORS & CONVENTION BUREAU** (801 SW US Hwy 101; 541/994-8378, 800/452-2151) for an overview.

RESTAURANTS

Bay House / ★★★★

5911 SW US HWY 101, LINCOLN CITY; 541/996-3222
Though the Bay House has suffered the pains of an inconsistent past, owner Steve Wilson has ushered in a new era for this well-heeled destination on the south edge of town. Set on the banks of Siletz Bay, it's traditional, with tabletop candlesticks providing just enough light to read the inspired menu of Pacific Northwest meals. Chef Jesse Otero steers a menu that changes daily, featuring tender beef, local fish, and organic veggies in preparations that are fresh flavored and elegant. As always, the wine list is book-thick and *Wine Spectator*–approved. *$$$–$$$$; AE, DIS, MC, V; no checks; lunch, dinner every day; full bar; reservations recommended; www.bayhouserestaurant.com; south end of town.* &

Blackfish Café / ★★★

2733 NW US HWY 101, LINCOLN CITY; 541/996-1007
Since opening in 1999, this coastal treasure has offered an unusual blend of affordable, first-rate meals without the foodie fuss. Owned and operated by husband-wife dynamos Rob and Mary Pounding, Blackfish leads with the expertise of Rob, who for years ran the four-star, four-diamond cuisine at Salishan Lodge (see review under Gleneden Beach). Emphasizing fresh catches, vegetables, and good bread (baked fresh at Rockfish Bakery, which the Poundings opened in 2004), the menu changes each season but consistently shines. Still, Blackfish keeps it real with a stylish but comfy dining room ambience. *$$–$$$; AE, MC, V; no checks; lunch, dinner Wed–Mon (Thurs–Mon in winter), brunch on holidays; beer and wine; reservations recommended; www. blackfishcafe.com; north end of town.* ♿

LODGINGS

Inn at Spanish Head / ★★

**4009 SW US HWY 101, LINCOLN CITY;
541/994-1617 OR 800/452-8127**
Carved from a steep cliffside, this resort hotel boasts great views and premium beach access. These 125 individually owned condo units serve as vacation rentals, meaning each has its own style and decor. All are fresh and tidy, with floor-to-ceiling windows and access to an outdoor pool, a Jacuzzi, a small gym, and a game room. One-bedroom suites are the roomiest, though even the smaller bedroom and studio units have kitchenettes and elbow room. Check out the top-floor restaurant and lounge for curve-of-the-earth views stretching from Cascade Head to Siletz Bay. *$$$–$$$$; AE, DC, DIS, MC, V; checks OK; www.spanishhead.com; south end of town.*

Gleneden Beach

More an oversize wayside than a thriving town, Gleneden Beach is most known as the landmark for Salishan Lodge, a well-heeled resort accompanied by tony boutiques and art galleries. The outpost also features **EDEN HALL** (6675 Gleneden Beach Loop Rd; 541/764-3825), a stage for local music and theater, and the adjoining **SIDE DOOR CAFE** (541/764-3825), a bistro housed in Gleneden's old brick and tile factory.

LODGINGS

Salishan Lodge & Golf Resort / ★★★★

**7760 N US HWY 101, GLENEDEN BEACH;
541/764-2371 OR 888/SALISHAN**
A pioneer in swanky lodging, this sprawling resort—built in 1965—spans 750 acres on both sides of US Highway 101. And while Salishan has seen both heydays and decline, a recent multimillion-dollar renovation is working

NORTHERN OREGON COAST SPAS

When it's time to be soothed, smoothed, and renewed, wander off the beach and into a spa. Luxury day spas are rolling out all along the Northern Oregon Coast, though not quite at the pace of their urban neighbors located inland.

Serene music and a spare, Zen-like decor create a gentle ambience at **CANNON BEACH SPA** (232 N Spruce; 503/436-8772; www.cannonbeachspa.com), a top-tier spot for the ultimate unwind. Of the variety of Japanese-style treatments, the most indulgent splurge is the seemingly straightforward but rewarding Soku foot soak. A hot footbath is infused with therapeutic salts and comes with a massage.

At **DESERT SPRINGS NATURAL HEALING SPA** (422 SW 10th St, Newport; 541-574-9887; www.dshealing.com), the emphasis is all natural. From a tidy spa overlooking the Yaquina Bay, owner and herbalist Norma Anderson delivers alternative treatments such as candle waxing, energy release, reiki, and raindrop therapy. Body treatments are equally earthy.

Just when you think Salishan Resort can't get any better, they roll out a 9,000-square-foot $3.5 million spa. The **SPA AT SALISHAN** (7760 US Hwy 101, Gleneden Beach; 541/764-4300; www.salishan.com) rounds out the top-shelf amenities at this leading destination. Overlooking Siletz Bay, the contemporary building blends cedar, stone, and natural light. The indulgent menu includes seven styles of massage, a host of wraps, scrubs, manicures, and pedicure treatments. Like everything else at Salishan, relaxation carries a price.

Situated on the rocky shores of Yachats, the Overleaf Lodge has always offered a powerfully close ocean experience. With the addition of the **OVERLEAF SPA** (north end of Yachats; 541/547-4880; www.overleaflodge.com) in 2006, that invigorating beauty is now complemented with relaxation. The new 3,000-square-foot spa boasts saunas, steam baths, Vichy showers, Jacuzzis, and an exercise center. The third-story facility—easily offering the best views of any Oregon coast spa—overlooks the mighty Pacific and the 804 Trail that hugs the coastline.

—Drew Myron

hard to restore its good name. All the upscale elements are in place: a Scottish-style golf course (redesigned in 2004), tennis courts, boutiques, art galleries, three restaurants, a 10,000-bottle wine cellar, an indoor pool, a fitness center, a full-service spa (see sidebar), and 205 guest rooms tucked among forested grounds. Even with the massive overhaul, an attitude of highbrow detachment prevails. *$$$–$$$$; AE, DC, DIS, MC, V; checks OK; www. salishan.com; on US Hwy 101.*

Depoe Bay

Small but mighty, Depoe Bay has the world's smallest harbor: 350 feet wide, 750 feet long, and only 8 feet deep at mean low tide. Roughly 100 vessels moor at this harbor year-round, with many more boats visiting during the summer. Navigating the short and narrow basalt channel is daunting at best, and the journey to sea is tricky for even the most skilled sailor.

A huge seawall runs the length of the downtown core, providing optimum ocean views and sea-spray experiences. Waves run beneath lava beds, building enough pressure to spout water as high as 60 feet into the air.

Depoe Bay is billed as the whale-watching capital of the world, and a resident pod of gray whales call these waters home. The **DEPOE WHALE WATCHING CENTER** (119 SW US Hwy 101; 541/765-3304) is in the center of town. **DOCK-SIDE CHARTERS** (541/765-2545 or 800/733-8915) offers fishing expeditions and whale-watching tours.

A line of shops along US Highway 101 peddles the typical tourist jumble of taffy and T-shirts. Skip the clutter and look to the sea.

RESTAURANTS

Oceanus / ★★

177 US HWY 101, DEPOE BAY; 541/765-4553
In a pocket-size town, it's a coup to find two top-shelf restaurants side by side. Both Oceanus and Tidal Raves (see review) are graced with stellar oceanfront settings and over-the-top views. Oceanus, the newer of the two, is a small, quiet, and relaxed family-owned business. The menu is a seafood statement, with eclectic preparations and variations. For an optimum experience, reserve a table along the wall of windows. *$$–$$$; AE, MC, V; lunch, dinner Tues–Sun; beer and wine; reservations recommended; north end of town, west side of hwy.*

Tidal Raves / ★★

279 NW US HWY 101, DEPOE BAY; 541/765-2995
Straddling the gap between flip-flop casual and highbrow fussy, Tidal Raves fills the niche for moderately priced fresh seafood in a picturesque setting. Carved out of a cliffside cove, the views alone are worth the stop. Swirling surf crashes against rocks below, and at sunset the beauty is blinding. Thankfully, the food—chockablock with seafood choices—hits the mark. Thai-grilled tiger shrimp is a signature dish, and the cioppino earns accolades too. It's easily the best restaurant in town, so reservations are critical. *$$–$$$; AE, MC, V; local checks only; lunch, dinner every day (winter hours vary); beer and wine; reservations recommended; on west side of hwy.*

LODGINGS

Channel House Inn / ★★

35 ELLINGTON ST, DEPOE BAY; 541/765-2140 OR 800/447-2140
It's not especially luxurious, and the boxy exterior isn't a real charmer, but Channel House scores points for sheer drama. A true cliffhanger, the 12-room inn overlooks the narrow channel into Depoe Bay harbor. Waves crash against the rocky shoreline, and every room boasts ocean views. All 12 rooms—ranging from singles to more spacious suites—have private baths, and most have private decks and fireplaces. For a real treat, book a suite with a private outdoor spa. Romance has its price. Here, the language of love is spoken with cash. *$$$–$$$$; AE, DIS, MC, V; checks OK; www.channel house.com; south end of town.*

Newport

One of the coast's most popular tourist destinations, Newport—at first glance—is an unending stream of strip malls and stoplights. Wade through the commercial chaos to uncover the coastal gems tucked on side streets and out-of-the-way spots. In short, avoid US Highway 101. Instead, check out the artsy **NYE BEACH HISTORIC DISTRICT** (west of US Hwy 101, on 3rd St), where boutiques share the neighborhood with the **NEWPORT PERFORMING ARTS CENTER** (777 W Olive St; 541/265-2787) and the **NEWPORT VISUAL ARTS CENTER** (777 NW Beach Dr; 541/265-6540). As the name implies, this area offers easy access to an expansive stretch of unspoiled but popular beach.

Head to the east side of US Highway 101 for the **HISTORIC BAYFRONT**, where a working harbor bustles with a dizzying array of fishing fleets, souvenir shops, seafood markets, chowder houses, and a (cheesy) wax museum.

Two lighthouses grace this town: **YAQUINA HEAD OUTSTANDING NATURAL AREA AND LIGHTHOUSE** to the north (off US Hwy 101; 541/574-3100) and **YAQUINA BAY LIGHTHOUSE** (536 Bay Front St; 541/265-5679) to the south. Newport also boasts two aquariums: **HATFIELD MARINE SCIENCE CENTER** (2030 S Marine Science Dr; 541/867-0100), an Oregon State University marine research facility, and the world-class 29-acre **OREGON COAST AQUARIUM** (2820 SE Ferry Slip Rd; 541/867-3474).

RESTAURANTS

Blu Cork / ★★★

613 SW 3RD ST, NEWPORT; 541/265-2257
This hip wine bar opened in 2005 and brought a bit of Portland's Pearl District to Nye Beach. Warm, earthy hues, white tablecloths, a granite bar, and live music have got us swooning. Every weekend, this casually classy spot packs guests enjoying mid- to high-end wines, live music (local, polished jazz ensembles and folk artists), and delicious small-plate appetizers. A real family

affair, the Blu Cork grooves with the guidance of winophile Jonathon Trusty and his parents, Deborah and Bob. *$–$$; MC, V; no checks; dinner Wed–Sat; beer and wine; no reservations; in Nye Beach.* &

Local Ocean Seafoods / ★★★

213 SE BAY BLVD, NEWPORT; 541/574-7959
Zip past the clatter of tourist traps and head to Local Ocean Seafoods for fresh, affordable seafood with a harbor view and relaxed, modern vibe. This casually sophisticated fish market–restaurant serves simple but inspired headliners like fish tacos, teriyaki tuna kebabs, and roasted-garlic crab chowder. This high-energy spot opened in 2005 and shines as Newport's only modern architecture. Postmodern meets industrial cool with glass walls, stainless-steel accents, and exposed ductwork. In the summer, the glass doors slide open for alfresco dining. *$–$$; MC, V; local checks only; lunch, dinner every day; beer and wine; no reservations; www.localocean.net; east end of bayfront.*

La Maison Bakery and Café / ★★★

315 SW 9TH ST, NEWPORT; 541/265-8812
Fresh flowers, white linens, warm woods, and colorful walls set the mood at this French-country café. Tucked a few blocks east of US Highway 101, this intimate spot has just 10 tables and a bursting dessert case. Breakfast and lunch are delicious surprises at this hidden and surprisingly affordable find. Crepes are stuffed with artichokes, tomatoes, and cheese. Breakfast sandwiches feature homemade, oversize English muffins. Lunch shines too. Feast on roast pork, grilled chicken salad, or soups. *$–$$; MC, V; local checks only; breakfast, lunch Mon–Sat; beer and wine; no reservations; east side of hwy, near 10th and Lee sts.*

Saffron Salmon / ★★

859 SW BAY BLVD, NEWPORT; 541/265-8921
Dining in Newport poses a conundrum with little middle ground: Settle for mediocre diner food, or break the bank for a pricey but gourmet meal? Saffron Salmon is worth the splurge. Situated on the end of a pier (slightly removed from the row of ticky-tacky bayfront shops), this upscale restaurant offers walls of windows, contemporary design, and this-close views of Yaquina Bay. The best seats, secured with a reservation, are along the window where you'll see fishing fleets and sea lions. In the evening, couples can cozy up with dim lighting and a small but gourmet menu focused on locally harvested seafood, organic vegetables, and Oregon wines. *$$–$$$; DIS, MC, V; checks OK; lunch, dinner Thurs–Tues; beer and wine; reservations recommended; south end of bayfront.*

LODGINGS

Sylvia Beach Hotel / ★★

267 NW CLIFF ST, NEWPORT; 541/265-5428 OR 888/795-8422
With 33 guest rooms named after famous writers, this Nye Beach treasure is perfect for the literati. Though there are no televisions, radios, or phones, there's plenty of time to savor good books. The four-story hotel is situated on a 45-foot bluff above the ocean, just steps from the beach and trendy restaurants and boutiques. Built in 1910 and renovated in the 1980s, Sylvia is growing a bit long in the tooth. The well-loved hotel deserves a bit of freshening. *$$–$$$; AE, MC, V; checks OK; www.sylviabeachhotel.com; oceanfront, on Cliff St.* &

Tyee Lodge / ★★★

4925 NW WOODY WAY, NEWPORT; 541/265-8953 OR 888/553-8933
It's a relief to discover Tyee Lodge, a secluded bed-and-breakfast that skips the theme rooms and Victorian fuss in favor of relaxed, quiet comfort and great ocean views. Nestled in the trees on a cove overlooking Agate Beach, it has five rooms that feature ocean views, private baths, fireplaces, comfy chairs, and mints at the bedside. Guests are greeted with warm cookies and complimentary wine and beer. Owners Brenda and Monty Roberts are attentive but not cloying. And breakfast is a candlelit, three-course affair. *$$$; AE, DIS, MC, V; checks OK; www.tyeelodge.com; very north end of town.*

Waldport

Overshadowed by busy Newport to the north and quirky Yachats to the south, Waldport is an unsung seaside town with its own quiet beauty. The lovely Alsea River Bay, for example, is an estuary offering great clamming and fishing. Boats and equipment can be rented at **DOCK OF THE BAY MARINA** (1245 Mill St; 541/563-2003). On sunny days, hundreds of sea lions sunbathe on the sand spit beneath the stately **ALSEA BAY BRIDGE**. Built in 1937 and restored in 1991, the bridge is a beautiful example of the coast's many historic spans (see sidebar). At the south end of the bridge, the **ALSEA BAY BRIDGE INTERPRETIVE CENTER** (620 NW Spring St; 541/563-2002) presents museum-quality photos and displays of the area's transportation history.

Near the port, stop at the **SALTY DAWG BAR & GRILL** (375 Port St; 541/563-2555) for broasted chicken. Head to **ESPRESSO 101 BAKERY & DELI** (180 US Hwy 101; 541/563-3621) for hot coffee, fresh doughnuts, and local gossip.

RESTAURANTS

Vickie's Big Wheel Drive In / ★

US HWY 101 AND SPRING ST, WALDPORT; 541/563-3640
It's no showstopper from the outside, but this two-table-and-a-counter surprise is a local fave. Vickie Banes, the affable owner, drives this 1950s-era
joint, alternately taking turns at the grill and the takeout window or working
the tables (chrome and formica, of course). The entire menu (posted behind
the bar) is no-frills. The best bet is the burger basket, a thick and juicy patty
with a party of fries. Milk shakes are good too. But avoid high noon, when
the tiny place is squeezed elbow to elbow. *$; no credit cards; local checks only;
lunch, early dinner Mon–Sat; no alcohol; no reservations; north end of town
at foot of bridge.*

LODGINGS

Cliff House Bed and Breakfast / ★★

1450 SW ADAHI RD, WALDPORT; 541/563-2506
This popular bed-and-breakfast is a four-room historic home perched on a
cliff overlooking a beautiful stretch of wide, sandy beach. All the makings for
romance are in place, including a 65-foot-long oceanfront deck with hot tub.
Massages (by appointment) are administered on the private gazebo overlooking the ocean. Innkeepers Sharon and Keith Robinson have decorated with
teddy bears and antiques (four-poster beds, ornate chandeliers, and the like).
For minimalists, the decor may invoke a touch of "cutesy" claustrophobia.
*$$$; MC, V; checks OK; www.cliffhouseoregon.com; south end of town, 1
block west of hwy.*

Yachats

Small but active, Yachats is a funky, inclusive town tucked between a lush forest
and the rugged, rocky shore. Crashing waves can be heard from just about any
place in this town nestled against the earth's edge.

This village of just 650 residents—and steadily growing—is surrounded by
natural wonders and boasts three state parks: **YACHATS OCEAN ROAD STATE
NATURAL SITE, YACHATS STATE PARK,** and **SMELT SANDS STATE RECREATION
SITE**—here the **804 TRAIL** traverses north along rocky cliffs to spill onto an 8-mile
stretch of wide, sandy beach. Just 2 miles south, **CAPE PERPETUA SCENIC AREA**
(2400 US Hwy 101; 541-547-3289) is a temperate rain forest with 26 miles of
hiking trails. Nearby **HECETA HEAD LIGHTHOUSE** (800/551-6949) shines as the
brightest light on the coast. The neighboring **SEA LION CAVES** (91560 US Hwy
101; 541/547-3111) is the largest sea cave in the world. It plummets 208 feet
below the ground and is as wide as a football field.

Shopping is limited but on the rise. Check out the **WINE PLACE** (US Hwy 101 and 4th St; 541-547-5275) for an impressive selection; **JUDITH'S KITCHEN TOOLS** (next to Clark's Market; 541/547-3020); and Raindogs (162 Beach St; 866/RAIN-DOG), a modern boutique of inspired home and life decor.

RESTAURANTS

The Drift Inn / ★★★

124 US HWY 101, YACHATS; 541/547-4477

Once a dark, smoky bar for locals, the Drift Inn replaced Lester's bar and has packed a steady breakfast, lunch, and dinner crowd ever since. The down-to-earth spot (with a wonderfully attentive, if not hippy-esque, staff) is a cozy enclave reminiscent of TV's friendly neighborhood joints, à la *Cheers*. In many ways, this family-friendly spot is the centerpiece of counterculture Yachats. The eclectic menu—burgers, salads, pasta, steaks—is combined with nightly live music for a groovy vibe. Though weekends and summer season deliver crowds, the bar-side wait is bearable. *$–$$$; MC, V; checks OK; breakfast, lunch, dinner every day; full bar; no reservations; www.the-drift-inn. com; center of town.*

Green Salmon Coffee House / ★★

220 US HWY 101, YACHATS; 541/547-3077

Though the name conjures images of moldy fish, the Green Salmon is nothing but fresh and natural. Here, "green" refers to environmental practices such as solar power and low-flush toilets, along with organic coffee, plus eggs and produce harvested from local farms. Owners Deb Gisetto and Dave Thomas keep this counter-service café earthy with standouts like panini sandwiches on hearty whole-grain bread and Deb's Famous Oats (a generous bowl of warm oats and granola drizzled with honey and steamed milk). Since opening in 2005, this local hangout has hummed. *$; no credit cards; checks OK; breakfast, lunch Tues–Sun; no alcohol; no reservations; at 2nd St.* &

La Serre / ★

160 W 2ND ST, YACHATS; 541/547-3420

Once the crown—and only—jewel for fine dining in Yachats, La Serre has suffered in recent years from inconsistent meals and spotty service. Still, this experience of soft lights and relaxed dining is worth the risk. When it's good, it's very good. The menu features seafood, steaks, pasta, and crepes. For a cozy meal, skip the dining room and head for the comfy lounge, complete with bar seating, couches, and fireside dining. *$$–$$$; AE, MC, V; local checks only; dinner Wed–Mon; full bar; reservations recommended; at 2nd St.*

LODGINGS

Ocean Haven / ★

94770 US HWY 101, YACHATS; 541/547-3583
If remote is the new luxury, Ocean Haven—a two-story, five-room inn on the edge of the earth—takes the getaway lead. Located 8 miles south of Yachats and just minutes from Cape Perpetua's old-growth forest, here every room boasts oceanfront drama. Though the decor is not fancy, it is tidy, and the rates are affordable. Eco-focused owners Bill James and Christie DeMoll have banned pets, smoking, and Hummers. There are no phones, televisions, or Internet, either. Even the minigrocery is stocked with organic meals, with proceeds going to ocean-conservation groups. *$$; AE, DIS, MC, V; no checks; www.oceanhaven.com; 8 miles south of town.*

Overleaf Lodge / ★★★

2055 US HWY 101, YACHATS; 541/547-4880 OR 800/338-0507
This three-story, 54-room hotel hugs the rocky coastline and offers ocean-front drama from every room. The surf practically churns at your bedside, and the neighboring walking trail yields tide-pool explorations. Easily the most modern of all Yachats accommodations, the Overleaf—with whirlpool tubs, soft robes, fireplaces, and picture windows—is targeted for couples seeking a seaside escape. While the rooms are all tastefully decorated in earth tones, there is a somewhat processed quality that feels more corporate chain than comfy lodge. An expansion in 2006 provided additional rooms, an exercise room, and a 3,000-square-foot spa (see sidebar). *$$$–$$$$; AE, DIS, MC, V; no checks; www.overleaflodge.com; north end of town.* &

Shamrock Lodgettes / ★★★

2055 US HWY 101, YACHATS; 541/547-3312 OR 800/845-5028
It's the parklike oceanfront setting that makes the Shamrock shine. This gem is situated on five serene acres at the mouth of Yachats Bay, where the river meets the sea. Rooms spill onto a sandy beach and the picturesque bay. Accommodations are a mixed bag of 1950s-era knotty-pine cabins and mod-ern motel rooms (many with kitchenettes). The guest-room decor is equally eclectic, ranging from kitschy cabin to colorful contemporary. An expansion in 2006 added two new cabins with large decks, kitchenettes, fireplaces, and peeks of the Pacific. *$$–$$$$; AE, MC, V; no checks; www.shamrocklodgettes. com; south of bridge.*

SOUTHERN
OREGON COAST

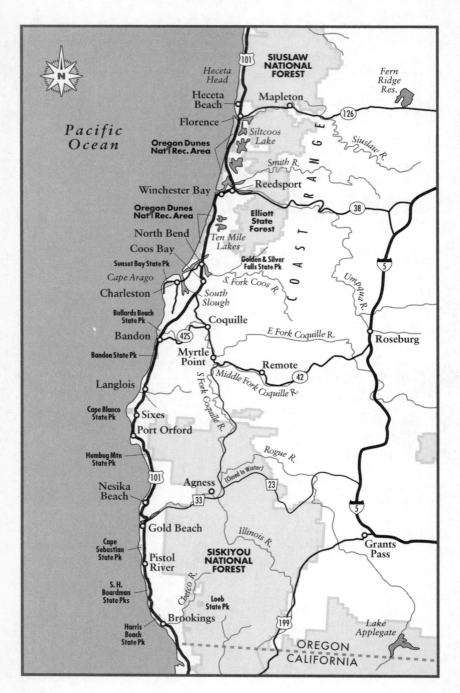

Pacific Ocean

SIUSLAW NATIONAL FOREST

Heceta Head

Heceta Beach

Mapleton

Florence

Fern Ridge Res.

Oregon Dunes Nat'l Rec. Area

Siltcoos Lake

Smith R.

Siuslaw R.

Winchester Bay

Reedsport

Oregon Dunes Nat'l Rec. Area

North Bend

Coos Bay

Sunset Bay State Pk

Cape Arago

Charleston

Elliott State Forest

Ten Mile Lakes

Golden & Silver Falls State Pk

S. Fork Coos R.

South Slough

Bullards Beach State Pk

Coquille

E Fork Coquille R.

Roseburg

Bandon

Bandon State Pk

Myrtle Point

Remote

Langlois

S Fork Coquille R.

Middle Fork Coquille R.

Cape Blanco State Pk

Sixes

Port Orford

Humbug Mtn State Pk

Rogue R.

Agness

(Closed in Winter)

Nesika Beach

Gold Beach

Cape Sebastian State Pk

Illinois R.

SISKIYOU NATIONAL FOREST

Grants Pass

Pistol River

S. H. Boardman State Pks

Chetco R.

Loeb State Pk

Harris Beach State Pk

Brookings

Lake Applegate

OREGON
CALIFORNIA

COAST RANGE

Umpqua R.

SOUTHERN OREGON COAST

Unexplored, unbelievable. Put simply, the south coast is unspoiled. Isolated from urban cores and largely undeveloped, this 150-mile stretch of stunning coastline is marked by just a handful of small communities. The eight major towns are historic seaports situated near the mouth of rivers. Given their distance from urban centers (eight-hour drives from either Portland or San Francisco), these cities are not as dependent on tourism as north coast towns. The south coast thrives—and sometimes struggles—with its remote location.

ACCESS AND INFORMATION

US HIGHWAY 101 follows the Pacific coastline from Washington to Southern California, linking most of the towns along the Southern Oregon Coast. From Interstate 5, four scenic, paved, two-lane roads follow rivers west to the south coast: from Eugene, **STATE ROUTE 126** follows the Siuslaw River to Florence; from Drain, **STATE ROUTE 38** follows the Umpqua River to Reedsport; from Roseburg, **STATE ROUTE 42** follows the Coquille River to Bandon and Coos Bay; and from Grants Pass, **US HIGHWAY 199** follows the Smith River, then cuts through the redwoods and dips into Northern California near the Oregon border south of Brookings.

Air service between Portland and North Bend is offered on **HORIZON AIR** (800/547-9308). **GREYHOUND** (800/231-2222; www.greyhound.com) offers limited bus service.

Florence

Unlike the trademark rugged coastline to the north, Florence marks the northern edge of a sweeping sand-dune landscape. The **OREGON DUNES NATIONAL REC-REATION AREA** (541/ 750-7234) begins here: 32,000 acres of mountainous sand dunes that stretch 40 miles south to Coos Bay. To get the real flavor of this unique ecosystem, head to the **OREGON DUNES OVERLOOK** (on US Hwy 101, 11 miles south of town).

Once you're oriented, venture to **SAND MASTER PARK** (87542 US Hwy 101, Florence; 541/997-6006), the world's first sandboard park. Or head to **JESSIE M. HONEYMAN STATE PARK** (US 101, 3 miles S of Florence; 800/551-6949; www.oregonstateparks.org/park_134.php), the second-largest overnight campground in the state, with 2 miles of sand dunes. Sand isn't the only terrain here. Several large freshwater lakes provide premium fishing, kayaking, and boating. Sandboard and kayak rentals are available at **CENTRAL COAST WATERSPORTS** (1901 US Hwy 101; 541/997-1812).

DARLINGTONIA BOTANICAL WAYSIDE (5 miles north of town, on east side of US Hwy 101) is a bog featuring *Darlingtonia californica*, pitcher plants with unusual burgundy flowers that bloom in May and devour insects.

In recent years, Florence has exploded as a retirement destination. A moderate climate, reliable health-care facilities, and a small-town pace has drawn senior

SOUTHERN OREGON COAST THREE-DAY TOUR

DAY ONE: After staying the night at **HECETA HEAD LIGHTHOUSE**, belly up for the seven-course breakfast, then head to the **SEA LION CAVES**, a natural habitat with ocean panoramas. Back in Florence, stroll through the riverfront shops in **OLD TOWN** and savor a lunch of burgers and sandwiches on the riverfront deck at **TRAVELER'S COVE** (1362 Bay St; 541/997-6845) before hitting **JESSIE M. HONEYMAN STATE PARK** to sandboard and swim. Tired but satisfied, enjoy an evening drive south along US Highway 101 toward Coos Bay, stopping in North Bend for dinner at **CAFE MEDITERRANEAN** before settling in at the **COOS BAY MANOR HOUSE BED & BREAKFAST**.

DAY TWO: After breakfast at Coos Bay Manor, continue south to the harbor village of Charleston, southwest of Coos Bay on Cape Arago Highway. Pack some picnic fixings at **SEA BASKET** (3502 Kingfisher Rd; 541/888-5711) before heading to **SUNSET BAY** and **SHORE ACRES STATE PARKS**. After your oceanside

citizens making Florence their new home. At the same time, the town is growing as an affordable, family-focused vacation spot. While US Highway 101 is strewn with a strip mall–like atmosphere, the city itself is actually dotted with out-of-the-way gems. The best of these finds are in **OLD TOWN**, a district of unique restaurants and shops along the **SIUSLAW RIVER**.

RESTAURANTS

Pomodori's / ★★★

1415 7TH ST, FLORENCE; 541/902-2525
When John Bartow and Jeffrey Lindow took over the popular Pomodori's in 2005, they didn't miss a beat. This charming spot off the beaten path enjoys a robust local following. And though *pomodori* is Italian for "tomatoes," you won't find any sloppy red sauce here. Chef John has a deliberate but delicate touch, turning out Northern Italian–Mediterranean–style dishes that lean on basil, pine nuts, sun-dried tomatoes, kalamata olives, and white-wine infusions. The focus is pure, fresh flavor, as evidenced in a range of seafood, chicken, pork, and beef innovations. Lunch features equally satisfying, though more casual, fare. *$$–$$$; MC, V; no checks; lunch, dinner Tues–Sat; full bar; reservations recommended; off US Hwy 101.* &

Thai Talay / ★★

2515 US HWY 101, FLORENCE; 541/997-7227
From the four-lane bustle of US Highway 101, Thai Talay doesn't boast much curb appeal. Those willing to risk the strip-mall appearance are rewarded with the south coast's best Thai dishes, served up in a tidy, no-fuss setting.

explorations and lunch, head south to Bandon, where golfers will want to play the world-class courses at **BANDON DUNES GOLF RESORT**, while others can tool through **OLD TOWN** shops and riverfront or take in a tour of the **CRANBERRY BOGS**. Enjoy an early dinner at **WILD ROSE**, then unwind at **A BANDON INN**.

DAY THREE: Stop at **2 LOONS CAFE** (120 2nd St; 541/347-3750) for coffee and pastries before heading south for a hike along Cape Blanco. On the way, stop at the **LANGLOIS MARKET & DELI** (48444 US Hwy 101; 541/348-2476) for picnic fixings. Hike at **CAPE BLANCO STATE PARK**, the westernmost point along the Oregon coast, then refuel with a picnic and take in the lighthouse, historic house, and rugged shoreline. For those ready for a real getaway, continue just a short way south to Port Orford for dinner at **PORT ORFORD BREADWORKS**, then relax at **WILDSPRING GUEST HABITAT**. Or venture farther south to Gold Beach and head for the **TU TU' TUN LODGE**, an elegant Rogue River resort, with a stop for dinner first at **CROW'S NEST** or **SPINNER'S**.

The thick menu—nearly 100 options—presents so many choices and nearly any pick is a fine one. The curries are always a good bet, though they tend to be hot, so order accordingly. Also try the Tom Kha, a rich coconut-milk soup with lemongrass, chili, cilantro, and more. The unassuming spot is so popular that it has spawned additional restaurants in Bandon and Newport. *$–$$; MC, V; no checks; lunch, dinner Tues–Sun; beer and wine; no reservations; north end of town.* &

Waterfront Depot Restaurant & Bar / ★★

1252 BAY ST, FLORENCE; 541/902-9100
Tucked along the Siuslaw River in Old Town, this treasure dates back to 1913 when it served as the train depot for nearby Mapleton. Transformed into a restaurant in 2004, its historic flavor was retained by keeping the original wood flooring and adding an elegant pub decor of deep brown and purple hues. A comfy wood bar consumes nearly half the busy dining room, and it is the perfect perch for sampling more than 30 wines or gourmet martinis. Locals pack this place every night—drawn, no doubt, by the impressive tapas menu, affordable entrées, and the sit-and-stay-awhile vibe. *$–$$; MC, V; local checks only; dinner every day; full bar; reservations recommended; on Bay Street in Old Town.*

BEACONS OF LIGHT

The Oregon Coast boasts numerous historic lighthouses standing as icons along the Pacific shore. In varying sizes, statures, and working conditions, the beacons serve as reminders of the state's treacherous maritime past. Most offer walking tours, interpretive trails, and—best of all—fantastic views.

CAPE DISAPPOINTMENT, near Astoria, is the oldest lighthouse in the Northwest, built to warn boaters of the dangerous entrance to the Columbia River. Even with the lighthouse's beacon, hundreds of ships were lost in what is called the "graveyard of the Pacific."

TILLAMOOK ROCK LIGHTHOUSE sits on a rock outcrop 2 miles offshore (the state's only offshore lighthouse) visible from both Seaside and Cannon Beach. Though decommissioned in 1957, the light has a second, er, life as a columbarium (a place where cremated remains are stored).

Standing just 38 feet tall, CAPE MEARES LIGHTHOUSE (10 miles west of Tillamook on the Three Capes Scenic Loop) is the shortest in Oregon, though it sits more than 200 feet above the ocean. When it was lit, its beacon was visible for more than 23 miles. A modern beacon has replaced the old beacon (which sits just behind the new one), though the original sentinel still operates as an interpretive center.

Newport has two lighthouses. YAQUINA HEAD LIGHTHOUSE, rising a stately 93 feet, is the tallest on the Oregon coast and stands 162 feet above sea level. A major face-lift in 2006 keeps this Newport lighthouse in working order. The

LODGINGS

Edwin K Bed and Breakfast / ★★

1155 BAY ST, FLORENCE; 541/997-8360 OR 800/833-9465

Florence is a black hole for good motels, but a handful of bed-and-breakfasts nicely fill the gap. A top pick is the Edwin K, a tidy Craftsman-style home set against the Siuslaw River on the western edge of Old Town. Built in 1914 (by one of Florence's founders), the formal home shines with Douglas fir details, antiques, wool rugs, and chandeliers. All six guest rooms have private baths. A roomy one-bedroom apartment and a spacious two-bedroom cottage are also available. Innkeepers Marv and Laurie VandeStreek serve a five-course breakfast on china and crystal. *$$$; DIS, MC, V; checks OK; www.edwink. com; on Bay St on west end of Old Town.*

nearby **YAQUINA BAY LIGHTHOUSE**, located on the north end of the Yaquina Bay State Recreation Site, provides a nautical backdrop but was in service for only a few years before being replaced by Yaquina Head Lighthouse.

Located on a cliffside, the picturesque **HECETA HEAD LIGHTHOUSE** north of Florence shines the brightest light on the Oregon coast. The historic assistant lightkeeper's house now operates as an interpretive center and bed-and-breakfast (see review).

The **UMPQUA RIVER LIGHTHOUSE** looms above the entrance to Winchester Bay—a midsize working harbor. The 65-foot tower contains a distinctive lens that emits a red and white flash. Tours of the lighthouse and adjacent museum are offered in the summer.

CAPE ARAGO LIGHTHOUSE, located 12 miles southwest of North Bend and Coos Bay, emits a unique foghorn. Though the lighthouse is not open to the public, views are good from Sunset Bay State Park south of the lighthouse.

Although it was decommissioned in 1939, the **COQUILLE RIVER LIGHTHOUSE** near Bandon was restored in 1979 to serve as an interpretive center. Park staff and volunteers offer year-round tours of the tower watch room.

CAPE BLANCO LIGHTHOUSE, 9 miles north of Port Orford, towers as the most westerly point in the continental United States. The oldest standing lighthouse on the Oregon coast, its dramatic clifftop location provides a watch tower for wildlife viewing below.

—Drew Myron

Heceta Lighthouse Bed & Breakfast / ★★★

**92072 US HWY 101, BETWEEN FLORENCE
AND YACHATS; 541/547-3696**

Set on a rugged cliffside 400 feet above the ocean, Heceta Head's lighthouse beams the brightest beacon on the Oregon coast. The historic Victorian home here is one of the last remaining lightkeeper's cottages on the West Coast, and it now operates as an interpretive center by day and a B and B by night. With its six cozy rooms, stellar ocean views, and walking trails that lead to the lighthouse and beach, staying here is a rare and special experience. There are no TVs or phones, but the romance factor is high, particularly with nighttime access to the lighthouse. The Mariner rooms offer the best views and privacy. And breakfast is a decadent, two-hour, seven-course affair. *$$$; AE, DIS, MC, V; no checks; hecetalighthouse.com.*

Gardiner, Reedsport, and Winchester Bay

Once bustling with mill activity, this trio of small towns now sags with the decline of the timber industry. The saving grace is the area's new perspective on the advantages of a recreation-guided economy, boosted by the 50-mile stretch that comprises the spectacular **OREGON DUNES NATIONAL RECREATION AREA**. Here, the coastal landscape gives way to surreal 500-foot-high rolling dunes and beach grass with a forest boundary. As a "designated ATV area," the region roars with RV parks and three- and four-wheeler enthusiasts.

In Reedsport, the **UMPQUA DISCOVERY CENTER MUSEUM** (409 Riverfront Way, Reedsport; 541/271-4816) features a weather station and exhibits. The **UMPQUA RIVER LIGHTHOUSE** (1020 Lighthuse Way, Winchester Bay; 541/271-4631) looms above the entrance to Winchester Bay—a midsize working harbor. The 65-foot tower contains a distinctive lens that emits a red and white flash. Tours of the lighthouse and museum are offered May though September.

North Bend, Coos Bay, and Charleston

The most industrial communities on the coast—North Bend, Coos Bay, and Charleston—blend together to create the somewhat nondescript bay area. Sadly, the area suffers from a numbing sprawl of traffic, prolific retail chains, tired sawmills, and rusted shipyards lining what could one day be a stunning waterfront draw. Still, for those looking to counter the north coast's heavy tourism vibe, the Bay Area is evidence of an active, working coast as the regions make the slow transition from a resource extraction–based economy to a service- and recreation-oriented one.

The town of Coos Bay—at 15,000 residents, the coast's largest city—is situated slightly inland with the bay wrapping both sides of the city, providing extensive waterfront, albeit underutilized and unappreciated. High-end homes and major renovations are increasingly emerging along the highlands and shorelines of Coos Bay neighborhoods.

Despite the buzz of sprawl, the area is not without its natural wonders. A string of state parks line the dramatic shore: traveling south of the Cape Arago Highway, your first stop is **SUNSET BAY STATE PARK** (12 miles southwest of Coos Bay; 541/888-3778). It offers year-round camping and has a bowl-shaped cove with 50-foot cliffs on either side. A few miles south, **SHORE ACRES STATE PARK** (541/888-3732) boasts a cliffside botanical garden with an impressive display of native and exotic plants. Continuing south, **CAPE ARAGO STATE PARK** (541/888-3778) overlooks the **OREGON ISLANDS NATIONAL WILDLIFE REFUGE** (541/867-4550), home to seabirds, seals, and sea lions.

RESTAURANTS

Cafe Mediterranean / ★★

1860 UNION ST, NORTH BEND; 541/756-2299
Celebrity chef Rachel Ray filmed her famed "$40 a Day" segment at this friendly, family-style café in historic North Bend. And it's no wonder. Chef-owner Sami Abboud—a former Lebanese pop star who emigrated to the United States in the late 1990s—serves up the real deal: gyros, spanakopita, kebabs, lentils, and—the best bet—chicken *shawerma* sandwich. In a city lacking dining diversity, this relaxed café is a welcome change from the typical fish-and-chips fare. Abboud also owns Euros, a more formal dining option in Coos Bay. *$–$$; MC, V; no checks; lunch, dinner Mon–Sat; beer and wine; no reservations; www.cafemediterranean.net; at California St.*

LODGINGS

Coos Bay Manor Bed and Breakfast / ★

955 S 5TH ST, COOS BAY; 541/269-1224 OR 800/269-1224
A family-friendly B and B is a rare find; most attempt a romantic ambience with strict no-kidlet policies. This stately Victorian welcomes mannered children and pets—and at no extra charge. Still, this grand 1912 colonial-style home is not a romper room. Set on a beautifully landscaped residential street with waterfront views, the home sparkles with tall ceilings, spacious rooms, a baby grand piano, and antiques. There are five rooms (three with private baths), including a family suite that adjoins two rooms. In warm weather, hosts Pam and Bill Bate serve breakfast on the second-floor balcony. *$$$; AE, MC, V; checks OK; www.coosbaymanor.com; 4 blocks above waterfront.*

The Old Tower House Bed and Breakfast / ★★

476 NEWMARK AVE, COOS BAY; 541/888-6058
This historic Gothic Revival–style home built in 1872 is situated in the appealing historic Empire District (a once-bustling area that seems to be showing signs—albeit slow—of reemergence). In the main house, the three guest rooms share two baths, while a more spacious cottage tucked behind the home has its own private entry. Innkeepers Tom and Stephanie Kramer celebrate the past with a decor heavy in antiques and lace, and they serve a gourmet breakfast (crème brûlée french toast, for example) on the veranda or in the formal dining room overlooking the bay. *$$–$$$; DIS, MC, V; checks OK; www.oldtowerhouse.com; take Charleston exit from downtown.*

Bandon

In recent years, Bandon has been called "the town that golf discovered." And it's true that the three world-class golf courses at **BANDON DUNES GOLF RESORT** on the north end of town (see review)—along with the nine-hole **BANDON FACE ROCK GOLF COURSE** (3235 Beach Loop Rd; 541/347-3818)—have created a micro-economy within a town of not quite 3,000 residents. Located at the mouth of the **COQUILLE RIVER**, Bandon is booming.

Evidence is everywhere. Top-tier hotels and specialized inns now cater to a more sophisticated traveler. **OLD TOWN**, a historic district along the Coquille River, is teeming with bistros, cafés, and shops. And to the south, the **OCEAN SPRAY CRANBERRY COOPERATIVE** and other farmers are flush with bogs producing millions of dollars worth of cranberries each year. The prolific crop has ranked Bandon as the state's cranberry capital. The **CRANBERRY BOGS**, with their vivid burgundy hue, are big business and an unusual source of agri-entertainment. The annual **BANDON CRANBERRY FESTIVAL** (541/347-9619) is held in September. Tours and tastings are available at **FABER FARMS** (off Hwy 42 at 54980 Morrison Rd; 541/347-1166). And the **GARDEN PARTY** (east of town on SR 42 S; 541/347-3020) is a cranberry farm serving pie and tea in a serene garden setting.

Along with economic health, Bandon offers a majestic, moody coastline best accessed from the south jetty in town or from **FACE ROCK VIEWPOINT** on **BEACH LOOP ROAD**. The scenic route parallels the ocean with views of the weather-sculpted rock formations and is an excellent alternative to congested US Highway 101. Two miles north of Bandon, **BULLARDS BEACH STATE PARK** (541/347-2209) offers trails that lead to uncrowded beaches. From Bullards, stroll to the **COQUILLE RIVER LIGHTHOUSE**, built in 1896, decommissioned in 1939, and now the subject of a major restoration.

RESTAURANTS

Alloro Wine Bar & Restaurant / ★★

375 2ND ST, BANDON; 541/347-1850
Debuting in 2006, snappy Alloro wows this seaside town with old-world Italian meals and top-shelf wines in a contemporary setting. Appropriately situated in Old Town, this small but tony *enoteca* is the work of owners Jeremy Buck (chef) and Lian Schmidt (wine steward), who both studied in Florence, Italy. Stepping away from the spaghetti standards, the menu boasts a bevy of homemade pastas and innovative fish, chicken, and beef dishes. Lian helps guests navigate the wine options, including many of Oregon's best vintners. *$$–$$$; MC, V; local checks only; lunch, dinner Wed–Sun; beer and wine; reservations recommended; www.allorowinebar.com; Hwy 101 and 2nd St.*

Wild Rose / ★★

130 CHICAGO ST, BANDON; 541/347-4428
Like a garden in harvest, Wild Rose brims with fresh food in a small but lively space. You won't find any weeds in this tidy Old Town spot, though if you did they would be edible and organic. Taking the reins in 2004, owners Daniel and Lynn Flattley have maintained, if not increased, Rose's top ranking. Daniel works the front of the house, while Lynn prepares accomplished meals of seafood, pasta, and beef, as well as all the breads, soups, and desserts. Daily

HISTORIC BRIDGES

More than a means to get from one side to the other, Oregon's historic bridges—more than 200 across the state—are stunning architectural achievements.

Twenty of these historic beauties are concentrated along US Highway 101, providing critical and picturesque passage along the Oregon coast's dramatic 362-mile stretch. Oregon's own engineer, Conde B. McCullough, is credited with more than 500 bridges, including the series of 1930s-era bridges along US Highway 101.

McCullough created stunning spans that solved architectural challenges without sacrificing beautiful design. The elegant bridges are characterized by a variety of graceful arches, striking spires, and stately art deco details. A coastal drive offers a wonderful bridge tour. Though there are too many to mention here, a few highlights include the following.

The **YAQUINA BAY BRIDGE**, in Newport, has five concrete support decks with a high-soaring steel arch. A pedestrian plaza with winding stairways offers lookouts.

The **CAPE CREEK BRIDGE** near Heceta Head Lighthouse north of Florence features numerous columns and arches reminiscent of Roman aqueducts. The bridge stands 104 feet above the creek below.

The **SIUSLAW RIVER BRIDGE** is a steel drawbridge with beautiful art deco details. It is best viewed from Old Town Florence.

The **COOS BAY BRIDGE** (dedicated posthumously to Conde McCullough) is a cantilever truss bridge stretching a mile. When built in 1936, it ranked as the longest bridge in the Oregon highway system.

Want to know more? The **ALSEA BAY BRIDGE INTERPRETIVE CENTER** (at foot of bridge, Waldport; 541/563-2002) offers an impressive, museum-quality exhibit of Oregon's bridge legacy.

—Drew Myron

specials, such as crab ravioli or grilled salmon, are fresh caught and delicious. *$$–$$$; AE, DIS, MC, V; checks OK; dinner Thurs–Mon; full bar; reservations recommended; midblock on Chicago St.*

LODGINGS

A Bandon Inn / ★★½
56131 TOM SMITH RD, BANDON; 541/347-7000
At A Bandon Inn (get the wordplay?), guests enjoy the typical hotel swag but with personalized inn attention. Though aimed at the golfer, this new four-room getaway also offers extra amenities for nongolfers. Along with its

own putting green, the swanky digs include a private lake, an indoor pool, a Jacuzzi, and a masseuse on call. The small-scale resort located on a bluff overlooking the Coquille River sports a clean, contemporary lodge design with floor-to-ceiling windows for panoramic views. *$$$–$$$$; AE, DIS, MC, V; checks OK; www.abandoninn.com; south of Bandon Dunes, east of US Hwy 101.*

Bandon Dunes Golf Resort / ★★★☆

57744 ROUND LAKE DR, BANDON; 541/347-4380 OR 888/345-6008
Hailed as one of North America's finest golf resorts, Bandon's three Scottish-style links courses—situated along 23 miles of windswept dunes and shoreline—rank on *Golf Magazine*'s list of "Top 100 in the World." Three restaurants, two bars, and a variety of accommodations keep guests rested, fed, and on the green. The main lodge (mostly single rooms, some with views) is austere. A series of cottages tucked throughout the expansive grounds provide a more comfortable stay. Geared to a sports-minded male clientele, the place lacks the typical resort-level appointments, most notably a swimming pool, a spa, or in-room robes. *$$$–$$$$; AE, DC, DIS, MC, V; no checks; www.bandondunesgolf.com; north end of town.* &

Bandon Ocean Guesthouse Bed and Breakfast / ★★

87147 BEACH LANE, BANDON; 541/347-5124 OR 888/335-1076
Combining contemporary design with ocean views, Ocean Guesthouse (formerly Beach Street Bed and Breakfast) gives communal accommodations a good name. Eschewing the typical lace-and-tchotchke decor, hosts Sidney and Edel Zeller offer six guest rooms in their spacious, cedar-shingled home just 100 yards from the shore. In a nod to the sister city of Bandon, Ireland, rooms bear Irish names. All have private baths, and most boast fireplaces, Jacuzzi tubs, and private decks. Donegal is the roomiest, with ocean views and a private deck. Breakfast is served in the sunny dining room beside the eight-foot fireplace. *$$$; MC, V; no checks; www.bandonocean.com; ½ mile from Beach Loop Rd.* &

Port Orford

Easily likened to an early Big Sur, Port Orford seems to stand in its own private world of quiet. But even tiny Port Orford is facing development pressures as its majestic beauty and remote location gain recognition. Once a working town of lumbermen, ranchers, and fishermen, the area is steadily attracting second-homeowners and retirees.

It's not difficult to see the appeal. **CAPE BLANCO LIGHTHOUSE** in **CAPE BLANCO STATE PARK** (5 miles north of town, 6 miles west of US Hwy 101; 541/332-6774) is the oldest lighthouse and the most westerly point in the Lower 48—and the windiest station on the coast. The lighthouse, 245 feet above the ocean, and the small interpretive center are open seasonally to the public. West of the light station, a path leads to the end of the cape. The nearby **HUGHES HOUSE** (541/332-0248; www.hugheshouse.org; tours Apr–Oct) was home to the area's first non-Native settlers. **HUMBUG MOUNTAIN STATE PARK** (5 miles south of town off US Hwy 101; 541/332-6774) features a steep switchback trail to a top-of-the-world panorama at the summit.

Port Orford is one of Oregon's only true **OCEAN HARBORS**. Because the port is unprotected from strong southerly winds, fishing boats can't be moored in the harbor. Instead, fishing boats are lifted in and out of the turbulent ocean with a five-story hoist. Visitors are welcome to this unique open water port with dramatic ocean views, and fresh seafood is available right off the boat (on Dock Rd, 1 block west of Hwy. 101).

The gigantic rock promontory of **BATTLE ROCK** (center of town) dominates the waterfront shoreline. The rock marks the site of the mid-19th-century battle between the first landing party of white settlers and local Native Americans. Past the rock, a trail winds down the hillside and to the beach.

RESTAURANTS

Port Orford Breadworks / ★★

190 6TH ST, PORT ORFORD; 541/332-4022
Here, ocean vistas, red-and-white-checked tablecloths, candles burning from Chianti bottles, and affable hosts create a beachy Italian bistro vibe. After years of baking bread for scores of restaurants, Breadman (as he is called) and his wife, Nancy, hung up the dough duties in 2004 to launch their own eatery. Serving rustic Italian lunches and dinners, Breadworks features trattoria-style meals. Patrons choose from just three entrées—clam linguine, cheese ravioli, or osso buco, for example—that change weekly. The ocean views are the best in town. *$$–$$$; MC, V; checks OK; lunch Wed–Sat, dinner Wed–Sun; beer and wine; reservations recommended; www.portorfordbreadworks.com; across from Battle Rock Park.*

LODGINGS

WildSpring Guest Habitat / ★★★★

92978 CEMETERY LOOP, PORT ORFORD; 866/333-9453
Situated on the remote and rugged southern coast, this secluded 5-acre resort induces a tranquil, reverent pace. With just five cabins, it's a getaway small in scale but large in spirit. Meander hiking trails through acres of forest, relax in meditation alcoves, stroll through the walking labyrinth, or unwind in the open-air slate spa overlooking the Pacific. Built in 2004, the cabins are nestled under a canopy of trees and boast an elegant mix of sumptuous bedding, earthy hues, warm woods, and plush seating. Rather than TVs or telephones, cabins are equipped with relaxing music, soft robes, and forgiving light. *$$–$$$$; AE, MC, V; no checks; www.wildspring.com; south end of town.* &

Gold Beach

At its worst, Gold Beach has been called a strip mall set in a gorgeous place. At its best, the small but sprawling city serves as gateway to some of the state's best fishing, hiking, and white-water recreation.

Named for the old gold found here in the 19th century, Gold Beach is renowned as the town at the ocean end of the Rogue River. The shiny nuggets are gone, but the **ROGUE RIVER** still has plenty of riches for anglers. Today salmon, steelhead, and trout draw enthusiasts from all over the country.

Many visitors head inland to the 180,000-acre **KALMIOPSIS WILDERNESS AREA** (in the Siskiyou National Forest, between Gold Beach and Brookings). Maps are available at the **U.S. FOREST SERVICE** office (125 S Ellensburg Ave; 541/247-3600). Jet-boat trips are a popular way to explore the backcountry. Guides offer insight and stop to observe wildlife along the 60- to 100-mile journey up the Rogue. Outfits include **JERRY'S ROGUE RIVER JETS** (800/451-3645) and **MAIL BOAT HYDRO JETS TRIPS** (800/458-3511).

For hikers, the **OREGON COAST TRAIL** (800/525-2334) traverses headlands and remote beaches between Gold Beach and Brookings. A portion of the trail winds up and over **CAPE SEBASTIAN** (3 miles south of town, off US Hwy 101; 800/551-6949) at **CAPE SEBASTIAN STATE PARK**.

In town there are just a few choice restaurants. Upscale shopping is limited, though **GOLD BEACH BOOKS** (29707 Ellensburg Ave; 541/247-2495) offers two stories of new and used books.

RESTAURANTS

The Crow's Nest Restaurant and Lounge / ★

29850 US HWY 101, GOLD BEACH; 541/247-6837
Walk into Crow's Nest, and the bartender's got a smile and a question: beer or ashtray? Either or neither is all good at this local watering hole. Get it here: fishing reports, weather warnings, cold brews, and fresh halibut fish-and-chips. Sure, the bar and adjoining poolroom can get smoky and loud, but the cheap eats here—enjoyed against a surprising ocean view—sure beat the bloated prices at much of the area's "fine dining" choices. Looking for an elegant, well-heeled meal? Keep walking. Wanna kick back with good grub? Roost here. $–$$; MC, V; *local checks only; lunch, dinner every day; full bar; no reservations; downtown, west side of US Hwy 101.*

Spinner's Seafood, Steak & Chophouse / ★★

29430 ELLENSBURG AVE (US HWY 101), GOLD BEACH; 541/247-5160
In an attempt to hit all markets, Spinner's packs its menu with multiple choices: burgers, pasta, salmon, lobster, prime rib, filet mignon, and more. Many times the effort makes the mark, though often the results hover at average. But the setting is stellar, which no doubt explains the cars packing the lot every night. Set on the west side of US Highway 101, here every table boasts an ocean view and the sunset panorama sets a romantic mood.

Location—with views—is the golden nugget for this town's most popular spot. *$$–$$$; AE, MC, V; checks OK; lunch, dinner every day; full bar; reservations recommended; north end of town.*

LODGINGS

Ireland's Rustic Lodges / ★★

29330 ELLENSBURG AVE, GOLD BEACH;
541/247-7718 OR 877/447-3526

In a seaside town with limited public-beach access, snagging a room with a view—and a path to the beach—ranks high on the priority list. With its collection of log cabins, suites, and beach houses, Ireland's fits the bill. Situated on 19 acres of oceanfront property (it shares space with Gold Beach Inn next door), this popular spot features a parklike setting ideal for families to play. For the best views, book an upstairs suite with a fireplace and ocean vistas. But for retro charm, knotty pine cabins—though viewless—top the list. *$$–$$$$; AE, DIS, MC, V; no checks; www.irelandsrusticlodges.com; center of town.*

Tu Tu' Tun Lodge / ★★★★

96550 NORTH BANK ROGUE, GOLD BEACH;
541/247-6664 OR 800/864-6357

Set on the grassy banks of the Rogue River 7 miles inland, Tu Tu' Tun (pronounced too-TOOT-in) is a rare resort: it perfectly balances contemporary lodge decor with a tranquil outdoor setting. This is a second-generation family business; hosts Dirk and Laurie Van Zante lovingly tend the lodge built and designed by Dirk's stepfather in 1970. But in no way is this elegant hideaway dated. Among the coast's spendiest accommodations, this handsome, well-designed lodge offers 16 rooms, two suites, and two cottages—with nary a misstep among them. *$$$–$$$$; MC, V; checks OK; www.tututun.com; US Hwy 101 to Nesika Beach, then 7 miles inland along Rogue River.*

Brookings

You know you're near the California border when palm trees dot the landscape. Just 6 miles north of California, Brookings is often referred to as the Banana Belt of the Pacific Northwest, thanks to its sunny and temperate year-round climate. Winter weather is noticeably milder here than on the moody north coast. Retirees have flocked to this southern spot, and spendy new homes line the hillsides.

Unlike most of the Oregon coast towns dependent on tourism, Brookings still hums with an economy based in lumber, fishing, and service-oriented jobs. In addition, the area is North America's top provider of **EASTER LILY** bulbs. These factors create a bustling town of industry that is sadly short on fine dining and lodgings.

But the surrounding natural beauty makes this a vacation-worthy stop. To the north lie **SAMUEL H. BOARDMAN** and **HARRIS BEACH STATE PARKS** (1655

US Hwy 101; 541/469-2021). To the east are the lush **SISKIYOU MOUNTAINS**, divided by the Chetco and Winchuck rivers. Ancient redwood forests populate the south.

AZALEA PARK (just east of US Hwy 101) is great picnic spot and home to fragrant azaleas, wild strawberries, fruit trees, and violets. **MYRTLEWOOD**—pride of the Southern Oregon Coast—grows in groves at **LOEB STATE PARK** (8 miles east of town, North Bank River Rd; 541/469-2021). **REDWOOD NATURE TRAIL** is a 1-mile loop trail just a half mile past the park on the north bank of Chetco River Road.

The **PORT OF BROOKINGS HARBOR** (16408 Lower Harbor Rd; 541/469-2218) is home to commercial fishermen as well as **PLEASURE BOATERS AND SPORT FISHERMEN**. Public boat ramps and slips are available. A small public fishing pier is located near the Coast Guard station on Boat Basin Road.

RESTAURANTS

Suzie Q's Fine Dining / ★

613 CHETCO AVE, BROOKINGS; 541/412-7444
Suzie Schwarz opened this homey 10-table affair in 2004, and though she calls it "fine dining," the setting is more Mayberry than Montmartre. A gas fireplace, a pastry case of homemade goodies, and an espresso bar make things cozy. The place is always abuzz, and an attentive staff keeps the meals moving. Breakfast and lunch are best bets. The dinner menu, while expansive, seems overpriced for the setting, though the wine list is impressive. *$-$$$; MC, V; local checks only; breakfast, lunch, dinner Tues–Sat; beer and wine; reservations recommended; downtown, west side of US Hwy 101.*

LODGINGS

Chetco River Inn / ★★

21202 HIGH PRAIRIE RD, BROOKINGS; 541/251-0087 OR 800/327-2688
Eighteen miles inland and a world away, this backcountry getaway commands peace and quiet. Situated on 35 acres of private forest bordered on three sides by the wild and scenic Chetco River, this lodge defines unplugged, operating entirely on solar power, a generator, batteries, and propane. The five guest rooms and a cottage are comfortably decorated and offer varying mountain, river, and garden views. Serenity gets a boost from the inn's fragrant lavender gardens. A pristine outdoor setting—combined with rare solitude—makes this inn a real find. *$$$; MC, V; checks OK; www.chetcoriverinn. com; half-hour drive up North Bank Rd.*

SOUTHERN OREGON
AND THE CASCADES

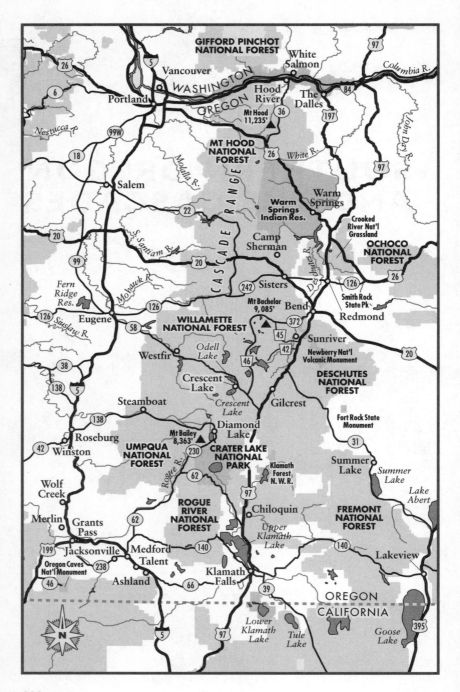

SOUTHERN OREGON AND THE CASCADES

The Cascade Mountain Range forms a massive north-to-south ridge through Oregon. These broad mountains are dominated to the east by a second, younger chain of magnificent volcanic peaks that tower over the old guard.

The Cascades—including Mounts Jefferson, Washington, Bachelor, Sisters, and Broken Top—split Oregon into two distinct regions: one wet and one dry.

ACCESS AND INFORMATION

A major north-south highway runs along each side of the Cascades: **INTERSTATE 5** on the west, and **US HIGHWAY 97** on the east. **US HIGHWAY 26**, the main east-west route between Portland and Eastern Oregon's desert, crosses the Cascades south of Mount Hood and connects with US Highway 97. Routes to Bend, the largest town on the east side of the Cascades, depart from Salem on **STATE ROUTE 22**, from Albany on **US HIGHWAY 20**, and from Eugene on **STATE ROUTE 126** (via McKenzie Pass). From Eugene, follow **STATE ROUTE 58** (via Willamette Pass) to US Highway 97 at the halfway point between Bend and Klamath Falls. The most scenic route to the east side of the mountains, open only in summer, is the narrow **OLD MCKENZIE HIGHWAY (SR 242)** from Eugene. Farther south, Crater Lake is accessible from Roseburg on **STATE ROUTE 138** (via Diamond Lake) and from Medford on **STATE ROUTE 62**. The most southerly routes are from Medford on **STATE ROUTE 140** and from Ashland on the **GREEN SPRINGS HIGHWAY (SR 66)**.

Flights between Portland and Bend-Redmond, Klamath Falls, and Medford are offered daily on **HORIZON AIR** (800/547-9308; www.horizonair.com) and other carriers. **AMTRAK** (800/USA-RAIL; www.amtrak.com), bound for California from Portland, crosses Willamette Pass into Klamath Falls, bypassing Southern Oregon with the exception of a stop in tiny Chemult.

Roseburg and the Umpqua River Valley

There are nearly a dozen wineries in this valley; take Interstate 5 south of Eugene to get here. Some of our favorites include **ABACELA WINERY** (12500 Lookingglass Rd; 541/679-6642; www.abacela.com), **GIRARDET** (895 Reston Rd; 541/679-7252; www.girardetwine.com), **HENRY ESTATE WINERY** (687 Hubbard Creek Rd, Umpqua; 541/459-5120 or 800/782-2686; www.henryestate.com), **HILL CREST VINEYARD** (240 Vineyard Lane; 541/673-3709; hillcrestvineyard.com), **SPANGLER VINEYARDS** (491 Winery Lane; 541/679-9654), and **PALOTAI VINEYARD AND WINERY** (272 Capital Lane; 541/464-0032).

Timber still plays a role in Roseburg, where you can find artifacts at the **DOUGLAS COUNTY MUSEUM OF HISTORY AND NATURAL HISTORY** (exit 123 off I-5, at fairgrounds; 541/957-7007; www.co.douglas.or.us/museum). Stop at family-

OREGON CASCADES THREE-DAY TOUR

DAY ONE: From Portland, head out early on Highway 26, stopping to learn about Native American history at the **MUSEUM AT WARM SPRINGS**. Continue south to Bend for lunch at the **DESCHUTES BREWERY & PUBLIC HOUSE**. Take a quick stroll through downtown and **DRAKE PARK** overlooking **MIRROR POND** before checking in at the **INN OF THE SEVENTH MOUNTAIN**. Pick up the **DESCHUTES RIVER TRAIL** from the inn's nature trail for a hike to Dillon or Benham Falls in summer, or venture up the road toward **MOUNT BACHELOR** for a late-afternoon Nordic ski at **VIRGINIA MEISSNER SNO-PARK** (14 miles west of Bend on Cascade Lakes Hwy; get required permit at local ski shops) in winter. After a soak in the inn's hot tub, head downtown for drinks and dinner at **MERENDA RESTAURANT AND WINE BAR**. Groove on over to the **GROVE CANTINA** for dancing and dessert.

DAY TWO: After checking out, savor coffee and a pastry at **NANCY P'S BAKING COMPANY** (1054 NW Milwaukee Ave, Bend; 541/322-8778), then sprint across the street to grab a healthy assortment of organic deli food to go at **DEVORE'S GOOD FOOD STORE AND WINE SHOP**. In summer, drive the one-lane road off County Road 21 to **PAULINA PEAK** for a view of the **NEWBERRY CALDERA, PAULINA AND EAST LAKES**, and the **BIG OBSIDIAN FLOW**; year-round, visit the **HIGH DESERT MUSEUM**. Continue south on US Highway 97

run **KRUSE FARMS** (532 Melrose Rd; 541/672-5697 or 888/575-4268; www.krusefarms.com; Apr–Jan, except holidays).

The humans are the only caged animals at the **WILDLIFE SAFARI** (SR 99, 4 miles west of I-5 via exit 119; 541/679-6761 or 800/355-4848; www.wildlifesafari.org) as they drive through 600 acres packed with species like cheetahs and giraffes.

K&R'S DRIVE INN (25 miles north of Roseburg, exit 148 off I-5; 541/849-2570) dishes out huge scoops of Umpqua ice cream and incomparable malts—try the wild blackberry; the parking lot is full from before noon till after dark.

RESTAURANTS

Roseburg Station Pub & Brewery / ★

700 SE SHERIDAN ST, ROSEBURG; 541/672-1934

You know what you're going to get at McMenamins, and this is no different in Roseburg, where the brothers have brought their robust ales, pub grub, and peculiar art to yet another historic site: Roseburg's 90-year-old train depot. This brick fortress is an oasis in the summer heat, with its covered

to either State Route 138 in summer for the north entrance to **CRATER LAKE NATIONAL PARK** or to State Route 62 just north of Klamath Falls in winter to the park's south entrance. Drink in the heady blue of Crater Lake as you enjoy a picnic on the rim. Drive westward on State Route 62 and then Interstate 5 to Ashland and check in at cozy **COWSLIP'S BELLE**. Walk through **LITHIA PARK** on your way to an early dinner at **LELA'S CAFÉ** before making a mad dash to the **OREGON SHAKESPEARE FESTIVAL** for an eight o'clock performance. Walk the four blocks back to your turned-down bed, and fall into a deep slumber.

DAY THREE: Get some laps in at the Ashland Racquet Club swimming pool (courtesy of your inn) before a leisurely breakfast back at Cowslip's Belle. Then pack your cooler with ice before heading north on State Route 99 for a self-guided wine and farm tour, starting with **RISING SUN FARMS** and **HARRY AND DAVID'S COUNTRY VILLAGE** in Medford. Detour north on Interstate 5 to the **ROGUE VALLEY CREAMERY**, then shoot south on Hanley Road to **VALLEY VIEW WINERY'S TASTING ROOM** in Jacksonville. Take a stroll through the shops on **HISTORIC CALIFORNIA STREET** and visit the **JACKSONVILLE MUSEUM**. Have a bite at **BELLA UNION** before heading west on State Route 238 and south on US Highway 199 to **FORIS VINEYARDS WINERY**. Catch the last tour of the day at **OREGON CAVES NATIONAL MONUMENT** before returning north to Grants Pass for dinner at **RIVER'S EDGE** and the final night's stay at **FLERY MANOR**.

patio overlooking the tracks for the Southern Pacific Railroad's now-defunct Shasta Route. *$; AE, DIS, MC, V; local checks only; lunch, dinner every day; full bar; no reservations; www.mcmenamins.com; downtown.* &

LODGINGS

Seven Feathers Hotel and Casino Resort / ★★

146 CHIEF MIWALETA LANE, CANYONVILLE; 800/548-8461
Owned by the Cow Creek Band of the Umpqua Tribe, this resort houses the most luxurious hotel on Oregon's I-5 corridor. Funded by 1,000-plus slots and gaming tables, the 147-room hotel (with indoor swimming pool and spa) is a bargain on weekdays. Choose a package that includes a room, breakfast, and a round at the 18-hole Myrtle Creek championship course (541/863-GOLF). The dramatic crystal-chandeliered Camas Room offers fine Northwest cuisine and an exceptional Sunday brunch. *$$; AE, DIS, MC, V; local checks only; lunch, dinner every day; full bar; www.sevenfeathers.com; 25 miles south of Roseburg.* &

Wolf Creek Inn / ★

100 FRONT ST, WOLF CREEK; 541/866-2474
Hollywood actors flocked here in the 1920s; it was purchased by the state in 1975 and is now on the National Register of Historic Places. Rooms upstairs have antique beds. The downstairs dining room, open to nonguests for lunch and dinner, features the best of both coasts, with Northwest fare and New York–style pizza. *$$; MC, V; local checks only; closed Mon–Tues Oct–May; www.thewolfcreekinn.com; 20 miles north of Grants Pass, exit 76 off I-5.* &

North Umpqua River

From Roseburg traveling east toward Diamond Lake and Crater Lake National Park, State Route 138 follows the **WILD AND SCENIC–DESIGNATED NORTH UMPQUA RIVER**. The emerald green waters of the North Umpqua are famous worldwide among fly fishers, attracting the rich and famous for nearly a century. Today the area also attracts hikers and mountain bikers to the **NORTH UMPQUA TRAIL**, which follows the river for more than 70 miles. Spectacular hikes, like the one at **FALL CREEK FALLS** (milepost 32 on SR 138), show off the North Umpqua Forest's old-growth canopy.

LODGINGS

Steamboat Inn / ★★

42705 N SR 138, STEAMBOAT; 541/498-2230 OR 800/840-8825
On the banks of the North Umpqua River sits this homey fishing lodge. Eight small cabins share a common veranda that parallels the river; each (somewhat cramped) unit has knotty pine walls and a bathroom with a soaking tub. Remarkably good family-style dinners are served in the main building by reservation; breakfast and lunch are in the café. In spring, winemakers and chefs make special meals. *$$$; MC, V; checks OK; Sat–Sun Mar–Apr and Nov–Dec, closed Jan–Feb; www.thesteamboatinn.com; 38 miles east of Roseburg.*

The Rogue River Valley

The **ROGUE RIVER** is one of most beautiful and wild rivers in Southern Oregon. Percolating out of crystal clear springs in Crater Lake National Park, the river flows from the Cascades to the Coast Range through miles of wilderness. It forms canyons, white water, and pools before spilling into the Pacific Ocean, carrying loads of steelhead and king salmon. Many rustic lodges along the river cater specifically to fly fishers and rafters. Grants Pass and nearby Merlin offer the best fishing and rafting.

Two companies offer guided river tours. **HELLGATE JETBOAT EXCURSIONS** (966 SW 6th St, Grants Pass; 541/479-7204 or 800/648-4874; www.hellgate. com) departs from the **RIVERSIDE INN** (971 SE 6th St, Grants Pass; 541/476-6873 or 800/334-4567; www.riverside-inn.com) in Grants Pass. **ORANGE TORPEDO**

TRIPS (209 Merlin Rd, Merlin; 541/479-5061; www.orangetorpedo.com) conducts popular white-water trips.

Grants Pass

The town of Grants Pass may seem as though it offers little in the way of culture or charm. But take the time to stop in its historic downtown, and you'll find some quaint and long-standing businesses, as well as a few upscale shops.

Pop into the **BLUESTONE BAKERY & COFFEE CAFÉ** (corner of 6th and D sts; 541/471-1922) for intensely rich desserts. To find out about other fun activities, stop at the **GRANTS PASS & JOSEPHINE COUNTY CHAMBER OF COMMERCE** (198 SW 6th St; 541/955-7144) downtown.

RESTAURANTS

River's Edge / ★★★

1936 ROGUE RIVER HWY (SR 99),
GRANTS PASS; 541/479-3938
There are some advantages in the Californization of Southern Oregon, and River's Edge is one of them. Transplant Kelly Hatch has graced the culinary scene with plates like Macadamia Nut Encrusted Halibut and Stuffed Meatloaf. The enthusiastic service, elegant decor, and sweeping river view don't hurt, either. *$$–$$$; AE, MC, V; no checks; lunch, dinner every day; full bar; reservations recommended; www.riversedgerestaurant.net; Grants Pass exit off I-5.* &

Summer Jo's / ★★

2315 UPPER RIVER RD LOOP, GRANTS PASS; 541/476-6882
Sitting on a 6-acre organic farm, this cheery country restaurant serves entrées like salmon with sorrel sauce or rosemary-encrusted rack of lamb with apple-mint chutney. Try the excellent Epicurean Adventure Tasting Menu and a selection from the *Wine Spectator* award–winning wine list. *$–$$; AE, MC, V; local checks only; breakfast, lunch Wed–Sun, dinner Wed–Sat (closed Jan 1–mid-Feb); full bar; reservations recommended; www.summerjo.com; exit 58 off I-5.* &

LODGINGS

Flery Manor / ★★

2000 JUMPOFF JOE CREEK RD, GRANTS PASS;
541/476-3591 OR 541/471-2303
This spacious, modern home set on 7 acres of wooded mountainside became a B and B in 1996. Owners John and Marla Vidrinskas have added water features, hammocks, and a gazebo. Inside, the showpiece is the Moonlight Suite, favored by honeymooners. A second suite and three other rooms are elegantly furnished with period decor. Marla serves a healthy three-course breakfast in the formal dining room. *$$–$$$; MC, V; checks OK; www.flerymanor.com; 10 miles north of town, Hugo exit (exit 66) off I-5.* &

Rogue Forest Bed & Breakfast / ★★☆

12035 GALICE RD, MERLIN; 541/472-1052
The Rogue Forest B and B was built by a river-rafting pioneer. Now that it's been converted to a B and B, the suite in the main house plus a cabin offer a getaway in the woods. Features include private decks, outdoor Jacuzzi, and luxurious linens. The on-site Rogue Forest River Company offers rafting trips. *$$$; MC, V; checks OK; www.rogueforestbnb.com; 16 miles west of I-5, via Merlin exit (exit 61).*

Oregon Caves National Monument

Cave Junction, 28 miles southwest of Grants Pass on US Highway 199, is home to two of Oregon's better wineries: **FORIS VINEYARDS WINERY** (654 Kendall Rd; 541/592-3752 or 800/84FORIS; www.foriswine.com) and **BRIDGEVIEW VINE-YARDS & WINERY** (4210 Holland Loop Rd; 541/592-4688 or 877/273-4843; www.bridgeviewwine.com). Both have tasting rooms open every day.

About 20 miles east of Cave Junction, on State Route 46, is **OREGON CAVES NATIONAL MONUMENT** (19000 Caves Hwy; 541/592-2100; www.nps.gov/orca; tours every day, hourly mid-Mar–Nov, every 15 minutes late June–Aug), an active marble cave filled with glistening mineral formations and wet with moon milk, set among redwoods at 4,000 feet elevation. If you tour the caves, come prepared for cool temperatures and strenuous climbing (500 steps).

OREGON CAVES LODGE (541/592-2100; May–Oct) is completely hand built and somewhat unusual: this shaggy 22-room lodge is built across a ravine and has a stream running through the dining room.

LODGINGS

Out 'n' About Treesort / ★

300 PAGE CREEK RD, CAVE JUNCTION; 541/592-2208
This out-on-a-limb B and B has 18 structures swinging from the trees, including 12 lodging units ranging from the Tree Room Schoolhouse Suite for six to the Peacock Perch for two. Tree-musketeers can engage in ropes courses, horseback riding, and even craft making. Full breakfast is included. Book early; summer reservations go fast. The resort also offers tours and tree house–building workshops. *$$; MC, V; checks OK; www.treehouses.com; 10 miles southeast of Cave Junction near Takilma.*

Medford

While Southern Oregon's largest city may not win any beauty contests, Medford has achieved national recognition for its shapely pears, due to the efforts of Harry and David's, a local mail-order giant. **HARRY AND DAVID'S COUNTRY VILLAGE** (1314 Center Dr; 541/776-2277; www.harrydavid.com) offers "seconds" from gift packs; it's the departure point for tours (877/322-8000) of the complex, also home to **JACKSON & PERKINS** (www.jacksonandperkins.com), the world's largest rose growers.

The international award–winning cheeses of the **ROGUE VALLEY CREAMERY** (311 N Front St, Central Point; 541/665-1155) can be tasted at their factory in Central Point, a small burg a couple miles outside of Medford. Check out their new **ITALIAN MARKETPLACE & CAFÉ** (211 N Front St), one block away.

If you're heading toward Ashland from Medford, make one more stop, at the **RISING SUN FARMS** tasting room (5126 S Pacific Hwy, Phoenix; 541/535-8331), to stock up on picnic supplies, like their Pesto–Dried Tomato Cheese Torta.

The **CRATERIAN GINGER ROGERS THEATER** (23 S Central Ave; 541/779-3000; www.craterian.org) is Medford's showpiece, a downtown performing arts center with a 742-seat theater that opened in 1997. The 1924 building originally called the Craterian functioned as a vaudeville and silent-movie house. Why is it now named for Ginger Rogers? The actress owned a ranch on the nearby Rogue River for many years, once danced on the Craterian stage, and in the last years before her death helped raise money for the theater's $5.3 million renovation.

For dining in Medford proper, try **PORTERS** (147 N Front St; 541/857-1910) in the old train station, with patio dining. For fine dining, we recommend **CAFÉ DEJEUNER** (1108 E Main St; 541/857-1290), and for Thai food go to **ALI'S THAI KITCHEN** (2392 N Pacific Hwy; 541/770-3104), a humble spot north of town with good, inexpensive fare.

LODGINGS

Under the Greenwood Tree / ★★★☆

3045 BELLINGER LN, MEDFORD; 541/776-0000
Recently acquired by Joe and Barbara Lilley, this stately 1862 home epitomizes the quintessential bed-and-breakfast. Expansive lawns, rose gardens, 300-year-old trees, a gazebo, birds, llamas, and antique farm buildings provide a country setting. Cozily furnished with antiques, the common rooms and four rooms invite guests to wind down. Popular for weddings, the B and B has a dance floor under the stars. Joe's penchant for baking means you're treated to a three-course country-gourmet breakfast, as well as afternoon tea with homemade bread and muffins. *$$–$$$; AE, DIS, MC, V; checks OK; www.greenwoodtree.com; exit 27 off I-5.* &

Jacksonville

Resembling a set from your favorite Western, Jacksonville is one of the prettiest places in the Northwest. The town has relied heavily on its good looks and historic merit for survival since the Pacific Railroad bypassed the town and laid rails through Medford, a few miles east. Because the **APPLEGATE VALLEY** was well suited for orchards, miners picked up their ploughs when the gold rush ended. Much of the original 19th-century city, declared a National Historic Landmark in

1966, has been restored; Jacksonville now boasts more than 100 historic homes and buildings, several along **CALIFORNIA STREET**.

The **JACKSONVILLE MUSEUM** (206 N 5th St; 541/773-6536; www.sohs.org), in the stately 1883 Italianate courthouse, follows the history of the Rogue River Valley and displays works by Peter Britt (see Britt Festival). In the adjacent children's museum, kids walk through miniature pioneer settings. Walking trails thread around old gold diggings in the hills; the longest (3 miles) is **RICH GULCH HISTORIC TRAIL** (trailhead off 1st and Fir sts), an easy climb to a panoramic view. Also stroll through the 1875 "country Gothic" **BEEKMAN HOUSE AND GARDENS** (on east end of California St; 541/773-6536).

VALLEY VIEW WINERY (1000 Upper Applegate Rd; 541/899-8468 or 800/781-WINE; www.valleyviewwinery.com) offers tastings in Ruch, 6 miles southwest of Jacksonville on State Route 238, and in Jacksonville, at their **VALLEY VIEW WINERY TASTING ROOM** (125 W California St; 541/899-1001 or 800/781-9463).

The **BRITT FESTIVAL** (541/773-6077 or 800/882-7488; www.brittfest.org; June–Sept), an outdoor music-and-arts series, is held on the hillside field where Peter Britt, a famous local photographer and horticulturist, once lived. It's now the area's biggest draw in summer, with 70,000 visitors.

RESTAURANTS

Bella Union / ★★

170 W CALIFORNIA ST, JACKSONVILLE ; 541/899-1770
In a town of stately mansions and proper English decor, the bustling Bella Union continues its reputation as a dependably good meal in a casual environment. In the original century-old Bella Union Saloon, this restaurant has everything from pizza and pasta to gourmet dinners and picnic baskets. Proprietor Jerry Hayes, a wine fancier, pours a wide variety. *$$; AE, DIS, MC, V; no checks; lunch, dinner every day, brunch Sun; full bar; reservations recommended; www.bellau.com; downtown.*

Jacksonville Inn / ★★

175 E CALIFORNIA ST, JACKSONVILLE;
541/899-1900 OR 800/321-9344
Ask a native to name the area's best restaurant, and the answer is often the Jacksonville Inn. The staff is considerate, and the antique-furnished dining room, housed in the original 1863 building, is intimate. Jerry Evans maintains one of the best-stocked wine cellars in Oregon. Reserve in advance, especially during the Britt Festival. You can also stay in one of their eight upstairs rooms, complete with breakfast. *$$$; AE, DC, DIS, MC, V; checks OK; breakfast, dinner every day, lunch Tues–Sat, brunch Sun; full bar; reservations recommended; www.jacksonvilleinn.com; downtown.*

McCully House Inn / ★★

240 E CALIFORNIA ST, JACKSONVILLE;
541/899-1942 OR 800/367-1942
McCully House, a Gothic Revival mansion, was built in 1860 for Jacksonville's first doctor. Two elegant dining rooms and patio seating draw raves for ambience, as does the Northwest menu. Lodging options include inn rooms and nearby cottages, houses, or the honeymoon suite; all include continental breakfast. *$$$; AE, DIS, JCB, MC, V; checks OK; dinner every day Memorial Day–Labor Day, Tues–Sat off-season (closed Jan); full bar; reservations recommended; www.countryhouseinns.com; downtown.* ᵶ

Talent

RESTAURANTS

New Sammy's Cowboy Bistro / ★★★

2210 S PACIFIC HWY (SR 99), TALENT; 541/535-2779
Proprietors Vernon and Charlene Rollins have cultivated a huge foodie following, despite their lack of advertising or a real sign (look for a weak flashing light next to the highway). Because the bistro has just six tables, you'll have to secure reservations months in advance. Elaborate menu options are served à la carte or within a set three-course dinner. Vernon stocks the cellar with thousands of West Coast and French wines. *$$$; MC, V; checks OK; dinner Thurs–Sun (Fri–Sat in midwinter); beer and wine; reservations required; 3 miles N of Ashland on SR 99.*

Ashland

The remarkable success of the **OREGON SHAKESPEARE FESTIVAL** (see "Oregon Shakespeare Festival and the Ashland Theater Scene") since 1935 has transformed this sleepy town into one with, per capita, the region's best tourist amenities. The festival draws more than 370,000 people throughout the eight-month season, filling its theaters to an extraordinary 85 percent capacity on average. The town of 20,000 still has its soul: for the most part, it seems a happy little college town, set amid lovely ranch country.

Designed by the creator of San Francisco's Golden Gate Park, **LITHIA PARK** runs for 100 acres behind the outdoor theater; there's an ice-skating rink in winter. **SCHNEIDER MUSEUM OF ART** (1250 Siskiyou Blvd; 541/552-6245) at the south end of the Southern Oregon University campus is the best art gallery in town. **WEISINGER'S OF ASHLAND WINERY** (3150 Siskiyou Blvd; 541/488-5989; www.weisingers.com) and **ASHLAND VINEYARDS** (exit 14 off I-5; 541/488-0088; www.winenet.com) are worth a stop.

Get picnic supplies at the **ASHLAND COMMUNITY FOOD STORE** (237 N 1st St; 541/482-2237; www.ashlandfood.coop), a busy member-owned co-op. Swim at the **ROGUE RIVER RECREATION AREA** or **APPLEGATE RIVER**. Less than an hour's drive up scenic Dead Indian Memorial Road are two lake resorts: **HOWARD PRAIRIE LAKE RESORT** (3249 Hyatt Prairie Rd; 541/482-1979; www.howard prairieresort.com) and **LAKE OF THE WOODS** (950 Harriman Rd, Klamath Falls; 541/949-8300; www.lakeofthewoodsresort.com), open seasonally. **SKI ASHLAND** (1745 SR 66; 541/482-2897; www.mtashland.com), on nearby Mount Ashland, 18 miles south of town, offers 22 runs for all classes of skiers (usually Thanksgiving–mid-Apr).

RESTAURANTS

Amuse Restaurant / ★★★

15 N FIRST ST, ASHLAND; 541/488-9000
The French expression *amuse-bouche*, or "fun for the mouth," appropriately provides the name for this elegant restaurant. Husband-and-wife team Erik Brown and Jamie North bring years of experience at notable Napa Valley restaurants. Their French-inspired dishes make extensive use of organic produce and meats, served in eye-appealing compositions. More than 150 wines represent the Northwest and France. For dessert, try North's deep-fried pastry lavished in whipped cream and berry jam. *$$$; AE, DC, DIS, MC, V; local checks only; dinner Tues–Sun summer, Wed–Sun off-season; beer and wine; reservations recommened; www.amuserestaurant.com; 1 block from plaza.* &

Breadboard Restaurant & Bakery / ★

744 N MAIN ST, ASHLAND; 541/488-0295
Diners return again and again to this unassuming eatery on the edge of town for dependable and hearty home cooking. Covered patios have gorgeous views of the rolling hills. The sizable menu appeals to vegetarians and carnivores alike. In the morning, try a tofu scramble with fresh salsa, chicken-fried steak, or sourdough pancakes with a side of crispy bacon. Breads, muffins, and pastries are served with homemade jam. *$; MC, V; local checks only; breakfast, lunch every day (closed holidays); no alcohol; no reservations; 1 mile north of town.* &

Chateaulin / ★★★

50 E MAIN ST, ASHLAND; 541/482-2264
The opening of Chateaulin more than 30 years ago marked the beginning of Ashland's surprisingly refined culinary scene today. Down the walkway from Angus Bowmer Theater, this café bustles during Shakespeare season, with theater crowds gathered for fine French cuisine. House specialties are pâtés and veal dishes, but all the dishes are impressive. An inside door leads to its sister business, a wine and gourmet shop. *$$; AE, DIS, MC, V; checks OK; dinner every day in summer; full bar; reservations recommended; www.chateaulin. com; down walkway from Angus Bowmer Theater.* &

Cucina Biazzi / ★★

568 E MAIN ST, ASHLAND; 541/488-3739
Beasy McMillan has owned several successful restaurants in Ashland over the years, but this traditional Tuscan-style trattoria is her best-loved to date. Four-course dinners are served on white linen in what was once the living room in this former residence. As tempting as it may be, don't fill up on the antipasto—fresh pasta portions are substantial, followed by a fish or meat entrée, a perfectly dressed green salad, and a rich dessert. *$$$; MC, V; checks OK; dinner every day; full bar; reservations recommended; near fire station.*

Lela's Café / ★★★

258 A ST, NO. 3, ASHLAND; 541/482-1702
Owner Lela Sherdon originally started a bakery, which grew into a small café and is now one of the better places in Ashland. Each dish offers a series of delights to the tongue—chicken liver mousse with Calvados *gelle*, brioche, and sweet onion marmalade is just one delicious option. Ordering a smattering of small plates and wines is suggested, as is saving room for dessert. *$$–$$$; MC, V; local checks only; lunch, dinner Tues–Sun summer, Tues–Sat off-season; reservations recommended; www.lelascafe.com; close to train tracks.* &

Monet / ★★★

36 S 2ND ST, ASHLAND; 541/482-1339
This gentrified French restaurant is the talk of Ashland. Favorite dishes include shrimp sautéed in white wine and Pernod or beef tenderloin flambéed in Cognac, then served in a four-peppercorn cream sauce. The chef goes out of his way to make interesting vegetarian choices, such as La Crique Ardechoise, a country potato dish with garlic and parsley. Dine outdoors if you can. *$$$; DIS, MC, V; local checks only; dinner Tues–Sun summer, Tues–Sat off-season (closed Jan–mid-Feb); full bar; reservations recommended; www.restaurant monet.com; just off Main St.*

The Peerless Restaurant / ★★★

265 4TH ST, ASHLAND; 541/488-6067
Crissy Barnett's reputation for doing things in style can definitely be said about her restaurant, adjacent to her boutique hotel. The Peerless has the best atmosphere in town. The menu is Northwest, with tropical influences. Try the wine flights on Tuesday nights. *$$$; AE, DIS, MC, V; checks OK; dinner Tues–Sat (closed Jan); reservations recommended; between A and B sts.* &

LODGINGS

Chanticleer Inn / ★★★

120 GRESHAM ST, ASHLAND; 541/482-1919 OR 800/898-1950
Ellen and Howie Wilcox have spared no expense updating the six rooms in this beautiful 1920 Craftsman, using antiques, designer fabrics, and classic bathroom fixtures to create a pleasing French provincial effect. Each room

has a view of the Cascade foothills or a private patio entrance with a garden view. A gourmet breakfast, as well as afternoon wine, sherry, port, and home-made cookies, is included. *$$$; AE, MC, V; checks OK; www.ashlandbnb. com; 2 blocks from library, off Main St.*

Country Willows Inn / ★★★

1313 CLAY ST, ASHLAND; 541/488-1590 OR 800/945-5697
Set on 5 acres of farmland outside of town, this 1896 home affords peace and quiet, plus a lovely view of the hills. Chuck and Debbie Young offer a variety of rooms, suites, and cottages. Breakfast, presented on a pretty sunporch, features organic juices and unique egg dishes. Besides a hot tub and swimming pool, you'll see the Youngs' ducks, geese, and goats. *$$–$$$; AE, DIS, MC, V; checks OK; www.countrywillowsinn.com; 4 blocks south of Siskiyou Blvd.* &

Cowslip's Belle / ★★★

159 N MAIN ST, ASHLAND; 541/488-2901 OR 800/888-6819
Named after a flower in *A Midsummer Night's Dream*, this 1913 Crafts-man bungalow is cheery. Rooms in the main house are traditional, while a Craftsman-style addition offers more privacy. Request the suite with spa tub, twisted-juniper bed frame, and balcony overlooking the mountains. Turn-down service, a full breakfast, and an Ashland Racquet Club pass complete a pretty picture. *$$$; no credit cards; checks OK; www.cowslip.com; 3 blocks north of theaters.* &

Mount Ashland Inn / ★★★

550 MOUNT ASHLAND RD, ASHLAND;
541/482-8707 OR 800/830-8707
Wind your way up Mount Ashland Ski Road, and you discover a huge, two-story log cabin, crafted from incense cedars from the surrounding 40-acre property where Chuck and Laurel Biegert have created five suites for absolute comfort. Enjoy spectacular mountain views from the dining room. An out-door spa and sauna, cross-country skis, snowshoes, and mountain bikes are available, as is a multicourse breakfast (for extra). Expect snow November through April. *$$$; DIS, MC, V; checks OK (for deposit only); www.mtashland inn.com; follow signs to Mount Ashland Ski Area.*

Peerless Hotel / ★★★

243 4TH ST, ASHLAND; 541/488-1082 OR 800/460-8758
In Ashland's Historic Railroad District, the original hotel that stood here was saved from disrepair by owner Crissy Barnett. The hotel's six B and B units are now decorated in an exotic style, with antiques and whimsical murals that make you feel as though you're in different continents. High ceilings and luxurious, oversize bathrooms are trademarks. Suite 3 features a bath with two claw-foot tubs and a glassed-in shower. A four-course gourmet break

OREGON SHAKESPEARE FESTIVAL
AND THE ASHLAND THEATER SCENE

Established in 1935, the **OREGON SHAKESPEARE FESTIVAL** is among the oldest and largest professional regional theater companies in the United States. OSF presents an eight-month season of 11 plays—by Shakespeare, as well as classic and contemporary playwrights—in repertory in three unique theaters. In the outdoor **ELIZABETHAN THEATER**, which seats 1,200, famous and authentic nighttime productions of Shakespeare plays are staged (three each summer). The two indoor theaters—the intimate **NEW THEATRE** and the **ANGUS BOWMER THEATRE** (mid-Feb–late Oct)—includes comedies, classics, romances, new works, and dramas. The festival is dark on Mondays.

Offstage, visit the **EXHIBIT CENTER**, where you can clown around in costumes from plays past. Company members give informal free **NOON TALKS** about life at OSF, as well as backstage tours for a fee. Before the plays on the Elizabethan stage, the free **GREEN SHOW** (June–Oct) is a lively and colorful program of dance and music in the festival courtyard, with three different shows nightly, some with themes to match the night's outdoor play. Music and dance concerts are also held across the street in **CARPENTER HALL** (noon Wed and Sat in Aug).

Current playbill and ticket information for OSF (last-minute tickets in summer are very rare) are available at the **FESTIVAL BOX OFFICE** (15 S Pioneer St; 541/482-4331; www.osfashland.org; open every day except holidays).

Ashland is also home to the **OREGON CABARET THEATER** (1st and Hargadine sts; 541/488-2902; www.oregoncabaret.com; Feb–Dec), now in its 20th year, presenting musicals and comedies accompanied by a full dinner and dessert menu, beer, and wine. Opened in 2002, **OREGON STAGE WORKS** (191 A St; 541/482-2334; www.oregonstageworks.org; Mar–Oct) stages creative and challenging productions of American playwrights.

—Annissa Anderson

fast is served in Crissy's Peerless Restaurant (see review) across the garden. *$$$–$$$$; AE, DIS, MC, V; checks OK; www.peerlesshotel.com; between A and B sts.* &

Romeo Inn / ★★★

295 IDAHO ST, ASHLAND; 541/488-0884 OR 800/915-8899
A sign in one room of this 1932 Cape Cod home reads "The perks are best here"—an appropriate summary, given the many ways Don and Deana Politis enhance their guests' stays. The inn, located in a charming hillside neighborhood,

is impeccably kept. Breakfast is an elaborate affair. Complimentary cookies are offered, along with a patio with hot tub and swimming pool. *$$$; DIS, MC, V; checks OK; www.romeoinn.com; south of Siskiyou Blvd.*

Klamath Falls

For decades, the wide-open spaces around this city of 19,000 (called "K Falls" by locals) attracted only ranchers and farmers, lured by the 1902 Reclamation Act that offered homesteads to veterans. Recent droughts brought water issues to a boil when the Endangered Species Act—drafted in part to protect coho salmon in Upper Klamath Lake—restricted irrigation, leaving farmers high and dry. While the feds work on creative solutions, Klamath Falls is hardly going down the drain. Oregon's "City of Sunshine" redeveloped downtown and is promoting the area's natural beauty; tourism and real estate are on the rise, and the town now sports several hotel chains.

The **FAVELL MUSEUM OF WESTERN ART AND INDIAN ARTIFACTS** (125 W Main St; 541/882-9996; www.favellmuseum.com) is a true western museum. **KLAMATH COUNTY MUSEUM** (1451 Main St; 541/883-4208) exhibits the region's volcanic geology. The **BALDWIN HOTEL MUSEUM** (31 Main St; 541/883-4207; June–Sept), in a spooky 1906 hotel, retains many fixtures of the era. The **ROSS RAGLAND THEATER** (218 N 7th St; 541/884-0651 or 888/627-5484; www. rrtheater.org), a onetime art-deco movie theater, now presents more than 60 plays each year.

UPPER KLAMATH LAKE lies on the remains of a larger ancient lake system and, at 143 square miles, is the largest lake in Oregon; it's fine for fishing and serves as bird nesting grounds. The Williamson River, which flows into the lake, yields plenty of trout. The **VOLCANIC LEGACY SCENIC BYWAY** (State Route 140) runs alongside the lake and through the beautiful Wood River valley.

The Klamath Indian Tribe, a confederation of the Klamath, Modoc, and Yahooskin Natives who have occupied the region for thousands of years, opened their **KLA-MO-YA CASINO** (on US Hwy 97, Chiloquin; 541/783-7529 or 888/552-6692; www.klamoya.com) just a few miles north of the Klamath Falls Airport.

RESTAURANTS

Bel Tramonto / ★

6139 SIMMERS AVE, KLAMATH FALLS; 541/884-8259
Located on an unlikely strip several minutes' drive from downtown, Bel Tramonto is nonetheless worth seeking out. The restaurant's previous interior was completely remodeled by owners Chris and Carrie King and painted to reflect the Tuscan-style menu. The four courses are offered à la carte, but there's also a prix-fixe option. Homemade pastas and hearty meat and fish dishes are complemented by a selection of affordable Italian wines. *$$–$$$; AE, DIS, MC, V; local checks only; dinner Tues–Sat; full bar; reservations recommended; corner of S 6th and Patterson sts.*

LODGINGS

Running Y Ranch Resort / ★★

5500 RUNNING Y RD, KLAMATH FALLS;
541/850-5500 OR 888/850-0275

The $250 million Running Y Ranch Resort provides recreation and real estate services along with its 85-room lodge, Arnold Palmer 18-hole golf course, restaurant, café, and condo development on 9,000 acres on Klamath Lake. Though rooms in the lodge are lacking in decor, they are spacious, and many have views onto the golf course and beautiful surrounds. A spa, a sports and fitness center, a pool, a sauna, a hot tub, an ice rink, and biking trails keep you busy. *$$–$$$$; AE, DC, DIS, MC, V; checks OK; www.runningy. com; 10 miles west of town.*

Lakeview

At nearly 4,800 feet elevation, Lakeview calls itself the "Tallest Town in Oregon." While most of Lake County exceeds 4,300 feet elevation, this prehistoric lake basin is more noteworthy for its hot springs and fabulous hang gliding. **HUNTER'S HOT SPRINGS** (US Hwy 395, 2 miles north of town; 800/858-8266) has two pools—the outdoor pool is perfect for stargazing—with direct hookups to geyser springs that blow every 40 seconds at Old Perpetual.

Paragliding championships are held above Lakeview at **BLACK CAP LAUNCH** (follow signs in Lakeview for Hang Glider Port), which offers tremendous views for those without wings. A popular gliding site is Tague's Butte on **ABERT RIM**, a massive fault scarp that stretches 30 miles and towers 2,000 feet over Lake Abert.

WARNER CANYON SKI AREA (10 miles north of Lakeview; 541/947-5001) offers 17 weeks of skiing each year, beginning in mid-December, with no lines for the 700-foot vertical chair lift. A modest ski lodge has a small restaurant.

For authentic campfire cuisine and western-style cabins, visit the **WILLOW SPRINGS GUEST RANCH** (Clover Flat Rd, Lakeview; 541/947-5499; www. willowspringsguestranch.com), a working cattle ranch that generates its own power. The wood-fired hot tub overlooks acres of meadows.

Summer Lake

In the heart of **OREGON'S OUTBACK** lies Summer Lake, bordered by the Fremont National Forest and marshland. One of Oregon's largest bird refuges, **SUMMER LAKE WILDLIFE AREA** (541/943-3152) is here. For archaeology hounds, there are more petroglyphs found throughout Lake County than in the rest of Oregon and Washington combined.

Hiking in the **GEARHART MOUNTAIN WILDERNESS** to the south, fly-fishing the many rivers and reservoirs, and cycling the almost-deserted paved roads in the **FREMONT NATIONAL FOREST** are just a few options.

Summer Lake itself mostly recedes in summer, but don't worry: you can still get wet. Head to **SUMMER LAKE HOT SPRINGS** (milepost 92, SR 31; 877/492-8554), a historic bathhouse where for $5 you can soak all day.

The **LODGE AT SUMMER LAKE** (53460 SR 31; 541/943-3993), housed in Paisley's former dance hall, serves three home-style meals a day year-round. **SUMMER LAKE STORE** (37580 SR 31; 541/943-3164), a mom-and-pop grocery store, and a small pioneer museum nearby are usually open.

LODGINGS

Summer Lake Inn / ★★★

47531 SR 31, SUMMER LAKE; 541/943-3983 OR 800/261-2778
Everything in the design of this inn capitalizes on the area's expansiveness, offering colorful sunrises and miles of unobstructed views of marsh, lake, and desert from every vantage point. Six luxurious cabins sport wraparound decks, kitchens, and raised Jacuzzi tubs; three original cabins under a shared roof offer more economical options. Dinner in the inn's dining room is by reservation; breakfast baskets are available upon request. You can fish and canoe in the private pond in summer; birding and walking trails are available year-round. *$$$; MC, V; checks OK; dinner Sun–Wed; www.summerlakeinn. com; between mileposts 81 and 82.*

Silver Lake

North of Silver Lake, watch for the cutoff to **FORT ROCK STATE MONUMENT** (26 miles north and east of Silver Lake off Hwy 31; 541/388-6055). Here you'll find remnants of an ancient volcanic blast, where Klamath Indians found refuge when Mount Mazama exploded 6,800 years ago. In one of Fort Rock's caves, archaeologists found what they believe to be the oldest shoes on record: a pair of woven sandals that date back 10,000 years.

RESTAURANTS

Cowboy Dinner Tree / ★

EAST BAY RD, SILVER LAKE; 541/576-2426
This rustic line shack–turned–steak house surprises many who first arrive on its doorstep, but word of the legendary cowboy dinner helps them through the creaky wooden doors. Come hungry, because the dinners truly are huge. Diners choose from either a whole smoked chicken or a hunk of aged and dry-rubbed grilled steak, served with a mountain of accompaniments. Basic, woodstove-heated cabins are also available for the weary. *$–$$; no credit cards; checks OK; dinner Fri–Sun Nov–May, Thurs–Sun June–Oct; no alcohol; reservations required; www.cowboydinnertree.com; 4 miles off SR 31 at milepost 47.*

Crater Lake National Park

Heading north from Klamath Falls on US Highway 97, then west on State Route 62, you'll reach the south entrance to **CRATER LAKE NATIONAL PARK**. Some 7,700 years ago, 10,000- to 12,000-foot-high Mount Mazama was the Mount St. Helens of its day. It blew up and left behind a 4,000-foot-deep crater—now a lake filled by rainwater and snowmelt.

With the water plunging to depths of 1,932 feet, it's the deepest lake in the United States—and probably the bluest. A prospector searching for gold found this treasure in 1853; in 1902 it was designated a national park, the only one in Oregon. Crater Lake National Park is extraordinary: the impossibly blue lake, eerie volcanic formations, a vast geological wonderland. The **STEEL INFORMATION CENTER** (near south entrance at park headquarters; 541/594-3000; www. nps.gov/crla) is a good stop year-round; in summer, a second visitor center operates in **RIM VILLAGE**. Visitors can camp at **MAZAMA VILLAGE CAMPGROUND** or book a room at the 40-unit **MAZAMA VILLAGE MOTOR INN** (541/830-8700); plan early, as space fills fast. The 33-mile **RIM DRIVE** along the top of the caldera offers many vistas; the two-hour boat ride from Cleetwood Cove out to Wizard Island requires a short but strenuous hike back to the parking lot. In winter, only the south and west entrance roads are open. Then, cross-country skiing and snowshoe walks are popular.

LODGINGS

Crater Lake Lodge / ★★

> **RIM DR, CRATER LAKE NATIONAL PARK; 541/830-8700**
> Originally built in 1909, the historic wood-and-stone building, perched at 7,000 feet on the rim of the caldera, was weakened by decades of heavy snowfall. Now restored, the summer lodge has 71 guest rooms, all with great views. Best are the eight with claw-foot bathtubs in window alcoves. Guests should reserve right away in the lodge-style dining room; if it's full, choose between two restaurants: at nearby Rim Village or Mazama Village. *$$$; DIS, MC, V; checks OK; closed mid-Oct–mid-May; www.craterlakelodge.com; via SR 138 (north) or SR 62 (south).*

Diamond Lake and Mount Bailey

MOUNT BAILEY ALPINE SKI TOURS (off SR 138, just north of Crater Lake; 541/793-3348 or 800/446-4555; www.mountbailey.com) offers true backcountry skiing, with experienced, safety-conscious guides and snow cats instead of helicopters to take you to the top of this 8,363-foot ancient volcano. **DIAMOND LAKE RESORT** (800/733-7593; www.diamondlake.net), headquarters for the guide service, is great for sports.

Cascade Lakes Area

The 100-mile scenic **CASCADE LAKES HIGHWAY** (SR 58) tour requires several hours and a picnic lunch; mountain views and fishing resorts are tucked along the way. Most scenic are **SPARKS AND ELK LAKES**; both offer great boating and swimming. **HOSMER LAKE** is a favorite for canoeing and fishing (only with a fly), while **LAVA LAKE** offers fishermen live-bait options. **ODELL AND DAVIS LAKES**, near Willamette Pass on State Route 58, mark the southern end of the tour that winds its way north, eventually following the Deschutes River on Century Drive to Bend.

Odell Lake

LODGINGS

Odell Lake Lodge and Resort

E ODELL LAKE ACCESS OFF SR 58, CRESCENT LAKE;
541/433-2540 OR 800/434-2540
This shoreside resort is ideal for the fisher, hiker, and skier in all of us. Cast for mackinaw, rainbow, or kokanee trout in summer, or sink into a good book in the library in winter. Request Room 3, a corner suite warmed with knotty pine paneling and lake and stream views, or spend the few additional dollars to get a lakeside cabin. The restaurant is open year-round for three meals a day. *$$; DIS, MC, V; checks OK; www.odelllakeresort.com; 30 miles from Oakridge on SR 58, take E Odell Lake exit.* &

Sunriver

More than a resort, Sunriver is an organized community with 1,500 residents. The unincorporated town sprawls over 3,300 acres, and its own runway for private air commuting does brisk business. Sunriver's specialty is big-time escapist vacationing, and the resort (see review) has all the facilities to keep you busy all week long, year-round.

For members and resort guests, a two-level indoor club and spa provides tennis courts, a lap pool, and a full slate of services, from massages to aromatherapy. Summer offers golf (three 18-hole courses), tennis (28 courts), rafting, canoeing, fishing, swimming (three pools, two complexes of hot tubs), biking (30 miles of paved trails), and horseback riding. In winter the resort is home base for skiing (Nordic and alpine), ice-skating, and snowmobiling.

Dining in Sunriver includes **MEADOWS AT THE LODGE**, a showplace for Sunday brunch. Seasonally, resort guests can make dinner reservations at the **GRILLE AT CROSSWATER**, an exclusive members-only restaurant. Elsewhere, choose anything from Chinese to pizza. The **TROUT HOUSE** at the Sunriver Marina is a mainstay for dinners and Sunday brunch.

LODGINGS

Sunriver Lodge & Resort / ★★★☆

I CENTER DR, SUNRIVER; 541/593-1000 OR 800/801-8765
Families have been coming to Sunriver Resort from all over for more than two decades. The outdoor recreation options make it the perfect active getaway, with a vast range of accommodations. For the best bargain, request one of the large homes through the lodge reservation service and split expenses with another family; included are club and pool access. Couples choose Lodge Village rooms for an economical choice or splurge on luxurious River Lodges rooms. *$$$–$$$$; AE, DIS, MC, V; checks OK; www.sunriver-resort.com; 15 miles south of Bend.*

Bend and Mount Bachelor

Bend is the largest city in Central Oregon, located on the sunny side of the Cascades. The formerly sleepy high-desert town, founded on timber a century ago, is now indisputably Oregon's tourism showcase. A recent study conducted by the state's tourism office quantified the town's popularity, showing that of six days spent in the state, visitors spend more than half (3.2 days) in Central Oregon. Many visitors have come here to stay, doubling the population of Bend in the last 10 years to its current status of more than 70,000 people.

If the long snow season on nearby **MOUNT BACHELOR** (see separate section, below), the centerpiece of Central Oregon's alpine playground, isn't enough to lure you in winter, then the more than 35 golf courses, plentiful hiking and bike trails, river rafting, access to more than 300 high lakes, and world-class fishing and climbing will suffice in summer. And with more than 220 days of sunshine and a mild climate, Bend and its environs afford some form of outdoor recreation year-round, attracting multisport aficionados and some of the nation's top triathletes (see Sports and Recreation).

Bend

The town was appropriately named, just over a century ago, for its location at a bend in the Deschutes River. Today, the **DESCHUTES RIVER TRAIL** has access points from downtown to well past the **INN OF THE SEVENTH MOUNTAIN** (see review) that allow visitors to experience more than 10 miles of trails, lava formations, and a series of waterfalls (see Parks). In warmer months, raft outfitters take customers through the more prominent sections of rapids, while do-it-yourselfers brave the calmer stretches.

The **BEND PARKWAY**, a raised highway that lets passers-through avoid US Highway 97's 10 miles of uninspired strip development, allows access to the historical town center, which thrives just to the west. To the southwest is the **OLD MILL DISTRICT** (see Shopping), a former timber mill torn down and replaced with a sleek glass-and-split-rail complex of restaurants, shops, and galleries on the

Deschutes riverbank. Apropos to the "new" Bend, the mill district's previously abandoned smokestacks building, seen from higher spots around town, now houses an **REI** store (380 Powerhouse Dr; 541/385-0594; www.rei.com). Across the river, the **LES SCHWAB AMPHITHEATER** (see Performing Arts and Nightlife) seats 7,500 for concerts. To the east of downtown is the newly thriving **MID-TOWN** area surrounding **PILOT BUTTE**. Farther east, the ponderosas and deciduous plantings close to the river give way to juniper and sage, all but invisible for the quickly sprouted housing developments there.

ACCESS AND INFORMATION

Air service to Central Oregon is funneled into **ROBERTS FIELD AIRPORT** (15 miles north of Bend, in Redmond), which is serviced by Alaska/Horizon, United, and SkyWest airlines with direct flights from Portland, Seattle, San Francisco, Los Angeles, and Salt Lake City. There are also two private airports, one in Sunriver and one in Bend. Several national **CAR RENTAL** companies have locations in the airport, and a few more have Bend storefronts. **GREYHOUND** (1315 NE 3rd St; 541/382-2151) offers daily bus service to major Oregon cities.

Tourism information can be found at the **BEND VISITOR AND CONVENTION BUREAU** (917 NW Harriman St; 541/382-8048; www.visitbend.com) or at the **CENTRAL OREGON VISITORS ASSOCIATION** (661 SW Powerhouse Dr; 800/800-8334; www.visitcentraloregon.com).

MAJOR ATTRACTIONS

Heading north from Summer Lake on State Route 31 or Klamath Falls on US Highway 97, the road to Bend passes through **NEWBERRY NATIONAL VOLCANIC MONUMENT** (between La Pine and Bend on both sides of US Hwy 97; 541/593-2421 or 541/383-4771; www.fs.fed.us), a 56,000-acre monument in the Deschutes National Forest that showcases geologic attractions tens of thousands of years old. Within the **NEWBERRY CRATER**, 13 miles east of US Highway 97 on Forest Road 21, lie the Big Obsidian Flow, Paulina Falls, and East and Paulina lakes; each lake includes a small resort. The 7,985-foot **PAULINA PEAK**, accessible by road in summer, provides an excellent vantage point over the features within the collapsed caldera, which spans 500 square miles. Tour **LAVA RIVER CAVE**, a mile-long lava tube (on US Hwy 97, 13 miles south of Bend). As you descend into the dark depths, you'll need a warm sweater. **LAVA LANDS VISITOR CENTER** at the base of Lava Butte (12 miles south of Bend; 541/593-2421; closed in winter) is the interpretive center for the miles of lava beds. Drive—or, when cars are barred, take the shuttle—up Lava Butte, formed by a volcanic fissure, for a dramatic view. Seasons for Newberry attractions vary depending on snowfall (generally mid-May–Sept).

The **HIGH DESERT MUSEUM** (59800 S US Hwy 97, 4 miles south of Bend; 541/382-4754; www.highdesert.org) is an outstanding educational resource and nonprofit center for natural and cultural history. This modern structure, built from pine and lava rocks, is set on 20 acres of natural trails. Outdoor exhibits offer replicas of covered wagons, a sheepherder's camp, a settlers' cabin, and an old sawmill; three river otters, three porcupines, and about a half-dozen raptors are in residence (presentations daily). The museum also has an extensive collection of Columbia Plateau Indian artifacts.

MUSEUMS AND GALLERIES

The **MIRROR POND GALLERY** (875 NW Brooks St; 541/317-9324; www. mirrorpondgallery.org) is a showcase for community art sponsored by **ARTS CENTRAL** (www.artscentraloregon.org), the regional arts council for Central Oregon. The **BEND GALLERY ASSOCIATION** (www.bendgalleries.com) is a 14-member association that hosts the popular **FIRST FRIDAY GALLERY WALK** each month, complete with free biodiesel-powered shuttle bus. Several art galleries are also scattered throughout the Old Mill District (see Shopping); some are included on the bus tour.

WORKING WONDERS CHILDREN'S MUSEUM (520 SW Powerhouse Dr, Ste 624; 541/389-4500; www.workingwonders.org; Thurs–Mon) gives kids a hands-on learning experience. Downtown, visit the **DESCHUTES HISTORICAL CENTER** (NW Idaho and Wall sts; 541/389-1813), which features regional historical facts and interesting pioneer paraphernalia.

PARKS

The **BEND METRO PARKS & RECREATION DISTRICT** (www.bendparks andrec.org) manages 2,375 acres of parks in Bend, including 48 miles of trails. The showcase is the much-photographed **DRAKE PARK** which features 11 acres bordering the Deschutes River on **MIRROR POND. SHEVLIN PARK** less than 3 miles west of downtown, is perfect for picnics and outdoor fun. The district also operates **JUNIPER SWIM & FITNESS**. Portions of the **DESCHUTES RIVER TRAIL** within the city limits are managed by the district, which is currently at work building a fully connected river trail between **TUMALO STATE PARK** (see below) and the **MEADOW DAY-USE AREA**. Once it's complete, the trail system will encompass 19 miles of trails. **BIG SKY PARK**, Bend's newest sport park, features soccer and baseball fields, a BMX track, walking trails, and a dog park.

Also visit **PILOT BUTTE STATE SCENIC VIEWPOINT** (just east of downtown on US Hwy 20; 541/388-6055), a red-cinder-cone park with a mile-long road to a knockout vista on top. Just northwest, along the Deschutes River, **TUMALO STATE PARK** (541/382-3586) offers both day-use and camping options with yurt, tent, or RV spots.

SHOPPING

Bend is full of high-end shops. Shoppers should focus on downtown and the Shops at the Old Mill. **DOWNTOWN,** locally owned and unique stores include art galleries; gift, clothing, and shoe boutiques; children's toy and apparel shops; and specialty food, wine, and chocolate stores. Downtown Bend shops

---

PEDAL POWER IN THE OREGON CASCADES

From mountains to rolling hills to high desert, Central and Southern Oregon are awesome for mountain biking and road cycling.

If you're a biker, maintained trails in the **DESCHUTES NATIONAL FOREST** around Bend and Sisters, **UMPQUA NATIONAL FOREST** around Roseburg, **SISKIYOU NATIONAL FOREST** south of Grants Pass and Ashland, and **ROGUE RIVER NATIONAL FOREST** between Ashland and Klamath Falls are havens for two-wheeled recreation. The **FREMONT NATIONAL FOREST** outside Summer Lake and Lakeview, and many other meandering and scenic byways in similarly less-populated counties, provides peaceful routes for road cyclists.

Thanks to both public-trail access and efforts by mountain bikers to create their own trail systems, trail options around Bend are seemingly limitless to visitors. **CENTRAL OREGON TRAIL ALLIANCE** (www.cotamtb.org), a volunteer-based mountain-bike-trail advocacy group, and its founders have steadily maintained many of the area's bike trails that link to the national forest trail networks. **PHIL'S TRAIL**, a local's favorite, offers several loop options for a variety of skill levels. Make sure to pick up a **FREE TRAIL MAP** in bike stores or at the trailhead before heading out. Family rides are common on the easier trails at **SHEVLIN PARK** or from several access points on the **DESCHUTES RIVER TRAIL** off Century Drive. Road cycling is most popular on the **CASCADE LAKES HIGHWAY** (open only in

---

are also in walking distance of several of the best restaurants (see reviews) and picturesque Drake Park overlooking Mirror Pond.

At the **SHOPS AT THE OLD MILL** (www.theoldmill.com), there's an outdoor promenade of top-of-the-line chain stores, just steps from the Deschutes River. There's also a few small shops, restaurants, and a cinema.

Located outside of these groupings are a few mentionable local's favorites. The **IRON HORSE** (210 NW Congress St; 541/382-5175) is an eclectic antique store in a historic neighborhood, just blocks from downtown. For specialty food and wine, visit **DEVORE'S GOOD FOOD STORE AND WINE SHOP** (1124 NW Newport Ave; 541/389-6588) or the upscale **NEWPORT MARKET** (1121 NW Newport Ave; 541/382-3940) across the street.

PERFORMING ARTS AND NIGHTLIFE

Central Oregon's mild temperatures and many days of sunshine make it ideal for outdoor concerts. The famous **CASCADE FESTIVAL OF MUSIC** (www.cascademusic.org) is the longest-running and largest cultural musical event in Bend, held in Drake Park every summer in late August. Musicians perform a different theme nightly under large tents.

summer and fall). **SUNRIVER RESORT**, south of Bend, also offers miles of paved bike trails.

The **NORTH UMPQUA TRAIL**, paralleling the **NORTH UMPQUA RIVER** between Diamond Lake and Roseburg, is a multi-use trail more than 70 miles long, with combinations of out-and-back and loop rides for intermediate to advanced mountain bikers on mostly single track over rolling terrain through old-growth forest.

Outside of Grants Pass, the Siskiyou National Forest is fast becoming a draw for more-experienced mountain bikers. A number of trails in the **GALICE AND ILLINOIS VALLEY RANGER DISTRICTS** provide challenging and lengthy loop routes, best tackled in spring and fall due to hot summer temperatures.

Ashland's bike-trail advocacy group is **SOUTHERN OREGON MOUNTAIN BIKE ASSOCIATION** (www.somba.org), a good source for local bike shops, online trail maps for purchase, and general mountain-biking goings-on. Popular rides in the area are on the **APPLEGATE LAKE LOOP** close to town or the easier **FISH LAKE AND HIGH LAKES TRAILS** in the Rogue River National Forest off State Route 140 toward Klamath Falls.

Several paved highways in the Fremont National Forest west of Summer Lake are prime for road cycling in summer and autumn months. This vastly undiscovered part of the **OREGON OUTBACK** yields very little vehicle traffic so services are sparse, requiring good planning but delivering great rewards.

—Annissa Anderson

The scenic **LES SCHWAB AMPHITHEATER** (www.bendconcerts.com), overlooking the Deschutes River in the Old Mill District, is host to many famous artists and offers the free **SUMMER SUNDAYS CONCERT SERIES**, featuring local bands. The **ATHLETIC CLUB OF BEND** (61615 Athletic Club Dr; 541/385-3062; ww.athleticclubofbend.com) holds its **CLEAR SUMMER NIGHTS** concerts every summer, bringing well-known artists to an intimate setting. The renovated **TOWER THEATRE** (835 NW Wall St; www.tower theatre.org) downtown regularly presents concerts, as well as the **BEND FILM FESTIVAL** (www.bendfilm.org).

Bend's stage theaters offer an array of productions. The **CASCADES THEATRICAL COMPANY** (48 NW Greenwood Ave; 541/389-0803) presents six main-stage productions yearly, with an all-volunteer production crew and cast. The **SECOND STREET THEATER** (220 NE Lafayette Ave; 541/312-9626) is a local repertory company that produces seven professional shows annually.

For a complete listing, pick up the *Source* (www.tsweekly.com), the local alternative free weekly. Much of the indoor live music listed will show at either the **DOMINO ROOM** (51 NW Greenwood Ave; 541/388-1106) or the **GROVE CANTINA** (1033 NW Bond St; 541/318-8578).

SPORTS AND RECREATION

Bend is home to several annual sporting events that draw competitors and spectators from all around the globe. The **POLE PEDDLE PADDLE** (www. pole-pedal-paddle.com), held every May, is a race that involves alternating between downhill and cross-country skiing at Mount Bachelor, cycling, trail running, canoeing or kayaking, and sprinting to the finish line at Les Schwab Ampitheater. The **PACIFIC CREST TRIATHLON** (www.racecenter.com/ pacificcrest) in June attracts top athletes from across the nation to what is fast becoming one of the West's top training grounds. The preeminent **CASCADE CYCLING CLASSIC** (www.cascade-classic.org) in July is the longest-running stage racing event in North America. The five-day event spans the entire Central Oregon landscape from the formidable McKenzie Pass to the popular and exciting downtown criterium. The **BEND MARATHON** (www.bend-marathon.com) in October attracts runners who welcome the high desert's clear autumn weather.

The **BEND ELKS BASEBALL CLUB** (www.bendelks.com) excites fans all summer long at their home games staged at **VINCE GENNA STADIUM** (SE 5th St and Roosevelt Ave). **GOLF COMPETITIONS** occur from midspring to late fall every year at many of the more than 35 public and private courses (www. visitbend.com) in Central Oregon.

RESTAURANTS

Alpenglow Café / ★

1133 NW WALL ST, BEND; 541/383-7676

The glow they're referring to is probably the warm feeling you'll have after eating their mountainous breakfast (served all day). Orange juice is fresh squeezed, bacon and ham are locally smoked, and all breads are homemade. Chunky potato pancakes, made with cheddar and bacon, are served with homemade applesauce or sour cream. Entrées come with a pile of home fries and coffee cake or fresh fruit. *$; AE, DIS, MC, V; local checks only; breakfast, lunch every day; no alcohol; no reservations; www.alpenglowcafe.com; at Greenwood Ave.* &

Ariana / ★★★

1304 NW GALVESTON AVE, BEND; 541/330-5539

In a bungalow that previously housed Bend's favorite coffee house, Ariana's Mediterranean-inspired dining got off to a confusing start. Once word got around that the restaurant, rather than being an overpriced Greek eatery, offers one of the most flavorful meals in town, chef/co-owners Ariana Asti, Andres Fernandez, and Glenn Asti have been kept hopping. Best here are the Steak alla Florentina, served with truffled *frites*, and ridiculously light Spinach and Ricotta Cannelloni with both Parmesan sauce and very fresh marinara. *$$$; AE, MC, V; local checks only; dinner Tues–Sat; full bar; reservations recommended; www.arianarestaurantbend.com; Westside.* &

Deschutes Brewery & Public House / ★★★

1044 BOND ST, BEND; 541/382-9242
The Deschutes Brewery, nationally recognized for its handcrafted ales, has been a stop for most visitors since 1988. With the addition of chef Gene Soto, the pub's menu offerings quickly changed from palatable to damn good. Nightly (and lunch) specials rival those of the fancier restaurants, but people sharing a table can alternately be munching on scrumptious Buffalo wings, the Brewery Burger, or Sweet and Spicy Baked Mac and Cheese. Service here is the best in town. *$–$$; AE, MC, V; checks OK; lunch, dinner every day; beer and wine; no reservations; www.deschutesbrewery.com; off Greenwood Ave.* &

Hans / ★★

915 NW WALL ST, BEND; 541/389-9700
In Bend for 22 years, Hans is a tried-and-true favorite for both lunch and dinner. A casual, bright café with hardwood floors and big windows, Hans continues to offer a refreshingly low-key atmosphere and amazing consistency in the selection of tasty pizzas, pastas, and German specialties. Blackboard specials from the lunch menu constantly delight, as do creative salads, the venerable Hans Burger, and high-quality deli sandwiches. A pastry case with layered cakes and cookies sold separately tempts even the strong-willed. *$$; MC, V; local checks only; lunch, dinner Tues–Sat; full bar; reservations recommended; www.hansrestaurant.com; downtown.* &

Merenda Restaurant and Wine Bar / ★★★

900 NW WALL ST, BEND; 541/330-2304
Chef-owner Jody Denton offers rustic Riviera-inspired comfort food with simple, high-quality ingredients—at competitive prices. Though spacious, both the restaurant and wine bar fill up quickly, so be prepared to wait if you don't have a reservation. The menu includes pasta, pizza, and meat dishes, and a nightly wood-fired special. For small plates, try the stuffed figs or Spanish white anchovies. Wine flights are popular here, as is happy hour. *$$–$$$; AE, DC, DIS, MC, V; local checks only; lunch, dinner every day; full bar; reservations recommended; www.merendarestaurant.com; downtown.* &

Pine Tavern / ★★

967 NW BROOKS ST, BEND; 541/382-5581
With 70 years of history and a reputation for quality, the Pine Tavern is all you want in a dinner house: good food, service, atmosphere, and value. Request a table by the window overlooking Mirror Pond, and marvel at the 200-year-old tree growing through the tavern floor; outdoor dining is also available. Oregon Country Beef prime rib is the restaurant's specialty. Hearty sourdough scones and honey butter are served first but are worth saving for dessert. *$$; AE, DIS, MC, V; checks OK; lunch Mon–Sat, dinner every day; full bar; reservations recommended; www.pinetavern.com; downtown.* &

Victorian Café / ★★

1404 NW GALVESTON AVE, BEND; 541/382-6411
The converted house-turned-café off a Westside roundabout can be easily identified even without the big wooden sign. Every weekend, and many weekdays, patient would-be diners wait outside for the best breakfast in Bend. John Nolan's venture takes breakfast upscale, catering to the connoisseur with his nine types of eggs Benedict and his adventurous takes on standard fare like potato hash and omelets. The house recipe Bloody Mary is not to be missed. *$; DIS, MC, V; local checks only; breakfast, lunch every day; no reservations; off NW 14th Ave.*

LODGINGS

Inn of the Seventh Mountain / ★★

18575 SW CENTURY DR, BEND; 541/382-8711 OR 800/452-6810
This inn, which offers the closest accommodations to Mount Bachelor, is popular with families, no doubt due to the vast choice of activities and the reasonable prices. An ice rink, a sauna, three hot tubs, a water slide, and a heated swimming pool vie for guests' attention, along with tennis, horseback riding, biking, skating, rafting—you get the picture. With the opening of Seasons Restaurant in 2005, guests should now plan to stay in for dinner and the fantastic Sunday brunch. *$$–$$$; AE, DIS, MC, V; checks OK; www.innofthe7thmountain.com; 7 miles west of downtown.* &

McMenamins Old St. Francis School / ★★★

700 NW BOND ST, BEND; 541/382-5174 OR 877/661-4228
Open in 2005, this artfully restored campus adds a new dimension to the spectrum of Bend lodgings. Classrooms in this 1936 Catholic schoolhouse have been magically transformed into uniquely and historically decorated guest rooms. Also available are a 10-bed hostel for the budget minded and four rental cottages for group getaways. The prime downtown location is made even more desirable by the three on-site pubs, and free for hotel guests are a movie theater and Turkish-style soaking pool complete with stunning tile murals. *$–$$$; AE, DC, DIS, MC, V; no checks; www.mcmenamins.com; downtown off Franklin Ave.* &

Mount Bachelor Village Resort / ★★★

19717 MOUNT BACHELOR DR, BEND;
541/389-5900 OR 800/452-9846
What advantages this development has over some of its neighbors is spacious rooms. We prefer the newer units, where the color scheme is modern and light, and soundproofing helps mute the thud of ski boots. Some rooms look out at the busy road, but the River Ridge Suites overlook the spectacular Deschutes River. Amenities include outdoor Jacuzzis, seasonal outdoor heated pool, tennis courts, a 2.2-mile nature trail, and complimentary access

to the exclusive Athletic Club of Bend. *$$$; AE, DIS, MC, V; checks OK; www.mtbachelorvillage.com; toward Mount Bachelor off Century Dr.* &

Phoenix Inn Suites / ★

300 NW FRANKLIN AVE, BEND; 541/317-9292 OR 888/291-4764
Huge, spotless rooms and an informative and friendly staff make this all-suite hotel with 117 units popular with both business and pleasure-seeking travelers. Request a room with a mountain view. There's a pool, Jacuzzi, and fitness center, but the best things about this inn are its prized downtown location and affordability. There's a continental breakfast buffet in a comfortable dining room. *$$–$$$; AE, DC, DIS, MC, V; checks OK; www.phoenixinnsuites. com; downtown.* &

Pine Ridge Inn / ★★☆

1200 SW CENTURY DR, BEND; 541/389-6137 OR 800/600-4095
Perched on the edge of the river canyon off Century Drive, this privately owned 20-suite inn is smaller than neighboring resorts but big on privacy, luxury, and views of the Deschutes River. Innkeepers Judy and Don Moilanen are personable, pampering guests with wine or microbrew tastings each afternoon, turndown service, and homemade complimentary breakfasts each morning. Budget tip: Six rooms facing the parking lot are less expensive. *$$$–$$$$; AE, DC, DIS, MC, V; checks OK; www.pineridgeinn.com; just before Mount Bachelor Village.* &

Rock Springs Guest Ranch / ★★

64201 TYLER RD, BEND; 541/382-1957 OR 800/225-3833
From June through September and on holidays, the emphasis here is on family vacations, weddings, and reunions. The rest of the year, it's a top-notch conference center. In summer, day counselors supervise kids in day-long special programs while adults hit the trail, laze in the pool, play tennis or sand volleyball, or ride one of 70 horses stabled on-site. Digs are comfy knotty pine cottages with fireplaces set amid ponderosa pines alongside a small, secluded lake. *$$$; AE, MC, V; checks OK; www.rocksprings.com; 8 miles north of Bend off US Hwy 20.* &

Mount Bachelor

MOUNT BACHELOR SKI AREA (22 miles southwest of Bend, on Century Dr; 541/382-7888 for ski report or 800/829-2442; www.mtbachelor.com) is now under the ownership of Powdr Corp., based in Park City, Utah. It's one of the largest ski areas in the Pacific Northwest, with **7 HIGH-SPEED LIFTS** (10 lifts in all) feeding skiers onto 3,100 vertical feet of groomed and dry-powder slopes. Snowboarders and skiers can enjoy a full park with rails and jumps, a minipark for beginners, and the **SUPERPIPE**—a 400-foot-long half-pipe with 17-foot walls. The **TUBING PARK** has a surface lift and five groomed runs. The **SKIER'S PALATE**

CENTRAL AND SOUTHERN OREGON'S PUB COUNTRY

The recreation towns of Southern and Central Oregon now also serve as a mecca for enterprising microbrewers. Here are some of our favorites.

In Bend, the **DESCHUTES BREWERY & PUBLIC HOUSE** is the standard that many microbreweries strive for. Makers of award-winning Black Butte Porter, Bachelor Bitter, and Cascade Golden Ale, Deschutes is the second-largest Oregon producer of bottled beer. Though beer connoisseurs will have already sampled their bottled brews, tasting a seasonal beer on tap or a cask ale is an altogether different, and memorable, experience. For a brewery tour and tasting, visit their **BREWING FACILITY AND MOUNTAIN ROOM** (901 SW Simpson Ave; 541/385-8606).

BEND BREWING COMPANY (1019 NW Brooks St; 541/383-1599) showed up on the scene in 1995. Lesser-known to tourists, with consequently shorter wait times for a table, the BBC carved its niche as a local's spot. Favorites like Elk Lake India Pale Ale, Outback Old Ale, and Metolius Golden Ale can be enjoyed overlooking Mirror Pond from the outdoor patio in summer.

SILVER MOON BREWING (24 NW Greenwood Ave; 541/388-8331) began as a home-brew shop and was licensed in 2001 as a tasting room. Among owner-brewer Tyler Reichert's best brews are Bridge Creek Pilsner, Badlands Bitter, and Snakebite Porter.

The **LODGE AT CASCADES LAKES BREWING COMPANY** (1441 SW Chandler Ave; 541/388-4998) is conveniently located when you're coming from Mount

(at midmountain Pine Marten Lodge) serves excellent lunches; **SCAPOLO'S** (on lodge's lower level) features Italian cuisine. Skiing usually closes in mid-May, and the slopes reopen July 1 for summer sightseeing. High-season amenities include a ski school, racing, a day care, rentals, and a Nordic lodge with trails groomed for both classic and skate skiing.

Sisters and the Deschutes River Area

From Bend, US Highway 20 heads northwest to Sisters, and from Sisters, State Route 126 goes east to Redmond; together with US Highway 97, these roads form a triangle in an area rich with rivers and parks. North from Madras on US Highway 26 is the Warm Springs Indian Reservation. And through it all runs the **DESCHUTES RIVER**, designated a scenic waterway north of the town of Warm Springs.

Bachelor and the Cascades Lakes Highway. Brews here are a salute to local wonders, with names like Monkey Face Porter, Pine Marten Pale Ale, and 20-Inch Brown.

The **BROTHERS MCMENAMIN** most recently joined the fray with their much-lauded renovation of the **OLD ST. FRANCIS SCHOOL** (see review. In Roseburg, their **ROSEBURG STATION PUB & BREWERY** (see review) brought a train station back to life.

In Southern Oregon, **WILD RIVER BREWING & PIZZA COMPANY** has locations in Cave Junction (249 N Redwood Hwy; 541/592-3556), and Grants Pass (595 NE E St; 541/471-7487). Year-round as well as seasonal ales are brewed on-site in the Grants Pass pub.

Ashland, leading the culinary way in Southern Oregon, wouldn't have any less than the **STANDING STONE BREWING COMPANY** (101 Oak St; 541/482-2448), leaders in restaurant energy conservation. Besides turning out good-tasting ales, the Amarotico brothers have created an energy-efficient and sustainable way to run their high-production restaurant.

Klamath Falls' first microbrewery has been in operation for 13 years. **MIA & PIA'S PIZZERIA & BREWHOUSE** (3545 Summers Lane; 541/884-4880) is a family-style brew pub with, appropriately, 13 beers on tap. The **CREAMERY BREW PUB & GRILL** (1320 Main St; 541/273-5222), with 12 of their own regular and seasonal ales on tap, has been up and running since 2005, when the original creamery building was renovated into a brewing spot and restaurant.

—Annissa Anderson

Redmond

Often overlooked in favor of its big sister to the south (Bend), Redmond offers a nice alternative base for exploring the Sisters region. About 6 miles north of Redmond, east of Terrebonne, some of the finest rock climbers gather to test their skills on the buff and magenta tuff and rhyolite cliffs of **SMITH ROCK STATE PARK** (off US Hwy 97; 541/548-7501). Year-round camping is available.

Experience a train robbery over Sunday brunch on the **CROOKED RIVER DINNER TRAIN** (4075 NE O'Neil Rd; 541/548-8630; www.crookedriverrailroad.com) as it ambles up the 38-mile Crooked River valley between Redmond and Prineville. Three-hour scenic excursions include white-tablecloth dinner service and sometimes have special themes, such as western murder-mystery theater and cowboy cookouts. Reservations required.

LODGINGS

Inn at Eagle Crest / ★★

1522 CLINE FALLS RD, REDMOND; 541/923-2453 OR 800/MUCH-SUN
Yet another golf resort in Central Oregon? The difference here is that golfers enjoy oddly milder weather just 20-some miles north of Bend. Private homes at this full resort rim the 18-hole golf course, and visitors choose from hotel rooms or condominiums. The resort has two recreation centers, with a variety of court sports, pools, and spa facilities, as well as trails, an equestrian center, and playfields. The food at the resort's formal Niblick & Greene's is apropos to its clubby atmosphere. *$$; AE, MC, V; checks OK; www.eagle-crest.com; 5 miles west of Redmond.* &

Sisters

Named after the three mountain peaks—Faith, Hope, and Charity—that dominate the horizon, this little community is becoming a mecca for tired urbanites looking for a taste of cowboy escapism. On a clear day (about 250 a year here), Sisters is exquisitely beautiful. Surrounded by mountains, trout streams, and pine and cedar forests, this small town capitalizes on the influx of winter skiers and summer camping and fishing enthusiasts. Though the town population is about 1,000, more than 7,500 live in the surrounding area on sage and ponderosa ranchettes.

In the early 1970s, Sisters developed its western theme, but it's grown much more sophisticated of late. The town, built on about 30 feet of pumice dust spewed over centuries from the nearby volcanoes, has added mini-mall shopping clusters with courtyards and sidewalks to eliminate blowing dust. There are several large art galleries, locally owned curio shops, an excellent fly-fishing shop—the **FLY FISHER'S PLACE** (151 W Main Ave; 541/549-3474; www.theflyfishersplace.com), and even freshly roasted coffee, at **SISTERS COFFEE COMPANY** (273 W Hood Ave; 541/549-0527).

Mixed sentiment about the pseudowestern storefronts aside, Sisters' economy thrives on the attention from tourists. Sisters hosts 56,000 visitors for each of four shows during June's annual **SISTERS RODEO**. In July, the town also has the world's largest outdoor quilt show, the longtime **SISTERS OUTDOOR QUILT SHOW**, with 800 quilts hanging from balconies and storefronts. Call the **VISITOR CENTER** (541/549-0251) for information.

With an easy walk to every store in town, Sisters has become known as a great place to shop. Among many locally owned and unique stores is the famous quilt and gift shop **STITCHIN' POST/WILD HARE** (311 W Cascade St; 541/549-6061), a must-see for the crafts crowd, and eclectic **BEDOUIN** (143 E Hood Ave; 541/549-3079), with its walk-through neighbor **NAVIGATOR NEWS**, an art gallery–coffeehouse.

Though the restaurant-to-visitor ratio is unexpectedly low, two good bakeries can be found downtown. The **SISTERS BAKERY** (251 E Cascade St; 541/549-0361) makes old-fashioned doughnuts, pastries, and pies. For an ever-so-slightly healthier option, **ANGELINE'S BAKERY & CAFÉ** (121 W Main Ave; 541/549-1922) offers bagels and sandwiches.

RESTAURANTS

Bronco Billy's Ranch Grill and Saloon / ★

190 E CASCADE ST, SISTERS; 541/549-RIBS

Formerly known as the Hotel Sisters Restaurant, this bar and eatery serves, unsurprisingly, ranch cooking. Owners John Keenan and John Tehan have succeeded in re-creating the look of a first-class 1900 hotel, with a touch of *Hee Haw!* and *Haunted House* thrown in for entertainment value; full-size straw-stuffed dolls in period dress occupy the corners. The upstairs hotel rooms are now private banquet rooms. The covered patio is a good hangout for drinks in summer. *$$; MC, V; checks OK; lunch, dinner every day in summer, lunch Sat–Sun, dinner every day in winter; full bar; reservations recommended; at Fir St.* &

Jen's Garden / ★★

403 E HOOD AVE, SISTERS; 541/549-2699

When Jen's Garden opened spring 2005, food lovers from Black Butte Ranch to Tumalo breathed a huge sigh of relief. Chef-owners T. R. and Jennifer McCrystal fill a previously empty niche of fine dining in Sisters with their French provincial–inspired restaurant. The intimate cottage cuisine stars finely prepared à la carte and prix-fixe menu options that change weekly, with items like grilled pork tenderloin with roasted shallot–applejack demi-glace over white beans and pears. *$$$; MC, V; local checks only; dinner Wed–Sun; beer and wine; reservations recommended; www.intimatecottagecuisine.com; at Larch St.*

LODGINGS

Black Butte Ranch / ★★★☆

US HWY 20, BLACK BUTTE RANCH; 541/595-6211 OR 866/901-2961

With 1,800 acres, this recreation wonderland remains the darling of Northwest resorts. Rimmed by the Three Sisters mountains, the ranch draws families year-round to swim, ski, fish, golf, bike, boat, ride horses, and play tennis. The best way to make a reservation is to state the size of your party and whether you want a home or condo. Tables at the Lodge Restaurant (Wed–Sun in winter) are tiered so everyone can appreciate the meadow panorama beyond. *$$$; AE, DIS, MC, V; checks OK; www.blackbutteranch.com; 8 miles west of Sisters.* &

Camp Sherman

This tiny settlement midway between Sisters and Santiam Pass is lush and green despite raging fires in summer 2003. Reservations are recommended at the popular **KOKANEE CAFE** (25545 SW Forest Service Rd 1419; 541/595-6420; April–Oct).

LODGINGS

Metolius River Resort / ★★

25551 SW FOREST SERVICE RD 1419, CAMP SHERMAN; 541/595-6281 OR 800/81-TROUT
Not to be confused with the lower-priced, circa-1923 Metolius River Lodges across the bridge, these 11 upscale cabins on the west bank have large decks and river-rock fireplaces. Most have bedroom lofts, furnished kitchens, river-facing decks, cable television, and barbecues. Because the pricey cabins are privately owned, interiors differ, but most include luxurious lodge-style furnishings and all are meticulously maintained. Management prohibits group rentals and pets to maintain a tranquil atmosphere. *$$$; AE, DIS, MC, V; checks OK; www.metoliusriverresort.com; 5 miles north of US Hwy 20.*

Warm Springs

Many travelers pass through the **WARM SPRINGS INDIAN RESERVATION** on their way south to Bend or north to Mount Hood. To visitors, the area is most well known for the sulfur-free hot springs near the Warm Springs River—the center of **KAH-NEE-TA HIGH DESERT RESORT & CASINO** (see review), on the reservation nestled below the barren Mutton Mountains. Even if you're not spending the night, be sure to stop and visit the incredible **MUSEUM AT WARM SPRINGS** (541/553-3331; www.warmsprings.biz/museum). It includes a stunning exhibit of a Wasco wedding ceremony, a contemporary art gallery, and a gift shop.

LODGINGS

Kah-Nee-Ta High Desert Resort & Casino / ★★

100 MAIN ST, WARM SPRINGS; 541/553-1112 OR 800/554-4786
A peaceful getaway 11 miles from US Highway 26, the resort's accommodations are diverse, including houses, RV spaces, 20 tepees, and a 30-room motel in the village. The lodge and casino building has sweeping views, but the 139 rooms are otherwise unremarkable. The main lodge's fine dining room is the Juniper Room; the Chinook Room offers buffet service and food to go. An 18-hole golf course and tennis courts are on-site; all guests can access the hot springs mineral pool. *$$–$$$; AE, DC, DIS, MC, V; checks OK; www.kah-nee-taresort.com; 11 miles north of Warm Springs on SR 3.* &

EASTERN OREGON

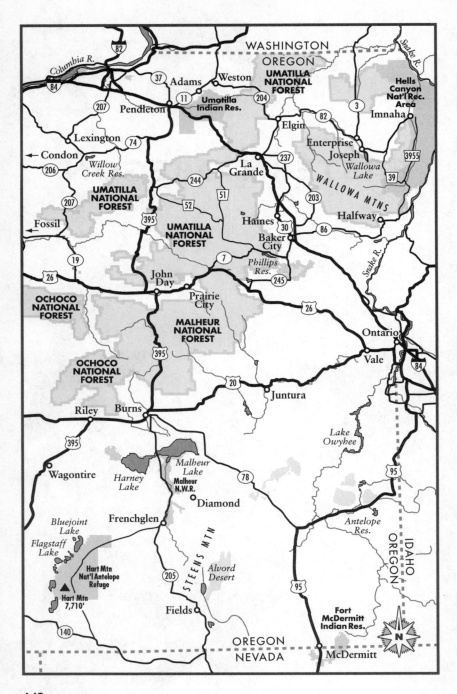

142

EASTERN OREGON

Eastern Oregon is an undiscovered treasure, full of old cow towns and some of the state's highest mountain peaks, in the Wallowa Mountains. Here lies Hells Canyon, North America's deepest river gorge. The Blue Mountains and the Malheur National Wildlife Refuge are just a few of the backdrops.

Summers here are long and dry, perfect for hikes or bike rides. A day trip from Pendleton to Joseph has some of the state's best views.

ACCESS AND INFORMATION

Traveling from Portland in the west or Boise in the east, **INTERSTATE 84** runs through Eastern Oregon. Pendleton, La Grande, and Baker City all sit on I-84, making them good starting places for exploring this area. **US HIGHWAY 395** runs north and south from Pendleton to Burns, cutting through the Umatilla, Malheur, and Ochoco national forests. **US HIGHWAY 26** connects Redmond in Central Oregon to Ontario near the Oregon-Idaho state line, with **US HIGHWAY 20** from Bend running a similar, more southerly route to Ontario.

During the winter, check for road closures, since I-84 crosses the Blue Mountains at more than 4,000 feet and the U.S. highways often accumulate huge snowdrifts. **THE OREGON DEPARTMENT OF TRANSPORTATION** (503/588-2941 or 800/977-6368; www.oregon.gov/ODOT) and the travel Web site **TRIP CHECK** (www.tripcheck.com) have up-to-date road reports.

Amtrak has a train from Eugene to Ontario on US Highway 20 and Greyhound travels I-84 from Portland to Boise, Idaho. Buses between Eastern Oregon towns are operated by several smaller carriers, such as **COMMUNITY CONNECTIONS** (541/523-6591) in Enterprise and Joseph and **PEOPLE MOVER** (800/527-2370) in John Day. If you're flying, **HORIZON AIR** (www.horizonair.com) goes from Portland to Pendleton and from Seattle to Walla Walla, Washington.

Pendleton

Dubbed "Round-Up City" after the famous rodeo it hosts every September (see "Adult Spring Break—In Pendleton"), Pendleton is Eastern Oregon's largest city, with a bustling downtown. Locals take pride in their farms, ranches, and wool, which fuel the economy.

PENDLETON WOOLEN MILLS (1307 SE Court Pl; 541/276-6911; www.pendleton-usa.com) was founded here in 1909. Buy some discounted blankets or take a tour of the mills. **PENDLETON UNDERGROUND TOURS** (37 SW Emigrant Ave; 541/276-0730 or 800/226-6398) is a 1½-hour tour of the city's past, including its 1890s underground poker rooms and brothels.

ARMCHAIR BOOKS (39 SW Dorion Ave; 541/276-7323) has a huge selection of books by local authors. Stop by **HAMLEY'S AND COMPANY** (30 SE Court Ave; 541/278-1100; www.hamley.com), longtime makers of saddles and leather, to

---

NORTHEASTERN OREGON THREE-DAY TOUR

DAY ONE: Get the day rolling in Pendleton with coffee and a pastry at the **GREAT PACIFIC WINE AND COFFEE COMPANY**. Walk over to **ARMCHAIR BOOKS** and read up on the rich history of rough-and-tumble Umatilla County. Grab a meatball sub on fresh-baked bread at **COMO'S** (39 SE Court Ave; 541/278-9142) and then check out the **PENDLETON UNDERGROUND TOUR** before stopping off at **HAMLEY'S AND COMPANY** for some authentic western shopping. Drive over to the **TAMASTSLIKT CULTURAL INSTITUTE** to learn more about the Confederated Tribes of the Umatilla, or rent a bike from the **PEDALER'S PLACE** (318 S Main St; 541/276-3337) and explore the old highways that connect Pendleton with numerous small towns. End the night with a delicious meal at **RAPHAEL'S**. Stay at the **PARKER HOUSE BED AND BREAKFAST**.

DAY TWO: Make the trip northeast on Highway 11 to Weston and eat a cowhand's breakfast at the **LONG BRANCH CAFÉ & SALOON** (201 E Main St; 541/566-3478). Drive east through the Blue Mountains and into the Wallowa Mountains on Highway 204 to Elgin, and then hop on Highway 82 east to

---

see a western art gallery and watch saddle makers. The **TAMASTLIKT CULTURAL INSTITUTE** (72789 Hwy 331; 541/966-9748), which tells the story of Oregon from the Native point of view, has great art exhibits.

RESTAURANTS

Great Pacific Wine and Coffee Company / ★

403 S. MAIN ST, PENDLETON; 541/276-1350
A great place to drink coffee and read, share a bottle of wine, or listen to live music. Owners Carol Hanks and Ken Schulberg serve a limited menu, focusing on snacks like veggies and hummus and gourmet sandwiches. Pendleton's only bistro, "GP" is decorated with elegant hardwood floors and rustic brick walls. Great Pacific also serves local microbrews on tap, as well as by the bottle. *$; AE, DIS, MC, V; checks OK; breakfast, lunch, dinner Mon–Sat; beer and wine; reservations recommended (except Fri); at SE Emigrant Ave.* &

Raphael's / ★★★

233 SE 4TH ST, PENDLETON; 541/276-8500 OR 888/944-CHEF
This is the place for exquisite dining in Eastern Oregon. Located in the historic Raley House—home of Round-Up founder Roy Raley and, later, Pendleton mayor Joe McLaughlin—this living history lesson has been turned into a true dining experience by owners Raphael and Rob Hoffman. Whether you eat in front of the green marble fireplace or on the back deck, you can really taste the West. Besides the basic steaks and seafood, Oregon marionberry

Enterprise. The drive, just under two hours, highlights some of the state's most scenic areas. Stop in at the **TERMINAL GRAVITY BREWERY** for a beer and some of the best pub food you'll ever have. If you can put down your IPA, head down to Joseph, just 6 miles south. Before checking into the **BRONZE ANTLER B&B**, stroll down Main Street and admire the seven bronze sculptures that populate Joseph's downtown. Stop by the **ASPEN GROVE GALLERY** (602 N Main St; 541/432-9555) or the **VALLEY BRONZE OF OREGON** before calling it a night.

DAY THREE: Wake up early and take in the beauty of **WALLOWA LAKE**. Go on an early hike through the **EAGLE CAP WILDERNESS AREA** or enjoy a lakeside picnic with goods from the **WILDFLOUR BAKERY** back in town. For an Alps-like view, take the **WALLOWA LAKE TRAMWAY** to the top of Mount Howard. Adventure seekers can take their mountain bikes on the tram and ride the 5-mile trail back down to the lake. If extreme sports aren't your thing, have lunch at the **SUMMIT GRILL** (59919 Wallowa Lake Hwy; 541/432-5331) and enjoy a leisurely after-lunch stroll that showcases views of four states. End your day—and trip—with a meal at the **WALLOWA LAKE LODGE**.

elk chops and rattlesnake-and-rabbit sausage are big hits. *$$; AE, DIS, MC, V; checks OK; dinner Tues–Sat; full bar; reservations recommended; www. raphaelsrestaurant.com; between Court Pl and Dorian Ave.* &

LODGINGS

The Parker House Bed & Breakfast / ★★★

311 N MAIN ST, PENDLETON; 541/276-8581 OR 800/700-8581
One night at the Parker House easily turns into two. Overlooking the Umatilla River and Pendleton's downtown, this pink stucco mansion is the nicest place in town. An English garden and front porch with white chairs are a major contrast to the wheat fields and rodeo rowdiness. Ask for the Gwendolyn or Mandarin Room, both of which have balcony access. *$$; MC, V; checks OK; www.parkerhousebnb.com; cross Umatilla River to N Main St.*

Adams

RESTAURANTS AND LODGINGS

Bar M Ranch / ★★

58840 BAR M LANE, ADAMS; 541/566-3381 OR 888/824-3381
Located 31 miles east of Pendleton, this working ranch is nestled along the Umatilla River in the foothills of the Blue Mountains. Guests can do everything from trout fishing to soaking in the Bingham Hot Springs. During the

summer, ranch hands lead horseback rides through the ranch's 2,500 acres. If you're in the area for just a day, call ahead and have lunch—the scenic drive to the Bar M alone is worth the trip. *$$$; MC, V; checks OK; reservations recommended (dining); www.barmranch.com; drive 13 mi after crossing over tracks at Bar M sign at Bingham Rd.* &

La Grande

Home of Eastern Oregon's only four-year college, Eastern Oregon University, La Grande offers an eclectic mix of shops and restaurants that only a college town can provide.

THE OPAL ROSE GALLERY (209 Depot St; 541/962-7912 or 866/304-7912) sells the works of Northwest artists—everything from photography to hand-made jewelry. **SUNFLOWER BOOKS** (1114 Washington St; 541/963-5242) is a great place to pick up something to read and have some coffee.

RESTAURANTS

Foley Station / ★★

1114 ADAMS AVE, LA GRANDE; 541/963-7473

This is *the* place for breakfast. The Belgian waffles and huevos rancheros are perfect-looking. If you come later, try their happy hour in the intimate bar; the pan-fried halibut and organic burgers are a bargain, washed down with one of Oregon's many microbrews. *$$; AE, DIS, MC, V; checks OK; breakfast, lunch, dinner every day; full bar; reservations recommended; www.foleystation. com; between 4th and Depot sts.* &

Ten Depot Street

10 DEPOT ST, LA GRANDE; 541/963-8766

Ten Depot, a longtime local favorite, is a good place to get a feeling for this town. The dining room, in an old brick building with antique furnishings, is nice, but it's more fun to eat dinner in the bar, with its beautiful carved-wood back. During the week, the blue plate specials are a deal. Dinners range from a two-fisted (half-pound) burger to chicken-and-pesto pasta to prime rib (the house specialty). *$$; AE, MC, V; checks OK; lunch, dinner Mon–Sat; full bar; reservations recommended; 2 blocks west of Adams Ave.* &

LODGINGS

Stange Manor / ★

1612 WALNUT ST, LA GRANDE; 888/286-9463

The winding staircase in this 1920s Georgian mansion, which was once owned by a lumber baron, is a masterpiece, and the sunroom is a great spot for collecting your thoughts. Choice quarters is the master bedroom, but the maid's room and the guest room are fine too—this is La Grande's nicest place

ADULT SPRING BREAK—IN PENDLETON

During the third week in September, Daytona Beach and Cancun can't hold a candle to Pendleton. More than 30,000 visitors flock to this small but proud town of 15,000 for what can only be described as an adult spring break—the **PEND-LETON ROUND-UP**. Main Street actually shuts down for an entire week, filled with **LIVE MUSIC** every night. A notable Nashville star (Terri Clark in 2005 and Sarah Evans in 2006) usually kicks off the madness with a Saturday-night concert before the Professional Bull Riders (PBR) Classic opens the rodeo scene Monday and Tuesday nights. Accompanied by fireworks and rock music, 40 cowboys each night ride the world's toughest bulls.

Wednesday is the official start of the Round-Up, and the crowds gradually increase each day before the Round-Up begins. Grounds are limited to standing-room only for Saturday's finale. While the bucking broncs and angry bulls in the arena may seem wild, it's nothing compared to what happens in the famous **LET 'ER BUCK ROOM** beneath the south grandstands. Serving only liquor and open only during the time of the rodeo (noon–5pm) the Let 'er Buck Room quickly becomes as hedonistic as any out-of-control frat party. It's not unusual to see a good-natured cowgirl literally give a young farmhand the shirt off her back.

The fun continues after the rodeo, as local watering holes like the Rainbow and Crabby's fill up from dusk till 2 am. Besides the chance to bump boots with a sexy "buckle bunny" or handsome bull rider, the Round-Up is one of the world's best rodeos. All the competitors are world-class athletes, and the community effort to stage a week of celebration is truly spectacular. Cowboy or not, anyone looking for an experience out of this world should take in the Round-Up at least once in their lifetime.

—Beau Eastes

to stay, after all. Chef-owner Carolyn Jensen serves a mean breakfast, so be prepared to eat a late lunch. *$$; MC, V; checks OK; www.stangemanor.com.*

Condon

LODGINGS

Hotel Condon / ★

202 S MAIN ST, CONDON; 541/384-4624 OR 800/201-6706
The restored Hotel Condon—built in 1920 and renovated in 2001—gives travelers a classy lodging option in the middle of Oregon's wheat country.

HORSE TRAILS

One of the best opportunities east of the Cascades is the chance to saddle up and explore the marvels of the West on horseback.

Near Pendleton, the **BAR M RANCH** offers day rides along the Umatilla River, with overnight rides in nice weather. Near Condon, just outside the town of Fossil, the **WILSON RANCHES RETREAT BED & BREAKFAST** lets guests help with cattle drives and branding. On the 9,000-acre ranch, visitors can see an array of wild animals.

At Wallowa Lake, the **EAGLE CAP WILDERNESS PACK STATION** (800/681-6222) provides rides in the state's largest wilderness area. Hikers can hire the packers to drop them off at hard-to-reach locations and arrange for them to return a few days later. In southeastern Oregon, the **STEENS MOUNTAIN PACKERS** (800/977-3995) take visitors as high as 7,000 feet along old deer trails near the town of Frenchglen. With all these gorgeous settings, most riders plan their next trips before they're even finished with the one they're on.

—Beau Eastes

Five-course meals and lunch specials are served in the dining room throughout the week. Guests can spend the day fishing for bass and steelhead in the nearby John Day River or enjoy a scenic cycling route alongside one of the West's last undammed rivers. *$; AE, DIS, MC, V; checks OK; www.hotel condon.com; at 2nd St.* &

Fossil

LODGINGS

Wilson Ranches Retreat Bed & Breakfast / ★★

16555 BUTTE CREEK RD, FOSSIL; 541/763-2227 OR 888/968-7698
About 2 miles northwest of Fossil, this ranch takes you back to the Old West. Visitors can work with Phil Wilson in the fields, herding cattle, or branding calves to get the feel of life on the ranch. The Wilson's 9,000-acre spread is also perfect for a mountain biking, horseback riding, and hiking getaway. With its proximity to the John Day River, the Wilson is one of the best family lodging options out here. *$; AE, DIS, MC, V; checks OK; www.wilsonranches retreat.com; 2 mi northwest of Fossil on Butte Creek Rd.*

Wallowa Mountains and Hells Canyon

This is the ancestral home of Chief Joseph; he fled from here with a band of Nez Perce to his last stand near the Canadian border. Although Chief Joseph's remains are interred far from his beloved land of the winding water, he saw to it that his father, Old Chief Joseph, was buried here, on the north shore of Wallowa Lake.

HELLS CANYON NATIONAL RECREATION AREA (35 miles east of Joseph; 541/426-5546; www.fs.fed.us/hellscanyon/) encompasses the continent's deepest gorge, an awesome trench cut by the Snake River through sheer lava walls.

Enterprise

RESTAURANTS

Terminal Gravity Brewery / ★

803 SCHOOL ST, ENTERPRISE; 541/246-0158

Oregonians have high expectations for their microbrews, and Terminal Gravity doesn't disappoint. Their IPA is the company's most sought-after brew, but their stout and ESG are also great. The brewery itself is a traveler's haven, with pickup volleyball games in the summer and lively discussions among an eclectic crowd in the winter. The food is better-than-average pub fare, with local produce and a revolving menu. *$; no credit cards; checks OK; dinner Thurs–Sat; beer and wine; no reservations; south end of town.*

Joseph

It's not surprising that the town of Joseph, given its proximity to both Hells Canyon and the Eagle Cap Wilderness, has long been a hub for outdoor sports. No one could have predicted that this isolated town of 1,300 would also become a thriving center for art—but that's what it is now.

In 1982 a local businessman opened a foundry where artists could have sculptures cast in bronze. The foundry's success attracted artists from around the world. Today Joseph is home to two working foundries and a dozen galleries, showcasing mostly traditional art.

Joseph's art scene is centered on Main Street, where you'll see places to eat and a few old-timers like the hardware store and lumberyard. The street is also filled with lampposts, paving-stone sidewalks, and large bronze sculptures. Stop by the **MANUEL MUSEUM** (400 N Main St; 541/432-7235) for John Wayne memorabilia and Civil War objects. Other notable galleries include **INDIGO GALLERY** (504 S Main St; 541/432-5202) and **VALLEY BRONZE OF OREGON** (307 W Alder St; 541/432-7551; www.valleybronze.com).

Some call **WALLOWA LAKE STATE PARK,** just south of Joseph on the lakeshore, one of the most beautiful state parks in the country. It has a swimming beach and a boat launch. It's near trailheads that lead into the **EAGLE CAP WILDERNESS AREA,** which is filled with glacier-ripped valleys, high mountain lakes, and marble peaks. And it's home to **ALPENFEST**, a major September festival.

Scoot to the top of 8,200-foot Mount Howard on the **WALLOWA LAKE TRAMWAY** (59919 Wallowa Lake Hwy; 541/432-5331; www.wallowalake tramway.com), a gondola that ascends to 2 miles of hiking trails with views of Hells Canyon, the Wallowas, and Idaho's Seven Devils. Maps are available at the **WALLOWA MOUNTAINS VISITOR CENTER** (88401 Hwy 82, Enterprise; 541/426-5546).

As you hike, let a llama lug your gear with **HURRICANE CREEK LLAMA TREKS** (541/432-4455 or 800/528-9609; www.hcltrek.com; June–Aug). A day's hike takes you 4 to 8 miles, and meals are included. Sign up for a morning horseback ride or an extended wilderness pack trip at the **EAGLE CAP WILDERNESS PACK STATION** (see "Horse Trails").

Don't let winter stop you from exploring the Wallowas. Head into the back-country for a few days of guided telemark skiing with **WING RIDGE SKI TOURS** (541/426-4322 or 800/646-9050; www.wingski.com). Experienced guides lead you to a rustic cabin or a tent shelter, next to a wood-fired sauna tent.

RESTAURANTS

Old Town Café

8 S MAIN ST, JOSEPH; 541/432-9898
Locals and tourists pack this place, which has a modern-day, western chat 'n' chew atmosphere. Get a seat in the garden and enjoy your lunch or the break-fast burritos smothered in homemade salsa. *$; MC, V; checks OK; breakfast, lunch Fri–Wed; beer and wine; no reservations; downtown.*

Wildflour Bakery / ★

600 N MAIN ST, JOSEPH; 541/432-7225
Come here for berry scones or a sandwich on the deck. Their breads are organic, and many meals are vegetarian. *$; no credit cards; checks OK; break-fast, lunch Wed–Sun; no alcohol; no reservations; north end of town.* ♿

LODGINGS

The Bronze Antler Bed & Breakfast / ★

309 S MAIN ST, JOSEPH; 541/432-0230 OR 866/520-9769
Locals helped restore the interior of this cozy lodge to its past glory when Bill Finney and Heather Tyreman took over, giving it a homey Eastern Oregon feel. The Chief Joseph Room has a panoramic view of the Wallowa Moun-tains, but when the sun sets, the Sawtooth Room is the place to be. Bill and Heather are quick to share their favorite hiking trail or the best dish at any restaurant in the county, giving guests a true insider's view into Joseph. Chil-dren over 12 are welcome. *$$; AE, DIS, MC, V; checks OK; www.bronzeantler. com; at 4th Ave.*

Wallowa Lake Lodge / ★

60060 WALLOWA LAKE HWY, JOSEPH; 541/432-9821
Many of the guest rooms at the Wallowa Lake Lodge are quite small, but that shouldn't matter: you're here to hike the trails and knock around downtown Joseph. That said, the lake-view rooms with balconies have more space, and evenings are often spent sprawled in front of the lobby's stone fireplace anyway. If you plan to stay longer than a night, the lakeside cabins are best. *$$; DIS, MC, V; checks OK; www.wallowalake.com; near state park.*

Imnaha

LODGINGS

Imnaha River Inn / ★★

73946 RIMROCK RD, IMNAHA; 541/577-6002 OR 866/601-9214
Built by Nick and Sandy Vidan in 2000, this 7,000-square-foot log cabin looks like a Lincoln Log project come to life. An hour north of Joseph, the Imnaha River Inn is alone in the wilderness. You'll see bighorn sheep from the front deck, overlooking an untouched landscape. The Elk Room looks onto the Imnaha River; the Bear Den has a picturesque view of the Imnaha River Canyon. A truly unique destination. *$$; no credit cards; checks OK; www. imnahariverinn.com.* &

Halfway

Halfway, on the southern slopes of the Wallowas, is even more isolated than Joseph but just as pretty. Its green valley is filled with old barns and hay fields, until the meadows steepen and rise to mountain peaks.

HELLS CANYON begins at **OXBOW DAM**, 16 miles east of Halfway. For spectacular views of the **SNAKE RIVER**, drive from Oxbow to Joseph (take Hwy 86 to Forest Rd 39, summers only). Get maps from the U.S. Forest Service **RANGER STATION** in Pine (541/742-7511), 1½ miles outside Halfway. Outfitter **WALLOWA LLAMAS** (36678 Allstead Lane; 541/742-2961; www.wallowallamas.com) leads three- to seven-day trips into the Eagle Cap Wilderness, with the animals lugging your gear. For those who would rather experience the raging river up close, **HELLS CANYON ADVENTURES** (4200 Hells Canyon Dam Rd; 541/785-3352; www. hellscanyonadventures.com) in Oxbow arranges jet-boat or white-water raft tours leaving from Hells Canyon Dam.

LODGINGS

Pine Valley Lodge / ★★

163 MAIN ST, HALFWAY; 541/742-2027
A wacky good spirit came to Halfway with the arrival of Babette and Dale
Beatty. They've put together a quirky collection of restored lodge rooms and
guest houses on one side of Main Street and a restaurant and gallery on the
other. Babette was the first *Sports Illustrated* swimsuit-edition cover girl,
in 1963, and from the breakfast area you'll see the vintage issue displayed
upstairs. If their Halfway Supper Club is serving dinner, jump at the chance to
eat there. *$$; no credit cards; checks OK; www.pvlodge.com; downtown.*

Baker City and Haines

Baker City has had good fortune. In 1861 gold was found in the nearby Blue
Mountains. By the beginning of the 20th century, Baker City was home to 6,700
people—more than lived in Boise. But as the mines died out, so did the people. In
the 1960s, the Geiser Grand Hotel had shut its doors, and travelers passed right
through town. Then good fortune struck again.

The Bureau of Land Management chose Flagstaff Hill, 4 miles north of town,
for its **NATIONAL HISTORIC OREGON TRAIL INTERPRETIVE CENTER** (Hwy 86,
Baker City; 541/523-1843; open every day; $5 per adult, $10 per carload) in 1992.
The museum drew more than 500,000 visitors in its first 18 months, and its suc-
cess started a little tourism boom. Three years later, the Geiser Grand Hotel shone
after a $6 million makeover, and the museum's popularity continues.

But, like most Eastern Oregon towns, Baker City is not "touristy." There are
no trendy restaurants, shopping is limited, and nightlife is not exactly hopping.
Come here for the history and scenery. After checking out the Oregon Trail center,
take the 75-minute round-trip hike to the trail itself. Living-history camps outside
the center give insight into one of the largest peacetime migrations ever. Plan on a
half day or so to fully explore.

When you're back downtown, stop at **BELLA** (2023 Main St; 541/523-7490),
a popular downtown market. And don't miss the architecture—more than 100
buildings are listed in the National Register of Historic Places.

A restored narrow-gauge steam train, the **SUMPTER VALLEY RAILWAY** (541/894-
2268; www.svry.com), makes the short run between McEwen, just west of
Phillips Lake, and Sumpter from Memorial Day through September. **ANTHONY
LAKES SKI AREA** (20 miles west of North Powder on Forest Rd 73; 541/856-
3277) has good powder snow, one chair lift, cross-country trails, and snow-cat
skiing. In the same area, see elk on the horse-drawn wagon tours of the **ELK-
HORN WILDLIFE AREA**.

RESTAURANTS

Barley Brown's Brewpub / ★

2190 MAIN ST, BAKER CITY; 541/523-4266
Downtown Baker City's biggest dinners come from this family-friendly restaurant—only half its space is the bar. The menu features pasta and steak. The brewery makes a full line of beers with cute names, including Tumble Off Pale Ale and seasonal brews such as Sled Wreck Winter Ale. Weekends often feature live music. *$; AE, DC, DIS, MC, V; checks OK; dinner Mon–Sat; full bar; no reservations; at Main and Church sts.*

Haines Steak House / ★

910 FRONT ST, HAINES; 541/856-3639
There's no mistaking that you're in cattle country, so get ready to chow down on a giant steak. Don't stray from beef here—it's well selected, well cut, and well cooked (rare, natch). *$$; AE, DC, MC, V; checks OK; lunch Sun, dinner Wed–Mon; full bar; reservations recommended; on old Hwy 30.*

LODGINGS

Geiser Grand Hotel / ★★

1996 MAIN ST, BAKER CITY; 541/523-1889 OR 888/434-7374
This hotel, an 1889 National Historic Landmark, was completely shut down for 25 years, but after a 1993 restoration, it's shining. Locals swear the Geiser Grand is haunted, and a *New York Times* writer even reported that she felt a "presence" there sitting on her bed. But don't let that stop you. Each of the 30 rooms has a crystal chandelier—need we say more? Get a cupola suite; they're a splurge, but the mountain and downtown views are worth it. The dining area, where you'll get mainly meat-and-potatoes fare, has a huge stained-glass skylight. *$$; AE, DIS, MC, V; checks OK; www.geisergrand.com; at Washington Ave.*

John Day

John Day looks like just another cow town, but its surroundings are loaded with history. It's just off the Oregon Trail, and before the 1860s, the region was packed with gold. **KAM WAH CHUNG MUSEUM** (250 NW Canton St; 541/575-0028; open Sat–Thurs, May–Oct) was the stone-walled home of an early 20th-century Chinese herbalist and doctor.

JOHN DAY FOSSIL BEDS NATIONAL MONUMENT is one of the world's greatest fossil collections, with three dispersed units. Colorfully banded hills are seen at the Painted Hills Unit; an ancient fossilized forest is featured at the Clarno Unit; and fascinating geological layers are viewed at the Sheep Rock Unit. Stop by the **VISITOR CENTER AND MUSEUM** near the Sheep Rock Unit (Hwy 19, 10 miles northwest of Dayville; 541/987-2333; open 9am–5pm every day).

LODGINGS

The Ponderosa Guest Ranch / ★★★

PO BOX 190, SENECA; 541/542-2403
Get ready to cowboy up at the Ponderosa Guest Ranch, a real working cattle ranch with up to 4,000 animals. Guests partake of fun activities like assisting a bovine cesarean, branding, or driving cattle to mountain pastures. Sound a little intimidating? Go check out the wildflowers or look for antelope, bears, groundhogs, eagles, sandhill cranes, cinnamon ducks, and sage hens. Hearty ranch fare, included in the price, is served family style. *$$$; MC, V; checks OK; 3-night min; www.ponderosaguestranch.com; on Hwy 395, halfway between John Day and Burns.*

Prairie City

LODGINGS

Strawberry Mountain Inn / ★

E HWY 26, PRAIRIE CITY; 541/820-4522 OR 800/545-6913
A welcome retreat for families, the Strawberry Mountain Inn sits approximately 10 miles away from Strawberry Lake. Owners Bill and Linda Harrington have set up a playground for the little ones that complements the pool table and hot tub for adults. The house features five rooms; stay in the Blue Room, with its bay window opening up to the mountain. *$$; AE, MC, V; checks OK; www.stawberrymountaininn.com; just east of downtown.*

Southeast High Desert

MALHEUR NATIONAL WILDLIFE REFUGE (on Hwy 205, 37 miles south of Burns; 541/493-2612) is one of the country's major bird refuges—187,000 acres of wetlands and lakes. Spring is the best time to see a wide variety of birds; more than 130 species rest on the refuge. The **REFUGE HEADQUARTERS** (32 miles southeast of Burns on south side of Malheur Lake; 541/493-2612) provides maps.

Burns

The town of Burns, once the center of impressive cattle kingdoms, is still a market town, albeit a quiet one. **CRYSTAL CRANE HOT SPRINGS** (on Hwy 78, Crane, 25 miles southeast of Burns; 541/493-2312) is a good place to take a break from driving and swim in the hot-springs pond or soak in a water trough turned hot tub.

RESTAURANTS

Pine Room Cafe

543 W MONROE ST, BURNS; 541/573-6631
This may be Burns's fanciest restaurant, but that doesn't mean you have to take your cowboy hat off at the dinner table. Besides the expected hand-cut steaks, popular entrées include the chicken artichoke and fish dishes. Expect a true western environment. *$$; MC, V; local checks only; dinner Tues–Sat; full bar; reservations recommended; at Egan Ave.* &

LODGINGS

Sage Country Inn / ★

351½ W MONROE ST, BURNS; 541/573-7243
Set well back from the main drag through Burns, the Sage Country Inn is a comfortable base for a southeastern Oregon adventure. All three rooms in this 1907 Georgian Colonial are pretty different; the Cattle Baron's Room is manly, and the Court Street Room is, shall we say, flowery. Each room has antiques and books on local history and ranchers' witticisms. Read up and save your questions for breakfast—the owners can tell you all about the history of southeastern Oregon. *$$; MC, V; checks OK; www.sagecountryinn. com; at S Court Ave.*

Diamond

LODGINGS

Hotel Diamond

12 MILES EAST OF HWY 205, DIAMOND; 541/493-1898
When you drive into Diamond, the first things you see are dilapidated stone buildings. Buzz by, and you might mistake Diamond for a ghost town; however, its few residents keep the looming ghosts at bay. The Diamond Hotel, which doubles as a general store, has eight rooms. Dinners include a family-style meal if the house is full or cheeseburgers if it's not. An old attached icehouse is now Frazier's, a tiny pub named after the owners' great-grandparents, who managed the hotel 100 years ago. *$; MC, V; checks OK; www. central-oregon.com/hoteldiamond; closed winter (call for exact dates); 12 mi east of Hwy 205.*

Frenchglen

This beautiful little town (population about 15) 60 miles south of Burns is a favorite stopover for those visiting the **MALHEUR NATIONAL WILDLIFE REFUGE** or **STEENS MOUNTAIN**. Steens rises gently from the west to an elevation of 9,670 feet and then drops sharply to the Alvord Desert in the east. A road goes all the way to the ridgetop (summers only), and another makes a long loop around Steens—passing the vast borax hardpan of the former Alvord Lake, numerous hot springs, and, near the northeastern end of the route, good fishing in Mann Lake. Contact the **BUREAU OF LAND MANAGEMENT** (Hwy 20W, Hines; 541/573-4400) just southwest of Burns for information about Steens Mountain (see "Horse Trails").

It's a rough but scenic ride from Frenchglen to the 275,000-acre **HART MOUNTAIN NATIONAL ANTELOPE REFUGE** (541/947-3315). Turn west off Highway 205 and follow Rock Creek Road to the visitor center, where you can learn about recent wildlife sightings. Pronghorn are frequently noted, and bighorn sheep live east of the headquarters on the steep cliffs that form the western boundary of fault-block Hart Mountain. No visit here is complete without a long dip in the local hot spring. It's south of the visitor center in the campground—very rustic and absolutely free.

LODGINGS

Frenchglen Hotel / ★

HWY 205, FRENCHGLEN; 541/493-2825
One of the handful of historic hotels owned by the Oregon state parks department, the Frenchglen is a small, white frame American Foursquare–style building that dates back to the mid-1920s. Nothing's very square or level here, and that's part of the charm. Eight small, plain bedrooms don't have TVs and telephones; all rooms share baths. Many of the guests are birders, and the lobby is stocked with field guides. Ranch-style dinner is one seating only, with mandatory reservations. *$; MC, V; checks OK; closed mid-Nov–mid-Mar; www.oregonstateparks.org/park_3.php; 60 miles south of Burns.*

SEATTLE
AND ENVIRONS

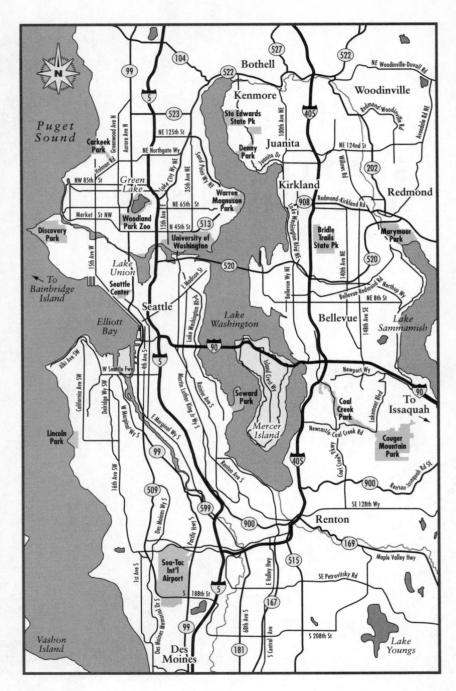

SEATTLE AND ENVIRONS

Gone are the days when the Emerald City was synonymous with grunge music, plaid flannel, and Boeing airplanes. These days, software and coffee have replaced 747s; Microsoft, Amazon.com, and Starbucks now rule as some of the region's largest employers.

The continued success of Bill Gates' empire and other companies has brought an unexpected benefit to this city on Puget Sound: a wealth of support for cultural venues. The Seattle Symphony hosts hundreds of concerts each year in its $118 million Benaroya Hall. Marion Oliver McCaw Hall—the gleaming home for the internationally acclaimed Seattle Opera and Pacific Northwest Ballet—opened in 2003. Frank O. Gehry designed the 2004 Experience Music Project; he credits a smashed Jimi Hendrix guitar as inspiration for the museum building's controversial psychedelic-colored, curving exterior that can be identified from miles away.

Even the most standard city buildings have gotten in on the 21st-century design action: the Seattle Public Library's downtown building garnered worldwide attention when it opened in 2004, thanks to its unusual glass-and-metal design by Pritzer Prize–winning Dutch architect Rem Koolhaas. (The geometric building, striking from the outside, is even more surprising inside: escalators, staircases, and hallways are painted hot pink, lime green, and fire engine red.)

All these new additions—including the boutiques and high-end stores that line downtown's Fifth and Sixth avenues—are interspersed along the urban grid with some of the city's most historic areas: the century-old Pike Place Market and Pioneer Square, home to turn-of-the-19th-century architecture and Old West–style saloons.

The neighborhoods surrounding downtown also display the yin-and-yang of historic-meets-modern: The fishing-industry stronghold of Ballard now boasts lounges next door to hole-in-the-wall bars; the eccentric and artistic "republic of Fremont"—complete with a sculpture of a troll eating a Volkswagen—hosts hip boutiques and new apartments. Other bustling 'hoods include Capitol Hill, where students and bohemian types populate coffee shops and funky secondhand stores; trendy Belltown with expensive high-rise condos overlooking Elliott Bay, boutiques, and see-and-be-seen nightlife; and stately Queen Anne, named for its Victorian architecture, with a charming hilltop avenue lined with shops and the city's icon, the 605-foot-tall Space Needle.

Seattle's neighbors to the east are also diverse, from the minimetropolis of Bellevue—which continues to expand with upscale shopping centers and restaurants—to corporate Redmond (home to Microsoft) and the tony lakefront city of Kirkland.

Meanwhile, some things haven't changed. The area's geography—which keeps natives from moving and attracts immigrants and outdoor lovers—is still one of the most stunning in the United States. The Olympic Mountains rise to the west across Puget Sound; the Cascades rule the eastern horizon; on a clear day Mount Rainier rises high in the south; and water bodies—Elliott Bay, Lake Union, Lake Washington—hug the city on three sides. Locals and visitors take advantage of the beautiful surroundings by boat, by bike, or on foot during much of the year,

SEATTLE THREE-DAY TOUR

DAY ONE: Start your day in **PIKE PLACE MARKET** like a local in the bountiful land of the liquid bean: coffee at the oldest **STARBUCKS**. You'll appreciate the fuel as you explore the Market's fruits, teas, baked goodies, eclectic jewelry, and enormous flower bouquets. Listen to street performers, then purchase a half-price day-of-show ticket for that evening's stage entertainment from **TICKET/TICKET**. Descend to the waterfront and refuel with a seaworthy lunch at **IVAR'S** (Pier 54; 206/467-8063) outdoor fish bar, letting animated seagulls swoop any leftover fries from your hand. Take advantage of the panoramic views of the city, Mount Rainier, and the occasional whale-spotting with an **ARGOSY CRUISE** (Pier 56; 206/623-1445). Rest at the **INN AT THE MARKET** before dinner at **DAHLIA LOUNGE**. Then it's a walk to the Fifth Avenue Theatre or Benaroya Hall. Cab back for a nightcap in **CAMPAGNE**'s bar before tucking in.

DAY TWO: Have tea and a toasty crumpet from the **CRUMPET SHOP** (1503 1st Ave; 206/682-1598) in the market before heading over to lower Queen Anne for an overview of the city from the top of the **SPACE NEEDLE**. Then walk around **SEATTLE CENTER** and visit the **EXPERIENCE MUSIC PROJECT** and **CENTER HOUSE** (305 Harrison St; 206/684-7200) for a snack. To enjoy the outdoors, rent a kayak and paddle around in Lake Union. For great shopping, go to Belltown,

thanks to the area's temperate climate. (A raincoat is often required from October to May, when the region lives up to its soggy reputation.)

ACCESS AND INFORMATION

Telling nightmare traffic stories has become something of a competitive sport in Seattle. It doesn't require dramatic license: A recent national study pegged Seattle as having the second-worst traffic jams in the nation (behind Los Angeles). And though a long-awaited light-rail system should alleviate some of the carbon-monoxide crush, it's not set to go online until 2009. In the meantime, the best defense is patience and street smarts. Most of Seattle is divided into avenues (starting with First near the waterfront) running north-south and streets running east-west (many are one way downtown).

    INTERSTATE 5 is the main north-south arterial; two east-west arterials connect it to Eastside communities (such as Bellevue) via two floating bridges: **INTERSTATE 90** (south of downtown) and **STATE ROUTE 520** (north of downtown); the major Eastside north-south highway is **INTERSTATE 405**. Numerous smaller highways connect the neighborhoods, such as **STATE ROUTE 99** (Pacific Highway S/Aurora Avenue N), which parallels I-5 to the west; **STATE ROUTE 522**, which connects I-5 and I-405 at the north end of

have lunch at **MACRINA BAKERY & CAFÉ**, then shop along First Avenue and purchase an outfit for your night on the town. Have dinner at the **METROPOLITAN GRILL** (820 2nd Ave; 206/624-3287), famous for its steaks. Enjoy a concert at the swanky **TRIPLE DOOR** (216 Union St; 206/838-4333). Finish off the evening with drinks at the **ALIBI ROOM** (85 Pike St, Ste 410; 206/623-3180).

DAY THREE: Grab a "very French" pastry at **LE PANIER** (1902 Pike Pl; 206/441-3669) in the market, then head to **PIONEER SQUARE** for an **UNDERGROUND TOUR** and a taste of old Seattle culture. Browse the extensive collections of the homey **ELLIOT BAY BOOK COMPANY**. A short walk to the **INTERNATIONAL DISTRICT** and **UWAJIMAYA VILLAGE** will satiate any hunger pains with rice bowls and sushi rolls from its food court. A deeper understanding of Seattle's international culture can be had at the **SEATTLE ASIAN ART MUSEUM** in **VOLUNTEER PARK** on Capitol Hill. After touring the exhibits, head outside to climb the park's water tower, offering sweeping Puget Sound and city views. Stay on Capitol Hill for a romantic dinner at **1200 BISTRO** (1200 E Pike St; 206/320-1200) or a garlic-laden meal at Lebanese **KARAM'S** (340 15th Ave E; 206/324-2370). Save your sweet tooth for the 1920s-styled, Frank Sinatra–meets–Seattle grunge hangout **B & O ESPRESSO** (205 Belmont Ave E; 206/322-5028), where you can also indulge in a nightcap.

Lake Washington; and **STATE ROUTES 509 AND 599**, alternate routes south to the airport.

Getting to downtown from **SEATTLE-TACOMA INTERNATIONAL AIRPORT** (17801 Pacific Hwy S, SeaTac; 206/431-4444; www.portseattle.org/seatac) is a 35-minute straight shot north on Interstate 5, but try to avoid rush hours (7–9:30am and 4:30–7pm). **GRAY LINE AIRPORT EXPRESS** (206/626-6088; www.graylineofseattle.com) runs airport passengers to and from major downtown hotels (about $10.25 one way, $17 round trip). **TAXIS** from the airport cost $35–$40; by law, however, taxis *to* the airport from downtown Seattle charge a lower flat fee (though some cabbies might need reminding). Large **CAR RENTAL** agencies have locations near the airport, in downtown Seattle, and in the outlying suburbs.

AMTRAK (King St Station, 3rd Ave S and S Jackson St; 800/USA-RAIL; www.amtrak.com) and **GREYHOUND** (811 Stewart St; 800/231-2222; greyhound.com) are downtown.

METRO TRANSIT (206/553-3000; transit.metrokc.gov) has more than 300 bus routes and connects with bus services from greater Puget Sound to the north and south (Pierce Transit and Sound Transit). Metro buses are free until 7pm downtown (between waterfront and I-5, and Jackson and Battery sts). The **WATERFRONT STREETCAR** (part of Metro) serves the waterfront,

Pioneer Square, and the city's Chinatown–International District, for now by bus; it's due to recontinue the streetcar in summer 2007. For off-road transport, ride the space-age **MONORAIL**, which glides between downtown's **WESTLAKE CENTER** (Pine St and 4th Ave, 3rd floor) and the Seattle Center in two minutes. For a water-focused day trip, catch a **WASHINGTON STATE FERRY** (Colman Dock, Pier 52; 206/464-6400 or 888/808-7977; www.wsdot. wa.gov/ferries/) to nearby islands and across Puget Sound.

SEATTLE'S CONVENTION AND VISITORS BUREAU has a **CITYWIDE CONCIERGE CENTER** at the Washington State Convention and Trade Center (7th Ave and Pike St, main floor next to escalators; 206/461-5888; www.see seattle.org), where you can get help buying tickets, making reservations, and getting information. In summer, visit the **OUTDOOR KIOSKS** at Seattle Center and Pioneer Square for visitor information.

Seattle

Seattle reigns as the cultural capital of the Pacific Northwest, thanks to a thriving arts, restaurant, and entertainment scene. Venues host world-class musicians, contemporary artists, Broadway-bound plays, and acclaimed dance troupes.

MAJOR ATTRACTIONS

Even first-time visitors can probably rattle off the big must-sees in Seattle: **PIKE PLACE MARKET** (Pike St and 1st Ave), **PIONEER SQUARE** (along 1st and 2nd aves, between James and S Jackson sts; www.pioneersquare.org), and the **SPACE NEEDLE**, which anchors a corner of another major attraction—the **SEATTLE CENTER** (301 Harrison St; 206/684-8582; www.seattlecenter.com), between Denny Way and Mercer Street, between First Avenue N and Fifth Avenue N. Born out of the 1962 World's Fair, the more than 80-acre park is home to arts and athletics venues—such as **MARION OLIVER MCCAW HALL** and **KEY ARENA**—as well museums including the **PACIFIC SCIENCE CENTER** (200 2nd Ave N; 206/443-2880; www.pacsci.org), with interactive, kid-friendly exhibits and an IMAX theater.

Life on and in Puget Sound is the focus of interactive exhibits at **ODYSSEY, THE MARITIME DISCOVERY CENTER** (2205 Alaskan Way, Pier 66; 206/374-4000; www.ody.org) and the **SEATTLE AQUARIUM** (1483 Alaskan Way, Pier 59; 206/386-4320; www.seattleaquarium.org), which boasts a 400,000-gallon Underwater Dome full of swimming salmon and sharks. Come close to more than 1,000 animal species at the lovely **WOODLAND PARK ZOO** (5500 Phinney Ave N; 206/684-4800; www.zoo.org). In Pioneer Square, the hokey-but-fun **UNDERGROUND TOUR** (610 1st Ave; 206/682-4646; www. undergroudtour.com) teaches visitors about Seattle's unusual and occasionally scandalous history.

MUSEUMS AND GALLERIES

The 42-foot-tall *Hammering Man* kinetic sculpture presides over the expansion of the **SEATTLE ART MUSEUM** (100 University St; 206/654-3100; www. seattleartmuseum.org), home to impressive Asian, African, and Northwest Coast art collections, as well as national traveling exhibits. While the museum is closed during construction, much of the collection is being displayed in the art deco **SEATTLE ASIAN ART MUSEUM** (1400 E Prospect St; 206/654-3100; www.seattleartmuseum.org) in Capitol Hill's Volunteer Park. SAM also just opened the new 9-acre **DISCOVERY SCULPTURE PARK** (2901 Western Ave), with artworks and views of Elliott Bay. The **HENRY ART GALLERY** (15th Ave NE and NE 41st St; 206/543-2280; www.henryart.org), on the University of Washington campus, is known for its photography collection and excellent contemporary art exhibits. (Maya Lin presented her first West Coast exhibit here in 2006.) First Hill's once-stodgy **FRYE ART MUSEUM** (704 Terry Ave; 206/622-9250; www.fryeart.org) has been redesigned, adding exhibits and music and film events.

CANLIS GLASS (3131 Western Ave, Ste 329; 206/282-4428; www.canlis glass.com) is a new studio and gallery filled with J. P. Canlis's ocean-inspired glass sculptures. J. P.'s grandfather, Peter, founded Canlis, the restaurant. To find work by glass pioneers like Dale Chihuly, visit the well-Foster/White Gallery (1331 5th Ave.; 206/622-2833). Stonington Gallery (119 S Jackson St; 206/405-4040) exhibits contemporary Native American jewelry, textiles and other artworks. For more galleries, see Shopping.

The **CHILDREN'S MUSEUM** (Seattle Center; 206/441-1768; www.the childrensmuseum.org) encourages exploration of other cultures with hands-on exhibits, such as a global village featuring child-sized dwellings from Japan, Ghana, and the Philippines. **WING LUKE ASIAN MUSEUM** (407 7th Ave S; 206/623-5124; www.wingluke.org) examines the Asian-American experience in the Northwest, including the internment of Japanese Americans during World War II. Bankrolled by Microsoft cofounder Paul Allen, the eye- and ear-popping **EXPERIENCE MUSIC PROJECT** (Seattle Center; 206/770-2700; www.emplive.com) celebrates rock 'n' roll and its history. The **SCIENCE FICTION MUSEUM AND HALL OF FAME** (206/SCI-FICT; www. sciencefictionexperience.com) opened in the same building in 2004. The **BURKE MUSEUM OF NATURAL HISTORY AND CULTURE** (17th Ave NE and NE 45th St; 206/543-5590; www.burkemuseum.org) on the UW campus harbors the Pacific Northwest's only dinosaurs—snap a shot of Junior sitting on the 5-foot-tall sauropod thigh bone. Twenty-six full-size airplanes are suspended in midair at the **MUSEUM OF FLIGHT** (9404 E Marginal Wy S; 206/764-5720; www.museumofflight.org).

PARKS AND GARDENS

Seattle offers hundreds of acres of scenic parks to explore. Local favorites include **DISCOVERY PARK** (3801 W Government Way; 206/386-4236) in Magnolia, the largest wilderness expanse in the city, with miles of trails, a

SEATTLE-AREA BIG SALES EVENTS

Why pay retail when you can shop really big sales events throughout the year? No matter what your interest, you're bound to find something to love at these annual sales in the Seattle area. Book lovers line up early to buy used books from the **FRIENDS OF THE SEATTLE PUBLIC LIBRARY**(7400 Sandpoint Wy NE; 206/523-4053; www.splfriends.org) during mid-April and mid-September at Magnuson Park. Cooks salivate over **CITY KITCHENS'** (1527 4th Ave; 206/382-1138) annual sale in Seattle, which runs from the last week of August through the end of September. **NORDSTROM'S** (locations citywide) eagerly awaited Half-Yearly Sales for women and children take place in June and November. Men get their chance in late December and mid-June. But the legendary—and biggest—sale of the year is the Nordstrom Anniversary Sale in July.

Outdoor enthusiasts run to the **REI** (222 Yale Ave N; 206/223-1944; www.rei.com) Anniversary Sale at the beginning of May. Gardeners delight in the **SWANSON'S NURSERY** (9701 15th Ave NW; 206/782-2543; www.swansons

beach, an 1881 lighthouse, and sweeping Sound views. **WASHINGTON PARK ARBORETUM** (2300 Arboretum Dr E; 206/543-8800) has 200 wooded acres along Lake Washington's Ship Canal, with walking and running trails and a Japanese garden. **VOLUNTEER PARK** (1247 15th Ave E; 206/684-4075) on Capitol Hill features a 1912 conservatory full of hothouse plants, a sculpture by Isamu Noguchi, and a view from the top of the water tower. **GAS WORKS PARK** (N Northlake Way; 206/684-4075) on Lake Union is where Seattleites go to fly a kite and to watch boaters crisscross the lake. Joggers, dog walkers, and strollers make the 2.8-mile loop around **GREEN LAKE** (www.cityofseattle.net/parks/).

SHOPPING

It's true that most Seattleites favor fleece, Gore-Tex, and jeans over business suits and high heels. But casual no longer equates with frumpy in this cosmopolitan city.

The downtown core along Fifth and Sixth avenues hosts fashionable outposts including **BETSEY JOHNSON** (1429 5th Ave; 206/624-2887; www.betseyjohnson.com), **BARNEYS NEW YORK** (1420 5th Ave; 206/622-6300; www.barneys.com), America's first **BGN PARIS** (1525 6th Ave; 206/344-4040; www.bgn.fr), and **MARIO'S** (1513 6th Ave; 206/223-1461; www.marios.com), a huge designer store known for men's suits and women's top labels. Stunning couture by Seattle local **LULY YANG** can be found downtown (1424 4th Ave; 206/623-8200; www.lulydesign.com).

nursery.com) Early Spring Sale, during the last two weeks of February for bare-root shrubs and perennials, and the Fall Sale, during the month of September for discounts on trees, shrubs, and more. Wine connoisseurs can stock up at **SEATTLE CELLARS** ' (2505 2nd Ave; 206/256-0850; www.seattlecellars.com) twice-yearly sales in February and August.

Between the big sales events, for those willing to wander outside of the Seattle city limits, there are several always-on-sale options at three Puget Sound outlet malls: **CENTRALIA FACTORY OUTLETS** (exit 82 from I-5, 1342 Lum Rd; 360/736-3327; www.centraliafactoryoutlet.com) including Levi's, London Fog, Corningware, and Vitamin World; **PRIME OUTLETS BURLINGTON** (exit 229 from I-5, 448 Fashion Wy; 360/757-3549; www.primeoutlets.com), with Coach, Eddie Bauer, Liz Clairborne, and Mikasa; and the **FACTORY STORES AT NORTH BEND** (exit 31 from I-90, 461 South Fork Ave SW; 425/888-4505; www.premiumoutlets.com) where you'll find Black & Decker, Dressbarn, Haggar, and Toy Liquidators, among many others.

—Kate van Gelder

The neighboring upscale shopping centers **PACIFIC PLACE** (600 Pine St; 206/405-2655; www.pacificplace.com) and **RAINIER SQUARE** (between 4th and 5th aves and Union and University sts; 206/373-7119; www.rainiersquare.com) house hundreds of national chains—Escada, Coach, Tiffany & Co., Louis Vuitton, Furla—as does the more standard **WESTLAKE CENTER** (4th Ave and Pine St; 206/467-3044; www.westlakecenter.com). Founded-in-Seattle **NORDSTROM** (500 Pine St; 206/628-2111; www.nordstrom.com) offers floors of classy merchandise and excellent customer service—including free personal shoppers.

Hipsters flock to stylish boutiques like **NUVO MODA** (1307 1st Ave; 206/684-6886) and denim den **RIVETED** (1113 1st Ave; 206/624-5326; www.rivetedjeans.com) along First and Second avenues. Other trendy shops include newcomer **ILLI** (2113 Westlake Ave; 206/973-3487), featuring classy but sexy styles by up-and-coming designers.

Also downtown, tourists and locals alike head to **PIKE PLACE MARKET** (1st Ave between Virginia and Union sts) for fresh produce, local crafts, and foodie goods: French kitchenware from the original **SUR LA TABLE** (84 Pine St; 206/448-2244), handcrafted cheese from **BEECHER'S** (1600 Pike Pl; 206/956-1964; www.beechershandmadecheese.com), roasted beans from perked-first-in-the-market **STARBUCKS** (1912 Pike St; 448-8762; www.starbucks.com).

But shopping options in Seattle are as diverse as its neighborhoods. Fashionistas shop the once gritty, now trendy **BELLTOWN**, just north of downtown, for its many stylish boutiques and home decor stores stocked full of designer merchandise like Jonathan Adler goods at **VELOCITY ART AND DESIGN** (2118 2nd Ave; 866-781-9494; www.velocityartanddesign.com).

Historic **PIONEER SQUARE**, anchoring the south end of downtown, features an eclectic trove of **ART GALLERIES**; the tree-lined streets fill with art lovers each month during the popular **FIRST THURSDAY GALLERY WALK** (Pioneer Square Community Association; 206/667-0687; www.pioneersquare. org/firstthursday.html). The neighborhood also offers many bookstores, from niche to mainstream, including local independent **ELLIOTT BAY BOOK COMPANY** (101 S Main St; 206/624-6600; www.elliottbaybook.com), which houses more than 150,000 tomes on its wooden shelves.

Books in Japanese, Asian goods, and unusual foods can be found just east of Pioneer Square in **CHINATOWN–INTERNATIONAL DISTRICT'S UWAJIMAYA** (600 5th Ave S; 206/624-6248; www.uwajimaya.com), the largest Asian grocer and gift store in the Pacific Northwest.

Gift and clothing boutique **LIPSTICK TRACES** (303 E Pine St; 206/329-2813) and retro home-furnishing shop **AREA 51** (401 E Pine St; 206/568-4782) are right at home on funky Capitol Hill; all types of pedestrians—students, tattooed musicians, young professionals—can be seen strolling the area's main drag of **EAST BROADWAY**. Also popular with students and a diverse crowd, the **UNIVERSITY DISTRICT** surrounding the University of Washington campus offers shops full of goods decorated with the school's Husky mascot and the open-air **UNIVERSITY VILLAGE** (NE 45th St and 25th Ave NE; 206/523-0622; www.uvillage.com), home to Crate & Barrel, Abercombie & Fitch, Pottery Barn, medi-spa **CALIDORA** (2613 NE University Village; 206/522-2613) and designer lingerie shop **ZOVO** (4612 26th Ave. NE; 206/525-9686).

Quirky **FREMONT**, north of the ship canal, offers artsy shops, niche bookstores, and small boutiques along Fremont Avenue and 35th Street. One of our favorite places to visit isn't quite a shop, it's a chocolate factory: **THEO CHOCOLATE** (3400 Phinney Ave N; 206/632-5100) gives public tours and samples of their goodies made from organic cocoa beans—in the old Red Hook Brewery building.

To the west, the Scandinavian stronghold of **BALLARD** has unique boutiques like international folk art gallery **LA TIENDA** (2050 NW Market St; 206/297-3605), furniture stores, and cafés—some reflect the neighborhood's heritage, others cater to stylish locals now frequenting the area.

Small boutiques and cozy coffeehouses, including the Latin American–inspired **EL DIABLO** (1811 Queen Anne Ave; 206/285-0693), line the top of **QUEEN ANNE** Avenue. The much busier south base of the Queen Anne neighborhood is home to bars, restaurants, and the Seattle Center, with numerous attractions and gift shops.

PERFORMING ARTS

Theater/Dance

Seattleites avidly support the arts. Parents take their children to the ballet and symphony; new plays open to full houses throughout the year. Many New York producers try out shows here before taking them to Broadway. The big three playhouses are **A CONTEMPORARY THEATRE**, better known as **ACT** (700 Union St; 206/292-7676; www.acttheatre.org), **INTIMAN THEATRE** (Seattle Center; 206/269-1900; www.intiman.org), and **SEATTLE REPERTORY THEATRE** (Seattle Center; 206/443-2222; www.seattlerep.org). The musical toasts of Broadway, as well as those headed there, star at the ornate **5TH AVENUE THEATRE** (1308 5th Ave; 206/625-1900; www.5thavenuetheatre. org). The historic **PARAMOUNT THEATRE** (911 Pine St; 206/443-1744; www. theparamount.com) also hosts touring productions and national headliners. Imaginative and surprisingly sophisticated productions play out at **SEAT-TLE CHILDREN'S THEATRE** (Seattle Center; 206/441-3322; www.sct.org). **TEATRO ZINZANNI** (6th Ave and Battery St; 206/802-0015; dreams.zinzanni. org) offers an extravagant cirque-meets-cabaret experience and a five-course meal by famed chef Tom Douglas. Classics are the core of the city's premiere dance company, the **PACIFIC NORTHWEST BALLET** (Seattle Center; 206/441-2424; www.pnb.org); an annual holiday favorite, *The Nutcracker*, features spectacular Maurice Sendak sets.

Music

Music of all genres—from alternative rock and reggae to chamber and classi-cal—can be heard in Seattle, the hometown of Pearl Jam, Nirvana, and Dave Matthews. The **SEATTLE SYMPHONY** (200 University St; 206/215-4747; www.seattlesymphony.org), under the baton of Gerard Schwarz, has an elegant downtown home in Benaroya Hall. The acclaimed **SEATTLE OPERA** (Seattle Center; 206/389-7676; www.seattleopera.org), guided by Speight Jenkins, brings first-rate productions to Marion Oliver McCaw Hall. Jazz clubs include classy **DIMITRIOU'S JAZZ ALLEY** (2033 6th Ave; 206/441-9729; www.jazzalley.com) and cozy **TULA'S** (2214 2nd Ave; 206/443-4221; www. tulas.com).

Some of the city's most anticipated festivals revolve around music. The **NORTHWEST FOLKLIFE FESTIVAL** (Seattle Center; 206/684-7300; www. nwfolklife.org) showcases a melting pot of talent—from African marimba players to American fiddlers—over Memorial Day weekend. **BUMBERSHOOT** (Seattle Center; 206/281-8111; www.bumbershoot.org), over Labor Day weekend, hosts headliner acts ranging from Beck to Tony Bennett. And jazz artists, representing bebop to swing, make the rounds of local clubs for the **EARSHOT JAZZ FESTIVAL** (206/547-9787; www.earshot.org) in October.

GET BEAUTIFUL IN SEATTLE

It's time to get pampered and lovely. Where do you go? These are some of our favorite spots.

If you want a world-class haircut, call **SEVEN SALON** (downtown Seattle and Bellevue; 206/903-1777; www.7salon.com). You'll feel like you're in New York's SoHo. Celebrities flock to this salon, which features giant Buddha heads, blaring Euro lounge and rock music, and sexy black-clad stylists. A more intimate spot is the **SEAN STATTON SALON** (206/292-1181; www.seanstattonsalon.com), hidden downstairs at the Sorrento Hotel (see review). Have an appetizer or a glass of wine while Statton layers your locks; he's a master at curly hair.

For pampering, go to **GENE JUAREZ SALON & SPA** (607 Pine St; 206/326-6000; www.genejuarez.com). Our favorite is their rainfall shower, infused with essential oils. You'll want to stay for hours. If you want a one-stop shop, this gigantic spa—with locations around the city—is it. **HABITUDE AT THE LOCKS** (2801 NW Market St; 206/782-2898) in Ballard is a Northwest-inspired spa known for its great body treatments.

If you want more than just some pampering, stop by **CALIDORA** (University Village; 206/522-2613; www.calidora.com). They're experts on the medical

Literature/Film

Seattle's literate population happily supports the annual **SEATTLE ARTS AND LECTURES** series (206/621-2230; www.lectures.org), which brings prominent authors to town. **TOWN HALL** (1119 8th Ave; 206/652-4255; www.town hallseattle.org) hosts international writers, politicians, and journalists in a historic building with stained-glass windows and wooden benches.

The **SEATTLE INTERNATIONAL FILM FESTIVAL** (206/324-9996; www. seattlefilm.org) features hundreds of international films at various theaters in a packed three-week marquee that begins in late May; the well-attended event also includes discussions with actors and filmmakers.

Check the free weeklies, *Seattle Weekly* and *The Stranger*, for event listings. Most tickets are sold through **TICKETMASTER** (206/292-ARTS; www. ticketmaster.com); **TICKET/TICKET** sells half-price, day-of-show tickets in three locations (401 Broadway Ave E, Pike Place Information Booth, and Pacific Place; 206/324-2744).

NIGHTLIFE

Although Seattle doesn't offer the dynamic after-dark scene of some equally sized U.S. cities, night owls can find fun in the city's urban neighborhoods. Some of the best nightspots are in Belltown and on Capitol Hill, a favorite

stuff—Botox, laser hair removal, restylane. They even have a computer that shows you how bad (or good, if you're lucky) your skin really is. It measures everything from pore size to sun damage. Meghan at **RED** (1925 3rd Ave; 206/256-6214; www. redseattle.net) gives the best facials, ever. On the Eastside, **CADDELL'S LASER & ELECTROLYSIS CLINIC** (Bellevue; 425/998-0181; www.caddellslaserclinic.com) is the best. Owner Debbie Caddell has been removing hair for decades.

If you're not ready for permanent hair removal, the **SWEET SPOT SUGARING STUDIO** (473 N 36th St; 206/632-3602; www.sweetspotonline.net) might be your thing. Instead of wax, owner Lara Olsha uses an ancient blend of sugar and lemon—still used in the Middle East—to whisk those hairs away. She specializes in Brazilian bikinis—for both men and women. The **WAXING BOUTIQUE** (914 65th St NE; 206/524-6616; www.thewaxingboutique.com) takes it all off, too. Owner Melissa Avila also applies makeup with an airbrush machine—so it goes on perfectly.

On your way in or out of the city, spruce up your nails with a 15-minute manicure at the **BUTTER LONDON** kiosk at SeaTac Airport (Central Terminal, Concourse B; www.butternails.com; no appointments). Or get a mani and pedi from ultrahip, ultrafun **FRENCHY'S** (3131 E Madison St; 206/325-9582; www. frenchysdayspa.com).

Getting gorgeous in this town has never been so easy.

with Seattle's gay and lesbian population. Hot spots on the hill range from the high-energy dance beats at **NEIGHBORS** (1509 Broadway Ave; 206/324-5358) to the retro chic of the **BALTIC ROOM** (1207 Pine St; 206/625-4444) and the **CENTURY BALLROOM** (915 E Pine St, 2nd floor; 206/324-7263), a former theater offering swing and salsa dancing. Belltown's lounges and hybrids include the live-music club-café **CROCODILE CAFÉ** (2200 2nd Ave; 206/441-5611), which once hosted local bands like Nirvana, and the high-tech dance floor and high-class pool hall of **BELLTOWN BILLIARDS** (90 Blanchard St; 206/448-6779). Near the Pike Place Market, the **ZIG ZAG CAFÉ** (1501 Western Ave; 206/625-1146) is famous for its extraordinary bartenders. Queen Anne abounds with sexy lounges, such as **Q** (1625 Queen Anne Ave N; 206/281-1931), with its chocolate mint–laced mojito and suede cushions; the **PARAGON** (2125 Queen Anne Ave N; 206/283-4548), which gets packed and often has live music; and **TINI BIGS** (100 Denny Way; 206/284-0931), famous for its martinis, a new late-night menu (with items like mini duck corndogs), and weekend "bloodshot brunch."

Downtown, all-ages rock shows are held at the largely volunteer-run **VERA PROJECT** (1916 4th Ave; 206/956-VERA), which is slated to move to Seattle Center in 2007; national headliners have appeared at the **SHOWBOX** (1426 1st Ave; 206/628-3151; www.showboxonline.com) since 1938. In Fremont, hipsters listen to live music at **TOST** (513 N 36th St; 206/547-0240), and in

Ballard, the **TRACTOR TAVERN** (5213 Ballard Ave NW; 206/789-3599) books folk, alt-country, and bluegrass acts, among others. If you just want a beer, stop at **BROWERS CAFÉ** (400 N 35th St; 206/267-1200), with its enormous selection; check out its Belgian Beer Week in June and Hops Fest in August.

For those who want to dance the night away, Belltown's futuristic **VENOM** (2218 Western Ave; 206/448-4887), with a DJ who spins tunes from a capsule in the middle of the floor, and the massive **TRINITY NIGHTCLUB** (111 Yesler Way; 206/447-4140; www.trinitynightclub.com) in Pioneer Square are the best bets.

SPORTS AND RECREATION

Even when they don't win pennants, the **SEATTLE MARINERS** (206/346-4000; www.mariners.mlb.com) have a hit on their hands with open-air **SAFECO FIELD** (between Royal Brougham Way and S Atlantic St; 206/346-4003), popular even with nonbaseball fans, thanks to its public tours. **QWEST FIELD** (formerly Seahawks Stadium) next door, opened in fall 2002 as home for the Paul Allen–owned **SEATTLE SEAHAWKS** (206/682-2800; www.seahawks.com) and also hosts the **SEATTLE SOUNDERS** (206/622-3415 or 800/796-KICK; www.seattlesounders.net). The **UNIVERSITY OF WASHINGTON HUSKIES** (Husky Stadium, 3800 Montlake Blvd NE; 206/543-2200; www.gohuskies. com) thrill rabid fans from their Lake Washington–backed gridiron. Seattle's pro women's basketball team, the WNBA's **SEATTLE STORM** (206/283-DUNK; www.wnba.com/storm/), tips off in the **KEY ARENA** (305 N Harrison St, Seattle Center) in summer; the **SEATTLE SUPERSONICS** (206/283-DUNK; www.nba.com/sonics/) dominate the arena November through April.

Plenty of outdoor venues appeal to amateur athletes. In-line skaters and bikers work up a sweat along the 14-mile **BURKE-GILMAN TRAIL**, a stretch of blacktop running from north Lake Union to the Eastside along the northwest shore of Lake Washington. Along the trail, the **BICYCLE CENTER** (4529 Sand Point Way NE; 206/523-8300) rents bikes and skates. For a map of Seattle bike routes, contact the city **BICYCLE AND PEDESTRIAN PROGRAM** (206/684-7583; www.seattle.gov/transportation/bikeprogram.htm). Kayakers, rowers, and canoeists ply the waters of **LAKE UNION** and **LAKE WASHINGTON**. Rent a kayak from **NORTHWEST OUTDOOR CENTER** (2100 Westlake Ave N, Ste 1; 206/281-9694 or 800/683-0637; www.nwoc.com) or a canoe at the **UNIVERSITY OF WASHINGTON WATERFRONT ACTIVITIES CENTER** (206/543-9433; depts.washington.edu/ima/IMA.wac.html). Outdoor enthusiasts of all stripes flock to the two-level flagship **REI** store (222 Yale Ave N; 206/223-1944 or 888/873-1938; www.rei.com), which, along with an abundance of equipment, houses an indoor climbing wall, an outdoor mountain bike–hiking test trail, and the U.S. Forest Service's **OUTDOOR RECREATION INFORMATION CENTER** (206/470-4060; www.nps.gov/ccso/oric.htm) for trip planning.

RESTAURANTS

Agua Verde Cafe & Paddle Club / ★★☆

1303 NE BOAT ST, SEATTLE; 206/545-8570

Even on the grayest days, this waterfront café feels like sun-drenched Baja, thanks to brightly colored walls and a deck overlooking Portage Bay. Around lunch expect a crowd; on sunny afternoons, paddlers who've rented kayaks from the club downstairs arrive for après-workout margaritas. The menu features Baja classics—fish tacos, salads, ceviche—and plenty of vegetarian plates. We love the *taco de mero*, grilled halibut and shredded cabbage. *$; DIS, MC, V; checks OK; lunch, dinner Mon–Sat; full bar; reservations recommended; www.aguaverde.com; University District.* &

Campagne / ★★★☆

86 PINE ST, SEATTLE; 206/728-2800

Tucked away in a Pike Place Market courtyard, Campagne's candlelit room with cherry-wood floors and yellow walls reminds you of southern France. Chef Daisley Gordon's menu blends Northwest influences into French fare— think wild mushrooms with house-made gnocchi or roasted leg of lamb with chickpea purée and red pepper, and artichoke and red-wine relish. The hazelnut crème brûlée with a Breton sable cookie is heaven. Downstairs is the slightly lower priced, but no less popular, Café Campagne (206/728-2233). *$$$; AE, DC, MC, V; no checks; lunch Mon–Fri, dinner every day; full bar; reservations recommended; campagnerestaurant.com; in the courtyard of Inn at the Market.* &

Canlis / ★★★★

2576 AURORA AVE N, SEATTLE; 206/283-3313

A locals' favorite for special occasions thanks to its beautiful interior and attentive service, family-owned Canlis has been offering impeccable fine dining since 1950. Dubbing itself the "birthplace of Northwest cuisine," Canlis serves dishes like escargot in puff pastry, oysters live on the half shell, or wild Pacific king salmon with hazelnut-caper butter. The much-lauded wine list has options ranging from $30 to $1,000 a bottle. Expect to be treated like royalty, and to pay accordingly, in this dining destination with live piano music and an incredible view of Lake Union. *$$$$; AE, DC, DIS, MC, V; checks OK; dinner Mon–Sat; full bar; reservations required; www.canlis.com; just south of Aurora bridge.* &

Carmelita / ★★★

7314 GREENWOOD AVE N, SEATTLE; 206/706-7703

Here is a vegetarian restaurant that even a carnivore can love, thanks to an innovative, tasty menu and attention to detail (back patio dwellers can wrap themselves in blankets provided by the restaurant). Art fills this restaurant owned by visual artists Kathryn Newmann and Michael Hughes. Find entrées like leek and Gruyère tart with frisée salad, caper vinaigrette, and potato

SEATTLE RESTAURANTS WITH A VIEW

The Cascade and Olympic mountains, Lake Union, Puget Sound, and Lake Washington offer ideal settings for outdoor adventures. But you don't have to board a boat or strap on your hiking shoes to take in the scenery. At many area restaurants, spectacular views come with every meal.

SALTY'S ON ALKI (1936 Harbor Ave; 206/935-4715) spreads a huge weekend brunch buffet with heaping piles of fresh crab and salmon, tables covered with desserts, dueling chocolate fountains, and made-to-order crepes, pasta, and omelet stations. Salty's waterfront location on Elliott Bay in West Seattle and interior wall-to-wall windows are equally over-the-top. Through the glass, see the downtown Seattle skyline, ferries and freighters underway, and even sea lions napping on concrete pilings.

Across the bay, **ANTHONY'S PIER 66** (2201 Alaskan Way; 206/448-6688) offers an elevated perch for jaw-dropping views of Seattle's working waterfront and the Olympic Mountains. This top-floor restaurant serves Asian-influenced fresh seafood dishes like sake-steamed ginger Penn Cove mussels. Pacific Northwest standards—halibut, planked wild chinook salmon—also complement the view. **ANTHONY'S BELL STREET DINER** (206/448-6688) beneath is a more casual option, great for families.

A few piers north, at Pier 70, **WATERFRONT SEAFOOD GRILL** (2801 Alaskan Way; 206/956-9171) offers a panoramic view of Elliott Bay, the Magnolia bluffs,

galette or pizza with cauliflower pesto, fresh mozzarella, Romano, pickled peppers, and broccoli sprouts. *$$; MC, V; local checks only; dinner Tues–Sun; beer and wine; reservations recommended; carmelita.net; Phinney Ridge.* ♿

Cascadia Restaurant / ★★★⯪

2328 1ST AVE, SEATTLE; 206/448-8884

Chef-owner Kerry Sear uses regional foods and flavors to create deliciously simple fare that he serves in a lovely (and quite formal) dining room with a waterfall window. The menu features such à la carte options as carmelized spice-rubbed king salmon or roasted organic chicken with black truffles. Three seven-course tasting menus, with one for vegetarians, are also available. The bar is famous for its addictive miniburgers. *$$$$; AE, DC, DIS, MC, V; no checks; dinner Mon–Sat; full bar; reservations recommended; www. cascadiarestaurant.com; Belltown.* ♿

and the Space Needle. The eclectic menu, with global inspirations from the Mediterranean and Asia, includes items like Maine lobster with truffle sauce or rack of lamb and lobster mashed potatoes. Sit on the huge deck if you can.

Just above Pike Place Market, the romantic and intimate **CHEZ SHEA** (94 Pike St; 206/467-9990) provides Elliott Bay views through semicircular windows. Choose options from the seasonal Northwest four-course prix-fixe menu or the seven-course chef's tasting menu.

Tourist-pleaser **PALISADE** (2601 W Marina Pl; 206/285-1000), at the north end of the waterfront, offers a stunning 180-degree view of the yachts in its neighboring marina, as well as Elliott Bay, Alki Point, and the Seattle skyline; waitstaff occasionally interrupt diners to point out colorful sunsets or harvest moon risings. But this restaurant popular with prom goers and special-occasion celebrants doesn't just offer beauty outside its windows; its decor includes a Japanese garden with bonsais and orchids and a flowing stream populated with koi and lobsters (which can become your dinner). The fare matches the waterfront setting: Check the daily fresh sheet for entrées like Alaskan halibut stuffed with Dungeness crab or the grilled king salmon.

On Lake Washington, **THIRD FLOOR FISH CAFÉ** (205 Lake St, Kirkland; 425/822-3553) is among the best on the Eastside. Its sweeping water and mountain views provide a lovely backdrop for Mediterranean-influenced seafood dishes like wild sturgeon with a shiitake mushroom vinaigrette.

—Kristin Harrison

Central Cinema / ★

1411 21ST AVE, SEATTLE; 206/686-6684

Enjoy dinner and a movie at Seattle's coolest eatery and cinema. Features, independent films, and kid-friendly flicks make up the fun choices. (Think original *Willy Wonka* and *The Goonies*.) Forget the popcorn (even though they do have it): order wine or pitchers of beer, pizzas, calzones, salmon burgers, or desserts like crème brûlée. You'll sit in comfy booths among exposed-brick walls. *$; MC, V; no checks; dinner Wed–Sun; beer and wine; no reservations; www.central-cinema.com; Central District.* &

Chinook's at Salmon Bay / ★★

1900 W NICKERSON ST, SEATTLE; 206/283-4665

At Fisherman's Terminal, this restaurant with industrial decor—steel countertops, visible ventilation ducts—pairs well with the bustle of the working marina seen through large windows. Order from the daily special sheet with offerings like wild king salmon or garlic-baked prawns. There's a great all-you-can-eat tempura bar—don't miss the fat, tender *panko*-coated onion rings. Chinook's is known for its warm wild-blackberry cobbler. *$$; AE, MC, V; checks OK; breakfast Sat–Sun, lunch, dinner every day; full bar; no reservations; www.anthonysrestaurants.com; in Interbay.* &

Cremant / ★★★☆

1423 34TH AVE, SEATTLE; 206/322-4600
This French restaurant is a culinary newcomer, but the kitchen talent has decades of experience. Start with a glass of Cremant, a French sparkling wine. Then dive into the divine French onion soup with a layer of Gruyère, the flavorful bacon-wrapped country pâté, and Salad d' Endive loaded with Roquefort and walnuts. Whatever you do, get the *pomme frites*. The place can get loud; service is exemplary. *$$$; MC, V; no checks; dinner every day; full bar; reservations recommended; Madrona.* &

Crush / ★★★

2319 E MADISON ST, SEATTLE; 206/302-7874
In a stylishly renovated 1903 Tudor-Victorian house, chef Jason Wilson serves seasonal "modern American" fare. Items on a menu that changes weekly may include slow-braised short ribs with potato purée or peppered rare ahi tuna with pork belly–braised beans. Other specialties include house-made chocolates and gourmet cheeses. Dress to impress: Crush is quite a scene. *$$; AE, DIS, MC, V; no checks; dinner Tues–Sat; full bar; reservations recommended; www.crushonmadison.com; west end of Madison Valley.* &

Dahlia Lounge / ★★★☆

2001 4TH AVE, SEATTLE; 206/682-4142
Owned by celebrity chef Tom Douglas, this famous restaurant—Tom Hanks ate here in *Sleepless in Seattle*—is sophisticated yet comfortable. The menu changes daily, but expect dishes like veal sweetbreads, roasted monkfish with sweet-corn sauce and chanterelle-mushroom hash, squash ravioli, or Oregon Country Beef flatiron steak. The Dungeness crab cakes and coconut cream pie deserve their iconic status, as does the bag of dessert doughnuts fried to order. *$$$; AE, DC, DIS, MC, V; local checks only; lunch Mon–Fri, dinner every day; full bar; reservations recommended; www.tomdouglas.com; downtown.* &

El Gaucho / ★★★

2505 1ST AVE, SEATTLE; 206/728-1337
Playboy magazine named El Gaucho one of the best steak houses in America. Patrons, seated on comfy banquettes in the senate-style dining room, feast on prepared-tableside Caesar salad or Bananas Foster and any number of (trademarked) Angus beef prime cuts served with classic sides. In the bar, a well-heeled crowd sips martinis or wine from a lauded list. The Pampas Room downstairs, open for dancing and drinking on Friday and Saturday, offers the full El Gaucho menu. A new El Gaucho opens in Bellevue in fall 2007. *$$$$; AE, DIS, MC, V; checks OK; dinner every day; full bar; reservations recommended; elgaucho.com; Belltown.* &

Elliott's Oyster House / ★★★

1201 ALASKAN WAY, PIER 56, SEATTLE; 206/623-4340
Elliott's annual Oyster New Year in November is a world-class all-you-can-slurp pig-out. But this more than 30-year-old oyster house—with updated nautical decor and windows overlooking tourist-boat docks—offers more than hundreds of bivalves. Innovative alternatives include Dungeness crab served hot and spicy or troll-caught wild king salmon. The crab cakes, with rock shrimp and a beurre blanc blended with blood-orange juice, are exceptional. *$$$; AE, DC, DIS, MC, V; checks OK; lunch, dinner every day; full bar; reservations recommended; www.elliottsoysterhouse.com; waterfront.* &

Eva Restaurant and Wine Bar / ★★★

2227 N 56TH ST, SEATTLE; 206/633-3538
James Hondros and spouse-chef Amy McCray have transformed a well-windowed, warm-wooded room into an elegant, first-rate bistro. Panfried oysters rolled in the crumbs of pappadams (Indian flatbread) and served with a raita sauce and cilantro pesto typify the originality of the menu. The desserts are flawless, and Hondros's well-chosen wine list has plenty of bottles in the $30 range—and nearly a dozen good half bottles. *$$; AE, MC, V; checks OK; dinner Tues–Sun; full bar; reservations recommended; Green Lake.* &

Flying Fish / ★★★☆

2234 1ST AVE, SEATTLE; 206/728-8595
Even on nights when neighboring Belltown joints are quiet, Flying Fish always seems to be busy. Chef-owner Christine Keff serves delicious, fresh seafood to hip urbanites in a stylish dining room with tangerine-colored walls. Entrée choices, all organic, range from lobster ravioli with yellow-foot mushrooms to a heap of crispy fried calamari with a honey jalapeño mayonnaise. Keff encourages large parties to opt for the sold-by-the-pound sharing platters. *$$; AE, DC, MC, V; local checks only; dinner every day; full bar; reservations recommended; www.flyingfishseattle.com; Belltown.* &

Harvest Vine / ★★★☆

2701 E MADISON ST, SEATTLE; 206/320-9771
Joseph Jimenez de Jimenez's shareable Spanish tapas draw raves from locals and visiting celeb chefs. Start with a glass of fino sherry and order *platitos* from more than two-dozen seasonally inspired options. Simply superb are the grilled sardines with lemon and the tender octopus with grilled potatoes. The chef's wife and award-winning pastry *patrona*, Carolin Messier de Jimenez, innovates classic Spanish and Basque desserts. Be advised: Harvest Vine takes reservations only for parties of eight or more, so waits can be long. *$$; MC, V; checks OK; dinner Tues–Sat; beer and wine; no reservations; Madison Valley.* &

Hing Loon / ★

628 S WELLER ST, SEATTLE; 206/682-2828
While the decor equates with a cafeteria, the service here is friendly and attentive, and the cheap Chinese food is delicious. Read from the handwritten paper menus on the walls to order dishes like salt-and-pepper tofu, lamb and mushroom hot pots, and a myriad of excellent seafood. (The full menu is more than seven pages long.) If you are overwhelmed by the options, you can't miss with any of Hing Loon's noodle dishes. *$; MC, V; no checks; lunch, dinner every day; beer and wine; no reservations; Chinatown–International District.* &

Il Terrazzo Carmine / ★★★

411 1ST AVE S, SEATTLE; 206/467-7797
More than a few consider this Seattle's best Italian restaurant. Seattle's rich and famous dine here at tables with a background of European draperies. The biggest attraction is the menu: cannelloni filled with veal and spinach bubbling with ricotta; fettuccine tossed with house-smoked salmon, mushrooms, and peas. Tiramisu is decadent. A guitarist plays classical music most nights. *$$$; AE, DC, DIS, MC, V; no checks; lunch Mon–Fri, dinner Mon–Sat; full bar; reservations recommended; www.ilterrazzocarmine.com; Pioneer Square.* &

Kingfish Café / ★★½

602 19TH AVE E, SEATTLE; 206/320-8757
The Coaston sisters serve sassy Southern classics in a stylish, casual space with sepia-tinted photos from the family album—including one of distant cousin Langston Hughes—adorning the walls. They take no reservations, so expect lines. It's worth it for the likes of Jazz It Slow Gumbo, catfish cakes with green-tomato tartar sauce, or the famous buttermilk fried chicken. Save room for red velvet cake or strawberry shortcake. *$$; MC, V; checks OK; lunch Wed–Mon, dinner Mon, Wed–Sat, brunch Sun; beer and wine; no reservations; East Capitol Hill.* &

La Carta de Oaxaca / ★

5431 BALLARD AVE NW, SEATTLE; 206/782-8722
This small, bustling restaurant with communal tables and black-and-white photographs on the walls serves some of the best Mexican food in Seattle. Start with chips and your pick of dips from the salsa bar. Entrée portions are just larger than tapas size; best bets include the halibut tacos, chicken in a sweet mole negro, and sausage and potato *molotes* (fried tortillas) Be prepared: Waits can be long. Margaritas or cerveza from the corner bar help pass the time. *$; AE, DIS, MC, V; checks OK; dinner Mon–Sat; full bar; no reservations; Ballard.*

Lampreia / ★★★★

2400 1ST AVE, SEATTLE; 206/443-3301
This restaurant has a near-cultish following. From most seats in the spare dining room, diners can see chef-owner Scott Carsberg in the kitchen five nights a week. Carsberg is often described as a minimalist; many consider him a genius. Menu descriptors reflect his simple approach: "lentils from Verona served as a salad with guinea hen terrine" or "thin sheets of pasta filled with foie gras in beef consommé." Service, as directed by Carsberg's wife, Hyun Joo Paek, is seamless and reverential. *$$$; AE, MC, V; no checks; dinner Tues–Sat; full bar; reservations recommended; www.lampreiarestaurant.com; Belltown.* &

Lark / ★★★

926 12TH AVE, SEATTLE; 206/323-5275
Bring a group of friends to this subtly elegant Capitol Hill spot with exposed wood beams and sheer curtains and plan to stay a while. The delicious seasonal offerings are intended for sharing, but you may want to hoard every bite of dishes such as baby beets with sherry vinegar and tangerine oil, flatiron steak with parsley salad and blue cheese, or halibut cheeks with stone-ground grits. The no-reservations policy (except for large groups) can cause a crush at the tiny bar. Have patience; the meal will be worth the wait. *$$$; MC, V; checks OK; dinner Tues–Sun; full bar; no reservations; south Capitol Hill.* &

Le Gourmand / ★★★

425 NW MARKET ST, SEATTLE; 206/784-3463
Le Gourmand's tucked-away, vintage-brick building doesn't quite fit one's image of what an upscale restaurant should be, but the interior, with a wall of trees, hollyhocks, and lupines, is lovely. The owners have created a calm, intimate dining space, simply appointed to show off Bruce Naftaly's fine French-Northwestern fare. Dinner consists of appetizer, entrée, and salad (in true European style, the salad follows the main course). Depending on the time of year, you might enjoy earthy nettle soup at the beginning of your meal or delicate leek and onion tarts crowned with juniper berries. The pretty people stop for cocktails and small plates at the adjoining Sambar, with its outdoor patio. *$$$; AE, MC, V; local checks only; dinner Wed–Sat; beer and wine; reservations recommended; Ballard.* &

Macrina Bakery & Café / ★★

2408 1ST AVE, SEATTLE; 206/448-4032
Seattleites head here for their favorite treats: fresh breads, pastries, cakes, and espresso. Homemade bread pudding with fresh fruit and cream or house-made granola make great starts to a day; lunch offerings include salads and sandwiches on fresh bread. The cozy café's founder, Leslie Mackie, reveals baking secrets in her *Macrina Bakery and Café Cookbook*. A second location is on Queen Anne (615 W McGraw St; 206/283-5900). *$; MC, V; local checks only; breakfast, lunch Mon–Fri, brunch Sat–Sun; beer and wine; no reservations; www.macrinabakery.com; Belltown.* &

Malay Satay Hut / ★★☆

212 12TH AVE S, SEATTLE; 206/324-4091

After a fire at this strip-mall restaurant in Seattle's Little Saigon in 2001, its fans fretted that this flavor hub where Malaysia meets China, India, and Thailand might be gone forever. But the location has reopened, and the Hut is back to serving flavorful curries, wontons, stir-fries, and satays. Order the *roti canai*, Indian flatbread served with a potato-chicken curry sauce or Buddha's Yam Pot, a chicken, shrimp, and vegetable stir-fry in a deep-fried basket of grated yams. There's a second Malay Satay Hut in Redmond (15230 NE 24th St; 425/564-0888). *$; MC, V; no checks; lunch, dinner every day; beer and wine; reservations recommended; Chinatown–International District.* &

Matt's in the Market / ★★★

94 PIKE ST, 3RD FLOOR, SEATTLE; 206/467-7909

Matt's is tucked in a tiny space on the third floor of the Corner Market Building. Chef Erik Canella turns out food that's not only well crafted but also some of downtown's freshest—cooks shop the market twice a day. Seafood is the best bet here: try the rare-seared albacore, filé gumbo, or clams and mussels in an ouzo-infused broth. Owner Matt Janke occasionally manages to squeeze musicians in to play live jazz. *$$; MC, V; no checks; lunch, dinner Mon–Sat; beer and wine; reservations recommended; Pike Place Market.*

Mike's Chili Parlor / ★

1447 NW BALLARD WAY, SEATTLE; 206/782-2808

It's no wonder Mike's has been around for 85 years. The meaty, hearty, and flavorful chili pairs well with a cold beer. Expect a very casual atmosphere: it's a tavern. Order chili served over hand-cut homemade french fries, pasta, hot dogs, or hamburgers, or choose the "big ass bowl of chili." Mike Semandiris's great-grandfather opened the tavern when he first came to America from Greece. Regulars are mostly area industrial workers. Sit on the back patio if you can. *$; cash only; lunch, dinner Mon–Sat; full bar; no reservations; Ballard.*

Monsoon / ★★☆

615 19TH AVE E, SEATTLE; 206/325-2111

Like the wind after which this restaurant was named, the menu here changes seasonally. Don't miss signature appetizers: spring rolls stuffed with Dungeness crab; tamarind soup with chicken and gulf shrimp. Share the five-spice flank steak with Chinese celery and hothouse tomatoes or the seared scallops with bok choy and black-bean sauce. Vegetable dishes, such as the oven-baked Asian eggplant, also satisfy. Waits can be long, and the dining room is noisy when full. *$$; MC, V; no checks; lunch Tues–Fri, dinner Tues–Sun; beer and wine; reservations recommended; www.monsoonseattle.com; east Capitol Hill.* &

The Oceanaire Seafood Room / ★★★

1700 7TH AVE, SEATTLE; 206/267-2277
This is a classic fish house, part of a national chain, with 30 daily-changing seafoods. Service is flawless in this dining room with decor inspired by a 1940s steamship. Look for all the fish-house classics—oysters Rockefeller, fish-and-chips—but don't miss chef Kevin Davis's innovative dishes like herb-crusted sturgeon. Everything's à la carte, which can make this an expensive outing, but half orders of the side dishes feed four. The towering inferno of a baked Alaska is also enormous. *$$$; AE, B, DC, DIS, JCB, MC, V; checks OK; lunch Mon–Fri, dinner every day; full bar; reservations recommended; www. oceanaireseafoodroom.com; downtown.* &

Ovio Bistro / ★★

4752 CALIFORNIA AVE SW, SEATTLE; 206/935-1774
Shing and Ellie Chin opened this urban bistro in 2002; their first restaurant is now a West Seattle fine-dining favorite. Chef Tony LaVelle creates boldly flavored, innovative fare: Bubba's Fennel and Mint Salad, sea scallop pot pie, or grilled lobster french toast with sun-dried tomato butter. Warm chocolate cake with a *dulce de leche* center and served with strawberry sauce and vanilla ice cream makes a grand finale. *$$$; DIS, MC, V; local checks only; dinner Mon–Sat; full bar; reservations recommended; www.oviobistro.com; at Edmunds St.* &

Palace Kitchen / ★★

2030 5TH AVE, SEATTLE; 206/448-2001
The mural on this restaurant's south wall is a tip-off to owner Tom Douglas's goal here: The 17th-century period piece depicts scullery maids and castle servants feasting on roast meats while guzzling red wine in the "palace kitchen." To join in the fun, order shareables like the spicy grilled chicken wings. For a more formal supper, try the *plin*, tender raviolis with chard and sausage, or one of the night's specials from the applewood grill. *$$$; AE, DC, DIS, MC, V; checks OK; lunch Mon–Fri, dinner every day; full bar; reservations recommended; www.tomdouglas.com; Belltown.* &

Ray's Boathouse / ★★☆

6049 SEAVIEW AVE NW, SEATTLE; 206/789-3770
Regional seafood dominates the menu at this Seattle institution on Shilshole Bay. Fishing trollers and sailboats pass by the windows of the candelit dining room and add to the nautical decor. Its seafood, like the signature Chatham Strait black cod, is usually wild and always fresh. Upstairs, Ray's Café, with a popular patio, serves lower-priced, lighter fare. Choices include fish-and-chips, burgers, or clam linguine. Make reservations for weekday lunch in the café. *$$$; AE, DC, DIS, MC, V; checks OK; dinner every day, lunch, dinner every day (café); full bar; reservations recommended; www.rays.com; Ballard.* &

Rover's / ★★★★

2808 E MADISON ST, SEATTLE; 206/325-7442
"Chef in the Hat" Thierry Rautureau has won the hearts of Seattleites with his divine French fare; foodies from afar also make pilgrimages to his nationally renowned restaurant and unpretentious dining room. Rautureau uses stocks, reductions, herb-infused oils, and purées to enhance steamed Maine lobster, breasts of quail, or the requisite foie gras—offerings that may be on one of the three prix-fixe menus (one vegetarian). Sommelier Cyril Frechier manages the 5,500-bottle collection. Dining in the courtyard, weather permitting, is enchanting. *$$$$; AE, DC, MC, V; checks OK; dinner Tues–Sat; beer and wine; reservations required; www.rovers-seattle.com; Madison Valley.* &

Saito's Japanese Cafe & Bar / ★★★⯪

2120 2ND AVE, SEATTLE; 206/728-1333
On any given night in this smart Belltown place, you might see the Japanese ambassador or Mariners superstar Ichiro Suzuki. They come for Saito-san's sushi, arguably the best in town. The fish is fresh and cut thicker than you'll usually find in Seattle, and hot items are innovative. Try the butter *itame*, a geoduck sauté with sugar snaps and shiitakes. Save room for the house-made ice cream sampler, with green tea, mango, or sweet plum flavors. *$$$; AE, DIS, E, MC, V; no checks; lunch Tues–Fri, dinner Tues–Sat; full bar; reservations recommended; www.saitos.net; Belltown.* &

Salumi / ★★

309 3RD AVE S, SEATTLE; 206/621-8772
In this little wedge of Italy near the King Street train station, Armandino Batali (the father of famed New York chef Mario Batali) cures his own *coppa*, three kinds of salami, lamb or pork prosciutto, spicy *finocchiona*, and citrusy *soppressata*, a lamb and orange sausage. The meatball sandwich, piled high with sautéed peppers and onions, is a locals' favorite. Expect lines out the door and limited seating at communal tables during lunch. *$; AE, MC, V; checks OK; lunch Tues–Fri, dinner Sat; beer and wine; reservations required (dinner); Pioneer Square.* &

Santorini Pizza & Pasta / ★★

11001 35TH AVE NE, SEATTLE; 206/440-8499
This neighborhood pizza and pasta joint is packed every night. The Greek-American Apostolou family make you feel at home, and their food is hearty and comfortable. The Greek salad is perfect, and the pastas are satisfying, but it's the pizzas that really shine here. Try specialties like the Aegean with chicken, garlic, pesto, fresh spinach, onions, sun-dried tomatoes, and feta cheese or the Islander with shrimp, fresh mushrooms, and tomatoes. *$; AE, DC, DIS, MC, V; checks OK; dinner Mon–Sat; beer and wine; no reservations; www.santorinipizza.com; Wedgwood.* &

Tamarind Tree / ★★

1036 S JACKSON ST, STE A, SEATTLE; 206/860-1404
Upscale ambience and buzz-inducing beverages provide big Vietnamese value in the heart of Little Saignon. The modern decor—dark wood with bright punches of color—makes for a refined setting where you wouldn't think you could use your hands as utensils. But that's what makes it so fun. When the wonderful-smelling Thang Long yellow fish comes to your table with all the accompaniments—rice crackers, roasted peanuts, lettuce, carrots, and fresh herbs—don't hesitate to make a little burrito with a lettuce leaf and throw in the turmeric-seasoned fish. *$; MC, V; no checks; lunch, dinner every day; full bar; no reservations; Chinatown–International District.* &

Via Tribunali / ★★

913 E PINE ST, SEATTLE; 206/322-9234
Owned by the coffee guru behind Caffe Vita, this sexy joint with exposed-brick walls oozes all things Italian, from ingredients shipped from Italy to the language of the menu. At a wood-fired brick oven, a pizzaiola creates authentic thin-crust Neapolitan pies. Pizza options include classics like the simple Margherita with hunks of cheese and tomatoes or the "Via Tribunali" with buffalo mozzarella cheese, ricotta, and provolone. *$; AE, MC, V; no checks; dinner Wed–Sun; full bar; no reservations; Capitol Hill.* &

Vios Café & Marketplace / ★★☆

903 19TH AVE E, SEATTLE; 206/329-3236
The name is Greek for "life," and this communal spot bustles with lively energy. Thomas Soukakos's eatery and Mediterranean market serves espresso, homemade goodies like coffee cake, and Greek-inspired fare like lamb burgers and hummus. Sandwiches are excellent; try the succulent fennel-braised pork. The sleek space welcomes children with open arms—its walls are decorated with photos of kids—and offers them a (play) room of their own. *$; AE, MC, V; local checks only; breakfast, lunch, dinner Tues–Sat; beer and wine; no reservations; east Capitol Hill.* &

Voila! / ★★

2805 E MADISON ST, SEATTLE; 206/322-5460
Our French friends say that Voila! tastes just like home, and we believe them. This is a casual neighborhood bistro, with Dijon mustard–colored walls, a grand mirror, and French posters. Chef-owner Laurent Gabrel sometimes comes out and chats with diners. Try the *tagliatelle aux champignons des bois*—wild mushrooms and pasta. French classics like coq au vin and *boeuf bourguignon* are excellent here. Servers can be inexperienced and don't always know the menu well. *$$$; AE, DC, MC, V; local checks only; dinner Mon–Sat; full bar; reservations recommended; Madison Valley.* &

Wild Ginger Asian Restaurant and Satay Bar / ★★½

1401 3RD AVE, SEATTLE; 206/623-4450
This landmark is wildly popular, though some cynicals say it's gotten too much hype. Owners Rick and Ann Yoder's culinary vision, inspired by time spent in Southeast Asia, changed the Seattle restaurant scene and pan-Asian cuisine everywhere. Wild Ginger offers a wide range of multiethnic dishes from Bangkok, Singapore, Saigon, and Jakarta. At the mahogany satay bar, order from a wide array of skewered selections, like the mountain lamb and Saigon scallop satay. *$$$; AE, DC, DIS, MC, V; no checks; lunch Mon–Sat, dinner every day; full bar; reservations recommended; downtown.* &

LODGINGS

Ace Hotel / ★★

2423 1ST AVE, SEATTLE; 206/448-4721
This futuristic, hostel-like hotel is a hipster's delight with white wood floors, white walls (some rooms have black-and-white Andy Warhol–like murals), and white robes. No down comforters here; low beds have simple wool French Army blankets. Small wall TVs, minibars, and CD players are in the 28 rooms (some don't have bathrooms; shared bathrooms are down the hall). There's no room service, but you'll have Belltown's eateries at your command. Rooms on First Avenue can be noisy. *$$–$$$; AE, DC, DIS, JCB, MC, V; checks OK; www.acehotel.com; between Battery and Wall sts.*

Alexis Hotel / ★★★

1007 1ST AVE, SEATTLE; 206/624-4844 OR 888/850-1155
This whimsical yet elegant boutique-style hotel has 109 rooms, including suites of various sizes. The decor in this pet-friendly hotel features original Pacific Northwest artwork. North-facing rooms have a view of Elliott Bay; First Avenue rooms may be a little noisy. Perks include shoe shines, a fitness room, an on-call masseuse, and the Aveda Day Spa. Live jazz and an evening wine tasting occur every Wednesday. The Library Bistro provides picnics to go and tours of Pike Place Market. *$$$–$$$$; AE, DC, DIS, JCB, MC, V; checks OK; www.alexishotel.com; downtown.* &

The Edgewater / ★★★

2411 ALASKAN WAY, PIER 67, SEATTLE;
206/728-7000 OR 800/624-0670
A waterfront landmark, the Edgewater is home to some of the Emerald City's most unusual claims to fame. It's the only Seattle hotel that juts over the water, and it's the only venue that once allowed customers—including the Beatles—to fish from its windows. All 234 rooms have fireplaces and log bed frames. The sleek Six Seven Restaurant & Lounge serves Northwest cuisine with pan-Asian influences and has stunning views of Elliott Bay, Puget Sound, and the Olympics. *$$$; AE, DC, DIS, MC, V; checks OK; www.edgewater hotel.com; waterfront.* &

11th Avenue Inn / ★★

121 11TH AVE E, SEATTLE; 206/669-4373 OR 800/370-8414

From the outside, this 1906 box-house looks like most other unassuming Capitol Hill residences from the turn of the 20th century. However, if you want to feel like a local, this cozy house has an ideal location between the park-filled, quirky coffee shops of residential Capitol Hill and the bustling city just a few blocks to the west. One step inside, and the bland exterior dissolves as you're quickly transported into the world of Jane Austen fantasy. The three-story converted home is adorned with wall tapestries, Victorian love seats, ornate wood furniture, and Oriental rugs. Breakfast is full service at a formally dressed 10-seat table, but owner Dave Williams insists that the 11th Avenue Inn is laid-back. *$$; MC, V; checks OK; www.11thavenueinn. com; at E Fir St.*

Fairmont Olympic Hotel / ★★★★

411 UNIVERSITY ST, SEATTLE; 206/621-1700 OR 800/441-1414

On the site of the original University of Washington, the only four-star hotel in Seattle offers exceptional pampering in a 1924 Italian Renaissance icon. Luxury can be found in each of the 450 rooms and in the venerable restaurant, the Georgian (206/621-7889). Amenities include twice-daily housekeeping service, complimentary shoe shine, town-car service, and high-speed Internet access. The Fairmont doesn't just pamper adults; it goes out of its way for children, providing them with a loaner Sony PlayStation, kid-sized bathrobes, and even babysitting service. *$$$$; AE, DC, DIS, JCB, MC, V; checks OK; www.fairmont.com/seattle; downtown.* ⅊

Hotel Andra / ★★★

2000 4TH AVE, SEATTLE; 206/448-8600

This 1926 building was recently transformed into the Hotel Andra, and it's luxurious. It's also simple: no spa, and a small gym. The 119 rooms and suites are spacious, but bathrooms are tiny. Sleek and modern, rooms are decorated with Swedish design in mind. Celebrity chef Tom Douglas's latest restaurant, Greek-inspired Lola (206/441-1430), is an added bonus, especially since you can eat their food in Andra's loft above the lobby. *$$$$; AE, DIS, MC, V; checks OK; www.hotelandra.com; Belltown.* ⅊

Hotel Max / ★★★

620 STEWART ST, SEATTLE; 206/728-6299 OR 866/833-6299

This is the artsy, funky, fun 163-room hotel in Seattle. Your room gets an original painting by a Northwest artist (read about them in the book in the honor bar) and a full-length photo on the door. There's even a "grunge floor," if that tells you anything. Rock 'n' roll plays in the lobby. Amenities are posh—a fitness center, 24-hour room service from Red Fin (206/441-4341) sushi downstairs, flat-screen LCD TVs, and special pillow and spiritual menus to personalize the experience. *$$$–$$$$; AE, DC, DIS, JCB, MC, V; no checks; www.hotelmaxseattle.com; downtown.*

Hotel Monaco / ★★★

1101 4TH AVE, SEATTLE; 206/621-1770 OR 800/945-2240
The Monaco's 189 rooms are boldly decorated in a blend of colorful stripes and florals in reds and yellows. Ten Mediterranean suites feature bathrooms with two-person Fuji jet tubs. Amenities include 24-hour room and business service, leopard-print bathrobes, evening wine tasting, a fitness center, and privileges at a health club. Monaco's personality extends to the Southern-inspired Sazerac restaurant (206/624-7755). Ask for a loaner goldfish, or bring Fluffy; it's the most pet-friendly hotel in town. *$$$–$$$$; AE, DC, DIS, JCB, MC, V; checks OK; www.monaco-seattle.com; downtown.* &

Hotel 1000 / ★★★⯪

1000 1ST AVE, SEATTLE; 206/957-1000 OR 877-315-1088
This new luxury hotel is high-tech and sophisticated. After your first visit, the hotel sets the preferred temperature and art preferences for your room. Just wave your key card to get in. Infrared-sensor technology tells staff if you're inside. The Golf Club features 50 "virtual" international PGA courses. The Hotel 1000 building includes 101 guest rooms, 19 suites, and 47 residences—not to mention a lobby room with an open fire pit, a spa, a reading area, and a fitness center. Swanky BOKA Kitchen + Bar (206/357-9000; www.boka seattle.com) is a contemporary "urban American" restaurant featuring tasting plates like Thai-spiced chicken lollipops and entrées like Maine lobster primavera. Don't miss the lighted, sculpted-glass bamboo installations by local artist J. P. Canlis. *$$$$; AE, DIS, MC, V; checks OK; www.hotel-1000seattle.com; downtown.* &

Hotel Vintage Park / ★★★

1100 5TH AVE, SEATTLE; 206/624-8000 OR 800/624-4433
From the lobby's plush velvet settees and leather armchairs to the Grand Suite's double-sided fireplace, the Vintage Park looks like the ideal spot to break out a smoking jacket. The 126 rooms are named after Washington wineries and vineyards; the hotel hosts a complimentary fireside Northwest wine tasting every evening. Nice touches include in-room fitness equipment, privileges at a local health club, and 24-hour room service, including lunch or dinner from the hotel's excellent Italian restaurant, Tulio (206/624-5500; www.tulio.com). *$$$; AE, DC, DIS, JCB, MC, V; checks OK; www.hotel vintagepark.com; downtown.* &

Inn at El Gaucho / ★★★

2505 1ST AVE, SEATTLE; 206/728-1133 OR 866/354-2824
In a city full of big hotels, you'll feel at home here. The Inn at El Gaucho is an all-suite, 18-room hotel above the restaurant (see review). Get the famous firey steak delivered to your bed, or savor your meal while sitting on the leather couch. Rooms feel like upscale bachelor pads—the only feminine touches are the fancy shampoo and conditioner. Cookies, a jazz CD,

and bottled water are nice bonuses. *$$$–$$$$; AE, MC, V; no checks; inn. elgaucho.com; Belltown.* &

Inn at the Market / ★★★☆

86 PINE ST, SEATTLE; 206/443-3600 OR 800/446-4484

Everything about the Inn at the Market oozes quintessential Seattle atmosphere: views of Elliott Bay and the Olympics from most rooms, close proximity to bustling Pike Place Market, and room service from country-French Campagne (see review). The 70 rooms are handsomely dressed in soft taupe, copper, and green and have floor-to-ceiling bay windows that open. West-facing windows have incredible views of Puget Sound. The rooftop deck is a must-see. *$$$–$$$$; AE, DC, DIS, JCB, MC, V; checks OK; www.innat themarket.com; Pike Place Market.* &

Mayflower Park Hotel / ★★★

405 OLIVE WAY, SEATTLE; 206/623-8700 OR 800/426-5100

Past and present come together at this handsome 1927 hotel set in the heart of the city's retail district. A member of the National Trust Historic Hotels of America, the Mayflower has a lobby decorated with antique Chinese artwork and furniture. The 171 rooms are fairly small but offer elegant dark-wood furniture and deep tubs. Amenities include free high-speed wireless Internet access and same-day laundry service. Cozy Andaluca (206/382-6999) serves Northwest-Mediterranean fare; you can also sip a martini at Oliver's. Valet parking. *$$–$$$; AE, DC, DIS, MC, V; checks OK; www.mayflowerpark.com; downtown.* &

Panama Hotel / ★★☆

605½ S MAIN ST, SEATTLE; 206/223-9242

This historic European-style hotel was built in 1910. Its 100 rooms have hardwood floors, antique furnishings, down comforters, lace curtains, and single sinks. Men's and women's baths, down the hall, are small but clean. Street-side rooms can be noisy. Ask for a tour of the basement to see the only remaining Japanese bathhouse left intact in the United States. There's no room service, but the adjacent Panama Hotel Tea & Coffee House serves snacks and tea. *$–$$; AE, MC, V; no checks; www.panamahotelseattle.com; Chinatown–International District.* &

Pensione Nichols / ★★☆

1923 1ST AVE, SEATTLE; 206/441-7125 OR 800/440-7125

The only bed-and-breakfast in Seattle's downtown core (just above the market), Pensione Nichols is furnished with antiques from the 1920s and '30s; 10 guest rooms share four bathrooms. A large, appealing common room on the third floor has a spectacular view of Elliott Bay; a bountiful continental breakfast—including fresh treats from the market—is served here. Be warned: The stair climb from street level is steep. *$$; AE, DC, DIS, MC, V; checks OK; www.pensionenichols.com; downtown.* &

EASY SEATTLE GETAWAYS

Aside from the obvious choices of Vancouver and Portland, which are two favorite and most worthy cities for a two- or three-day getaway from Seattle, the options around the Puget Sound area are innumerable, ranging from island to mountain to desert.

VASHON ISLAND: It's a 15-minute car-ferry ride from West Seattle to this bucolic, rural island, which has no hotels, no stoplights, and just one fast-food outlet. What it does have are beautiful parks, user-friendly B and Bs, miles of country roads for bike riding, an inner bay good for swimming in summer, and **BOB'S BAKERY** (17506 Vashon Hwy SW; 206/463-5666), a matchless mecca for muffins and other goodies. See the Puget Sound chapter for information.

LEAVENWORTH: OK, it's kitschy—faux Tyrolean architecture, men in lederhosen. But the mountain air is clean and invigorating, the hiking and biking are unsurpassed, and a little accordion music never hurt anyone. When was the last time you had a good wiener schnitzel? See the Central Cascades chapter for information.

VICTORIA: Hop on the *Victoria Clipper* for the three-hour catamaran ride to the Inner Harbour, then grab your overnight bags and walk to your room at the world-famous **EMPRESS** (see review) or one of dozens of ultradeluxe B and Bs. Foot power takes you to all the attractions in one of the world's most-visited small cities, which has shed its one-note Olde England persona. You don't even have to have afternoon tea. See the Victoria and Vancouver Island chapter for information.

YAKIMA VALLEY: Until recently, the world-class wines made here were not matched by the valley's dining and lodging options, but a new generation of small inns and bistros is changing that. It's just a two-hour drive from Seattle to Yakima, a bit more to the heart of the wine country in Sunnyside, and the sun shines almost every day. That's worth the drive alone. Be sure to drive through **TOPPENISH** to see the town's remarkable collection of murals. See the Southeast Washington chapter for information.

Sorrento Hotel / ★★★☆

900 MADISON ST, SEATTLE; 206/622-6400 OR 800/426-1265

When it opened at the turn of the 20th century, the Sorrento was a grand Italianate masterpiece holding court just east of downtown. Today, the beauty of the Sorrento is in details: elegant furnishings, Italian marble bathrooms, and the plush Fireside Room. The 76 rooms and suites are

TACOMA: Yes, Tacoma. The City that Seattle Looks Down On actually has a better set of public museums than its snobby bigger cousin—chief among them are the **WASHINGTON STATE HISTORY MUSEUM, GLASS MUSEUM**, and **TACOMA ART MUSEUM**. A drive along the bluffs facing Commencement Bay will remind you that Northwest fortunes were made here before Seattle ever prospered, that **POINT DEFIANCE PARK** is almost the equal of Vancouver's Stanley Park, and the **SPAR TAVERN** (2121 N 30th St; 253/627-8215) has the best pub food in Western Washington. See the Puget Sound chapter for information.

PORT TOWNSEND: One of the West's finest collections of heritage Victorian homes, many of them B and Bs, beckons visitors to this artsy-crafty community. Music is a summertime draw at **FORT WORDEN STATE PARK** and the **OLYMPIC MUSIC FESTIVAL** (in nearby Quilcene), and **SWEET LORETTE & CYNDEE'S BISTRO AND CAFE's** (see review) charming provençal atmosphere and food are divine. See the Olympic Peninsula chapter for information.

ASHLAND: It's a long way to drive (seven hours, if you're lucky going through Portland), but you can catch a 45-minute flight to Medford, pick up a rental car, and spend a weekend enjoying first-class theater, wonderful midpriced restaurants, and some of the best small inns in the West. In the town's lovely, European-style central district, Ashland Creek tumbles down from the mountains above, it's a 10-minute walk to everything, and the weather from May to September is blessedly warm and sunny. See the Southern Oregon and the Cascades chapter for information.

SUNRIVER: It's more like a California resort than a Northwest retreat, but this development near Bend is a splendid place for a family to take a weekend off. Bike riding, swimming, river floating, wildlife watching, horseback riding, golf, and just general lazing are all available within the resort village, and spur-of-the-moment calls often yield remarkably economical last-minute getaway packages. It's also a bit far to drive to but just a 45-minute flight from Sea-Tac. See the Southern Oregon and the Cascades chapter for information.

—Eric P. Lucas

comfortably luxurious in an old-fashioned way but offer amenities like free high-speed Internet access. The Hunt Club serves Northwest and Mediterranean cuisine. Complimentary town-car service takes guests downtown. The hidden Sean Statton Salon downstairs is excellent. *$$$$; AE, DC, DIS, JCB, MC, V; checks OK; www.hotelsorrento.com; First Hill.* &

W Seattle Hotel / ★★★☆

1112 4TH AVE, SEATTLE; 206/264-6000 OR 877/W-HOTELS
Dressed in postmodern art, velvet drapes, and oversize chess sets, the W's two-story lobby is one of those see-and-be-seen kind of places—especially when a DJ spins tunes once a month. The rest of the hotel lives up to its glam entryway. Taupe and black rooms are stylishly simple with stainless steel– and glass-accented bathrooms, goose-down comforters, and Zen-inspired water sculptures. You don't have to go far for great food—just cross the lobby to Earth & Ocean (206/264-6060). *$$$$; AE, DC, DIS, JCB, MC, V; checks OK; www.whotels.com; downtown.* ᴋ

Watertown / ★★

4242 ROOSEVELT WAY NE, SEATTLE; 206/826-4242 OR 866/944-4242
The upscale sister hotel of the University Inn just two blocks south, the more luxurious Watertown was built in 2002. The 100 studios and suites in this nonsmoking hotel have free high-speed Internet access, microwaves, refrigerators, coffeemakers, and TVs that swivel to face the bathroom. The hotel has a fitness center, a general store, and underground parking and offers a free shuttle service to Seattle attractions. Thoughtful touches include loaner bicycles and board games or spa amenities delivered to your room. *$$; AE, DC, DIS, MC, V; checks OK; www.watertownseattle.com; University District.*

The Westin Seattle / ★★☆

1900 5TH AVE, SEATTLE; 206/728-1000 OR 800/WESTIN-1
The Westin's twin cylindrical towers have a '60s-era look, but the spacious guest rooms provide some of the best views in the city, especially above the 20th floor. The gargantuan size of the hotel (891 rooms and 34 suites) contributes to some lapses in service, but rooms are comfortable. You'll also find a large pool and whirlpool tub with city view and an exercise room. *$$$$; AE, DC, DIS, JCB, MC, V; checks OK; westin.com; downtown.* ᴋ

The Eastside

The suburbs—and suburban cities—on the east side of Lake Washington across from Seattle are collectively known as "the Eastside." They include Bellevue, Redmond, Kirkland, Woodinville, and Issaquah. The **EAST KING COUNTY CONVENTION & VISITORS BUREAU** (425/455-1926; www.eastkingcounty.org) has the lowdown on Eastside goings-on.

Bellevue

Washington's fourth-largest city has cast off its shopping-mall image. Its newly impressive downtown skyline is populated by glass high-rises as well as a few cultural attractions. The **MEYDENBAUER CENTER** (11100 NE 6th St;

425/637-1020; www.meydenbauer.com) hosts myriad arts performances, and the **BELLEVUE ARTS MUSEUM** (510 Bellevue Way NE; 425/519-0770; www.bellevueart.org) presents exhibits of regional arts, crafts, and design. The **ROSALIE WHYEL MUSEUM OF DOLL ART** (1116 108th Ave NE; 425/455-1116) displays more than 3,000 dolls.

Big companies are here: Drugstore.com, T-Mobile, and Expedia.com. But shopping is still the main attraction. The Bellevue Collection includes three high-end shopping centers with hundreds of stores: **BELLEVUE SQUARE** (between NE 4th and NE 8th sts; 425/454-8096; www.bellevuesquare.com), packed with a triple-decker Nordstrom store and Crate & Barrel, plus 200 shops and restaurants; kitty-corner is glitzy **BELLEVUE PLACE** (10500 NE 8th; 425/453-5634); and across the street is the new 310,000-square-foot **LINCOLN SQUARE** (800 Bellevue Way; 425/454-7400), with numerous restaurants, a high-end billiards parlor, and a 16-screen movie theater. Farther east, find family-oriented **CROSSROADS SHOPPING CENTER** (15600 NE 8th; 425/644-1111; www.crossroadsbellevue.com).

In fall 2007, watch for the first tower of the $1.2 billion **WASHINGTON SQUARE** (near Lincoln Square) development, yet another sign that things are happening in this Eastside city. It includes five condominium towers, townhomes, an office building, a hotel, shops and restaurants, a terraced outdoor plaza, a meeting and events center, and an athletic club and health spa. The **HILTON BELLEVUE** (300 112th Ave SE; 425/455-1300) also has recently emerged, having undergone a multimillion-dollar renovation and conversion (it was formerly the Doubletree).

For more-intimate shopping, check out shops like the new **POSH ON MAIN** (10245 Main St, Ste 103; 425/454-2226) in Old Bellevue. Posh has luxe women's shoes, à la New York. The 19-acre **DOWNTOWN PARK** (10201 NE 4th St, just south of Bellevue Square), with a waterfall and promenade, offers shoppers a nature break. Other parks include **BELLEVUE BOTANICAL GARDEN** (12001 Main St; 425/452-2750), **ENATAI BEACH PARK** (3519 108th Ave SE; 425/452-6885), where you can go canoeing and kayaking; and **NEWCASTLE BEACH PARK** (4400 Lake Washington Blvd SE), with swings, slides, and swimming.

RESTAURANTS

Mediterranean Kitchen / ★★

103 BELLEVUE WAY, BELLEVUE; 425/462-9422

If you love garlic, this is your place. Owner Bassam Aboul Hosn calls regulars by name at his Lebanese restaurant. It's no wonder they keep coming back: His garlic sauce is addictive. Order the *shish tawook*, chicken served over yellow rice alongside authentic hummus and salad. Beef, lamb, or chicken kebabs are also delicious. Vegetarian options include stuffed grape leaves and *fatoush* (a salad featuring toasted pita). The Seattle location (366 Roy St; 206/285-6713), run by Bassam's father, is equally good. *$$; AE, MC, V; no checks; lunch Mon–Sat, dinner Sun–Thurs; reservations recommended; www. medkitchen.com; NE 1st Ave and Bellevue Way.* &

Seastar Restaurant and Raw Bar / ★★★☆

205 108TH AVE NE, BELLEVUE; 425/456-0010
A local favorite for seafood, this fine-dining restaurant is owned by chef John Howie, who was executive chef at Seattle's Palisade for nearly a decade. Seattle celebrities eat here, and it's no wonder. Try the multilevel raw-bar sampler: Hawaiian ahi *poke*, California roll, and scallop ceviche. On the hot side, we like flash-seared diver sea scallops with tropical fruit chutney and the Kauai shrimp wrapped in *saifun* noodles. Howie is also a pioneer of alder and cedar-plank cooking. Offerings for red meat lovers—like a 9-ounce Snake River Farms Kobe beef grilled rib-eye—are also delicious. *$$$; AE, DC, DIS, MC, V; local checks only; lunch, dinner every day; full bar; reservations recommended; www.seastarrestaurant.com; at NE 2nd St.* &

Trader Vic's / ★★☆

700 BELLEVUE WAY NE, #50, BELLEVUE; 425/455-4483
This new outpost of the popular chain—famous for the Mai Thai its founder claimed to create in 1944—features all the elements that kept loyal patrons coming back decades ago. Don't be fooled by the bland exterior; the interior is every bit as upscale tiki hut as the Vic's of the '70s. (Some would say it's as kitsch as ever.) Elegantly prepared Polynesian-inspired classics fill the menu: crab Rangoon, bongo bongo soup with spinach and Pacific oysters, Indonesian rack of lamb. *$$$; AE, DC, MC, V; no checks; lunch, dinner every day; full bar; reservations recommended; www.tradervics.com; in Lincoln Square, adjacent to the Westin Hotel.* &

LODGINGS

Bellevue Club Hotel / ★★★

11200 SE 6TH ST, BELLEVUE; 425/454-4424 OR 800/579-1110
One of the most elegant hotels in the area, the Bellevue Club is part hotel, part upscale athletic club. The 67 rooms feature sunken tubs and original works by Northwest artists, as well as cherry-wood furniture custom-made on Whidbey Island. Some rooms overlook the tennis courts; others open to terra-cotta patios. Oversize limestone-and-marble bathrooms—with spalike tubs—are perfect for postworkout soaks. The club offers fine dining at Polaris Restaurant (425/637-4608) and casual fare at Splash. *$$$–$$$$; AE, DC, DIS, MC V; checks OK; bellevueclub.com; at 112th Ave SE.* &

Westin Bellevue / ★★★

600 BELLEVUE WAY NE, BELLEVUE; 425/638-1000
Swanky, hip, sexy, and elegant: that's how people describe this new hotel in the center of activity. The 337 rooms have all the Westin amenities, including 32-inch flat-screen TVs and "heavenly beds." Take in views of Mount Rainier, the Seattle skyline, and Lake Washington. Sixteen grand deluxe rooms have big four-fixture bathrooms, high ceilings, and private decks. The indoor lap pool has an outdoor deck and a workout "powered by Reebok."

Dine in their Manzana Rotisserie Grill, or have a drink in Cypress. *$$$$;*
AE, DC, DIS, JCB, MC, V; local checks only; www.westin.com/bellevuewa; in
Lincoln Square. &

Redmond

Once a bucolic valley farming community, Redmond today is a sprawling McTown
of freeway overpasses, offices (Microsoft, Nintendo, and Eddie Bauer are head-
quartered here), subdivisions, and retailers, including the open-air, 100-plus-shop
REDMOND TOWN CENTER AND CINEMAS (16495 NE 74th; 425/867-0808;
www.redmondtowncenter.com). Some of Redmond's pastoral roots remain. It's
not dubbed the bicycle capital of the Northwest for nothing: bikers can pedal the
10-mile **SAMMAMISH RIVER TRAIL** or check out races on the 400-meter **MARY-
MOOR VELODROME** (2400 Lake Sammamish Pkwy; 206/675-1424; marymoor.
velodrome.org). In summer, 522-acre **MARYMOOR PARK** (6046 W Lake Sammamish Pkwy NE; 206/296-2966) draws crowds for picnics. The **CONCERTS AT
MARYMOOR** series (6046 W Lake Sammamish Pkwy NE; 206/628-0888; concert-
satmarymoor.com) hosts a popular summer program that has featured artists from
Norah Jones to Ringo Starr.

RESTAURANTS

Pomegranate / ★★☆

18005 NE 68TH ST, REDMOND; 425-556-5972
Well-known caterer Lisa Dupar and her husband opened this restaurant with
families in mind, and they succeeded in making a place where both kids and
adults can have fun. The catering kitchen adjoins the restaurant, so kids can
watch the action. Parents drink Key lime pie martinis, kids drink alcohol-free
coconutty "*loco coladas,*" and everyone feasts on the American flatbreads
topped with tequila rock shrimp with roasted garlic, cilantro, and sliced red
jalapeños. *$$–$$$; AE, DIS, MC, V; checks OK; lunch every day, dinner Tues–
Sat, brunch Sat–Sun; full bar; reservations recommended; pomegranatebistro.
com; across from Chalet Grocery on Redmond Way.* &

Kirkland

Sure, there's a crunch of expensive condos and traffic here, but this beautiful town
tucked into the eastern shore of Lake Washington has avoided the Eastside's typical strip-mall syndrome. People *stroll* here among congenially arranged eateries,
galleries, and boutique retailers. In summer, sidewalks fill with locals and tourists,
as do **PETER KIRK PARK** (202 3rd St) and the **KIRKLAND MARINA** (25 Lake Shore
Plaza), where you can catch an **ARGOSY** (206/623-1445; www.argosycruises.
com; Apr–Sept) boat for a lake cruise. Welcome downtown additions include the
402-seat **KIRKLAND PERFORMANCE CENTER** (350 Kirkland Ave; 425/893-9900;
www.kpcenter.org). Even the obligatory mall, **KIRKLAND PARKPLACE** (6th St and

Central Wy; 425/828-4468), doesn't spoil the townscape—it's several blocks east of the waterfront.

For a casual bite, try **WILDE ROVER IRISH PUB & RESTAURANT** (111 Central Way; 425/822-8940; www.wilderover.com); its chef is a United Kingdom native, and the traditional shepherd's pie is the real deal. Two decks, live music, and pool tables keep things lively. Two new stylish boutiques worth checking out are **MANHATTAN** (122 Lake St S; 425/576-1065; www.boutiquemanhattan.com) and **PROMESSE** (128 Central Way; 425/828-4259; www.shoppromesse.com).

RESTAURANTS

Cafe Juanita / ★★★☆

9702 NE 12TH PL, KIRKLAND; 425/823-1505

This well-regarded restaurant in a converted white-brick house serves Northern Italian fare. The execution by Holly Smith is precise; the presentation, flawless. A professional waitstaff brings cuisine that changes with the seasons. Grilled octopus with fennel might start a meal, as could a pear salad with pine nuts, Parmigiano-Reggiano, and white truffle oil. The dessert list is formidable and irresistible, with select cheeses or Valrhona chocolate–truffle cake with vanilla gelato, espresso sauce, and crisp almond wafer. *$$$; AE, MC, V; no checks; dinner Tues–Sun; full bar; reservations recommended; www.cafejuanita.com; at the corner of 97th Ave NE.* ♿

Mixtura / ★★☆

148 LAKE ST S, KIRKLAND; 425/803-3310

This new Peruvian restaurant is causing a positive stir in Kirkland. Its owner, Emmanuel Piqueras, gained national attention with his Peruvian cuisine at Andina in Portland. Here, he serves mostly tapas in this space decorated in shades of graphite, with open views of both the kitchen and the big parking lot outside. Try the beef-heart *anticuchos* skewers or the *Pulpito Crocante*—marinated octopus served in a small dish with olive tapenade. *$$$; AE, DIS, MC, V; checks OK; dinner every day; full bar; reservations recommended; just south of Kirkland Ave.* ♿

Yarrow Bay Grill / ★★☆

1270 CARILLON PT, KIRKLAND; 425/889-9052

Chef Vicky McCaffree serves pan-Asian fare in an upstairs dining room with great Lake Washington views and elegant decor. Try dishes like the Seven-Spice Seared Ahi and Thai Seafood Stew, with a coconut milk–lemongrass broth, or a seared pork tenderloin with grilled nectarine chutney. New Mexico corn ravioli further stretches the geographical perspective. The Beach Café (425/889-9052) just below is a more economical option. *$$$; AE, DC, DIS, JCB, MC, V; no checks; dinner every day; full bar; reservations recommended; www.ybgrill.com.* ♿

LODGINGS

The Woodmark Hotel on Lake Washington / ★★★

1200 CARILLON PT, KIRKLAND; 425/822-3700 OR 800/822-3700
The only hotel nestled on the shoreline of Lake Washington, this four-story brick building is just steps from a marina and a shoreline path popular with joggers. Many celebrities stay here. One hundred guest rooms, about half with stunning lake views, offer a relaxing retreat of cream-colored furnishings. "Raid the pantry" when the restaurant lays out a complimentary late-night buffet. The hotel's restaurant, Waters (425/803-5595; www.watersbistro.com), features Northwest cuisine. The spa here is not-to-miss. *$$$–$$$$; AE, DC, JCB, MC, V; checks OK; www.thewoodmark.com; at Lakeview Dr.* &

Woodinville

Oenophiles and hopheads love this little Eastside town. **CHATEAU STE. MICHELLE** (14111 NE 145th St; 425/488-1133; chateaustemichelle.com), the state's largest winery, offers daily tastings and tours as well as popular summer concerts on its lovely 87-acre estate. Across the street, **COLUMBIA WINERY** (14030 NE 145th St; 425/488-2776; columbiawinery.com) also has daily tastings and weekend tours. Or wet your whistle at one of the state's first microbreweries, **REDHOOK ALE BREWERY** (14300 NE 145th St; 425-483-3232; redhook.com), which, along with daily $1 tours (including a souvenir glass and plenty of samples), has a pub with tasty grub and live music Friday and Saturday.

RESTAURANTS

The Herbfarm / ★★★★

14590 NE 145TH ST, WOODINVILLE; 425/485-5300
This is a must-experience restaurant for anyone who loves gourmet dining and pampering service. Nationally renowned chef Jerry Traunfeld creates seasonal menus that feature local produce and herbs—many grown in the Herbfarm's gardens. A nine-course prix-fixe dinner may include dishes like tempura squash blossoms stuffed with goat cheese, pea flan with caviar, herb-crusted lamb, and a selection of small treats like lemon-thyme espresso truffles. This is a coveted destination; reservations usually need to be booked months in advance. *$$$$; AE, MC, V; checks OK; dinner Thurs–Sun; beer and wine; reservations required; theherbfarm.com; off Hwy 202.* &

LODGINGS

Willows Lodge / ★★★↟

14580 NE 145TH ST, WOODINVILLE; 425/424-3900 OR 877/424-3930
Willows Lodge is a quintessential Northwest hotel, combining casual grace with a recycling aesthetic unique to the region. A 1,500-year-old cedar stands sentinel near the entry, and 100-year-old reclaimed Douglas fir forms the

two-level lobby. The 88 rooms at this luxe lodge have balconies or patios, rock-lined fireplaces, and stereo/DVD/CD systems (borrow CDs and DVDs at the front desk). Other lodge amenities include a spa, a Japanese garden, and complimentary breakfast. The renowned Herbfarm Restaurant (see review) occupies its own site on the grounds. *$$$$; AE, DC, DIS, JCB, MC, V; checks OK; willowslodge.com; across from Redhook Brewery.* ♿

Issaquah

Though every so often a cougar shows up in this wealthy Cascade-foothills suburb 15 miles east of Seattle, Issaquah is pleasantly mild mannered. Historic **GILMAN VILLAGE** (317 NW Gilman Blvd; 425/392-6802; www.gilmanvillage.com), composed of refurbished old farmhouses, offers an agreeable day of poking about in its 40 or so shops and restaurants. The **VILLAGE THEATRE** (120 Front St N and 303 Front St N; 425/392-2202; www.villagetheatre.org) entertains with mostly original, mainly musical productions at two downtown theaters. While you're there, try **FINS BISTRO SEAFOOD RESTAURANT** (425/392-0109) in the same building. Another fun spot is **XXX DRIVE-IN** (98 NE Holly St; 425/392-1266), with burgers, shakes, and root beer.

Seattleites cross the Interstate 90 bridge in packs during summer weekends to "scale" the Issaquah Alps, which have miles of hiking trails from easy to challenging; the **ISSAQUAH ALPS TRAILS CLUB** (425/392-6660; issaquahalps.org) offers organized day hikes. Drop in the first weekend of October for **ISSAQUAH SALMON DAYS** (425/392-7024; www.salmondays.org), a celebration—including food, crafts, music, and a parade—marking the return of the salmon that surge up Issaquah Creek.

Seattle-Tacoma International Airport

LODGINGS

Hilton Seattle Airport Hotel / ★★☆

17620 INTERNATIONAL BLVD, SEATAC; 206/244-4800 OR 800/HILTONS
A renovation doubled the size of this well-run hotel to a total of 396 rooms (7 suites). Rooms are set around two landscaped courtyards. The hotel has a pool, an indoor-outdoor Jacuzzi, a fitness room, and a 40,000-square-foot conference center. A 24-hour business center caters to worker bees. The hotel's restaurant, Spencer's for Steaks and Chops (206/248-7153), serves all meals. Room service is 5am to midnight, but the complimentary airport shuttle is 24 hours. *$$–$$$; AE, DC, DIS, JCB, MC, V; checks OK; www.hilton.com; corner of S 176th St and Pacific Hwy S.* ♿

PUGET SOUND

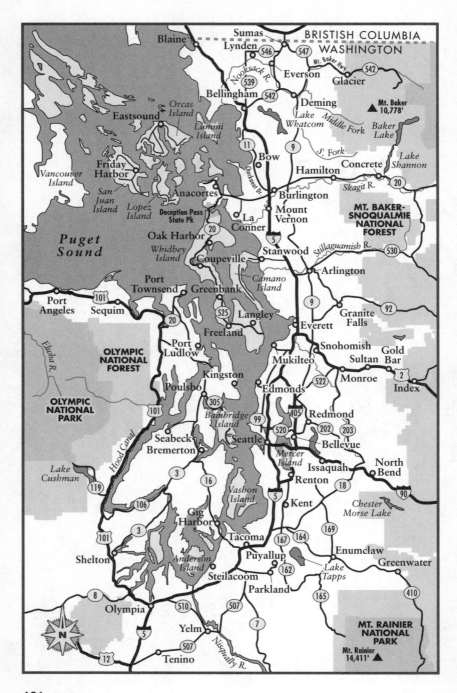

PUGET SOUND

The Puget Sound region is one of Washington's most idyllic areas. From the gardens in Blaine's Peace Arch Park at the Canadian Border to the state's capital campus in Olympia, each of the cities and towns along the Interstate 5 corridor, and the islands on the Sound, has a unique identity.

ACCESS AND INFORMATION

Fly into **SEATTLE-TACOMA INTERNATIONAL AIRPORT** (17801 Pacific Hwy S, SeaTac; 206/433-5388; www.portseattle.org/seatac/)—13 miles south of Seattle and 16 miles north of Tacoma—and you have easy access to **INTERSTATE 5**. You'll need a car to best explore the region; most **CAR RENTAL** agencies have outlets at Sea-Tac Airport.

Train travel offers a different view. **AMTRAK** (King Street Station, 303 S Jackson St, Seattle; 206/382-4125 or 800/USA–RAIL; www.amtrak.com) has daily runs between Portland, Seattle, and Vancouver, British Columbia, with stops including Everett and Bellingham.

WASHINGTON STATE FERRIES (Pier 52, Seattle; 206/464-6400 or 800/843-3779; www.wsdot.wa.gov/ferries/) access the San Juan Islands, Whidbey, Vashon, and other islands in Puget Sound.

Edmonds

This quintessential seaside city with its waterfront boardwalk and flower-lined streets is just 15 miles north of Seattle via Interstate 5. City streets and neighborhoods burst into color every summer for the annual "Edmonds in Bloom" competition. A stroll along the waterfront or in **BRACKETT'S LANDING PARK** (just north of the ferry landing) offers a clear view of the Olympic Mountains.

Arts are an integral element here, with a ballet, orchestra, symphony, and theater groups, which help host the **EDMONDS ARTS FESTIVAL** (www.edmondsartsfestival.com) each June. Antique lovers will find more than 200 shops at the **AURORA ANTIQUE PAVILION** (24111 SR 99, Ste 201; 425/744-0566; www.antiquepav.com) and nearly 100 dealers at the **TIMES SQUARE ANTIQUE MALL** (10117 Edmonds Way; 425/670-0770). For all other shipping, don't miss the quaint shops downtown.

A train station and nearby **EDMONDS HARBOR INN** (130 W Dayton; 800/441-8033; www.nwcountryinns.com/edmonds/) make this pleasant town an overnight destination as well. The **SHELL CREEK GRILL & WINE BAR** (526 Main St; 425/775-4566; www.shellcreekgrill.com) specializes in Southwest cuisine, and **CHANTERELLE'S** (316 Main St; 425/774-0650) is known for its addictive tomato bisque. Find information at the **EDMONDS CHAMBER OF COMMERCE** (121 5th Ave N; 425/670-1496; www.edmondswa.com).

Everett Area

Timber and fishing once supported this Snohomish County seat north of Seattle. Mansions along Grand and Rucker avenues are reminders of the days when timber barons ruled. Today, Naval Station Everett and the Port of Everett form the core of the growing economy in North Everett, which juts into the Snohomish River and Port Gardner Channel. Boeing's Paine Field facility occupies a major portion of the south end. US Highway 2 heads east over the Cascades from Everett, and ferries float west from Mukilteo, just south of Everett.

Mill Creek

Often called suburban nirvana, this tidy, country-club community northwest of Edmonds and south of Everett includes several **PARKS** (www.cityofmillcreek. com). One of the city's best-loved restaurants is nestled in Mill Creek Town Center, on State Route 527 east of exit 183 off Interstate 5. **ZINNIA** (15130 Main St; 425/357-0512; www.zinniawa.com) offers lunch-goers generous salads and sandwiches, and evening diners choose from vegetarian dishes to wild game.

Mukilteo

Mukilteo, on the southwest edge of Everett via State Routes 525 and 526 west of Interstate 5, is probably best known for the Mukilteo-Clinton ferry that grants access to Whidbey Island, Deception Pass, and the Olympic Peninsula. The restored 1906 lighthouse at **LIGHTHOUSE PARK** (follow signs from I-5) a block from the ferry dock is worth seeing. For a quick bite, dart into **IVAR'S** (720 Front St; 425/742-6180; www.ivars.net) next to the ferry terminal. Information is available through **SNOHOMISH COUNTY TOURISM BUREAU** (909 SE Everett Mall Way, Ste C300, Everett; 425/348-5802 or 888/338-0976; www.snohomish.org).

RESTAURANTS

Charles at Smugglers Cove / ★★

8340 53RD AVE W, MUKILTEO; 425/347-2700
Chef Claude Faure and his wife, Janet, turned this landmark building—a 1929 speakeasy set on a bluff above Possession Sound—into an elegant restaurant. A terrace overlooks the sound in this French country–style eatery. Dishes such as veal chop with tarragon and *poulet aux crevettes* (breast of chicken with prawns) grace the classically French menu. Save room for crepes suzette or Grand Marnier soufflé. *$$$; AE, MC, V; local checks only; lunch Tues–Fri, dinner Mon–Sat; full bar; reservations recommended; www. charlesatsmugglerscove.com; at SR 525 and 526.* &

Diamond Knot Brewery & Alehouse / ★

621 FRONT ST, MUKILTEO; 425/355-4488
This rustic tavern across from the Mukilteo ferry dock is a neighborhood secret. Get a steak or seafood delivered on a sizzling stone slab. You cook the meat to your liking, a piece at a time. It's a bit of work and a lot of fun. Even if you opt for a burger or pizza, pair it with a pint of nitrogen-infused ale. *$$; MC, V; no checks; lunch, dinner every day; beer and wine; www.diamondknot. com; on left at approach to ferry-dock parking lot.* &

LODGINGS

Silver Cloud Inn / ★★

718 FRONT ST, MUKILTEO; 425/423-8600
This waterfront inn adjacent to the Mukilteo ferry is built over the water, and half its 70 rooms have spectacular Puget Sound views. The location is ideal—fishing and crabbing at the beach in back, picnics at the park in front, and restaurants down the street. Rooms include microwaves and refrigerators; some have jetted tubs and fireplaces. Eat your continental breakfast in the cozy sitting room off the lobby. *$$–$$$; AE, DIS, MC, V; checks OK; www.silvercloud.com; exit 189 from I-5.* &

Snohomish

Rather than lamenting its urbanization, the town of Snohomish (on State Route 9 south of US Highway 2 east of Everett) is living up to its moniker as the "Antique Capital of the Northwest." Antique shops fill downtown. The **STAR CENTER MALL** (829 2nd St; 360/568-2131; www.myantiquemall.com/starcenter) is the largest, with nearly 200 dealers; a restaurant, **COLLECTOR'S CHOICE** (360/568-1277), is on the lower level. After you scour that mall, work your way up and down First Street around the corner. Take tea at **MRS. PENNYCOOKE'S TEA ROOM** (922 1st St; 360/568-5045) and opt for the ginger scones. On the Snohomish River side of the street, **TODO MEXICO** (1101 1st St; 360/862-0210) is a good choice. For fine dining, **SEBASTIAN'S** (924 1st St; 360/568-3928; www.sebastiansjazz.com) offers steaks, seafood, and pasta; **MARDINI'S** (101 Union Ave; 360/568-8080; www. mardinis.com) is all about Mediterranean food.

In this town—the Snohomish County seat—you can also get in the air, with the **AIRIAL HOT AIR BALLOON COMPANY** (10123 Airport Way; 360/568-3025; www.airialballoon.com), **SKYDIVE SNOHOMISH** (9912 Airport Way; 360/568-7703; www.skydivesnohomish.com), or a ride from **HARVEY FIELD** (9900 Airport Way; 360/568-1541; www.snohomishflying.com). And once you return to earth, don't miss the new **BEE HIVE DAY SPA** (629 1st St; 360/568-2740) with treatments like the barista coffee buzz and worker bee polisher.

Learn more from the **SNOHOMISH COUNTY TOURISM BUREAU** (see Mukilteo).

Everett

In Everett, at the junction of Interstate 5 and US Highway 2, the impressive downtown **EVERETT EVENTS CENTER** (2000 Hewitt Ave; 866/332-8499; www.everetteventscenter.com), with a 10,000-seat capacity, is home to the **SILVERTIPS** (425/252-5100; www.everettsilvertips.com), Everett's Western Hockey League franchise team, and the **EVERETT HAWKS** (866/383-4295; www.everetthawks.com), a National Indoor Football League team. The **EVERETT AQUASOX** (3802 Broadway; 425/258-3673; www.aquasox.com) is a single-A, short-season farm team for the Seattle Mariners.

But there's more to Everett than sports. The **ARTS COUNCIL OF SNOHOMISH COUNTY** (1507 Wall St; 425/257-8380; www.artscouncilofsnoco.org) features a dazzling display of Pilchuck glass. The **EVERETT PERFORMING ARTS CENTER** (2710 Wetmore Ave; 425/257-8600 box office or 888/257-3722; www.village theatre.org/epac) hosts events. The **FUTURE OF FLIGHT AVIATION CENTER & BOEING TOUR** (exit 189 west from I-5 to SR 526, follow signs; 425/438-8100 or 800/464-1476; www.futureofflight.org) offers a 60-minute tour of the plant where Boeing jets are assembled. Tours run every day and fill early; purchase tickets online.

For information, contact the **EVERETT CHAMBER OF COMMERCE** (11400 Airport Rd, Ste B; 425/257-3222; www.everettchamber.com).

RESTAURANTS

Alligator Soul / ★

2013-1/2 HEWITT AVE, EVERETT; 425/259-6311
When this colorful Cajun restaurant changed hands and received a makeover, so did the menu. Fortunately, the comfort foods—jalapeño corn bread, fried catfish, and sweet potato–pecan pie—made the cut. But dinner now includes more New Orleans–style dishes like alligator tail, ham hocks, and black-eyed peas or pulled pork. Sunday brunch is another addition. Wednesday through Saturday evenings, listen to zydeco, jazz, and blues bands. *$$; DC, DIS, MC, V; no checks; lunch, dinner Tues–Sat; beer and wine; reservations recommended; www.thealligatorsoul.com; near Broadway, across from arena.*

Emory's on Silver Lake / ★

11830 19TH AVE SE, EVERETT; 425/337-7772
A former roadhouse on a country lake, Emory's sits in the middle of southeast suburban Everett, offering aged steaks and seafood—such as salmon, halibut, and cannelloni with Dungeness crab—as well as pasta, salads, and burgers. The Key lime cheesecake is worth the splurge. Emory's has an easygoing pub-style charm, lake views, and deck dining. After your meal, explore the dock. *$$; AE, DIS, MC, V; no checks; lunch Mon–Fri, dinner every day; full bar; reservations recommended; www.emorys.com; on SR 527 north of exit 186 off I-5.* &

Pita King / ★★

2210 37TH ST, EVERETT; 425/258-4040
This Middle Eastern bakery is the only place in Western Washington where you can get fresh, hot *manakeesh*—Lebanese pizzas topped with *za'tar*, a blend of thyme, olive oil, sesame, and sumac. Also pick up fresh pita bread and spinach, cheese, and meat pies made to order, all in the authentic stone oven. The grocery portion of the bakery features treats like olives, feta cheese, halal (similar to "kosher") meats, and baklava. A member of the gracious Alaeddine family will greet you with traditional Lebanese hospitality. *$; MC, V; checks OK; breakfast, lunch every day; no alcohol; no reservations; www. pitakingbakery.com; exit 192 off I-5.* &

LODGINGS

The Inn at Port Gardner / ★★

1700 W MARINE VIEW DR, EVERETT; 425/252-6779 OR 888/252-6779
Talk about quiet. This place is truly that, and there's not much to do within walking distance except stroll along the marina or eat next door at Lombardi's Italian Restaurant. But the Inn at Port Gardner is nice. Thirty-three rooms are done up in neutral tones, some overlooking the water. Some rooms have sweeping mountain views, too. Suites are worth the price, and all rooms include continental breakfast. The lobby's fireplace and art make it a nice place to lounge. *$$–$$$; AE, DC, DIS, MC, V; local checks only; www.inn atportgardner.com; exit 193 off I-5.*

Stanwood

Pastoral Stanwood, west of Interstate 5 on State Route 532, once was a thriving port on the Stillaguamish River, which you can easily imagine from the mural on the **STANWOOD CINEMAS PAVILION** (6996 265th St NW). Today, this still largely agricultural community northwest of Everett is noted for **KAYAK POINT GOLF COURSE** (15711 Marine Dr NE; www.kayakpoint.com), consistently ranked one of "America's Top 50 Public Golf Courses" by *Golf Digest*. Grab a bite at the golf resort's **FIRE CREEK GRILL** (360/652-9676), or drive back to town for a sandwich at the **COOKIE MILL** (9808 SR 532; 360/629-2362) before you cross the bridge to Camano Island. For dinner, **MAXIME'S GLOBAL CUISINE** (10007 270th NW; 360/629-6002) is the locals' favorite.

Stanwood is also known for the 54-acre campus of internationally renowned glass-art **PILCHUCK SCHOOL** (206/621-8422; www.pilchuck.com), founded in 1971 by Dale Chihuly and others. Spring tours and a summer open house (admission $30) give visitors a chance to see artists at work.

Learn more from the **STANWOOD CHAMBER OF COMMERCE** (8725 271st St NW; 360/629-0562; www.stanwoodchamber.org).

Camano Island

Less than 2 miles west of Stanwood on State Route 532 and an hour's drive north of Seattle, this 18-mile-long island still has that "away from it all" feel. Beach access is plentiful at **CAMANO ISLAND STATE PARK** (southwest end of island; 360/387-3031; www.parks.wa.gov/alpha.asp), where the day-use area has picnic shelters; camping is also available. You can also comb beaches at two small county parks: **UTSALADY BAY** at the north end and **CAVALERO BEACH** on the southeast side of the island. Some of Washington's best bird-watching is here.

The island also boasts an 18-hole golf course, galleries, and restaurants, including the **CAMANO** (170 E Cross Island Rd; 360/387-9972) and **ISLANDERS ESPRESSO & EATERY** (848 N Sunrise Blvd, Bldg D). The 18-hole **CAMALOCH GOLF COURSE** (326 N East Camano Dr; 360/387-3084) also has a deli. Visit the island over Mother's Day weekend and take in the **CAMANO ARTS ASSOCIATION STUDIO TOUR** (360/387-7146; www.camanoarts.org).

Find information at the **CAMANO ISLAND CHAMBER OF COMMERCE** (578 N Camano Dr; 360/629-7136; www.camanoisland.org).

LODGINGS

Camano Island Inn / ★★

1054 S WEST CAMANO DR, CAMANO ISLAND; 360/387-0783 OR 888/718-0783
Each of the six rooms in this luxurious waterfront inn has a private deck and water view. It's not unusual to spot whales, seals, sea lions, and sea otters. Rooms have oversize showers; some have jetted tubs. Beds have down comforters and pillows. Curl up in front of the fireplace or take breakfast in bed. A paved path provides beach access; kayaks are available; massages can be arranged. *$$; AE, DIS, MC, V; checks OK (in advance); www.camanoisland inn.com; exit 212 from I-5, follow SR 532 west onto island.* &

Whidbey Island

Whidbey Island has done something remarkable over the past 30 years: It has preserved its integrity as an island. Old values and old growth have not been completely sacrificed to new growth. Shoreline beauty is available for miles at a time. Prairies, pasture, meadows, and woods can be roamed in peace and quiet. The citizenry has preserved **GREENBANK FARM** and the 22-square-mile historic **EBEY'S LANDING NATIONAL HISTORIC RESERVE** (162 Cemetery Rd, Coupeville; www.nps.gov/ebla), as well as the small-town character of Coupeville and Langley. The art scene here rivals Seattle in quality, and the literary arts are first-class, too. The **WHIDBEY WRITER'S CONFERENCE** (www.writeonwhidbey.com) draws people nationwide. Whidbey Island is officially the longest island in the United States (even if it does have a bridge at its north end). When you visit, slow down and enjoy.

B and Bs are a flourishing art form on Whidbey; at last count there were at least 140. They range from cozy rooms in a family home to over-the-top elegance, luxury, and privacy. The town of Oak Harbor is kid friendly with a waterfront park, a local drive-in movie theater, a comic shop, and fast-food outlets. There are five **STATE PARKS** (www.parks.wa.gov) on Whidbey, which make for great family hikes and beach walks. All but Joseph Whidbey State Park have camping.

ACCESS AND INFORMATION

You can drive to the north end of Whidbey Island by taking Interstate 5 north from Seattle, turning west on **STATE ROUTE 20** to Anacortes, and following it south over the Deception Pass bridge onto the island, where the highway continues south to Keystone. The ferry to Clinton on the south end of the island leaves from Mukilteo (see Everett Area section) approximately every half hour and takes about 20 minutes; from the mainland, **STATE ROUTE 525** continues north on Whidbey to State Route 20. There's also a ferry between Keystone, about midway up the west side of Whidbey, and Port Townsend on the Olympic Peninsula (where State Route 20 continues south). The Keystone ferry's schedule is less frequent, the lines can be long, and the ferry is sometimes waylaid by the tides and weather. Best to check ahead with **WASHINGTON STATE FERRIES** (206/464-6400 or 888/808-7977; www.wsdot.wa.gov/ferries). Whether you're car-free on purpose or by necessity, Whidbey has **ISLAND TRANSIT** (360/678-7771 or 360/321-6688; www.islandtransit.org), a fare-free bus system. A great tourism Web site is www.whidbeycamanoislands.com.

Clinton

This town is the gateway to the island via ferry. Whether you're an experienced kayaker or not, **WHIDBEY ISLAND KAYAKING COMPANY** (360/321-4683 or 800/233-4319) rents kayaks at five locations. If you're into leather, **ACE LEATHER GOODS, INC.** (8930A State Hwy 525; 360/341-2699) has great clothes and more.

RESTAURANTS

J. W. Desserts / ★

KEN'S KORNER MALL, CLINTON; 360/341-1827
If your idea of the perfect lunch is a superb bowl of soup followed by a piece of the most decadent chocolate espresso cake (sans flour) ever conceived, then J. W. Desserts is a must-stop. The decor is European bistro-chic, with a touch of Northwest and East Coast vintage travel, and a cozy fireplace corner has couches. Soups change daily; when seafood chowder shows up, it's a word-of-mouth celebration. The chef-owner, John Auburn, used to create celebrity cakes for celebrity occasions. Now he feeds the locals, and they love it. So does he. *$; MC, V; checks OK; breakfast, lunch Tues–Sat; wine only; no reservations; www.jwdesserts.com; 2 miles on SR 525 from Clinton ferry dock, turn right into Ken's Korner.*

WHIDBEY ISLAND THREE-DAY TOUR

DAY ONE: Approach Whidbey from the south via the Mukilteo-Clinton ferry, then grab a latte and bagel once you're on the island by driving 2 miles to **KEN'S KORNER**, the mini-mall with attitude, and finding **KIICHLI'S BAGEL BAKERY**. Also stock up on sandwiches here, then visit **J. W. DESSERTS** for their flourless chocolate cake—these are your picnic rations for your south-end explorations. Drive west a few miles to get aired out at **SOUTH WHIDBEY STATE PARK**'s (www.parks.wa.gov) beach, then enjoy your picnic in the woods above. Spend the afternoon at the shops in **LANGLEY**. Afterward, find your B and B: If you love tall trees, head to the **EAGLES NEST INN** in Langley. If you love Italy, go west to **A TUSCAN LADY** in Freeland. If you love Northwest elegance, it's the **CLIFF HOUSE**, also in Freeland. After settling in, return to Clinton for dinner at **TRATTORIA GIUSEPPE**. For a nightcap, head to the **BEACHFIRE GRILL** (5023 Harbor Hills Dr, Freeland; 360/331-2363) a few miles north at Holmes Harbor, where you can play golf the next morning.

DAY TWO: After breakfast at your B and B, walk through meditative paths at the **EARTH SANCTUARY**, just outside Freeland, and linger in the labyrinth. Head to **BAYVIEW CORNER** and poke around the shops in the Cash Store Building,

Trattoria Giuseppe / ★★

KEN'S KORNER MALL, CLINTON; 360/341-3454
This place is a surprise. The decor, in all its high-ceiling and arched Tuscan *taverna* aplomb, is not exactly what you'd expect to see behind the Ken's Korner facade. The food is a surprise, too. The pollo Gorgonzola with penne pasta is a local favorite, and the seafood dishes get raves. Their standard Italian fare for dessert, Crema al Caramello, ranks way up there in creamy pleasure. Live classical and jazz piano on Saturdays. *$$; AE, MC, V; checks OK; dinner every day; full bar; reservations recommended; www.trattoriagiuseppe.com; 2 miles on SR 525 from Clinton ferry dock, turn right into Ken's Korner.*

LODGINGS

The Chinook Retreat Center / ★★

WHIDBEY INSTITUTE, CLINTON; 360/341-3404
The Chinook Retreat Center at the Whidbey Institute, on 70 lovely acres of forests and meadows, offers quiet cabins. Heron, Hermitage, Bag End, and Mushroom are smaller and don't have bathrooms or kitchens—those are in a separate building nearby. Each cabin has one bed and electricity, but that's about it. Bag End has a meditation loft and small wood stove. The Farmhouse, with seven bedrooms, and Granny's, with two bedrooms, offer more

then drive north a few miles to **GERRY'S KITCHEN** in Freeland for lunch. After lunch, visit **MEERKERK GARDENS** (3531 Meerkerk Lane, Greenbank; 360/378-1912) on the way to **GREENBANK FARM** (Wonn Rd and Hwy 25; 360/678-7700; www.greenbankfarm.com) to browse antique shops, sample fine cheeses, and have afternoon tea and loganberry pie at Whidbey Pies Café (360/678-1288). Check in to your night's lodgings: If you love log cabins in the woods, it's the **GUEST HOUSE LOG COTTAGES** in Greenbank. If you like historical flavor near the water, it's the **FORT CASEY INN**. Then head into **COUPEVILLE** and spend the afternoon with some good shopping, or play pool at **TOBY'S TAVERN**. Eat dinner at the **OYSTERCATCHER**, then watch the sunset from **FORT CASEY STATE PARK**'s (3 miles south of Coupeville) beaches before calling it a night.

   DAY THREE: Return to Coupeville for breakfast at **GREAT TIMES WATERFRONT COFFEE HOUSE**, then visit **EBEY'S LANDING NATIONAL HISTORIC RESERVE** and **FORT EBEY STATE PARK** (395 Fort Ebey Rd; 360/678-4636). Head north to Oak Harbor for lunch at **FLYERS** or grab picnic fixings at Seabolts Smokehouse and head out to **JOSEPH WHIDBEY STATE PARK**. Then drive north to take a hike at **DECEPTION PASS STATE PARK** before returning to Oak Harbor for dinner at **KASTEEL FRANSSEN**. To end your tour, stay at the welcoming **COMPASS ROSE** B and B in Coupeville.

amenities. If you don't want to cook or eat out, chef Patti Howard, the Casual Gourmet, oversees meal plans. *$–$$; AE, MC, V; checks OK; www.whidbey institute.org; 2 miles north on SR 525 from Clinton ferry; turn left at Cultus Bay Rd, go ½ mile to Campbell Rd, turn right, go 0.2 mi, look for sign on left.*

Langley

The Langley area was first established in 1880 when Jacob Anthes purchased 120 acres of forest to harvest cordwood for steamers. The town, on a side road north of State Route 525 just north of Clinton, was incorporated in 1913 and named after Seattle Judge J. W. Langley, who invested in the original woodcutting business. These days, it is the most sophisticated little town on Whidbey. Classy art galleries, fine cuisine, elegant accommodations, and intriguing shops abound. But Langley still sports its small-town virtues. The much-loved 1930s **CLYDE THEATRE** (217 1st St; 360/221-5525; www.theclyde.com) has movies for $5. The **SOUTH WHIDBEY HISTORICAL MUSEUM** (321 2nd St; 360/221-2101; open weekends) is inspiring. The views don't hurt either. And there's a pier, a waterfront park, and pocket beaches.

   A new addition to Langley's shops is **GREGOR RARE BOOKS** (197 A 2nd St, Langley; 360/221-8331; www.gregorbooks.com). The **MOONRAKER** (209 1st

St; 360/221-6962) has a collection of Northwest titles; **GOLDEN OTTER USED BOOKS** (124 2nd St; 360/221-8929) is also good. Get cool clothes at the **COTTAGE** (210 1st St; 360/221-4747), **IN THE COUNTRY** (315 1st St; 360/221-8202), and **BIG SISTER** (208 1st St; 360/221-7056). Island time can be measured by a visit to Herb Helsel at **LANGLEY CLOCK AND GALLERY** (220 2nd St; 360/221-3422). He once had a motorcycle shop; now he fixes vintage clocks and is "open by chance and appointment." All things old and interesting, including Virginia, abound at **VIRGINIA'S ANTIQUES AND GIFTS** (206 1st St; 360/221-7797). At the **GOOD CHEER THRIFT SHOP** (114 Anthes Ave; 360/221-6465; www.goodcheer.org), original art can be discovered amid castoffs. Art is also found at **LOWRY-JAMES RARE PRINTS** (101 Anthes Ave; 360/221-0477).

At last count, there were 10 galleries in town, including **GASKILL/OLSON** (301 1st St; 360/221-2978; www.gaskillolson.com), where the sculpture of Georgia Gerber is on display. When you need a break, stroll **SEAWALL PARK**, below First Street, where you'll encounter Gerber's sculpture of a boy and a dog. Her life-size bronze pig is a famous landmark in Seattle's Pike Place Market. The handblown glass in Langley is distinctive. George Springer, a glass artist for more than 30 years, can be found at his **HELLEBORE GLASS STUDIO** (308 1st St; 360/221-2067; www. helleboreglass.com). **MUSEO PICCOLO GALLERY** (215 1st St; 360/221-7737) also features glass art. The **ARTIST'S GALLERY COOPERATIVE** (314 1st St; 360/221-7675) includes everything from the sublime to the ridiculous. **ART WALKS** (www. visitlangley.com) are on the first Saturday of each month.

Everything chocolate can be had at the **CHOCOLATE FLOWER FARM AND THE GARDEN SHED** (5040 Saratoga Rd (farm); 224 1st St (shop); 360/221-4464; www.chocolateflowerfarm.com). Quaff microbrews at the **DOG HOUSE** (230 1st St; 360/221-9996); wines are offered at the Osenbach family–operated **WHIDBEY ISLAND WINERY** (5237 S Langley Rd; 360/221-2040; www.whidbeyislandwinery. com). Great foods are available at **ISLAND GOURMET AND GIFT SHOPPE** (221 2nd St; 360/221-3626; www.islandgourmetgifts.com). There are too many good places to eat in this little town, including **LANGLEY VILLAGE BAKERY** (221 2nd St; 360/221-3525), where the locals rave about the pesto pizza and the three-milk cake—which actually translates into cream in all its manifestations. Before or after a movie at the Clyde, stop in at **MIKE'S PLACE COFFEEHOUSE AND CREAMERY** (219 1st St; 360/221-6575), which comes complete with a restaurant in the back; locals lounge in the front. The locals love **VILLAGE PIZZERIA** (108 1st St; 360/221-3363)—one East Coast transplant is rapturous about their meatball sandwich. A north island resident drives down to eat banana-bread French toast at the **BRAE-BURN** (197 D 2nd St; 360/221-3211).

Langley has **MYSTERY WEEKEND** in February, the **CHOOCHOKUM ARTS FESTIVAL** in July, **DJANGOFEST** (gypsy jazz) in September, and a **COFFEE FEST** in April. For information, contact the **SOUTH WHIDBEY CHAMBER OF COMMERCE** (208 Anthes Ave, Langley; 360/221-6765; www.southwhidbeychamber.com).

RESTAURANTS

Café Langley / ★★

113 1ST ST, LANGLEY; 360/221-3090
Since 1989 the brothers Garibyan have been holding court with the tastiest Mediterranean fare in the region. From marinated-eggplant sandwiches to tasty lamb shish kebabs, this storefront café has cuisine sparkling with creativity in an atmosphere of comfy elegance. The hummus is creamy beyond delicious; the Northwest salmon and halibut are beautifully prepared; the Mediterranean seafood stew is rich with mussels, shrimp, salmon, and scallops. Russian cream with raspberry sauce is a signature dessert. *$$–$$$; AE, MC, V; checks OK; dinner every day (Tues–Sun in winter); full bar; reservations recommended; downtown.*

The Edgecliff / ★★

510 CASCADE AVE, LANGLEY; 360/221-8899
It's the view that first gets your attention in this restaurant on a bluff overlooking Puget Sound and the Cascades. It's elegant inside, too. Chef Micah Noack, born and raised in Coupeville to the north, started here early in 2006 after a stint at the Fish Bowl down the street. His kalamata olive–encrusted rack of lamb is an attention getter, as are the seared scallops with orange vinaigrette. The butternut-squash ravioli come with a brown butter–brandy sauce, caramelized walnuts, roasted garlic, and fresh sage. *$$$; AE, DIS, MC, V; checks OK; lunch, dinner every day; full bar; reservations recommended; on the cliff near the north end of 1st St.*

The Fish Bowl / ★★☆

317 2ND ST, LANGLEY; 360/221-6511
Despite its modest exterior, the Fish Bowl offers extravagant seafood and service. Maureen and Roy Cooke opened the doors in 2001, and the locals haven't stopped lining up since. Chef David Bagley oversees a menu that includes oysters with champagne-vinegar mignonette and crab cakes served with truffled mushroom and asparagus risotto. Strawberries sautéed in a cabernet sauce with a dash of freshly ground pepper and a bed of vanilla ice cream makes for a distinctive finish. *$$–$$$; AE, DIS, MC, V; checks OK; dinner every day (Tues–Sun in winter); full bar; reservations recommended; www.fishbowlrestaurant.com; downtown.*

LODGINGS

Ashingdon Manor / ★★★

5023 LANGLEY RD, LANGLEY; 360/221-2334 OR 800/442-4942
This elegant B and B does not give itself away at first glance. It's not on the water, it's not in the woods, and you can see it from the road. Inside, however, its artistic grace and old-world charm seduce even the most avid outdoor lover to consider moving permanently indoors. Breakfast, prepared by

Jennifer Johnson, who was the chef-owner at Seattle's once revered Chez Nous, is signature gourmet. *$$$; AE, MC, V; checks OK; www.ashingdon-manor.com; 2 miles north on SR 525 from Clinton ferry, turn right on Langley Rd, go 2 more miles.* &

Chauntecleer House, Dove House, and the Potting Shed / ★★★★

5081 SARATOGA RD, LANGLEY; 360/221-5494 OR 800/637-4436

Bunny Meals has visions of places and perfection, and she somehow manages to make them come true. These three cottages are too cute for words—and even if you don't like cute, you'll love these luxurious accommodations. The Dove House has touches of the Southwest throughout. The Potting Shed is for gardeners. The chicken-themed Chauntecleer has a magnificent view. All have kitchens, bedrooms, and are fully appointed with all things colorful. This is a very happy, pricey place to rest your body and revive your spirit. *$$$$; AE, MC, V; checks OK; www.dovehouse.com; just north of Langley.*

Country Cottage of Langley / ★★

215 6TH ST, LANGLEY; 360/221-8709

This place is actually six cottages, all with gardens outside and Jacuzzis inside. Some have water views. Each is distinct in decor, from nautical to floral. Breakfast might be eggs Benedict, quiche, or a three-cheese omelet with baked goods ranging from German pancakes and Dutch babies to ginger scones and breakfast bread pudding. You can eat in your cottage, in the innkeepers' dining room, or perhaps out in the gazebo. *$$$; MC, V; no checks; www.acountrycottage.com; a few minutes walk from downtown.*

Eagles Nest Inn / ★★★

4680 SARATOGA RD, LANGLEY; 360/221-5331

Tall trees and trails abound in this landscape where the rooms are a sanctuary within a sanctuary. This octagonal home sits on a hill surrounded by woods. Nature is reflected throughout in wall murals, paintings, photographs, and sculpture. It's quiet here. Each of the four rooms offers a pretty setting with a private bath. The best is the Eagle's Nest, an eight-sided penthouse suite rimmed with windows (and a balcony) giving a 360 degree view of the water and forest. The chocolate chip cookies are famous, and there's a library lounge complete with a refreshment center. Innkeepers Joanne and Jerry Lechner love the place, and it shows. *$$–$$$; DIS, MC, V; checks OK; www.eaglesnestinn.com; 2 miles north of Langley.*

Inn at Langley / ★★★★

400 1ST ST, LANGLEY; 360/221-3033

This place is over the top in good taste, so if you want to stay at everyone's "best of the best," go for it. It's all true. We'll spare you the accolades; just check out the Web site. The 26 state-of-the-art rooms all have views, fireplaces, and original art. The superb dinners are available only on weekends (which can start on Thursdays in the summer). Is the "best chef in Seattle," Matt Costello, now the best chef in Langley? You'll have to ask the locals. *$$$$; AE, DIS, MC, V; no checks; www.innatlangley.com; downtown Langley.*

Saratoga Inn / ★★★

201 CASCADE AVE, LANGLEY; 360/221-5801 OR 800/698-2910
A Cape Cod inn with a Puget Sound view, the Saratoga is elegant and trendy with its big wrap-around porch, fireplaces in its 15 rooms, most with views, and careful detail to wood and stone. Teddy bears on the beds and the big cookie jar in the lobby cozy up the place. There's gourmet breakfast in the dining room and afternoon hors d'oeuvres in the parlor. *$$–$$$; AE, MC, V; no checks; www.saratogainnwhidbeyisland.com; 2-minute walk from downtown.*

Bayview Corner

In 1999 Nancy Nordhoff (a National Women's History Project award winner in 2006) invested in 22 acres of commercial land at historic Bayview Corner, just off State Route 525, about halfway between Clinton and Freeland. Since 1924 the Cash Store Building has been a general store, a gas station, a feed store, a food co-op, an art store, and a pet laundry. It's now home to eclectic shops and restaurants, all celebrating local and environmental sensibilities guided by the **GOOSEFOOT COMMUNITY FUND** (www.goosefoot.com). **BAYVIEW ARTS** (360/321-8414), under the eye of Mary Ann Mansfield, has impressive art. **EVENTUALLY** (360/321-5338)—actually the name of the shop—creatively redefines the very concept of recycled. You can rent bikes at the **HALF LINK BICYCLE SHOP** (360/331-7980). The longest-running **FARMERS MARKET** on the island is at Bayview every Saturday March through September (www.bayviewfarmersmarket.com).

Freeland

Okay, so Freeland has a brand-new shopping center—this doesn't mean the old Freeland isn't as funky and friendly as ever. The same family of feisty females runs the **FREELAND CAFÉ** (1642 E Main St; 360/331-9945; www.whidbey.com/freelandcafe), where you can get breakfast all day as well as Virina's famous teriyaki sauce. This really is a local, no-frills joint. For good food with a frill or two, go to **GERRY'S KITCHEN** (1675 Main St; 360/331-4818) across the street. The **ISLAND TEA COMPANY** (1664 Main St; 360/331-6080; www.islandteacompany.com) is a cottage tea shop. If you need to knit, check out **KNITTY PEARL'S** (1686 Main St; 360/331-2212; www.knittypearls.com).

Just outside Freeland, off Newman Road, is the **EARTH SANCTUARY** (360/321-5465; www.earthsanctuary.org), where eco-artist Chuck Pettis has transformed sacred inspiration into 75 acres of earthy delight. The prayer wheels, stones, and meditative paths are calming. A $7 donation lets you walk a labyrinth, stand with sacred stones, or spin a high-tech Tibetan prayer wheel containing 1.3 trillion prayers. There's also a small retreat house.

Right across the street from the road to the Earth Sanctuary is **ISLAND GLASS** (2062 E Newman Rd; 360/321-4439; Sat–Sun 10am–5pm), where Robert Adamson retreated after many years jetting around the world teaching the art of glassblowing. There's a small shop with affordable handblown glass art.

LODGINGS

À la Provence B and B / ★

5717 MUTINY BAY RD, FREELAND; 360/331-6086 OR 866/694-9643
Notable because of its very family-friendly garden cottage (with its stocked kitchen, luxurious bedroom, and a bunk room) and proximity to the beach, À la Provence also has a Sunset B and B Suite with a private entrance. Lynda Minter, owner and innkeeper, describes herself as "an Iowa farm girl," so there's gardening going on, which translates into U-pick lavender and organic produce. The willow tree by the pond in back is glorious. *$$$; MC, V; checks OK; www.alaprovence.com; 10 miles north of Clinton, left at Fish Rd in Freeland, right at Mutiny Bay Rd.*

A Tuscan Lady / ★★

619 DOLPHIN DR, FREELAND; 360/331-5057
It's hard to be fully prepared for this lush and extravagant place. The extraordinary attention to detail inside and out makes A Tuscan Lady a complete getaway, even if you don't make it to the nearby beach. The gardens and the rooms are full of color and design. Artist-owner Darla Duchessa has poured her creative heart into this Italian holiday experience. The separate villa, which sleeps six, comes complete with a light-filled cathedral loft, with beds in each corner in honor of Darlene's four daughters, who always want to sleep in the same room. The big, private bedroom is a romantic hideaway in the heart of the villa. *$$–$$$; MC, V; checks OK; www.atuscanlady.com; call for directions.*

The Cliff House / ★★★↯

727 WINDMILL RD, FREELAND; 360/331-1566 OR 800/297-4118
Twenty-five years ago, Peggy Moore knew just what she was doing when she had Arne Bystrom design the exquisite Cliff House, with its central atrium, sunken living room, stone fireplace, spa tubs, and breathtaking views of sea, sky, and mountains. It's still a luxury to experience a private getaway in this unique A-frame with its original art, native rugs, and rare Indian baskets. There's a trail down to the private beach. The quaint and cozy Seacliff Cottage is less expensive and more playfully decorated, with a deck overlooking the water and a kitchenette. Peggy, who lives in a house on the premises, sets a beautiful breakfast table in each of the houses. Very pricey, very worth it. *$$$$; no credit cards; checks required (in advance); www.cliffhouse.net; go out Bush Pt Rd to Windmill Rd.*

Greenbank

It didn't take long for the locals to take action when **GREENBANK FARM** (765 E Wonn Rd; 360/678-7700; www.greenbankfarm.com) suddenly seemed doomed to become a 700-home development. Within weeks, private and public money and passion combined to save the 522-acre farm. Once the largest loganberry farm in the country, Greenbank Farm is now home to everything from the Greenbank Car Show to the Burning Word Poetry Festival to the Loganberry Festival, as well as galleries, a cheese shop, and a weekly **FARMERS MARKET** on Sunday May through September.

LODGINGS

Guest House Log Cottages / ★★

24371 SR 525, GREENBANK; 360/678-3115 OR 800/997-3115
These are real log cabins in the woods, furnished with such care that you feel like you've come home to some long-lost memory. The five cabins, each with all the conveniences of a small house, are tended with personal charm, comfy furnishings, and antiques. The large, private lodge overlooking the pond boasts a 24-foot-tall stone fireplace. It's your own private dream home where you can meditate alone in the jetted tub in a solarium or play in the Jacuzzi for two with a view. There's a swimming pool in summer for all the guests. *$$$; MC, V; checks OK; www.guesthouselogcottages.com; 1 mile south of Greenbank Store.*

Coupeville

Like any old town worth its history, Coupeville wages a war with itself over visitors—which is a good thing. Visually, historical preservation prevails, even if galleries and shops are shiny and new. Coupeville fills up on festival occasions, some of which involve kites, art, and water, so plan ahead.

It's **GRAY WHALE** country around here for a few months each year. Mid-March to May, they can be seen from the island's east shore on Saratoga Passage. Penn Cove mussels are harvested from here for good cause. In March the **PENN COVE MUSSEL FESTIVAL** (www.centralwhidbeychamber.com) offers bluegrass music, mussel-shell jewelry, cheap good beer, and bowls of mussels. And yes, the **ISLAND COUNTY HISTORICAL SOCIETY MUSEUM** (902 NW Alexander St; 360/678-3310; www.islandhistory.org) really does have the largest collection of woolly-mammoth bones in the Puget Sound area.

For refreshments, stop at the patio at **GREAT TIMES WATERFRONT COFFEE HOUSE** (12 NW Front St; 360-678-5860) or at **KNEAD & FEED** (4 NW Front St; 360-678-5431). **CHRISTOPHER'S** (23 NW Front St; 360/678-5480) is also a local favorite for seafood and steaks. **TOBY'S TAVERN** (8 NW Front St; 360/678-4222) helps keep the town well supplied with good brews and pub grub.

Get information from the **CENTRAL WHIDBEY CHAMBER OF COMMERCE** (302 N Main St; 360/678-5434; www.centralwhidbeychamber.com), as well as two other **WEB SITES** (www.coupevillelodging.com, www.cometocoupeville.com).

RESTAURANTS

The Oystercatcher / ★★★

901 GRACE ST, COUPEVILLE; 360/678-0683

The word on this small, intimate restaurant with no official front door is "go, eat, and go again." The small and imaginative menu changes frequently, according to the inspiration of chef-owner Susan Vanderbeek. Her experience shows on the plate, in the wine glass, and throughout this tiny restaurant with an enormous reputation. Hopefully, the mussel and oysters hors d'oeuvres and the flourless chocolate torte stay put, no matter the season. *$$; MC, V; checks OK; dinner Wed–Sun; beer and wine; reservations required; behind* Coupeville Examiner *office.*

LODGINGS

The Anchorage Inn / ★

807 MAIN ST, COUPEVILLE; 360/678-5581 OR 877/230-1313

Owners-innkeepers Dave and Dianne Binder love what they are doing so much that they teach the art of innkeeping as well as practice it at the Anchorage Inn. Dave even folds the breakfast napkins into unique origami shapes reflecting the theme or mood of the day. It's fun here. This new "old" Victorian has seven lavishly appointed rooms, most with water views, all with cheery charm and private baths. Savor Diane's hearty breakfast—and don't forget to ask Dave about Wiley. *$$; DIS, MC, V; checks OK; www. anchorage-inn.com; a block from waterfront.*

Captain Whidbey Inn / ★★

2072 W CAPTAIN WHIDBEY INN RD, COUPEVILLE; 360/678-4097 OR 800/366-4097

This lovable old log inn dates back to 1907, which is both the good and the not-so-good news. It's good if you like rustic knotty pine, bohemian ambience, 12 rooms with a view, and a bar in which Hemingway would happily reincarnate. It's not so good if your own private bathroom is nonnegotiable on your vacation checklist. But fear not: there are four sparsely furnished cottages with fireplaces and baths, plus 13 lagoon rooms—the best choices—with private baths and verandahs. The problem is that the walls are thin; avoid those above the bar. As of this writing, longtime owner John Stone was selling, but it's on the National Register of Historic Places, so it's destined to be preserved and is worth a visit. If Captain John's still in charge, check into an afternoon sail on the *Cutty Sark. $$; DIS, MC, V; checks OK; www. captainwhidbey.com; off Madrona Way on Penn Cove.*

Compass Rose / ★

508 S MAIN ST, COUPEVILLE; 360/678-5318 OR 800/237-3881
If you're very lucky, Captain Marshall Bronson will give you a tour of his backyard library where everything from rare books to antique "blood-letting" instruments deck the walls. "We have a divine time," says his wife, Jan, of being hosts of a two-room B and B that feels like it belongs in the movies. Funny and in love with Whidbey after their many years of hosting foreign dignitaries, the Bronsons are as charming as the 1890 Queen Anne Victorian they have filled with treasured antiques. *$$; MC, V; checks OK; www. compassrosebandb.com; just south of SR 20.*

Fort Casey Inn / ★

1124 S ENGLE RD, COUPEVILLE; 360/678-8792
Overlooking Puget Sound, Fort Casey Inn is right next door to Fort Casey State Park, with its bunkers, beaches, lighthouse, and cannons that were fired only in practice. The row of nine fully restored Georgian Revival houses, each with its own two-bedroom duplex B and B (breakfast is stocked in the kitchen), comprises the inn. Now owned by Seattle Pacific University, the inn also overlooks Crockett Lake, a bird sanctuary. Its history is reflected in the decor, which ranges from tied-rag rugs to old military photographs. *$–$$; MC, V; checks OK; www.fortcaseyinn.com; 2 miles west of Coupeville.*

Morris Farmhouse B & B

105 W MORRIS RD, COUPEVILLE; 360/678-0939 OR 866/440-1555
This grand old farmhouse has a bright red dining room and Georgia O'Keeffe prints on the walls. "We Celebrate Diversity," it says on the B and B's flyer. The six rooms and family suite are casual and comfortable. The great gathering room is about as welcoming as it gets. Owners-innkeepers Katherine Heibult and Margaret Johnson have kept the restored charm of the place and added an informality that is instantly welcoming. *$–$$; AE, MC, V; checks OK; www.morrisfarmhouse.com; 2½ miles south of Coupeville.*

Oak Harbor

This Navy town, with its transient military population, takes a lot of heat from the more "granola"-minded (in Oak Harbor–speak) islanders to the south. The truth is, along with the town's fast-food joints, big-box stores, traffic jams, and high decibels from low-flying naval planes, the nearby base preserves open space, provides jobs, and adds diversity. The Navy base even has a friendly, low-fee golf course with a view that's open to the public. Besides, if you're taking the kids along, they like the planes, burgers, and family-friendly accommodations.

CITY BEACH PARK, along the bay at the south end of town, has playground equipment, a saltwater lagoon to swim in, and ice cream at the windmill. Eat burgers at **FLYERS** (32295 SR 20; 360/675-5858), then head off to the **BLUE FOX**

DRIVE-IN THEATRE AND BRATTLAND GO-KARTS (1403 Monroe Landing Rd; 360/675-2794) for fun and nostalgia. There's a great video arcade here, too.

Oak Harbor is working hard to restore the historic qualities of its old town. On Pioneer Way, close to the harbor, there are three antique shops within two blocks, including **SHADY LADIES ANTIQUES** (Old Town Mall; 830 SE Pioneer Way; 360/679-1902), which specializes in everything from fine and funky furniture to costume and estate jewelry. Check out **WHIDBEY WILD BIRD** (Old Town Mall; 830 SE Pioneer Way; 360/279-2572), the **WIND & TIDE BOOKSHOP** (790 SE Pioneer Way; 360/675-1342), and **EILEEN'S CREATIVE KITCHENWARE** (860 SE Pioneer Way; 360/679-1902).

The locals swear by the Greek food at **ZORBAS** (841 SE Pioneer Way; 360/279-8322), the tasty multiethnic dishes at **ERAWAN THAI AND SUSHI** (885 SE Pioneer Way; 360/679-8268), and the salmon and chowder at **SEABOLTS SMOKEHOUSE** (31640 SR 20, Ste 1; 360/675-6485).

Three miles west of Oak Harbor is **JOSEPH WHIDBEY STATE PARK** (888/226-7688; day use only Mar–Sept) with a great beach. **DECEPTION PASS STATE PARK** (www.parks.wa.gov) is only 9 miles north. Even though it's the most-visited park in the state, with more than 4,000 acres, 19 miles of saltwater shoreline, and 35 miles of trails, solitude is only a hike away. Don't forget the trails on the north side of the much-photographed bridge that connects Whidbey to Fidalgo Island.

RESTAURANTS

Kasteel Franssen (Auld Holland Inn) / ★

33575 SR 20, OAK HARBOR; 360/675-0724

The trademark windmill, as well as the European fare and the local following, still prevail at Joe and Elisa Franssen's iconic Oak Harbor restaurant. Chef and co-owner Scott Fraser of Vancouver, British Columbia, was trained in French cooking and includes caribou and pheasant along with the favorite sautéed beef tenderloin served with brandy dijonnaise cream sauce. Adjacent to the restaurant, the Auld Holland Inn has 34 rooms with antiques, some with hot tubs; rates include continental breakfast. *$$; AE, MC, V; checks OK; lunch, dinner every day; full bar; reservations recommended; www.auld hollandinn.com; ½ mile north of town.*

LODGINGS

The Coachman Inn / ★

32959 SR 20, OAK HARBOR; 360/675-0727

The Coachman Inn at the north end of town makes a great base for a family weekend of exploring on Whidbey. Although it's on the main road and has a motel look to its various buildings, the inn has quiet rooms in the back with a mountain view, minikitchens, a pool, private entrances, and great rates. On the free-breakfast menu, there's sausage and gravy as well as cereals. *$–$$; AE, MC, V; checks OK; www.thecoachmaninn.com; at Midway Blvd.*

The Skagit Valley

As you travel north of Everett on Interstate 5, the expanse of the Skagit Valley is always a bit of a visual surprise as you cast off the ridge at Starbird Road and plummet quickly down to the valley floor (be aware that the Washington State Patrol love this spot for catching speeders). Come March, and lasting roughly into mid-June, the fields are transformed into sheets of wondrous color when daffodils, tulips, and irises take the stage. The countryside is ideal for bicyclists, but beware the throngs of visitors during the annual **TULIP FESTIVAL** (360/428-5959; www.tulipfestival.org; usually late Mar–early Apr). Contact the **MOUNT VERNON CHAMBER OF COMMERCE** (117 N 1st St, Ste 4; 360/428-8547; www.mount vernonchamber.com) for information.

Conway

RESTAURANTS

Conway Pub & Eatery / ★★

18611 MAIN ST, CONWAY; 360/445-4733

The menu here is classic Northwest tavern fare. The decor is rustic saloon. The atmosphere is one big, happy family. And the sign over the door reads, "Peace, love & joy to all who enter here." That sums up all you need to know about this legendary establishment, and a trip to the Skagit Valley is not complete without a stop here, even if it's just to buy a souvenir T-shirt. If you're planning on grazing your way through La Conner, at least try "the best oysters this side of the Mississippi." *$; AE, DIS, MC, V; checks OK; lunch, dinner every day; full bar; reservations recommended; exit 221 off I-5.*

La Conner

La Conner was founded in 1867 by John Conner, a trading-post operator who named the town after his wife, Louisa A. Conner. Over the years, the town became a haven for nonconformists, always with a smattering of artists and writers, including Mark Tobey, Morris Graves, Guy Anderson, and Tom Robbins. This free-spirited attitude contributes to the harmony that exists between the Swinomish Nation on the Fidalgo Island side of the channel and the Skagit-side community, creating a cultural richness exceptional for a town the size of La Conner. Merchants have crafted a unique American bazaar here. **HELLAMS VINEYARD** (109 N 1st St, Ste 101; 360/466-1758), La Conner's only specialty wine and beer shop, fits right into the bohemian atmosphere with tastings and dinner cruises through nearby Deception Pass.

Partake of tasty wood-fired pizzas and fine ales at **LA CONNER BREWING COMPANY** (117 S 1st St; 360/466-1415). Sample Spanish-Mediterranean fare at the **DULCE PLATE** (508 Morris St; 360/466-1630). Enjoy ambience and nostalgia at

SEEDS: A BISTRO & BAR (623 Morris St; 360/466-3280) in the historic Tillinghast Seed Company building. **KERSTIN'S** (505 S 1st St; 360/466-9111) does marvelous European-style dishes.

GACHES MANSION (703 S 2nd St; 360/466-4288; www.laconnerquilts.com), home of the not-to-be-missed Quilt Museum, is a wonderful example of American Victorian architecture, with period furnishings and a widow's walk that looks out on the entire Skagit Valley. The **MUSEUM OF NORTHWEST ART** (121 S 1st St; 360/466-4446; www.museumofnwart.org; Tues–Sun) is a regional gem. Each November, the community hosts the **ARTS ALIVE** festival (360/466-4778 or 888/642-9284; www.laconnerchamber.com).

RESTAURANTS

Calico Cupboard / ★★☆

720 S 1ST ST, LA CONNER (AND BRANCHES); 360/466-4451
The Calico Cupboard is a specialty café with a tradition of hearty breakfasts and soup-and-salad lunches. But don't stop there: the pastries earned the Calico "Best Bakery in Skagit County" awards for many years. Expect standing-room-only crowds on Tulip Festival weekends in March and April. Buy your goodies from the take-out counter and find a sunny bench by the water. Two other Calicos are in Anacortes (901 Commercial Ave; 360/293-7315) and Mount Vernon (121-B Freeway Dr; 360/336-3107). $; MC, V; checks OK; breakfast, lunch every day; beer and wine; no reservations; www.calico cupboardcafe.com; downtown La Conner, on the main drag.

Nell Thorn Restaurant & Pub / ★★☆

205 WASHINGTON ST, LA CONNER; 360/466-4261
Relative newcomer Nell Thorn's, with its focus on local and organic foods and artisan breads, has settled in as a local hit. The rustic-elegant charm in its location next to the La Conner Country Inn is a delight. Two levels offer dining options to fit your mood: cozy pub downstairs, quieter loft upstairs. Start with bread and a warm olive appetizer or the very popular endive salad with apple vinaigrette and goat cheese. Try the pork tenderloin, troll-caught salmon, or rack of lamb, then finish with the signature Skagit Mud Brownie. $$–$$$; AE, MC, V; lunch Thurs–Sun (seasonally), dinner Tues–Sat; full bar; reservations recommended; www.nellthorn.com; 1 block off 1st St.

Palmer's on the Waterfront / ★★★☆

512 S 1ST ST, LA CONNER; 360/466-3147
With sage green walls and high-gloss ivory woodwork, the spacious digs of La Conner's only waterfront fine-dining restaurant are enhanced by expansive views of the Swinomish Channel; there's also a deck. Dinner reflects a flair for French continental cuisine (à la the Northwest), with an emphasis on the art of sauté. Begin with the Wicked Escargot appetizer and the Crunchy Montrachet Salad while you deliberate on entrées ranging from the classic (roasted London broil) to the exotic (spicy calamari penne). Martinis are a specialty.

$$; AE, MC, V; local checks only; lunch, dinner every day; full bar; reservations recommended; www.nwcuisine.com; left off Morris St at 1st St.

LODGING

The Heron Inn & Watergrass Day Spa / ★★

117 MAPLE AVE, LA CONNER; 360/466-4626 OR 877/883-8899
Welcome to one of the prettiest hostelries in town, with 12 jewel-box rooms. Relax on one of three outside decks with more views of mountains, or slip into the garden hot tub. Splurge on Room 32, with a gas fireplace, a spacious sitting area, and a wonderful view of the Skagit Valley and Cascades. The day spa has two treatment rooms. The owners also have two other unique properties in La Conner: the Heron's Nest (www.heronlodging.com) and the Heron Waterside (www.heronwaterside.com). *$$; AE, MC, V; checks OK; www.theheron.com; east edge of town.*

Hotel Planter / ★★☆

715 S 1ST ST, LA CONNER; 360/466-4710 OR 800/488-5409
Operating as a hotel since 1907 and a designated National Register of Historic Places property, this Victorian-style brick establishment has played host to the most famous (and infamous) characters of La Conner's colorful past. Current owner Don Hoskins created a tasteful blend of past (original woodwork staircase and entrance) and present (private baths and armoire-hidden TVs in all 12 of the rooms). A gazebo-covered hot tub in the courtyard is for all to enjoy. *$$; AE, MC, V; checks OK; www.hotelplanter.com; south end of Main St.*

Skagit Bay Hideaway / ★★★☆

17430 GOLDENVIEW AVE, LA CONNER;
360/466-2262 OR 888/466-2262
This luxury waterfront hideaway features a Northwest shingle-style cottage divided into two identical suites. Watch the sun setting over Skagit Bay from your rooftop spa, or enjoy the view in your living room, complete with fireplace. In the morning, a full gourmet breakfast is served en suite. Bathroom showers are, literally, a blast, with double heads and multiple body sprays that will make you feel as if you just stepped into a waterfall. *$$$; AE, DIS, MC, V; checks OK; www.skagitbay.com; 1½ miles west of La Conner across Rainbow Bridge on Fidalgo Island.*

The Wild Iris / ★★

121 MAPLE AVE, LA CONNER; 360/466-1400 OR 800/477-1400
This 16-room inn with spacious suites feels a bit "country." Under new ownership, 9 rooms are deluxe suites featuring gas fireplaces, oversize jetted tubs, and panoramic Cascade and farmland views from decks or balconies. Most standard rooms, which we don't recommend, face the parking lot and seem a bit cramped. *$$$; AE, MC, V; checks OK; www.wildiris.com; east edge of town.* ♿

Mount Vernon

Mount Vernon is the "big city" of surrounding Skagit and Island counties. Like many of the small cities sprinkled throughout the Puget Sound basin, it is experiencing growth and a rise in its real estate prices as Seattle's urban sprawl inches closer and closer. Still, Mount Vernon maintains its small-town flavor.

Browse **SCOTT'S BOOKSTORE** (121 Freeway Dr; 360/336-6181) in the historic Granary Building. Pick up some goodies from the **SKAGIT VALLEY FOOD CO-OP** (202 S 1st St; 360/336-9777). Or drop into the **SKAGIT RIVER BREWING COMPANY** (404 S 3rd St; 360/336-2884) for pub grub. Afterward, check out the burgeoning crop of retail merchants along Main Street. **IL GRANAIO** (100 E Montgomery St, Ste 110; 360/419-0674), Mount Vernon's answer to authentic Italian cuisine, is a great place to wind down.

RESTAURANTS

The Porterhouse / ★

416 W GATES, MOUNT VERNON; 360/336-9989

After years of working the demanding Seattle restaurant scene, Silas and Elise Reynolds stumbled on an opportunity to help open the Rockfish Café in Anacortes. They headed north and never looked back. Now they've created the warm environment of a British Isle public house through a sophisticated pub menu and their signature rotating beer selection. Make this your stop for a casual meal, a game of darts, a pint of porter, and a dose of genuine small-town hospitality. *$–$$; MC, V; no checks; lunch, dinner Mon–Sat; beer and wine; porterhousepub@gmail.com; just off corner of Main.*

LODGINGS

White Swan Guest House / ★★

15872 MOORE RD, MOUNT VERNON; 360/445-6805

Change comes even to the most venerable of establishments. In the case of Peter Goldfarb's White Swan Guest House, that change occurred in 2006 after nearly 19 years of operating three rooms in his main "Grannie's farmhouse" plus a separate cottage. The White Swan Guest House is now just the charming two-story cottage, featuring an open first floor with kitchen and an upstairs queen-bedded room. Enjoy a sunny afternoon on the deck in a comfortable Adirondack chair, and bring binoculars and bikes. This is country escapism at its finest. On Fir Island 6 miles southeast of La Conner. *$$; MC, V; checks OK; www.thewhiteswan.com; call for directions.*

The San Juan Islands

The San Juan Islands, an archipelago of 743 islands at low tide and 428 at high tide, are breathtakingly beautiful. The islands are a hiker's, kayaker's, wildlife lover's, and bird watcher's year-round playground: more than 275 species of birds have been sighted, and 50 pairs of eagles nest here.

Only four islands are accessible by Washington State ferry (see Access and Information below): Lopez, Orcas, San Juan, and Shaw. To best serve yourself, the place, and the community, savor the San Juans off-season. And don't worry about the weather. Because the islands get half the rainfall of Seattle, the typical Northwest gloom does not take hold. Rarely is there an entire day without sun. Fall lasts nicely throughout October, and spring can begin in February. Even the winter months are lovely. The low winter light spreads silver across sea and sky, and the quiet has deep appeal.

With ferry-fare increases and seasonal surcharges, it's pricey in the summer, plus the ferry lines are long and lodgings booked full. There's one exception, however: There's a great summer day trip to be had by walking on the ferry to Friday Harbor, getting a $15 day pass for the seasonal **SAN JUAN TRANSIT** (www.sanjuantransit.com), and spending the day exploring San Juan island stop by stop. You can get to Lime Kiln State Park, Pelindaba Lavender Farm, the alpaca farm, English Camp, and Roche Harbor. Arrive early enough in the day to make the most of the hourly pickups at each place.

EMILY'S GUIDE & MAPS (800/448-7782; www.emilysguides.com) are a great resource. The **SAN JUAN ISLANDS VISITORS BUREAU** (www.visitsanjuans.com) Web site is excellent. For news, there's another Web site (www.sanjuanislander.com) to check out.

ACCESS AND INFORMATION

The San Juan Islands are served year-round by the **WASHINGTON STATE FERRIES** (206/464-6400 or 800/843-3779; www.wsdot.wa.gov/ferries/) from Anacortes (see section below). In the summer, getting your car on a ferry out of Anacortes can mean a three-hour-plus wait. Cars pay only westbound, so if you plan to visit more than one island, arrange to go to the farthest first (San Juan) and explore your way east.

Summer options for those who don't want to drive Interstate 5 to Anacortes include the high-speed **VICTORIA CLIPPER** (2701 Alaskan Wy, Seattle; 206/448-5000; www.victoriaclipper.com), which travels daily in season from downtown Seattle to Friday Harbor. **KENMORE AIR** (425/486-1257 or 866/435-9524; www.kenmoreair.com) has floatplane flights to the islands from Lake Union north of downtown Seattle and from north Lake Washington in Kenmore. **SAN JUAN AIRLINES** (800/874-4434; www.sanjuanairlines.com) offers flights from Boeing Field, Bellingham, and Anacortes.

The **AIRPORTER SHUTTLE** (866/235-5247; www.airporter.com) gets

---

SAN JUAN ISLANDS THREE-DAY TOUR

DAY ONE: Get an early morning ferry from **ANACORTES** to **FRIDAY HAR-BOR** and head out to **ROCHE HARBOR VILLAGE** (10 miles from town) to have lunch at the **LIME KILN CAFÉ** or out on the deck at the **MADRONA GRILL**. Stroll the **ARTISTS VILLAGE** and the **WESTCOTT BAY RESERVE SCULPTURE PARK** before taking the five-minute drive along West Valley Road to the **SAN JUAN ISLAND NATIONAL HISTORIC PARK'S ENGLISH CAMP**. Then take **MITCHELL BAY ROAD** to the scenic **WESTSIDE ROAD** where during the summer months the orca whales can often be seen feeding. Stop at **LIME KILN POINT STATE PARK** for a whale update at the lighthouse. On your way south, take a left on **WOLD ROAD** and drive a quarter mile to **PELINDABA LAVENDER FARM**, particularly lovely in the summer months. (The farm's products are also for sale at their shop in downtown Friday Harbor, so do a quick drive-by for a look at lavender and opt time-wise for whales if they're in local waters.) Continue south down **BAILER HILL ROAD** to **FALSE BAY ROAD**, turn right, and find your way to **CATTLE POINT ROAD**. Turn right again and go about a mile to **OLD FARM ROAD**. Turn right and then go left on **STARLIGHT WAY** to **OLYMPIC LIGHTS** B and B. Check in, relax, then take the short way (10-minute drive) back to **FRIDAY HARBOR** for pasta at **VINNY'S** (165 West St; 360/378-1934) before turning in for the night.

---

you from Sea-Tac Airport to the ferry terminal in Anacortes. The **ISLAND AIRPORTER** (360/378-7438; www.islandairporter.com) offers direct service between Friday Harbor and Sea-Tac Airport.

Anacortes

Anacortes, the gateway to the San Juans, is itself on an island: Fidalgo. Though most travelers rush through town on their way to the ferry, there are lots of reasons to stick around: One is great parks, including the 2,800-acre **ANACORTES COMMUNITY FOREST LANDS** (www.friendsoftheacfl.org); **WASHINGTON PARK** (360/293-1927 for campsite availability), less than a mile west of the ferry terminal, is another treasure. For Anacortes culture, **ART WALKS** (www.anacortesart.com) are the first Friday of each month. Historic **MURALS** deck the walls throughout town. **FESTIVALS** range from quilts to cars to jazz; check out the Web site (www.anacortes.org) for event information.

Seafaring folks should poke around **MARINE SUPPLY AND HARDWARE** (202 Commercial Ave; 360/293-3014); established in 1913, it's packed with marine

DAY TWO: Wake up to breakfast at the inn and then a walk to neighboring **AMERICAN CAMP**. Stop at the visitor's center and take time to explore some of the trails along the shore or up on the hillside before heading to **FRIDAY HARBOR** and an afternoon ferry to **ORCAS ISLAND**. (No fare required for eastbound ferries.) Park your car in line early and save time for lunch at the **BACK DOOR KITCHEN** (400-b A St; 360/378-9540) and a shopping stroll through town before the ferry leaves.

DAY THREE: On Orcas Island, check in to the **OUTLOOK INN** in Eastsound for the night. Stroll the shops and galleries in town and have dinner at **CHRISTINA'S**. If there's time, check out the movie at the **SEA VIEW THEATRE** (A St; 360/376-5724). After breakfast with the locals at **VERN'S** (246 Main St; 360/376-2231), overlooking the water, take a drive up **MOUNT CONSTITUTION** in **MORAN STATE PARK** for the view and, if there's time, a short hike. (Get trail info at park headquarters.) Follow the morning's excursion with lunch at the **CAFÉ OLGA**, in Olga, where there's a fine art gallery as well as fine food. Get a late afternoon ferry to **LOPEZ ISLAND** (no fare required) and check in to the **MACKAYE HARBOR INN**. Go for a bike or kayak ride (compliments of the inn) and then out for dinner at the **BAY CAFÉ**. Enjoy a relaxed morning at the inn, then visit Lopez Village on your way to the ferry to **ANACORTES**. (Still no fare required eastbound.) To recover from your three days of island pleasure, check in at the **MAJESTIC INN & SPA** in Anacortes for a spa session and a good night's sleep before re-entering life-at-large.

items as well as reclining ceramic frogs in polka-dot bikinis. For the other kind of yarn, **ANA CROSS STITCH** (713 Commercial Ave; 360/299-9010) is a favorite. They offer knitting cruises out of La Conner, too. History buffs can visit the **ANACORTES MUSEUM** (1305 8th St; 360/293-1915; www.anacorteshistorymuseum. org). If kayaking is your passion, **ISLAND OUTFITTERS** (2403 Commercial Ave; 360/299-2300 or 866/445-7506; www.seakayakshop.com) offers tours out of **CAP SANTE MARINA** (360/293-0694; www.portofanacortes.com). Take a kayak lesson or rent one for a San Juan weekend; reservations are necessary.

Casual eateries abound. A local favorite spot for breakfast, burgers, and fish-and-chips is **SAN JUAN LANES STORK'S RESTAURANT** (2821 Commercial Ave; 360/293-7500), at the local bowling alley. **GERE-A-DELI** (502 Commercial Ave; 360/293-7383) is a friendly hangout with good homemade food. **CALICO CUPBOARD** (901 Commercial Ave; 360/293-7315) is an offshoot of the popular café-bakery in La Conner. You'll find artisan breads and more at **LA VIE EN ROSE FRENCH BAKERY AND PASTRY SHOP** (418 Commercial Ave; 360/299-9546; www.laviebakery.com) and decadent donuts at the **DONUT HOUSE** (2719 Commercial Ave; 360/293-4053), open all day every day for any 3am cravings. The bakery at **THE STORE** (919 37th St; 360/293-2851) specializes in huge muffins; there's also a deli.

For local brews, try the **ROCKFISH GRILL AND ANACORTES BREWERY** (320 Commercial Ave; 360/588-1720; www.anacortesrockfish.com). Nearly next door, the **STAR BAR CAFÉ** (416½ Commercial Ave; 360/299-2120) is the healthy-fare hangout. The **GREEK ISLANDS** (2001 Commercial Ave; 360/293-6911), **ESTE-BAN'S MEXICAN RESTAURANT** (1506 Commercial Ave; 360/299-1060), **MOLTO BENE** (710 Commercial Ave; 360/293-9014 or 360/293-2457), and **TOYKO JAPANESE RESTAURANT** (818 Commercial Ave; 360/293-9898) bring international fare to life.

If you're aiming for an early ferry, a good and reasonable overnight choice is the **SHIP HARBOR INN** (5316 Ferry Terminal Rd; 360/293-5177 or 800/852-8568; www.shipharborinn.com), right next to the terminal. It has a comfortable mix of refurbished and spotless motel-style rooms and cabins-with-a-view. Consider staying in Anacortes and day-tripping to the San Juans and Whidbey Island.

RESTAURANTS

Flounder Bay Café / ★

2201 SKYLINE WAY, ANACORTES; 360/293-3680
This waterside café in Skyline Marina on the southwest shore of town has boldly colored sails hanging from the ceiling and fresh, seasonal seafood on the plate. The Sunset Suppers are favorites with the locals. There's live jazz on Sunday evenings and warm-season dinner cruises. *$$; AE, DIS, MC, V; local checks only; lunch Mon–Sat, dinner every day; full bar; reservations recommended; www.flounderbaycafe.com; at Skyline Marina, west of town.*

Il Posto / ★★★

2120 COMMERCIAL AVE, ANACORTES; 360/293-7600
Il Posto is the new Italian restaurant in town, and thanks to chef Marcello Giuffrida, it's the real thing. But don't just stop for a quick bite on the way to the ferry. A long evening's dalliance with the food and wine—starting out with the Carpaccio di Melanzine (grilled eggplant with goat cheese, honey mustard, carmelized onions, pine nuts, and balsamic glaze) and ending with any dessert on the menu—is worth staying overnight for. *$$–$$$; AE, DIS, MC, V; local checks only; dinner Wed–Mon; full bar; reservations recommended; at 21st St on way into town.*

LODGINGS

Heron House Guest Suites / ★★★

11110 MARINE DR, ANACORTES; 360/293-4477 OR 866/212-6510
Tucked away on the west side of Anacortes, Heron House is just a skipping stone away from Deception Pass and Mount Erie. The uncommonly plush Common Room has a huge stone fireplace to go with the huge view. Big breakfasts, too. Of the four rooms, the Nautical and the Pacific Rim have spa tubs and fireplaces. All have king beds and private baths. *$$–$$$; MC, V;*

local checks only; www.heronhouseguestsuites.com; past ferry terminal, turn left on Anaco Dr, which becomes Marine Dr.

Majestic Inn & Spa / ★★★

419 COMMERCIAL AVE, ANACORTES; 360/299-1400
A few years ago, a fire ravaged the newly renovated beauty of this grand, historic 1889 hotel, but it keeps on rising from the ashes. The hotel architecture is meticulously restored turn-of-the-century. The rooms, with their flat-screen TVs, crisp contemporary furniture, and polished bathrooms, make for a great relaxation zone after a trip to the spa. Try the Cocoon, a hydrothermal body capsule body treatment, followed, perhaps, by Amaretto Biscotti Torte with Caramel Sauce from the restaurant. *$$$; AE, DIS, MC, V; checks OK; www.majesticinnandspa.com; downtown in old town Anacortes.*

Lopez Island

Lopez Island, the flat and friendly isle famous for drivers who wave, is also bike-friendly. Its 30-mile circuit is fairly level and suitable for the whole family. The Tour de Lopez, the last weekend in April, is typically Lopezian: low-key and noncompetitive. The only time this island gets competitive is on the Fourth of July, when they pride themselves on one of the largest private fireworks shows in the state.

You can rent a bike from **LOPEZ BICYCLE WORKS** (2847 Fisherman Bay Rd; 360/468-2847; www.lopezbicycleworks.com); you can also rent kayaks there (www.lopezkayaks.com) mid-April to October. Rent kayaks and take guided tours through **CASCADIA KAYAK TOURS** (360/468-3008; www.cascadiakayaktours.com). Agate Beach, Shark Reef Park, and Otis Perkins Park give great beach access; you can camp at 80-acre **ODLIN COUNTY PARK** (on right, about 1 mile south of ferry dock; 360/468-2496) or 130-acre **SPENCER SPIT STATE PARK** (on left, about 5 miles south of ferry dock; 888/226-7688; www.parks.wa.gov).

Lopez Village, 4 miles south of the ferry dock on the west shore near Fisherman Bay, has **CHIMERA** (Lopez Village; 360/468-3265; www.chimeragallery.com), with island glass, pottery, and paintings. **ISLANDS MARINE CENTER** (Fisherman Bay Rd; 360/468-3377; www.islandsmarinecenter.com) is a full-service marina with 100 slips. This is also where you buy fishing and crabbing licenses.

A favorite food stop is **HOLLY B'S BAKERY** (Lopez Village; 360/468-2133; Apr–Nov), famous for her cinnamon rolls. The **LOVE DOG CAFÉ** (Lopez Village; 360/468-2150) features Italian food, pizza, and a view. **VITA'S WILDLY DELICIOUS** (Lopez Village; 360/468-4268) is precisely that: gourmet to go—wine, too. **BUCKY'S** (Lopez Village; 360/468-2595) serves steaks as well as seafood; **CAFFE LA BOHEME** (Lopez Village; 360/468-2294) has Ruth Reichl's favorite coffee, Graffeo; and **ISABEL'S ESPRESSO** (Lopez Village; 360/468-4114), on the grassy knoll, serves organic coffee. The **GALLEY RESTAURANT AND LOUNGE** (Fisherman Bay Rd; 360/468-2713) used to be the local beer joint; with its inventive menu and reasonable prices, it's the best family-friendly, year-round restaurant on Lopez.

LOPEZ ISLANDER RESORT (Fisherman Bay Rd; 360/468-2233 or 800/736-3434; www.lopezislander.com), next door to the marina, is great for families.

RESTAURANTS

The Bay Café / ★★★

9 OLD POST RD, LOPEZ VILLAGE; 360/468-3700
After all these years, the Bay Café still has its great reputation as well as its great view. Its spacious, modern digs are close to the beach, but it still retains its eclectic flair. The Bay Café is a come-as-you-are kind of place. The food, however, is always well dressed. The oft-changing menu might include steamed mussels, Oregon bay-shrimp cakes, or grilled tofu with chickpea-potato cakes. *$$; AE, DIS, MC, V; checks OK; dinner every day (Thurs–Sun in winter); full bar; reservations recommended; www.bay-cafe.com; junction of Lopez Rd S and Lopez Rd N in village.*

LODGINGS

Edenwild Inn / ★

132 LOPEZ RD, LOPEZ ISLAND; 360/468-3238 OR 800/606-0662
This modern Victorian-style manse, complete with garden and arbor, is nestled right in Lopez Village, which means easy access to the bookstore next door and the beach down the road. There are eight rooms, all with views of gardens or bays or both. Some rooms have fireplaces, some have king-sized Victorian sleigh beds, all have private baths. Relaxing lounging areas are inside and out. *$$–$$$; AE, MC, V; checks OK; www.edenwildinn.com; in Lopez Village.* &

Inn at Swifts Bay / ★★

856 PORT STANLEY RD, LOPEZ ISLAND;
360/468-3636 OR 800/903-9536
A Tudor retreat on laid-back Lopez? Yup, complete with wing chairs and tons of books and movies. The flora and fauna and saltwater vistas make going outside nice, too. There's a secluded hot tub down a stone path at the edge of the forest. Breakfast might be hazelnut waffles with fresh berries and crème fraîche, crab cakes, or orange-cinnamon bread-pudding French toast with cinnamon-custard sauce. Innkeepers will arrange a ride from the ferry. Five beautiful rooms, including three suites, have queen-sized beds with down comforters. *$$–$$$; MC, V; checks OK; www.swiftsbay.com; 2 miles south of ferry landing.*

Lopez Farm Cottages and Tent Camping / ★

555 FISHERMAN BAY RD, LOPEZ ISLAND; 360/468-3555
Only on Lopez Island could you find upscale camping with no RVs or electronic music allowed. No kids under 14 either, unless you reserve all 10 campsites. And no dogs. What you do get is a lovely, private farmland setting, a

bathhouse, Adirondack chairs, a table, a hammock, and a flat spot for your tent. There's something about this place that feels just right. The cottages are cheerful "Northwest Scandinavian." There's a Jacuzzi for cottage guests, who also get breakfast delivered in a basket. $–$$; MC, V; checks OK; www.lopez farmcottages.com; about 3 miles from ferry, 1 mile from village. &

MacKaye Harbor Inn / ★★

949 MACKAYE HARBOR RD, LOPEZ ISLAND; 360/468-2253 OR 888/314-6140 This tall white Victorian, built in 1927, was the first house on Lopez to boast electricity, which means its tradition of hospitality is well honed. The wide veranda looking out over beach grasses and bay is nice. The Harbor Suite is our choice, with fireplace, private bath, and enclosed sitting area facing the beach. Rent a kayak or borrow a mountain bike, head off, and return to fresh cookies. If you bike from the ferry, be warned: The closest restaurant is 6 miles back in town (although the Islandale Store is but a mile away). Four acres of gardens add to the charm. $$–$$$; MC, V; checks OK; www.mackaye harborinn.com; 12 miles south of ferry landing.

Orcas Island

Orcas was named after the Spanish explorer Revilla Gigedo de Orcasitas. You can't miss 2,407-foot Mount Constitution, the centerpiece of **MORAN STATE PARK** (800/233-0321; www.parks.wa.gov/alpha.asp). It was Washington's first state park. From the old stone tower at the summit, which was built by the Civilian Conservation Corps in 1936, you can see from Vancouver to Mount Rainier and everything between. The park is 13 miles northeast of the ferry landing. Get a campsite through a **CENTRAL RESERVATION SERVICE** (888/226-7688; www.parks.wa.gov).

The man for whom the park is named was shipbuilding tycoon Robert Moran. His old mansion is now the focal point of **ROSARIO RESORT & SPA** (see review), just west of the park. Even if you don't stay at the resort, the mansion, decked out in period memorabilia, is worth a stop. Its enormous pipe organ is still used for performances.

There are bikes for rent from **DOLPHIN BAY BICYCLES** (at ferry landing; 360/376-4157; www.rockisland.com/~dolphin) or **WILD LIFE CYCLES** (in Eastsound; 360/376-4708). A new service is the seasonal **ORCAS SHUTTLE** (360/376-7433; www.orcasislandshuttle.com), offering regular bus service around the island as well as taxi and car rental. The $10-per-day bus pass is a great deal. Walk-ons stay at the **ORCAS HOTEL** (at ferry landing; 360/376-4300 or 888/672-2792) and do day trips.

The village of Eastsound is on the water's edge on the bridge of land between the two horseshoe halves of Orcas. It's a good 8 miles from the ferry, so unlike Friday Harbor on San Juan Island, which gets a lot of ferry foot traffic, Eastsound is quieter. On Saturdays, the **ORCAS FARMERS MARKET** (North Beach Rd, Eastsound; www.orcasislandfarmersmarket.org; May–Sept) has everything from tarot readings to organic beef. Walkable Eastsound's shops and galleries are distinctive. **TRES FABU** (238 North Beach Rd, Eastsound; 360/376-7673) has chic, funky clothes. Darvill's Book Store (296 Main St, Eastsound; 360/376-2135) also has lattes-with-a-view; next door, **DARVILL'S RARE PRINT SHOP** (360/376-2351; www.darvillsrareprints.com) has antique prints. The **ORCAS CENTER** (downtown Eastsound; 360/376-2281; www.orcascenter.org) has entertainment.

ROSES BAKERY & RESTAURANT (382 Prune Alley, Eastsound; 360/376-5805) has gourmet groceries. Locals eat at **CHIMAYO'S** (Our House Mall, North Beach Rd, Eastsound; 360/376-6394) for affordable flavors of New Mexico. They go to **ORCAS HOME GROWN** (8B North Beach Rd, Eastsound; 360/376-2009) for fair-trade coffee and veggie juices, **PORTOFINO'S** (upstairs on A St, Eastsound; 360/376-2085) for pizza, and **MAIN STREET BAKERY** (corner of Main and North Beach Rd, Eastsound; 360/376-5345) for soups, sandwiches, and pastries.

In town, the historic **OUTLOOK INN** (171 Main St, Eastsound; 360/376-2200 or 888/688-5665) has everything from European-style rooms with shared baths to luxury suites with Jacuzzis; the **NEW LEAF CAFÉ** is onsite. For family gatherings, retreats, and reunions, a few minute's walk from Eastsound is **HEARTWOOD HOUSE** (360/317-8220; www.heartwoodhouse.com). For family-friendly cabins on the beach, check out **BEACH HAVEN RESORT** (North Beach; 360/376-2288; www.beach-haven.com) and **WEST BEACH RESORT** (West Beach; 360/376-2240; www.westbeachresort.com).

RESTAURANTS

Bilbo's Festivo / ★★

310 A ST, EASTSOUND; 360/376-4728
Bilbo's, under the tender, loving cooking care of Cy Fraser for 30 years, was recently sold to loyal, long-time employees who are intent on preserving the menu and the ambience. The cozy adobe feeling, with its Mexican tiles, fireplace, and Navajo and Chimayo weavings, includes a generous garden courtyard with highly varnished cedar tables and wraparound benches. The vegetables are broiled to intensify the flavor of the superb sauces. Summer lunch is served grilled-to-order outdoors. *$$; MC, V; local checks only; lunch every day June–Sept (Sat–Sun Apr–May), dinner every day; full bar; reservations recommended; at North Beach Rd.*

Café Olga / ★

11 PT LAWRENCE RD, OLGA; 360/376-5098
It's a bit of a drive to Olga Junction but worth the experience, which includes the Orcas Island Artworks, a gallery that shares this renovated barn with the café. It's all local work, and artists take turns behind the counter. The popular café features home-style cooking, including fish of the day and local oysters, sandwiches, and huge salads. For dessert, try the terrific blackberry pie or the tiramisu. *$; MC, V; local checks only; lunch, dinner every day (Wed–Mon off-season; closed Jan–early Feb); beer and wine; no reservations; at Olga Junction.*

Christina's / ★★★⯪

310 MAIN ST, EASTSOUND; 360/376-4904
Perched over Eastsound above a 1930s gas station overlooking the water, Christina's is a blend of country-style locale and urban sophistication. Christina Orchid's classic continental food has kept patrons returning for more than 26 years. Local oysters are routinely on the menu. King salmon might come with scallops and Jack Daniels cream sauce; filet of beef could arrive with horseradish potato gratin. Christina's is a destination restaurant well worth the drive, the ferry, and the stairs. Try her new cookbook, a huge hit. *$$$; AE, DC, MC, V; checks OK; dinner every day (Thur–Mon in winter); full bar; reservations recommended; www.christinas.net; at North Beach Rd.*

Inn at Ship Bay / ★★★

326 OLGA RD, EASTSOUND; 360/376-5886 OR 877/276-7296
Originally homesteaded in the 1860s, this orchard farmhouse, now home to the inn's dining room, was a cornerstone of local agriculture. The owners, Geddes and MaryAnna Martin, still have apple, pear, and plum orchards. Geddes, the chef, makes ice cream and serves it atop delicious flourless chocolate cake. His other specialties include handcrafted foods, such as ricotta ravioli and seafood. Eleven deluxe rooms have comfortable pillow-top beds and bay views. *$$$; AE, DC, DIS, MC, V; checks OK; dinner every day (Tues–Sun Mar–Apr, Oct–Nov; closed Dec–Jan); full bar; reservations recommended; www.innatshipbay.com; east of Eastsound.* &

LODGINGS

Cascade Harbor Inn / ★★

1800 ROSARIO RD, EASTSOUND; 360/376-6350 OR 800/201-2120
The inn shares its vistas of pristine Cascade Bay and beach access with sprawling Rosario Resort next door. Forty-five modern units—some studios with Murphy beds, some two-queen rooms, some in between—have decks and water views, and many configure into multi-unit suites with full kitchens. Continental breakfast included in summer. *$$–$$$; AE, DIS, MC, V; checks OK; www.cascadeharborinn.com; just east of Rosario Resort.*

Deer Harbor Inn and Restaurant / ★★

33 INN LANE, DEER HARBOR; 360/376-4110 OR 877/377-4110
Over the years, owners Pam and Craig Carpenter have shored up this rustic old lodge, built in 1915 in an apple orchard overlooking Deer Harbor on the lovely southwest side of the island. Lodge rooms are small, with peeled-log furniture. The newer cabins are cozy, with log furniture, knotty pine walls, woodstoves or fireplaces, and private hot tubs. The Pond Cottage is our favorite, with two bedrooms, two bathrooms, and a kitchen. Dinners are served nightly in the lodge's rustic dining room. *$$–$$$; AE, MC, V; checks OK; www.deerharborinn.com; from ferry landing, follow signs past West Sound.* &

Doe Bay Resort & Retreat / ★★

DOE BAY, NEAR OLGA; 360/376-4278

Doe Bay, long an island destination of hippies and other eccentrics, is making yet another comeback. The resort has 33 acres of waterfront, and it's back in stride with retreat programs and fine meals, as well as an eclectic array of reasonable accommodations ranging from tent spaces to wood-stove cabins to cozy cottages. (A yurt, anyone?) Chef Marissa Canters has a vegetarian vision that includes shiitake mushroom pâté and hazelnut toast points, as well as chocolate pot pie. *$–$$; MC, V; checks OK; www.doebay.com; about 40 minutes from ferry, 3 miles past Olga.*

The Inn on Orcas Island / ★★★

114 CHANNEL RD, DEER HARBOR; 360/376-5227 OR 888/886-1661

Part Nantucket cottage, part English manor house, this stunning inn at the edge of Deer Harbor is a labor of love for owners Jeremy Trumble and John Gibbs. The two former Southern California art-gallery owners showcase collections of English paintings, needlepoint, and china. The art alone is worth a visit; the six manor rooms, all with water views, are worth at least six visits, and the 6 acres are worth year-round exploration. There's also a carriage house and a waterside cottage. *$$$–$$$$; AE, MC, V; checks OK; www.the innonorcasisland.com; from ferry landing, follow signs past West Sound.* ₲

Otters Pond B&B / ★★

100 TOMIHI DR, EASTSOUND; 888/893-9680

Otter's Pond B&B, close to Moran State Park, is quiet-on-quiet. There's only one TV on the premises, and shoes are removed inside. Owners Carl and Susan Silvernail are purposeful about providing a serene retreat in their five-room B and B. Each room has its own bathroom, and the hot-tub bathhouse is partially enclosed with Japanese-style screens. All is meditative across the pond. A five-course gourmet breakfast followed by bird-watching could easily be your day's activity. *$$$; DIS, MC, V; no checks; www.otterspond.com; off Olga Rd.*

Rosario Resort & Spa / ★★★

1400 ROSARIO RD, ROSARIO; 360/376-2222 OR 800/562-8820

This waterfront estate is listed in the National Register of Historic Places. Teak floors, mahogany paneling, original furnishings, and Tiffany accents give a feel for the home's illustrious past. Its expansive grounds look over the water, and there's nostalgia in this long unchanged vista. Many of the 116 rooms, each with a cheery upscale country style, are up a steep hill (use the nonstop van service). Most offer bay views. The mansion is home to a museum, music room, and restaurant. Don't miss the organ recital. There are also spa services, a pool, kayaks, and a dive shop. *$$$; AE, DC, DIS, MC, V; checks OK; www.rosario.rockresorts.com; from Eastsound, 3 miles east on Olga Rd.* ₲

Spring Bay Inn / ★★★

464 SPRING BAY TRAIL, OLGA; 360/376-5531

Sandy Playa and Carl Burger are youthful retired state park rangers, and their love of natural places graces this inn with a taste of the real Northwest. On 57 wooded seafront acres adjacent to Obstruction Pass State Park, Spring Bay Inn offers a big dose of the great outdoors. Wildlife abounds, and so do creature comforts. Of the four rooms, all with private baths and fireplaces, the light-filled Treetop room is one of the most uplifting spaces we've seen. Coffee, muffins, and fruit are delivered to each door in the morning—sustenance for a free kayak tour guided by your hosts. Soak under the stars in the bay-side hot tub. *$$$; DIS, MC, V; checks OK; www.springbayinn.com; Obstruction Pass Rd to Trailhead Rd, left onto Spring Bay Trail.*

Turtleback Farm Inn / ★★★

1981 CROW VALLEY RD, EASTSOUND; 360/376-4914 OR 800/376-4914

At Turtleback Farm, amid trees and ponds, you get the feeling that not much has changed here in a long, long time. With the nearby Turtleback Mountain up for sale and the locals scrambling to save it, this bucolic setting might not last forever. But the inn continues to be one of the best B and Bs around. Bill and Susan Fletcher love Crow Valley, and it shows. There are seven rooms, with views, in the Farmhouse. The four expansive suites with vistas in the new Orchard House feature fir flooring, trim, and doors; Vermont casting stoves; and spacious baths with large claw-foot tubs and showers. *$$$–$$$$; AE, DIS, MC, V; checks OK; www.turtlebackinn.com; 6 miles from ferry.* &

San Juan Island

Arriving on San Juan Island means floating into Friday Harbor, which is the good news and the bad news. It's good because you have immediate access to food and lodgings. It's bad because you have to find your way past real estate offices and trinket traders to find the island's heart.

Historically, the island was summer home to Native Americans who fished and gathered food in the sheltering islands. Europeans then brought sheep farming, followed by orchards, agriculture, and commercial fishing.

San Juan Island also had a contested history that saw joint occupation by both British and American troops. The acrimony started in 1859 when an American farmer shot a British farmer's pig. The dispute was eventually settled in 1872 by Kaiser Wilhelm. The Pig War that never actually happened became history and eventually resulted in **SAN JUAN ISLAND NATIONAL HISTORIC PARK** (www.nps. gov/sajh), covering more than 1,700 acres at two distinct sites, **AMERICAN CAMP** at the southern end of the island and **ENGLISH CAMP** to the north.

From May through September the endangered orca whales cruise waters on the island's west side. Watching them from shore is worth the wait. They pass near **LIME KILN POINT STATE PARK** (www.parks.wa.gov) where there are trails, picnic spots, and a lighthouse usually staffed with a whale researcher in the summer. The

WHALE MUSEUM in Friday Harbor (62 1st St; 360/378-4710 or 800/946-7227; www.whalemuseum.org) is wonderful.

A short walk uptown is the **SAN JUAN ISLAND HISTORICAL MUSEUM** (405 Price St, Friday Harbor; 360-378-3949; www.sjmuseum.org). For an end-of-the-day respite, sip wine at **SAN JUAN VINEYARDS** (3136 Roche Harbor Rd; 360-378-9463; www.sanjuanvineyards.com). **WESTCOTT BAY SCULPTURE PARK** (Roche Harbor; 360/370-5050; www.wbay.org) has acres of art on the island's north end. If you visit in the summer, **ISLAND STAGE LEFT** (www.islandstageleft. org) has excellent outdoor Shakespeare productions at Roche Harbor, and it's free (donations appreciated).

The **COUNTY FAIR** (www.sanjuancountyfair.org) during the third weekend in August is one of the most eclectic fairs in the state. The **FARMERS MARKET** sets up on Saturdays May to mid-October at the courthouse parking lot in Friday Harbor. **PELINDABA LAVENDER FARM** (www.pelindaba.com) has a festival in July and an eating and gathering place in town. For a few hours of scenic quiet, ride the interisland ferry circuit (free to walk-ons).

A side benefit to an off-season visit is the blues music scene. At the local Italian restaurant **BELLA LUNA** (175 1st St, Friday Harbor; 360/378-4118), blues musicians show up on Wednesday. Some are old pros, and the place rocks. In true island style, however, it's early to bed: the music ends at 9pm. There's a similar gathering of jazz musicians on Sunday. In the summer, there's live music at the Port of Friday Harbor, on the grounds of the historical museum, and at Roche Harbor, where there's an ongoing art fair.

ISLANDS STUDIOS (270 Spring St, Friday Harbor; 360/378-6550; www. islandstudios.com; year-round) features local artists. **WATERWORKS GALLERY** (Argyle and Spring sts, Friday Harbor; 360/378-3060; www.waterworksgallery. com) represents some of the finest artists in the San Juan Islands. **DOLPHIN ARTS** (165 1st St, Friday Harbor; 360/378-3531) has original designs and locally made jewelry. **DAN LEVIN** (50 1st St, Friday Harbor; 800/234-5078) is renowned for his fine gold and silver craftsmanship. There are four bookstores in town, including **SERENDIPITY** (223 A St, Friday Harbor; 360/378-2665), in an old historic house.

The best diving in the archipelago is here (some claim it's the best cold-water diving in the world); **ISLAND DIVE & WATER SPORTS** (in Friday Harbor; 360/378-2772 or 800/303-8386; www.divesanjuan.com) has rentals, charters, and instruction. You can rent bicycles year-round at **ISLAND BICYCLES** (380 Argyle St, Friday Harbor; 360/378-4941; www.islandbicycles.com) and **KAYAKS** from late spring through early fall (www.crystalseas.com, www.bonaccord.com, www.leisurekayak.com). There's car rentals at **M&W** (725 Spring St, Friday Harbor; 800/323-6037; www.sanjuanauto.com), and in the summer great bus service and tours with **SAN JUAN TRANSIT** (at Cannery Landing at ferry terminal, Friday Harbor; 360/378-8887 or 800/887-8387; www.sanjuantransit.com).

There's no shortage of food in Friday Harbor. Locals stand by the authentic Thai dishes at the **GOLDEN TRIANGLE** (140 1st St; 360/378-3560); breakfast at the **BLUE DOLPHIN** (185 1st St; 360/378-6116); dinner or lunch—usually with onion rings—on the deck at **DOWNRIGGERS** (10 Front St; 360/378-2700); good local brews at the **FRONT STREET ALEHOUSE** (1 Front St; 360/378-2337); and fish-and-chips at the **HUNGRY CLAM** (205 A St; 360/378-3474). **HERB'S** (80 1st St; 360/378-7076) is the local tavern for good basic burgers, pool, and karaoke on Wednesday nights. **STEPS WINE BAR AND CAFÉ** (140 1st St; 360/378-5959) offers a touch of trendy. **MARILYN'S GARDEN PATH CAFÉ** (135 2nd St; 360/378-6255) is where locals go for lunch. The **BACK DOOR KITCHEN** (400 A St; 360/378-9540) is a local secret for both lunch and dinner tucked away in a nursery garden behind a warehouse at the end of Web Street. Finding it is half the fun.

At **ROCHE HARBOR VILLAGE** (Roche Harbor; 360/378-5757; www.rocheharbor. com), chef Bill Shaw keeps the menus lively and consistently good at all three restaurants: The **LIME KILN CAFÉ** is open year-round (in winter only for breakfast and lunch). Fine dining at **MCMILLAN'S** is available all year (Thurs–Sun in winter). In the summer, the **MADRONA BAR AND GRILL** has lively deck dining.

There's a range of places to stay in Friday Harbor. **WAYFARER'S REST BACK-PACKER'S HOSTEL** (35 Malcolm St; 360/378-6428; www.rockisland.com/ ~wayfarersrest) is rustic and friendly. The motelish **ORCA INN** (770 Mullis St; 360/378-6184 or 877/541-6722; www.theorcainn.org) is reasonable, has kitchens, and often has rooms available in the summer. On the other end of the historic spectrum, the 1898 **TUCKER HOUSE** (260 B St; 360/378-2783 or 800/965-0123; www.tuckerhouse.com), a block from the ferry dock, is family- and pet-friendly and comfortable. So is the **FRIDAY HARBOR INN** (410 Spring St; 360/378-4000 or 800/793-4765; www.fridayharborinn.com), where kids can swim in the pool and parents can get a massage at **LAVENDERA DAY SPA** (360/378-3637; www. lavenderadayspa.com). For an independent stay in a downtown Friday Harbor suite, complete with Annie Howell Adams original art, antiques, bedrooms, and kitchen, check out **NICHOLS STREET SUITES** (85 Nichols St; 866/374-4272; www.lodging-fridayharbor.com).

For camping, there's **LAKEDALE RESORT AT THREE LAKES** (4313 Roche Harbor Rd; 360/378-2350 or 800/617-2267; www.lakedale.com), which has everything from tent sites to a luxury lodge. Camping is also available at **SAN JUAN COUNTY PARK** (50 San Juan Park Dr; 360/378-8420; www.co.san-juan. wa.us); at **SNUG HARBOR MARINA RESORT** (1997 Mitchell Bay Rd; 360/378-4762; www.snugresort.com), and right next door at **MITCHELL BAY LANDING** (2101 Mitchell Bay Rd; 360-378-9296; www.mitchellbaylanding.com), where you can rent kayaks.

RESTAURANTS

Duck Soup Inn / ★★☆

50 DUCK SOUP LANE, FRIDAY HARBOR; 360/378-4878

For more than 30 years, Gretchen Allison has served special food in this serene setting with its rustic cottage, gardens, fireplace, and pond views. The focus of the ambitious menu is on seafood; specialties include applewood-smoked oysters and grilled fish. House-baked bread, a bowl of perfectly seasoned soup, and a large salad accompany ample portions. Leave room for white chocolate–banana cream pie. *$$; DIS, MC, V; checks OK; dinner*

*Wed–Sun (closed in winter); beer and wine; reservations recommended; www.
ducksoupinn.com; 5 miles northwest of Friday Harbor.*

The Place Bar & Grill / ★★★

I SPRING ST, FRIDAY HARBOR; 360/378-8707
The soothing waterside view, friendly atmosphere, and splendid menu make
for a memorable experience. Chef-owner Steven Anderson features a rotating world of cuisines, focusing on fish and shellfish. Try the mushroom sauté
appetizer with artichoke hearts and warm goat cheese or the black-bean
ravioli with tequila shrimp. This is a family affair: in summer, up to five
Andersons are working. *$$–$$$; MC, V; local checks only; dinner every day
(Tues–Sat in winter); full bar; reservations recommended; at foot of Spring St.*

Vinny's / ★★

165 WEST ST, FRIDAY HARBOR; 360/378-1934
Vinny's is an upbeat, sophisticated, Tuscan-style eatery offering Italian classics and daily fresh seafood specials. The pasta dishes are generous; for a
"hot" meal experience, split a caesar salad and an order of the "Pasta from
Hell," a combo of garlic, pine nuts, raisins, and bell peppers in a spicy cream
sauce. There's an island-style laid-back feel and a harbor view. *$$–$$$; MC,
V; local checks only; dinner every day; full bar; reservations recommended;
downtown off 1st St.*

LODGINGS

Beaverton Valley Farm B&B / ★★

4144 BEAVERTON VALLEY RD, SAN JUAN ISLAND; 360/378-3276
A few miles out of town, this classic 1907 farmhouse comes complete with
free-ranging chickens, a lamb, cats, and a dog. It's relaxed here, with an
eco-friendly emphasis. Owner Natasha Frey, raised on the island, is young
for an innkeeper, but she and partner Dave Kinnaman are world-traveled,
and their version of hospitality includes privacy and independence as well
as floral comforters and feather beds. The four comfy rooms all have private
baths, and there's a log cabin with a kitchenette. *$$; MC, V; checks OK; www.
beavertonvalley.com; at mile marker 4.*

Dragonfly Inn / ★

4770 ROCHE HARBOR RD, SAN JUAN ISLAND; 360/378-4287
During his professional life, Robert Butler developed a love of Japanese art
and culture, and he's translated this passion into the Dragonfly Inn. With its
deep *ofero* tubs in each of the four guest rooms, elegant screens, and stone-
work, the place is reminiscent of a Zen forest retreat. Butler offsets this asceti-
cism with robust hospitality and skill in the kitchen, where guests can chat
with him while he prepares a gourmet Asian fusion breakfast complete with
crème fraîche wasabi. *$$$; MC, V; checks OK; www.thedragonflyinn.com; 5
miles out on Roche Harbor Rd.*

Friday Harbor House / ★★★

130 WEST ST, FRIDAY HARBOR; 360/378-8455 OR 866/722-7356
The plain architecture of Friday Harbor House belies its posh interior. It's serene; 23 guest rooms are decorated in muted modern tones and have gas fireplaces and huge jetted tubs positioned to absorb both the fire's warmth and the harbor view. Some rooms have tiny balconies; not all offer full waterfront views. The view dining room (open to the public for dinner) maintains the inn's quixotic cool, warming considerably when you take your first bite of Dungeness crab cakes. *$$$$; AE, DIS, MC, V; checks OK; www.fridayharbor house.com; from ferry, left on Spring St, right on 1st St, right on West St.* &

Friday's Historic Inn / ★★

35 1ST ST, FRIDAY HARBOR; 360/378-5848 OR 800/352-2632
This elegantly renovated 1891 historic building is an oasis in the center of town. Of the 15 rooms, the best is the Eagle Cove, a third-floor, water-view perch with a deck, kitchen, double shower, and Jacuzzi. Some (economy) rooms share baths. All are graciously furnished. Heated bathroom floors and fresh-baked cookies in the afternoon are just two thoughtful touches. There are no grounds here, yet you can retreat to the outdoor deck and patio. *$$– $$$; MC, V; checks OK; www.friday-harbor.com; 2 blocks from ferry.* &

Harrison House Suites / ★★★

235 C ST, FRIDAY HARBOR; 360/378-3587 OR 800/407-7933
Farhad Ghatan sold his wonderfully renovated Craftsman inn to Anna Maria de Freitas and Adam Pass, two East Coast transplants who are equally comfortable in the new kitchen and in deep waters (they are both certified scuba instructors). Both left corporate craziness to take up B and B madness, and they love it. Anna makes fresh cookies daily. There are suites with decks, rooms with views, and gardens around every corner. Kayaks as well as mountain bikes are available for guest use. Fresh-baked breads are served each evening; mornings, it's fresh scones. There is no charm left unturned. *$$–$$$$; AE, DIS, MC, V; checks OK; www.harrisonhousesuites.com; 2 blocks from downtown.*

Highland Inn / ★★★

WEST SIDE, SAN JUAN ISLAND; 360/378-9450 OR 888/400-9850
Helen King, former owner of the famous Babbling Brook Inn in Santa Cruz, moved north and built the inn of her dreams on San Juan Island. Her two suites are huge, with sitting rooms, fireplaces, and marble bathrooms with jetted tubs and steam-cabinet showers. Drink in views of the Olympic Mountains, Victoria, and Haro Strait from the 88-foot-long covered veranda. In the afternoons, King serves tea along with her signature white- and dark-chocolate-chip cookies. *$$$$; AE, MC, V; checks OK; www.highlandinn.com; call for directions.*

Juniper Lane Guesthouse / ★

1312 BEAVERTON VALLEY RD, FRIDAY HARBOR; 360/378-7761
This guest house combines local chic, global sensibilities, avant-garde decor, and a pastoral landscape. There are practical backpacker bunk rooms, elegant private rooms, a kitchen, a common room, do-it-yourself breakfast, outdoor patios, and a fire pit, all within walking distance of town. Young owner-manager Juniper Maas was born and raised on the island, traveled the world, and returned to refurbish her dream guest house. She has created a truly unique environment for travelers of every age and inclination. *$–$$; MC, V; checks OK; www.juniperlaneguesthouse.com; on the edge of Friday Harbor, 1 mile from the ferry.* &

Lakedale Resort at Three Lakes / ★★★

**4313 ROCHE HARBOR RD, SAN JUAN ISLAND;
360/378-0944 OR 800/617-2267**
What's surprising about Lakedale Resort is that it's right in the middle of the island rather than on the water; it works as both a campground and a luxury lodge; and its peace and beauty make you want to stay put, especially in the quiet off-season when the 82 acres of lakes and forests cast their meditative spell. For romance, the lodge is grand; the 10 rooms have slate fireplaces, balconies, and lake views. For families, the log cabins, with two bedrooms, two bathrooms, and kitchens make a great getaway. There are group sites for camping as well as hiker- or bicycle-only sites. *$–$$$; AE, DIS, MC; checks OK; www.lakedale.com; 4.5 miles from the ferry landing.* &

Lonesome Cove Resort / ★★

416 LONESOME COVE RD, FRIDAY HARBOR; 360/378-4477
A fixture on the island since the 1940s, this 10-acre resort has been loyally and lovingly protected throughout the years. The six classic hand-built log cottages are still 40 feet from the water's edge, and the summer sunsets are glorious. There have been no fancy changes, and the fireplaces still burn real wood. It's hard to find places that stop time and remind us that life existed before cell phones, computers, and stock portfolios. This is one of them. *$$–$$$; MC, V; checks OK; www.lonesomecove.com; take Roche Harbor Rd 9 miles north to Lonesome Cove Rd.* &

Olympic Lights / ★★

146 STARLIGHT WAY, FRIDAY HARBOR; 360/378-3186
The south end of San Juan Island has some of the most glorious beaches and woods on the island. This four-room B and B, light-filled and romantic, sits on the edge of it all. Lea and Christian Andrade play marimba in a band when they're not here. They live in a cottage next door, so guests have full run of what was once the Old Johnson Farmhouse. In summer, the gardens bloom in abandon. Breakfast omelets are courtesy of the inn's chickens and its herb garden. *$$–$$$; no credit cards; checks OK (in advance); www.olympiclights. com; south end of island.*

Roche Harbor Resort / ★★★

ROCHE HARBOR RD, SAN JUAN ISLAND;
360/378-2155 OR 800/451-8910

There are few places in the region that take you back in time like a visit to Roche Harbor Resort. The centerpiece, the ivy-clad Hotel de Haro, was built in 1886. History buffs relish the piecework wallpaper and period furnishings; the creaky, uneven floorboards; and the thought that Teddy Roosevelt was once a guest. The view from the entry takes in the flower garden, cobblestone waterfront, and bay. The hotel offers 20 rooms; only 4 have private bathrooms. A fine-dining restaurant, café, and casual eatery are on the grounds (see section introduction). Recent additions include posh vacation houses, luxury suites, and an artists' village. *$$–$$$$; AE, MC, V; checks OK; www. rocheharbor.com; on waterfront at northwest end of island.*&

Sakya Kachod Choling / ★★

PO BOX 3191, AT HANNAH RD, FRIDAY HARBOR; 360/378-4059

This Tibetan Buddhist retreat center was designed to blend the architecture of both Tibet and the Northwest. Inside, master Tibetan craftsmen painted the shrine-room walls with murals of museum quality. There are two single-bed retreat rooms and a kitchen and bathroom to share. The trees, mossy knolls, Mount Baker vista, and peace and quiet invite reflection and meditation. You don't have to be a Buddhist to come. Meals are an additional cost. *$; MC, V; checks OK; www.sakya-retreat.net; west side of island.*

Wharfside B&B / ★★

K DOCK, STE 13, FRIDAY HARBOR; 360/378-5661 OR 800/899-3030

If nothing lulls you to sleep like the gentle lap of the waves, the *Wharfside*'s for you. Two staterooms on the 60-foot sailboat are nicely finished with queen-sized beds, with the compact precision that only boat living can inspire. Enjoy the huge breakfast on deck and watch boaters head to sea. *$$$; AE, MC, V; checks OK; www.slowseason.com; in marina just north of ferry terminal.*

Bellingham and Area

Bellingham is the metropolitan hub of northwestern Washington, on the shores of Bellingham Bay and flanked by the foothills of majestic Mount Baker. Numerous small towns flank Bellingham in the transition zone from the Skagit Valley to this thriving city on the Nooksack River.

Chuckanut Drive

This famous 17 miles (State Route 11) between Burlington in the Skagit Valley and Bellingham on the bay is one of the prettiest drives in the state. On a gorgeous long summer evening, it may be *the* prettiest. It winds through lush farmlands, then clings to Chuckanut and Blanchard mountains with westerly views over Samish Bay. If you're in the driver's seat, however, keep both hands on the wheel and your eyes on the narrow, winding road. Take advantage of the numerous turnouts so you can linger a bit longer over the magnificent vistas—and get impatient locals off your bumper. Watch out for cyclists, who use Chuckanut as a training ride. Access **CHUCKANUT DRIVE** (www.chuckanutdrive.com) either northbound (exit 231 off I-5, Burlington) or do it in reverse, southbound (from Fairhaven Pkwy, exit 250 off I-5, Bellingham)—take Fairhaven Parkway to 12th Street and turn left.

As you buzz along the mostly straight, flat stretch northbound between Burlington and Bow, it's hard to believe Interstate 5 is only minutes away to the east. Removed from traffic, you'll discover orchards, oyster beds, slow-moving tractors, and migratory bird action. As if by design, art galleries and antique shops are at convenient intervals. On the drive's south end is **KARMA PLACE** (3533 Chuckanut Dr, Bow; 360/766-6716), with its serene Japanese garden, art gallery, tearoom, bamboo nursery, and antique shop. For a fascinating detour, visit the **PADILLA BAY NATIONAL ESTUARINE RESEARCH RESERVE** and the newly remodeled **BREAZEALE INTERPRETIVE CENTER** (1043 Bayview-Edison Rd, west of Chuckanut Dr; 360/428-1558; www.inlet.geol.sc.edu/PDB; 10am–5pm Wed–Sun) Nearby **BAYVIEW STATE PARK** (360/757-0227; www.parks.wa.gov/parkpage) has overnight camping, rustic cabins, and beachfront picnic sites.

BLAU OYSTER COMPANY on Samish Island (11321 Blue Heron Rd, 7 miles west of Edison via Bayview-Edison Rd and Samish Island Rd; 360/766-6171; www.blauoyster.com; 8am–5pm Mon–Sat) has been selling oysters since 1935; follow signs to the shucking plant. You'll also find oysters at **TAYLOR SHELLFISH FARMS** (2182 Chuckanut Dr, Bow; 360/766-6002; www.taylorshellfish.com), open every day in summer.

LARRABEE STATE PARK (off Chuckanut Dr, 7 miles south of Bellingham; 360/902-8844; www.parks.wa.gov) was one of Washington's first state parks. The Interurban Trail, once the electric rail route from Bellingham to Mount Vernon, is now a 5-mile trail connecting three parks on Chuckanut Drive: Larrabee State Park to Arroyo Park to Fairhaven Park in Bellingham. The **CHUCKANUT GALLERY** (700 Chuckanut Dr, Bellingham; 360/734-4885) on the drive's north end has a nice sculpture garden.

Edison

This compact, historic burg (circa 1869) west of Chuckanut Drive is on the comeback from its early heyday as a logging and agricultural hub. Its cluster of Victorian homes is being spruced up, and the "business district"—mainly along Caines Court—now offers an eclectic mix: the **EDISON EYE GALLERY** (360/766-6276), **FREDA LOKO "WORLD ARTS"** (360/766-4420), **SLOUGH FOOD** (360/766-4458), and the **BREAD FARM** (360/757-0362). The familiar standbys are still there, too: the **FARM TO MARKET BAKERY** (14003 Gilmore Ave; 360/757-0362), the **OLD EDISON INN** on the corner (5829 Caines Ct; 360/766-6266), the **EDISON CAFÉ** on the east end of town (5797 Main Ave; 360/766-6940), and the **LONGHORN SALOON & GRILL** (5754 Caines Ct; 360/766-6330) in the center of things.

Bow

Just east of Edison on State Highway 11 is Bow, a town in Samish Bay.

RESTAURANTS

The Oyster Bar on Chuckanut Drive / ★★★

2578 CHUCKANUT DR, BOW; 360/766-6185

This restaurant with its intriguing history and loyal following continues to make steady improvements to its cliffhanging location and fails to disappoint even the most discerning diner. The view remains nothing short of spectacular, the fare is gourmet, and the wine cellar maintains its award-winning collection. Entrées might be a generous cedar-planked fillet of wild salmon or a perfectly cooked filet mignon. *$$$; AE, MC, V; local checks only; lunch, dinner every day; beer and wine; reservations recommended; www.theoysterbaron chuckanutdrive.com; closer to Bellingham end of Chuckanut Dr.*

The Rhododendron Café / ★★

5521 CHUCKANUT DR, BOW; 360/766-6667

The Rhododendron Café can be the start of or the end to a delightful afternoon on Chuckanut Drive. It may not have the view of other eateries, but the commitment to quality and creativity here makes this a delicious stop. Once the site of the Red Crown Service Station in the early 1900s, the "Rhody" now serves homemade soup (chowder is excellent) and a tasty portobello burger. Lightly breaded and panfried Samish Bay oysters—the specialty of the area—are delicious. A nightly seafood stew has an ethnic or seasonal theme. Seating is intimate and tables fill up fast, so call ahead. *$$; AE, MC, V; checks OK; breakfast Sat–Sun, lunch, dinner Wed–Sun (closed late Nov–Jan); beer and wine; reservations recommended; www.rhodycafe.com; at Bow-Edison junction.*

LODGINGS

Benson Farmstead Bed & Breakfast / ★★☆

10113 AVON-ALLEN RD, BOW;
360/757-0578 OR 800/441-9814

This 17-room restored 1914 farmhouse surrounded by gardens is filled with antiques and Scandinavian memorabilia. Four upstairs rooms (all with private baths) have antique beds and quilts. A cottage-style family suite is out back; there's also a suite by the waterfall garden. Jerry and Sharon Benson cook a country breakfast and sometimes serve desserts in the evening. Don't be surprised to hear music in the air; the Benson family are talented singers, pianists, and violinists. If you prefer accommodations closer to La Conner, the Bensons have a beach-front log home on Skagit Bay for rent too. *$$; MC, V; checks OK; www.bbhosts.com/bensonbnb; exit 232 west off I-5.*

Chuckanut Cabins / ★★★

3164 CHUCKANUT DR (BAYHOUSE), BOW
2360 OYSTER CREEK LANE (DECKHOUSE), BOW; 360/766-6901
Both these beautiful cottages have expansive views over Samish Bay and the San Juan Islands. In the Bayhouse, enjoy the view in bed with the added glow of the gas fireplace. At the Deckhouse, take advantage of the outdoor, very private (bathing-suit optional) hot tub. Champagne on arrival, breakfast in your cabin, a collection of classic movies, and guest robes are just some thoughtful extra touches. *$$$; AE, MC, V; checks OK; www.chucaknutcabins. com; 10 miles south of Bellingham.*

Samish Point by the Bay / ★★

4465 SAMISH POINT RD, BOW;
360/766-6610 OR 800/916-6161
Theresa and Herb Goldston's unique and very tranquil getaway on their 40-acre waterfront estate at Samish Island's west end offers miles of wooded trails, more beach access than the local state park, mountain views, and unparalleled solitude. Their three-bedroom cottage has a gas fireplace in the living room and a hot tub on the back deck. It accommodates up to six. It is a veritable private reserve all yours during your stay. The kitchen is stocked with continental breakfast fixings. *$$–$$$; AE, MC, V; checks OK; www.samishpoint.com; exit 236 off I-5, west through Bow and Edison to Samish Island.*

Bellingham

Western Washington University is here, so Bellingham is definitely a college town. But that's not all. The Bellwether on the Bay development on Squalicum Harbor—which includes the mini–grand hotel (see review)—will soon be joined by an even more ambitious plan as the Georgia-Pacific property is slowly dismantled and cleaned up, paving the way for much-needed waterfront places.

Opened in May 2006, the Depot Market Square provides a home for the beloved **BELLINGHAM FARMERS MARKET** (www.depotmarket.org) on the site of the historic railroad depot. The **WHATCOM MUSEUM OF HISTORY AND ART** (121 Prospect St; 360/676-6981; www.whatcommuseum.org) has at its centerpiece a massive 1892 Romanesque structure used as a city hall until 1940. Check out the **SYRE EDUCATION CENTER** (201 Prospect St; 360/676-6981 ext. 205) down the block and the **WHATCOM CHILDREN'S MUSEUM** (227 Prospect St; 360/733-8769) a few doors north. A short walk away is the **AMERICAN MUSEUM OF RADIO & ELECTRICITY** (1312 Bay St; 360/738-3886; www.americanradiomuseum.org).

The summer **BELLINGHAM FESTIVAL OF MUSIC** (360/676-5997 or 800/335-5550; www.bellinghamfestival.org; late July–mid-Aug) is an institution, featuring more than two weeks of orchestral, chamber, and jazz performances. The **MOUNT BAKER THEATRE** (104 N Commercial St; 360/734-6080; www.mountbaker-theatre.com), built in 1927 and renovated in 1995, is home to the **WHATCOM**

SYMPHONY ORCHESTRA (www.whatcomsymphony.com) and hosts other events. The SKI-TO-SEA RACE (360/734-1330; www.bellingham.com/skitosea) attracts teams from all over the world to an annual seven-event relay on Memorial Day weekend.

Outdoors, downtown Bellingham and Fairhaven are completely linked by trail. SEHOME HILL ARBORETUM (Bellingham Parks and Recreation, 360/676-6985; www.ac.wwu.edu/~sha/), adjacent to the WWU campus, sports more than 3 miles of trails with prime views. WHATCOM FALLS PARK (1401 Electric Ave; 360/676-6985) has more than 5 miles of trails overlooking waterfalls. BIG ROCK GARDEN PARK (2900 Sylvan St, near Lake Whatcom; 360/676-6985; Apr–Oct) is a woodland of garden art and sculpture.

Bellingham's restaurant scene has picked up over the years. For swanky and spendy, there's NIMBUS (119 N Commercial St; 360/676-1307), aptly named for its location at the top of the Towers, or GIUSEPPE'S ITALIAN RESTAURANT (1414 Cornwall St; 360/714-9100) in gorgeous new digs. BOUNDARY BAY BREWERY (1107 Railroad St; 360/647-5593) downtown is a popular hangout that serves a delicious lamb burger. Ethnic favorites are BUSARA THAI CUISINE (404 36th St, in Sehome Village; 360/734-8088), CASA QUE PASA for Mexican (1415 Railroad Ave; 360/738-8226), OSAKA (3207 Northwest Ave; 360/676-6268) for its superb sushi, and LUCKY PANDA (2311 James St; 360/738-2888) for exceptional Chinese. CALLALOO CARIBBEAN KITCHEN (1212 N State St; 360/676-JERK) is a fresh breeze with an interesting menu and whimsical interior. Stop in at MEDITER-RANEAN SPECIALTIES (505 32nd St, in Viking Plaza; 360/738-6895) for fantastic Greek, Italian, and Middle Eastern foods.

If you haven't been to FAIRHAVEN (www.fairhaven.com) lately, you may not recognize it: new construction is everywhere. Once a separate town that was the result of a short-lived railroad boom in 1889, the Fairhaven Historic District retains its old-time charm and offers plenty of exploring. The MARKETPLACE (Harris and 12th sts) houses shops in refurbished splendor. Crafts, galleries, coffeehouses, bistros and bars, trendy boutiques, bookstores, a charming garden, and a lively evening scene are all contained within several blocks. VILLAGE BOOKS (1200 11th St; 360/671-2626; www.villagebooks.com) is Northwest Washington's largest independent bookstore, also housing the popular COLOPHON CAFÉ (360/647-0092; www.colophoncafe.com), PAPER DREAMS (360/676-8676), and BOOK FARE (360/734-3434), a quiet coffee spot.

The cruise terminal at the end of Harris Street houses the southern terminus of the ALASKA MARINE HIGHWAY SYSTEM (355 Harris Ave; 360/676-8445 or 800/642-0066; www.dot.state.ak.us/amhs/); here, travelers begin the three-day coastal journey through the famed Inside Passage. Between May and September, the SAN JUAN ISLAND COMMUTER (888/734-8180; www.islandcommuter.com) operates daily between Bellingham, Orcas Island, and San Juan Island. VICTORIA SAN JUAN CRUISES (360/738-8099 or 800/443-4552; www.whales.com) offers overnight cruise and whale-watching packages to Victoria. The AMTRAK (www.amtrak.com) station is next door.

RESTAURANTS

Bistecca Italian Steakhouse / ★★

4156 MERIDIAN ST, BELLINGHAM; 360/647-1060

The location is anything but glamorous, the signs are poor, and parking is not obvious. Despite these glaring shortcomings, at Bistecca ("steak" in Italian) chef Marc Eilberg is working quiet magic on various meat cuts and handmade pastas while training a novice staff on the art of properly prepared—and presented—food in the European tradition. Diverse wine list. *$$–$$$; AE, MC, V; no checks; dinner every day; full bar; reservations recommended; above Meridian Grill on corner of Westerly Rd.*

Du Jour Bistro and the Vines Wine Shop / ★★

1319 CORNWALL AVE, BELLINGHAM; 360/714-1161

The merger of two businesses is usually not as convenient as it turned out for owners Mike Peterson and Becki Lawson. A wall came down and voila! Du Jour Bistro was born. It partners with the Vines Wine Shop, where your meal can be accompanied by a bottle off the rack next to your table (with a modest corkage fee). The menu is French, with such delights as beef tenderloin with a port–mission fig demi-glace or duck breast with honey-lavender glaze. *$–$$; MC, V; checks OK; lunch, dinner Mon–Sat; beer and wine; reservations recommended; www.thevinesdujour.com; heart of downtown.*

Pacific Café / ★★★

100 N COMMERCIAL ST, BELLINGHAM; 360/647-0800

The Pacific is one of Bellingham's most consistent and innovative gems. Anchoring the southwest corner of the remodeled Mount Baker Theatre building, this café's ambience is civilized, and service is superb. Co-owner Robert Fong's Hawaiian background and years of travel in Europe, India, China, and Thailand influence the sophisticated menu, which relies on the freshest of ingredients—ahi directly from Hawaii and organic Oregon beef, to name a few. The abstract watercolors and quiet jazz make for a romantic evening. *$$; AE, MC, V; local checks only; lunch Mon–Fri, dinner Tues–Sat; beer and wine; reservations recommended; www.thepacificcafe.com; at Champion St downtown.*

Pepper Sisters / ★★

1055 N STATE ST, BELLINGHAM; 360/671-3414

Innovative Southwestern fare is served here. Cheerful service, a great location in a vintage brick building, and a wide-awake kitchen have made Pepper Sisters an institution. The grilled king salmon taco in a soft blue-corn tortilla with accents of kalamata olives, garlic, chipotle aioli, and fresh arugula is a wildly popular regular blackboard special. *$; MC, V; checks OK; dinner Tues–Sun; beer and wine; reservations recommended; south of downtown.*

LODGINGS

The Chrysalis Inn & Spa / ★★★

804 10TH ST, BELLINGHAM; 360/756-1005 OR 888/808-0005
Commanding prime waterfront real estate north of Fairhaven, the Chrysalis Inn & Spa keeps quietly racking up the accolades. Designed in an Asian-Northwest motif, the Chrysalis has 43 rooms (9 of which are luxury suites), each with oversize tubs, window seats, fireplaces, and water views. The spa offers numerous choices for pampering. Fino's, their sophisticated wine bar–restaurant, is a terrific afternoon spot that also serves a free breakfast buffet for inn guests. *$$$–$$$$; AE, DC, DIS, MC, V; checks OK; www.the chrysalisinn.com; Fairhaven Pkwy exit off I-5.*

Fairhaven Village Inn / ★★

1200 10TH ST, BELLINGHAM; 360/733-1311 OR 877/733-1100
This small boutique hotel is the only overnight accommodations in the Fairhaven Historic District, with walkable access to the unique dining, shopping, and entertainment options in this popular Bellingham destination. Each of the 22 spacious guest rooms has a bay view, a fireplace, robes, and high-quality bedding. *$$–$$$; AE, DC, DIS, MC, V; checks OK; www.fairhaven villageinn.com; exit 250 from I-5, follow Old Fairhaven Pkwy.*

Hotel Bellwether / ★★★★

1 BELLWETHER WAY, BELLINGHAM; 360/392-3100 OR 877/411-1200
Bellingham's own small "grand" hotel is located on the waterfront near downtown overlooking Bellingham Bay with terrific sunset views from most of the 68 rooms. Gas fireplaces, soaking tubs (also with views), and a rich decor of imported Italian furniture further enhance the Bellwether's splendor. At day's end, enjoy turn-down service with fine chocolates atop your Hungarian down pillow and Austrian bed linens. For the ultimate in seclusion, rent the dramatic three-story Lighthouse Suite, complete with champagne and caviar. *$$–$$$$; AE, DC, DIS, MC, V; local checks only; www.hotel bellwether.com; exit 256 off I-5, turn right on Squalicum Way, which becomes Roeder Ave.*

Schnauzer Crossing / ★★★

4421 LAKEWAY DR, BELLINGHAM;
360/734-2808 OR 800/562-2808
Still reigning as a superior bed-and-breakfast, this contemporary home overlooking Lake Whatcom is a labor of love by Donna and Monty McAllister. Aside from the three rooms, it's the Japanese-style grounds with koi pond, meditation garden, wisteria arbor, hammock, and hot tub that make the experience so special. Breakfast is Donna's specialty. The three resident schnauzers are the top dogs here. *$$$–$$$$; DIS, MC, V; checks OK; www.schnauzer crossing.com; exit 253 off I-5.*

Lummi Island

Sentinel to the entrance of Bellingham Bay, Lummi is one of the most overlooked islands of the San Juans. It's serviced by a tiny **FERRY** (360/676-6730; www. co.whatcom.wa.us/publicworks/ferry) that leaves Gooseberry Point at 10 minutes past the hour on weekends, more frequently on weekdays. It's cheap and quick. The ferry returns from Lummi on the hour on weekends, every 20–40 minutes on weekdays.

LODGINGS

The Willows Inn / ★★★

> **2579 WEST SHORE DR, LUMMI ISLAND;**
> **360/758-2620 OR 888/294-2620**
> Owners Judy Olsen and Riley Starks keep things interesting at this old favorite inn–turned–food resort. The main house has four rooms with private baths; two have private entrances. A small cottage has a terrific view; a two-bedroom house with gas fireplace and whirlpool tub looks out to the water from a deck. Weekend dinners are served year-round. On summer Sundays, it's "spot prawns and margaritas on the deck." The Taproot pub is a local hot spot in the afternoons. Ask about picnic boat excursions. $$$; AE, MC, V; checks OK; www.willows-inn.com; north on Nugent Rd for 3½ miles.

Ferndale

Tiny Ferndale (population 9,000) started as a voting precinct in the mid-1800s, blossomed briefly as a potential Whatcom County seat in the latter part of the 19th century, and endured the failings of an overzealous civic promoter. Today Ferndale is a pleasant community proud of its historical contributions. Notable attractions include **PIONEER PARK** (adjacent to downtown; 360/384-4302) with its log structure exhibits, living-farm **HOVANDER HOMESTEAD PARK** (5299 Nielsen Ave; 360/384-3444), and **TENNANT LAKE NATURAL HISTORY INTERPRETIVE CENTER** (5236 Nielsen Ave; 360/384-3064), a spectacular sanctuary.

Ferndale is surprisingly blessed with an overabundance of eateries. Just within the three-block stretch that constitutes the heart of downtown, you'll find at least six different choices. Contact the **FERNDALE CHAMBER OF COMMERCE** (5683 2nd Ave; 360/384-3042) for information.

RESTAURANTS

Poor Siamese Café / ★★★

> **5683 3RD AVE, FERNDALE; 360/312-9433**
> Poor Siamese Café, in its petite, brick-fronted space, is sensory overload—in the best of senses. Curry dishes are so rich and creamy that even chopsticks stand up unassisted. The deft use of basil, lemongrass, and lime leaves coax their flavors into bursting with freshness. A myriad vegetables—carrots,

spinach, baby corn, tomatoes, bell peppers, broccoli, and bamboo shoots, to name a few—are the foundation for all entrées and noodle dishes, with a choice of meat or seafood added. The "spicy" scale ranges from 1 to 4; go for 2½, and nobody gets hurt. Takeout is an option. *$–$$; no credit cards; local checks only; lunch, dinner Mon–Sat; beer and wine; reservations recommended; just off corner of Vista Dr.*

Lynden

This community, noted for its immaculate yards and colorful gardens, adopted a Dutch theme in tribute to its early settlers. To sample it, visit the **DUTCH BAKERY** (421 Front St; 360/354-3911) and **HOLLANDIA RESTAURANT** (655 Front St; 360/354-4133), in Lynden's unusual shopping mall—there's a stream running through it. The **EASTSIDE MARKET & DELI** (1011 E Grover St; 360/354-2246) specializes in Dutch foods, and the **DUTCH VILLAGE INN** (655 Front St; 360/354-4440) is a bed-and-breakfast with lodging in a windmill; the six guest rooms are named after Dutch provinces. Golfers can head north of town to **HOMESTEAD FARMS GOLF RESORT** (115 E Homestead Blvd; 800/354-1196; www.homestead farmsgolf.com), a championship course with a full clubhouse, a challenging 18-hole par-71 putting course, a restaurant, deluxe condominiums, and a new hotel. For more information, visit the town's **WEB SITE** (www.lynden.org).

Blaine

The northernmost city along the Interstate 5 corridor, Blaine is the state's most popular and beautiful border crossing into British Columbia. Home to the grand International Peace Arch Monument, which spans the U.S.-Canadian border, the surrounding park borders on two bays: Semiahmoo on the U.S. side, Boundary on the Canadian side. The park is filled with gardens and sculptures. Each June, there's a Peace Arch celebration.

In Blaine itself, there aren't many places to stay, though one is pretty famous: **SEMIAHMOO RESORT-GOLF-SPA** (see review). East of town, **SMUGGLER'S INN B&B** (9910 Canada View Dr; 360/332-1749) is a rambling replica Victorian gem on the border with expansive views.

LODGINGS

Semiahmoo Resort-Golf-Spa / ★★★

9565 SEMIAHMOO PKWY, BLAINE; 360/318-2000 OR 800/770-7992
Sharing its unique proximity on Semiahmoo Spit with a 1,100-acre wildlife preserve, Semiahmoo Resort offers golf, acres of wooded trails, waterfront, and views west to the sea and the San Juans and east to Drayton Harbor. Long a favorite of escapists from Seattle and Vancouver, the resort has a spa, a fitness center, a pool, racquetball, and tennis. The 198 rooms have classy earth-tone furnishings, and most have water views and fireplaces.

Guests will enjoy the five restaurants, café, and two award-winning golf courses. *$$$–$$$$; AE, DC, DIS, MC, V; checks OK; www.semiahmoo. com; exit 270 off I-5.*

Tacoma, Olympia, and the South Sound

Heading south from Seattle, Interstate 5 takes you to the state's third-largest city, Tacoma, which has become a destination for museum lovers. Thirty miles farther to the south is the state's picturesque bay-side capital of Olympia. Scattered among these metropolises are intriguing small communities along Puget Sound.

Vashon Island

It almost feels accidental to find an idyllic island like this where locals still tell time by the tides, and shops and restaurants are mostly family-owned. The lack of neon and billboards is refreshing on this hilly island where art, agriculture, and alpacas are plentiful. Most restaurants and stores are in Vashon Center, the halfway point on this 12-mile-long island, but art galleries are peppered throughout its length. Beach access can be a challenge, but when you find it, you'll probably catch a glimpse of marine mammals skirting the shore.

Island arts are displayed at the **BLUE HERON ART CENTER** (19704 Vashon Hwy SW; 206/463-5131; www.vashonalliedarts.com) and at **SILVERWOOD GALLERY** (23927 Vashon Hwy SW; 206/463-1722; www.silverwoodgallery.com). Gardeners like **DIG FLORAL & GARDEN** (19028 Vashon Hwy SW; 206/463-5096; digfloralandgarden.com). The adjacent two-story house is **MADIGAN'S** (19028 Vashon Hwy SW; 206/463-0080), a fine gifts and furniture store. Rent sea kayaks and receive instruction or guided trips at **VASHON ISLAND KAYAK COMPANY** (Jensen Acres boathouse at Quartermaster Harbor; 206/463-9257; www.puget soundkayak.com). Walkers will enjoy the garden shows, gallery walks, and celebrations like the Strawberry Festival in July.

Access Vashon via **WASHINGTON STATE FERRIES** (206/464-6400 or 800/843-3779; www.wsdot.wa.gov/ferries/), which reach the north end from downtown Seattle (foot passengers only) or West Seattle (the Fauntleroy ferry) or the south end from Tacoma via the Tahlequah ferry at Point Defiance. You can ferry to one end, drive to the other, and connect Seattle and Tacoma with nary a moment on Interstate 5.

Find more information at the **VASHON CHAMBER OF COMMERCE** (19001 Vashon Hwy SW; 206/408-8057 or 206/463-6217; www.vashonchamber.com).

RESTAURANTS

Ferrara on Vashon / ★★☆

17526 VASHON HWY SW, VASHON ISLAND; 206/463-4455
This gorgeous restaurant offers some of the finest dining on Vashon. Burgundy touches provide contrast to the black-and-white interior and uniforms

of the knowledgeable staff. The effect of a softly illuminated bar is doubled on an arched and mirrored wall. The ricotta gnocchi are mouth-watering. Anywhere else, this setting might be stuffy, but on a tiny island where most folks know each other, the atmosphere is friendly and inviting. $$–$$$; AE, MC, V; checks OK; dinner Tues–Sat; full bar; reservations recommended; www. ferraraonvashon.com; at Bank Rd in downtown Vashon Center. ≼

The Hardware Store / ★

17601 VASHON HWY SW, VASHON ISLAND; 206/463-1800
This 1890s-era building has served many uses, but the one most people remember is its incarnation as a hardware store, so it made sense to keep the name. The shell of the building is original; almost everything else is updated and a little hip. The restaurant provides gallery space, hand-mixed drinks, and food prepared at an exhibition grill. The packed house confirms the wisdom of offering old favorites (meatloaf and mashed potatoes) and new ventures (Penn Cove mussels seared with bacon, shallots, and apple). $–$$; AE, B, DC, E, JCB, MC, V; local checks only; breakfast Sun, lunch Thurs–Tues, dinner Wed–Mon; full bar; reservations recommended (dinner); www.ths restaurant.com; at Bank Rd in downtown Vashon Center. ≼

Tacoma

The "City of Destiny" is Washington's third-largest municipality, with the country's seventh-busiest port and one of the nation's largest city parks (Point Defiance). Tacoma also is home to three universities, two military installations, and a world-class zoo. Yet increasingly this city is noticed for the revitalization of its downtown core and its emergence as a cultural destination. The transformation of Tacoma has been described as a renaissance, but "restoration" seems a more fitting adjective. Several historic buildings in the downtown warehouse district have been converted from industrial use to hip residential and commercial functions, such as the University of Washington's Tacoma campus. Today you'll find museums, theaters, art galleries, boutiques, and many fine restaurants.

The $63 million **MUSEUM OF GLASS INTERNATIONAL CENTER FOR CONTEMPORARY ART** (1801 E Dock St; 866/468-7386; www.museumofglass.org) displays cutting-edge glass art and shows how it's made in the 180-seat amphitheater Hot Shop. The Antoine Predock–designed **TACOMA ART MUSEUM** (1701 Pacific Ave; 253/272-4258; www.tacomaartmuseum.org) makes art accessible through hands-on activities, lectures, and interpretations of exhibits. **UNTITLED**, the museum café, offers an assortment of soups, sandwiches, and salads, as well as beer and wine, to museum visitors and passersby. The **WASHINGTON STATE HISTORY STATE MUSEUM** (1911 Pacific Ave; 888/238-4373; www.washington history.org) occupies the arched brick building created to complement the old train station, **UNION STATION** (17th St and Pacific Ave), which now houses the **FEDERAL COURTHOUSE** and a spectacular public display of Dale Chihuly glass art. **JOB CARR'S CABIN** (2350 N 30th St; 253/627-5405; www.jobcarrmuseum.org)

is a tiny Old Town museum that marks the city's birthplace. The **WORKING WATERFRONT MUSEUM** (705 Dock St; 253/272-2750; www.wwfrontmuseum. org) is a work in progress with boats on display. The free **KARPELES MANUSCRIPT MUSEUM** (407 S G St; 253/383-2575; www.rain.org/~karpeles), with changing exhibits of famous documents, is across from **WRIGHT PARK** (Division and I sts), a city park with a 1908 glass-and-steel conservatory.

Three theaters downtown comprise the **BROADWAY CENTER FOR THE PER-FORMING ARTS** (901 Broadway Plaza; 253/591-5894; www.broadwaycenter. org): the restored 1,100-seat **PANTAGES THEATER** (901 Broadway Plaza), the **RIALTO THEATER** (310 S 9th St), a former old movie house, and the contemporary and colorful **THEATER IN THE SQUARE** (915 Broadway).

The **UNIVERSITY OF WASHINGTON TACOMA** branch campus (1900 Commerce St; 253/692-4000 or 800/736-7750; www.tacoma.washington.edu) is an excellent example of the use of reconditioned historic buildings. Stately homes and cobblestone streets in the north end are often used as sets by Hollywood moviemakers. One example is **STADIUM HIGH SCHOOL** (6229 S Tyler St; 253/571-1325), a turreted chateau originally built to be a luxury hotel.

Tacomans love the outdoors, and there are several ways to get your share of fresh air. **RUSTON WAY WATERFRONT** (between N 49th and N 54th sts) is a popular 2-mile seawall-sidewalk dotted with restaurants. **LAKEWOLD GARDENS** (12317 Gravelly Lake Dr SW, Lakewood; 253/584-3360 or 888/858-4106; www. lakewold.org) is 10 minutes south of Tacoma (exit 124 off I-5 to Gravelly Lake Dr) on a beautiful 10-acre site overlooking Gravelly Lake.

POINT DEFIANCE PARK (northwest side of Tacoma, call for directions; 253/305-1000), located on the northwest tip of Tacoma that reaches into Puget Sound, is a 700-acre largely old-growth forest. The wooded 5-mile drive and parallel hiking trails open up periodically for sweeping views of Gig Harbor, Vashon Island, and Brown's Point. The park is a gardener's delight with rose, rhododendron, Japanese, and Northwest native gardens. Inside the park, **CAMP 6** is a railroad village with a working steam engine, and **FORT NISQUALLY** is a reconstruction of the original Hudson Bay Company fort built in 1833. But the jewel in the crown of this park is **POINT DEFIANCE ZOO & AQUARIUM** (5400 N Pearl St; 253/591-5335; www.pdza.org). This Pacific Rim–themed facility features creatures from countries bordered by the Pacific Ocean.

The **TACOMA DOME** (2727 E D St; 253/572-3663; www.tacomadome.org), one of the world's largest wooden domes, is regularly booked for trade fairs, concerts, and sports shows. **CHENEY STADIUM** is a first-class ballpark best known as the home of the **TACOMA RAINIERS** (2502 S Tyler St; 253/752-7707; www. tacomarainiers.com), the triple-A affiliate of the Seattle Mariners.

Tacoma offers many restaurants and cafés, but a few favorites downtown include **ALTEZZO** (1320 Broadway Plaza, in Sheraton Tacoma Hotel; 253/572-3200; www.sheratontacoma.com), with Italian cuisine; **OVER THE MOON CAFÉ** (709 Opera Alley—aka Ct C; 253/284-3722; www.overthemooncafe.com) for old-fashioned American food; **PACIFIC GRILL** (1502 Pacific Ave; 253/627-3535; www.pacificgrilltacoma.com) for a dressy night on the town; and **RAVENOUS** (785 Broadway; 253/572-6374), where every dish pleases. Two notable pubs are

TACOMA THREE-DAY TOUR

DAY ONE: Start with breakfast at the **BROADWAY GRILL** (1320 Broadway Plaza; 253/572-3200) on the fourth floor of the **SHERATON TACOMA HOTEL** (www.sheratontacoma.com). Plan to be at the **WASHINGTON STATE HISTORICAL MUSEUM** as soon as it opens so you can spend the morning browsing its three floors. Head north on Pacific Avenue and up Ninth Avenue to Broadway for lunch at **RAVENOUS**. Go back down the hill to marvel at the **TACOMA ART MUSEUM** and be amazed at the possibilities of glass at the **MUSEUM OF GLASS INTERNATIONAL CENTER FOR CONTEMPORARY ART**. Check in at the Sheraton and catch your breath with a glass of wine in the Lobby Atrium. Feast downtown at **SEA GRILL**.

DAY TWO: Enjoy breakfast at the Broadway Grill, then continue museum touring at the **KARPELES MANUSCRIPT MUSEUM**. Cross the street and visit the **SEYMOUR BOTANICAL CONSERVATORY** (316 S G St; 253/591-5330) in **WRIGHT PARK**. Drive back down the hill to the **WORKING WATERFRONT MUSEUM**, then drive south on Dock Street to the **BLUE OLIVE ULTRA LOUNGE & BISTRO** for lunch. Make arrangements in advance for the guided tour, then drive less than 13 miles to **LEMAY: AMERICA'S CAR MUSEUM** (423 152nd St E; www.lemaymuseum.com), where 400 vintage vehicles await. Return downtown to check into the **MARRIOTT COURTYARD** and indulge in a massage in the hotel's **AVANTI SPA** (1506 Pacific Ave; 253/682-2005). Have dinner at **INDOCHINE**. Consider taking in a show at one of three downtown theaters in **BROADWAY PLAZA** (www.broadwaycenter.org).

DAY THREE: Enjoy breakfast at the Marriott, then visit **POINT DEFIANCE ZOO & AQUARIUM**—a living museum. Have lunch at the **LOBSTER SHOP** (4015 Ruston Way; 253/759-2165), then walk the 2-mile **RUSTON WAY WATERFRONT** promenade. Return to the Marriott for a relaxing swim before dining downstairs at **PACIFIC GRILL** (1502 Pacific Ave; 253/627-3535).

the **HARMON** brew pub (1938 Pacific Ave; 383-2739) and the **SWISS PUB** (1904 S Jefferson Ave; 253/572-2821), where you can choose from 36 drafts.

Besides the Sheraton Tacoma (1320 Broadway Plaza) and Courtyard by Marriott (see review) downtown—and the Silver Cloud Inn (2317 N Ruston Way) on the waterfront—Tacoma offers several quality B and Bs and inns.

Learn more at the **TACOMA–PIERCE COUNTY CONVENTION AND VISITOR BUREAU** (1119 Pacific Ave, 5th floor; 253/627-2836; www.traveltacoma.com).

RESTAURANTS

Asado / ★★⯪

2810 6TH AVE, TACOMA; 253/272-7770

Cowhide-backed booths, enormous longhorns, and the aroma of mesquite wood set the tone for experiencing "Cucina Argentina"—a savory combination of French, Italian, and Spanish flavors. *Asado* means "roasted meat," and Black Angus beef is prized here, but seafood, pork, and chicken are also grilled to perfection. Many of the entrées are accented with delectable sauces and salsas such as *chimichurri*. The staff is competent and confident; trust their recommendations. *$$–$$$; AE, DC, DIS, JCB, MC, V; checks OK; dinner every day; full bar; reservations recommended; www.asadotacoma.com; between Pine and Anderson sts.* &

Blue Olive Ultra Lounge & Bistro / ★★

1715 DOCK ST, TACOMA; 253/383-7275

The focal point of this ultracool spot on Thea Foss Waterway is a brilliant neon-blue bar dividing the pan-Asian restaurant from the lounge. During early evening, the scene is mellow under cream-colored pomander lights absorbed by burnished copper walls. Seating near the picture windows affords a grand view of Mount Rainier. The energy increases at about 9pm, with live bands on Friday nights and DJs on others. *$$–$$$; AE, B, DC, DIS, E, JCB, MC, V; local checks only; lunch Wed–Sat, dinner every day; full bar; reservations recommended; www.blueolive.net; next door to Museum of Glass.* &

El Gaucho / ★★★

2119 PACIFIC AVE, TACOMA; 253/272-1510

The dramatic entrance to this glamorous steak house promises a perfect evening, and the El Gaucho team delivers. Tableside-tossed caesar salad, chateaubriand for two, and showy flaming shish kebabs are trademark items on the pricey menu. Tables in the sunken dining room are closer to the red tufted bar, grand piano, and open grill, but a table on the mezzanine lets you enjoy a view of it all. *$$$; AE, DIS, MC, V; checks OK; dinner every day; full bar; reservations recommended; www.elgaucho.com; in museum district.* &

Indochine / ★★

1924 PACIFIC AVE, TACOMA; 253/272-8200

Half a block before you reach the ornate doors of this exotic Southeast Asian restaurant, you'll smell basil, curry, and jasmine. On your first visit, sit at one of the Brazilian cherrywood tables beside the reflecting pond. The menu is overwhelming, so zero in on the house specialties: the best Thai, Vietnamese, and Chinese recipes combined to create treasures like the Black Sea—a mound of seafood tossed with nutty *kala masala* and coconut milk over black rice. A second, smaller, dressed-down location (2045 Mildred St W, Fircrest; 253/564-9409) is also reliable. *$$–$$$; AE, MC, V; no checks; lunch, dinner Mon–Sat; full bar; reservations recommended; just before 21st St.* &

Sea Grill / ★★★

1498 PACIFIC AVE, STE 300, TACOMA; 253/272-5656

Sea Grill is owned by the same folks who own El Gaucho and the Waterfront Seafood Grill in Seattle. Glass walls and copper-leaved chandeliers adorn the spacious dining room that flows into a circular bar. Come here for seafood and steaks: the all-out indulgence is Seafood Bacchanalia. Steaks are prepared on an open-pit charcoal grill in the exhibition kitchen. Stay long enough for someone to order the Mount Rainier Volcano: this version of baked Alaska, complete with chocolate lava, is flambéed tableside. *$$$–$$$$; AE, B, DC, DIS, E, JCB, MC, V; checks OK; lunch Mon–Fri, dinner Mon–Sat; full bar; reservations recommended; www.the-seagrill.com; at 15th St.* &

21 Commerce / ★★

21ST AND COMMERCE STS, TACOMA; 253/272-6278

This swank restaurant in the historic warehouse district now sports a brushed-chrome bar and tables along floor-to-ceiling windows. Behind the bar, birchwood booths rest against the original exposed-brick wall. Inside this contrasted setting, chef Donny Wong's creative team orchestrates Asian fusion surprises like the Thai chicken quesadilla and hoisin barbecue salmon. Other highlights are the crab cakes and scallops in a sweet-and-sour sesame sauce. Martinis are a draw, with 21 to choose from. *$$–$$$; AE, MC, V; checks OK; dinner Tues–Sat; full bar; reservations recommended; www.21martinis. com; downtown.* &

LODGINGS

Marriott Courtyard / ★★

1515 COMMERCE ST, TACOMA; 253/591-9100

Warm reds and golden hues are accented with black scrollwork in this cozy hotel that brings 156 more rooms within walking distance of three museums and downtown's finest restaurants. Business guests appreciate the library and in-room technology features. Families enjoy the indoor pool and adjacent $5 million city park and amphitheater. Avanti Spa, designed to resemble an Ital ian village, shares hotel space on two floors. *$$$; AE, DC, DIS, MC, V; checks OK; www.marriott.com/seatd; exit 133 from I-5 to city center, exit at 15th St, uphill a block, left on Commerce St.* &

Thornewood Castle B&B / ★★★

8601 N THORNE LANE, LAKEWOOD; 253/584-4393

You'll feel like royalty in this enormous Gothic-Tudor manor where richly paneled rooms are furnished with leather sofas, antique chests, and portraits of aristocrats. This mansion on 4 acres was the setting for the miniseries *Rose Red* by Stephen King. Eight of the 22 bedrooms are now used as guest rooms. Most have stained-glass windows, some have fireplaces, others have soaking

tubs. The half-acre Olmstead-designed English garden is lovely. *$$$–$$$$;*
AE, DIS, MC, V; checks OK (in advance); www.thornewoodcastle.com; exit
123 from I-5 to Thorne Lane.

The Villa / ★★

705 N 5TH ST, TACOMA; 253/572-1157 OR 888/572-1157
This large Mediterranean-style villa can fool you into thinking the sun is shin-
ing even on cloudy days. Five colorful rooms trimmed in white add to the
faraway feeling, but you're actually only 2 miles from downtown. There's foot-
thick walls between rooms, luxurious downy beds and fireplaces, and wine on
the tiled patio bordered by flowers. Breakfast can be delivered, or join others at
the rustic table in the sunny dining room. *$$$–$$$$; AE, DIS, MC, V; checks
OK; www.villabb.com; exit 133 from I-5 to city center, at G St.* ⅖

Gig Harbor

The tranquility of this picture-perfect fishing village will undoubtedly be disturbed
by the addition of a second Narrows bridge. While it's hard to say how many
motorists will leave State Route 16 to venture into downtown Gig Harbor, boat
traffic is expected to remain as busy as ever. Good anchorage and various moorage
docks continue to attract gunwale-to-gunwale pleasure craft. The harbor is still
the life of the town, and you'll find bookstores, boutiques, bakeries, and a wild-
birdfeed store along Harborview Drive, which almost encircles the bay.

Sea-kayaking classes from **GIG HARBOR KAYAK CENTER** (8809 N Harborview
Dr; 253/851-7987 or 888/429-2548) are fun; rental boats are available, and you
can explore the bay in a few hours or sign up for a tour that takes you farther.

Gig Harbor is a good place for celebrations. An arts festival in mid-July, a
maritime festival in June, and a Scandinavian Fest in October are main events, but
check the events calendar at the **GIG HARBOR CHAMBER OF COMMERCE** (3302
Harborview Dr; 253/851-6865; www.gigharborchamber.com) for others. The
Saturday **GIG HARBOR FARMERS MARKET** (www.gigharborfarmersmarket.com;
mid-Apr–Oct) overflows.

KIMBALL ESPRESSO (6950 Kimball Dr; 253/858-2625) is a nice place for a
snack, and it doubles as a gallery. Several restaurants along the harbor offer quick
bites and sit-down dinners. Locals love **BRIX 25** (7707 Pioneer Way; 253/858-6626;
www.harborbrix.com), **EL PUEBLITO** (3226 Harborview Dr; 253/858-9077), and
JUDSON STREET CAFÉ (3114 Judson St; 253/858-1176). The **MARITIME INN**
(3212 Harborview Dr; 253/858-1818; ww.maritimeinn.com) is in the heart of
downtown but can be noisy. The **BEST WESTERN WESLEY INN** (6575 Kimball Dr;
253/858-9690 or 888/462-0002; www.wesleyinn.com) up the hill has a pool.

PENINSULA GARDENS NURSERY (5503 Wollochet Dr NW; 253/851-8115)
southwest of town is fun to explore. Just outside Gig Harbor there are three parks
with beaches where clam digging is sometimes allowed: **KOPACHUCK STATE PARK**
(follow signs from SR 16; 253/265-3606), **PENROSE POINT STATE PARK**, and

JOEMMA STATE PARK, both on the Key Peninsula (south of SR 302, west of SR 16 at Purdy). You can also easily reach the beach at the Purdy Spit.

RESTAURANTS

The Green Turtle / ★★

2905 HARBORVIEW DR, GIG HARBOR; 253/851-3167
This unassuming, fun, and funky little restaurant is still considered one of Gig Harbor's finest. Asian, French, and Northwest combinations like Dungeness crab–stuffed mahi mahi and ginger- and wasabi-topped yellowfin ahi are our favorites. You wouldn't guess from the humble parking lot that the view from the deck, and even inside the dining room, is the best in the harbor. *$$–$$$; AE, DIS, MC, V; checks OK; lunch Mon–Fri, dinner Tues–Sun; beer and wine; reservations recommended; www.thegreenturtle.com; past Tides Tavern away from downtown.* &

Tides Tavern / ★

2925 HARBORVIEW DR, GIG HARBOR; 253/858-3982
The Tides is a landmark in Gig Harbor—which probably accounts for the overpriced fare. People come by boat, seaplane, and car to this gathering place on the water. The stellar pub fare is responsible for the packed house most nights, especially on the deck in summer. An older crowd dominates during lunch, but the younger set turns out in numbers at night. In fact, the energy level elevates around the pool table, on the deck, and in front of the television. Live bands on the weekends add to the excitement. *$–$$; AE, MC, V; checks OK; lunch, dinner every day; beer and wine; reservations recommended; www.tidestavern.com; downtown.*

LODGINGS

The Inn at Gig Harbor / ★★

3211 56TH ST NW, GIG HARBOR; 253/858-1111
This serene Craftsman-style inn with 64 rooms and suites is just 2 miles from the Narrows bridge, but it feels miles away from the fray. Eight types of rooms are available, including king suites with Jacuzzis, queen suites with fireplaces, and kitchenette units. Views of Mount Rainier are a bonus in the back, but it's quieter in front. Spend a few minutes looking at the black-and-white historic photos of Gig Harbor on the walls of each level. The theme flows into the Heritage Inn Restaurant, where you should have a bowl of the award-winning clam chowder. *$$–$$$; AE, DC, DIS, JCB, MC, V; checks OK; www.innatgigharbor.com; 2 miles west of Narrows bridge, exit 10, left above overpass, right at Pt Fosdick Dr, 1 mile up on right.* &

Puyallup

This farm town is best known as the place where you "do the Puyallup." Few would argue that the Western Washington Fair has brought fame and fortune to this rapidly growing town, but an unfortunate by-product is traffic congestion. State Route 161 to the south is frenetic, so head east up the valley to Sumner and the White River (State Route 410) or to Orting, Wilkeson, and Carbonado (State Routes 162 and 165). If your destination is Mount Rainier through this gateway, State Route 410 leads to Chinook Pass and State Routes 162 and 165 lead to the Carbon River and Mowich Lake entrances.

The **EZRA MEEKER MANSION** (312 Spring St; 253/848-1770; www.meeker mansion.org; 12pm–4pm Wed–Sun) is the finest original pioneer mansion left in Washington. Its builder and first occupant, Ezra Meeker, introduced hops to the Puyallup Valley. His lavish 17-room Italianate house (circa 1890) has been beautifully restored.

Puyallup is big on old-time seasonal celebrations; it hosts two of the Northwest's largest: April's **DAFFODIL FESTIVAL AND PARADE** (253/863-9524) and September's Western Washington Fair—better known as the **PUYALLUP FAIR** (110 9th Ave SW; 253/841-5045; www.thefair.com)—one of the nation's biggest fairs, with food, games, rides, and premier touring bands. The **PUYALLUP DOWNTOWN FARMERS MARKET** (www.puyallupmainstreet.com) is held Saturday mornings at **PIONEER PARK** (corner of Pioneer and Meridian sts) and runs through the growing season (usually late May–Sept).

Learn more about Puyallup at the **CHAMBER OF EASTERN PIERCE COUNTY** (47 E Pioneer St; 253/845-6755; www.puyallupchamber.com).

Parkland

Located between Puyallup and Lakewood on State Route 512, this suburb south of Tacoma is home to Pacific Lutheran University.

RESTAURANTS

From the Bayou / ★★

508 GARFIELD ST, PARKLAND; 253/539-4269
Four former school friends from Louisiana launched this Parkland restaurant, which has claimed a loyal following. The smoked-salmon cheesecake appetizer is unexpectedly addictive. Then there's a tantalizing array of Cajun food such as gumbo and alligator. Even the stuffed-halibut entrée—or praline cream pie—is worth the trip. The setting is a bonus, too, with zydeco music and black-and-white photos of Acadian villages. $–$$; AE, DIS, V; checks OK; lunch, dinner Tues–Sat; beer and wine; reservations recommended; www.fromthebayou. com; SR 512 E exit from I-5, then Pacific Ave exit to Parkland. &

Marzano's / ★★

516 GARFIELD ST, PARKLAND; 253/537-4191

People drive from miles around to experience Lisa Marzano's Italian specialties. It's not unusual to have to book two or three weeks out on weekends. Outside seating on two deck areas is a plus; opt for deck seating when the weather cooperates. For entrées, try the tortellini Aurora or gnocchi Veronese. Finish with the *canola rustica. $$; AE, DIS, MC, V; checks OK; lunch Tues–Fri, dinner Tues–Sat; beer and wine; reservations recommended; SR 512 exit from I-5, adjacent to Pacific Lutheran University.* &

Steilacoom and Anderson Island

This little community at the edge of the water was once a Native American village, then became Washington Territory's first incorporated town, in 1854. Steilacoom prides itself on its heritage and encourages walking tours of its historic homes. Many of the houses include placards that list the construction date and original owners' names. The **STEILACOOM TRIBAL MUSEUM** (1515 Lafayette St; 253/584-6308) is a turn-of-the-19th-century church overlooking the South Sound islands and the Olympic range. October's **APPLE SQUEEZE FESTIVAL** (www.steilacoom. org/museum/) and midsummer's Salmon Bake, with canoe and kayak races, are good reasons to pay a visit. **PIERCE COUNTY FERRIES** (253/798-2766 recording; www.co.pierce.wa.us/) run from here to Anderson Island. Reach Steilacoom via Steilacoom Boulevard off Interstate 5 at exit 128. Visitor information is at **CITY HALL** (1717 Lafayette St; 253/851-1900; www.steilacoom.org).

LODGINGS

Anderson House on Oro Bay / ★★

12024 ECKENSTAM-JOHNSON RD, ANDERSON ISLAND; 253/884-4088

A visit to this country inn has all the hallmarks of a trip to grandma's house: hardwood floors, patchwork quilts, a breezy porch, and the smell of fresh-baked bread. Four rooms, all with private baths, are available in this farmhouse. For decompressing, there's the garden, the pasture, and the 200 acres of woods. You can fish, comb the beach, bicycle, or play nine holes at the nearby Riviera Community Club. Call for a pickup at the ferry landing, or use the dock if you're arriving by water. *$$–$$$; MC, V; checks OK; www. non.com/anderson/house; call for directions.*

Olympia

This tidy and unpretentious capital city is an undiscovered gem. Walkers love the paths around the grounds of the capital campus and Capitol Lake, along the Puget Sound waterfront, and through downtown. Excellent restaurants, a thriving arts community, and the renowned Evergreen State College contribute to Olympia's appeal.

The state capital's centerpiece—visible from the freeway—is the classic dome of the **WASHINGTON STATE LEGISLATURE BUILDING** (416 14th Ave; 360/902-8880). This striking Romanesque structure houses the office of the governor and other executives. Hourlong guided tours are offered every day; maps are provided for self-guided tours; tours of the red-brick **GOVERNOR'S MANSION** are on Wednesday afternoons (360/902-8880; reservations required). The **STATE CAPITOL MUSEUM** (211 W 21st Ave; 360/753-2580; www.wshs.org/wscm) houses a permanent exhibit documenting the state's political past. The **WASHINGTON STATE LIBRARY** (6880 Capitol Blvd S, Tumwater; 360/753-5592; www.statelib.wa.gov) is open to the public during business hours. Downtown, on Seventh Avenue between Washington and Franklin streets, you'll find the restored **OLD CAPITOL**, with pointed towers and high-arched windows.

The **WASHINGTON CENTER FOR THE PERFORMING ARTS** (on Washington St between 5th Ave and Legion Way; 360/753-8586; www.washingtoncenter.org) is home to more than a dozen performance groups. Across Fifth Avenue, the **CAPITOL THEATER** (206 E 5th Ave; 360/754-5378) provides a forum for the active **OLYMPIA FILM SOCIETY** (360/754-6670; www.olyfilm.org) and locally produced plays and musicals.

A few blocks from the heart of downtown, **CAPITOL LAKE** offers picturesque vantage points of the capitol and grassy areas for picnics and play, as well as a trail that encircles most of the lake. After a walk, treat yourself to award-winning peach cobbler at the **SOUTHERN KITCHEN RESTAURANT** (601 Capitol Way S) in the Ramada Inn, fitted between the lake and **HERITAGE PARK** in the town square.

Toward the harbor, the colorful **OLYMPIA FARMERS MARKET** (near Percival Landing; 360/352-9096; www.farmers-market.org; Thurs–Sun Apr–Oct, Sat–Sun Nov–Dec up to Christmas) displays produce, flowers, and crafts from all over the South Sound. The waterfront park at **PERCIVAL LANDING** (700 N Capitol Way) is the site of several harbor festivals.

In another part of downtown, adjacent to City Hall, is the serene **YASHIRO JAPANESE GARDEN** (off Plum St exit from I-5), honoring one of Olympia's sister cities. The historic heart of the area—Olympia, Lacey, and Tumwater—is **TUMWATER FALLS** (exit 103 off I-5), where the Deschutes River flows into Capitol Lake. A nice walk along the river takes you past waterfalls.

THE EVERGREEN STATE COLLEGE (2700 Evergreen Pkwy NW; 360/866-6000; www.evergreen.edu), west of Olympia on Cooper Point, offers a regular schedule of plays, films, experimental theater, and special events. The library and pool are open to the public.

The Nisqually Delta, an outlet of the Nisqually River that forms at the foot of a Mount Rainier glacier, is the area's finest nature preserve. It enters Puget Sound just north of Olympia at the **NISQUALLY NATIONAL REFUGE** (exit 114 off I-5, follow signs; 360/753-9467; www.fws.gov/nisqually). A 5-mile hiking trail follows an old dike around the delta.

More information is at the **OLYMPIA–THURSTON COUNTY VISITOR AND CONVENTION BUREAU** (1600 E 4th Ave; 360/704-7544 or 877/704-7500; www.visitolympia.com).

RESTAURANTS

Cielo Blu / ★★

514 CAPITOL WAY S, OLYMPIA; 360/352-8007
This new eatery from the owners of the former Capitale Restaurant exudes energy, which may be why it's a favorite for legislators. The coppery-orange and green decor is a nice complement to the intense Asian, Italian, and Spanish creations like black bean ravioli topped with chipotle-lime cream, tomatillo salsa, and cilantro crème. Another spicy treasure is the cilantro crusted grilled prawns with capellini and a creamy chile vinaigrette. Many of the sauces and garnishes are spicy. *$$; AE, B, DC, DIS, E, JCB, MC, V; checks OK; lunch Tues–Fri, dinner Mon–Sat; full bar; reservations recommended; www. cieloblufusion.com; near 5th Ave.* &

The Mark / ★★⯪

407 COLUMBIA ST, OLYMPIA; 360/754-4414
Red velvet draperies, black leather booths, and leopard-print upholstery give this chic restaurant and nightclub attitude and style. This is the kind of place writers love during the day. Businesspeople come for lunch, and at night, all types enjoy the live music inside and a DJ outside. But the food, which emphasizes French and Spanish cheeses, olives, and breads, is the draw for those who appreciate sophisticated fare. The handmade pastas are excellent, and pappardelle with artichoke is a favorite. *$$–$$$; AE, DIS, MC, V; checks OK; lunch, dinner Thurs–Sat; full bar; reservations recommended; www.the markolympia.com; between 4th and 5th aves.* &

Ristorante Basilico / ★★

507 CAPITOL WAY S, OLYMPIA; 360/570-8777
The affection Olympia has for the two Italian men who own and operate this restaurant is mutual, evidenced by the exchange of hearty hugs patrons give and receive. Word-of-mouth recommendations are spreading like wildfire as visitors to this warm, friendly ristorante discover how simply elegant Northern Italian cuisine can be. Filet mignon, seasoned only with truffle salt, is tender. Hand-rolled pasta offerings include Maltagliati All'Antica con Pesto, with only a hint of garlic. *$$–$$$; AE, B, DC, DIS, E, JCB, MC, V; checks OK; lunch, dinner Mon–Sat; full bar; reservations recommended; between 5th Ave and Legion Way.* &

Trinacria / ★★

113 CAPITOL WAY S, OLYMPIA; 360/352-8892
You can easily imagine Lady and the Tramp taking a table nearby to enjoy their plate of spaghetti in this sweet restaurant. Eugenio Aliotta, the Sicilian owner of this pizzeria, has been a legend in Olympia since 1989, but few outsiders know about his light hand with pizza and pasta. The favorite is his Sicilian pizza, folded over like a large calzone. The traditional ragù and Parmesan is simple and delicious. The Italian music near the kitchen is loud, so

sit near the front. *$–$$; no credit cards; checks OK; lunch, dinner Tues–Sat; beer and wine; reservations recommended; at 4th Ave.* &

Waterstreet Café / ★★

610 WATER ST SW, OLYMPIA; 360/709-9090
Like the mix that is Olympia, this café and bar facing Capitol Lake caters to a variety of interests. Pale ale and pizza share table space with pinot noir and filet mignon. The setting is laid-back, despite upscale decor: calla lilies and candlelight, ornate chandeliers and Oriental rugs. The menu includes café staples kicked up a notch: we loved the shrimp empanadas. Sauces are abundant, like the tomato-arugula purée adorning lobster ravioli with tiger shrimp. *$$–$$$; AE, B, DC, DIS, E, JCB, MC, V; checks OK; lunch, dinner every day; full bar; no reservations; www.waterstreetcafeolympia.com; behind Ramada Inn, facing Capitol Lake.* &

LODGINGS

Fertile Ground Guesthouse / ★

311 9TH AVE SE, OLYMPIA; 360/754-0389
This B and B is making its mark in the South Sound as an excellent example of green lodgings. During your stay with owners Karen Nelson and Gail Sullivan, you'll experience organic cotton linens on futons, organic soaps and shampoos, and an all-organic breakfast. The room downstairs has a shower, and the larger upstairs room offers a roomy claw-foot bathtub. Take time to explore their enormous herbicide- and pesticide-free garden, where they'll harvest ingredients for breakfast: waffles with fruit, huevos rancheros, or omelets with eggs from their free-range chickens—and free-trade coffee, of course. *$$; MC, V; checks OK; www.fertileground.org; between Adams and Franklin sts across from library.*

Yelm and Tenino

Yelm is home to the **OUTBACK BOUTIQUE** (207 1st St S; 877/458-4618; www. outbackboutique.com), an oasis of antiques, linens, gifts, clothes, and personal indulgences displayed in dozens of creative settings under one large roof, easily identifiable by the purple and white striped awning. If you're on your way to Mount Rainier, **ARNOLD'S COUNTRY INN** (717 Yelm Ave E; 360/458-3977) serves breakfast, lunch, and dinner. This still rural but steadily growing area south of Olympia on State Route 507 is known for **WOLF HAVEN** (3111 Offut Lake Rd, Tenino; 360/264-4695; www.wolfhaven.org), a sanctuary for captive-born wolves that offers public tours. Tenino is also known for the country-dining destination **ALICE'S RESTAURANT** (19248 Johnson Creek Rd SE; 360/264-2887; www.alicesdinners.com).

OLYMPIC AND KITSAP PENINSULAS

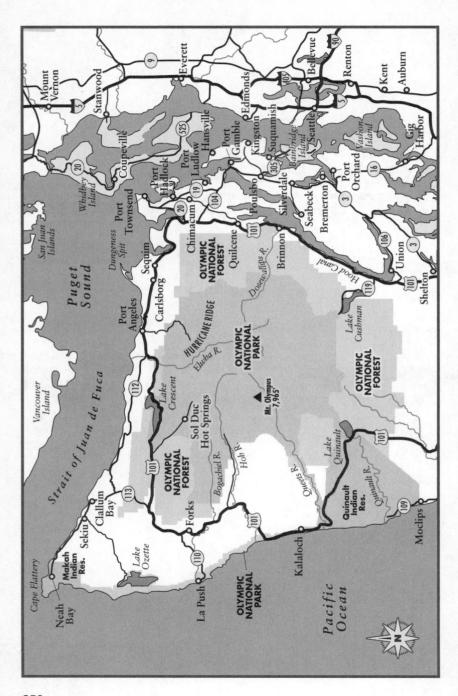

OLYMPIC AND KITSAP PENINSULAS

The wonders of the Olympic and Kitsap peninsulas draw visitors from all over the world. The scenery throughout the entire 5,000 square miles of the peninsulas is diverse. In Kitsap County, you'll see up-and-coming Bremerton, get caught up in Poulsbo's Scandinavian atmosphere, and ponder history through the dollhouse homes in the historic mill town of Port Gamble. Then cross the Hood Canal Bridge to the Olympic Peninsula's farmland, forests, crashing swells, and the charming town of Port Townsend.

United States Highway 101 wraps snugly around an empire built and ruled by Mother Nature. In the center, Olympic National Park is home to 1,200 plant species, 300 bird species, and 70 different kinds of mammals. The park's mountainous terrain blends with an ocean landscape and a temperate rain forest, giving the impression of three parks rolled into one. More than 5 million people every year come to soak in the hot springs, wander the forest, hug the 250- to 500-year-old fir and cedar trees, and sneak a peek at wildlife adept at the art of camouflage.

ACCESS AND INFORMATION

The best route to the Kitsap and Olympic peninsulas is the **WASHINGTON STATE FERRIES** (206/464-6400 or 800/843-3779; www.wsdot.wa.gov/ferries), which run regularly between downtown Seattle and Bremerton on the Kitsap Peninsula or Bainbridge Island, gateway to both peninsulas. Ferries also dock in Port Townsend (from Keystone on Whidbey Island) on the Olympic Peninsula, in Kingston (from Edmonds) on the Kitsap Peninsula, and in Southworth (from Fauntleroy in West Seattle), near Port Orchard on the Kitsap Peninsula.

You can also drive around Puget Sound on **INTERSTATE 5** through Tacoma to reach the Kitsap Peninsula via the Narrows Bridge or through Olympia and Shelton to reach the Olympic Peninsula.

You can reach Port Angeles on the Olympic Peninsula by boat from Victoria, British Columbia. The MV *Coho*, operated by **BLACK BALL TRANSPORTATION** (360/457-4491; www.ferrytovictoria.com), runs daily with a 1½-hour crossing; the much quicker **VICTORIA EXPRESS** (360/452-8088 or 800/633-1589; www.victoriaexpress.com) is a foot-passenger ferry that runs daily, summer and fall.

Public bus transportation between communities is available through **KITSAP TRANSIT** (360/373-BUSS or 800/501-RIDE), **JEFFERSON COUNTY TRANSIT AND WEST JEFFERSON TRANSIT** (360/385-4777 or 800/371-0497), **CLALLAM TRANSIT SYSTEM** (360/452-4511 or 800/858-3747), and **MASON COUNTY TRANSIT AUTHORITY** (360/426-9434 or 800/281-9434).

Small planes land at airports in Bremerton, Jefferson County, Shelton, Sequim, and Port Angeles. The largest airline to serve the peninsula is **HORIZON AIR** (800/547-9308; www.horizonair.com), which lands at Fairchild International Airport in Port Angeles.

For information, contact the **PORT TOWNSEND CHAMBER OF COMMERCE VISITOR INFORMATION CENTER** (2437 E Sims Way; 360/385-2722 or 888/ENJOYPT; www.ptchamber.org) or the **NORTH OLYMPIC PENINSULA VISITOR & CONVENTION BUREAU** (360/452-8552 or 800/942-4042; www.olympicpeninsula.org/) in Port Angeles.

Bainbridge Island

Some people consider Bainbridge an extension of Seattle—it's just a 30-minute ferry ride away. Once a major logging port, it's now a haven for city professionals, writers, and artists. It makes a pleasant tour by car or bike, during which you can see some farms, waterfront homes, and spectacular cityscapes—especially from **FAY-BAINBRIDGE STATE PARK** (Sunrise Dr NE; 888/226-7688) on the northeast corner of the island. The wooded and waterfront trails in **FORT WARD STATE PARK** (along Rich Passage, 6 miles from ferry terminal; 888/226-7688), on the south end of the island, make a nice afternoon stroll.

BLOEDEL RESERVE (7571 NE Dolphin Dr; 206/842-7631; www.bloedel reserve.org) is 150 acres of gardens, woods, meadows, and ponds. Plants from all over the world make the grounds interesting to tour at any time of the year.

For a relaxing day, ride the ferry and walk up to the **BAINBRIDGE ISLAND WINERY** (8989 Day Rd E; 206/842-9463; www.bainbridgevineyards.com), then walk into downtown, take in the shops, have coffee at **PEGASUS ESPRESSO HOUSE** (206/842-6725), and float back to Seattle.

RESTAURANTS

Madoka / ★★★⯪

241 WINSLOW WAY W, BAINBRIDGE ISLAND; 206/842-2448
This is a new pan-Pacific restaurant on a quiet street. Its chef left some top Seattle restaurants for a more laid-back lifestyle, and he's found it here. Visit Madoka for dishes like Penn Cove mussels steamed with green curry, coconut milk, and basil or a seafood risotto with prawns and salmon. The golden wall at the door contrasts with the restaurant's spare black interior. Overlapping red and orange spirals cover the cushions, and there's a red wall on the stairs to the upper loft dining area. Sumptuous. *$$$; AE, MC, V; no checks; lunch Wed–Sat, dinner Wed–Mon; full bar; reservations recommended; www. madokaonbainbridge.com; downtown Winslow.*

Kitsap Peninsula

The Kitsap Peninsula, between the larger Olympic Peninsula and the mainland, is roughly defined by Puget Sound (and Bainbridge and Vashon islands) on the east and by Hood Canal on the west. Connected to the Olympic Peninsula by a small stretch of land at the southern end of Hood Canal, the Kitsap Peninsula links to the mainland of Western Washington via the Tacoma Narrows Bridge. The Hood Canal Bridge connects Kitsap's northern end to the Olympic Peninsula.

Belfair

This small town on the northern side of the narrow belt of land connecting the Kitsap and Olympic peninsulas is on State Route 3 between Shelton and Port Orchard.

LODGINGS

Selah Inn / ★★

NE 130 DULALIP LANDING, BELFAIR; 360/275-0916
Just a stone's throw from crystal-clear Hood Canal, Selah Inn is great for couples, families, and events. Rent the main inn (four bedrooms), two cottages (two bedrooms with kitchens), an apartment rental (one bedroom with kitchenette), or the beachfront Canal House (three bedrooms). It all feels like home—except for the seals and oysters. Dinners are available. *$$–$$$; MC, V; checks OK; www.selahinn.com; southern end of Hood Canal.*

Port Orchard

This small town on Sinclair Inlet has a busy marina and a quaint waterfront feel. The main boardwalk on Bay Street is lined with antique shops, restaurants, and art galleries. **SIDNEY ART GALLERY AND MUSEUM** (202 Sidney Ave; 360/876-3693) and **BETHEL AVENUE BOOK COMPANY** (1140 Bethel Ave; 360-876-7500) are two good stops. The **PORT ORCHARD FARMERS MARKET** (Marina Park, 1 block from Bay St; 360/871-5463; Sat late Apr–Oct) grows each year.

   KITSAP FERRY COMPANY (360/377-7279; www.kitsapferryco.com) operates a daily foot ferry between downtown Port Orchard and the main ferry terminal at Bremerton. Or take the Fauntleroy ferry from Seattle to Southworth and drive State Route 160 west. Otherwise, drive north on State Route 3 from Shelton or north on State Route 16 from Tacoma.

RESTAURANTS

Cosmos Ristorante & Delicatessen / ★★

1821 LUND AVE, PORT ORCHARD; 360/895-3138
This Italian restaurant is next door to an office supply store in a bright pink building. But overlook that. Cosmos features rustic Italian food—with recipes from the co-owner's Italian mom—in the front of the building and a well-stocked gourmet deli (closed Sunday) in back. Portions are huge and delicious, and the atmosphere is cozy. *$$; MC, V; local checks only; lunch Mon–Sat, dinner every day; full bar; reservations recommended; www.cosmos deli.com; south side of Port Orchard.*

OLYMPIC PENINSULA THREE-DAY TOUR

DAY ONE: Begin in Port Townsend. First, stop by the **VISITORS CENTER** on State Route 20 and pick up maps of the vicinity. Then start your day off right at the **TYLER STREET COFFEE HOUSE** and indulge in one of the hand-twisted cinnamon braids and a cup of coffee. Walk it off by visiting the shops along Water Street, especially the **ANCESTRAL SPIRITS GALLERY** for authentic aboriginal and tribal arts and crafts. Next, take a driving tour—one map details a route and points out 72 Victorian structures to admire. Grab gourmet picnic food at **PROVISIONS** (939 Kearney St; 360/385-4541; www.provisionspt.com) and head to **FORT WORDEN STATE PARK**. Interact with sea creatures at the touch tanks at the **MARINE SCIENCE CENTER** before picnicking on the beach, then take a beach walk and explore the old gun batteries of the fort. Head back downtown to catch an early movie at the **ROSE THEATRE**, a refurbished architectural gem with undeniably the best popcorn anywhere. Have dinner at the **WILD COHO**, where dishes feature the in-season bounty of the Northwest. Spend the night at the impeccably furnished **JAMES HOUSE** bed-and-breakfast.

DAY TWO: After your B and B breakfast, stop by **SWEET LAURETTE & CYNDEE'S BISTRO AND CAFÉ** for French pastries to enjoy on the road. Head out of town on State Route 20 to US Highway 101 west toward Sequim. Take the Sequim Avenue exit into downtown Sequim and head to **MIKE'S BIKES** (150 W Sequim Bay Rd; 360/681-3868). Rent a mountain bike or city cruiser and hit the trails! Mike's is located adjacent to the **OLYMPIC DISCOVERY TRAIL** (360/683-7180;

One Ten Lounge / ★★★

110 HARRISON AVE, PORT ORCHARD; 360/895-3079
Frank Sinatra plays in the background, and the cha-cha sound of shaken martinis fills the air. This hip, new 1930s-style martini lounge is already a favorite. More than 30 cocktails are served, with fresh-squeezed ingredients and superior spirits. Notables are the Kamikaze and chocolate fudge martini. Small nibbles are served, but come here for the spirits, not the food. *$; MC, V; no checks; appetizers only every day; full bar; no reservations; downtown Port Orchard.*

LODGINGS

Reflections Bed and Breakfast Inn / ★★

3878 REFLECTION LANE E, PORT ORCHARD; 360/871-5582
This inn overlooking Sinclair Inlet has gardens with visiting birds, a gazebo, and a hot tub. Heirloom quilts grace the beds, and the house is filled with

www.olympicdiscoverytrail.com), one of the most popular trails in the area for recreational cycling. The car-free trail, much of it built on old railroad grade, stretches 22 miles to Port Angeles through farmland and forests. On your ride, check out an impressive local bird exhibit and get information on the flora and fauna of the Olympic Peninsula at the **DUNGENESS RIVER AUDUBON CENTER AT RAILROAD BRIDGE PARK** (2151 W Hendrickson Rd, Sequim; 360-681-4076). Stop at **SUNNY FARMS COUNTRY STORE**, *the* spot for picnic food, only a short detour from the trail about halfway between Sequim and Port Angeles. After a full day of biking, return to Sequim and check in at **COLETTE'S BED AND BREAKFAST** for true Northwest luxury, then drive to Port Angeles and go to dinner at **BELLA ITALIA**.

DAY THREE: After your breakfast at Colette's, continue west on US Highway 101 toward Forks. Stop in at **SOL DUC HOT SPRINGS** for a relaxing soak, and grab a bite for lunch in their lodge before you leave. Keep heading west on US Highway 101 and take State Routes 113 and 112 past Clallam Bay. Turn southwest onto the Hoko-Ozette Road for 21 miles until you reach the **OZETTE RANGER STATION**. There you will find wooded boardwalk trails, the **CAPE ALAVA TRAIL** and the **SAND POINT TRAIL**, which weave 3 miles through dense forest and high meadows leading to the beach. Be prepared to see seals, deer, eagles, otters, and perhaps whales. After your hike, drive back to US Highway 101 and continue south to Forks. Make a quick stop for groceries and head to the **SHADY NOOK COTTAGE**, where you can cook your own dinner and sleep.

colonial antiques. There are four guest rooms (two with private baths), and the owner serves a formal, multicourse breakfast. *$$; MC, V; no checks; www.reflectionsbnb.com; east of Port Orchard off Beach Dr.* &

Bremerton

Things are happening in this Navy town. Just on the cusp of being cool, Bremerton is experiencing an influx of people looking for metropolitan comforts without the traffic and smog. It's got a brand-new convention center, hotel, and city government center, and luxurious waterfront condominiums are replacing parking lots. It's no longer a secret: *Money* magazine calls it a future hot spot, and Mayor Cary Bozeman's ideas keep businesses pouring in. The once-dead downtown is perking up, with new restaurants slated soon.

The boardwalk has views of the **USS TURNER JOY** (300 Washington Beach Ave; 360/792-2457), and **BREMERTON'S NAVAL MUSEUM** (402 Pacific Ave; 360/479-7447) depicts the region's shipbuilding history. You can find the first Revolutionary

War submarine at the **NAVAL UNDERSEA MUSEUM** (10 Dowell St, Keyport; 360/396-4148; www.keyportmuseum.cnrnw.navy.mil).

For information on the **FIRST FRIDAY ART WALK** (downtown Bremerton), contact the **MADE IN BREMERTON STORE** (408 Pacific Ave; 360/782-1500). The **ADMIRAL THEATER** (515 Pacific Ave; 360/373-6743), a historic 1942 movie house, is the place to catch a live show. The **BOAT SHED** (101 Shore Dr; 360/377-2600), at the end of the Manette Bridge, is a great waterfront restaurant that's perfect for families.

Reach Bremerton by ferry from downtown Seattle's Pier 52. If you're driving from Poulsbo or Shelton, take State Route 3. From Tacoma or Seattle, take I-5 South to Highway 16, crossing the Tacoma Narrows Bridge.

RESTAURANTS

Anthony's Home Port Bremerton / ★★★

20 WASHINGTON AVE, BREMERTON; 360/337-5004
This is the first upscale restaurant Bremerton's seen in years. We know it's a 23-restaurant chain, but its fresh seafood is solid, and the view of Sinclair Inlet is stunning. Stop here for wild king salmon, local oysters, and Dungeness crab. *$$$; AE, MC, V; no checks; breakfast Sun, lunch, dinner every day; full bar; reservations recommended; www.anthonys.com; right off ferry dock.*

La Fermata / ★★★

2204 E 11TH ST, BREMERTON; 360/373-5927
Dark wood, warm candlelight, and sparkling wine glasses set the stage for intimate meals here, not to mention the fireplace, the bar, and fresh flowers adorning the tables in this tiny date spot. Besides ambience, La Fermata delivers flavor—Northern Italian with a Northwest twist. The menu changes monthly and includes seasonal greens and heirloom tomatoes in summer. *$$$; AE, MC, V; checks OK; dinner Tues–Sat; beer and wine; reservations recommended; across Manette Bridge.*

Simon August / ★★

1100 PERRY AVE, BREMERTON; 360/377-7357
This new fresh-food market and restaurant has baked goods, seasonal and organic produce, and grab-and-go meals like polenta, salad, and sandwiches. You'll know it when you arrive in Manette, Bremerton's cutest neighborhood. Crates of fresh produce are displayed on the sidewalk in front. Sit inside for a true European vibe. Owners Tim Waibel and Chris Bortisser hope to create a village feel. Also check out Augustino's (1223 McKenzie Ave; 360/377-7317), Waibel and Bortisser's new Mediterranean-Portuguese restaurant. *$; AE, DC, MC, V; checks OK; lunch, dinner Tues–Sun; beer and wine; no reservations; east of Manette Bridge.*

LODGINGS

Hampton Inn & Suites Bremerton / ★

150 WASHINGTON AVE, BREMERTON; 360/405-0200

Along with Anthony's and the new Bremerton Harborside Conference Center came this no-frills hotel. Rooms are big, simple, and comfortable, with views of the water; your stay includes free breakfast. *$$$; AE, DC, MC, V; no checks; hamptoninn.hilton.com; right off ferry dock.*

Illahee Manor / ★★★

6680 ILLAHEE RD NE, BREMERTON; 360/698-7555

This 6-acre property overlooking Port Orchard Bay has been in the same family since 1922. Five large rooms, each with a soaking tub and one with a sauna, are in the main house, and there are two cottages. Rooms are comfortable and decorated with antiques. A cascading waterfall tumbles throughout the property, where you'll see grazing llamas and deer. Take a trail to the beach after you enjoy the three-course breakfast prepared by a French-trained chef. *$$$; AE, DC, MC, V; checks OK; www.illaheemanor.com; across Manette Bridge in east Bremerton.*

Seabeck

This tiny community is on the east shore of Hood Canal northwest of Bremerton, near Scenic Beach State Park. Reach the town via Seabeck Highway from State Route 3.

LODGINGS

Willcox House / ★★★

2390 TEKIU RD, SEABECK; 360/830-4492 OR 800/725-9477

Clark Gable was a guest at this 10,000-square-foot mansion. Built in 1930 by Col. Julian Wilcox and his wife, Constance, the Wilcox House is full of history. Decorated in 1930s art deco, it could be the set of a silver-screen classic movie. Surrounded by towering trees, it overlooks Hood Canal 9 miles south of Seabeck; the grounds have ponds and English-style gardens. Breakfast is homemade, with many courses, and prix-fixe dinners are also available. *$$$; MC, V; checks OK; www.willcoxhouse.com; call for directions.*

Silverdale

North of Bremerton sits Silverdale, a shopping-mall city with a suburban feel, just off State Route 3.

RESTAURANTS

Bahn Thai / ★★☆

9811 MICKELBERRY RD, SILVERDALE; 360/698-3663
Traditional Thai-style cushions are popular here. Customers remove their shoes, cross their legs, and partake of exotic dishes. Bahn Thai serves authentic Thai flavors—bamboo strips, basil, lemongrass, galangal, and kaffir lime leaves. Choose from many vegetarian options and six different curries. *$; AE, DC, MC, V; local checks only; lunch Mon–Fri, dinner every day; beer and wine; no reservations; ½ block north of Bucklin Hill Rd.* &

Breezy Hill Bistro / ★★

3611 NW BUCKLIN HILL RD, SILVERDALE; 360/698-7197
This little bistro offers rich and creative French flavors—duck confit with a red wine poached pear, apple and Brie soup. The only thing lacking is ambience. The food's presentation is fab, but the dining room in a converted house with office carpet and vinyl benches just doesn't quite work. *$$$; AE, MC, V; no checks; lunch Tues–Fri, dinner Tues–Sat; beer and wine; reservations recommended; in West Silverdale off Silverdale Way.*

Waterfront Park Bakery & Café / ★★

3472 NW BYRON ST, SILVERDALE; 360/698-2991
Locals rave about this place, and many admit to making it a twice-a-day destination. Opened 15 years ago, Waterfront's motto is "The center of the known universe for Coffee and Comfort." It's kind of true. Everything here is made from scratch: fresh-baked pastries, crab-asparagus quiche, wraps, soups, sandwiches, and cookies. *$; MC, V; local checks only; breakfast, lunch Mon–Sat; no alcohol; no reservations; www.waterfrontbakery.com; old town Silverdale.*

LODGINGS

Silverdale Beach Hotel / ★★

3073 NW BUCKLIN HILL RD, SILVERDALE;
360/698-1000 OR 800/544-9799
This hotel recently went from rundown to renovated; now the entryway is bright and welcoming. The only thing keeping this hotel from a better rating is the size of the 151 rooms. Family fun includes a large indoor pool facing the water, a fitness center, a sauna, and tennis courts. *$$$; AE, DC, MC, V; no checks; www.silverdalebeachhotel.com; right off Silverdale Way.*

Suquamish

Suquamish is on the Port Madison Indian Reservation, via State Route 305 from either Bainbridge Island (follow signs past Agate Passage) or Poulsbo. The **SUQUAMISH MUSEUM** in the **TRIBAL CENTER** (15838 Sandy Hook Rd NE; 360/598-3311) is devoted to Puget Sound Salish Indian culture. Chief Sealth's (for whom Seattle was named) grave is located nearby in **OLD MAN HOUSE STATE PARK** (360/598-3311; www.stateparks.com).

Poulsbo

Known as "little Norway," Poulsbo has a history that is still apparent. Its architecture is modeled after the fjord villages of Norway; signs reading "Velkommen til Poulsbo" line Front Street, the main drag (aka State Route 305). The **LIBERTY BAY PARK**, downtown on the waterfront, is a great place to picnic. Rent a kayak from **OLYMPIC OUTDOOR CENTER** (18971 Front St; 360/697-6095 or 800/592-5983).

Pick up a book at **LIBERTY BAY BOOK** (18881-D Front St NE; 360/779-5909) and head to **POULSBOHEMIAN COFFEEHOUSE** (19003 Front St; 360/779-9199) to hang out in comfy living-room chairs. Stop by **CASA LUNA OF POULSBO** (18830 Front St; 360/779-7676) and get a mammoth burrito to go; appease your sweet tooth at **BOEHMS CHOCOLATE** (18864 Front St NE; 360/697-3318) or **SLUYS BAKERY** (18924 Front St NE; 360/779-2798).

RESTAURANTS

Molly Ward Gardens / ★★★

27462 BIG VALLEY RD, POULSBO; 360/779-4471
"The very best ingredients, simply prepared" is the motto of this intimate restaurant located on the outskirts of Poulsbo. Surrounded by organic gardens, this place has a whimsical bohemian feel and an eclectic collection of antique chandeliers. Every table is different. The menu—organic greens, local seafood, natural meats—is a rolling whiteboard that changes daily. Patio seating in the summer. *$$$; MC, V; checks OK; lunch Wed–Sat, dinner Tues–Sun, brunch Sun; full bar; reservations recommended; www.mollywardgardens. com; approx 3 miles south of Hood Canal Bridge off SR 3.*

Mor Mor Bistro Bar / ★★★

18820 FRONT ST NE, POULSBO; 360/697-3449
Mor Mor, which means "grandmother" in Norwegian, was recently opened by a young husband-and-wife team; black-and-white photos of the couple's grandmothers in their youth hang on the walls. The atmosphere is sophisticated but comfortable. Flavors and presentation are stellar. Try the grilled Oregon natural cheeseburger served on "Sluys Poulsbo Bread," fresh three-cheese ravioli, organic greens, and Quinault Bay razor clams. Head upstairs

and check out the Far-Mor ("grandfather") Wine Studio. *$$$; AE, MC, V; no checks; lunch, dinner Wed–Mon; full bar; reservations recommended; www. mormorbistro.com; west end of Front St.*

LODGINGS

Manor Farm Inn / ★★

26069 BIG VALLEY RD NE, POULSBO; 360/779-4628
Manor Farm is exactly that—a small gentleman's farm with horses, pigs, sheep, cows, chickens, and a trout pond. Each of seven rooms has a wood-burning fireplace, a private porch, and a king-sized bed. Four-course breakfasts are served (open to the public); guests who want to sleep in can get a tray of hot scones delivered to their door before breakfast. *$$$; AE, MC, V; checks OK; www.manorfarminn.com; off SR 305, half hour from Bainbridge ferry.*

Port Gamble

This picture-postcard town located on State Route 104 between Kingston and Hood Canal was built in the mid-19th century by the Pope & Talbot timber company. More than a dozen Victorian houses line the main street (Rainier Avenue), and a nice collection of shops make this a worthy place to peruse.

PORT GAMBLE MUSEUM (32400 Rainier Ave, in back of Port Gamble General Store; 360/297-8074) provides an in-depth history of the town. **RUGOSA ROSE** (32319 NE Rainier Ave; 360/297-2604) is a full-service florist. Give in to luxury at the **SPA AT PORT GAMBLE** (House 10, Rainier Ave; 360/297-8889).

PORT GAMBLE GENERAL STORE (32400 NE Rainier Ave; 360/297-7636) is packed with camping and fishing supplies; beer, wine, and a café are in back. **TEA ROOM AT PORT GAMBLE** (32279 Rainier Ave; 360/297-4225) is a nice place.

Hansville

Hansville, at the north end of Hansville Road NE via State Route 104 near Kingston, has a couple of the prettiest, most accessible, and least-explored beaches on the Kitsap Peninsula. **POINT NO POINT**, marked by a lighthouse, is great for a family outing. Follow the road from Hansville to the west, and you'll reach **CAPE FOULWEATHER** (via NE Twin Spits Rd). The short trail through the woods can be tough to find, so look for the Nature Conservancy sign on the south side of the road.

Hood Canal and NE Olympic Peninsula

US Highway 101 hugs the west side of Hood Canal through tiny towns with names like Lilliwaup, Duckabush, and Union; vacation homes line the miles of scenic shoreline. Sample the wines at **HOODSPORT WINERY** (N 23501 US Hwy 101; 360/877-9894).

Shelton

Once serious timber country—this logging community still sells thousands of Christmas trees a year—these days, Shelton is reinventing itself as a tourist destination. Located on US Highway 101 between Olympia and Hood Canal, Shelton sits on the shore of Oakland Bay, a far southwestern reach of Puget Sound.

Popular hangout **LYNCH CREEK FARM AND FLORAL** (331 W Railroad Ave; 360/426-8615) is a café and home decor store rolled into one. **SAGE BOOK STORE** (116 W Railroad Ave; 360/426-6011) has a fireplace, making it a cozy spot to browse. **LA FACTOR DAY SPA** (117 N 8th St; 360/427-3189), a recently opened full-service spa, is not what you'd expect in Shelton.

This stretch of highway also serves as the jumping-off spot for many recreational areas in the Olympic National Forest, including **LAKE CUSHMAN STATE PARK** (7211 N Lake Cushman Rd, Hoodsport).

RESTAURANTS

Travaglione's Ristorante Italiano / ★★

825 FRANKLIN ST, SHELTON; 360/427-3844
Pasta made in-house from an Italian family recipe makes this place a must-visit destination on the Olympic Peninsula. Set in a bright 1930s house with Craftsman windows and wood floors, it's bright in daytime and intimate at night. The menu has "violis" stuffed with Dungeness crab, portobello mushrooms, or butternut squash; spaghetti with handmade meatballs; linguine; and lasagne. Owner Cheryl Travaglione will make you feel at home. *$$; AE, DC, MC, V; checks OK; lunch Mon–Fri, dinner Wed–Sun; beer and wine; reservations recommended; downtown West Shelton on Franklin St.*

Xinh's Clam & Oyster House / ★★☆

221 W RAILROAD AVE, STE D, SHELTON; 360/427-8709
Chef Xinh Dwelley, a five-time West Coast oyster-shucking champion, is a magician in the kitchen. This is one of the best little clam and oyster houses on the Olympic Peninsula. Diners come from Tacoma and Seattle for some of the Northwest's freshest seafood, paired with Vietnamese flavors; the mussels in curry sauce is delicious. *$$; AE, MC, V; checks OK; dinner Tues–Sat; beer and wine; reservations recommended; downtown Shelton.*

SOMETHIN' ABOUT OYSTERS

Tom Robbins likened eating an oyster to French-kissing a mermaid. Hemingway lost the "empty feeling" after a famous oyster meal. Shakespeare believed the world was his oyster which with sword he would open.

There is something about oysters.

"They are a sexy animal," agrees Bill Whitbeck, author of *The Joy of Oysters* and known by many in the Northwest as Oyster Bill. "They have an aura about them that is intriguing."

That intrigue has been alive and well in the Northwest for decades: Washington is home to the continent's largest concentration of oyster farms and is the biggest oyster-growing state in the United States. Many of our state's oysters come from Hood Canal, a 60-mile-long finger-shaped inlet between the Olympic Peninsula and the Kitsap Peninsula. The saltwater canal is lined with oyster farms—Quilcene, Hama Hama, and Dabob oysters—as well as public tidelands for recreational harvesting.

One single oyster filters up to 60 gallons of water each day; it is no coincidence that Hood Canal has famously clean water. These busy bivalves play a major role in maintaining the ecological balance in the waters where they grow.

Union

North of Shelton on State Route 106, Union sits on the south shore of Hood Canal's "hook," between Belfair and US Highway 101.

RESTAURANTS

Robin Hood / ★★

6790 SR 106, UNION; 360/898-4400
A stopover since the early 1930s, this stone and log structure has functioned as a dance hall and tavern, drugstore, and B and B. These days, it is a popular gathering place for good food—in the front restaurant—and brew out back in the cavelike pub. The dining room has high-beamed ceilings and a fireplace; large windows overlook a creek. The restaurant menu has high-quality seafood, steak, and free-range poultry. The pub has gourmet pizza and organic hamburgers. *$–$$$; AE, DC, MC, V; checks OK; dinner Wed–Sun; full bar; reservations recommended; www.therobinhood.com; ¼ mile west of Alderbrook Resort.*

"They actually use oysters in certain areas to bring back water quality," points out Whitbeck, who sports a bumper sticker that says "Oysters are habitat forming." As oyster demand increases, the demand and necessity for clean water swells, too.

Recently Washington's only native oyster, the Olympia oyster, has started making a comeback. The Olympia, named after the Olympic Peninsula, grew in Puget Sound for thousands of years. As pollution increased, they died off. Now they are being reintroduced by a handful of peninsula growers. Check out **TAYLOR SHELLFISH** (www.taylorshellfishfarms.com) and the **OLYMPIA OYSTER COMPANY** (www.olympiaoyster.com). Oyster experts say the health of this little bivalve is an indicator of the health of Washington's waters.

"Oysters taste like the sea," says Whitbeck, who makes it his business to introduce "virgin slurpers" to the joy of oysters. "When an oyster is fresh, it tastes like clean salt water." Whitbeck's favorite and recommended way to eat an oyster is naked.

"I mean the oyster," he says with a smile. "With a nice chilled glass of steely white wine."

For oyster beach seasons, call the **DEPARTMENT OF HEALTH SHELLFISH HOTLINE** (800/562-5632).

—Ritzy Ryciak

LODGINGS

Alderbrook Resort and Spa / ★★★★

10 E ALDERBROOK DR, UNION; 360/898-2200 OR 800/622-9370
Alderbrook strikes the perfect balance between rustic and luxurious. The main entry has large log beams, rugged rock walls, and 20-foot windows that overlook Hood Canal and the Olympic Mountains. Established in 1913, the resort was recently renovated. Guest rooms have slate tile, soaking tubs, and daybeds. Each of the 16 beach-front cottages has its own fireplace. In addition to a full-service spa, there's a fitness center, a saline swimming pool enclosed in glass, and a restaurant with local fare. $$$$; AE, MC, V; no checks; www. alderbrookresort.com; south end of Hood Canal.

Quilcene

Quilcene, on US Highway 101 between Shelton and Sequim, overlooks Dabob Bay on Hood Canal, just south of the Hood Canal Bridge and State Route 104. Every summer weekend, this popular eastern access point to the Olympic Mountains holds concerts by the internationally acclaimed, Seattle-based Philadelphia String Quartet and world-class artists at the **OLYMPIC MUSIC FESTIVAL** (11 miles west of

Hood Canal Bridge on SR 104, then ¼ mile south of Quilcene exit; 206/527-8839; www.olympicmusicfestival.org). Nearby, **MOUNT WALKER** (5 miles past Quilcene Ranger Station, 295142 Highway 101 S; 360/765-2200), a 6-mile hike or drive, has views of Puget Sound.

Port Ludlow

In the late 1800s, this port was a mill town known for shipbuilding. Just north of the Hood Canal Bridge and State Route 104 and east of State Route 19, the port town overlooks the mouth of Hood Canal at Admiralty Inlet in Puget Sound.

LODGINGS

The Resort at Port Ludlow / ★★☆

I HERON RD, PORT LUDLOW; 360/437-0411 OR 877/805-0868
Noted as a New England–style resort, this lodging on Port Ludlow is an ideal destination. Today, all blue-collar remnants of the port's past have been replaced with luxury. The resort has a marina, hiking trails, hotel and condo accommodations with Olympic Mountain views, and a golf course that's a designated Audubon Cooperative Sanctuary. The hotel's Fireside restaurant has noteworthy local cuisine. *$$$; AE, MC, V; checks OK; www.portludlow resort.com; 6 miles north of Hood Canal Bridge on west side of canal.*

Port Hadlock

From Port Ludlow, the back road to Port Hadlock hugs the shoreline of Oak Bay. Port Hadlock is on State Route 116, a more direct route east of State Route 19 between State Route 104 and Port Townsend, at the south end of Port Townsend Bay. The false-front, Old West–style buildings in Port Hadlock sport bright colors. **VILLAGE BAKER** (10644 Rhody Dr; 360/379-5310) specializes in artisan breads and pastries. Local events include Hadlock Days in July and musical performances at nearby Fort Flagler State Park (see Marrowstone Island section).

RESTAURANTS

Ajax Café / ★★☆

21 N WATER ST, PORT HADLOCK; 360/385-3450
Hanging hats frame the windows of this colorful restaurant with bright blue walls and polka-dotted chairs. Customers try on the hats while they wait. Live music on the weekend makes this a rockin' spot. Ajax was recently bought by three women who started here as waitresses. The menu has stayed true to its roots: macadamia nut–encrusted halibut, Oregon Country Beef steaks and ribs, and the fishermen's stew. *$$; MC, V; local checks only; lunch, dinner every day (Tues–Sun in winter; closed Jan); beer and wine; reservations recommended; www.ajaxcafe.com; on waterfront, off Oak Bay Rd.*

Chimacum Café / ★

9253 RHODY DR, CHIMACUM; 360/732-4631
This establishment in the tiny town of Chimacum, just 8 miles south of Port Townsend, is well worth a stop on your way to or from PT (as locals call it). This is the kind of family-friendly place where the waitresses call you "Hon." Locals sit at the old-time counter swigging mugs of coffee with their meals. People come from miles around for one of their rotating Sunday dinners, such as old-fashioned turkey with accompaniments for under $10. Try the homemade pies. *$; DC, MC, V; checks OK; breakfast, lunch, dinner every day; no alcohol; no reservations; south side of SR 19, between Cenex store and post office.*

Marrowstone Island

Long ago, Marrowstone Island's enterprise was turkey farming. Today locals farm oysters and harvest clams. Just 20 minutes southeast of Port Townsend, via State Route 116 east of Port Hadlock and Indian Island, Marrowstone offers a slower pace.

FORT FLAGLER STATE PARK (10541 Flagler Rd; 360/385-1259) is an old coastal fortification where seals and gulls hang out at the end of the sand spit, across Admiralty Inlet from Whidbey Island. Pick up a bag of oysters at the historic **NORDLAND GENERAL STORE** (5180 Flagler Rd; 360/385-0777) or rent a boat and paddle around at **MYSTERY BAY STATE PARK** (on west side of Marrowstone Island; 360/902-8844).

LODGINGS

Beach Cottages on Marrowstone / ★

10 BEACH DR, NORDLAND; 360/385-3077 OR 800/871-3077
This rustic resort is set on 10 acres bordering a tidal estuary. It has eight cabins with views of the Olympics and Mount Rainier. Cabins have equipped kitchens, Tempur-Pedic beds, and woodstoves for heat (wood, kindling, and newspaper are provided). Bring a good book, a pair of binoculars, and a bathing suit. *$$; MC, V; checks OK; www.beachcottagegetaway.com; right at "Welcome to Marrowstone" sign off SR 116.*

Port Townsend

Port Townsend's inhabitants (about 8,300 of them) have done an amazing job of preserving the history of this Victorian town, incorporating an abundance of cultural and artistic events and offering some of the finest dining on the Olympic Peninsula. Along with the area's scenic mountains, sparkling waters, beaches, trails, parks, and nearby forests, it all adds up to Northwest paradise.

Historically, settlers came in the mid-1800s and built more than 200 Victorian homes; foreign consuls off ships added a cosmopolitan flavor. When mineral deposits petered out, the railroad was never built, so the elite investors left. Port Townsend became a land of vanished dreams and vacant mansions in the late 1890s, leaving it in an architectural time warp. It is these original buildings with wraparound views that lie at the heart of the town's charm in the National Historic Landmark District.

It wasn't until the 1970s that the area's cheap homes and relatively remote location began to draw new residents. Now the days of bargain real estate are long gone. But the magnificent buildings and views remain, the quirky entrepreneurial and artistic spirit of the community is thriving, and the town attracts thousands of tourists.

In a town once filled with bed-and-breakfast inns, now they are a dying breed. Once affordable homes in the '70s, they're now million-dollar babies that regularly go on the market. Most buyers who have that kind of cash aren't the type to be slinging hash for boarders. Instead, they're converting them into private homes. But there are still a few stellar B and Bs in Port Townsend, along with vintage hotels and unique accommodations.

ACCESS AND INFORMATION

Port Townsend sits at the north end of the Quimper Peninsula on **STATE ROUTE 20**, which continues east of here on Whidbey Island and southwest of here to its terminus at US Highway 101 on Discovery Bay. You can also reach Port Townsend by the **KEYSTONE FERRY** (206/464-6400; www.wsdot. wa.gov/ferries) from Whidbey Island, though the sailing can be interrupted by wind and tides in stormy weather.

The town is generally divided into Downtown and Uptown. Downtown was originally the commercial area, rowdy at night and rife with brothels. Uptown was where gentlemen built their homes. The ladies of the house went to the waterfront, so a shopping district arose. In reality, the town is so small it doesn't matter. But locals make this distinction if you're asking directions. Ask for the map at the **VISITORS CENTER** (2437 E Sims Way; 360/385-2722).

MAJOR ATTRACTIONS

Except for some unavoidable suburban sprawl on the outskirts of town, the streets and buildings are much the same as they were a century ago. The Visitors Center map has a driving tour of 74 historical points, including many of the ornate homes and buildings. Don't miss the Carnegie Library, U.S. Post Office, and Jefferson County Courthouse. The **ROTHSCHILD HOUSE** (on Taylor St between Jefferson and Franklin sts; www.jchsmuseum.org/Rothschild/house.html) is Washington's smallest state park, measuring 50 by 200 feet. The Greek Revival–style house with a garden is open seasonally for tours.

Among other points of interest is **MANRESA CASTLE** (7th and Sheridan sts; 360/385-5750 or 800/732-1281; www.manresacastle.com), built in 1892 for Charles and Kate Eisenbeis, prominent members of the early Port Townsend business community. Its design is similar to some of the castles in the

Eisenbeis's native Prussia. Today the castle is a hotel and restaurant. **HALLER FOUNTAIN** (Washington and Taylor sts) is where Galatea, Port Townsend's brazen 1906 goddess, lives. Visit the **JEFFERSON COUNTY HISTORICAL SOCIETY** (210 Madison St; 360/385-1003) for a fascinating museum in the original city hall.

One of several parks, **CHETZEMOKA PARK** (Jackson and Blaine sts) is a memorial to the S'Klallam Indian chief who became friends with the first white settlers. It has a charming gazebo, picnic tables, tall Douglas firs, and a grassy slope down to the beach.

FORT WORDEN STATE PARK (200 Battery Way; 360/385-4730; www. fortworden.org) offers everything from beach-front walks to lodging to cultural events. Along with sister forts on Marrowstone and Whidbey islands, it was part of the defense system established to protect Puget Sound more than a century ago. The 433-acre complex overlooking Admiralty Inlet now incorporates turn-of-the-20th-century officers' quarters—where you can stay overnight (see review)—campgrounds, gardens, a theater, and a concert hall. The setting may look familiar to those who saw the movie *An Officer and a Gentleman*, which was filmed here. Within the park is the **MARINE SCIENCE CENTER** (360/385-5582; www.ptmsc.org), where you can touch sea animals and later catch a cruise to nearby **PROTECTION ISLAND NATIONAL WILDLIFE REFUGE** (at mouth of Discovery Bay), the region's largest seabird rookery. The park is also home to **CENTRUM** (360/385-3102; www.centrum. org), which sponsors concerts, workshops, and festivals throughout the year (see "Fun in Port Townsend").

If you want a break from sightseeing, take in a movie at the restored 1907 **ROSE THEATRE** (235 Taylor St; 360/385-1089; www.rosetheatre.com). Two local wineries offer tastings: **FAIR WINDS WINERY** (1984 Hastings Ave W; 360/385-6899; www.fairwindswinery.com) and **SORENSEN CELLARS LTD.** (274 Otto St, Ste S; 360/379-6416; www.sorensencellars.com).

Outdoorsy types have options ranging from beachcombing and hiking to kayaking, mountain biking, whale watching, and golfing. The **DISCOVERY BAY GOLF CLUB** (7401 Cape George Rd; 306/385-0704, www.discoverybay golfclub.com) is 5 miles south of downtown Port Townsend. The club has 18 holes and views of Discovery Bay, the Olympics, and the Cascades.

SHOPPING

While there are places here that sell the obligatory tourist T-shirts and shot glasses, the town also has an eclectic variety of galleries that carry fine art, crafts, and Native arts; stores with kitchenwares, antiques, and gifts; and some unusual indie shops.

Among the colorful places that line Water Street, you'll find some standouts, including the **WINE SELLER** (940 Water St; 360/385-7673; www.pt wineseller.com), which stocks wines, microbrews, and cigars. **SUMMER HOUSE DESIGN** (930 Water St; 360/344-4192) carries new home accents with retro design, plus contemporary handbags and Chinese paper lanterns. The **PERFECT SEASON** (918 Water St; 360/385-9265) is a gardener's delight.

WILLIAM'S GALLERY (914 Water St; 360/385-3630; www.williams-gallery.com) carries water fountains, copper and ceramic fish, watercolors, jewelry, and functional pottery. The **GREEN EYESHADE** (720 Water St; 360/385-3838; www.thegreeneyeshade.com) is a charming kitchenwares and gift shop; for noncooks, there's a substantial selection of jewelry. **EARTHENWORKS GAL-LERY** (702 Water St; 360/385-0328; www.earthenworksgallery.com) carries beautiful contemporary arts and crafts.

On the west side of Water Street is **ANCESTRAL SPIRITS GALLERY** (701 Water St; 360/385-0078; www.ancestralspirits.com), with artifacts and art from aboriginal peoples. Music aficionados go to **QUIMPER SOUND** (901 Water St; 360/385-2454; www.quimpersound.com), an old-school record shop.

Not all shopping is on Water Street; Washington Street has the **PORT TOWNSEND ANTIQUE MALL** (802 Washington St; 360-379-8069)—the best place for vintage and antique finds, and **DOLCE LA BELLE** (842 Washington St, Ste 102; 360/385-2969; www.dolcelabelle.com), steps away from the fleece and conservative fashions offered on Water Street; it has a refreshing collection of Northwest independently designed skirts, vintage hand-dyed lingerie, and silk-covered journals. Lawrence Street features **BADD HABIT** (1005 Lawrence St; 360/385-3101, www.baddhabit.com), which is more than a hip T-shirt shop: they say 100 percent of the profits go to a nonprofit that provides funding for substance abusers. **PETALS** (1031 Lawrence St; 360/385-5289; www.ptpetals.com) is the most charming floral and gift shop in town. Owner Denise Blanchard set up shop in an old Lawrence Street gas station, circa 1920.

In the Boat Haven area, near State Route 20 and Haines Place, is **WASTE NOT WANT NOT** (304 10th St; 360/379-6838), which deals in decades of discards, from old-fashioned farmhouse sinks to salvaged windows.

RESTAURANTS

Fins Coastal Cuisine / ★★☆

1019 WATER ST, PORT TOWNSEND; 360/379-3474
This sophisticated restaurant has white tablecloths, open-beamed ceilings, and beautiful views of Port Townsend Bay. Seafood is the star here: Starters include chilled Hood Canal oysters on the half shell, clam chowder, and Dungeness crab cakes. Don't miss the house specialties, like salmon with tarragon mustard or Portuguese fisherman's stew. Lunch is upscale: Kobe beef burgers topped with horseradish cheese sauce, wild salmon gyros in pita bread. A quiet wine bar adjacent to the restaurant has an extensive selection. *$$$; AE, DC, MC, V; local checks only; lunch, dinner every day; full bar; reservations recommended; www.finscoastalcuisine.com; between Tyler and Polk sts.*

FUN IN PORT TOWNSEND

The Port Townsend calendar is jam-packed with events and outings all year-round. Some of the most popular are:

The **VICTORIAN FESTIVAL** (360/379-0668; www.victorianfestival.org) in March has Victorian fashion and many other events. The **ANNUAL KITCHEN TOUR** is in April. The **RHODY FESTIVAL GRAND PARADE** (www.rhody festival.org) is in May. The **SECRET GARDEN TOUR** is in June. The **FESTIVAL OF AMERICAN FIDDLE TUNES** and the **JAZZ PORT TOWNSEND FESTIVAL** (360/385-3102; www.centrum.org) are in July. The **PORT TOWNSEND COUNTRY BLUES FESTIVAL CONCERT** (360/385-3102; www.centrum.org) is in August. September features the **ANNUAL WOODEN BOAT FESTIVAL** (360/385-3628; www.woodenboat.org), **PORT TOWNSEND FILM FESTIVAL** (www.ptfilmfest.com), and **FALL HOMES TOUR** (www.ptguide.com/homes tour). Contact the **VISITORS CENTER** (2437 E Sims Way; 360/385-2722) or check out the **WEB SITE** (www.ptguide.com) for dates.

—Kathy Schultz

Fountain Café / ★★☆

920 WASHINGTON ST, PORT TOWNSEND; 360/385-1364

Locals like to think this diminutive restaurant with its European bistro ambience is a secret, but it's not. Patrons can't keep from spreading the word. The space has nine tables and four seats at the old wooden counter. Try warm salads with potatoes, prosciutto, and sautéed veggies topped with pesto dressing and pine nuts. For dinner, try the divine roasted walnut and Gorgonzola penne or the Zuppa Pesce, a fresh fish soup with mussels, clams, prawns, and vegetables in a savory saffron wine broth. *$$; MC, V; checks OK; lunch, dinner every day; beer and wine; reservations recommended; between Tyler and Taylor sts.*

Galatea Cafe & Tapas Bar / ★☆

842 WASHINGTON ST, PORT TOWNSEND; 360/385-5225

The tapas at this simply decorated restaurant are tasty, but be sure to order a winning house margarita or martini. Try the marinated olives with anchovies and fresh herbs and the flavorful carne asada with peppers and Argentine spices. Fat prawns might be wrapped in prosciutto, topped on saffron risotto cakes, or tucked in quesadillas. On weekends, crowds gather for their signature paella. Courtyard seating is available next to the Haller Fountain. *$$; MC, V; checks OK; dinner Wed–Sat, brunch Sun; full bar; reservations recommended; www.galateacafe.com; between Taylor and Adams sts.* &

Hanazano Asian Noodle / ★★☆

225 TAYLOR ST, PORT TOWNSEND; 360/385-7622
Bamboo accents and Japanese fish art decorate the walls of this small restaurant. It's a good spot for tasty noodle dishes and culinary entertainment. Sit at the large *jatoba* wood counter and watch owner Kaori Hull throw soft egg noodles, vegetables, and pork into big pans of splattering oil for *yakasoba*. The *champon* soup is filling and delicious, stocked with noodles, seafood, pork, and vegetables in a spicy broth. Teriyaki chicken is a favorite standby. Sake is de rigeur. *$; MC, V; local checks only; lunch, dinner Tues–Sat; wine only; reservations recommended; corner of Washington St.*

Lanza's Ristorante / ★★

1020 LAWRENCE ST, PORT TOWNSEND; 360/379-1900
You'll feel like family in this Italian restaurant. The friendly service, classic dishes, and generous portions add up to a homey atmosphere. Start with the heaping antipasto platter. Traditionalists love the spaghetti with the famous family meatballs or sausage. The Seafood Lorraine is loaded with, well, seafood. Pizzas can be made to order with crusts ranging from thin and crispy to thick. Canines visit the back door, where Lori Lanza hands out special meatballs. Save room for Grandma Glory's Italian wedding cake, an angel food with rich frosting and a hint of almond and coconut. *$$; MC, V; checks OK; dinner Mon–Sat; beer and wine; reservations recommended; between Polk and Tyler sts.*

The Salal Café / ★★

634 WATER ST, PORT TOWNSEND; 360/385-6532
Late risers needn't worry about missing out on this café's hearty breakfast: it's served until 2pm. On weekends, patrons spill out onto the sidewalk to gain entrance to the dining room with its countryish decor or to the atrium in back. With more than 50 breakfast items, choosing can be daunting. Some suggestions: homemade biscuits and gravy or the crispy-thin blueberry crepes topped with whipped cream. Choose the salmon crepe for lunch, or one of the generous salads. *$; MC, V; checks OK; breakfast, lunch every day; beer and wine; reservations recommended; between Madison and Quincy sts.*

Silverwater Café / ★★

237 TAYLOR ST, PORT TOWNSEND; 360/385-6448
This corner restaurant in the turn-of-the-20th-century Elks Building is always busy. During lunch you'll find hearty burgers, grilled chicken sandwiches with artichoke hearts, and wild coho salmon salad. The café is a favorite for business lunches. Meat eaters love the New York pepper steak doused with green peppercorn and mushroom sauce, but vegetarians also have several choices. Many dishes here are seasoned with their special spice blends. For light fare and superb cocktails, head upstairs to Mezzaluna, a quiet bar in the mezzanine. *$$; MC, V; checks OK; lunch Mon–Sat, dinner every day; full bar;*

reservations recommended; www.silverwatercafe.com; between Tyler and Adams sts.

Sweet Laurette & Cyndee's Bistro and Café / ★★★

1029 LAWRENCE ST, PORT TOWNSEND; 306/385-4886
The lemony-lime-colored walls and bright floral and candy-striped café curtains give this place a charming Provençal atmosphere. Every meal is divine. In the café, order the moist brioche stuffed with apricots and almonds, fluffy provençal omelets, or Frenchman's Toast. For lunch, the roast–pork loin sandwich perfectly blends flavors of caramelized onions, Gorgonzola, and green apples. Dinner is no less amazing. Try the flavorful and supertender beef short ribs or the pan-seared duck breast. *$$–$$$; MC, V; local checks only; breakfast, lunch every day, dinner Wed–Sun, brunch Sun; beer and wine; reservations recommended; www.sweetlaurette.com; between Polk and Tyler sts.* &

Tyler Street Coffee House / ★★★

215 TYLER ST, PORT TOWNSEND; 360/379-4185
Tim Roth runs this family operation where all the dough is handmade from scratch. This place is usually packed. If you try nothing else, indulge in one of the cinnamon twists made from croissant dough sandwiched with almond butter, sprinkled with cinnamon sugar, double twisted, baked, and glazed. At lunch you'll be treated to four kinds of soups (try the mulligatawny) and sandwiches that include a killer egg salad. *$; no credit cards; local checks only; breakfast, lunch Tues–Sat; no alcohol; no reservations; at Water St.*

The Wild Coho / ★★★

1044 LAWRENCE ST, PORT TOWNSEND; 360/379-1030
Painted in earthy colors, this intimate restaurant is for gourmands serious about Northwest cuisine. Jay Payne, a former Seattle chef, is creative with his use of wild coho salmon, duck, oysters, Dungeness crab, and meats. One menu staple is wild coho salmon with sweet-potato crust, chive butter, and spiced tomato relish. Thursday is "Small Plates" night ($5–$7 each); it's the best way to taste the bounty. *$$$; MC, V; checks OK; dinner Tues–Sat; full bar; reservations recommended; www.wildcoho.com; between Polk and Tyler sts.* &

LODGINGS

The Bishop Victorian Hotel and Gardens / ★★☆

714 WASHINGTON ST, PORT TOWNSEND; 800/824-4738
Victorian character, great service, and a fine location make this hotel number one among the vintage hotels in town. At more than a century old, it's kept its grandeur but has been updated with creature comforts. Just one block off the busy Water Street strip, it has lovely manicured gardens, an ornate reception area with a fireplace, and Victorian antiques and period lighting throughout.

Of the 16 rooms, only one lacks a view of the water or town. Parking is free. Your room key gives you access to an athletic club. *$$–$$$; AE, DIS, MC, V; checks OK; www.rainshadowproperties.com/bishop; between Adams and Quincy sts.* ♿ (1 room)

Chevy Chase Beach Cabins / ★★

3710 S DISCOVERY RD, PORT TOWNSEND; 360/385-1270
This beach-front property is about 8 miles from downtown Port Townsend. The seven cabins accommodate everyone. The property has views of Discovery Bay and Vancouver Island, miles of private beach front (including a sand-dollar bed yielding thousands in the summer), and a swimming pool circa 1951. Cabins, all with kitchens, range from cozy studios to the roomy "Clubhouse." Cabin No. 4 has the best view. They feature Victorian reproduction furniture and range in size from two to eleven bedrooms. There is no food on the premises, so bring your own. *$$–$$$$; MC, V; checks OK; www. chevychasebeachcabins.com; at Cape George Rd.*

Fort Worden State Park / ★

200 BATTERY WAY, PORT TOWNSEND; 360/344-4400
Within Fort Worden State Park are 33 former officers' quarters dating back to 1904. These two-story homes offer spacious lodgings, each with a complete kitchen. The most coveted one-bedroom lodging is Bliss Vista, perched on the bluff, with a fireplace and romantic appeal. Alexander's Castle, a minimonument with a three-story turret, is charming in its antiquity, sequestered away from the officers' houses. RV and tent sites are also onsite, near the beach or tucked into the woods. Make summer reservations well in advance. The Commons houses a coffee shop and café, open daily. *$$; MC, V; checks OK; www.fortworden.org; 1 mile north of downtown.*

Holly Hill House / ★★★

611 POLK ST, PORT TOWNSEND; 360/385-5619
A picture-perfect Victorian home built in 1872, this bed-and-breakfast has water views, a rocking chair porch, and lush gardens with almost 100 rose-bushes. An inviting parlor with period antiques, comfy leather furniture, and a fireplace beckons, as do homemade chocolate-walnut cookies. All five rooms have private baths, heavenly beds, and charming rooms, each with its own personality. The favorite is the romantic Colonel's Suite, which has a huge picture window with water, mountain, and town views. *$$–$$$; MC, V; local checks only; at Clay St.*

The James House / ★★★⯪

1238 WASHINGTON ST, PORT TOWNSEND; 800/385-1238
This gorgeous 1889 Victorian perched on a bluff overlooking Puget Sound is truly the best of the B and B bunch. The welcoming owner, Carol McGough, has managed to spare the chintz rather than spoil the elegant house. Each of the 10 rooms has a view and a private bathroom. They feature antiques such

PORT TOWNSEND SNACKS AND LIBATIONS

Besides all the great restaurants reviewed in this chapter, there are other fun pit stops in Port Townsend:

Try the **ELEVATED ICE CREAM & CANDY SHOP** (627-631 Water St, Port Townsend; 360/385-1156; www.elevatedicecream.com), an old-fashioned candy shop that features more than 20 ice cream flavors and makes fresh fruit Italian ices, shakes, malts, and ice cream pies.

Two watering holes worth noting are on Water Street: Locals congregate at **SIRENS** (823 Water St, Port Townsend; 360/379-1100), a bar hidden up three long flights of stairs. It has magnificent views of the bay, a funky mishmash of Victorian furniture, a pool table, and live music. The menu features a little of everything. **WATER STREET BREWING & ALE HOUSE** (639 Water St, Port Townsend; 360/379-6438; www.waterstreetbrewing.com) is a friendly establishment with an impressive beer collection and upscale pub fare. The main bar is spacious, as is the dining room in back. A provocative 8-foot by 15-foot mural of a voluptuous nude ravished by impish creatures hangs in the bar, a payment made in the early '70s for a sizable bar tab. Upstairs is a large pool hall. Every weekend there's live music ranging from blues and jazz to rock and jam bands.

Uptown is **PROVISIONS** (939 Kearney St, Port Townsend; 360/385-4541; www.provisionspt.com), a delicatessen and specialty food market. Go there for gourmet picnic food or takeout specialties.

—Kathy Schultz

as mahogany sleigh beds. Chef Donna Kuhn has been delighting guests for more than a decade with breakfasts such as baked spiced pears and cranberry and white chocolate–chip scones. Stay at the separate modern Bungalow on the Bluff. *$$–$$$$; AE, DIS, MC, V; checks OK; www.jameshouse.com; between Fillmore and Harrison sts.* ⅃ (Bungalow on the Bluff)

Palace Hotel / ★

1004 WATER ST, PORT TOWNSEND; 800/962-0741

The 1889 Romanesque-style Palace Hotel is in the midst of the shopping and historic district downtown. Eighteen rooms, nearly all with private bathrooms, are furnished with period antiques and a distinct Victorian decor. Room 3, also known as Marie's Room (the madam of the house until the mid-1930s), is on a view corner of the hotel, retaining the ex-bordello atmosphere in its original shades of burgundy and forest green. The hotel is decked out come the holiday season. Long flights of stairs can be a difficult ascent for some. Off-street parking is a plus, but noise from overexuberant tourists can be a minus. *$–$$$; AE, DIS, MC, V; checks OK; www.palacehotelpt.com; at Tyler St.*

The Swan Hotel / ★

216 MONROE ST, PORT TOWNSEND; 800/824-4738
This hotel's excellent location and solicitous service make for a pleasant night's stay, whether you choose one of the compact and cozy cabins or a room in the main structure. Just steps from Puget Sound, the cabins are rustic on the outside but immaculate and comfy on the inside. The decor is homey and fresh, and each has amenities such as coffee service and a small fridge. Cabin No. 2 is the only one with a gas fireplace. The main hotel wouldn't win any decorating contests, but half of the eight rooms have decks with water views. A spacious two-level penthouse sleeps up to 10. *$$–$$$; AE, DIS, MC, V; checks OK; www.theswanhotel.com; between Water and Washington sts.*

Sequim and the Dungeness Valley

Popular with retirees and young families, Sequim (pronounced "skwim") is quickly becoming *the* place to be on the Olympic Peninsula. The sun shines 306 days a year here, and annual rainfall is only 16 inches, because Sequim sits in the middle of the rain shadow cast by the Olympic Mountains. The downtown area, off US Highway 101 above Sequim Bay, is busy and full of hip shops.

On Sequim Bay near Blyn, a few miles east of Sequim, the S'Klallam Indians operate the unique **NORTHWEST NATIVE EXPRESSIONS** art gallery (1033 Old Blyn Hwy; 360/681-4640; www.jamestowntribe.org/gallery.htm). Across the highway stands the **SEVEN CEDARS** (270756 US Hwy 101; 800/4LUCKY7; www.7cedarscasino.com), a mammoth gambling casino with valet parking.

For Olympic Mountain ice cream, made on the peninsula, great coffee, and local artwork, visit the **BUZZ** (128 N Sequim Ave; 360/683-2503)—or, in Port Angeles, **ITTY BITTY BUZZ** (110 E 1st St; 360/565-8080). **CEDARBROOK HERB FARM** (1345 S Sequim Ave; 360/683-7733; www.cedarbrookherbfarm.com), Washington's oldest herb farm, has a large variety of plants and a gift shop. **SUNNY FARMS COUNTRY STORE** (262461 US Hwy 101, Sequim; 360/683-8003), halfway between Sequim and Port Angeles, is the place to go for organic produce, deli food, and hanging plants.

The July **LAVENDER FESTIVAL** (877-681-3035; www.lavenderfestival.com) has put Sequim on the map as the lavender capital of North America—more than 30,000 people attend. **DUNGENESS SPIT** (6 miles northwest of Sequim; 360/457-8451), one of the world's longest natural sand spits, has a national wildlife refuge for birds near its start. A walk down the narrow 5½-mile beach leads to a remote lighthouse.

For information, contact the **NORTH OLYMPIC PENINSULA VISITOR & CONVENTION BUREAU** (800/942-4042; www.northwestsecretplaces.com) or **DESTINATION SEQUIM** (360/683-6197; www.visitsun.com).

RESTAURANTS

Oak Table Café / ★

292 W BELL ST, SEQUIM; 360/683-2179

Famous for their 3-inch-high apple pancakes, the Oak Table is the breakfast place in Sequim. The dining room is fittingly "oaky"—wood floors, tables, and chairs—and owner Billy Nagler and his family provide great service. Egg dishes are paired with everything from vegetables to Hollandaise sauce; the crepes are decadent; and the buttermilk pancakes are notably fluffy. Chestnut Cottage, also owned by the Nagler family (and also in Port Angeles), has a similar menu. *$; AE, DC, MC, V; checks OK; breakfast every day, lunch Mon–Sat; no alcohol; no reservations; www.oaktablecafe.com; at 3rd Ave.* &

Old Mill Café / ★★★

721 CARLSBORG RD, SEQUIM; 360/582-1583

Elk antlers and 10-foot cross-cut saws hang on the walls. In the 1920s, this spot was the local tavern frequented by workers from the mill across the street. Recently renovated and reopened, this always-packed café is known for its home-made food, huge portions, and down-home feel. Logger burgers, house-smoked ribs, Dungeness crab cakes, organic greens, and free-range eggs are served here. On Sunday, breakfast is served all day. *$$; MC, V; checks OK; breakfast, lunch, dinner every day; full bar; no reservations; at the corner of Spath Rd.*

LODGINGS

Colette's Bed and Breakfast / ★★★

339 FINN HALL RD, SEQUIM; 360/457-9197 OR 877/457-9777

The entry-room of this eco-friendly and very luxurious B and B has pan-oramic windows that look out at the Strait of Juan de Fuca—don't be sur-prised if you see bald eagles flying outside. There are two rooms in the main house and five private cottages, all with two-person Jacuzzi tubs, fireplaces, and views of the strait. Bedsheets are 400-thread-count. Hosts Lynda and Peter Clark serve a five-course gourmet breakfast. *$$$; AE, MC, V; no checks; www.bbonline.com/wa/colettes/; ½ mile from Sequim.*

Lost Mountain Lodge / ★★★

303 SUNNY VIEW DR, SEQUIM;
360/683-2431 OR 888/683-2431

This lodge leaves no luxury stone unturned. Appetizers are served upon arrival, and homemade lattes can be frothed on request. The main lodge has three private suites with wide-screen TVs, crème de la crème of toiletries, and 400-thread-count sheets on the king-sized beds. An outdoor hydrotherapy spa overlooks a pretty pond. The gourmet breakfast is full of choices: frittata, fruit, yogurt, sweet bread. The nearby upscale Guest House and Farm House are ideal for families. *$$$–$$$$; AE, DC, MC, V; checks OK; www.lostmountain lodge.com; 3 miles west of Sequim.* &

Port Angeles and the Strait of Juan de Fuca

US HIGHWAY 101 parallels the Strait of Juan de Fuca beyond Sequim through Port Angeles and along Lake Crescent to Sappho, where the highway turns south toward Forks. But STATE ROUTE 112 hugs the shoreline more closely, extending west through tiny communities including Clallam Bay, Sekiu, and Neah Bay.

Port Angeles

Port Angeles, the largest natural deep-water harbor north of San Francisco, is a launch spot to Victoria, British Columbia (see Access and Information at beginning of this chapter), and the northern gateway to OLYMPIC NATIONAL PARK (360/565-3130; www.nps.gov/olym). The park, as big as Rhode Island, with a buffer zone of national forest surrounding it, has the largest remaining herd of Roosevelt elk, which occasionally create "elk jams" along US Highway 101. OLYMPIC RAFT AND KAYAK SERVICE (360/452-1443 or 888/452-1443) offers trips down the Elwha and Hoh rivers.

In downtown Port Angeles, stop by PORT BOOK AND NEWS (104 E 1st St; 360/452-6367). Newly opened ELIZABETH AND COMPANY (106 E 1st St; 360/452-5222) has coffee, pastries, and wi-fi Internet access. STAR'S BAKERY (710 S Lincoln St; 360/457-3279), near the library, is a good place to buy picnic food. Browse SWAIN'S GENERAL STORE (602 E 1st St; 360/452-2357) for everything else.

In and around Port Angeles, several small and notable wineries dot the map: CAMARADERIE CELLARS (334 Benson Rd; 360/417-3564; www.camaraderie cellars.com), LOST MOUNTAIN WINERY (3174 Lost Mountain Rd; 360/683-5229; www.lostmountain.com), BLACK DIAMOND WINERY (2976 Black Diamond Rd; 360/457-0748; home.wavecable.com/~bdwinery), and OLYMPIC CELLARS WINERY (255410 US Hwy 101 E; 360/452-0160; www.olympiccellars.com).

The OCTOBER DUNGENESS CRAB & SEAFOOD FESTIVAL (www.crabfestival. org) showcases the foods and traditions of the Olympic Peninsula. PORT ANGELES VISITORS CENTER (877/456-8372; www.portangeles.org) has information.

RESTAURANTS

Bella Italia / ★★★

118 E 1ST ST, PORT ANGELES; 360/457-5442
Bella Italia is a culinary gem on the Olympic Peninsula. Renowned for its wine list (more than 500 selections), fresh seafood, and local organic produce, this is where the locals go for dinner. The restaurant is warmly lit, and dining tables and booths are intimate and comfortable. Olympic Coast Cuisine, their daily specials sheet, has "fresh catch" options that come from different parts of the peninsula, such as Quilcene oysters and Neah Bay salmon. The

wine bar is a nice spot for an evening drink. *$$$; AE, DC, MC, V; checks OK; dinner every day; full bar; reservations recommended; www.bellaitaliapa.com; between Laurel and Lincoln sts.* &

Joy's Wine Bistro / ★★★

1135 E FRONT ST, PORT ANGELES; 360/452-9449
Joy's, owned by the Siemion family, is a new hot spot in Port Angeles. We're talking bright: glowing orange walls, bright red chairs, hand-painted table-tops. Joy Siemion, a New York–trained chef, has worked in restaurants on both the East and West coasts. Mom Barbara Gooding grinds the wheat berries for the bread. The roasted-chicken sandwich has smoked mozzarella, roasted tomatoes, Cajun mayo, and chicken pulled from the bone. *$$; AE, DIS, MC, V; local checks only; lunch every day, dinner Tues–Sat; beer and wine; reservations recommended; www.portangeleswinebistro.com; east side of Port Angeles.*

Sabai Thai / ★★★

903 W 8TH ST, PORT ANGELES; 360/452-4505
Sabai, meaning "comfortable and enjoyable" in Thai, is the perfect way to describe this new Port Angeles restaurant. Traditional hand-painted Thai fans span the ceiling, and carved bamboo light fixtures hang above each table. Chef-owner Victor Posten was born and raised in Bangkok. Andaman Pearl (named for the western Thai ocean) is a popular dish of stir-fried seafood paired with Thai basil, lime leaves, lemongrass, and Victor's homemade curry sauce. *$$; DC, MC, V; local checks only; dinner Mon–Sat; beer and wine; reservations recommended; west Port Angeles.*

Toga's Northwest & International Cuisine / ★★

122 W LAURIDSEN BLVD, PORT ANGELES; 360/452-1952
Toga's, named after chef Toga Hertzog, is known for its *jaegersteins* ("hunter stones") that come from Germany's Black Forest. These are large ceramic platters heated to 500 degrees and brought to individual tables, where diners cook varied meats to their liking. The decor inside the old house is a bit stiff, but people return for the flavors. Toga learned to cook in Germany; the menu has dishes like sauerbraten and beef stroganoff. Northwest selections—macadamia-coconut-crusted salmon or crab cakes—are also available. *$$$; AE, DC, MC, V; checks OK; dinner Tues–Sat; beer and wine; reservations recommended; west end of Port Angeles, right off US Hwy 101.*

LODGINGS

Five SeaSuns / ★

1006 S LINCOLN ST, PORT ANGELES; 360/452-8248 OR 800/708-0777
This B and B, a 1926 Dutch Colonial house, is centrally located, wireless, and classy but comfortable. The main house has four rooms with private baths—each is decorated to depict a season. The Carriage House, a separate house

with a kitchenette, is the fifth season (Indian Summer). A 7:30am wake-up knock is followed by homemade breakfast at 8:30am. Fresh cookies are available every afternoon. *$$–$$$; AE, DC, MC, V; checks OK; www.fiveseasuns. com; corner of E 10th St.*

Lake Crescent

Crystal-clear Lake Crescent, part of Olympic National Park, is home to rainbow trout and steelhead, Beardslee trout, and the famous Crescenti trout. US Highway 101 wraps around the south shore of this 600-foot-deep lake—so closely that drivers can see jumping fish. East Beach is on a road off the highway; 10 miles away, Fairholm Store and boat launch are on the far west end of the lake. Rental boats are available. Ask about the easy 1-mile hike to 90-foot Marymere Falls.

LODGINGS

Lake Crescent Lodge / ★

416 LAKE CRESCENT RD, PORT ANGELES; 360/928-3211
Built 85 years ago, this lodge was once known as Singer's Tavern. The main building has a grand veranda that overlooks the deep lake waters, a restaurant, and a relaxed bar. Upstairs rooms are noisy and rustic—and the bathroom is down the hall. Motel rooms are the best buy. A cluster of tiny, basic cabins, each with porch and fireplace, can be fun and charming—though remember that they were built in 1937, when President Franklin Roosevelt came to visit. *$$–$$$; AE, DC, MC, V; no checks; partially closed mid-Oct– Apr; www.lakecrescentlodge.com; 20 miles west of Port Angeles.* &

Sol Duc Hot Springs

The Quileute Indians called the area Sol Duc—"sparkling water." In the early 1900s, **SOL DUC HOT SPRINGS** (Sol Duc Rd, 28 miles west of Port Angeles; 360/327-3583 or 866/476-5382; every day mid-March–Oct; $10.75/person) became a mecca for affluent travelers. Today, part of Olympic National Park, the pools' naturally enriched mineral water is a popular spot for achy hikers and those in search of relaxation. The concrete pools aren't pretty to look at, but the surrounding old-growth trees make up for the basic facilities. One-hour massages ($65) are also available.

LODGINGS

Sol Duc Hot Springs Resort / ★★

SOL DUC RD, PORT ANGELES; 360/327-3583 OR 866/4SOLDUC
Accommodations here are rustic: 32 small carpeted cabins, each with a private bath and two double or queen beds. Up to four guests can share a cabin. Favorites are those with river-facing porches. There are no TVs. Camping

and RV sites are also available. The Springs Restaurant serves breakfast and dinner in summer (limited hours in spring and fall); a deli is open midday through the season. *$$$; AE, DC, MC, V; checks OK; closed Nov–Feb; www. visitsolduc.com; a few miles west of Lake Crescent, turn off US Hwy 101 onto Sol Duc Rd, then drive 12 miles south.*

Clallam Bay and Sekiu

Clallam Bay and nearby Sekiu, on State Route 112 along the Strait of Juan de Fuca, are the places to fish and watch whales. **CHITO BEACH RESORT** (in Clallam Bay; 360/963-2581; www.chitobeach.com) has cabins on the beach, a communal bonfire, and an edible herb garden. **STRAITSIDE RESORT** (in Sekiu; 360/963-2100; www.straightsideresort.com) is a hideaway ideal for families.

Twenty-one miles south of Sekiu is **LAKE OZETTE**, the largest natural body of freshwater in the state, part of Olympic National Park. At the north end of the lake is the **OZETTE RANGER STATION** (end of Hoko-Ozette Rd; 360/963-2725), a campground, and trailheads. The **CAPE ALAVA TRAIL** and the **SAND POINT TRAIL** each lead 3 miles to beaches, Cape Alava, the tiny Ozette Indian Reservation, the Indian Village Trail, ancient Indian petroglyphs, and views of **FLATTERY ROCKS NATIONAL WILDLIFE REFUGE** offshore. At Cape Alava you can see the coastal cliffs where a tidal erosion in the 1960s exposed a 500-year-old Native American village—once covered by a mud slide—with homes perfectly preserved. The archaeological dig was closed in 1981 after 11 years of excavation. Artifacts are on display in Neah Bay (see below).

Neah Bay

This is the end of the road, literally: State Route 112 ends at this small waterside town on the northern edge of the Makah Indian Reservation. A road leads to Cape Flattery. The Makah allow public access across their ancestral lands—a half-mile walk on a new boardwalk to land's end: 60-foot sheer cliffs with flying eagles overhead. Gray whales are often seen in April and May. Outlooks offer views of Tatoosh Island and the entrance to the Strait of Juan de Fuca. Sandy Hobuck Beach is open for picnics and surfing.

The **MAKAH CULTURAL AND RESEARCH CENTER** (Front St, Neah Bay; 360/645-2711) has wonderful exhibits, including artifacts from the Ozette digs (see Clallam Bay and Sekiu section above). **HOBUCK BEACH RESORT** (360/645-2339) has campsites and cabins. Farther on, the Tsoo-Yas Beach (pronounced "sooes") is also accessible; pay the landowners a parking fee. **PORT ANGELES VISITORS CENTER** (877/456-8372; www.portangeles.org) has information.

Forks and the Hoh River Valley

The Hoh Rain Forest in Olympic National Park is the wettest location in the contiguous United States: average annual rainfall is 133.58 inches. There are more than 3,000 species of plant life here—including the rain forest monarch and a giant Sitka spruce more than 500 years old and nearly 300 feet tall. **HOH VISITORS CENTER** (Hoh River Rd; 360/374-6925) and campground are 30 miles southeast of Forks. One- to three-day hikes up the Hoh River Trail offer incredible hiking; the longer trip to Glacier Meadows and access to Mount Olympus is best mid-July–October. Stop in at **PEAK 6 ADVENTURE STORE** (4883 Upper Hoh Rd; 360/374-5254) for all your gear needs.

Forks

This little town and very independent community on US Highway 101 on the west end of the Olympic Peninsula is a salt-of-the-earth kind of place. It is also a launch spot for Olympic National Park. Four rivers flow near Forks, making it a key fishing destination.

OLYMPIC SPORTING GOODS (190 S Forks Ave; 360/374-6330) can recommend fishing guides and provide license information. Check out the **FIVE-DAY TRIPS GUIDE** (800/443-6757; www.forkswa.com/5day) for the west side of the peninsula. The **TIMBER MUSEUM** (1421 S Forks Ave; 360/374-9663) tells the story of the West End's logging heritage, and **WEST WIND GALLERY** (120 N Sol Duc Way; 360/374-7795) is a must-visit.

FORKS VISITORS CENTER (1411 S Forks Ave; 360/374-2531 or 800/44-FORKS; www.forks-web.com/fg/visitorscenter.htm) has information and free wireless Internet access 24 hours a day.

LODGINGS

Eagle Point Inn / ★★

384 STORMIN' NORMAN LANE, FORKS; 360/327-3236
One of the most impressive places to stay near the Olympic rain forest, Eagle Point Inn rests on 5 acres in a bend of the Sol Duc River. This spacious log lodge has a stone fireplace made of rocks from the Sol Duc River. Down comforters cover the rooms' queen-sized beds, and a hearty breakfast is served. The owners live nearby in what was the original lodge, leaving you just the right amount of privacy. $$$; *no credit cards; checks OK; www.eaglepointinn. com; 10 miles north of Forks.*

Quillayute River Resort / ★

473 MORA RD, FORKS; 360/374-7447
Built in 1958 for fishermen, this newly renovated motel situated on the banks of the Quillayute River was closed for more than 20 years and recently reopened. There are five riverside suites, each furnished with a propane

"fireplace" and original 1950s kitchen stove, refrigerator, and cabinets. Each suite has a river view and an adjoining private garage. Hiking, kayaking, and other outdoor activities keep the family busy. *$$–$$$; AE, DIS, MC, V; checks OK; www.qriverresort.com; 10 miles west of Forks.*

Shady Nook Cottage / ★

81 ASH AVE, FORKS; 360/374-5497
Just a few blocks from downtown Forks, these three guest cottages are surrounded by a beautiful English garden full of bright flowers. Innkeeper Deannie Hoien, an accomplished stained-glass artist, continually updates the decor with her creations. Down comforters and handmade quilts create a welcoming charm. Cottages come equipped with full kitchens, microwaves, and TVs. *$$; no credit cards; checks OK; closed Dec–Mar except by arrangement; www.shadynookcottage.com; at N Forks Ave turn west, go 2 blocks, turn right onto Ash Ave.*

La Push and Pacific Ocean Beaches

The Dickey, Quillayute, Calawah, and Sol Duc rivers merge and enter the ocean near La Push. Miles of protected wilderness coastline (part of Olympic National Park)—the last stretch remaining in the United States outside of Alaska—extend to the north and south. La Push, at the end of State Route 110 west of US Highway 101, is home to the Quileute Indians, a small community that still revolves around its fishing heritage.

QUILEUTE OCEANSIDE RESORT (at La Push; 360/374-5267 or 800/487-1267; www.quileuteoceanside.com), one of the only nearby lodgings, is the place to go to watch whales. It's on First Beach, part of the Quileute Indian Reservation.

Other nearby beaches are part of **OLYMPIC NATIONAL PARK** (800/833-6388; www.nps.gov/olym). Hike 0.8 mile to remote **SECOND BEACH** (visit at low tide). **THIRD BEACH**, a 1.4-mile hike, is more crowded with surfers and whale watchers; from here, hikers can continue south to a trailhead near the Hoh River. **RIALTO BEACH**, north of La Push on Mora Road, is a 0.1-mile walk from the parking area on a paved trail; from here, hikers can continue north to trailheads at Lake Ozette.

About 25 miles south of Forks, US Highway 101 reaches the Pacific shoreline at **RUBY BEACH** (400 yards off US Hwy 101), offering ocean glimpses and easier beach access for a 10-mile stretch. Ruby Beach has excellent views of Destruction Island; nearby, a trail leads to the world's largest western red cedar.

WARNING: All ocean beaches can be extremely dangerous due to fluctuating tides and unfordable creeks during periods of heavy rain.

LODGINGS

Kalaloch Lodge / ★★

157151 US HWY 101, FORKS; 866/525-2562
The most impressive feature of this lodge is the incredible ocean view. Kalaloch Lodge, right off US Highway 101, has campgrounds and more than 60 lodging options, including cabins, rooms, and suites. The fireplace log cabins, with stacked log walls and Franklin woodstoves, are rustic and cozy. Kalaloch's restaurant (breakfast, lunch, dinner every day) has "Northwest sustainable food"—Penn Cove mussels from Whidbey Island, grass-fed beef, and halibut fish-and-chips. $$–$$$; AE, DIS, MC, V; checks OK; www. visitkalaloch.com; 35 miles south of Forks.

Lake Quinault

Lake Quinault, at the inland apex of the Quinault Indian Reservation, is usually either the first or the last stop on US Highway 101's scenic loop around the Olympic Peninsula. The north shore of the lake surrounded by firs is part of Olympic National Park, the south shore is surrounded by Olympic National Forest, and fishing is memorable. The north-shore and south-shore roads are connected by a gravel road and bridge over the Quinault River, making for a wonderful drive past campgrounds and trailheads.

RAIN FOREST RESORT VILLAGE (516 South Shore Rd, Quinault; 800/255-6936; www.rainforestresort.com) on Lake Quinault has lodgings; the adjoining **SALMON HOUSE RESTAURANT**, open to the public, is a nice choice for dinner. **QUINAULT RANGER STATION** (South Shore Rd, Quinault; 360/288-2525) just east of Lake Quinault Lodge provides information.

LODGINGS

Lake Quinault Lodge / ★★

SOUTH SHORE RD, QUINAULT; 360/288-2900
OR 800/562-6672 (WA AND OR ONLY)
Set in the middle of the Olympic rain forest, this grand old lodge built in 1926 was modeled after Yellowstone's Old Faithful Inn. The lobby has a towering brick fireplace and French doors that open to views of the lake—guests gather in leather sofas to relax. Decor is basic. The lodge features small rooms (only half with a view of the lake; all have private baths) and also several detached cabins. There's a sauna, pool, game room, boats, and hiking trails. Lodge cuisine is Northwest country. There are often too many conventioneers around (mainly in the winter), but somehow the old place manages to exude some of the quiet elegance of its past. $$–$$$; AE, DIS, MC, V; checks OK; www. visitlakequinalt.com; east off US Hwy 101 at milepost 125.

NORTH CASCADES

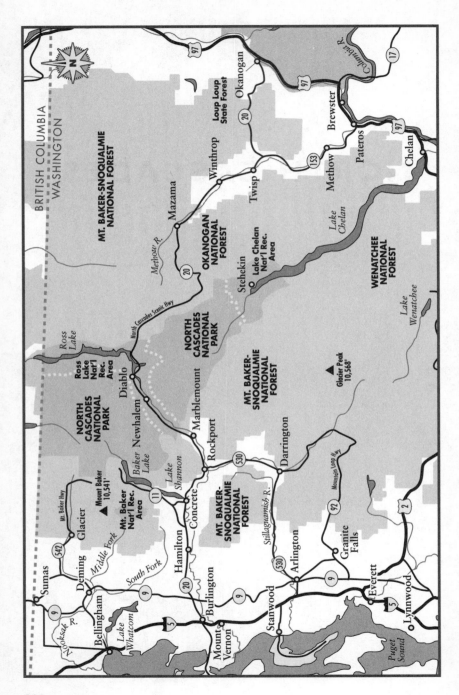

NORTH CASCADES

Raw beauty and ruggedness have been the North Cascades' calling card; often referred to as the North American Alps, the area has remained basically unchanged over the years. The region encompasses Mount Baker to the north, the North Cascades Scenic Highway, the Methow Valley just east of the Cascade Mountain range, and the popular playground of Lake Chelan.

ACCESS AND INFORMATION

There are no airports or train stations here. The North Cascades Scenic Highway (State Route 20) begins in the valley of the Skagit River and rises gradually toward the North Cascade Mountains. The road winds through the heart of North Cascades National Park, skirting the emerald waters of Ross Lake before descending into the remote high desert of the Methow Valley.

State Route 20, running west to east, begins near Sedro-Woolley at exit 230 off Interstate 5, some 65 miles north of Seattle. It eventually connects with Twisp. East of the Cascades, the Twisp-Chelan leg is connected by State Route 153 and US Highway 97.

Snow closes the North Cascades Highway each winter, typically on the east side near Mazama and near Diablo on the west. This stretch is usually blocked from mid-November to mid-April. In winter, Puget Sound visitors travel to the Methow Valley by crossing the Cascades via the longer, more southerly routes of US Highway 2 or Interstate 90.

For information, contact **NORTH CASCADES NATIONAL PARK SERVICE** (810 SR 20, Sedro-Woolley; 360/856-5700; www.nps.gov/noco/) or the **LAKE CHELAN CHAMBER OF COMMERCE AND VISITOR INFORMATION CENTER** (PO Box 216, Chelan; 800/4-CHELAN; www.lakechelan.com).

Mount Baker

The **MOUNT BAKER HIGHWAY** (State Route 542) begins in Bellingham and parallels the sparkling Nooksack River, passing several Christmas-tree farms and little towns like Deming and Glacier, to reach two of the state's most impressive sights: 10,778-foot Mount Baker and 9,131-foot Mount Shuksan. Extreme skiers and snowboarders from all over the world journey to **MOUNT BAKER SKI AREA** (end of SR 542; 360/734-6771, 360/671-0211 snow conditions; www.mtbakerskiarea. com), 56 miles east of Bellingham. The mountain has the highest average annual snowfall—595 inches—in North America. The region has a range of lodgings, including cabins through **MOUNT BAKER LODGING** (800/709-SNOW; www. mtbakerlodging.com).

Just north of Maple Falls, the **BLACK MOUNTAIN FORESTRY CENTER** (360/599-2623; www.blackmountainforestry.com) is a nonprofit organization dedicated to forestry education. The museum features photographs, antique tools, and an adjacent working sawmill.

NORTH CASCADES THREE-DAY TOUR

DAY ONE: Start your day in the Puget Sound area with breakfast at the **FARM-HOUSE RESTAURANT** (13724 La Conner Whitney Rd, Mount Vernon; 360/466-4411) and then head eastbound on the **NORTH CASCADES SCENIC HIGHWAY** for a daylong drive. Pack a lunch or grab a burger at the **GOOD FOOD CAFÉ** (59924 SR 20, Marblemount; 360/873-9309) in Marblemount before making your first must-stop: the **NORTH CASCADES VISITOR CENTER** (SR 20, near milepost 120; 360/386-4495, ext. 11) in Newhalem. Enjoy the center's exhibits, then take a short, easy hike to view the Picket Range. Back in your vehicle, begin driving across the mountains, allowing at least two hours for stops. The overlooks at **DIABLO LAKE** and **WASH-INGTON PASS** have sweeping, panoramic vistas. Continue your drive into the Methow Valley and luxuriate for the night at **FREESTONE INN AT WILSON RANCH** in Mazama, where you'll also have dinner.

DAY TWO: After your complimentary breakfast at the inn, drive into Winthrop and take the morning to explore its western-theme atmosphere. For a historical overview of the area, stop at **SHAFER MUSEUM**. Stroll the main street's Old

---

Everson

RESTAURANTS

Black Forest Steak & Schnitzel House / ★★★

203 W MAIN ST, EVERSON; 360/966-2855
The front of the menu quotes the founder, Jack Niemann: "My culinary art is wasted on those who salt before they've tasted." Dining aficionados who are not put off by this directness will enjoy the best steaks in the county. The hunting-lodge interior looks as if there should be guest rooms right over-head—and you'll wish there were after you've indulged in a rich apple stru-del. The menu also features seven kinds of schnitzel. *$$; MC, V; no checks; dinner every day; full bar; no reservations; Sunset exit off I-5 onto SR 544, in downtown Everson.* &

Deming

RESTAURANTS

The North Fork / ★

6186 MOUNT BAKER HWY, DEMING; 360/599-BEER
How can you not enjoy a place that bills itself as a brewery, pizzeria, wed-ding chapel, and beer shrine? The hand-tossed, thin-crust pizza is good—and

West storefronts, antique stores, and blacksmith shop. Stop for lunch nearby at the **TOPO CAFÉ**, where you can enjoy healthy Asian cuisine. In the early afternoon, unwind at **PEARRYGIN LAKE STATE PARK**, where you can take a swim, rent a boat, or relax with a book under the shady pines. Dine at the exquisite restaurant at **SUN MOUNTAIN LODGE**, where you'll also spend the night.

DAY THREE: For breakfast, stop at Winthrop's **DUCK BRAND HOTEL & CANTINA**, where they serve huevos rancheros and fluffy omelets. Then start your drive to Chelan. The 56-mile trip takes about 1½ hours, but allow time to stop in Twisp to pick up snacks at **TWISP RIVER PUB** or **CINNAMON TWISP**, then visit the **CONFLUENCE GALLERY**. In Chelan, check in to **CAMPBELL'S RESORT ON LAKE CHELAN** and settle into a lakeside lawn chair on the lodge's sandy beach or indulge in a spa treatment. Explore the downtown area nearby. Enjoy dinner at **CAMPBELL HOUSE CAFÉ** and wind up the day with an evening stroll through **RIVERWALK PARK** (downtown, between the two city bridges).

NOTE: This trip is suggested only for spring, summertime, or fall, since portions of the North Cascades Highway are closed in winter.

inexpensive. You can build your own, and there's an ample supply of microbrews on tap. For those wishing to tie the knot, an on-site minister is available—really. The beer shrine consists of nearly a century's worth of empty bottles and cans. $; MC, V; local checks only; lunch Sat–Sun, dinner every day; beer and wine; no reservations; www.northforkbrewery.com; milepost 21 on SR 542. &

Glacier

RESTAURANTS

Milano's Restaurant and Deli / ★★

9990 MOUNT BAKER HWY, GLACIER; 360/599-2863
This is a great little stopping point on your way home from Mount Baker. Serving good Italian food, Milano's is the best bet for several miles. Tasty raviolis are stuffed with spinach or porcini mushrooms, and the linguine vongole is clam-packed. The dessert case includes chocolate truffles, Mount Baker apple pie, tiramisu, or cappuccino chocolate torte. If you're in a rush, grab a take-out sandwich. $$; MC, V; local checks only; breakfast Sat–Sun, lunch, dinner every day; beer and wine; reservations recommended; on Hwy 542 in Glacier.

LODGINGS

Inn at Mount Baker / ★★★

8174 MOUNT BAKER HWY, GLACIER; 360/599-1776
Everything about this classy chalet is elegant. Trimmed in fir with vaulted ceilings, the Inn at Mount Baker offers a spectacular view of the Cascade Mountains and Nooksack River. Each of the six rooms comes with feather beds, down duvets, extra-deep tubs, terry-lined robes, and fresh flowers. A massage therapist is also available. Enjoy the view from the large outdoor hot tub, as well as Bill's famous potato pancakes for breakfast. *$$$; AE, DIS, MC, V; no checks; www.theinnatmtbaker.com; just before milepost 28 on SR 542.*

North Cascades Scenic Highway

One of the nation's prettiest drives, the **NORTH CASCADES SCENIC HIGHWAY** (State Route 20) takes you past waterfalls and alpine meadows, mountain lakes and timber. Because of winter snowfall, a 36-mile stretch of this 140-mile road is closed each year—usually between mid-November and mid-April. In fact, some residents have turned the annual highway closure into a game: they bet on when State Route 20 will close for the year. Don't miss the turquoise-colored Diablo and Ross lakes, created by Seattle City Light's hydroelectric dam projects to harness the turbulent power of water.

The highway, the most northerly cross-state route, connects the damper west side of the Cascades with the semiarid and sunnier eastern portion of the state. Nearly a three-hour drive from I-5 to Okanogan, the road meanders and climbs from peaceful farmland and lush, thick evergreens to rugged mountains and immense glaciers via **RAINY PASS** and **WASHINGTON PASS**, then glides down into a wide-open pastoral valley and grassy meadowlands.

Marblemount

Every year, from December through February, bald eagles hold a convention along the Skagit River near Marblemount. Hundreds of these raptors feast on spawned-out salmon, easily viewable from State Route 20 between Marblemount and Rockport. Some of the best viewing is from the river, via a float tour. For information, contact **CHINOOK EXPEDITIONS** (800/241-3451; www.chinook expeditions.com), **WILDWATER RIVER TOURS** (800/522-WILD; www.wildwater-river.com), or the **MOUNT BAKER RANGER DISTRICT** (2105 SR 20, Sedro-Woolley; 360/856-5700).

North Cascades National Park

The North Cascades are sometimes called America's Alps. Like their European counterparts, these mountains possess extraordinary grandeur, along with a wildness that makes them a worldwide draw.

In 1968 a 505,000-acre section immediately south of the U.S.-Canadian border won national park status. The huge park contains jagged peaks draped in ice and 318 glaciers. Part of the Cascade Range, the peaks are not especially tall—the highest hover around 9,000 feet—but their vertical rise takes them from almost sea level into the clouds, making them steep-walled, enchanting to view, and, in many places, inaccessible.

Although the North Cascades Highway bisects the wilderness area and provides dramatic views, the range's inner sanctum contains no roads, no lodges or visitor centers. Fortunately, the adventurous have been given 386 miles of maintained trails to explore—and the rest can take solace in a scenic drive.

Access to the park, about a three-hour drive from Seattle, is via the North Cascades Scenic Highway (State Route 20). The main highway provides access to dozens of trails, including the **PACIFIC CREST NATIONAL SCENIC TRAIL**. Backpackers also hike into the park from Stehekin, at the north end of Lake Chelan. Hiking usually starts in June; snow commonly melts off by July. But summer storms are frequent; be prepared with rain gear. Expect four-legged company in the backcountry.

Backcountry camping requires a free permit, available at the **NORTH CASCADES NATIONAL PARK HEADQUARTERS** (2105 SR 20, Sedro-Woolley; 360/856-5700; www.nps.gov/noca/) or the **WILDERNESS INFORMATION CENTER** (7280 Ranger Station Rd, Marblemount; 360/873-4500). Both offices have park information.

Diablo and Ross Lakes

Ancient forests, abundant wildlife, and waterfalls abound in the Diablo and Ross lakes areas. Enjoy the **DIABLO LAKE ADVENTURE CRUISE** for panoramic views; visit the **NEWHALEM SKAGIT TOURS OFFICE** (500 Newhalem St, Rockport; 206/233-2709; June–Sept) for more information. Also of interest is the nonprofit North Cascades Institute's recently opened **ENVIRONMENTAL LEARNING CENTER** (360/856-5700, ext. 209), including a dining hall and an amphitheater.

The Methow Valley

Just east of the Cascades, State Route 20 makes a dramatic descent from rain forest into the sagebrush landscape of the Methow (pronounced "MET-how") Valley. The Methow harkens to the days of the Old West, from Winthrop's authentic western storefronts to the valley's working ranches and farms.

CROSS-COUNTRY SKIING THE METHOW

Bright winter sunshine, dry powder snow, jaw-dropping views of mountain peaks—add almost 200 kilometers of well-groomed trails, and you have one of the nation's premier cross-country ski destinations. Ski season begins in early December and continues through March. The **METHOW VALLEY SPORT TRAILS ASSOCIATION** (MVSTA; 800/682-5787; www.mvsta.com) maintains this vast network of trails, the second largest in the country. The system has four linked sections, many of which go directly past the valley's accommodations, so you can ski from your door.

The largest section surrounds Sun Mountain Lodge in Winthrop, where 70 kilometers of trail cut through rolling hills. Below it, the Community Trail snakes past farms and bottomland as it meanders from Winthrop to Mazama. Mazama's flat terrain and open meadows are ideal for novices.

The remaining section, called Rendezvous, is recommended for intermediate to expert skiers only. Set above the valley at 3,500 feet, trails pass through rugged forestland, where five huts are located for overnight stays. Each hut bunks up to eight people. **CENTRAL RESERVATIONS** (800/422-3048) has maps and information and makes the required reservations for the hut-to-hut system. Special trails are also set aside for snowshoers. Skiing at MVSTA trails requires trail passes, available at ski shops in the valley.

—Nick Gallo

Mazama

Thirteen miles north of Winthrop on State Route 20 is the tiny hamlet of Mazama (pronounced "ma-ZAH-ma"), where fly-fishing and cross-country skiing are the main attractions. Here, you'll find the quaint **MAZAMA STORE** (50 Lost River Rd; 509/996-2855). There's also a picnic area—and the only gas pump for 70 miles if you're traveling west over the mountains. The town also hosts the annual summertime **METHOW MUSIC FESTIVAL** (800/340-1458), a classical-music series.

RESTAURANTS

Freestone Inn / ★★★

17798 SR 20, MAZAMA; 509/996-3906 OR 800/639-3809

This classy restaurant features candlelit tables with an ever-changing menu. Breakfast includes cast-iron-skillet prime-rib hash, eggs provençal, or the Wilson Ranch country breakfast. At dinner, try the grilled Dungeness crab cakes, double-cut lamb chops, pan-seared New York steak, homemade fettuccine, or brook trout. Desserts feature apple–white cheddar crisp or burnt lemon custard tart. *$$$; AE, DC, DIS, MC, V; local checks only; breakfast every day, dinner Tues–Sun; beer and wine; reservations recommended; www.freestone inn.com; 1½ miles west of Mazama.* ⅃

LODGINGS

Freestone Inn at Wilson Ranch / ★★★

17798 SR 20, MAZAMA; 509/996-3906 OR 800/639-3809
Though selected several years ago by *Travel & Leisure* as one of the 25 great American lodges, the Freestone Inn has not rested on its laurels. This 21-room log lodge sits on 120 acres in the wilderness. A massive river-rock fireplace is the lobby centerpiece; a small library nook is nearby. Guest rooms are trimmed in pine and come with big fireplaces, bathrooms with soaking tubs, wrought-iron fixtures, and old black-and-white photographs. An outdoor hot tub is near Freestone Lake. There's also the luxurious Lakeside Lodge and 15 smaller cabins. *$$$; AE, DC, DIS, MC, V; local checks only; www.freestone inn.com; 1½ miles west of Mazama.* ⅃

Mazama Ranch House / ★

HCR 74, MAZAMA; 509/996-2040
Horses and kids stay free at these accommodations just behind the Mazama Store. The ranch house sleeps up to 13; there are also eight new suites and another cabin that fits four. The ranch features a barn, corral, and arena for overnighters who bring horses; city dwellers can rent their own from Early Winters Outfitting (800/737-8750; www.earlywintersoutfitting.com). *$$; MC, V; checks OK; www.mazamaranchhouse.com; just off Lost River Rd, across from Mazama Country Inn.* ⅃

Winthrop

The Western motif of this mountain town fits the sun-baked (or snow-covered) hills and wide-open sky. The old-fashioned storefronts and boardwalks feel a bit like you're visiting Tombstone, the famous Arizona gunslinging town. This is where most "tourism" takes place in the Methow Valley. Stop at the **SHAFER MUSEUM** (285 Castle Ave; 509/996-2712), housed in pioneer Guy Waring's 1897 log cabin on the hill behind the main street.

After you've had a big day outside, sip a beer at the **WINTHROP BREWING COMPANY** (155 Riverside Ave; 509/996-3183), in an old schoolhouse on the main street. **WINTHROP MOUNTAIN SPORTS** (257 Riverside Ave; 509/996-2886; www. winthropmountainsports.com) sells outdoor-activity equipment and supplies and rents bikes, skies, snowshoes, and ice skates. The **TENDERFOOT GENERAL STORE** (corner of Riverside Ave and SR 20; 509/996-2288) has anything else you might need. The 100-year-old **WINTHROP PALACE** (149 Riverside Ave; 509/996-2245; www.winthroppalace.com), a steak and seafood restaurant-lounge, is one of the town's oldest landmarks.

PEARRYGIN LAKE STATE PARK (509/996-2370) is a good swimming hole 5 miles north of town. A useful Web site is **CENTRAL RESERVATIONS** (800/422-3048; www.methowreservations.com), which allows you to find events like the **WINTHROP R&B FESTIVAL** in mid-July. For more details, there's also the valley's **VISITOR INFORMATION SOURCE** (888/463-8469; www.methow.com).

RESTAURANTS

Duck Brand Hotel & Cantina / ★

246 RIVERSIDE AVE, WINTHROP; 509/996-2129 OR 800/996-2129
Since opening 25 years ago, this funky Winthrop restaurant has been known as "the Duck." Its menu has evolved over the years, from Mexican and Italian dishes to an ever-changing selection that might include eggs McDuck for breakfast, a Fallbroker BLT for lunch, or filet mignon for dinner. There's a delicious bakery, and upstairs, the Duck Brand Hotel has six inexpensive and sparsely furnished rooms. *$$; AE, DC, DIS, MC, V; local checks only; breakfast, lunch, dinner every day; full bar; no reservations; www.methownet. com/duck; on main street.*

Sun Mountain Lodge / ★★★

**604 PATTERSON LAKE RD, WINTHROP;
509/996-2211 OR 800/572-0493**
The first thing you notice when entering the Sun Mountain Lodge Dining Room is the spectacular scenery. Every seat has a view from the nearly 3,000-foot elevation. In 2006 Sun Mountain Lodge received the Washington Wine Grand Award for Hotel Dining Room from the Washington Wine Commission and the *Seattle Times*. The menu includes beef tenderloin, mushrooms from the Cascades, and vegetables from the Sunny M Farm. You'll pay for the experience, but it's worth it. *$$$; AE, DC, MC, V; local checks only; breakfast, lunch, dinner every day; full bar; reservations recommended; www.sun mountainlodge.com; 9.6 miles southwest of Winthrop.* &

Topo Café / ★

253 RIVERSIDE AVE, WINTHROP; 509/996-4596
Yes, there is Asian cuisine in Winthrop. Visitors delight in the quiet charm of Topo Café. The interior is subtle and elegant, while the dishes feature healthy goodies like *edamame*, spring rolls, pho (Vietnamese soup), phad thai, spicy Singapore noodles, or Japanese *katsu* cutlet. *$$; MC, V; local checks only; dinner Mon–Sat; beer and wine; reservations recommended; www.methownet. com/topo; on main road.*

EXPERIENCE A PEACEFUL THRILL IN THE METHOW VALLEY

Kurt Oakley describes floating through the Methow Valley at 3,000 feet aboard a hot-air balloon as a "peaceful thrill." Kurt and his wife, Melinda, have hosted **MORNING GLORY BALLOON TOURS** (429 Eastside County Rd, Winthrop; 509/997-1700; balloonwinthrop.com) for the last decade. Offered year-round, the balloon tours usually depart an hour after sunrise, when winds are calmest. Kurt likes to say that he covers the "air show," while Melinda attends to the "ground show." She makes breads, scones, and cream cheese and provides drinks, especially the traditional champagne. After landing, a champagne picnic is held to celebrate your sky trek.

"The tradition of champagne and propane goes back a few hundred years in the ballooning industry," explains Kurt, who averages about 125 balloon trips annually. Many fond memories have been made a few thousand feet above sea level. A private flight for two features red-carpet treatment, including champagne in flight, a bouquet of flowers, and chocolates presented upon landing. "We've hosted a number of marriage proposals," says Kurt. "They never say 'no' at 3,000 feet!"

A certified commercial balloonist with the Federal Aviation Administration, Kurt contends that while Sun Mountain Lodge, at 3,000 feet above sea level, offers the best scenery on land, "We feature the best scenery in the sky."

With balloon excursions offered in winter, Kurt explains that mountain valleys frequently encounter temperature inversions when it's calm. Thus, it's not uncommon for upper air temperatures to be 10–15 degrees warmer than on the ground. And since the balloon moves gently with the wind, there is no wind-chill factor. The beauty of a winter balloon flight is the radiant heat provided by the balloon's burner. While Morning Glory provides the hot drinks, Mother Nature provides the scenery and sunshine.

—Rick Stedman

LODGINGS

Hotel Rio Vista / ★

285 RIVERSIDE AVE, WINTHROP; 509/996-3535 OR 800/398-0911

Stand on the private deck on any of the 29 rooms overlooking the confluence of the Chewuch and Methow rivers, and you quickly understand the hotel's name: it means "river view" in Spanish. The setting is just part of the appeal of this western-themed hotel just south of downtown—rooms are nicer than you'd expect of a hotel in the area. They also rent a lofted cabin that sleeps six, 10 minutes west of Winthrop. *$$; MC, V; checks OK; www.hotelriovista. com; on main road.*

Sun Mountain Lodge / ★★★☆

604 PATTERSON LAKE RD, WINTHROP;
509/996-2211 OR 800/572-0493
Sun Mountain Lodge is a luxury resort that offers 360 degrees of surrounding scenery, which is its hallmark. Perched on a hill 3,000 feet above the valley, this place is an outdoor-enthusiast's dream. It was the first destination cross-country ski resort in the Northwest; it is now the largest. All rooms are fabulous, but the Mount Robinson rooms are the newest, and they're stunning; sit in your whirlpool bath and gaze at the mountains. *$$$–$$$$; AE, DC, MC, V; checks OK; www.sunmountainlodge.com; 9.6 miles southwest of Winthrop.*

WolfRidge Resort / ★★

412-B WOLF CREEK RD, WINTHROP; 509/996-2828 OR 800/237-2388
Located about 5 miles from the highway, this collection of log buildings is everything a mountain retreat should be. You'll find 19 beautifully crafted one- and two-bedroom log townhouses, studios, and hotel-style rooms. The log four-plex building, for example, has a queen bed and single daybed, log beam ceiling, microwave, mini-fridge, and sliding glass doors opening onto a view balcony. There's an outdoor pool and a hot tub in a river-rock setting. Venture out on skis or bikes on the trails that run right outside your door. *$$–$$$; AE, MC, V; checks OK; www.wolfridgeresort.com; south of Winthrop, head up Twin Lakes Rd 1½ miles, turn right on Wolf Creek Rd, travel 4 miles to entrance on right.*

Twisp

Just a few miles south of Winthrop you'll find the town of Twisp, the state's sunflower capital; it's worth a stop. Meander along Glover Street, a block off the main road. You'll find several vibrant businesses, including **ANTLER'S SALOON & CAFÉ** (132 Glover St; 509/997-5693).

Other Twisp attractions include the **METHOW VALLEY FARMERS MARKET** (Methow Valley Community Center; Sat, Apr 15–Oct 15) and the **CONFLU-ENCE GALLERY & ART CENTER** (104 Glover St; 509/997-ARTS; www.confluence gallery.com). The **MERC PLAYHOUSE** (101 Glover St; 509/997-PLAY; www.merc playhouse.com) offers local productions. For a sweet tooth, don't miss the **CIN-NAMON TWISP** (116 Glover St; 509/997-5030; www.cinnamontwisp.com). For more information, contact the **TWISP VISITOR INFORMATION CENTER** (509/997-2926) or the **TWISP CHAMBER OF COMMERCE** (www.twispinfo.com).

RESTAURANTS

Twisp River Pub / ★

SR 20, TWISP; 888/220-3360 OR 509/997-6822
Overlooking its namesake, the Twisp River Pub—home of the Methow Brewing Company—often draws a crowd. The riverside deck and beer garden are

fabulous during the summer. Expect above-standard pub fare, fresh seafood, and a kids' menu. It's a loud place, especially with live music on the weekends and an open mic most Saturday nights. *$$; AE, DC, DIS, MC, V; checks OK; lunch, dinner every day (Wed–Sun in winter); full bar; no reservations; www. twispriverpub.com; right on highway.*

Pateros

LODGINGS

Amy's Manor Inn / ★★

435 SR 153, PATEROS; 509/923-2334 OR 866-269-7466
Built in 1928, this enchanting manor sits at the foot of the Cascades in an impressive stand of trees overlooking the Methow River. Stone fences line the property, and 5 acres of flower gardens produce bursts of color. Three country-French rooms share two bathrooms, and many weddings are held here. Don't miss the culinary creations of owner Pamela Ahl, who also teaches cooking classes. *$$; MC, V; checks OK; www.amysmanor.com; 5 miles north of Pateros.*

Lake Chelan

Over the years, Lake Chelan has been where everyone goes on vacation. It's no wonder. Since everyone from college kids to young families hangs out here, it's always fun.

Though new condos and homes have dotted the southern end of the lake near the town of Chelan, development hasn't stopped anyone from coming to enjoy the more than 300 days of sunshine annually. Sunny weather has also been the reason for the doubling of area wineries over the last year.

If it's peace and quiet you seek, take a boat ride to the very northern tip of the lake, where you'll find the settlement of Stehekin. Plying the waters of Lake Chelan is the **LAKE CHELAN BOAT COMPANY** (1418 W Woodin Ave; 509/682-4584 or 509/682-2224; www.ladyofthelake.com), featuring year-round tours. Hop aboard the 56-foot yacht that was owned by the late great Dean Martin, *Innamorata*. Dinner cruises are offered nightly. **CHELAN AIRWAYS** (1328 W Woodin Ave; 509/682-5065 or 509/682-5555; www.chelanairways.com) has direct flights to Stehekin in 30 minutes from Chelan.

The lake also has 13 boat-in campgrounds at **LAKE CHELAN STATE PARK** (888/226-7688 for reservations) and **TWENTY-FIVE MILE CREEK CAMPGROUND** (509/682-2576).

Chelan

Located at the southern tip of Lake Chelan, the small town of Chelan is an outdoor paradise. Families enjoy the city's **LAKESIDE PARK**, a 10-acre retreat. Kids love **SLIDEWATERS** (102 Waterslide Dr off US Hwy 97; 509/682-5751; www. slidewaters.com). Try the 420-foot, completely darkened tunnel called "Purple Haze." The park also has a 60-person hot tub, swimming pool, and toddlers aqua park. Rent boats and water-ski gear at **CHELAN BOAT RENTALS** (1210 W Woodin Ave; 509/682-4444).

For accommodations, try **CHELAN QUALITY VACATION PROPERTIES** (888/977-1748; www.lakechelanvacationrentals.com). **WAPATO POINT ON LAKE CHELAN** (1 Wapato Pt Way, Manson; 509/687-9511 or 888/768-9511; www.wapatopoint. com) offers a full-fledged resort in neighboring Manson.

Overlooking Lake Chelan is the newest dent in the landscape: the 6,000-acre Bear Mountain Ranch, with homesites available at Bandera and Hawk's Meadow. The prize attraction, though, is picturesque **BEAR MOUNTAIN RANCH GOLF COURSE** (509/682-5910).

If you really want to appreciate Chelan's history, visit the **LAKE CHELAN HISTORICAL SOCIETY MUSEUM** (204 E Woodin Ave; 509/682-5644). The **LAKE CHELAN CHAMBER OF COMMERCE** (800/4-CHELAN; www.lakechelan.com) is a good resource. The **RANGER STATION** at Chelan (428 W Woodin Ave; 509/682-2576) is open year-round.

RESTAURANTS

Campbell House Café / ★★

104 W WOODIN AVE, CHELAN; 509/682-4250
This is where you'll find Chelan's freshest seafood, dependable steaks, and acceptable pastas. Breakfast is also really popular here. Upstairs, the Second Floor Pub and Veranda is more casual. Order burgers and brews, then people watch on a warm evening. *$$$; AE, MC, V; checks OK; breakfast (café), lunch, dinner every day; full bar; reservations recommended (café), no reservations (pub); www.campbellsresort.com; downtown facing main street near lake.* &

LODGINGS

Best Western Lakeside Lodge & Suites / ★

2312 W WOODIN AVE, CHELAN; 509/682-4396 OR 800/468-2781
Nestled in the towering pines 2 miles south of Chelan on US Highway 97, the Best Western offers 95 rooms; top floor units have vaulted ceilings. Its location is awesome: next to Lakeside Park, with its public sandy beach and views of the North Cascades. There's also heated indoor and outdoor pools, two outdoor spas, and free continental breakfast. *$$$; AE, DC, DIS, MC, V; checks OK; www.lakesidelodge.net.* &

A MOONLIGHT SNOWSHOE WALK IN STEHEKIN

Stehekin is like no other place you'll ever visit.

National Geographic featured this secluded location in 1974, and its mystique still lingers, especially during the winter. Located at the northern tip of Lake Chelan, Stehekin is a 55-mile boat ride from the small Central Washington town of Chelan. Normally a summertime destination for hiking and fishing, Stehekin Lodge lures in the winter with moonlight snowshoeing treks.

A weekend snowshoeing package includes round-trip boat ride on the *Lady Express*, two nights' lodging, snowshoe rental, transportation to and from trails, breakfast for two, and a Saturday-night guided snowshoe walk.

On Friday, arrive at Stehekin Lodge after a two-hour boat ride. Check in to your modest room, then stop by the store and pick up your snowshoes. Then it's onto the bus and a drive to Rainbow Falls. This is followed by an hour's trek around Buckner Orchard.

Back at the lodge, hang out in the lounge area, enjoying the lake and mountain views. Downstairs, the restaurant transforms from modest breakfast joint to romantic dinner setting, complete with candlelight. Dinners are simple but good, often featuring steak or fish, fresh salads, and wines from Chelan. After breakfast on Saturday morning, get back on the bus for the 9-mile ride to Stehekin Valley Ranch. From here, snowshoers have several options. Most prefer the 3-mile walk along the Stehekin River to High Bridge.

Save energy for the moonlight snowshoe trek. After dinner, a bus takes you to the airstrip. Donning snowshoes, you tromp through the forest, then walk several hundred yards to a waiting bonfire. Sipping mulled wine and creating s'mores is the nighttime ritual, as is the camaraderie that develops. Memories are etched through all the silence, and the mystique of Stehekin remains with you long afterward.

—Rick Stedman

Campbell's Resort on Lake Chelan / ★★

104 W WOODIN AVE, CHELAN; 509/682-2561 OR 800/553-8225

The city's landmark resort hotel, built in 1901, now has a new spa. Featuring 1,200 feet of beach front, Campbell's is a family favorite with 170 rooms, many with kitchenettes, all with patios. There's also two heated outdoor pools, two outdoor hot tubs, and boat moorage and golf packages. Reservations are hard to come by in high season. *$$–$$$; AE, MC, V; checks OK; www.campbellsresort.com; on lake at end of main street near downtown.*

Kelly's Resort / ★★

12800 LAKESHORE RD, CHELAN; 509/687-3220 OR 800/561-8978
Located 14 miles uplake on the south shore of Lake Chelan, Kelly's has been a family getaway for six decades. It features cabins and modern condo units on the lake, where you'll lie out in the sun at least half the time. In the main building, find a small store, fireplace room, deck, and coffee bar. Did we mention the outdoor heated pool, smack-dab in the middle of the woods? *$$$–$$$$; AE, MC, V; checks OK; www.kellysresort.com; drive 14 miles west on S Lakeshore Rd.*

Stehekin

This tiny hamlet at the northern tip of Lake Chelan is reminiscent of a bygone era. You feel the pace is less hectic the moment you step off the boat. The other methods of reaching Stehekin include Chelan Airways' floatplane or on foot via hiking trails. This is the gateway to North Cascades National Park. One of the burg's highlights is the **STEHEKIN PASTRY COMPANY** (2 miles up the Stehekin Valley Rd from the boat landing; 800/536-0745), renowned for its cinnamon rolls.

Stehekin is an access point for trails in North Cascades National Park; a **NATIONAL PARK SERVICE SHUTTLE BUS** (509/682-2549; mid-May–mid-Oct) provides transportation from Stehekin to trailheads. Part of the national park complex is **NORTH CASCADES STEHEKIN LODGE** (509/682-4494; www.stehekin. com), a year-round lodge featuring 28 rooms, a restaurant, a store, and a rental shop for bikes, boats, skis, and snowshoes.

The **STEHEKIN VALLEY RANCH** (800/536-0745; www.courtneycountry.com) has been a mainstay for years. It's a great place to use as a base. Open during summer, the ranch rents 12 units; 7 are rustic tent-cabins. Including three hearty meals a day, prices range from $70 to $90 a night. **CASCADE CORRALS** (509/682-7742) arranges horseback rides and mountain pack trips. A new addition is **STEHEKIN RAINBOW LODGE** (RainbowLodge@stehekinvalley.net), at the base of 312-foot Rainbow Falls. The house, featuring suites and cabins, is built in plain view of the falls.

LODGINGS

Silver Bay Inn Resort / ★★

10 SILVER BAY RD, STEHEKIN;
509/682-2212 OR 800/555-7781 IN WASH. AND ORE.
Two big changes have occurred for Kathy and Randall Dinwiddie, the former Seattle-area teachers turned innkeepers of Silver Bay Inn Resort. This spectacular solar home is available only April–October, and there's now wireless Internet access. The four waterfront cabins all have kitchens. A regular on these pages since 1986, Silver Bay Inn has added a gift shop. The hot tub has a 360-degree view of the lake and surrounding mountains. *$$–$$$; MC, V; checks OK; www. silverbayinn.com; 1½ miles up Stehekin Valley Rd from boat landing.*

CENTRAL CASCADES

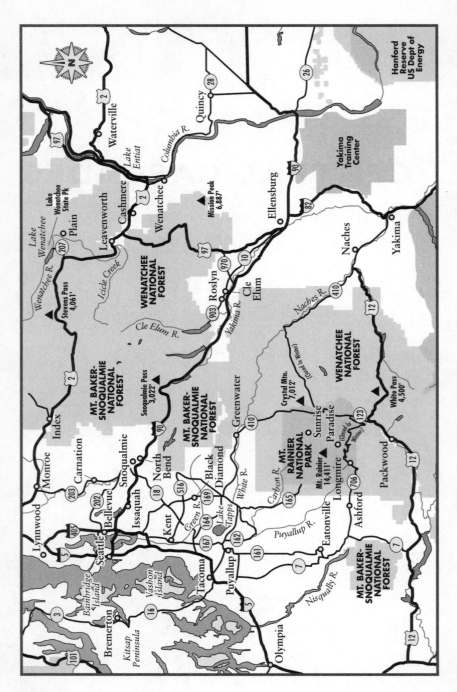

CENTRAL CASCADES

On clear days, commuters stuck in traffic on Western Washington freeways gaze east to the Central Cascades, where white peaks beckon in winter. In summer, the range's presence reminds why so many people live here. Year-round, blue-sky days reveal the always-snow-covered, stunning majesty of what is called, simply, "the mountain"—Mount Rainier.

The Cascades form a barrier between Eastern and Western Washington. The main cross-state routes of Interstate 90 (Snoqualmie Pass) and US Highways 2 (Stevens Pass) and 12 (White Pass) can get choked with snow, sometimes closing in winter.

The mountains around the Bavarian-style village of Leavenworth and north to the tiny village of Plain offer all-season getaways. The small towns of Cle Elum and Roslyn showcase their working-class roots next to their new neighbors: high-end Suncadia with its Arnold Palmer–designed golf course and 3,000-plus new homes being built.

From late spring to early fall, many Northwesterners head to "the mountain" to picnic in Paradise. Mount Rainier is an easy day trip from the Puget Sound area—or stay overnight in one of the lodgings nearby.

ACCESS AND INFORMATION

The scenic 400-mile **CASCADE LOOP** follows US Highway 2 east from Everett, crosses Stevens Pass to take in Leavenworth and Wenatchee, and heads north (see North Cascades chapter) to Lake Chelan, Winthrop, and the North Cascades Scenic Highway (State Route 20). The route can be accessed from Interstate 90 at Cle Elum by taking Highway 970 north to US Highway 97, which continues north. It joins US Highway 2 just east of Leavenworth. A brochure is available from the **CASCADE LOOP ASSOCIATION** (509/662-3888; www.cascadeloop.com).

The most popular east-west route across Washington, **INTERSTATE 90** connects Interstate 5 at Seattle with Ellensburg, Moses Lake, and Spokane (and beyond). A map of this multilane freeway is available from the **MOUNTAINS TO SOUND GREENWAY TRUST** (206/382-5565; www.mtsgreenway.org).

Lesser-known **US HIGHWAY 12** is a very scenic two-lane highway. Access Mount Rainier from the south by taking US Highway 12 to State Route 7, then north from Morton to Ashford and the Nisqually entrance. Or take Skate Creek Road north from Packwood on US Highway 12 to the Ohanapecosh entrance (closed in winter). Continuing east on US Highway 12 leads to White Pass Ski Resort, Yakima, and beyond.

It's a good idea to check **MOUNTAIN PASS REPORTS** (800/695-ROAD; www.wsdot.wa.gov/traffic/passes) before heading over the mountains in winter.

CENTRAL CASCADES THREE-DAY TOUR

DAY ONE: From Seattle, head north on Interstate 5, then east on US Highway 2 toward Leavenworth. Stop for a late breakfast at Sultan Bakery (711 Stevens Ave, Sultan; 360/793-7996) on the way, then tool over Stevens Pass and into the ersatz Bavarian village. Fuel up with lunch at **PAVZ CREPERIE**, then peruse the unique shops. If this is an adults-only getaway, check in at the romantic **RUN OF THE RIVER INN & REFUGE**, select from the assortment of bikes (free to use), and head out to nearby **HOMEFIRES BAKERY** (13013 Bayne Rd; 509/548-7362) for a snack, then continue to **SLEEPING LADY MOUNTAIN RETREAT** to admire the Dale Chihuly glass art before returning to town. If you've brought the kids, stay instead at the **ICICLE VILLAGE RESORT** and play minigolf or splash in the pool. Enjoy dinner at **CAFÉ MOZART**. Afterward, drive to **LEAVENWORTH SUMMER THEATER AT SKI HILL AMPHITHEATER** (Ski Hill Dr, Leavenworth; 509/548-2000; www.leavenworthsummertheater.org) to see *The Sound of Music* (make reservations in advance; it often sells out).

DAY TWO: After breakfast at your inn, head east on US Highway 2 to **SMALLWOOD'S HARVEST** (509/548-4196; www.smallwoodsharvest.com), a huge country mercantile, complete with a petting farm. Cruise along to Cashmere

US Highway 2 and Stevens Pass

US Highway 2 heads east-west across the state, from Interstate 5 at Everett to Spokane, winding up to Stevens Pass along the Skykomish River. **STEVENS PASS SKI AREA** (65 miles east of I-5 on US Hwy 2; 206/812-4510; www.stevenspass. com; late Nov–early Apr) is a favorite of Seattle-area skiers, offering downhill and cross-country skiing as well as snowshoeing; the **NORDIC CENTER** is located 5 miles east of the summit. Day lodges at the summit include a half-dozen casual eateries. From the pass, US Highway 2 drops down to the Wenatchee River. Along the way, the towns of Leavenworth, Cashmere, Wenatchee, and Waterville give travelers reason to stop.

Leavenworth

A former struggling mill town, self-styled in the 1960s as a Bavarian village, Leavenworth has more than found its niche: it's a theme town, called the "Ultimate Holiday Town USA" by the A&E channel.

Bavarian food, architecture, music, and festivals are the fabric of life here. Excellent lodging is plentiful, most with touches of Bavarian style. Popular festivals include the Washington State Autumn Leaf Festival, Oktoberfest, Christmas

and stop at **PIONEER VILLAGE** for history and **LIBERTY ORCHARDS** for Aplets and Cotlets. Have lunch at the **WALNUT CAFÉ** (106 Cottage Ave, Cashmere; 509/782-2022; www.thewalnutcafe.com), then continue to Wenatchee. Spend a leisurely afternoon enjoying **OHME GARDENS** and walking its 1-mile trail of stones and steps. Drive north to the small town of Waterville and check in at the **WATERVILLE HISTORIC HOTEL**. Explore the town on foot for a bit before taking the 25-mile drive back to Wenatchee for fine dining at **SHAKTI'S**.

DAY THREE: Have breakfast at the hotel in Waterville. Take US Highway 2 back south then west past Wenatchee and Cashmere, then take US Highway 97 and 970 south to Cle Elum. Stop at the **CLE ELUM BAKERY** or **PIONEER COFFEE ROASTING COMPANY** (121 Pennsylvania Ave; 509/674-4100) for refreshment. Drive to Roslyn to see where the TV show *Northern Exposure* was filmed in the 1990s. A walk through the **ROSLYN CITY CEMETERY** provides a glimpse of the many nationalities that lived here during the coal-mining days. Stop for a burger at the **ROSLYN CAFÉ** before leaving the old and settling in with the new at **SUNCADIA RESORT**. If you're feeling energetic, rent bikes to ride the trails, or end the day with a twilight round of golf on **PROSPECTOR GOLF COURSE**. Finish with dinner at the Inn at Suncadia's restaurant, the **GAS LAMP GRILLE**.

Lighting Festival, and Spring Bird Fest. Contact the Leavenworth Chamber of Commerce (see below) for information.

Explore the shops along Front Street. Stops include **DIE MUSIK BOX** (933 Front St; 509/548-6152 or 800/288-5883; www.musicboxshop.com); the **BAVARIAN CLOTHING COMPANY** (933 Front St; 509/548-2442), where you can custom-order genuine lederhosen or buy dirndls and capes; and **KRIS KRINGL** (907 Front St; 509/548-6867 or 888/KKRINGL; www.kkringl.com) for year-round Christmas shopping.

Cultural offerings are growing. The **HI STRUNG MUSIC & PICKIN' PARLOR** (923 Commercial St; 509/548-8663; www.histrungmusic.com) focuses on acoustic music. The **COMMUNITY COFFEE HOUSE** offers live music two Friday nights each month at the Chumstick Grange Hall (621 Front St; 509/548-7374; www.leavenworthcoffeehouse.com). Concerts at **ICICLE CREEK MUSIC CENTER** (7409 Icicle Rd; 509/548-6347 or 877/265-6026; www.icicle.org) highlight a range of styles.

In town, seek out the **MILLER FINE ARTS GALLERY** (210 Division St; 509/548-8010), or check out the **UPPER VALLEY MUSEUM**, co-located with the **BARN BEACH RESERVE** at the former Haus Lorelei B&B (347 Division St; 509/548-0181; www.wenatcheevalleymuseum.com/leavenworth). Visit the **LEAVENWORTH NUTCRACKER MUSEUM** (735 Front St; 509/548-4573 or 800/892-3989; www.

nutcrackermuseum.com; afternoons May–Oct, call for other times) to view 5,000 nutcrackers.

Boutique wineries continue to crop up (see "Columbia Cascade Wine Region: Touring and Tasting"). For a picnic, pair wine with cheese from the **CHEESE-MONGER'S SHOP** (633 Front St, Ste F; 509/548-9011; www.cheesemongersshop. com). Stop by the Front Street creperie, **PAVZ** (833 Front St; 509/548-2103; www. pavz.com), for a stylish, casual setting, or enjoy a glass of wine with your meal at **EDEL HAUS** (320 9th St; 509/548-4412 or 800/487-3335), one of the best places to dine alfresco.

Outdoor activities abound; check with the **LEAVENWORTH RANGER STATION** just off US Highway 2 (600 Sherbourne St, eastern edge of town; 509/548-6977) or the **LEAVENWORTH CHAMBER OF COMMERCE** (940 US Hwy 2; 509/548-5807; www.leavenworth.org) for information.

RESTAURANTS

Café Mozart / ★★★

829 FRONT ST, LEAVENWORTH; 509/548-0600

Nibble on schnitzel or pork medallions in this family-run dining retreat overlooking Front Street. Or splurge on the chateaubriand for two, a whopping 20-ounce Black Angus steak, served with grilled vegetables. For a gut-busting sampler of Bavarian specialties, order the Hofbrauhaus Platter for two. Don't miss the hot apple strudel with ice cream. The extensive "wine attic" can be viewed from the dining area, and live harp music and elegant decor add a romantic touch. The downstairs restaurant has a beer-hall atmosphere and serves heartier food. *$$$; AE, DIS, MC, V; local checks only; lunch, dinner every day (dinner only every day in winter); beer and wine; reservations recommended; www.cafemozartrestaurant.com; across from park.*

Visconti's Ristorante Italiano / ★★

636 FRONT ST, LEAVENWORTH; 509/548-1213

1737 N WENATCHEE AVE, WENATCHEE; 509/662-5013

Italian food is served up in a lively fine-dining atmosphere in the upper levels of Leavenworth's former brewery. Pizza and other delicious items—including savory mussels—come out of the wood-fired ovens. The homemade gelato shop Viadolce! opens at 6am. The Leavenworth Visconti's has a shorter menu than the original Visconti's, a fancy roadhouse on the main drag in Wenatchee. Both are popular and frequently packed, and both offer a kids menu. *$$; AE, DIS, MC, V; checks OK; lunch, dinner every day (Leavenworth), lunch Mon–Fri, dinner every day (Wenatchee); beer and wine; reservations recommended; www.viscontis.com; across from park (Leavenworth), US Hwy 2 where it becomes Wenatchee Ave (Wenatchee).*

COLUMBIA CASCADE WINE REGION: TOURING AND TASTING

Here's yet another region fabulous for wine.

In 2002 the **COLUMBIA CASCADE WINERY ASSOCIATION** (301 Angier Ave, Cashmere; 509/782-0708; www.columbiacascadewines.com) was formed to promote the wineries in the north-central region of the state, including ones as far north as Oroville and Mazama and south to Quincy.

The association now includes more than two dozen wineries, many new. This region has become the "in" place to visit, partially because there's already so much to do outdoors. Wineries were also a way for farmers to diversify from the economic ups and downs of growing apples and other fruit.

In Leavenworth, two annual festivals focus on wine—a wine walk in early June and wine tasting in August—and 10 tasting rooms are open year-round. There are six wineries in or near Leavenworth, including **BERGHOF KELLER** (11695 Duncan Rd; 509/548-5605; www.berghofkeller.com), which, appropriately, creates German-style wines. At **ICICLE RIDGE WINERY** (8977 North Rd; 509/548-7019; www.icicleridgewinery.com), the Wagoner family welcomes visitors to their log home and tasting room; in the summer, jazz concerts are held on-site.

Head east to Cashmere to visit the **COLUMBIA CASCADE WINE EXPERI-ENCE**, in Apple Annie's Antique Gallery (Eel Rd and US Hwy 2/97, Cashmere; 509-782-9463; 10am–6pm every day), a wine-tasting and sales facility operated by the Columbia Cascade Winery Association.

—Shelley Arenas

LODGINGS

Abendblume Pension / ★★★

12570 RANGER RD, LEAVENWORTH; 509/548-4059 OR 800/669-7634

Come here to leave everything behind. This Austrian chalet gets more popular by the minute. And no wonder: It's one of the most elegant, sophisticated inns in town, run by a gracious host. A sweeping staircase leads upstairs to the two best rooms, which have fireplaces, Italian marble bathrooms with two-person whirlpool tubs and his-and-hers sinks, and window seats with views. Outside is a patio hot tub. Breakfast is at your own pace in the pine-trimmed morning room; *abelskivers* (a pancake) are a specialty. *$$$; AE, DIS, MC, V; checks OK; www.abendblume.com; north on Ski Hill Dr at west end of town.*

Icicle Village Resort / ★★★

505 US HWY 2, LEAVENWORTH; 509/888-2776 OR 800/961-0162
It's not easy to find a kid-friendly place in Leavenworth that's fun, but here it is. This large Best Western has more than 90 rooms, yet it doesn't feel like a chain hotel. The modern condos can sleep six and have two bathrooms and a kitchen. The outdoor pool is open year-round (under a bubble in winter); there's also minigolf, a video arcade, and a movie theater. Check out the Black Bear Café & Coffee House and JJ Hills train-themed restaurant. *$$$; AE, DIS, MC, V; checks OK; www.iciclevillage.com; on US Hwy 2 near Icicle Rd.*

Mountain Home Lodge / ★★★

8201 MOUNTAIN HOME RD, LEAVENWORTH;
509/548-7077 OR 800/414-2378
This contemporary mountainside lodge offers a secluded escape-to-nature experience. Their motto is "children are seldom seen but often created." Outdoor activities shine in the winter. Most of the 10 themed rooms are on the small yet cozy side; for more space, splurge on a cabin. Room themes echo the region's nature and wildlife, including the Moose, Mountain Trout, Robin's Nest, and Timberline rooms. Hearty breakfasts and gourmet dinners ensure that guests stay energized for exploring their passions—indoors and out. *$$$$; DIS, MC, V; checks OK; www.mthome.com; off E Leavenworth Rd and US Hwy 2.*

Mountain Springs Lodge / ★★★

19115 CHIWAWA LOOP RD, LEAVENWORTH;
509/763-2713 OR 800/858-2276
Arriving at this high mountain lodge evokes images of coming home to the Ponderosa Ranch. Check in at Beaver Creek Lodge, which houses two Ralph Lauren–style suites and an excellent restaurant. Two 20-person-plus lodges and two smaller A-frame chalets face a sprawling lawn. This place is best for groups; enjoy the hot tubs and massive rock fireplaces. *$$$$; DIS, MC, V; checks OK; www.mtsprings.com; 14 miles northwest of Leavenworth, then 1 mile north of Plain.*

Natapoc Lodging / ★★★

12348 BRETZ RD, LEAVENWORTH;
509/763-3313 OR 888/NATAPOC
Natapoc offers an idyllic, classic "cabin in the woods" experience that is addictive to regulars. Choose from seven small or spacious log houses along the river. All have gas grills, TV/VCRs, and kitchens. You can fish, cross-country ski, or shop in Leavenworth. Or just sit on the deck and listen to the Wenatchee River or gaze at the stars as you slip into your hot tub. The larger lodges sleep up to 10, with home-away-from-home amenities that make them popular for families. *$$$$; AE, MC, V; checks OK; www.natapoc.com; 14 miles northwest of Leavenworth, then 2 miles north of Plain.*

Run of the River Inn & Refuge / ★★★★

9308 E LEAVENWORTH RD, LEAVENWORTH;
509/548-7171 OR 800/288-6491
This inn's gorgeous setting on the Icicle River practically ensures an at-one-with-nature experience. Six luxurious suites continue the nature theme, each with a river-rock fireplace, log bed, jetted tub, and cushy bathrobes. Spend the day on the large, private decks, or ride one of the tandem bikes. To feel as if you have the place to yourself, stay in the new Ravenwood Lodge, a two-story "cabin." Innkeepers Monty and Karen Turner are consummate hosts who also sell a breakfast cookbook. *$$$$; DIS, MC, V; checks OK; www. runoftheriver.com; 1 mile east of US Hwy 2.*

Sleeping Lady Mountain Retreat / ★★★

7375 ICICLE RD, LEAVENWORTH; 509/548-6344 OR 800/574-2123
This one-of-a-kind place is a quintessential Northwest retreat with an awareness of the environment and a devotion to the arts. At this former Civilian Conservation Corps camp, buildings are comfortably elegant, with Oriental rugs and woodstoves. The old chapel is now a theater. The 58 units are rustic yet elegant, with log beds. Two separate cabins include the Eyrie, with a whirlpool bath. There are two pools, a boulder-lined swimming pool open 24 hours seasonally, and a hot pool open year-round. You'll have an excellent meal in a (slightly disconcerting) buffet-style dining room. *$$$–$$$$; AE, DIS, MC, V; checks OK; www.sleepinglady.com; 2 miles southwest of Leavenworth.*

Cashmere

This little orchard town gives cross-mountain travelers who aren't in a Bavarian mood an alternative to Leavenworth. Western-style stores line the low-key main street; a river and a railroad border the town. The **CASHMERE MUSEUM** and **PIO-NEER VILLAGE** (600 Cottage Ave; 509/782-3230; www.cashmeremuseum.com) are worth a stop.

APLETS AND COTLETS have been produced in Cashmere for decades. Tour the plant at **LIBERTY ORCHARDS** (117 Mission St; 509/782-2191 or 800/231-3242; www.aplets.com). In an orchard off US Highway 2, 1 mile east of Cashmere, is **ANJOU BAKERY** (3898 Old Monitor Hwy; 509/782-4360).

Wenatchee

A visit to Wenatchee, very near the geographic center of Washington, also puts you in the heart of apple country, with the Apple Blossom Festival at the end of April. **OHME GARDENS** (just north of town on US Hwy 97A; 509/662-5785; www.ohme gardens.com) is a 9-acre Alpine retreat with cool glades and water features. It sits on a promontory 600 feet above the Columbia River, offering splendid views.

The **RIVERFRONT LOOP TRAIL** on the banks of the Columbia makes for a pleasant evening stroll or an easy bike ride; the 11-mile loop traverses both sides of the river (and crosses two bridges) from Wenatchee to East Wenatchee. The best place to join the trail is via a pedestrian overpass at the east end of First Street. The **WENATCHEE VALLEY MUSEUM AND CULTURAL CENTER** (127 S Mission; 509/664-3340; www.wenatcheevalleymuseum.com; 10am–4pm Tues–Sat) has permanent exhibits.

MISSION RIDGE (on Squilchuck Rd, 13 miles southwest of town; 509/663-6543; www.missionridge.com) offers some of the region's best powder, served by four chair lifts (including a quad lift installed in 2005). On the second or third Sunday in April, watch athletes compete in six grueling events in the **RIDGE-TO-RIVER RELAY** (509/662-8799; www.r2r.org).

The **WENATCHEE VALLEY CONVENTION & VISITORS BUREAU** (25 N Wenatchee Ave, Ste C111; 800/572-7753; www.wenatcheevalley.org) is a good source.

RESTAURANTS

Shakti's / ★★★

218 N MISSION, WENATCHEE; 509/662-3321 OR 888/662-3321
Former ballet dancer–turned–chef Shakti Lanphere and her mother, Renee, partnered to create this welcome oasis with linen tablecloths and soft lighting. Jazz on Wednesday adds to the supper-club feel. The food—such as braised rabbit or nightly risotto—highlights Northern Italian cuisine. You can get a great steak, too. Friendly, informed servers pamper you. *$$$; AE, MC, V; checks OK; dinner Tues–Sat; reservations recommended; www.shaktisfine dining.com; in Mission Square, downtown.*

The Windmill / ★★

1501 N WENATCHEE AVE, WENATCHEE; 509/665-9529
This former roadside diner looks offbeat, but it retains much of its simple charm, even after more than 75 years in business. Before your first dinner is over, you'll be planning a return. Meals are western American classics. There's seafood, too, but why mess with tradition? Stick with the meat. If the barbecued pork ribs are on the menu, indulge—they're worth it. *$$; MC, V; checks OK; dinner every day; beer and wine; reservations not accepted Fri–Sat; 1½ miles south of Wenatchee exit off US Hwy 2.*

LODGINGS

Coast Wenatchee Center Hotel / ★

201 N WENATCHEE AVE, WENATCHEE; 509/662-1234 OR 877/964-1234
This is the nicest hotel on the strip (a very plain strip, mind you, with numerous motels), with a city and river view. Connected to Wenatchee's convention center, it's popular with business travelers. The nine-story hotel has classic rooms with floral accents, upgraded in 2004. The Wenatchee Roaster and

Ale House, on the top floor, has a DJ. Swimmers enjoy outdoor and indoor pools. *$$; AE, DC, DIS, MC, V; checks OK; www.coasthotels.com or www. wenatcheecenter.com; center of town.*

The Warm Springs Inn / ★

1611 LOVE LANE, WENATCHEE; 509/662-8365 OR 800/543-3645
A winding drive bordered by orchards leads to the estatelike grounds of this three-story 1917 manor house. The pillared, ivy-covered entrance and dark-green-and-rustic-brick exterior lend majesty to this B and B. Six rooms are decorated with antiques. All have river views; a favorite is the blue and yellow room. Relax in the living room, watch movies in the sunroom, or walk to the river and claim a spot on the swing. *$$; AE, DIS, MC, V; checks OK; www.warmspringsinn.com; turn south off US Hwy 2 onto Lower Sunnyslope Rd, then right onto Love Lane.*

Waterville

Head 25 miles north of Wenatchee on US Highway 2 to reach the highest incorporated town in Washington. Waterville is home to several historic buildings. Learn about farming history and see a huge rock collection at the **DOUGLAS COUNTY HISTORICAL MUSEUM** (124 W Walnut St; 509/745-8435; Tues–Sun mid-May–mid-Oct).

Waterville Historic Hotel / ★★

102 E PARK ST, WATERVILLE; 509/745-8695 OR 888/509-8180
Step back in time at this gracious hotel that first opened its doors in 1903. Owner Dave Lundgren has been painstakingly restoring it since the late 1990s. Rooms are decorated with period furnishings; some have vintage cassette players with tapes of old radio shows. Two larger suites are great for families. Evenings, chat over complimentary beer and wine in the comfy lobby. *$–$$; AE, DIS, MC, V; checks OK; www.watervillehotel.com; closed Nov–Mar; downtown on US Hwy 2.*

Interstate 90 and Snoqualmie Pass

Carnation

Carnation is a verdant stretch of cow country nestled in the Snoqualmie Valley along bucolic State Route 203 (which connects I-90 to US Hwy 2 at Monroe). At **TOLT MACDONALD MEMORIAL PARK** (Fall City Rd and NE 40th St; 206/205-7532; www.metrokc.gov/parks/parks/toltmac.htm), trails and a suspension bridge provide a great picnic setting; campsites are available year-round.

Snoqualmie Valley farms produce great fruit and veggies. Go to the source at **REMLINGER FARMS** (on NE 32nd St, off SR 203; 425/333-4135; www.remlinger

farms.com), for U-pick south of Carnation. It's also a happening place for agri-entertainment, with the "Country Fair Family Fun Park" in summer; in October, kids love the farm's Pumpkin Harvest Festival.

Snoqualmie

The lovely Snoqualmie Valley is best known for its falls and its scenery. The 268-foot **SNOQUALMIE FALLS**, just up State Route 202 from Interstate 90 (parking lot next to **SALISH LODGE & SPA**; see review), is stunning. Use the observation deck or take a lightweight picnic down the 1-mile trail to the base.

The **NORTHWEST RAILWAY MUSEUM** (38625 SE King St; 425/888-3030; www.trainmuseum.org; every day year-round) runs a tour to the Snoqualmie Falls gorge from the towns of Snoqualmie and North Bend (most Sat–Sun Apr–Oct).

RESTAURANTS

The Dining Room at Salish Lodge & Spa / ★★★☆

6501 RAILROAD AVE SE, SNOQUALMIE;
425/888-2556 OR 800/272-5474
The views are breathtaking, but it's the food that really rocks. Literally. Don't miss the Snoqualmie River Hot Rocks, an appetizer of different fish cooked on sizzling stones. Even if you don't like fish, it's fun to watch. In fact, this place is all about the watching. Nearly everything is mixed in front of you, creating a unique fine-dining experience. Reserve the best table in house: a private room that juts out, providing a 180-degree view of the falls. Don't miss the legendary wine list, with 1,700 labels. For more casual fare, the little pub upstairs, the Attic, is a good bet. *$$$–$$$$; AE, DC, DIS, MC, V; checks OK; breakfast every day; dinner Tues–Sat; full bar; reservations recommended; www.salishlodge.com; exit 25 off I-90.*

LODGINGS

Salish Lodge & Spa / ★★★☆

6501 RAILROAD AVE SE, SNOQUALMIE;
425/888-2556 OR 800/272-5474
This is the perfect weekend getaway for Seattleites. It's rustic yet elegant. Don't miss the romantic, side-by-side, heated river-rock massage at the spa, which just won another national award. Salish has been around nearly 20 years; its rooms keep getting updated; and the sights and sounds of the waterfall make this a place you'll keep going back to. The rooms are spacious, complete with thoughtful details and our favorite, the swinging window that separates the bedroom from the romantic Jacuzzi tub. The lodge also arranges kayaking and rafting trips from your door. *$$$; AE, DC, DIS, MC, V; checks OK; www.salishlodge.com; exit 25 off I-90.*

North Bend

Zipping along on Interstate 90, exit 31 at North Bend looks like just a pit stop with gas stations, fast-food outlets, the last Starbucks before Snoqualmie Pass, and a plain outlet mall. But take the time to drive less than a mile north via Bendigo Boulevard into town, and you'll find some neat shops and restaurants—and less-expensive gas, too. **ROBERTIELLO'S** (101 W North Bend Way; 425/888-1803) serves excellent Italian food in the restored 1922 McGrath Hotel.

LODGINGS

Roaring River B&B / ★★

46705 SE 129TH ST, NORTH BEND;
425/888-4834 OR 877/627-4647

It's quite the find to discover such a secluded place less than an hour from city life, with reasonable rates to boot. Rhododendrons frame pathways at this retreat situated high above the Snoqualmie River, with views to match. The original home has one suite with a sauna; two other suites have whirlpool tubs and fireplaces. Herb's Place is a remodeled hunting cabin; crooked floors add to its charm. A breakfast basket is left at your doorstep. *$$$; AE, DIS, MC, V; checks OK; www.theroaringriver.com; exit 31 off I-90, about 4 miles northeast via North Bend Way and Mt Si Rd.*

Snoqualmie Pass

Four associated ski areas—**ALPENTAL, SUMMIT WEST, SUMMIT CENTRAL**, and **SUMMIT EAST**, collectively called the **SUMMIT AT SNOQUALMIE** (52 miles east of Seattle on I-90; 425/434-7669; www.summitatsnoqualmie.com)—offer the closest skiing for Seattleites, with a free shuttle that runs between the four areas on weekends, as well as the largest night-skiing program in the Northwest. Alpental is the most challenging; Summit West, with one of the largest ski schools in the country, has excellent instruction for all; Summit Central has some demanding bump runs and a great tubing hill; and the smallest, Summit East, is favored by cross-country skiers.

In summer, the transmountain pass is a good starting point for many hikes. Contact the **NORTH BEND RANGER STATION** (42404 SE North Bend Way; 425/888-1421; www.fs.fed.us/r6/mbs/about/snrd.shtml) for information. The **SUMMIT LODGE AT SNOQUALMIE PASS** (603 SR 906; 425/434-6300 or 800/557-STAY; www.snoqualmiesummitlodge.com) is your only choice for year-round lodging at the pass.

Roslyn

Modest turn-of-the-century homes in this onetime coal-mining town have become weekend places for city folk. But the main intersection still offers a cross section of the town's character. In Roslyn, once the set for the TV series *Northern Exposure*, fans will recognize the old stone tavern, the **BRICK** (100 W Pennsylvania Ave; 509/649-2643). Also familiar is the **ROSLYN CAFÉ** (201 W Pennsylvania Ave; 509/649-2763), popular for its American fare. The small **ROSLYN BREWING COMPANY** (208 W Pennsylvania Ave; 509/649-2232; Sat–Sun year-round, Fri–Sun in summer) is worth a visit.

At the **ROSYLN THEATER** (101 Dakota Ave; 509/649-3155), in a former mortuary, you can bring your dog. Down the road, behind the junkyard, you'll find **CAREK'S CUSTOM MARKET** (510 S "A" St; 509/649-2930), one of the state's better purveyors of fine specialty meats and sausages; try the beef jerky. The **ROSLYN CITY CEMETERY** pays homage to the ethnic diversity of the miners that settled here.

LODGINGS

Suncadia Resort / ★★★

3320 SUNCADIA TRAIL, ROSLYN; 866/904-6300
A mile from the working-class town of Roslyn, a high-end mountain resort development is underway. When it's finished, there will be more than 3,000 homes and condos on the 6,000-plus acres. First to open were the Inn at Suncadia and its restaurant, the Gas Lamp Grille, plus Prospector Golf Course. The small inn has sumptuous furnishings and a Northwest lodge design. The 14 rooms and 4 suites' stocked bookshelves, bathrooms with soaking tubs, and decks with rocking chairs help you relax. A pool and sports complex opens in summer 2007. More than 200 condos, many available for rental—open in 2008, then a village of shops and restaurants opens in 2009. *$$$$; AE, DC, DIS, MC, V; checks OK; www.suncadia.com; exit 80 from I-90, then follow signs.*

Cle Elum

This small mining town of about 2,000 parallels and is divided by Interstate 90 just east of Roslyn, with Cle Elum on one side of the freeway and South Cle Elum on the other. Freeway access at either end of town leads to First Street, Cle Elum's main thoroughfare, which makes the town a handy in-and-out stop. **CLE ELUM BAKERY** (1st St and Peoh Ave; 509/674-2233) is a longtime local institution, also popular with travelers. From one of the last brick ovens in the Northwest come baked goods such as *torchetti* (an Italian butter pastry rolled in sugar). Try **OWENS MEATS** (502 E 1st St; 509/674-2530) and **MAMA VALLONE'S STEAK HOUSE** (302 W 1st St; 509/674-5174). The latter offers cozy Italian dishes in a pleasant country-style home on the main street.

LODGINGS

Iron Horse B&B / ★

**526 MARIE AVE, SOUTH CLE ELUM;
509/674-5939 OR 800/2-2-TWAIN**
Iron Horse B&B is housed in a 1909 building originally for railroad employees. Now listed on the National Register of Historic Places, the bunkhouse, with eight rooms including a honeymoon suite, is furnished with reproduction antiques. Railroad memorabilia is on display. Four cabooses in the yard are fun for the kids. Owners Mary and Doug Pittis are restoring the South Cle Elum Train Depot in nearby Iron Horse State Park. The Depot Café opened there in summer 2006. *$$; MC, V; checks OK; www.ironhorseinnbb.com; adjacent to Iron Horse State Park Trail.*

Mount Rainier National Park

This majestic mountain is the symbol of natural grandeur in the Pacific Northwest, as well as one of the most awesome mountains in the world. Its dormant volcanic cone rises 14,411 feet above sea level, several thousand feet higher than other Cascade Range peaks. **MOUNT RAINIER NATIONAL PARK** (Tahoma Woods, Star Route, Ashford; 360/569-2211; www.nps.gov/mora; entrance fee $15 per automobile, $5 per person on foot, bicycle, or motorcycle) was created in 1889. The best way to appreciate Rainier is to explore its flanks: 300 miles of backcountry and trails lead to forests, glaciers, waterfalls, and meadows. Get required backcountry-use permits for overnight stays from the ranger stations at park entrances. Of the five entrance stations, the three most popular are described here; the northwest entrances—Carbon River and Mowich Lake—via long, unpaved roads aren't great for visitors.

State Route 410 heads east from Sumner through Enumclaw to the **WHITE RIVER ENTRANCE** (northeast corner) to the park and **SUNRISE VISITOR CENTER**, continuing on to Chinook Pass and connecting with either Cayuse Pass (State Route 123) or US Highway 12 near Naches. State Route 410 beyond the Crystal Mountain spur road is closed in winter, with no access to Sunrise and Cayuse and Chinook passes, which are closed in winter; take the loop trip via the passes, or the road to Sunrise, late May through October.

State Routes 7 and 706 connect Tacoma and Interstate 5 with the main **NISQUALLY ENTRANCE** (southwest corner) at **LONGMIRE**; the road continues east to State Route 123 between Cayuse Pass and White Pass. The road remains open during daylight hours in winter only from Longmire to **PARADISE**; carry tire chains and a shovel, and **CHECK CONDITIONS** by calling a 24-hour service (360/569-2211).

The **STEVENS CANYON ENTRANCE** (southeast corner) is on State Route 123, which connects State Route 410 and US Highway 12 via Cayuse Pass, closed in winter; in summer, **OHANAPECOSH** is a favorite stop.

SIDE TRIP TO HISTORY

Parents often like to inject some educational value into vacation trips; this side trip from Mount Rainier National Park offers history lessons cleverly disguised as "fun." If you're sans kids, you can still marvel at this glimpse into an earlier era.

From Mount Rainier's south side, head west on State Route 706 to the town of **ELBE** to see the **EVANGELISCHE LUTHERISCHE KIRCHE** (Highway 7). Built by German settlers in 1906, the 18-foot-by-24-foot clapboard "Little White Church" was once honored as the "Smallest Church in America" by *Ripley's Believe It or Not*. Also in Elbe, check out the **HOBO INN** (51630 SR 706 E; 360/569-2500), where you can sleep in one of eight cabooses, some nearly 100 years old.

During the summer and holidays, take a steam train ride through the foothills of Mount Rainier via the **MOUNT RAINIER SCENIC RAILROAD** (54124 Mountain Hwy E, Elbe; 888-STEAM-11; www.mrsr.com). Its depot is right next to the "Little White Church."

Just a few miles south of Elbe via State Route 7, take a left on Mineral Hill Road and follow it to the **MINERAL LAKE LODGE** (195 Mineral Hill Rd, Mineral; 360/492-5253; www.minerallakelodge.com). Built in 1906, this three-story log structure was once a wilderness retreat for the elite from Seattle and Tacoma. In the 1920s it was a sanatorium, and its storied past includes a time as a gambling

Black Diamond

This quiet, former coal-mining town is located on State Route 169 in Maple Valley, about 10 miles north of Enumclaw. The circa 1902 **BLACK DIAMOND BAKERY** (32805 Railroad Ave; 360/886-2741), with 26 kinds of bread, is worth a stop; it's also the last wood-fired brick oven in the area. The café is also good.

Greenwater

A tiny blink-and-you-miss-it community as you head east on State Route 410 to Crystal Mountain Ski Resort or Chinook Pass, Greenwater is a good place to stop for gas and espresso; check out the fun ski clothing store, **WAPITI WOOLIES** (58414 SR 410 E; 360/663-2268).

and drinking establishment. Today it's a cozy bed-and-breakfast with themed rooms creatively decorated by owner Ramona Sheppard.

Back on State Route 7, continue south to its intersection with US Highway 12 in the small town of **MORTON**. Here, two lumber mills are testament to the role that logging still plays, though greatly diminished from its heyday when there were more than 100 mills in the region. The importance of the railroads, which first came to the town in 1910, is also still evident.

In October 2005, the historic **MORTON TRAIN DEPOT** was moved to its new location on Fairhart Way. The street was named after Esper Fairhart, who immigrated to Morton from Kafarchima, Lebanon, in the early 1900s. Restoration efforts continue to make the building a fully functioning depot for the Mount Rainier Scenic Railroad and Tacoma Rail.

Travel west about 12 miles on US Highway 2 to the small town of **MOSSY-ROCK**, where the **EAST LEWIS COUNTY VISITOR CENTER** (118 State St; 360/983-3778; www.eastlewiscounty.com) provides information about recreational treasures, including two large lakes and camping. Just west of town, **DEGOEDE BULB FARM AND GARDENS** (409 Mossyrock Rd W; 360/983-9000; www.degoedebulb.com) has fields of blooming tulips in the spring and a lovely show garden to walk through year-round.

—Shelley Arenas

RESTAURANTS

Greenwater Lodge Coffee Shop / ★★

58106 SR 410 E, GREENWATER; 360/663-0290
In late 2005, new owners opened this restaurant in the historic 1917 lodge, and locals quickly made a beeline as restaurants are sparse in this region. Michele's fruit pies have become a favorite; pork chops are another specialty. The menu is heavy on comfort foods. More inventive dishes include steak stew with Moose Drool beer or cornmeal-dipped trout topped with fruit salsa. The kids menu and homestyle cooking make this a great place to bring the whole family. In summer, the large deck offers a closer connection to the forest setting by two rivers. *$–$$; DIS, MC, V; local checks only; breakfast Sat–Sun, lunch, dinner Tues–Sun; beer and wine; reservations recommended; 14 miles east of Enumclaw.* &

LODGINGS

Alta Crystal Resort / ★★

68317 SR 410 E, GREENWATER; 360/663-2500 OR 800/277-6475
This intimate mountain retreat has a cozy setting in the forest yet is convenient to both Crystal Mountain Ski Resort (10 miles east) and the northeast entrance to Mount Rainier National Park. The 24 one- and two-bedroom lodgings are condo-style with kitchens, and the pool and hot tub are open year-round. The Honeymoon Cabin is popular with couples. The bonfires, games, and other activities give the place a fun summer-camp flavor. *$$$–$$$$; MC, V; checks OK; www.altacrystalresort.com; about 12 miles east of Greenwater.*

Crystal Mountain

CRYSTAL MOUNTAIN SKI RESORT (off SR 410 just west of Chinook Pass, on northeast edge of Mount Rainier National Park; 360/663-2265; www.skicrystal. com), southeast of Enumclaw, is the state's best ski area and offers panoramic views at the top. There are runs for beginners and experts, plus fine backcountry skiing. And yes, there's even things to do here in summer. Besides the usual, try sunset dining at the state's highest restaurant, the Summit House (360/663-3003). Rent on-mountain condominiums from CRYSTAL MOUNTAIN LODGING (360/663-2558 or 888/668-4368; www.crystalmtlodging-wa.com) or hotel rooms from CRYSTAL MOUNTAIN HOTELS (360/663-2262 or 888/SKI-6400; www. crystalhotels.com).

Sunrise

Open only during summer, SUNRISE (6,400 feet) is the closest you can drive to Rainier's peak. The old lodge has no overnight accommodations but offers a VISITOR CENTER (northeast corner of park, 31 miles north of Ohanapecosh; 360/663-2425; www.nps.gov/mora/pphtml/facilities.html), snack bar, and mountain exhibits. Dozens of hiking trails begin here, such as the short one to a magnificent view of EMMONS GLACIER CANYON.

Eatonville

At Eatonville, just east of State Route 7, 17 miles south of Puyallup, the big draw is NORTHWEST TREK (on Meridian Ave/SR 161; 360/832-6117; www.nwtrek. org; every day mid-Feb–Oct, Sat–Sun and holidays Nov–mid-Feb; group rates available). Here visitors board small open-air trams for hourlong tours of the 435-acre grounds to see elk, moose, deer, bighorn sheep, and bison—the herd steals the show.

Ashford

If Ashford is the gateway to Paradise, then **WHITTAKER'S BUNKHOUSE** (30205 SR 706 E; 360/569-2439; www.whittakersbunkhouse.com) is the place to stop on the way to the very top—of Mount Rainier, that is. Rooms are basic (bunks available in summer) but plush compared to camping. There's an espresso café, too. Mount Tahoma Ski Huts, run by the **MOUNT TAHOMA TRAILS ASSOCIATION** (360/569-2451; www.skimtta.com), is Western Washington's first hut-to-hut ski trail system. It offers 50 miles of trails (20 groomed), three huts, and one yurt.

For expert advice, stop by the **MOUNT RAINIER VISITORS ASSOCIATION** booth (877/617-9950; www.mt-rainier.com; every day year-round), inside **WHITTAKER MOUNTAINEERING**'s office (30027 SR 706 E). You'll find a few small cafés in and near Ashford; we like **WILDBERRY** (37718 SR 706 E; 360/569-2379) for its pies; in spring, enjoy your slice out on the creekside picnic tables and watch for elk and deer. For the most unusual art around, don't miss Dan Klennert's **EX-NIHILO** (a Latin word meaning "something made from nothing") sculpture park (22410 SR 706 E, Elbe; 360/569-2280; May–Oct). His "Recycled Spirits of Iron" are just that—sculptures made of recycled iron.

LODGINGS

Altimeter Cabin / ★★★

34509 SR 706 E, ASHFORD; 360/569-2140 OR 866/267-6814

Built around 1900, this cabin offers a taste of mountaineering history from life as "the Guest House" on the property of famed mountaineer Lou Whittaker. The home and cabin housed mountain guides for years. Local couple Andrea Brannon and Ray Morford bought it from Whittaker a few years ago. They live in the main house and have restored the cabin with unique touches—Andrea is a glass artist, and her talents are evident throughout. The cozy cabin sleeps two in the loft, and up to two more on the futon. It has a claw-foot tub, kitchen, flat screen TV with DVD and Nintendo, wood stove, wi-fi, and no phone. Outdoors, there's a campfire, putting green, and a new hot tub sits where the original once stood. *$$$; MC, V; checks OK; www.altimetercabin.com; on north side of hwy just east of Skate Creek Rd.*

Stormking Spa and Cabins / ★★

37311 SR 706 E, ASHFORD; 360/569-2964
In recent years, the owners turned their former B and B, a historic 1890 homestead, into a pampering spa. Four secluded cabins are nestled in gorgeous forest settings. The Wolf and Raven cedar cabins are yurt-shaped, with skylights and river-rock rain showers; the Eagle features a two-person "greenhouse" shower. All three have gas fireplaces, outdoor hot tubs, and rustic elegance. These very private cabins include terry cloth robes and slippers. The Bear cabin has three bedrooms.. Continental breakfast is in all cabins except the Bear. *$$$; MC, V; checks OK; www.stormkingspa.com; 4½ miles east of Ashford.*

Longmire and Paradise

A few miles inside the southwestern park border, the village of **LONGMIRE** has the 25-room **NATIONAL PARK INN** (360/569-2275; www.guestservices. com/rainier), with tasteful, hickory-style furnishings; 19 rooms have private baths. A small **MUSEUM** with wildlife exhibits, a **HIKING INFORMATION CENTER** (360/569-4453; Apr–Sept), and **SNOWSHOE AND CROSS-COUNTRY SKI RENTALS** (360/569-2411) are nearby.

At 5,400 feet, **PARADISE** is the most popular destination on Rainier. You'll catch views of Narada Falls and Nisqually Glacier on the way to the parking lot and the **HENRY M. JACKSON MEMORIAL VISITOR CENTER** (just before Paradise; 360/569-2211, ext 6036). The center, housed in a flying saucer–like building, has a standard cafeteria and gift shop, nature exhibits and films, and a view from its observation deck. This visitor center is scheduled to be replaced with a new one in fall 2008. The unique and massive **PARADISE INN** (just past visitor center) was closed in 2005 for renovations after 88 years serving generations of park visitors; it is scheduled to reopen in summer 2008. Depending on the season, at Paradise you can picnic (best to bring your own fixings) among the wildflowers, explore the hiking trails (rangers offer guided walks), let the kids slide on inner tubes in the snow-play area, try a little cross-country skiing, or even take a guided snowshoe tromp.

White Pass

WHITE PASS SKI AREA (12 miles southeast of Mount Rainier National Park at summit of US Hwy 12; 509/672-3101; www.skiwhitepass.com) is an off-the-beaten-path ski destination offering downhill (with a high-speed quad lift) and cross-country skiing. Its base is the highest on the Cascade crest, at 4,500 feet. A Nordic center near the day lodge serves cross-country skiers with about 18 miles of trails. Summer hiking can be found in adjacent William O. Douglas and Goat Rocks wilderness areas. Lodging is available slope-side at the **VILLAGE INN CONDOMINIUMS** (509/672-3131). The nearby town of Packwood has several motels; we suggest **MOUNTAIN VIEW LODGE** (13163 US Hwy 12; 877/277-7192; www. mtvlodge.com) for comfy rooms—some with fireplaces—hot tub, and seasonal outdoor pool.

SOUTHWEST WASHINGTON

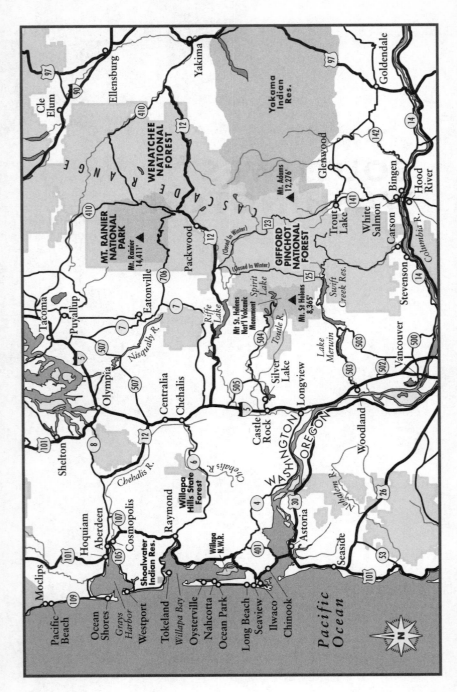

SOUTHWEST WASHINGTON

There is something for everyone in the southwest corner of Washington State. The mighty Columbia Gorge and its river create the area's southern border and the Pacific Ocean is its western delineation; to the north is the Chehalis River and to the east are Mounts Adams and St. Helens. It's no wonder Lewis and Clark thought they'd found paradise.

ACCESS AND INFORMATION

INTERSTATE 5 is the main freeway that runs through Southwest Washington (north-south), but the more scenic east-west Columbia Gorge **STATE ROUTE 14** (Vancouver to Bingen and US Highway 97 beyond), north-south Long Beach Peninsula **STATE ROUTE 103** (Ilwaco to Oysterville), north-south coastal **US HIGHWAY 101**, and coastal **STATE ROUTES 105 AND 109** near Grays Harbor make a better driving adventure. Coastal access from Interstate 5 is via **STATE ROUTE 4** (Longview to Long Beach Peninsula or US Highway 101), **STATE ROUTE 6** (Chehalis to Raymond–South Bend), or **US HIGHWAY 12** (north of Centralia through Aberdeen and Hoquiam to Ocean Shores).

AMTRAK rail service (800/USA-RAIL; www.amtrak.com) stops in **CEN-TRALIA** (210 Railroad Ave; 360/736-8653), **KELSO-LONGVIEW** (501 S 1st Ave; 360/578-1870), and **VANCOUVER** (1301 W 11th St; 360/694-7307) on their **COAST STARLIGHT** route. **GREYHOUND** (800/231-222; www.greyhound.com) bus service is available to Centralia, Kelso-Longview, and Vancouver.

Grays Harbor and Ocean Shores

A water wonderland for birds and people alike, this area encompasses 6 miles of coastline and 23 miles of freshwater canals and lakes. **BOWERMAN BASIN** (Airport Wy off SR 109), **GRAY'S HARBOR NATIONAL WILDLIFE REFUGE** (SR 109, 1½ miles west of Hoquiam; 360/753-9467), and **DAMON STATE PARK** (4½ miles south of the stone-pillar entrance into Ocean Shores on Pt Brown Ave) are great bird-watching areas. The new **OCEAN SHORES CONVENTION CENTER** (120 W Chance A La Mer Ave; 800/874-6737) is home to the area's **VISITOR CENTER**.

Elma

This little burg on US Highway 12 is about 20 miles east of Aberdeen, at the junction with highways that head east to US Highway 101 near Olympia.

RESTAURANTS

Saginaw's / ★

301 W MAIN ST, ELMA; 360/482-8747
Husband-and-wife team Scott and LouAnne Kendall created this cozy deli-diner as a way to share with others their passion for food. The place is filled with locals eating salads, soups, and sandwiches at lunch; dinners are pastas and meats. Never pass up their seafood cioppino when it's the special. Don't forget to have one of LouAnne's homemade bar cookies. *$–$$; AE, DIS, MC, V; local checks only; lunch Tues–Sat, dinner Tues–Sun; full bar; reservations recommended; at S 3rd St.* &

Aberdeen and Hoquiam

Blink, and you'll miss the street that separates these two towns located near the headwaters of Grays Harbor. Old Victorian homes grace hillsides, and their shared logging and maritime history is evident by the area's mills and fishing boats. When it's docked in its home port, don't miss visiting the reproduction of **ROBERT GRAY'S** *Lady Washington* (www.ladywashington.org). More-permanent structures are the **OLYMPIC STADIUM** (2811 Cherry St, Hoquiam) and the **SEV-ENTH STREET THEATRE** (313 7th St, Hoquiam; 360/537-7400). Built in 1937, the stadium is one of the few all-wooden ones remaining in the country. Go to **GRAYS HARBOR CHAMBER OF COMMERCE** in Aberdeen (506 Duffy St; 360/532-1924) for more information.

RESTAURANTS

Gabelli's / ★★★

116 W HERON, ABERDEEN; 360/533-6100
Aberdeen's beloved Pierre Gabelli is back. For 12 years, this Swiss-trained chef cooked Northern Italian cuisine at his popular restaurant, Parma. Now Pierre is again serving incredible food at affordable prices. Burgundy and gold, with warm lighting, create an intimate space reminiscent of a quaint European café. An abundance of pasta and a few meat entrées make ordering a challenge, but you'll never be disappointed. Gabelli's olive oil–garlic mix-ture is powerful, and Pierre's mom's *canoneini* (a puff pastry) is a must-have. *$$; AE, DIS, MC, V; local checks only; dinner Tues–Sat; beer and wine; reserva-tions recommended; downtown between S K and S Broadway sts.* &

Mallard's Bistro & Grill / ★

118 E WISHKAH ST, ABERDEEN; 360/532-0731
Ask chef-owner Niels Tiedt how the tremendous duck collection started, and he'll point to one particular poster. Ask him about the success of his 10-year-old restaurant, and he'll tell you about his 50-year love affair with food. This place is always packed, known for its large portions and more than 25

entrées. Special occasions are celebrated with the venerable duck call. *$$; MC, V; local checks only; dinner Tues–Sat; beer and wine; reservations recommended; between S I and S Broadway sts.* ᕦ

LODGINGS

Aberdeen Mansion Bed and Breakfast / ★★★

807 N M ST, ABERDEEN; 360/533-7079 OR 888/533-7079
Owners Al and Joan Waters sure know how to attract attention: Abderdeen Mansion is recognized in regional magazines as one of the premier bed-and-breakfasts. These two wow guests with their 100-year-old Queen Anne Victorian home. The three rooms, all with private baths, feature turn-of-the century furniture and fine antiques. The wraparound porch and turret are wonderful places to view the beautifully landscaped grounds. Enjoy a recently renovated game room, after-dinner desserts and drinks, a three-course gourmet breakfast, and conversations with your hosts. *$$$; AE, DIS, MC, V; no checks; www.aberdeenmansionbb.com; corner of W 5th St.*

Hoquiam's Castle Bed & Breakfast / ★★

515 CHENAULT AVE, HOQUIAM; 360/533-2005
After staying a night at this award-winning property, you'll feel as grand as the bed you slept in. With four royalty-themed and -decorated rooms, this B and B is over-the-top opulent. The King's Suite is ideal for that special romantic get-away. Three delightful women owners, Donna, Pat, and Kathy (a mother and her two daughters), have retained most of the home's original furnishings. Breakfast is served with fine china, and the vanilla ice cream french toast is delicious. Formal teas and afternoon tours are available for nonguests. *$$$; MC, V; no checks; www.hoquiamcastle.com; west on Emerson Ave, right on Garfield St, uphill to Chenault Ave.*

Ocean Shores

Crooner Pat Boone, who played golf here in the late 1960s, hoped to turn this coastal community into a destination resort town. It didn't happen. However, since the late 1990s there's been quite a buzz stirring up business and property values. The new **CONVENTION CENTER** (120 W Chance A La Mer Ave; 800/874-6737) will attract crowds as large as those seen at the **QUINAULT BEACH RESORT AND CASINO** (see review).

But there's more on this 6,000-acre peninsula than golf and gambling. Visit the home of the 2005 World Sport Kite Championship winners, **CUTTING EDGE KITES** (676 Ocean Shores Blvd NW; 800/379-3109) and pick up a good-looking wind toy and great kite-flying tips. **BJ'S FAMILY FUN CENTER** (752 Pt Brown Ave NE; 360/289-2702) and **PACIFIC PARADISE FAMILY FUN CENTER** (767 Minard Ave NW; 360/289-9537) offer bumper boats for kids and adults. Horse riding is a popular pastime, and **CHENNOIS CREEK HORSE RENTALS** (360/289-5591) and **NAN-SEA STABLES** (360/289-0194; www.horseplanet.com) offer rides on the beach.

Go shopping at **FUSIONS** (834 Pt Brown Ave NE; 360/289-2811), a gallery representing more than 70 Pacific Northwest artists, and at **JOAN OF ARTE** (740 Pt Brown Ave NE, Ste A; 360/289-2554), which has unique candles and self-help books. Also stop by **FLYING CATS** (114 E Chance A La Mer NE; 360/289-2287) for body-care products, and sample fruit curds and sip Irish tea next door at **MCCURDY'S CELTIC MARKETPLACE** (360/289-3955).

The **OCEAN SHORES CHAMBER OF COMMERCE AND VISITORS CENTER** (www.oceanshores.org) has a great Web site. A **TRAVEL AND TOURISM WEB SITE** (www.oceanshores.com) also has information.

RESTAURANTS

Palm's Restaurant / ★★

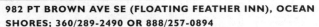

982 PT BROWN AVE SE (FLOATING FEATHER INN), OCEAN SHORES; 360/289-2490 OR 888/257-0894

The only canal-front restaurant in Ocean Shores, Palm's is an intimate, softly lit space with just six tables. Thai chicken curry puffs with a cucumber–cilantro relish or an artichoke–crab dip appetizer are good. The pan-seared rib-eye steak was a bit overdone, but its accompaniment, the delicious grape tomato–balsamic salsa, made it tasty. Outside seating on the private dock in summer. *$$; AE, DIS, MC, V; local checks only; breakfast Sat–Sun (by reservation only), dinner Fri–Sat (more days in summer); beer, wine, champagne cocktails; reservations recommended; www.floatingfeatherinn.com; 3.5 miles south of Ocean Shores' stone gate entrance.*

LODGINGS

Floating Feather Inn / ★★★

982 PT BROWN AVE SE, OCEAN SHORES; 360/289-2490 OR 888/247-0894

After 35 years in the travel industry, co-owner Nancy Dudacek-Milliman knows what it takes to run a first-rate B and B. From the moment you walk in, she and her husband, Roger, will make you feel at home. Located at the quiet end of town, the inn's four comfy rooms (stay in one of the two that overlook the canal rather than the street) have feather beds and down comforters. Breakfast scones are yummy, and the Ghirardelli chocolates and free movies are nice. The only thing that could be improved is larger, fluffier bath towels. *$$–$$$; AE, DIS, MC, V; local checks only; www.floatingfeatherinn. com; 3.5 miles south of Ocean Shores' stone gate entrance.* &

Quinault Beach Resort & Casino / ★★

78 SR 115, OCEAN SHORES; 360/289-9466 OR 888/461-2214

Don't let the frightening bright-purple foyer scare you away. Walk into the hotel's lobby, and you'll be rewarded with more-hospitable colors and classy decor. Although the 150 rooms are tastefully furnished and of reasonable size, some have an oddly placed gas fireplace in the middle of the room, which separates the bed from the sitting area. If you like to eat and gamble, you have three restaurants here to choose from and 16,000 square feet of casino to play in. A less risky venture is beachcombing out the front door. *$–$$$$; AE, DIS, MC, V; checks OK; www.quinaultbeachresort.com; west side of SR 115 on the beach.* &

Copalis

LODGINGS

Iron Springs Resort / ★

3707 SR 109, COPALIS; 360/276-4230

Families flock to this very rustic resort because of its impressive ocean views and great clam-digging and because of their desire to live with less for awhile. There's no television reception (movies are available) and no phones here, so you'll spend time on the beach and wooded trails just outside your door. Furnishings are minimal and funky, but the river-rock fireplaces are grand. Cabins 22–25 are best, since they're the newest. There's a steamy indoor pool; homemade cinnamon rolls greet you when you wake up. *$$; AE, DIS, MC, V; checks OK; www.ironspringresort.com; 3 miles north of Copalis Beach on SR 109.* &

Pacific Beach and Moclips

These two quiet towns along the northern end of State Route 109 have a smattering of cliff-hugging antiquated hotels, a restaurant with a priceless view, and a noteworthy museum. The **SANDPIPER RESORT** (4471 SR 109, Pacific Beach; 360/276-4580) and **OCEAN CREST RESORT** (4651 SR 109, Moclips; 800/684-8439) offer decent lodgings, and the latter also offers fine dining. A more reasonably priced eatery along this stretch of coastline is **PACIFIC TANGO** (61 Main St, Pacific Beach; 360/276-0102). The **MUSEUM OF NORTH BEACH** (4658 SR 109, Moclips; 360/276-4441) has an impressive collection.

Contact the **WASHINGTON COAST CHAMBER OF COMMERCE** (2616-A SR 109, Ocean City; 800/286-4552) for more information.

Westport and Grayland

These south-beach towns along this 18-mile stretch of coastline may be known for their charter fishing, cranberry bogs, and world-class surfing, but this area is quickly becoming something else: the hottest tourist destination on the Washington coast.

With new restaurants, oceanfront and marina condominiums, and a planned links-style 18-hole golf course, **WESTPORT** is trying to become the perfect getaway.

Places not to miss include the **WESTPORT MARITIME MUSEUM** (2201 Westhaven Dr; 360/268-0078), which offers tours of the **GRAYS HARBOR LIGHTHOUSE** (on W Ocean Ave). **WINDS OF WESTPORT** (320 Dock St; 360/268-1760) rents out electric and pedal-powered boats. One of the many charter fishing companies is **OCEAN CHARTERS** (2315 Westhaven Dr, Float 6; 800/562-0105).

GRAYLAND BEACH STATE PARK (925 Cranberry Rd; 360/267-4301) has excellent beachcombing and well-maintained yurts and camping sites. Two good shops are **POMEGRANATE** (1634 SR 105, Grayland; 360/267-0701) and the **ROSE COTTAGE** (1794 SR 105, Grayland; 360/267-0205), both offering unique gifts and home furnishings.

Check the **WESTPORT-GRAYLAND CHAMBER OF COMMERCE** (2985 S Montesano St; 800/345-6223; www.westportgrayland-chamber.org), **GRAYS HARBOR COUNTY TOURISM AGENCY** (800/621-9625; www.graysharbortourism.com), and a good **WEB SITE** (www.westportwa.com) for information.

RESTAURANTS

Anthony's Restaurant / ★★★⯪

421 E NEDDIE ROSE DR (THE ISLANDER RESORT), WESTPORT; 360/268-9166

You'll quickly discover why this new venue is the talk of the town: chef Mark Potovsky has spent more than 20 years in the finest Pacific Northwest restaurants. An archway leads you to an intimate dining area with white-linen tablecloths and handsomely dressed servers. The grilled pear, blue cheese, and prosciutto salad is your meal's perfect beginning. Apricot-glazed chicken and cranberry polenta are melt-in-your-mouth goodness. *$$$; AE, DIS, MC, V; local checks only; dinner every day; full bar; reservations recommended; www. westport-islander.com; off SR 105, follow Montesano St approx 4 miles, left on Westhaven Dr, follow to its end.* &

Half Moon Bay Bar & Grill / ★★★

421 E NEDDIE ROSE DR (THE ISLANDER RESORT), WESTPORT; 360/268-9166

This is a superb dining spot by the sea, overlooking the marina. Fresh fish is their forte—much of it caught just outside. Light jazz on weekends, live music on the deck in the summer, and a monthly Winemaker's Dinner keep the place abuzz. A combination of cozy booths and tables, warm earth tones, and Moroccan-style lanterns create a comfortable atmosphere. The Surf's Up caesar salad and Jetty Surf Melt will have you savoring every bite. *$–$$$; AE, DIS, MC, V; local checks only; breakfast, lunch, dinner every day; full bar; no reservations; www.westport-islander.com; off SR 105, follow Montesano St approx 4 miles, left on Westhaven Dr, follow to its end.* &

LODGINGS

Vacations by the Sea / ★★★☆

1600 W OCEAN AVE, WESTPORT; 360/268-1119 OR 877-332-0090

They may not be the prettiest, but these oceanfront condominiums have plush interiors and offer all the comforts of home. One- and two-bedroom rentals are so well maintained that you might feel terrible tracking in sand. Views are lovely: the ocean is just a few steps from your front door through the trail in the beach grass. Rock hunting is a blast here as beautiful orange-colored agates are in abundance. Access to the recreation center is included. *$$$–$$$$; AE, MC, V; checks OK; www.vacationsbythesea.com; off Montesano St, left on Ocean Ave.* ♿

Tokeland

Named after an Indian chief, this quiet bay community on the north shore of Willapa Bay south of Grayland hosts an extravagant Fourth of July celebration and has great fishing and crabbing off the small marina. The nearby **SHOALWATER BAY CASINO** (on Hwy SR 105 at Tokeland turnoff; 888/332-2048) is a hot spot.

LODGINGS

Tokeland Hotel / ★★

100 HOTEL RD, TOKELAND; 360/267-7006

This century-old structure teetered on the edge of collapse until it was restored by husband and wife Scott and Katherine White. Despite its creaky floors and shared bathrooms, this quaint, eighteen-room inn's antique furnishings and serene setting will tug at your heartstrings. Get one of the four rooms with a view of Willapa Bay if you can. The living room is a comfy place to settle in with a good book, a cup of tea, and the owners' dog, Whitey. An in-house restaurant serves decent, home-cooked food. *$–$$; DIS, MC, V; checks OK; www.tokelandhotel.com; Tokeland exit off SR 105, follow Hotel Rd 2 miles.* ♿

Long Beach Peninsula and Willapa Bay

The slender finger of land dividing Willapa Bay from the Pacific is famous for its 37-mile-long flat stretch of public beach, gentle marine climate, kite flying, clamming, and rhododendrons. Willapa Bay's Long Island, reachable only by boat, harbors a huge old-growth cedar grove. Some trees are more than 200 feet tall. The island is part of the **WILLAPA NATIONAL WILDLIFE REFUGE** (360/484-3482), with headquarters on US Highway 101, 10 miles north of Seaview. The **LONG**

BEACH PENINSULA VISITORS BUREAU (800/451-2542; www.funbeach.com) has an excellent Web site; the **WILLAPA CHAMBER OF COMMERCE** (360/942-5419; http://visit.willapabay.org) is also helpful.

Skamokawa

LODGINGS

Inn at Lucky Mud / ★★☆

44 OLD CHESTNUT DR, SKAMOKAWA; 360/482-8747 OR 800/806-7131
This place is in the middle of nowhere, and that's the point. Enjoy the view outside your window of the pond or an occasional herd of elk. Four spacious rooms each have their own bath and porch. You'll fall asleep to frog lullabies and awake to the smell of breakfast and strong coffee. Jessica's chocolate mud puffs are a surprise treat. *$$; DIS, MC, V; checks OK; www.luckymud.com; off SR 4 west of Longview, right onto Skamokawa Valley Rd, go 1.2 miles to fork, right onto E Valley Rd, follow it 4.9 miles, look for inn's sign, left at driveway, uphill, first house on right.*

Chinook

From primeval times to the present, fishing has loomed large in Chinook, located southeast of the Long Beach Peninsula on US Highway 101. Salmon was a dominant figure in the Native American cosmology and a staple of the local diet.

On Scarborough Hill, **FORT COLUMBIA STATE PARK** (1 mile southeast of Chinook on US Hwy 101; 888/226-7688; open every day) hosts a collection of restored turn-of-the-20th-century wooden buildings that once housed soldiers guarding the river mouth. The former commander's house is now a **MILITARY MUSEUM** (open mid-May–Sept). Rent the fully furnished two-bedroom Steward's House or five-bedroom Scarborough House; advance reservation required (800/360-4240). **ST. MARY'S CATHOLIC CHURCH** (at milepost 2 along US Hwy 101 just east of Chinook), which sits along the Columbia River, is worth a visit.

Ilwaco

Known as a salmon-fishing and -processing port and not much else a decade ago, Ilwaco's harbor is pulsating with new energy, particularly at **ILWACO HARBOR VILLAGE**, an array of galleries, restaurants, and shops. **SHOALWATER COVE GALLERY** (177 Howerton Way SE; 360/642-4020 or 877/665-4382) features local artist Marie Powell's watercolors. Savor chicken-basil sausage hoagies at the **CANOE ROOM CAFE** (161 Howerton Way SE; 360/642-4899). **OLE BOB'S SEAFOOD MARKET** (151 Howerton Way; 888/748-8156) is good for fresh oysters and crab, the **WADE GALLERY** (223 Howerton Way; 360/642-5092) for photography, and **NAUTICAL BRASS** (139 Howerton Way; 360/642-5092) for gifts. A seasonal **SATURDAY MARKET** (May–Sept) also happens here.

Ilwaco is still a charter-fishing hot spot. Two popular operators are **COHO CHARTERS** (237 Howerton Way SE; 360/642-3333; www.cohocharters.com) and **SEA BREEZE CHARTERS** (185 Howerton Way SE; 360/642-2300; www.seabreeze charters.net). Many charter operators also offer eco-tours. The **ILWACO HERITAGE MUSEUM** (115 SE Lake St; 360/642-3446; www.ilwacoheritagemuseum. org) features a good Lewis and Clark exhibit through 2007.

Nearby **CAPE DISAPPOINTMENT STATE PARK** (3 miles southwest of Ilwaco off US Hwy 101; 360/642-3078) is one of Washington's most popular attractions, with almost 2,000 acres stretching from **NORTH HEAD LIGHTHOUSE** to **CAPE DISAPPOINTMENT**, where another stately sentinel illuminates the Columbia River's mouth; both lighthouses are approachable by trail. Open all year, the park has yurts for comfortable winter stays and is home to the **LEWIS AND CLARK INTERPRETIVE CENTER** (360/642-3029; www.parks.wa.gov/lcinterpctr. asp), which affords visitors a retelling of the explorers' journey. But the biggest draw here is the view, the region's finest.

RESTAURANTS

Port Bistro Restaurant / ★★☆

235 HOWERTON AVE SE, ILWACO; 360/642-8447

With years of experience cooking in Seattle and Long Beach Peninsula restaurants, owner Jeff Marcus opened his own place. After spending time in this colorful eatery, you'll be glad he did. Marcus does delectable things to seafood. Fresh halibut tacos with chipotle sour cream are moist. The mango wine spritzer is refreshing and fruity, and the custom-made copper bar, open kitchen, and imaginative art make this a fun place to hang out. *$–$$; AE, MC, V; checks OK; lunch Tues–Fri, dinner Tues–Sat; beer and wine; reservations recommended; www.portofilwaco.com/paulys; waterfront along Ilwaco port.* ⅃

LODGINGS

China Beach Retreat / ★★★

222 CAPT ROBERT GRAY DR, ILWACO;
360/642-5660 OR 800/466-1896

This lovely hideaway by the bay is an ideal place to romance your sweetie. Three rooms match the beauty that surrounds this water wonderland. Upstairs rooms provide the best views; all have private baths, and the downstairs suite offers a two-person jetted tub. Stained glass windows and handmade tiles in the tubs are displays of art. The owners have added the Audubon Cottage, perfect for more privacy. Elaborate gourmet breakfasts are served 5 miles away at the charming Shelburne Inn (see review). *$$$–$$$$; AE, MC, V; checks OK; www.chinabeachretreat.com; ½ mile west of downtown.*

Seaview

Touted as an ocean retreat for Portlanders early in the 20th century (visitors arrived via river steamer, then transferred to a local railroad), Seaview now enjoys a legacy of older, stately beach homes, a pretty beach front, and some of the best dining and lodging on the Long Beach Peninsula. Nearly every road heading west reaches the ocean, and you can park your car and stroll the dunes. Don't miss the **WILD MUSHROOM FESTIVAL** in October.

RESTAURANTS

The Depot Restaurant / ★★★

1208 38TH PL, SEAVIEW; 360/642-7880
An old train station is now a fine-dining experience. Michael Lalewicz's Italian-French influences, coupled with local products, turn out mouth-watering combinations. The CrabMac appetizer is outstanding, as is the Depot House Greens salad. "Dine at the Source" by choosing the special seafood entrée caught that day. An open kitchen allows patrons to witness the magic. *$$; AE, DIS, MC, V; checks OK; dinner Wed–Sun; beer and wine; reservations recommended; www.depotrestaurantdining.com; on Seaview Beach approach.* &

42nd Street Café / ★★★

4201 PACIFIC HWY, SEAVIEW; 360/624-2323
When you enter this cozy roadside café, its friendly atmosphere will remind you of a festive family holiday. Named one of the top chefs by a regional magazine, Cheri Walker, along with her husband, Blaine, have made a fine-dining experience in a down-home place a reality. Service is prompt and pleasant. Decor is bright and cheery. 42nd Street has delectable sauces atop various seafood entrées. Bring home a jar of their yummy marionberry jam. *$–$$; MC, V; checks OK; breakfast, lunch, dinner every day; beer and wine; reservations recommended (dinner); www.42ndstreet.com; at 42nd St.* &

The Shoalwater Restaurant / ★★★½

4415 PACIFIC HWY, SEAVIEW; 360/642-4142
There are three very good reasons why awards and accolades for this 25-year-old establishment keep rolling in: owners Tony and Anne Kirschner and chef Lynne Pelletier. This team creates fresh seafood entrées and tantalizing desserts. Did we mention the best wine list on the Washington coast? Dark wood columns and beautiful stained-glass windows create a lush setting. *$$$; AE, DIS, MC, V; checks OK; lunch, dinner every day, brunch Sun; full bar; reservations recommended (dinner); www.shoalwater.com; at 44th St.* &

LODGINGS

The Shelburne Inn / ★★★

4415 PACIFIC WY, SEAVIEW; 360/642-2442 OR 800/466-1896
When you enter this nationally recognized inn, you'll feel immediately welcome. Lovingly crafted and maintained, the inn has 15 guest rooms full of exquisite antiques and old-world charm. Two suites offer fresh-baked cookies and in-room breakfast service if desired. You'll be talking about the five-course breakfast long afterward. A listing in the National Register of Historic Places makes this inn cherished. *$$$, AE, MC, V; checks OK; www.theshelburne inn.com; on SR 103 at N 45th.* &

Long Beach

The epicenter of peninsula tourist activity, Long Beach hosts throngs of summer visitors who browse the gift shops and arcades and wander the beach **BOARDWALK**—a pedestrian-only half-mile stroll with night lighting (wheelchairs and baby strollers welcome). The paved **LEWIS AND CLARK TRAIL** begins here, too.

A big draw is August's weeklong **INTERNATIONAL KITE FESTIVAL**, when the town swells to more than 50,000. Visit the **WORLD KITE MUSEUM AND HALL OF FAME** (112 3rd St NW; 360/642-4020; www.worldkitemuseum.com), or get in on the fun yourself by shopping at **LONG BEACH KITES** (115 Pacific Ave N; 360/642-2202 or 800/234-1033) or **OCEAN KITES** (511 Pacific Ave S; 360/642-2229).

For a tastier museum visit, check out the **CRANBERRY MUSEUM AND GIFT SHOP** (2907 Pioneer Rd; 360/642-5553; www.cranberrymuseum.com; every day Apr–Dec) and take a self-guided tour of the bogs. **ANNA LENA'S PANTRY** (111 Bolstad Ave E; 360/642-8585) has 20 or so varieties of fudge; it's also a quilters' destination. Grab a sandwich or a pizza to go at **SURFER SANDS** (1113 Pacific Hwy S; 360/642-7873).

CAMPICHE STUDIOS (101 Pacific Ave S; 360/642-2264) exhibits watercolors, pottery, and photos. Kitschy and fun, **MARSH'S FREE MUSEUM** (409 S Pacific Ave; 360/642-2188; www.marshsfreemuseum.com) features nationally famous Jake the Alligator Man, a mummified half-man, half-alligator who inspired a line of "Believe It Or Not"–style sportswear.

LODGINGS

Boreas Bed & Breakfast / ★★★

**607 N OCEAN BEACH BLVD, LONG BEACH;
360/642-8069 OR 800/642/8069**
When you meet owners Susie Goldsmith and Bill Verner, you'll understand why the glowing accolades about their B and B keep pouring in. Five generously sized rooms, each with a private bath, are colorful and artsy. Plush robes, signature dark chocolates, upscale bath products, and fresh flowers

LONG BEACH PENINSULA THREE-DAY TOUR

DAY ONE: Begin your day with breakfast at the **42ND STREET CAFÉ** in **SEAVIEW**. Drive south through Ilwaco to **CAPE DISAPPOINTMENT STATE PARK** and hike one of the coastal trails. Tour the **NORTH HEAD LIGHTHOUSE** or go for a dip at **WAKIKI BEACH**, the only swim-safe beach on the peninsula. Return inland to **ILWACO** to view the boats while lunching at the **PORT BISTRO RESTAURANT**. Check in to the **AUDUBON COTTAGE** at **CHINA BEACH RETREAT** and watch nature on the beach for the rest of the afternoon. Have dinner at the **SHOALWATER RESTAURANT** in Seaview.

DAY TWO: After a huge breakfast at the **SHELBURNE INN** (included with your previous night's lodgings), drive north to **LONG BEACH**. Go kite flying after visiting the **WORLD KITE MUSEUM**, or swing your club for a while at the **PENINSULA GOLF COURSE** (9604 Pacific Hwy, Long Beach; 360/642-2828). Have lunch at the **CRAB POT** (1917 Pacific Hwy S, Long Beach; 360/642-8870). Browse **SHOPS** along Pacific Highway, or stroll the **BOARDWALK**. Buy a T-shirt at

are extras. An impressive, three-course gourmet breakfast is served midmorning. After experiencing their luxurious and personable pampering, heck, you might ask Susie and Bill to come home with you. *$$$; AE, DIS, MC, V; checks OK; www.boreasinn.com; 1 block west of SR 103.*

Inn at Discovery Coast / ★★★

421 11TH ST SW, LONG BEACH; 360/642-5265 OR 866-843/5782
This boutique hotel is the epitome of luxury when it comes to oceanfront accommodations along the Long Beach Peninsula. The three-story, ultramodern inn has nine rooms, all with pine floors, neutral colors, and sleek furnishings. Some rooms have two-person jetted tubs while others have two-headed showers. You'll appreciate the down bedding and Aveda bath products, as well as the basket of breakfast goodies delivered to your door. *$$–$$$; AE, DIS, MC, V; checks OK; www.innatdiscoverycoast.com; left at Sid Snyder, go 4 blocks, left on Shoreview Dr, right on 11th St.* &

The Lighthouse / ★★☆

**12417 PACIFIC WAY, LONG BEACH;
360/642-3622 OR 877-220-7555**
There are actually two sets of accommodations on this unique property. The rustic roadside cabins built in the 1950s are cheaper, but the newer oceanfront condominiums located behind the older hotel are more elegant. The 30 tastefully decorated townhouse units are a stone's throw from the beach. One-, two-, and three-bedroom options, fully equipped kitchens, and an enclosed

FRANTIC FRED'S (310 Pacific Ave S, Long Beach; 360/642-3838), and indulge at SCOOPER'S ICE CREAM (101 N Pacific Ave, Long Beach; 360/642-8388). Leave crowds behind and check in to your evening's accommodations at the BOREAS BED & BREAKFAST. Relax before freshening up for dinner back in Seaview at the DEPOT RESTAURANT.

DAY THREE: Your morning meal at your B and B will get you started for the day. As you drive from Long Beach toward the northern tip of the peninsula, stop in Ocean Park at WEIR STUDIOS (2217 Bay Ave, Ocean Park; 360/665-6821) for fused-glass pendants and at WIEGARDT'S STUDIO GALLERY (2607 Bay Ave, Ocean Park; 360/665-5976) for watercolor paintings. Take the west-shore road to LEADBETTER POINT STATE PARK and spend the late morning bird-watching, beachcombing, and clam digging. Drive south through Oysterville and sit in the lovely OYSTERVILLE CHURCH (along Territory Rd) for a moment or two before going to Nahcotta for lunch at BAILEY'S BAKERY AND CAFÉ. Return to Ocean Park and check in to BLACKWOOD BEACH COTTAGES. Have dinner in Nahcotta at the ARK RESTAURANT.

swimming pool make this an ideal vacation spot for families. *$–$$$$; AE, DIS, MC, V; checks OK; www.lighthouseresort.net; 2½ miles north of Long Beach off SR 103, look for blinking lighthouse off to left.* &

Ocean Park, Nahcotta, and Oysterville

Just because these three communities are located in the quiet northern end of the Long Beach Peninsula doesn't mean they're not exciting. Check with the OCEAN PARK CHAMBER OF COMMERCE (888/751-9354; www.opwa.com) for local happenings. This area is great for clamming, beachcombing, golfing, and oyster eating. The NORTHWEST GARLIC FESTIVAL in June and the ROD RUN in September are two events not to be missed in Ocean Park.

Visit the WILLAPA BAY INTERPRETIVE CENTER in Nahcotta (next to the Ark Restaurant—see review; 360/665-4547; Sat–Sun in summer) to learn about the oyster industry. Stroll through OYSTERVILLE and imagine the slower-paced lifestyle of 100 years ago. Head out to LEADBETTER POINT STATE PARK (on Stackpole Rd) and bird-watch.

RESTAURANTS

The Ark Restaurant / ★★

273RD ST AND SANDRIDGE RD, NAHCOTTA; 360/665-4133

After 25 years, the Ark's ownership has changed. Its former owners garnered rave reviews in national media and penned four cookbooks. The dining room is a little too dolled up, with year-round holiday lights, but it has a stunning view of Willapa Bay. It still features tons of seafood, fried oysters from the bay, and wild blackberry cobbler from the Willapa Hills. Don't forget to walk through the herb and flower garden. *$$$; AE, DIS, MC, V; local checks only; dinner Tues–Sun (Thurs–Mon in winter), brunch Sun (summer and holidays); full bar; reservations recommended; www.arkrestaurant.com; on old Nahcotta dock, next to oyster fleet.*

Bailey's Bakery and Café / ★

26910 SANDRIDGE RD, NAHCOTTA; 360/665-4449
Owner Jayne Bailey's breakfast goodies are well worth the journey you'll make to her cheery roadside café at the northernmost end of the Long Beach Peninsula. Scones loaded with tart cherries or blueberries or a bowl of homemade granola are yummy. On Sundays, savor "Thunder Buns," the melt-in-your-mouth sticky buns. A daily soup special and a nice selection of sandwiches and salads are lunch fare. *$; no credit cards; checks OK; breakfast, lunch Thurs–Mon; no alcohol; no reservations; adjacent to Nahcotta Post Office.* &

LODGINGS

Blackwood Beach Cottages / ★★★☆

20711 PACIFIC WAY, OCEAN PARK; 360/665-6356 OR 888-376-6356
These 10 charming bungalows offer class and comfort in a private, forested setting. Cozy built-in nooks, fully equipped kitchens, and cookbooks make for memorable meals. Purchase a sweet-smelling candle and your favorite bottle of wine from their gift shop, then settle into your ocean or woodland view cottage. Mystic Cottage's beach decor is especially fun. You'll feel very spoiled here. *$$–$$$$; MC, V; checks OK; www.blackwoodbeachcottages. com; off SR 103 south of Klipsan Beach, just past milemarker 8.* &

Blue Bayou Inn / ★★☆

26811 DELL ST, NAHCOTTA; 360/665-0593
A relative newcomer to the Long Beach Peninsula, this property underwent a complete renovation in 2005 and opened two luxurious suites that year. With a private kitchenette and comfy living-room area, each suite has more than 550 square feet. Yummy picnic lunches are available with a two-night stay. Despite the suites being on the first level, bay views are available, and outdoor gas grills on the patio or deck make ideal spots for an evening barbecue. *$$$; MC, V; no checks; www.bluebayouinn.biz; off Sandridge Rd and 268th St.*

Moby Dick Hotel & Oyster Farm / ★★

25814 SANDRIDGE RD, NAHCOTTA; 360/665-4543
This unique nine-room hotel is eclectic. The exterior orange stucco walls are a pleasant prelude to what awaits inside: brightly painted rooms adorned with art and throw rugs. A heated-floor yurt and a dry-heat sauna are nice touches.

Most rooms have shared baths. Room 2 is our favorite, with its own soaking tub and sitting deck. Multicourse breakfasts are included in their restaurant (dinner Thurs–Mon; full bar; reservations recommended). *$$; AE, DIS, MC, V; checks OK; www.mobydickhotel.com; south of Bay Ave.* &

Centralia and Chehalis

Near each other on the Interstate 5 corridor south of Olympia, these two towns are close to State Route 6 west to Raymond and South Bend, and US Highway 12 east to White Pass, with access to Mount Rainier National Park. Take a walking tour or shop for antiques through historic Centralia or catch a **STEAM TRAIN RIDE** (360/748-9593; www.steamtrainride.com) in Chehalis. Visit the **LEWIS COUNTY CONVENTION AND VISITOR BUREAU** (1401 W Mellen St, Centralia; 800/525-3323; www.tourlewiscounty.com) for more information.

RESTAURANTS

The Shire Bar & Bistro / ★

465 NW CHEHALIS AVE, CHEHALIS; 360/748-3720
In this former men's club and tavern, you'll encounter their "eat, drink, and be merry" spirit. Owner Joel Wall has crafted a restaurant that offers fine food, live entertainment, and old-world charm. The bar alone is a sight to behold. Built in France in the late 1800s, this dark-wood beauty is where you'll want to sit on Thursday jazz nights; rock and blues are on Saturdays. Menus offer 20 different entrées ranging from burgers to prime rib. Try their Cajun-influenced cornmeal catfish sandwich or chicken gumbo, and get a taste of the true South. *$–$$; MC, V; local checks only; lunch Tues–Fri, dinner Tues–Sat; full bar; reservations recommended; www.theshirebarandbistro.com; at NW Pacific Ave.* &

Mount St. Helens
National Volcanic Monument

May 18, 1980, remains a vivid memory for most people in the Pacific Northwest since Mount St. Helens, one of the Cascade Range's most active volcanoes, erupted that morning. The explosion was heard as far away as British Columbia, and ash was carried for hundreds of miles. After being relatively quiet for 25 years, the mountain began to emit ash and steam in September 2005; the **JOHNSTON RIDGE OBSERVATORY** (milepost 52, SR 504; 360/274-2140) continues to be one of the most visited sites in Washington. Easiest access to reach the mountain is by taking the Castle Rock exit off Interstate 5 and traveling east on State Route 504. Known as the **SPIRIT LAKE MEMORIAL HIGHWAY**, this 52-mile road has five visitor centers en route to the mountain. Don't miss stopping at the **MOUNT ST.**

HELENS VISITOR CENTER (3029 Spirit Lake Hwy, Castle Rock; 360/274-0962) for more information about the 1980 eruption and the mountain's current volcanic activity.

Vancouver and Camas

Downtown Vancouver has undergone extensive urban revitalization, with its pride and joy being **ESTHER SHORT PARK** (W 8th and Columbia sts). Renovations are a welcome change for **UPTOWN VILLAGE** (along Main St) as well, with new businesses blending in with older ones.

The **VANCOUVER NATIONAL HISTORIC RESERVE TRUST** (360/992-1802) represents historic sites in the oldest and fourth-largest city of Washington. **FORT VANCOUVER** (612 E Reserve St; 360/696-7655), **OFFICERS ROW** (E Evergreen Blvd, between I-5 and E Reserve St), and **PEARSON AIR MUSEUM** (1115 E 5th St; 360/694-7026) are noteworthy places.

The **WATERFRONT RENAISSANCE TRAIL** (Columbia Way between Interstate 5 and SE Topper Dr, Vancouver) along the Columbia River is an ideal place to take a stroll, run, or ride a bike. **VANCOUVER LAKE PARK** (6801 NW Lower River Rd) and **LACAMAS LAKE** (2700 SE Everett Rd, just north of downtown Camas) are popular for water sports.

Annual festivals celebrate music, art, and food in the summer. The **FOURTH OF JULY FIREWORKS** display entertains thousands. The **TOURISM INFORMATION CENTER** (located in O. O. Howard House, 750 Anderson St, Vancouver; 877/600-0800) and the **SOUTHWEST WASHINGTON CONVENTION AND VISITORS BUREAU** (101 E 8th St, Vancouver; www.southwestwashington.com) offer information.

RESTAURANTS

Beaches Restaurant and Bar / ★★☆

1919 SE COLUMBIA RIVER DR, VANCOUVER; 360/699-1592
This popular eatery with great river views has been serving reasonably good food since 1995. You'll smell pizza in the wood oven as you enter; these and their lunch items are good, but dinner entrées often miss the mark. The good news is, you'll have room for the Key lime pie. The waiting area can be crowded, and the restaurant is noisy. An open kitchen, plentiful seating, a young staff, and free beach toys for kids create a festive family atmosphere. *$$–$$$; AE, DIS, MC, V; checks OK; lunch, dinner every day; full bar; reservations recommended; 1 mile east of I-5 bridge, along Columbia River.* &

Bortolami's Pizzeria / ★★☆

9901 NE 7TH AVE, VANCOUVER; 360/574-2598
This family-owned restaurant showcases two of Italy's greatest contributions: pizza and bicycles. While you dine on slices of your favorite pizza, delight in the eye-catching cycling paraphernalia on the walls. Children and parents alike will appreciate the fortlike play area for kids. The Rainbow Jersey

(Canadian ham and pineapple with marinara) is tasty. Or try the Domestique, which has chicken, roasted red peppers, and feta cheese. Create your own from among four different sauces and tons of toppings. *$$; AE, MC, V; checks OK; lunch, dinner every day; beer and wine; no reservations; www.bortolami. com; 99th St exit off I-5, go 1 block west.* &

Cinetopia/Vinotopia / ★★★

11700 SE 7TH ST, VANCOUVER; 360/213-2800 OR 877-608-2800
This is probably the country's most luxurious high-tech movie theater. Owner Rudyard Coltman's love of cinema created the "ultimate movie experience." Leather seats, the incredible sound technology, and 50-foot screens will leave you awestruck. And that's just the theater. There's also art, live entertainment, a wine bar, and a restaurant serving tasty tapas like scampi crostini and Dungeness crab with mango and avocado. And yes, you can take the restaurant food to your seat; three of the theaters have waiter service. *$$; AE, MC, V; checks OK; lunch, dinner every day; beer and wine; reservations recommended (restaurant); www.cinetopiatheaters.com; Mill Plain exit 28 off I-5, go 2 blocks east, right on SE 117th Ave.* &

Gray's at the Park Restaurant / ★★☆

301 W 6TH ST (HILTON VANCOUVER), VANCOUVER; 360/828-4343
After three years at the Portland Hilton, chef Nate Read made the move across the river to shake up Vancouver's restaurant and bar scene. Try Nate's specialty, the Five Hour Ragu, with veal, spicy Italian sausage, pancetta, tomatoes, and porcini mushrooms. Move on through the George Jetson–like bar with its retro furniture and beaded shimmer screens, and you'll enter the more tastefully decorated dining area with big booths and large windows. Opened since June 2005, this restaurant is one to keep your eye on. *$$–$$$, AE, DIS, MC, V; checks OK; breakfast, lunch, dinner every day; full bar; reservations recommended; www.graysatthepark.com; corner of Columbia and W 6th sts.* &

Hudson's Bar & Grill / ★★☆

17805 GREENWOOD DR (HEATHMAN LODGE), VANCOUVER; 360/816-6100 OR 888/475-6101
Media darling chef Marc Hosack has had some remarkable press. Using the freshest of Northwest ingredients, he crafts exciting dinner combinations like flatiron steak with apple, pear, and blue cheese bread pudding or seafood pasta with vodka-tomato-cream sauce. The Imperial Ranch Stock sirloin burger is a hands-down winner for lunch, but the salmon and vegetable pasta sauce was disappointing. Lofty ceilings, an open kitchen, and a huge fireplace create a comfortable space. *$$–$$$; AE, DC, DIS, MC, V; checks OK; breakfast, lunch, dinner every day; full bar; no reservations; www.hudsonsbarand grill.com; left on NE Greenwood Dr off of NE Parkway Dr.* &

A WALKABOUT IN ESTHER SHORT PARK

It's now possible to spend a day in downtown Vancouver and not run out of things to do, thanks to the revitalization of **ESTHER SHORT PARK** (W 8th and Columbia sts). The oldest town square in Washington is emerging because of new condominiums, restaurants, and shops. Enjoy breakfast at **GRAY'S ON THE PARK** (inside Hilton Vancouver, 301 W 6th St; 360/828-4343) before meandering through the shops that border the north and west sides of the park.

Check out **WILLOWS** (302 W 8th St; 360/993-1318), which offers upscale women's clothing, and **CONTESSA** (812 Columbia St; 360/993-5996), which has shoes and accessories for men and women. Kids enjoy hanging out at **KAZOO-DLES TOYS** (575 W 8th St; 360/699-9200), while adults are drawn to **ATHENS DAY SPA** (410 W 8th St; 360/695-4800).

Enjoy a **PICNIC LUNCH** in the summer while listening to a free afternoon concert in the park. Indulge your sweet tooth at **DOLCE GELATO** (535 W 8th St; 360-567-1001). Pick up fresh produce and other goodies at the year-round **FARMERS MARKET** (at W 8th and Esther sts).

—Lisa Evans

Roots Restaurant / ★★

19215 SE 34TH AVE, CAMAS; 360/260-3001
Don't let the unassuming storefront in a strip mall–like place prevent you from coming here. Roots has extraordinary dishes at affordable prices. The chicken sausage and mozzarella sandwich is flavorful, and the buttermilk onion rings are addicting. An open kitchen, an intimate bar, and a square dining area create a sociable atmosphere, but the humble decor makes the space appear a little cold. You'll praise the attentive waitstaff and the dark-colored curtains that obscure the dismal parking-lot view. *$$; AE, MC, V; no checks; lunch, dinner every day; full bar; reservations recommended; wwwroots restaurantandbar.com; Riverstone Marketplace Shopping Center.* &

Sheridan's Frozen Custard / ★★★

14389 SE MILL PLAIN BLVD, VANCOUVER; 360/260-8188
Sherry and Scott Ehle's two-year-old franchise has developed huge fans on both sides of the Columbia River. Ice cream connoisseurs will convert to this heavenly concoction with just one taste. Created in 1919 in New York, frozen custard has very little air whipped in, making it denser, smoother, and more decadent than ice cream. This sweet spot serves up sundaes, shakes, and con-cretes (chocolate or vanilla custard blended with your choice of topping), and offers free cones for dogs. *$; MC, V; no checks; dessert every day; no alcohol; no reservations; in parking lot of Mountain View Ice Arena.* &

Tommy O's / ★★

801 WASHINGTON ST, VANCOUVER; 360/694-5107
For 13 years, owner Tommy Owens has brought a touch of the Hawaiian Islands to downtown Vancouver. Formerly the Aloha Café, the bistro serves Pacific Rim cuisine with panache. Fresh halibut rolled in sweet macadamia nuts is moist and delicious. Seafood appetizers are tastier than the chicken or beef options. Surfing paraphernalia, Hawaiian music, and tropical table-cloths (white linens at dinner) add to the island charm. *$–$$$; AE, DIS, MC, V; local checks only; breakfast, lunch, dinner every day; full bar; reservations recommended; www.tommyosaloha.com; at 8th St.* &

LODGINGS

The Fairgate Inn / ★★★★

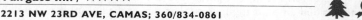

2213 NW 23RD AVE, CAMAS; 360/834-0861
A 15-year love affair with B and Bs and an amazing talent for design and decor helped Chris and Jack Foyt build this exquisite colonial mansion. Besides being an incredible place to stay, the inn hosts hundreds of weddings, meetings, and retreats. The foyer's grand Brazilian-cherry staircase leads to eight beautifully furnished, luxurious rooms each with a private bath and fireplace. Gorgeous hardwood furniture, high thread-count linens and a delicious gourmet breakfast leave long-lasting impressions. *$$$; AE, MC, V; checks OK; www.fairgateinn.com; exit 192 off SR 14, right on Brady Rd, right on 16th, right on 18th, left on Astor, right on 23rd (approx 4 miles NE of hwy).* &

Heathman Lodge / ★★★☆

7801 GREENWOOD DR, VANCOUVER; 360/254-3100 OR 888-475-3100
It really is an odd location for this beautiful hotel, but for the corporate traveler or for those wanting the illusion of a mountain getaway in the city, it works. Northwest Native American decor and design are prominently displayed throughout the property and its 121 guest rooms and 22 suites. A complimentary business center, meeting and banquet spaces, and an indoor heated pool with sauna and fitness room are here. Great meals aren't far away, as highly acclaimed Hudson's Bar & Grill (see review) is on-site. Despite being next to a busy shopping mall, it's the nicest place to stay on the east side of Vancouver. *$$–$$$$; AE, DC, DIS, MC, V; checks OK; www.heathmanlodge.com; near Thurston exit off SR 500.* &

Hilton Vancouver / ★★★

301 W 6TH AVE, VANCOUVER; 360/993-4500 OR 800-321-3232
The latest luxury hotel in Vancouver feels more like a boutique than a cor-porate behemoth. Part of the new convention center, it's not just smaller than the average Hilton, it's sexier. All 226 rooms offer Crabtree & Evelyn bath products and have specially made alarm clocks that play programmed music of your choice. Contemporary design and furniture, and paintings by

Northwest artists, are displayed throughout. A lofty entrance, beautifully colored carpets, and exquisite lighting display grand style. *$–$$$$; AE, MC, V; checks OK; www.vancouverwashington.hilton.com; corner of Columbia and W 6th sts.* &

Columbia River Gorge and Mount Adams

The **COLUMBIA GORGE INTERPRETIVE CENTER** (990 SW Rock Creek Dr; 509/427-8211 or 800/991-2338), on State Route 14 just west of Stevenson, has a nine-projector slide show that re-creates the gorge's formation.

Mount Adams and its surrounding area, 30 miles north of the Columbia via State Route 141, offer natural splendor largely overlooked by visitors, who seldom venture north from the gorge. Besides climbing to the summit of the 12,276-foot mountain—greater in mass than any of the five other major volcanic peaks in the Northwest—you can explore miles of trails in the **MOUNT ADAMS WILDERNESS AREA** and **GIFFORD PINCHOT NATIONAL FOREST**. Contact the **MOUNT ADAMS RANGER STATION** (2455 SR 141; 509/395-3400) in Trout Lake for information.

LODGINGS

Bonneville Hot Springs Resort and Spa / ★★★

1252 E CASCADE DR, NORTH BONNEVILLE; 509/427-7767 OR 866/459-1628 Grandeur is showcased in a lovely, though not flashy, way at this wooded resort. The great room is stunning with its big timbers and a river-rock fireplace. Richly colored linens, rugs, and furniture make the 74 spacious rooms and 4 suites warm and cozy. The best rooms are those with a hillside view and a hot tub on the balcony. An indoor pool and two Jacuzzis offer therapeutic mineral waters that are also used in the hotel's spa. Hospitality reigns supreme here. *$$$–$$$$; AE, DIS, MC, V; checks OK; www.bonnevilleresort. com; from SR 14, turn on Hot Springs Dr, right onto Cascade Dr.* &

Stevenson

Thanks to the city of **STEVENSON** (www.cityofstevenson.com), the **WI-FI PROJECT** provides free wireless Internet access downtown. Browse through women's clothing and gifts at **DUCK SOUP** (350 SW SR 14; 509/427-5136) and visit the studio of well-known watercolorist **MARILYN WOOD BOLLES** (509 NW 2nd St; 509/427-5930). **WALKING MAN BREWERY** (240 SW 1st St; 509/427-5520) and **BIG RIVER GRILL** (192 SW 2nd St; 509/427-4888) are ideal for a beer and a good meal. Two music festivals—**BLUES, BREWS, AND BARBEQUE** in June and the **BLUEGRASS FESTIVAL** in July—are hits. Stop by the **SKAMANIA COUNTY CHAMBER OF COMMERCE** (167 2nd Ave; 800/989-9178) to learn more.

RESTAURANTS

Bahma Coffee Bar / ★★

256 2ND ST, STEVENSON; 509/427-8700

Bahma, Hebrew for "place of comfort," is Stevenson's first and finest coffeehouse. Well-worn couches and lushly painted walls give a bohemian-renaissance feel to the space. The owners serve up more than a good cup of joe. Yummy breakfast and lunch items like scones, croissant sandwiches, soups, salads, and fruit smoothies are available. Check for live music on the weekends. *$; MC, V; checks OK; breakfast, lunch every day; beer and wine; no reservations; www.bahmacoffeebar.com; on SR 14, across street from AJ Market.* ৬

The Cascade Room / ★★★

**1131 SW SKAMANIA LODGE WAY (SKAMANIA LODGE),
STEVENSON; 509/427-7700 OR 800/221-7117**

This restaurant has a Greek chef, Emmanuel Afentoulis, whose heritage might inspire the large portions of his traditional fish and meat dishes. You'll get a view of the Columbia River, out-of-this-world salmon chowder, and heavenly desserts. Friday-night buffets and Sunday brunches are feasts fit for royalty. *$$–$$$; MC, V; no checks; breakfast, lunch, dinner every day; full bar; reservations recommended; www.skamania.com; just west of Stevenson, turn north onto Rock Creek Dr, left onto Skamania Lodge Way.* ৬

LODGINGS

Skamania Lodge / ★★★

**1131 SKAMANIA LODGE WY, STEVENSON;
509/427-7700 OR 800-221-7117**

Skamania is a destination resort in the middle of the Washington side of the Columbia Gorge. Sitting atop a bluff overlooking a valley and the river, the lodge's views are spectacular. A literal playground for the sports enthusiast, Skamania has a golf course, an indoor pool, tennis courts, and bikes. New management is changing the room decor and expanding the spa, but the overall Native American and Pacific Northwest atmosphere will remain in their 254 rooms, meeting spaces, and throughout the property. *$$$–$$$$; AE, DIS, MC, V; checks OK; www.skamania.com; just west of Stevenson, turn north onto Rock Creek Dr.* ৬

COLUMBIA GORGE THREE-DAY TOUR

DAY ONE: Have breakfast at **TOMMY O'S** in Vancouver and grab some picnic fixings at the Farmer's Market (at W 8th and Esther sts) before beginning your scenic, winding drive east on State Route 14. Stop at **BEACON ROCK STATE PARK** (34841 SR 14, Skamania; 509/427-8265; www.parks.wa.gov) and carefully walk the short, steep trail to the incredible river views at the top, then refuel with a picnic. Continue east to watch salmon and steelhead move up the fish ladder at **BONNEVILLE LOCK AND DAM** (off SR 14 at milepost 40; 509/427-4281; www.nwp.usace.army.mil/op/b). Return west a short way to North Bonneville and check in to the **BONNEVILLE HOT SPRINGS RESORT AND SPA**, swim in their therapeutic mineral pool, and then spend the rest of the afternoon in their spa. Venture just a few miles east and north to **SKAMANIA LODGE'S CASCADE ROOM** in Stevenson for dinner.

DAY TWO: Head east and check out the **COLUMBIA INTERPRETIVE CENTER MUSEUM** before stopping at **BAHMA COFFEE BAR** in Stevenson for breakfast. Walk to **BOB'S BEACH** (along Cascade Ave, ½ blk west of the city's dock,

---

Carson

LODGINGS

Carson Mineral Hot Springs Resort / ★★

372 ST. MARTIN RD, CARSON; 509/427-8292 OR 800/607-3678
The funk factor of this hundred-year-old resort is trying to turn fashionable. Gone are the cabins on the hillside. In their place is an imposing two-story structure that houses 28 rather unexciting rooms. New rooms with forested and river views, kitchenettes, and mineral-water Jacuzzi tubs will open in spring 2007—along with a golf course, spa, and restaurant. *$–$$; MC, V; checks OK; off SR 14, left at Carson Junction, 1 mile to 4-way stop, right onto Hot Springs Rd, left onto St. Martin Rd.* &

Carson Ridge Bed & Breakfast / ★★★

1261 WIND RIVER RD, CARSON; 509/427-7777 OR 877/816-7908
These seven colorful cabins are not rustic. Sitting against the foothills of the Cascades, they are ideal for couples: besides lying in the huge log beds, you can sit in a comfortable leather chair in front of the gas fireplace. Take a bath in the jetted tub. Nibble on the goodies in your welcome basket. Watch satellite TV. Breakfasts are served in a separate building. *$$$; AE, DIS, MC, V; no checks; off SR 14, left onto Carson Junction, 1.2 miles on left.* &

Stevenson) and marvel at windsurfers along the **COLUMBIA RIVER** before driving east to **WHITE SALMON** to do some serious retail **SHOPPING**. Have a snack or light lunch at **THE CREAMERY** (121 E Jewett Blvd, White Salmon; 509/493-4007) at some point during your spending spree. Head down the hill to **BINGEN** to sample Washington vintages at **GORGE WINE MERCHANTS** and then go next door and have dinner at **VIENTO'S**. Travel north up State Route 141 and head east to Glenwood, where you'll stay at the **FLYING L RANCH**.

DAY THREE: After a huge homemade breakfast at the ranch, drive the winding canyon roads southeast, parallel to the **KLICKITAT RIVER**, before connecting to State Route 142. Head east to Goldendale, visiting **GOLDENDALE OBSERVATORY STATE PARK** before stopping for Greek food and pastries for lunch at **ST. JOHN'S BAKERY, COFFEE & GIFTS**. Take US Highway 97 south to State Route 14 and make stops at the **STONEHENGE REPLICA**, **MARYHILL MUSEUM OF ART**, and **MARYHILL WINERY** before heading west to Lyle to check in to the **LYLE HOTEL** for the night. During the winter months, have dinner in the hotel's restaurant next to the wood stove. In the summer, enjoy your meal on their patio.

White Salmon and Bingen

High on a bluff overlooking the Columbia River, the towns of White Salmon and Bingen are the retail centers of Klickitat County. They're also in the heart of the **COLUMBIA RIVER GORGE NATIONAL SCENIC AREA**. The **WHITE SALMON RIVER** is one of the state's most popular rafting and kayaking destinations, April through October. Two of the best outfitters are **ZOLLER'S OUTDOOR ODYSSEYS** (1248 SR 141, located north of White Salmon on SR 141 at BZ Corner; 509/493-2641 or 800/366-2004; www.zooraft.com) and **WET PLANET** (860 SR 141, located north of White Salmon on SR 141, on right side of highway just before crossing river at Husum Falls; 509/493-8989 or 800/306-1673; www.wetplanetwhitewater.com).

At **RAY KLEBBA'S WHITE SALMON BOAT WORKS** (230 E Jewett Blvd; 509/493-4766), the staff can teach you how to make your own woodstrip-construction sea kayak or canoe. **NORTHWESTERN LAKE STABLES** (126 Little Buck Creek Rd, White Salmon; 509/493-4965) offers backcountry horseback-riding packages ranging from one hour to overnight.

If a less strenuous outing is in order, visit **WIND RIVER CELLARS** (196 Spring Creek Rd, Husum; 509/493-2324) or **GORGE WINE MERCHANTS** (218 W Steuben St, Bingen; 509/493-5333; www.gorgewinemerchants.com). Jewett Boulevard in White Salmon has several **SHOPS** worth checking out, including **WHITE SALMON GLASSWORKS** (105 E Jewett Blvd; 509/493-8400; www.whitesalmonglass.com), **COLLAGE OF THE GORGE** (111 E Jewett Blvd; 509/493-4483), and **NAYLOR ART** (157 E Jewett Blvd; 509/493-4567; www.naylorart.com).

The **MOUNT ADAMS CHAMBER OF COMMERCE** (milepost 65 on SR 14, 1 Heritage Plaza, White Salmon; 866/493-3630; www.mtadamschamber.com) has information.

RESTAURANTS

Viento's / ★★★

216 W STEUBEN ST, BINGEN; 509/493-0049

Chef and co-owner Kathy Watson left her job as a magazine editor to open this beautiful bistro and bar in the Columbia Gorge with her husband, Stu. They call their food "blowin' fresh cuisine." A savory surprise is the grilled romaine lettuce and Gorgonzola salad. An open kitchen and seating plan create a sociable space, but it's never noisy. Viento's is a rare gem in a small town. *$$–$$$; MC, V; checks OK; dinner Wed–Sun; full bar; reservations recommended; www.vientokitchen.com; on SR 14 at Alder St.* &

LODGINGS

Inn of the White Salmon / ★

172 W JEWETT BLVD, WHITE SALMON; 509/493-2335 OR 800/972-5226

Since 1990, owners Roger and Janet Holden have retained their inn's old-time charm. Although the antique furnishings and photographs are fascinating and the 16 rooms are bright, the dark hallways make it feel cloistered. It's not the best place for a romantic evening, but it's good for adventure-seekers who want a homey place to stay while exploring the gorge. An outdoor hot tub and wi-fi access are pluses. Breakfast is included with the room rate and is $15 for nonguests. *$$–$$$; MC, V; checks OK; www.innofthewhitesalmon. com; left off SR 14, 1½ miles uphill.*

Trout Lake

LODGINGS

Serenity's / ★★☆

2291 SR 141, TROUT LAKE; 509/395-2500 OR 800/276-7993

If you're seeking a serene setting in the woods, these four sweet chalet cabins are perfect. All cabins are nonsmoking and offer a gas-log fireplace as well as a "lite" cooking kitchen, which includes a small refrigerator, microwave, and coffee maker. Music and movies are available, but you'll appreciate the fact that there are no phones as the tranquil surroundings work their wonders. Windows in each cabin have lovely views of Mount Adams. Fresh flowers and chocolates are nice touches. Marcy Nordwall and Carmella DePersia are gracious hosts who have created a magical and memorable haven. *$$; MC, V; checks OK; www.serenitys.com; 23 miles north of White Salmon off SR 141.* &

Glenwood

LODGINGS

Flying L Ranch / ★★★

25 FLYING L LANE, GLENWOOD; 509/364-3488 OR 888-682-3267
Since 1997, owners Jacquie Perry and Jeff Berend and their brood of friendly
animals have made this sprawling mountain ranch east of Trout Lake a
homey haven. Distractions are easily left behind when TVs and phones are
absent. There are 29 beds distributed among the lodge, guesthouse, and three
cabins. Most rooms have their own baths, and a full-size kitchen is in the
lodge. Bird-watching, bike riding, and hot tubbing are the main draws. Volleyball and badminton, and a loop trail around the property, offer fun for the
entire family. Big breakfasts are likely to include huckleberry pancakes served
in the cozy kitchen house. Meadow and mountain views are gorgeous. *$$;
AE, MC, V; checks OK; www.mt-adams.com; east through Glenwood about ¼
mile toward Goldendale, turn north, proceed ½ mile to driveway on right.*

Lyle

LODGINGS

Lyle Hotel / ★★

100 7TH ST, LYLE; 509/365-5953 OR 800-447-6310
In the middle of seemingly nowhere, on State Route 14 east of White Salmon,
the Lyle Hotel provides Columbia Gorge adventure seekers an affordable
resting place. New owners Solea Kabakov and her husband, Chris Marlinga,
are making some wonderful changes to this quaint, 100-year-old hotel. The
antique furniture and colorful quilts adorn the 10 rooms. You'll share bath-
rooms, but you can make up for it by asking for a room with a river view.
The outdoor patio and restaurant (dinner Wed–Sun; beer and wine; reserva-
tions recommended) are sweet spots to enjoy a good meal and glass of wine.
*$; AE, DIS, MC, V; local checks only; www.lylehotel.com; 2 blocks south of
SR 14.* ⅙

Goldendale

Though Goldendale is the seat of Klickitat County, it's not a case of bright lights,
big city. This makes it the perfect location for **GOLDENDALE OBSERVATORY
STATE PARK** (602 Observatory Dr; 509/773-3141; www.parks.wa.gov; Wed–Sun
in summer, Sat–Sun by appointment in winter). Goldendale is 10½ miles north of
State Route 14 on US Highway 97.

On the way to visit the nearby **MARYHILL MUSEUM OF ART** (35 Maryhill
Museum Dr; 509/773-3733; www.maryhillmuseum.org; Mar–Nov), stop at the
MARYHILL WINERY (877/627-9445; www.maryhillwinery.com) next door. Both

are near the junction of State Route 14 and US Highway 97. About 2 miles east of the Maryhill Museum on State Route 14 is a life-size replica of England's neolithic **STONEHENGE**, built to honor fallen World War I soldiers from Klickitat County and as an antiwar memorial.

RESTAURANTS

St. John's Bakery, Coffee & Gifts / ★★★

2378 US HWY 97, GOLDENDALE; 509/773-6650

Stop at this little café and gift shop for the best Greek food you've ever had. Greek Orthodox nuns, who live at the monastery behind the café, spend their days praying and baking authentic delicacies like eggplant lasagne, spanako-pita, and baklava. Their shop also features religious items like icons and their homemade soaps, lotions, and candles. You'll know your money goes toward a good cause: the nuns, who never leave the monastery, are raising funds for a new church and living quarters. *$; MC, V; local checks only; breakfast, lunch Mon–Sat; no alcohol; no reservations; www.stjohnmonastery.org/store.html; between mileposts 23 and 24.*

SOUTHEAST
WASHINGTON

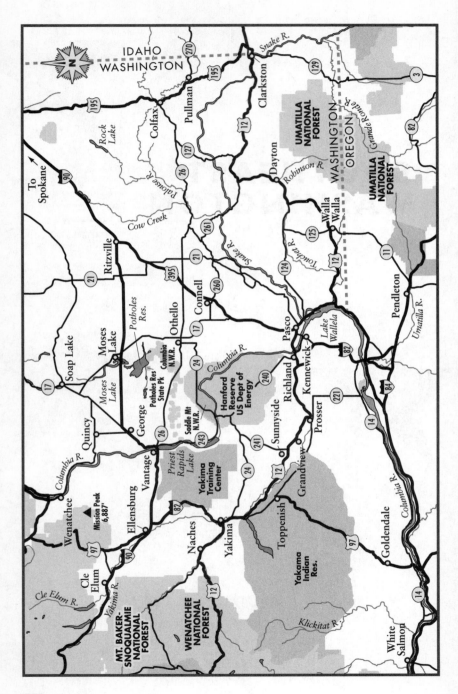

SOUTHEAST WASHINGTON

Southeast Washington is home to most of the state's 406 wineries and two major universities. Stretching from the Yakima Valley down through the Tri-Cities of Pasco, Kennewick, and Richland, Washington wine country also includes the Walla Walla Valley. This part of Washington isn't as evergreen as the rest of the state, but it's rich in wide-open spaces and agriculture.

ACCESS AND INFORMATION

Most people drive to Southeast Washington. Even if you fly, you'll need a car. **INTERSTATE 90** is the most practical route from Seattle, connecting at Ellensburg with **INTERSTATE 82**, which leads through the Yakima Valley to the Tri-Cities at the confluences of the Yakima, Snake, and Columbia rivers. From there, Walla Walla is an easy trip via Interstate 82 and **US HIGHWAY 12**.

From Portland, **INTERSTATE 84** or the two-lane **STATE ROUTE 14** on the Washington side leads to eastern Washington. If you're heading to Ellensburg or Yakima, turn north on **US HIGHWAY 97**. If your destination is the Tri-Cities, take Interstate 82/**US HIGHWAY 395**. It snows a lot in Central Washington, so carry tire chains and food between November 1 and April 1.

THE TRI-CITIES AIRPORT (3601 N 20th Ave, Pasco; 509/547-6352; www.portofpasco.org/aphome.htm) is served by Horizon Air, Delta, United Express, and SkyWest. **HORIZON AIR** (800/547-9308;www.horizonair.com) also serves the region's smaller airports, including Walla Walla, Yakima, and Moses Lake.

Most major car rental companies operate out of the Tri-Cities Airport. The **PASCO TRAIN STATION** (535 N 1st Ave) serves **AMTRAK** (509/545-1554 or 800/USA-RAIL; www.amtrak.com) and **GREYHOUND** (800/231-2222; www.greyhound.com). The local public transit company is **BEN FRANKLIN TRANSIT** (509/735-5100; www.bft.org). The **TRI-CITIES VISITOR AND CONVENTION BUREAU** (6951 W Grandridge Blvd; 800-254-5824; www.visittri-cities.com) is in Kennewick.

Columbia Basin

The Columbia Plateau is mostly rich agricultural land irrigated by the Columbia River Basin. More than 2,000 miles of canals water a million acres of fields.

Vantage and George

Sitting on a scenic stretch west of the Columbia just north of Interstate 90, Vantage offers a gorgeous view of the river. Have a picnic at the nearby **GINKGO PETRIFIED FOREST STATE PARK** (exit 36; 509/856-2700; www.parks.wa.gov), a dinosaur-inspired interpretive center that's open every day during the summer.

SOUTHEAST WASHINGTON THREE-DAY TOUR

DAY 1: Start your morning with breakfast at Ellensburg's **DAKOTA CAFÉ** (417 N Pearl St; 509/925-4783), followed by a stroll through downtown's shops. Head to Central Washington University and watch a **CHIMPOSIUM**. Next, drive the 30 miles to Yakima via the **CANYON RIVER ROAD**, stopping along the way to enjoy the scenery. Have a leisurely lunch at the **DEPOT RESTAURANT AND LOUNGE** in Yakima's North Front Street Historical District. Then take the **YAKIMA TROLLEY TO SELAH** and back (S 3ird Ave at Pine St; 509/249-5656; www.yakimatrolleys. org) in the summer. Listed on the National Register of Historic Places, it's one of the last turn-of-the-century interurban railroads left in the United States. Drive to the **WINE SHOP OF YAKIMA** (5110 Tieton Dr, Ste 260, Glenwood Square Mall; 509/972-2811) for an overview of the area's wine industry. Finally, drive east a short way and check in to **BIRCHFIELD MANOR COUNTRY INN** for the evening and enjoy dinner there.

DAY 2: Begin your day with a stroll along the 10-mile Yakima **GREENWAY**, a great walking and running path parallelling the Yakima River. For a yummy pastry and hot cup of coffee, visit **ESSENCIA ARTISAN BAKERY AND CHOCOLATERIE** (4 N 3rd St; 509/575-5570; www.essenciabakery.com) in downtown Yakima,

A small town named after the country's first president, George is just off Interstate 90 on the eastern bluffs above the Columbia. The quaint **MARTHA'S INN CAFÉ** (exit 149, 600 Frontage Rd; 509/785-3271) is a favorite stopping point in George. The area also boasts the naturally terraced **GORGE AMPHITHEATER** (www.hob.com/venues/concerts/gorge/) with a view overlooking the Columbia Gorge. Big names of all musical genres play here; arrive early to avoid traffic jams. Other caveats to be aware of: Restrooms are scarce, and locals are tiring of rowdy concertgoers. Call **TICKETMASTER** (206/628-0888; www.ticketmaster.com) for tickets. George is a three-hour drive from Seattle and two hours from Spokane. For those wanting to stay the night, two options are available: the **GORGE CAMPGROUND** (509/785-2267), which charges $35 per car per night, or the new **CAVE B INN AT SAGECLIFFE** (see review).

LODGINGS

Cave B Inn at Sagecliffe / ★★★

344 SILICA RD NW, QUINCY; 888/785-2283
Finally, a nice place to stay when you're at the Gorge—with an incredible view. The main lodge's curved roofline is reminiscent of the space age; a 30-foot-high rock fireplace anchors the main lobby. Each of the 12 cave-like rooms was built into a basalt hillside, and another 15 cliffhouses have

then jump in your car and head south on I-82 about 15 miles. Detour through **TOPPENISH** to view some of the 64 murals adorning city buildings, then head to the **YAKAMA NATION CULTURAL HERITAGE CENTER** and visit the museum. It's one of the few in the state run by Native Americans. Keep heading south and drive another 15 miles through Sunnyside, where you can visit **DARIGOLD'S DAIRY FAIR** and tour the cheese factory. Continue east about 35 miles and end your drive by checking in to the **COURTYARD RICHLAND COLUMBIA POINT**, overlooking the river. Before you turn in, have dinner at nearby **KATYA'S BISTRO & WINE BAR**.

DAY 3: Take another morning stroll along the **WATERFRONT TRAIL** right outside your hotel. After stopping at **GLORIA'S LA DOLCE VITA** (743 The Pkwy, Richland; 509/943-7400) for breakfast, head to the **COLUMBIA RIVER EXHIBITION OF HISTORY, SCIENCE & TECHNOLOGY**. Next, head east about 50 miles on US Highway 12 to Walla Walla. En route, stop at the **WHITMAN MISSION NATIONAL HISTORIC SITE**, where 19th-century missionaries and Native Americans clashed. Lunch in downtown Walla Walla at **GRAPEFIELDS**; then visit the historic buildings of the **FORT WALLA WALLA MUSEUM**. Check in to the restored 1928 **MARCUS WHITMAN HOTEL**, and finish your day with dinner at **CREEK TOWN CAFÉ**.

panoramic views of the river. Tendrils restaurant features regional fare from Sagecliffe's on-site organic gardens. The inn also offers a wine-tasting bar and culinary demonstration kitchen. The nearby Cave B Estate Winery has acres devoted to growing 14 varieties of grapes. *$$$$; AE, MC, V; checks OK; www. cavebinn.com; exit 143 from I-90.*

Ellensburg and Yakima Valleys

The Ellensburg and Yakima valleys stretch from the eastern foothills of the Cascades toward the Columbia River at Vantage. The region produces cattle, hay, and the most fruit trees in the country. Look for apples, mint, winter pears, and hops. Attractions here reflect this bounty, including the **AMERICAN HOP MUSEUM** (22 S "B" St, Toppenish; 509/865-4677) and the **CENTRAL WASH-INGTON AGRICULTURAL MUSEUM** (4508 Main St, Fullbright Park, Union Gap; 509/457-8735). The agriculture industry has drawn many migrant workers, resulting in a large Hispanic population and a culturally rich community. Visit the **YAKIMA VALLEY VISITORS AND CONVENTION BUREAU** (10 N 8th St; 800/221-0751; www.visityakima.com).

Ellensburg

In its early years, Ellensburg almost became the state capital. In 1890, Ellensburg lobbied for this honor until a fire hit its downtown and Olympia won the honor. Today hay and cowboys dominate this small town in the Kittitas Valley. For culture, look no farther than **CENTRAL WASHINGTON UNIVERSITY** (400 E 8th Ave; 509/963-2244; www.cwu.edu), where you'll find the serene Japanese Garden and the **SARAH SPURGEON GALLERY** (Randall Fine Arts Bldg; 509/963-2665), which holds art exhibits year-round. Another must-visit is the **CHIMPANZEE AND HUMAN COMMUNICATIONS INSTITUTE** (14th and "D" sts; 509/963-2244; www. cwu.edu/~cwuchci/), where humans and chimps communicate through American Sign Language (see sidebar). Annual events include the Western Art Show in May, Jazz in the Valley in late July, and the rodeo each Labor Day weekend.

Art can be found in Ellensburg off-campus as well. The **CLYMER MUSEUM AND GALLERY** (416 N Pearl St; 509/962-6416) honors John Clymer, Ellensburg's chronicler of the western frontier whose work appeared in the *Saturday Evening Post*. **GALLERY ONE** (408½ N Pearl St; 509/925-2670) sells regional crafts and displays contemporary art.

Ellensburg is also popular for skiing, rafting, hiking, or fly-fishing for trout. Contact the **ELLENSBURG CHAMBER OF COMMERCE** (609 N Main St; 888/925-2204; www.ellensburg-chamber.com) for details.

Locals recommend the **TAV** (117 W 4th Ave; 509/925-3939) because of the beautiful servers and reasonably priced burgers. Or try the funky **D&M COFFEE** on Main Street (408 S Main; 509/925-5313).

RESTAURANTS

Pearl's on Pearl Wine Bar & Bistro / ★★

311 N PEARL ST; ELLENSBURG; 509/962-8899
Pearl's is a local hangout with an ever-changing menu. Starters might include a sun-dried tomato tart, spicy lemon shrimp, or farfalle pasta with smoked salmon and sautéed veggies in champagne cream sauce; entrées featuring catfish, venison, or crab legs regularly appear. After dinner, enjoy cheesecake, or head to the bar for laid-back imbibing. *$$; MC, V; local checks only; lunch Sat–Sun, dinner every day; beer and wine; no reservations; www.pearlsonpearl. com; between 3rd and 4th aves.* &

The Valley Café / ★★

105 W 3RD AVE, ELLENSBURG; 509/925-3050
The Valley Café offers fine dining amid art deco decor, candlelit mahogany booths, and a 1930s back bar. Lunch favorites include sandwiches and salads—the lemon tahini dressing is marvelous—and quiche is a specialty. Dinners feature fresh seafood and Ellensburg lamb. Owner Greg Beach also owns the wine shop next door, so it's no surprise that the café's wine list is stellar,

TRAVELING BACK IN TIME

Immortalized in photos by Ansel Adams, the Yakima River Canyon Road is one of several Washington state scenic byways. This 25-mile stretch of breathtaking scenery along State Route 821 parallels the Yakima River, connecting the towns of Ellensburg and Yakima. Before I-82 was built, this was the main route, and its winding, narrow roadway still slows you down today. But enjoy taking your time: if you look sharp, you might see eagles, bighorn sheep, nesting hawks, falcons, deer, and elk.

Four primitive camping sites run by the Bureau of Land Management are great places to stop and soak in the scenery, watch rafters float by, or join the local fly fishers. The area is known as a blue-ribbon catch-and-release trout stream.

Each year, thousands of people visit the Yakima River Canyon to see the immense basalt cliffs, some rising more than 2,000 feet above the river. Depending on the season and the time of day, the colors of the steep rock change, enhanced by shadows, sun, clouds, and your own point of view.

Get really close by renting a rubber raft and floating part of the Yakima River. Stop at **RED'S FLY SHOP** (near mile marker 15 on Canyon Rd, Ellensberg; 509/929-1802; www.redsflyshop.com) for equipment rentals and details. You'll be floating on a class 1 river—so easy, it's almost like sitting in your bathtub. Besides camping, Red's also offers a few small cabins for rent. During the summer, human armadas can be seen floating the river.

Mother Nature's work doesn't get much better than this.

—Rick Stedman

with emphasis on Washington wines. Desserts include crème brûlée and fresh fruit pies. *$$; AE, DC, DIS, MC, V, checks OK; lunch, dinner every day; beer and wine; no reservations; near Main St.*

Yellow Church Café / ★

111 S PEARL ST; ELLENSBURG; 509/933-2233
Despite meals that sound religious—St. Benedict's Eggs, the Last Supper—a secular experience awaits you at the Yellow Church Café. This picturesque church was built for the German Lutherans in 1923 but has since served the community in a variety of ways: it's been a business office, a home, and an art gallery. The restaurant's owners are preacher's kids, so the location seems fitting. The Yellow Church Café has hardwood floors and balcony seating, and the menu includes basics such as steaks, seafood, chicken, and pasta. Written

CHIMPS CHATTER

Who ever knew chimps could do sign language? You can watch them sign to each other in Ellensburg. Using American Sign Language, chimps talk to each other and, yes, to humans at Central Washington University's **CHIMPANZEE AND HUMAN COMMUNICATION INSTITUTE** (CHCI).

It's all in the name of research. Begun in 1966, this is the first and longest running research project of its kind. Washoe and the other three signing chimpanzees—Loulis, Dar, and Tatu—have amazing sign language vocabularies. They gesture and vocalize.

At **CHIMPOSIUMS** (509/963-2244; 9:15am and 10:45am Sat, 12:30pm and 2:00pm Sun, Mar–Nov; $10/person, prepaid reservations recommended), the public can learn about free-living chimpanzee culture, threats to free-living and captive chimpanzees, and what the chimps are actually saying to each other. The workshop includes a guided observation of Washoe and her family.

—Rick Stedman

high on the wall, a quote won't let you forget where you are: "In an ordinary day, there are a thousand miracles." *$; AE, MC, V; local checks only; breakfast Sat–Sun, lunch, dinner every day; beer and wine; reservations recommended; www.yellowchurchcafe.com; at E 1st Ave.* &

LODGINGS

The Inn at Goose Creek / ★

1720 CANYON RD, ELLENSBURG; 800/533-0822

In spite of it being right next to I-90, the Inn at Goose Creek is remarkably comfortable and welcoming. With 10 themed rooms, there's something for everyone: the I Love Christmas room offers holiday spirit year-round, including music; the Ellensburg Rodeo room has a cowboy motif; and the All-Star Sports Fan room is a winner. For the romantic, the Victorian Honeymoon room comes with lace and a canopied bed. Be warned: A few rooms have a view of nothing more than the gas station next door. *$$; AE, MC, V; checks OK; www.innatgoosecreek.com; exit 109 off I-90.* &

Yakima

When approaching Yakima via I-82 from the north, you're greeted by a sign that reads "Yakima, the Palm Springs of Washington." Though the folks in Palm Springs haven't reciprocated that sentiment, Yakima still enjoys more than 300 days of sunshine annually. For first-time visitors, stop at exit 33, where you'll see the **NORTH FRONT STREET HISTORICAL DISTRICT** and several classy restaurants and shops. At the **DEPOT RESTAURANT AND LOUNGE** (32 N Front St; 509/469-4400), a renovated 1910 train station, you'll find great food (but slow service). Next door at Yakima Avenue and East "B" Street is a 22-car train that houses more restaurants and shops. The **YAKIMA VALLEY MUSEUM** (2105 Tieton Dr; 509/248-0747; www.yakimavalleymuseum.org) features pioneer equipment, costumes, a children's underground museum, and an old-fashioned soda fountain.

The **GREENWAY** (509/453-8280; www.yakimagreenway.org) is a 10-mile-long paved path for walkers and runners that stretches along the Naches and Yakima rivers from Selah Gap to Union Gap. The Greenway offers excellent views of wildlife, including bald eagles. Entrance points are at Sarg Hubbard Park (111 S 18th St), Sherman Park (E Nob Hill Blvd), Rotary Lake ("R" St), Harlan Landing (west side of I-82 between Selah and Yakima), and the east end of Valley Mall Boulevard.

Yakima has many places to stay; one of the nicest is the **HOLIDAY INN EXPRESS** (1001 E "A" St; 509/249-1000).

RESTAURANTS

Barrel House / ★★

22 N FIRST ST, YAKIMA; 509/453-3769
This swanky little restaurant has big city appeal, and a lot of class. The historic building where it's located was built in 1906 but feels new. Meals are simple but good. Dinner offerings include salmon, London broil, rosemary chicken, and grilled and marinated portobello mushrooms. *$$; MC, V; no checks; lunch Mon–Fri, dinner every day; beer and wine; no reservations; www. barrelhouse.net; near Yakima Ave.* &

Birchfield Manor Country Inn / ★★

2018 BIRCHFIELD RD, YAKIMA; 509/452-1960
Birchfield Manor offers French-country dining in an antique-filled room. The homey restaurant sits in a relaxed, pastoral setting. Entrées include double breast of chicken florentine or an authentic bouillabaisse. Five B and B rooms are above the restaurant, and six "cottage rooms" are in a separate building; some have fireplaces or two-person whirlpool tubs, and guests have access to an outdoor pool. *$$$; AE, DC, DIS, MC, V; checks OK; dinner Thurs–Sat; beer and wine; reservations recommended; www.birchfieldmanor.com; 2 miles east of Yakima, exit 34 off I-82 onto SR 24.* &

Café Melange / ★★

7 N FRONT ST, YAKIMA; 509/453-0571
Café Melange is an intimate and casual Mediterranean-influenced spot in the North Front Street Historical District. Favorites include shiitake tender

363

loin, smoked-salmon ravioli, and tapenade with Italian flat bread. *$$; MC, V; checks OK; lunch Mon–Fri, dinner Mon–Sat; beer and wine; reservations recommended; on Historic Front St, 1 mile west of I-82 at exit 33B.*

Carousel French Cuisine / ★★

25 N FRONT ST, YAKIMA; 509/248-6720
The Carousel is a fine French restaurant founded by two Belgians. Poland native Ewa Lichota now owns it and has maintained its elegant charm and French menu. Hors d'oeuvres include escargots and entrées such as coq au vin, *canard*, and bouillabaisse. *$$–$$$; DIS, MC, V; local checks only; dinner Tues–Sat; beer and wine; reservations recommended; on Historic Front St, 1 mile west of I-82 at exit 33B.*

Greystone Restaurant / ★★★

5 N FRONT ST, YAKIMA; 509/248-9801
The Greystone features fresh flowers on every table and soft lighting in a building that dates back to 1899. Its crab cakes have been a specialty for years, and entrées include rack of lamb, pan-seared salmon, and filet mignon. Don't leave without trying the hot Yakima apple cake. Served with hot rum caramel sauce and vanilla ice cream, it sets a new standard for desserts. *$$– $$$; DIS, MC, V; local checks only; lunch, dinner Mon–Sat; full bar; reservations recommended; at Yakima Ave.*

Santiago's Gourmet Mexican Cuisine / ★★

111 E YAKIMA AVE, YAKIMA; 509/453-1644
Santiago's has garnered numerous accolades since opening its doors in 1980. Start with chili con queso (chili and cheese sauce), then order a combination dinner from the selection named after prominent Mexican cities. The Cancun features a chicken burrito, black olive enchilada, and chicken taco. The Yakima apple pork mole is a local favorite, with Yakima apples and sliced pork loin covered with a sauce of chocolate, cinnamon, and spices. The most popular dinner items are steak or chicken picado, both served sliced and sautéed with vegetables. *$–$$; DIS, MC, V; checks OK; lunch, dinner Mon–Sat; full bar; reservations recommended on weekends; ¼ mile west of I-82 at exit 33B.*

LODGINGS

Orchard Inn Bed & Breakfast / ★★

1207 PECKS CANYON RD, YAKIMA; 509/966-1283 OR 866/966-1283
Two German innkeepers operate this unique B and B in the middle of a working cherry orchard. Located just minutes west of downtown Yakima, the Orchard Inn offers quiet and peaceful rooms, with private baths and jetted tubs. The separate B and B entrance offers a cozy living room with a library of books on travel, wine, cuisine, fishing, and music. This is a perfect four-season

destination. Fun, cherry-related products like chocolate-covered cherries and cherry jam are for sale. *$$; MC, V, checks OK; www.orchardinnbb.com; take 40th St exit off Hwy 12 for ¾ mile to Powerhouse Rd.*

A Touch of Europe B&B / ★★★

220 N 16TH AVE, YAKIMA; 888/438-7073
This Queen Anne Victorian was built in 1889 and opened as a B and B by owners Jim and Erika Cenci in 1995. Three antique-filled guest rooms have private baths and air-conditioning; the Prince Victorian Mahogany Room has a gas fireplace. Erika, the chef, was raised in Germany and has written several cookbooks. Her breakfast of cheeses and meats is served in the dining room or privately in the turret by candlelight. *$$; AE, MC, V; checks OK; www.winesnw.com/toucheuropeb&b.htm; exit 31 off I-82, west on Hwy 12.*

Naches

For information on hiking trails and other outdoor activities, stop at the Naches Ranger District (10237 U.S. Highway 12; 509/653-1400), where they provide maps and other details of the Okanogan and Wenatchee national forests.

LODGINGS

Whistlin' Jack Lodge / ★★

20800 SR 410, CHINOOK PASS; 800/827-2299
This 1957 mountain hideaway is ideal for hiking, alpine and cross-country skiing, fishing, or just escaping civilization. Weekend rates vary by room type: cottage, bungalow, or motel unit. Cottages, which have full kitchens and hot tubs, are close to the river and make great private retreats. Guests who want to dine out opt for motel rooms or bungalows. Whistlin' Jack's restaurant serves a specialty pan-fried trout, with live music on weekends. The lodge also has a convenience store and a 24-hour gas pump. *$$; AE, DIS, MC, V; local checks only; www.whistlinjacklodge.com; 40 miles west of Yakima via US Hwy 12 to Naches, then to Hwy 410.*

Toppenish

The town's best-known native son, western artist Fred Oldfield, has turned Toppenish's streets into an art gallery with more than 60 historical murals. These efforts by the **TOPPENISH MURAL SOCIETY** (5A Toppenish Ave; 509/865-6516) complement stores selling western gear, antiques, and art, making this a nice place for a walking tour and giving an authentic feel to summer rodeos.

The **YAKAMA NATION CULTURAL HERITAGE CENTER** (off US Hwy 97 and Buster Rd; 509/865-2800; www.yakamamuseum.com) includes a Native American museum and restaurant, reference library, gift shop, theater, and the 76-foot-tall Winter Lodge for banquets. Nearby is the tribal-run **LEGENDS CASINO** (580

SOUTHEAST WASHINGTON THREE-DAY WINE TOUR

When driving along Interstate 82 toward Washington wine country, you know you're there when you see the first huge sign just before exit 33: "Welcome to Washington Wine Country." You'll be in the center of the Yakima Valley's 40-plus wineries. Though Spring Barrel Tasting (last weekend in April) and Thanksgiving in Wine Country are two of the largest draws, any weekend during late spring and summer is good, especially if you don't want to deal with crowds. One of the best ways to visit them is in a limousine. Several limo companies, stretching from Yakima to the Tri-Cities, will map out a four-hour trip for you. Some favorites include **MOONLIT RIDE LIMOUSINE** (3908 River Rd, Yakima; 509/575-6846; www.moonlitride.com) and **PACIFIC LIMOUSINE** (Tri-Cities; 509/585-7717; www.limo01.com). If you're devising your own itinerary, here are some of the best places.

DAY ONE: Start your exploration in downtown Yakima at **KANA WINERY** (10 S 2nd St; 509/453-6611; www.kanawinery.com) and **YAKIMA CELLARS** (32 N 2nd St; 509/577-0461; www.yakimacellars.com), two wonderful tasting rooms. Next, head south on I-82 for about 9 miles and take exit 40 to visit **SAGELANDS WINERY** (71 Gangl Rd, Wapato; 509/877-2112; www.sagelandsvineyard.com), with spectacular views of the Yakima Valley and Mount Adams. Have a picnic lunch there. Stay on Yakima Valley Highway and drive up the hill to **WINDY POINT VINEYARDS** (420 Windy Point Rd, Wapato; 509/877-6824; www. windypointvineyards.com). One winery you can't miss is **PIETY FLATS** (2560 Donald-Wapato Rd, Wapato; 509/877-3115; www.pietyflatswinery.com). Their tasting room is in the 1911 Donald Fruit Mercantile Building, which feels like an old country store. Try their famous peach sundaes. After dinner in Sunnyside at **LA FOGATA MEXICAN RESTAURANT**, drive toward Grandview to spend the night at the **COZY ROSE PRIVATE COUNTRY SUITES**.

DAY TWO: After breakfast in your room, head south and stop at nearby **TUCKER CELLARS** (70 Ray Rd, Sunnyside; 509/837-8701; www.tuckercellars.

Fort Rd; 509/865-8800; www.yakamalegendscasino.com). **FORT SIMCOE STATE PARK** (open May–Sept), a frontier military post built in 1865, stands in desolate grandeur 30 miles west of Toppenish on the Yakama Indian Reservation. Off of Highway 97 in Toppenish (north or south bound), take Fort Simcoe Road west. Drive about 20 miles to the city of White Swan. In White Swan, watch for signs to Fort Simcoe State Park.

com), one of the state's oldest wineries. Your next stop is about 10 miles south in Prosser. Stop to taste wines at **SNOQUALMIE VINEYARDS** (660 Frontier Rd, Prosser; 509/786-2104; www.snoqualmie.com). At **HINZERLING WINERY** (1520 Sheridan Ave, Prosser; 509/786-2163 or 800/727-6702; www.hinzerling. com), you can have lunch featuring the best of fresh-from-the-garden regional cuisine and local wines. Then continue east 15 miles to Benton City, where you'll find more than a half dozen wineries clustered just off I-82 at exit 96. Be sure to stop at **SETH RYAN WINERY** (35306 N Sunset Rd, Benton City; 509/588-6780; www.sethryan.com) and **KIONA VINEYARDS** (44612 N Sunset Rd, Benton City; 509/588-6716; www.kionawine.com). Continue east some 20 miles to Pasco and check in to the **RED LION INN**, then go back across the river to have dinner in Richland at **TAGARIS WINERY** (844 Tulip Ln; 877/862-7999; www.tagariswines. com). The stylish tavern features a bistro and wine bar and serves gourmet pizzas and Pacific Northwest fare.

DAY THREE: After breakfast in the hotel, go back across the river again to taste a few varieties at **BARNARD GRIFFIN WINERY** (878 Tulip Ln, Richland; 509/627-0266; www.barnardgriffin.com) before leaving the Tri-Cities. Drive about 50 miles south and east to Walla Walla, stopping at the bright-yellow storefront of **CAYUSE VINEYARDS** (17 E Main St, Walla Walla; 509/526-0686; www.cayusevineyards. com) for some more sampling. Enjoy lunch across the street at **MERCHANTS LTD**. Afterward, take a short drive south of town to visit **BASEL CELLARS ESTATE WINERY** (2901 Old Milton Hwy, Walla Walla; 509/522-0200; www.baselcellars. com), then return to downtown and stop at **CANOE RIDGE VINEYARD** (1102 W Cherry St, Walla Walla; 509/527-0885; www.canoeridgevineyard.com), which specializes in classic merlot. After a stroll down Main Street, head a short way east and check in to the cozy **INN AT BLACKBERRY CREEK** (1126 Pleasant St, Walla Walla; 509/522-5233 or 877/522-5233; www. innatblackberrycreek.com). To round out your evening and three-day journey, return to downtown and dine in elegance at **26 BRIX RESTAURANT** before calling it a day.

Yakima Valley Wine Country

The Yakima Valley wine country stretches southwest from Yakima almost as far as the Tri-Cities, encompassing Zillah, Sunnyside, Grandview, Prosser, and Benton City. Washington has more than 400 wineries, with most of them out here along the Yakima River. There's an excellent Web site (www.wineyakimavalley. org) listing details (see "Southeast Washington Three-Day Wine Tour" for recommendations).

Zillah

RESTAURANTS

Squeeze Inn

611 1ST AVE, ZILLAH; 509/829-6226
Established in 1932, this Yakima Valley fixture was once a single 8-foot-wide storefront where customers had to squeeze in. Now it's more spacious, with plenty of room for locals to enjoy well-priced steak dinners that come with shrimp or fruit cocktail, bread, soup or salad, and a choice of baked potato, rice pilaf, pasta Alfredo, or garlic mashed potatoes. The music in the background is the best of the oldies, the decor is country farmhouse floral, and service is good. *$; MC, V; local checks only; lunch, dinner Mon–Sat; full bar; no reservations; on town's main street.* &

Sunnyside, Outlook, and Grandview

This is true farm country, with sights and aromas to match. If you need a snack, stop at **DARIGOLD'S DAIRY FAIR** (400 Alexander Rd, Sunnyside; 509/837-4321; open every day) for sandwiches, old-fashioned ice cream, free cheese samplings, and self-guided tours of the factory. Locals recommend the **SUNNY SPOT** (1850 Yakima Valley Hwy, Sunnyide; 509/839-7768) for breakfast.

RESTAURANTS

Dykstra House Restaurant / ★

114 BIRCH AVE, GRANDVIEW; 509/882-2082
Dykstra House, a 1914 mansion, makes bread from hand-ground whole wheat grown in the surrounding hills. Owner Linda Hartshorn takes advantage of local in-season produce, such as asparagus, in her entrées, but her specialty is dessert. Favorites are apple caramel pecan torte and Dykstra House chocolate pie, on the menu since she opened the place in 1984. *$$; AE, DC, DIS, MC, V; checks OK; lunch Tues–Sat, dinner Fri–Sat; beer and wine; reservations recommended; exit 75 off I-82.*

La Fogata Mexican Restaurant

1204 YAKIMA VALLEY HWY, SUNNYSIDE; 509/839-9019
This small, simple Mexican taqueria features rich coral walls and Michoacan specialties including posole, a stew of pork back and feet plus hominy. Less adventurous diners can't go wrong with excellent tacos and burritos. *$; MC, V; checks OK; breakfast, lunch, dinner Wed–Mon; full bar; no reservations; middle of town.*

Snipes Mountain Microbrewery & Restaurant / ★

905 YAKIMA VALLEY HWY, SUNNYSIDE; 509/837-2739

Snipes is expansive from every angle, and its huge stone fireplace and exposed rafters make the brew pub feel like a mountain lodge. The beers are brewed on-site, and the food is good steakhouse fare. Meals can be as fancy as you like, ranging from wood-fired pizza to hazelnut-crusted rack of lamb with mustard demi-glace. *$; AE, DIS, MC, V; checks OK; lunch, dinner every day; beer and wine; no reservations; www.snipesmountain.com; exit 63 or 69 off I-82.* &

LODGINGS

Cozy Rose Private Country Suites / ★

1220 FORSELL RD, GRANDVIEW; 800/575-8381

Owners Mark and Jennie Jackson offer four rooms, each with a private entrance, bathroom, fireplace, cable TV, and stereo. Splurge and get the Secret Garden Suite with a two-person Jacuzzi and king-sized bed. Breakfast is delivered to your room; typical fare includes french toast, omelets, and pecan pancakes. The Jacksons grow their own strawberries, herbs, and apples. They keep llamas on the property and are near a vineyard for a romantic walk. *$$–$$$; MC, V; checks OK; www.cozyroseinn.com; exit 69 off I-82.*

Outlook Guest House / ★

1320 INDEPENDENCE RD, OUTLOOK; 509/837-7651 OR 888/549-7244

This is the house where winemaker Joel Tefft raised his family, back before the landscape around it was planted with wine grapes. Each of the three rooms has a queen-sized bed and private bath—or you can rent the entire house, including the full kitchen and comfortable living and dining rooms. The Teffts supply you with coffee and continental breakfast basics, and you're just across the driveway from the Tefft Cellars winery. When tasting room hours are over, calm prevails. *$$; MC, V; checks OK; www.tefftcellars.com; exit 63 off I-82 and follow signs.*

Prosser

Who could resist a quick stop in Prosser, the "pleasant place with pleasant people"? Every day, the tasting room at **CHUKAR CHERRIES** (320 Wine Country Rd; 800/624-9544; www.chukar.com) gives out samples of local Bing and Rainier cherries.

LODGINGS

The Vintner's Inn at Hinzerling Winery / ★

1524 SHERIDAN AVE, PROSSER; 509/786-2163 OR 800/727-6702

If you'd like an insider's view of life in wine country, the Vintner's Inn is the place. The winery is one of the region's oldest, and this 1907 Victorian-style home has decades-old charm. Accommodations are quaint and comfortable; three bedrooms upstairs have private bathrooms. Downstairs, dinner is served, by reservation only, Fridays and Saturdays. The owner grows most of the herbs and vegetables used in the kitchen. *$$; DIS, MC, V; checks OK; www.hinzerling.com; just off Wine Country Rd.*

The Tri-Cities

The Tri-Cities' main attractions are the rivers, wineries, and golf courses. But the area also has an intriguing history, from Lewis and Clark's stop at what is now **SACAJAWEA STATE PARK** in Pasco to Kennewick's annual hydroplane races to Richland's role in ending World War II with top-secret atomic research at Hanford. The region is made up of three cities—Pasco, Kennewick, and Richland—and two counties (Benton and Walla Walla), but the **TRI-CITIES VISITOR AND CONVENTION BUREAU** (6951 W Grandridge Blvd, Kennewick; 800/254-5824; www.visittri-cities.com) pulls them together.

Richland

Richland was once a secret city, hidden away while the atomic-bomb workers did research in the 1940s. The **COLUMBIA RIVER EXHIBITION OF HISTORY, SCIENCE & TECHNOLOGY** (95 Lee Blvd; 509/943-9000; www.crehst.org) explains how the Tri-Cities area emerged during World War II when Hanford was created. **COLUMBIA RIVER JOURNEYS** (1229 Columbia Park Trail; 509/734-9941; www.columbiariverjourneys.com; May–Oct 15) offers jet-boat tours through Hanford Reach, a preserved section of the Columbia River. **ALLIED ARTS GALLERY** (89 Lee Blvd; 509/943-9815) displays local artists' work and sponsors an annual July art festival.

Dining opportunities here include not just Mexican cuisine but also an excellent Thai restaurant, the **EMERALD OF SIAM** (1314 Jadwin Ave; 509/946-9328).

RESTAURANTS

Atomic Ale Brewpub & Eatery / ★

1015 LEE BLVD, RICHLAND; 509/946-5465
The Atomic Ale Brewpub & Eatery is the Tri-Cities' first brew pub, founded in 1997. Besides standard pub fare, you can get wood-fired gourmet pizza or Atomic Ale red potato soup. Housed in a former A&W drive-in, the Atomic Ale Brewpub capitalizes on the area's nuclear history, with many historical photos adorning its walls. Beers have crazy names like Atomic Amber, Plutonium Porter, and Half-Life Hefeweizen. *$; AE, DIS, MC, V; checks OK; lunch, dinner Mon–Sat; beer and wine; no reservations; George Washington Way exit off I-82.* &

Katya's Bistro & Wine Bar / ★★

430 GEORGE WASHINGTON WAY, RICHLAND; 509/946-7777
Katya's is a hidden gem featuring Italian cuisine with a touch of French. Proprietor Stephen Hartley ensures that Katya's uses only certified Angus beef for its impressive list of entrées that include beef tenderloin, New York strip, rib-eye steak, steak Oscar, and Three City flatiron steak. The Chilean sea bass and rack of lamb are also delectable. Ukrainian borscht is a house specialty. Start with a spinach artichoke dip accompanied by warm kalamata olive bread. *$–$$; AE, DIS, MC, V; local checks only; dinner Mon–Sat; beer and wine; reservations recommended; between Davenport and Falley sts.*

LODGINGS

Courtyard Richland Columbia Point / ★

480 COLUMBIA POINT DR, RICHLAND; 509/942-9400
Location, location, location. When you have a beautiful hotel that's perched on the Columbia River, you have a great location. The Courtyard by Marriott is right across the street from the river—where many walk or jog the Waterfront Trail—and half a mile from golf links. The Courtyard has an indoor pool, fitness center, and comfortable lounge. Some rooms come with fireplaces. *$$; AE, MC, DIS, V; checks OK; www.marriott.com; George Washington Way exit off US Hwy 12 W.* &

Kennewick

Kennewick is the largest of the Tri-Cities, sharing a border with Richland and the magnificent Cable Bridge (lighted at night) with Pasco. It's a shopping town that has many malls, including Columbia Center. When you're done splurging, visit **COLUMBIA PARK** (between SR 240 and Columbia River; 509/585-4293). At the park's east end, near the US Highway 395 blue bridge, volunteers built the wooden castle–like **PLAYGROUND OF DREAMS**, with climbing structures and twisty slides. It's next to the **FAMILY FISHING POND**, where adults can teach children to catch and release. The park is the site of July's **COLUMBIA CUP** unlimited hydroplane races (509/547-2203; www.hydroracing.com). Winter sports fans focus on the **TRI-CITY AMERICANS** hockey team (509/736-0606), which plays at the **COLISEUM** (7100 W Quinault Ave; 509/783-9999).

RESTAURANTS

Casa Chapala / ★

107 E COLUMBIA DR, KENNEWICK; 509/586-4224
29 E BELFAIR PL, KENNEWICK; 509/783-8080
At Casa Chapala, in the east end of Kennewick, owners Lupe and Lucinda Barragan like things big: they put the place in the *Guinness Book of World Records* in 1999 for making the world's largest burrito. Their margaritas come in two sizes: grande and mucho grande. The food is authentic, with a

kids' menu and several low-fat options. *$; AE, DIS, MC, V; checks OK; lunch, dinner every day; full bar; no reservations; www.casachapala.com; east of N Washington St (Columbia Dr), just off Columbia Center Blvd (Belfair Pl).*

Pasco

Pasco has the most diverse population of the Tri-Cities and an economy based on light manufacturing and food processing. Historically a railroad town, Pasco is home to the **WASHINGTON STATE RAILROADS HISTORICAL SOCIETY MUSEUM** (122 N Tacoma St; 509/543-4159; www.wsrhs.org; open Sat Apr–Sept), which features old motorcars, railcars, and steam locomotives, including the state's oldest, the Blue Mountain, circa 1877.

Downtown is the **PASCO FARMERS MARKET** (4th Ave and Columbia St; 509/545-0738; open Wed and Sat May–Nov), one of the state's largest open-air produce markets. **SACAJAWEA STATE PARK** (off US Hwy 12) honors the remarkable Native American woman who accompanied the Corps of Discovery.

LODGINGS

Red Lion Hotel Pasco / ★

2425 N 20TH AVE, PASCO; 509/547-0701 OR 800/RED-LION
Four blocks from the Tri-Cities Airport, the Red Lion Hotel Pasco is also right next to Sun Willows Golf Course and Columbia Basin College. It's the region's largest hotel, with 279 standard rooms and a huge ballroom. It has two outdoor pools and an exercise room. The hotel's Vineyards Steak House restaurant features vintages from Tri-Cities wineries; the Grizzly Bar is a hot night spot. *$$; AE, DC, DIS, MC, V; checks OK; www.wescoasthotels.com; exit 12 off I-82/US Hwy 395.* ⓑ

Walla Walla and the Blue Mountains

The Walla Walla Valley is hot, not only meteorologically but also for its nationally known wines and sweet onions. And it's also an important historical area. In the early 1800s, the Lewis and Clark Expedition passed through, fur trappers set up Fort Walla Walla, and Dr. Marcus Whitman built a mission out here. Then smallpox hit area tribes, and a group of Cayuse men killed the missionaries in what's now known as the Whitman Massacre. The interpretive center at the **WHITMAN MISSION NATIONAL HISTORIC SITE** (7 miles west of Walla Walla along US Hwy 12; 509/529-2761; www.nps.gov/whmil) sketches out the story. The **WALLA WALLA VALLEY CHAMBER OF COMMERCE** (29 E Sumac St; 877-998-4748; www.wwchamber.com) has information.

Walla Walla

About a decade ago, this town was the place for some of the best wines in the country—but not for food. All that has changed, profoundly. Tourists are running to Walla Walla, wanting a taste of its merlot and cabernet sauvignon. Downtown bustles. The arts are big here, and the **WALLA WALLA SYMPHONY** (509/529-8020; www.wwsymphony.com) is the oldest symphony orchestra west of the Mississippi. Performances are held in **CORDINER HALL** (345 Boyer Ave) on the grounds of private **WHITMAN COLLEGE** (509/527-5176; www.whitman.edu). The **WALLA WALLA FOUNDRY** (405 Woodland Ave; 509/522-2114; www.wallawallafoundry.com) is a hub of art activity, where famous artists have come to cast sculptures. **FORT WALLA WALLA** (The Dalles Military Rd; 509/525-7703; www.fortwalla wallamuseum.org) has a museum featuring 14 historic buildings and a collection of pioneer artifacts.

RESTAURANTS

Creek Town Café / ★★

1129 S 2ND AVE, WALLA WALLA; 509/522-4777
Creek Town Café has quickly become one of Walla Walla's favorites, so expect a wait on weekends. A rock half-wall divides the room in two, and dark wood wainscoting complements framed historic photos. Dinner includes well-prepared seafood, meat, and pasta dishes that might range from turkey confit ravioli in butternut squash sauce to a flatiron whiskey steak with a kebab of roasted vegetables. Save your appetite for bread pudding or coconut cream pie. *$$; AE, DIS, MC, V; checks OK; lunch, dinner every day; beer and wine; reservations recommended; at E Morton St.* &

Grapefields / ★★

4 E MAIN ST, WALLA WALLA; 509/522-3993
Grapefields has a sophisticated bistro attitude, from the art deco bar to tasty tapas. The latter include toast manchego—bread grilled with manchego and served with a tomato-onion herb salsa—and Spanish sardines (not fishy at all) marinated in citrus, vinegar, garlic, and olive oil. The café menu offers a traditional charcuterie plate; a perfectly dressed ensalada verde topped with toasted walnuts, Gorgonzola, and Anjou pear; and hand-tossed pizzas. *$; AE, MC, V; checks OK; lunch Tues–Sat, dinner Tues–Sun; beer and wine; no reservations; just off 2nd Ave.*&

Merchants Ltd. / ★★

21 E MAIN ST, WALLA WALLA; 509/525-0900
Merchants has been a mainstay—especially for liberal-arts college students who come for the Wednesday-only spaghetti dinners—since 1976. The huge space across three storefronts serves healthy morning and midday meals. A full in-house bakery makes treats such as chocolate croissants and pizzas, while a well-stocked deli case serves picnic needs. Look for international

groceries, gourmet foodstuffs, organic coffee beans, and wines. *$; AE, DIS, MC, V; checks OK; breakfast, lunch Mon–Sat, dinner Wed; beer and wine; no reservations; 2nd St exit off US Hwy 12.* &

26 brix / ★★★

207 W MAIN ST, WALLA WALLA; 509/526-4075
The chef from the glamorous Salish Lodge near Seattle left to open 26 brix, a new fine dining restaurant where nearly every dish stars local products. Chef Mike Davis takes the area's famous sweet onions and makes caramelized sweet-onion consommé with onion ravioli, or he places asparagus from nearby Locati farms alongside a salmon dish. *$$–$$$; DIS, MV, V; local checks only; breakfast, lunch, dinner Sun, dinner Mon, Thur–Sat; beer and wine; reservations recommended; www.twentysixbrix.com; downtown.*

Whitehouse-Crawford ★★★

55 W CHERRY ST, WALLA WALLA; 509/525-2222
Here's another Walla Walla place that has a great Seattle-area chef: Jamie Guerin from Campagne. The restaurant is in a restored 1905 former planing mill. Tasty appetizers—try spicy calamari with ginger—pair well with local wines. Entrées have fun, unexpected twists, such as Southwest-style salmon with black beans, corn, and squash in a piquant tomato sauce, or pork smoked and served with grilled fresh figs, shallots, and spaetzle. Desserts are divine, including lemon verbena crème brûlée and twice-baked chocolate cake. *$$–$$$; AE, MC, V; checks OK; dinner Wed–Sun; full bar; reservations recommended; www.whitehousecrawford.com; downtown at 3rd Ave.* &

LODGINGS

Green Gables Inn / ★★

922 BONSELLA ST, WALLA WALLA; 888/525-5501
The title character from L. M. Montgomery's *Anne of Green Gables* series loved staying in guest rooms. Margaret and Jim Buchan incorporate that spirit in five rooms named for topics in the popular books, such as Idlewild, with a fireplace and Jacuzzi, and Dryad's Bubble, with a small balcony. The Carriage House is good for families; separate from the main house, it gives kids more room to run around. Full breakfast is served on fine china by candlelight. A wraparound porch and air-conditioning make for pleasant summer evenings. *$$–$$$; AE, DIS, MC, V; checks OK; www.greengablesinn.com; Clinton St exit off US Hwy 12.*

Inn at Abeja / ★★★

2014 MILL CREEK RD, WALLA WALLA; 509/522-1234
More than 100 years old, this 22-acre farmstead doubles as a working winery and luxurious retreat located east of town. Surrounded by the rolling Palouse Hills and the Blue Mountains, visitors can experience country tranquility with some modern conveniences. The Chicken House Cottage has vaulted

ceilings, a slate-tiled walk-in shower for two, and an airy full kitchen. Best is the two-story Summer Kitchen Cottage, with a deck overlooking the vineyards, a sky-lit bathroom, a king-sized bed, a claw-foot tub, and full kitchen and living room. *$$$–$$$$; MC, V; checks OK; www.millcreekbb.com/inn. htm; 1.6 miles east on US Hwy 12.*

Inn at Blackberry Creek / ★★

1126 PLEASANT ST, WALLA WALLA; 509/522-5233 OR 877/522-5233
Just around the corner from Pioneer Park and Whitman College is this charming 1912 farmhouse that has been restored by innkeeper Barbara Knudson, whose attention to detail—fresh cookies in the evening, flawlessly decorated rooms—makes for a pleasant stay. The three rooms feature peaceful views of the tree-lined property. The light-filled common area overlooks the lawns and invites you to play chess, thumb through magazines, or read in comfortable chairs. *$$; MC, V; checks OK; www.innatblackberrycreek.com; 4 blocks southeast of Pioneer Park.*

Marcus Whitman / ★★

6 W ROSE ST, WALLA WALLA; 866/826-9422
One of the largest structures in downtown Walla Walla, the elegant and historic Marcus Whitman has been restored by owner Kyle Mussman, who works hard to make the 1928 hotel part of the community, with events and special dinners such as sushi night. The best of the 91 comfortable rooms are suites in the original tower (the West Wing was added in the 1960s). Decorated in handsome, almost masculine colors, standard rooms don't have the same city views. *$–$$$; AE, MC, V; checks OK; www.marcuswhitmanhotel. com; at 2nd Ave.* &

Dayton

Dayton, a small farming town northeast of Walla Walla, is one of the state's first communities. Small wonder it's full of almost 90 Victorian-era buildings. Stop by the **DAYTON CHAMBER OF COMMERCE** (166 E Main St; 800/882-6299; www. historicdayton.com) for details. The **DAYTON HISTORICAL DEPOT** (222 E Commercial St; 509/382-2026; tours Tues–Sat), built in 1881, is the state's oldest remaining railroad station and is now a museum.

Don't miss the **MONTEILLET FROMAGERIE** (109 Ward Rd, 1½ miles west of Dayton; 509/382-1917; www.montecheese.com), where you can sample fresh goat and sheep cheese. Dayton is also known for easy access to **BLUEWOOD SKI RESORT** (22 miles south of Dayton via US Hwy 12; 509/382-4725; www. bluewood.com) in Umatilla National Forest in the Blue Mountains. It has clear skies, dry powder, and the second-highest base elevation (4,545 feet) in the state.

RESTAURANTS

Patit Creek Restaurant / ★★★

725 E DAYTON AVE, DAYTON; 509/382-2625

Patit Creek is a classic off-the-beaten-path discovery and a classy place to end a day of valley wine touring or skiing at Bluewood. Bruce and Heather Hiebert turned a 1920s service station into a 10-table restaurant famous for filets in green peppercorn sauce, chevre-stuffed dates wrapped in bacon, fresh vegetables, and huckleberry pie. *$$; MC, V; local checks only; lunch Wed–Fri, dinner Wed–Sat; beer and wine; reservations recommended; north end of town.* &

LODGINGS

The Purple House B&B Inn / ★

415 E CLAY ST, DAYTON; 800/486-2574

This 1882 house really *is* purple and has been a B and B since the late 1980s. Four rooms have modern amenities, including air-conditioning. Two have private baths. A separate carriage house is also on the premises. Innkeeper Christine D. Williscroft is a native of southern Germany, which shows in the inn's decor. The full breakfast might include strudel or crepes, served in a walled-in courtyard next to the private swimming pool. *$$; MC, V; checks OK; www.purplehouseBnB.com; 1 block off US Hwy 12.* &

The Weinhard Hotel / ★

235 E MAIN ST, DAYTON; 509/382-4032

This is a favorite place in the Walla Walla Valley. Fresh flowers and fruit greet guests in each room. Owners Dan and Ginny Butler restored the old Weinhard building (built as a saloon and lodge hall in the late 1800s) and filled it with elegant Victorian antiques that they collected from across the country. The 15 rooms have antique dressers, desks, and canopied beds. The Signature Room has a jetted tub. Inside the hotel is the recently updated Weinhard Café, serving tasty, inventive fare. *$$–$$$; AE, MC, V; checks OK; www.weinhard. com; downtown.* &

Pullman and the Palouse

Washington's golden Palouse region, next to Idaho and north of the Blue Mountains, is made up of rolling hills covered with wheat, lentils, and other crops. **KAMIAK BUTTE COUNTRY PARK** (13 miles north of Pullman on SR 27) is a good place for a picnic with a view of the hills. **STEPTOE BUTTE STATE PARK** (about 30 miles north of Pullman on US Hwy 195) is great for a panoramic view, but it's windy.

At **PALOUSE FALLS STATE PARK** (2 miles off SR 261 between Washtucna and Tucannon; 800/233-0321), the Palouse River roars over a basalt cliff higher than Niagara Falls, dropping 198 feet into a steep-walled basin on its way to the Snake

River. A hiking trail leads to an overlook above the falls, most spectacular during spring runoff. Camping and canoeing are allowed in **LYONS FERRY STATE PARK** (on SR 261, 7 miles north of Starbuck; 800/233-0321), at the confluence of the Palouse and Snake rivers; the park also has a public boat launch.

Pullman

The heart of the Palouse beats in Pullman, at the junction of US Highway 195 and State Route 27 near the Idaho border, and that heart is **WASHINGTON STATE UNIVERSITY** (visitor center: 225 N Grand Ave; 509/335-8633; www.wsu.edu). Established in 1892, WSU is where 17,000 die-hard Cougars live during the academic year. Your trip wouldn't be complete without sampling the ice cream or Cougar Gold cheese made at the WSU creamery, **FERDINAND'S** (Agriculture Science Bldg; 509/335-2141; open Mon–Fri). The $39 million Student Recreation Center, open to the public for a small fee, includes a large spa as part of the swimming complex.

The Student Book Corp., affectionately called the **BOOKIE** (700 NE Thatuna St; 509/332-2537; www.wsubookie.net), is a great place to browse or pick up Cougar paraphernalia. This place is jammed on home football weekends in the fall. There's also a second store: the **BOOKIE, TOO** (405 Stadium Way; 509/334-3661). If you visit one restaurant while in Pullman, make it the **COUGAR COTTAGE** (900 NE Colorado St; 509/332-1265), aka the Coug. This is a Pullman institution since 1932, and every frat boy and football player has done his penance there. For just hanging out, the **DAILY GRIND** (230 Main St; 509/334-9171) is a great place to grab coffee or sandwich.

Pullman is also known for its historical buildings, with brick masonry and early 1900s classical and Georgian architecture. Find more info at the **PULLMAN CHAMBER OF COMMERCE** (415 N Grand Ave; 800/365-6948; www.pullman.com).

RESTAURANTS

Hilltop Restaurant

920 NW OLSEN ST, PULLMAN; 509/334-2555

This steak house has an incredible view of the university and surrounding hills, a romantic vista complemented by linens and attentive service. Red meat is the specialty, from prime rib and steaks to Sunday's midday roast-beef family dinner. Homemade desserts include cheesecakes, mud pie, and chocolate truffles. Hilltop is connected to the three-story, 59-room Hawthorne Inn & Suites (928 NW Olsen St; 509/332-0928; www.pullman-wa.com/housing/motels/bestwest.htm), where it offers room service. *$$; AE, DIS, MC, V; checks OK; lunch Mon–Fri, dinner every day; full bar; no reservations; www.hilltoprestaurant.com; on Davis Way.*

Rico's Tavern

200 E MAIN ST, PULLMAN; 509/332-6566

This downtown institution has served up enough beer and jazz to rival any place in the Big Easy. On Fridays you'll find crowds enjoying a variety of jazz musicians. Sundays are a time for studying, and the high bookshelves invite you to stay awhile, even if you don't have a final to contend with. Food is basic pub fare. *$; AE, MC, V; local checks only; beer and wine; no reservations; downtown.*

Swilly's Café & Catering / ★★

200 NE KAMIAKEN ST, PULLMAN; 509/334-3395

Come here if you want to sit creekside among a nonstudent crowd. Local artwork covers the exposed-brick walls. It's an eclectic menu: Moroccan lamb, Thai shrimp, and grilled tenderloin are all served here. Or just stick with the good homemade soups, salads, sandwiches, burgers, and pastas. *$; AE, MC, V; checks OK; lunch, dinner Mon–Sat; beer and wine; no reservations; www.pullman-wa.com/food/swilly.htm; at NW Olson St.* &

LODGINGS

The Churchyard Inn B&B / ★

206 ST. BONIFACE ST, UNIONTOWN; 509/229-3200

The Churchyard Inn is next door to the historic St. Boniface Catholic Church in tiny Uniontown, 16 miles south of Pullman on US Highway 195. The three-story house was built as a parish in 1905 and converted to a convent in 1913, then to a B and B in 1995. Breakfast and beverages are served in the dining room with a view of the Palouse farmlands. *$$–$$$; MC, V; checks OK; www.churchyardinn.com; 2 blocks west of US Hwy 195.* &

SPOKANE AND NORTHEASTERN WASHINGTON

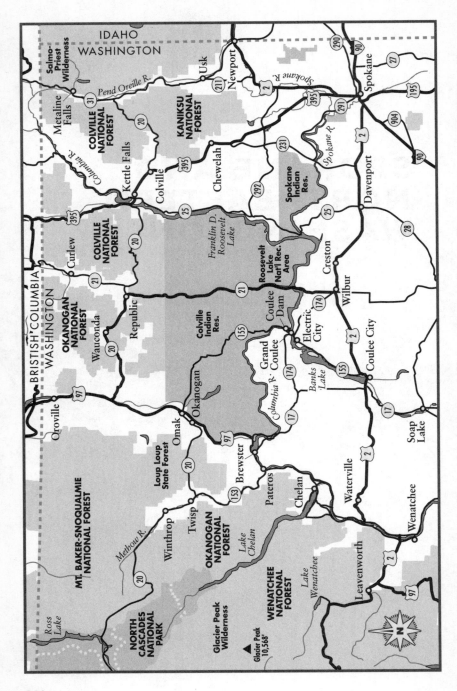

SPOKANE AND NORTHEASTERN WASHINGTON

Small towns and gorgeous countryside form the fabric of northeastern Washington. Kettle Falls lies to the north, deep in the Colville National Forest. On the shores of Lake Roosevelt to the west lie Coulee City and the historic Grand Coulee Dam. Small towns such as Davenport, Republic, Wilbur, and Newport are scattered throughout the wheatfields.

Spokane, the second largest city in the state, used to operate as a hub for the railroads, an industry still visible through Spokane's bustling downtown. Spokane is also home to the annual **BLOOMSDAY RUN**, held in May with more than 50,000 runners, and the spectacular **SPOKANE HOOPFEST**—a citywide three-on-three basketball tournament each June.

Aside from the numerous national forests, ski resorts, and spacious lakes, one of the most popular tourist attractions of northeastern Washington sits just across the Idaho border: the town of **COEUR D'ALENE**. The small city, located just 30 minutes east of Spokane, is built around the scenic Lake Coeur d'Alene and a quaint downtown. The town hosts festivals throughout the year; contact the **COEUR D'ALENE CHAMBER OF COMMERCE** (877/782-9232; www.coeurdalene.org) for details.

ACCESS AND INFORMATION

The fastest, most direct route to Spokane from Seattle is **INTERSTATE 90**; **US HIGHWAY 2** is another east-west route through northeastern Washington. North-south routes include **US HIGHWAY 97** on the eastern slope of the Cascades and **US HIGHWAY 395**, which runs through Spokane north to Colville. The **SPOKANE REGIONAL VISITOR CENTER** (201 W Main Ave; 509/747-3230 or 888/776-5263; www.visitspokane.com) is great.

Nine airlines—Alaska, America West, Big Sky, Canadian, Delta, Horizon, Northwest, Southwest, and United—serve **SPOKANE INTERNATIONAL AIRPORT** (W 9000 Airport Dr; 509/455-6455; www.spokaneairports.net), a 10-minute drive west of downtown.

AMTRAK's (800/USA-RAIL; www.amtrak.com) Empire Builder between Seattle and Chicago stops at Spokane's **INTERMODAL CENTER** (221 W 1st Ave). The **TRAILWAYS** bus system (509/838-5262; www.trailways.com) and **GREYHOUND** (509/624-5251; www.greyhound.com) also operate from that depot; buses also serve nearby Cheney.

SPOKANE THREE-DAY TOUR

DAY ONE: Kick your day off with a scone and a latte at the South Hill's **ROCK-WOOD BAKERY** (315 E 18th Ave; 509/747-8691) before walking to **MANITO PARK** a few blocks away. Spend the morning strolling through the park's European, Japanese, and rose gardens. Take a spin along **CLIFF DRIVE** to gaze at the old mansions and lovely views west as you head back downtown for a late lunch at **MIZUNA**. Explore the upscale shops at **RIVER PARK SQUARE** and browse the shelves of Spokane's favorite independent bookstore, **AUNTIE'S** (402 W Main Ave; 509/838-0206). For dinner, if you're still full from lunch, stop in to **BLUEFISH** for some light and spicy tuna rolls, or if your tummy's grumbling, try **MOXIE** next door. Gaze at the silent movies playing outside your window on the side of the Fox Theater as you nod off to sleep in style at the **MONTVALE HOTEL**.

DAY TWO: Wake up in your cozy bedroom and grab breakfast at the **DAVEN-PORT HOTEL**. Explore the historic mansions in the nearby Browne's Addition neighborhood before popping by the **NORTHWEST MUSEUM OF ARTS AND CULTURE** in the late morning. Nab a porch seat at the **ELK PUBLIC HOUSE**

Spokane

Always the bridesmaid and never the bride, Spokane is constantly living in the shadow of Seattle's cosmopolitan city lights. Though smaller, Spokane is hardly inferior. Much of the rich history that built Spokane is still very much a part of everyday life today. The homes of the city's forefathers still stand today: from the towering **GLOVER MANSION** (321 W Main Ave; www.glovermansion.com), which serves today as a popular event facility, to the historic homes of the **BROWNE'S ADDITION** neighborhood's (www.brownesaddition.org) streets.

Spokane is centered around the powerful Spokane River, the majestic Spokane Falls, and **RIVERFRONT PARK** (downtown; 800/336-PARK; www.spokane riverfrontpark.com), which was built around the river for Expo '74. The urban greenspace is home to an amusement park, the IMAX theater, and a breathtaking gondola ride. For the best view of the raging falls, a short ride on the gondola on a sunny day is well worth the small admission price. The park is also home to a 26-ton, 12-foot-high Radio Flyer wagon sculpture, a favorite of Spokane youngsters.

Riverfront Park also provides access to the 37-mile **CENTENNIAL TRAIL**, which links downtown Spokane to the **GONZAGA UNIVERSITY** campus (502 E Boone Ave; www.gonzaga.edu) and finally ends in Coeur d'Alene, Idaho. Gonzaga's **JUNDT ART MUSEUM** (202 E Cataldo Ave; 509/323-6611; www.gonzaga.edu) is worth a long look, with its cutting-edge art exhibits and original Dale Chihuly

and enjoy a hearty lunch. Rent a bike or skates at the downtown **RIVERFRONT PARK** and explore alongside the Spokane River. Before sunset, take a drive west and dip your toes in the historic waters of **MEDICAL LAKE**. Head over to nearby **CHENEY** for plate upon plate of Italian food at **LENNY'S ITALIAN & AMERICAN**. On your way back into Spokane, enjoy a nightcap at **CAVALLINO LOUNGE**, on the first floor of **HOTEL LUSSO**, where you'll stay for the night.

DAY THREE: Enjoy a classic breakfast at **FRANK'S DINER** before heading north to explore the beauty of **RIVERSIDE STATE PARK** and hike around the **BOWL AND PITCHER** lava formations. Then head back downtown and grab a burrito (we recommend the Veggie Thai) at **SLICK ROCK BURRITO** (827 W 1st Ave; 509/847-1234). Spend the afternoon strolling around the **GONZAGA UNIVERSITY** campus and contemplating the original Dale Chihuly artwork at the school's **JUNDT ART MUSEUM**. Head to the South Hill for dinner at **GORDY'S SICHUAN CAFÉ**, then venture into town for a play at **CENTERSTAGE** (1017 W 1st Ave; 509/747-8243) or a concert at **THE MET** (901 W Sprague Ave; 509/227-7638). Wash down the evening with a Peacock Punch at the **DAVENPORT HOTEL**'s Peacook Room before heading upstairs to your luxurious pad.

hanging glass chandelier. The impressive home of the Gonzaga University basketball team, the **MCCARTHEY ATHLETIC CENTER** (801 N Cincinnati St; www.gonzaga.edu) was completed in 2005.

On a drive through downtown Spokane, it's difficult to miss the brand-spanking-new **SPOKANE CONVENTION CENTER** (334 W Spokane Falls Blvd; 509/279-7000; www.spokanecenter.com), which is set to host the **2007 U.S. FIGURE SKATING CHAMPIONSHIPS** (www.spokane2007.com). Downtown Spokane also is home to the high-end shops of **RIVER PARK SQUARE** (N Post St and W Main Ave; www.riverparksquare.com) and some of the city's finest hotels and restaurants.

There is art nearly everywhere in the Lilac City. Visual art is at its prime at the modern **NORTHWEST MUSEUM OF ARTS AND CULTURE** (2316 W 1st Ave; 509/456-3931; www.northwestmuseum.org) and the small **LORINDA KNIGHT GALLERY** (523 W Sprague Ave; 509/838-3740; www.lorindaknight.com). Public art graces the downtown tunnels, park lawns, and building faces.

A drive through the tree-canopied neighborhoods of Spokane's South Hill is pleasant day or night; be sure to stop at **MANITO** (Grand Blvd and 18th Ave) and **CANNON HILL PARKS** (S Lincoln St and W 18th Ave) for a picnic. The **SOUTH PERRY DISTRICT** (www.southperry.com), one of the South Hill's most up-and-coming neighborhoods, is anchored by **THE SHOP** (924 S Perry St; 509/534-1647; www.theshop.bz), a cozy coffee joint in a refurbished gas station. It's known for acoustic music shows and delicious espresso. In summer, the owners open the nearby ice creamery, **THE SCOOP** (1004 S Perry St; 509/535-7171) and show free movies in The Shop's parking lot.

Spokane is a short drive from some of the region's best skiing. Nearby **MOUNT SPOKANE** (29500 N Mount Spokane Park Dr; 509/238-2220; www.mtspokane. com) is an hour's drive north of downtown. Hiking, biking, horseback riding, and camping during the warm months are just west of downtown in **RIVERSIDE STATE PARK** (9711 W Charles Rd, Nine Mile Falls; 509/465-5064; www.riverside statepark.org). Evening strolls, apple groves, fruit festivals, and endless pumpkin patches make for country fun at **GREEN BLUFF** (Day–Mount Spokane Rd and Green Bluff Rd; www.greenbluffgrowers.com), a community of family farms open during monthly festivals.

RESTAURANTS

Bittersweet Bakery and Bistro / ★★★

1220 S GRAND BLVD, SPOKANE; 509/455-8658
New to the Spokane scene but already a contender, Bittersweet Bistro appeals to all palates, with savory crepes in a pastel French setting. Though the crepes are $8 apiece, farm-fresh ingredients and gourmet cheeses make them worthwhile. Take in a cup of coffee, a snickerdoodle muffin, and the view of the nearby architectural delight St. John's Cathedral. *$$$; MC, V; checks OK; breakfast, lunch Mon–Sat; no reservations; Grand Blvd and 12th Ave.* &

Bluefish / ★★★★

830 W SPRAGUE AVE, SPOKANE; 509/747-2111
Dive into chef Ian Wingate's latest creation: the fishbowl-like Bluefish, lighted in hues of blue. Drool over the Kobe beef burger. Sushi here creatively blends simple elements to please aficionados and beginners alike. Service is professional, though on one visit a server seemed confused by a request of "vegan options." *$$; AE, DIS, MC, V; no checks; dinner Tues–Sat; full bar; no reservations; www.bluefishspokane.com; N Lincoln St and W Sprague Ave.* &

Chicken-n-More / ★★★

417½ W SPRAGUE AVE, SPOKANE; 509/838-5071
Spokane's authority on Southern soul food, Texas-bred owner Bob Hemphill runs this 1970s rec-room-like joint. It gets jammed at lunchtime, but the grub is worth the fuss. Chow on—ahem—chicken and more: fried chicken, ribs, jo-jos, and baked beans. On your way out, give Bob a holler. It's just that kind of place. *$; AE, DIS, MC, V; checks OK; lunch, dinner Mon–Fri; no alcohol; no reservations; across from Ridpath Hotel.* &

The Elk Public House / ★★★

1931 W PACIFIC AVE, SPOKANE; 509/363-1973
A summer supper at the Elk is the perfect end to a long day. It's known for a kicked-back atmosphere and not-so-average pub fare. Burgers gush caramelized onions, and chicken sandwiches melt in honey cream cheese. Opt for

the corn pasta salad as a side. When you can, have a drink at the bar and wait for a porch seat—you'll be glad you did. *$; AE, DIS, MC, V; checks OK; lunch, dinner every day; full bar; no reservations; www.wedonthaveone.com; W Pacific Ave and S Cannon St.* &

Frank's Diner / ★★

1516 W 2ND AVE, SPOKANE; 509/747-8798
10929 N NEWPORT HWY, SPOKANE; 509/465-2464
That massive train car you saw from the freeway in downtown Spokane or the north end? No accident; those are diners. Grab a seat at the bar and watch as the hilarious cooking staff carefully crafts your eggs, hash browns, and pancakes. Order the hotcakes, and be sure to get them with huckleberries. Add a thick, whip-topped milkshake. Pure delish. *$; DIS, MC, V; checks OK; breakfast, lunch, dinner every day; beer and wine; no reservations; www. franksdiners.com; downtown at S Walnut St; just past Northpoint Shopping Center on N Newport Hwy.* &

Gordy's Sichuan Café / ★★★★

501 E 30TH AVE, SPOKANE; 509/747-1170
Gordy's puts Spokane on the ethnic cuisine map. The bite-sized strip-mall storefront is a no–Web site, no-e-mail, no-reservation kind of place. Scarf Gan Pung Chicken, Savory Tofu, and Cashew Prawn Stir-fry. Pay attention to the specials chalkboard—often where Gordon Crafts' understanding of Sichuan cuisine shines. Save room for dessert; the ginger-orange ice cream is worth loosening your belt a notch. *$$; AE, MC, V; checks OK; lunch Tues–Fri, dinner Mon–Sat; beer and wine; no reservations; off Grand Blvd at 30th Ave.* &

Lenny's American & Italian / ★★★

1204 1ST ST, CHENEY; 509/235-6126
Sure, the name sounds strip-mall-ish, and the drive may seem a little far, but rest assured: Lenny's is the real deal. Italian owner and chef John Maticchio runs this simple, checkered-tablecloths place. The menu brags of every popular Italian dish: pasta, eggplant Parmesan, lasagne, fettuccine Alfredo, Italian sandwiches, and a few burgers, for good measure. There's no such thing as going hungry at Lenny's. *$$; MC, V; checks OK; dinner Mon–Fri; beer and wine; no reservations; Cheney–Four Lakes exit off I-90, in downtown Cheney.* &

Luna / ★★★★

5620 S PERRY ST, SPOKANE; 509/448-2383
Buried in the unlikeliest of Spokane's South Hill neighborhoods, Luna is difficult to find and easy to miss, but you'll never forget it after eating there. Food, wine, and service are at their very best in this candlelit atmosphere. Revel in the complexities of Luna's menu (such as Charred Lamb Rack with Juniper Berry Glace with Eggplant Risotto), but don't feel guilty sampling what's familiar: Applewood-Oven Pizzas, Coconut Curry Prawns, or the simple

SPOKANE'S HAUNTED HISTORY

Spokane is a city that thrives on memories, and history bursts from every street corner. Even today, longtime residents talk about the good old days of Expo '74, double features at the Fox Theater, and hamburgers and fries at Dick's (which still stands today, at Division Street and Third Avenue). Where there's history, there are sure to be ghost stories—and Spokane is full of both.

Start your ghost tour in Browne's Addition, where towering mansions beckon with windows and high, towerlike roofs. Rumors of a ghost in the **PATSY CLARK MANSION** (2208 W 2nd Ave) which now houses a law firm, ran rampant when a full-scale restaurant operated in the space. Ghosts supposedly haunted the wine cellar and were said to have thrown wine bottles across the cellar in protest of unsatisfactory varietals.

Ghost hunting in Spokane must include a stop at Gonzaga University's **MONAGHAN MANSION** (217 E Boone Ave), otherwise known at the school's Music Building. Built in 1898 for James Monaghan, the massive building is home to Spokane's creepiest tales. For years, students at Gonzaga reported stories

---

pasta dishes that hold tenure here. Café Marron, which opened in late 2005, is Luna's ugly stepchild—poor service and a pretentious menu. *$$$; AE, DIS, MC, V; checks OK; lunch, dinner every day, brunch Sun; full bar; reservations recommended; www.lunaspokane.com; on 57th Ave at Perry St.* &

Mizuna / ★★★

214 N HOWARD ST, SPOKANE; 509/747-2004

Meat lovers and veggie heads unite here over plates of upscale, gourmet cuisine in the coziest restaurant in town. Owner Sylvia Wilson boasts a gorgeous candlelit dining room and a polished, fun wait staff. A wine bar dominates half the space. Go light with the Vermont Cheddar and Apple Salad, or stuff yourself with the Vegetarian "Meatloaf" sandwich. Mizuna used to be all vegetarian, and dishes can still be made veg-friendly. Save plenty of room for tasty desserts. *$$$; AE, DIS, MC, V; checks OK; lunch Mon–Fri, dinner Mon–Sat; full bar; reservations recommended; www.mizuna.com; Howard St and Spokane Falls Blvd.* &

Moxie / ★★★★

816 W SPRAGUE AVE, SPOKANE; 509/456-3594

Get a seat by a window with a view of the tsunami mural next door for a date at Moxie. Chef Ian Wingate interprets traditional dishes with style: char-broiled chipotle-glazed meatloaf, seared prosciutto-wrapped scallops. *$$$; AE, DIS, MC, V; checks OK; lunch Mon–Fri, dinner Tues–Sat; full bar; reservations recommended; www.moxiemoxie.com; Lincoln St and Sprague Ave.* &

of pianos playing without pianists, eerie tunes echoing throughout the rooms, and doors slamming on their own. After a series of incidents, an exorcism was performed on the mansion in 1975—but students today claim that a presence still lurks here.

Like any burial ground, the **GREENWOOD CEMETERY** (19911 W Coulee Hite Rd) near Spokane Falls Community College is the subject of a popular haunted story. A staircase in the cemetery, nicknamed 1,000 Steps, is feared by the superstitious and ghost hunters alike. Tales say that no one can scale the entire flight of stairs without colliding with a sudden, unbearable sense of fear.

It seems everyone here has one spooky tale or another up their sleeves. Stories fly about haunting spirits in the corridors of the **DAVENPORT HOTEL** and mysterious noises in the **SPOKANE COUNTY COURTHOUSE** (1116 W Broadway). Whether or not you believe it, it's hard to say that Spokane's soot-covered downtown buildings, soaring South Hill mansions, and midtown alleyways don't at least *feel* a little haunted.

—Leah Sottile

Thai on 1st / ★★★

411 W 1ST AVE, SPOKANE; 509/455-4288

Thai on 1st is a sparkly gem in the city's drabbest area. It's the best Thai in Spokane—good and familiar. Decor is sparse, but the family that runs it makes you feel at home. Service and efficiency, aside from consistent, delicious food, is what this place is known for. Plates of phad thai or tongue-scalding curries satisfy a range of palates here. *$; MC, V; no checks; lunch Mon–Fri, dinner Mon–Sat; beer and wine; no reservations; 1st Ave and Washington St.* &

LODGINGS

The Davenport Hotel / ★★★☆

10 S POST ST, SPOKANE; 509/455-8888

The Davenport bathes any visitor in luxury, from the grand lobby and ballrooms to the decadent guest rooms and suites. Rooms range from standard suites to wet-bar-and-sitting-room spaces. The Palm Court is overpriced; opt for the surrounding restaurants. Davenport cuisine stands on the Sunday brunch—a larger-than-life meal held each week. The Peacock Room, a stunning stained-glass lounge, and Spa Paradiso are citywide favorites. *$$$$; AE, DC, DIS, MC, V; checks OK, www.thedavenporthotel.com; Post St and Sprague Ave.* &

Fotheringham House / ★★

2128 W 2ND AVE, SPOKANE; 509/838-1891
New owners in April 2006 brought with them an aesthetic of pampering guests in high style. The beautifully restored Queen Anne–style mansion is entirely and tastefully appointed with period antiques. The Garden Room overlooks an urban bird sanctuary. Stroll through the garden in summer and enjoy the lovely lavender display that lines the front walkway. Or enjoy Thursday high tea any time of year; the public is welcome. *$$; MC, V; checks OK; www.fotheringham.net; across from Coeur d'Alene Park.*

Hotel Lusso / ★★★

1 N POST ST, SPOKANE; 509/747-9750
Step into an intimate, romantic stay at Hotel Lusso—a pint-size hotel within walking distance of shopping, restaurants, and Riverfront Park. Rooms have oversize windows with downtown views. The 48 rooms include showers and baths surrounded by Italian marble. Guests are pampered with complimentary breakfast and hors d'oeuvres at the hotel's restaurant, Fugazzi. *$$$–$$$$; AE, DC, DIS, MC, V; checks OK; www.hotellusso.com; at Post St and Sprague Ave.* &

The Montvale Hotel / ★★★

1005 W 1ST AVE, SPOKANE; 509/747-1919
Contemporary and bursting with character, the Montvale provides the best lodging experience in the city. Built in 1899, the hotel was recently renovated to boast 36 luxury rooms. And we mean luxury: pillowy mattresses, flat-screen televisions, waterfall showerheads, and views of Spokane's Davenport arts district. Book a room overlooking the Fox Theater; at night you can catch silent movies as they are projected onto the theater's exterior. The Catacombs Pub—a German bierhaus–style place—is in the basement. *$$$; AE, DIS, MC, V; checks OK; www.montvalehotel.com; 1st Ave and Monroe St.* &

Pend Oreille and Colville River Valleys

The Pend Oreille valley remains an undiscovered secret to many northeastern Washington visitors, and that's just fine with those do who come here to enjoy the wild terrain, the wildlife, and the region's wide river, the Pend Oreille (pronounced "pon-der-RAY"). The river flows north to Canada, where it meets the Columbia just north of the border. The sparsely populated Colville River valley, home to tiny farming and logging communities, is also a haven for outdoor recreation, from fishing and boating to cross-country skiing and hunting.

The Pend Oreille

This northernmost corner of the state is generally considered a place to drive through on the way to Canada. In fact, it's nicknamed "the forgotten corner." But don't overlook this delightful region of the state—curve along Highway 20 as it heads north from US Highway 2 at Newport along the **PEND OREILLE RIVER**. The surrounding **SALMO-PRIEST WILDERNESS AREA** is home to grizzly bears, caribou, and bald eagles, among other elusive wildlife. Its 38 miles of hiking trails traverse 7,300-foot Gypsy Peak. To the west of the burg of Metaline Falls, north of Highway 20 on Highway 31, hikers can trek to the Kettle Crest, one of the best hikes in the region. You might see black bears, deer, coyotes, and birds on this 42-mile trip. The Colville branch of the U.S. Forest Service (765 S Main St, Colville; 509/684-7000) has some shorter loop trails that access the crest; their summer guided wildflower tours have become so popular that reservations are essential.

Colville and Kettle Falls Area

The working-class feel of a lumber town still personifies Colville and Kettle Falls, tight-knit blue-collar communities where you're likely to spot "Cream of Spotted Owl" bumper stickers on the logging trucks chugging down the road. The area is a jumping-off spot for exploring Lake Roosevelt to the southwest and the Okanogan to the northwest.

CHEWELAH, the first town as you head north of Spokane on US Highway 395, is home to the 18-hole challenging (and inexpensive) **GOLF AND COUNTRY CLUB** (2537 E Sand Canyon Rd; 509/935-6807; www.chewelahgolf.com). To the east is the tiny but friendly **49 DEGREES NORTH** ski area (3311 Flowery Trail Rd, Republic; 509/935-6649 or 866/376-4949; www.ski49n.com), 58 miles northeast of Spokane, which offers free beginner lessons.

Continuing north on US Highway 395, reach Colville, with a quaint Main Street of antique shops. Not far beyond is the town of Kettle Falls, on Lake Roosevelt. **CHINA BEND WINERY** (3751 Vineyard Way, Kettle Falls; 509/732-6123 or 800/700-6123; www.chinabend.com), north of Kettle Falls on Lake Roosevelt, grows organic grapes and has the northernmost vineyards in the state. The owners run a bed-and-breakfast from the winery; their breakfasts and dinners feature organic meals.

Grand Coulee Area

This wonderful area is grand indeed, from the landscape to the man-made Grand Coulee Dam erected to tame it. The **COLUMBIA RIVER** slices through northeastern Washington with a quiet power, the water rushing through enormous chasms. In prehistoric times, glacier-fed water created a river with the largest flow of water ever known. Today it's the second-largest river in the nation, traversing a basalt plateau of equally staggering scale.

Some 15 miles upstream of Grand Coulee Dam, the tiny **KELLER FERRY** (on Hwy 21; 800/695-7623, ext 511) shuttles across the Columbia dozens of times a day at no charge; the *Martha S.* holds just a dozen cars. The crossing takes 15 minutes to traverse the waterborne section of Highway 21, the link between the Colville Indian Reservation to the north of the river and the Columbia Plateau on the south. On the Grand Coulee side is a small store run by the Colville Tribe that sells fishing licenses and some groceries, and also rents boats.

For many years **LAKE ROOSEVELT**, the massive 150-mile-long reservoir created by Grand Coulee Dam, was untapped by the RV-on-pontoon fleets. Now several companies offer weekly (or weekend, for a hefty price) **HOUSEBOAT RENTALS**. Some of these vessels have deluxe features such as on-deck hot tubs, stereo systems, gourmet kitchens, and outdoor rinse-off showers. For rates and reservations, contact **ROOSEVELT RECREATIONAL ENTERPRISES** (800/648-LAKE; www. rrehousboats.com) or **LAKE ROOSEVELT RESORT & MARINA** (800/635-7585; www.lakeroosevelt.com).

Grand Coulee Dam

Clustered around Grand Coulee Dam are the towns of Grand Coulee, Coulee Dam, and Electric City. The **GRAND COULEE DAM** (509/633-9265 or 800/268-5332) is a marvel of engineering that harkens back to a time when man-made dams were the cutting edge of industrial design. Sometimes referred to as the eighth wonder of the world, the dam was conceived as an irrigation project that now supplies water to more than 500,000 acres of farmland. World War II gave it a new purpose: generating power for the production of plutonium at Hanford and aluminum for aircraft. As tall as a 46-story building and the length of a dozen city blocks, the dam was completed in 1942. The **VISITOR ARRIVAL CENTER** (open every day) features movies and exhibits; during summer months (end of May–Aug), the laser light show is a spectacular treat. Visit the **GRAND COULEE DAM AREA CHAMBER OF COMMERCE** (319 Midway Ave, Grand Coulee; 800/268-5332; www.grandcouleedam.org) for more information. If you're feeling lucky, stop in at the Colville Tribe's **COULEE DAM CASINO** (515 Birch St, Coulee Dam; 509/633-0766).

RESTAURANTS

La Presa / ★

515 E GRAND COULEE AVE, GRAND COULEE; 509/633-3173
This is authentic Mexican food, with 126 dishes on the menu. You'll get the standard Mexican plates, steaks, and seafood—and even chicken teriyaki. You won't go wrong with traditional favorites such as enchilada verde, made with fresh tomatillos. La Presa, which means "the dam," has a south-of-the-border feel, with velvet paintings and wool blankets. *$; DIS, MC, V; checks OK; lunch, dinner every day; full bar; reservations recommended; on Hwy 21, just up from dam.* ⅃

THE LIFE AQUATIC IN EASTERN WASHINGTON

When the ice has melted, the snowplows have been retired, and everyone's parkas have been packed away, Spokane is home to some of the most gorgeous springs, sweltering summers, and calm autumns in the state. These three seasons are when the sky makes way for breathtaking pink and gold sunsets, and when Spokane and northeastern Washington residents get the best of Mother Nature for her brutal winters in these parts. With an abundance of parks, rivers, trails, forests, and mountains, northeastern Washington is a warm-weather playground. But the most popular summertime excuse for missing work here is, "I'm heading to The Lake."

If you're staying in Spokane, one quick way to explore the lake life is to hop in the car and head out on I-90. West of town, take the Cheney–Four Lakes exit, and you can't miss some of the area's most understated lakes. **SILVER LAKE** sparkles in the summer under the afternoon sun, with a small beach and swimming area popular with local families. **MEDICAL LAKE** (both a town and a lake) was named by Native Americans for the water's medicinal qualities. Grab an ice cream cone in town, then walk the entire perimeter of the lake on a gorgeous paved hiking and biking path. East of Spokane, toward the Washington-Idaho border, take a dip in **LIBERTY LAKE** or spend the day outside at nearby **FISH LAKE**.

For a bigger rush, Spokane locals kayak along the **LITTLE SPOKANE RIVER** in north Spokane or brave the class I rapids of **HANGMAN CREEK** south of town.

If you have access to a boat—be it a paddleboat or motorboat—head west from Spokane toward **LAKE ROOSEVELT**. The 150-mile-long lake was created after the Columbia River was dammed in the 1940s, and it has since become one of the most popular lakes in the area for swimming, boating, and fishing. Practically in the shadow of the **GRAND COULEE DAM**, the lake's visitors can take a break from the sun and tour the facility, built in 1942.

—Leah Sottile

Soap Lake

The town of Soap Lake earned its name on a windy day, when frothy whitecaps dotted the surface of the nearby lake. Many believe the lake, known for its high content of soft minerals, has healing properties. Contact the **SOAP LAKE CHAMBER OF COMMERCE** (300 N Daisy St; 509/246-1821; www.soaplakecoc.org) for information on renting canoes and sailboats.

DRY FALLS, off Highway 17 north of Soap Lake, shows the power of ice. When glacial Lake Missoula overflowed its ice-age dam some 12,000 years ago, torrential floods headed west to the Pacific. The force of the water carved out what is now this ancient waterfall, 3½ miles wide and 400 feet high (by comparison,

Niagara Falls is 1 mile wide and 165 feet high). The **DRY FALLS INTERPRETIVE CENTER** (inside Sun Lakes State Park, 4 miles southwest of Coulee City on Hwy 17; 509/632-5583; open 10am–6pm every day, May–Sept) at the top of the canyon is a half mile from the scenic overlook.

SUN LAKES STATE PARK (888/226-7688; www.parks.wa.gov), downstream from the falls, offers all kinds of outdoor activities.

LODGINGS

Notaras Lodge / ★★

13 CANNA ST, SOAP LAKE; 509/246-0462
Notaras has 15 rooms in four huge log cabins, right on Soap Lake. In fact, the lake's mineral waters are on tap in the bathrooms, several of which have in-room whirlpools. Six rooms have lake views, so snag one of those if you can. Each room has a quirky theme: Luck of the Draw, for example, has a slot machine pull handle at the entrance. The owners run Don's Restaurant (14 Canna St; 509/246-1217; lunch Sun–Fri, dinner every day), which specializes in steak, seafood, and Greek entrées. *$–$$; MC, V; checks OK; www. notaraslodge.com; Soap Lake exit off Hwy 28, at Canna St.* &

Omak

Omak is a town of 4,000, 50 miles north of Grand Coulee on Highway 155. To reach downtown Omak, exit the highway from either direction on a business loop; the town isn't even visible from US Highway 97. Perhaps Omak's best-known draw, the **OMAK STAMPEDE** (509/826-1002 or 800/933-6625; www.omak stampede.org), climaxes with the famous and controversial Suicide Race, when riders race their horses 210 feet downhill at a 62-degree angle, plow through the Okanagon River, and cross 500 feet of Colville Indian land. The stampede routinely injures or kills horses. The stampede is part of a popular rodeo that stretches four days around the second weekend of August; during the stampede, Omak's population swells to 30,000.

While you're downtown, try **GRANDMA'S ATTIC** (12 N Main St; 509/826-4765) and **SISTERS** (13 N Main St; 509/826-1968), both cute gift shops. Besides knickknacks, Grandma's Attic has a mini–soda fountain.

VANCOUVER
AND ENVIRONS

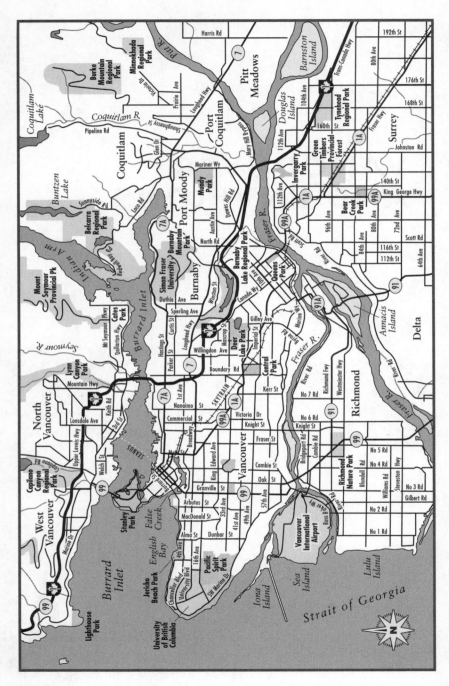

VANCOUVER AND ENVIRONS

Long a popular vacation spot, with its striking natural setting between the mountains and the sea, the Vancouver, Canada, area has recently been gripped by Olympic fever. The city and its surroundings (including the top-ranked ski-and-snowboard resort of Whistler) will host the 2010 Olympic Winter Games, and the region is in a frenzy of preparations. New construction is everywhere, from sports arenas to condo towers to a rapid-transit line linking the airport with downtown (scheduled for completion in 2009). Already a top destination for outdoor recreation, Vancouver will undoubtedly lure even more sports-enamored visitors as 2010 approaches, but urban planners are beefing up the region's cultural offerings as well. Canada's fastest-growing metropolis has already begun hosting pre-Olympic festivities that will grow more frequent as the big date draws near.

Vancouver may be preparing to welcome the world, but in recent decades immigrants, particularly from Asia, have helped transform the city into a vibrant gateway to the Pacific Rim. More than 30 percent of Vancouver's population is of Asian descent, and the city is home to some of the best Asian restaurants in North America, from simple noodle shops to spectacular Hong Kong–style banquet rooms. If you're craving freshly steamed dumplings, some of the best sushi on the continent, or bubble tea in a mind-bending array of flavors, you can find it all here.

In 2006 Vancouver voters elected Sam Sullivan as Canada's first quadriplegic mayor, further increasing this liberal city's already strong attitude of inclusiveness. Vancouver is living proof that a compassionate environment makes for a laid-back disposition.

ACCESS AND INFORMATION

VANCOUVER INTERNATIONAL AIRPORT (3211 Grant McConachie Way, Richmond; 9 miles/15 km south of downtown on Sea Island; 604/207-7077; www.yvr.ca) is a major international airport with daily flights to every continent. Look for First Nations artwork throughout the terminals. For advice and basic directions, newcomers can turn to an army of about 250 Green Coats, volunteer goodwill ambassadors for the airport authority. Several **CAR RENTAL** agencies are located on the ground floor of the three-level parking structure.

Weathered but still graceful, **PACIFIC CENTRAL STATION** (1150 Station St) is the local terminus of several bus and rail services. **GREYHOUND CANADA** (604/482-8747 or 800/231-2222; www.greyhound.ca) operates five buses daily between Vancouver and Seattle, with connections in Seattle to other U.S. points. **VIA RAIL** (888/842-7245; www.viarail.ca) is Canada's national passenger rail service. **AMTRAK** (800/872-7245; www.amtrak.com) trains make daily runs between Seattle and Vancouver. The **WHISTLER MOUNTAINEER** (604/606-8460 or 888/687-7245; www.whistlermountaineer.com) train runs to Whistler from North Vancouver, with a shuttle connection from downtown Vancouver hotels.

BC FERRIES (250/386-3431 or 888/223-3779; www.bcferries.bc.ca) serves the Vancouver area with boats to Victoria, the Gulf Islands, the Sunshine Coast, and points north. The ferry terminals are south of the city at Tsawwassen or northwest of town at Horseshoe Bay. **PACIFIC COACH LINES** (604/662-7575 or 800/661-1725; www.pacificcoach.com) operates a convenient bus-ferry-bus service between Vancouver's Pacific Central Station and downtown Victoria.

If you're driving, choose between two major highways. **HIGHWAY 99**, the main north-south highway connecting Vancouver to Seattle, leads south from the city across the fertile delta at the mouth of the Fraser River and connects with Washington State's Interstate 5. Highway 99 also connects Vancouver to the ski resort town of Whistler, about two hours north, and is known as the **SEA TO SKY HIGHWAY**. Transcontinental **HIGHWAY 1**, the main east-west highway, arrives from the east through the lower BC mainland and terminates in Vancouver; it runs along the south shore of the Fraser River. Another route is **HIGHWAY 7**, which runs east-west along the river's north shore.

Vancouver's weather is the mildest in Canada, thanks to ocean currents and weather patterns that bring warm, moist air in from the Pacific year-round. Spring comes early (by mid-March, usually); July and August are warmest; late summer and autumn days (through October) tend to be warm and sunny, with the occasional shower. Winter is rainy season—roughly November through March—but rain usually falls as showers or drizzle. Heavy continuous downpours are rare, as are thunderstorms and strong winds.

Vancouver

Vancouver is one of the few cities in the world where you can go snowboarding and golfing—or snowshoeing and sailing—on the same day. It's a relaxed, outdoorsy city, its walking paths and sidewalk cafés jam-packed at the first glimmer of sunshine. Along **ROBSON STREET**, the city's fashionable downtown shopping strip, a seemingly endless parade of shoppers includes locals and visitors from all over the world. Yet glance away from the opulence of the shops as you saunter along Robson, and you'll see, at the end of a side street, the peaceful waters of Burrard Inlet lapping at the shore. Beyond, the mountains on the North Shore glitter with snow for half the year.

No city is homogenous, particularly Vancouver. It's really an amalgam of neighborhoods, each with its own unique character. In **YALETOWN**, brick warehouses have been transformed into loft apartments, offices, chic shops, and trendy restaurants, while row after row of glittering condo towers line the shores of False Creek.

Home to one of North America's largest urban redevelopment projects, the **FALSE CREEK BASIN** is centered around the bustling—and must-see—market area and arts community on **GRANVILLE ISLAND**. Dynamic alternative cultures flourish in **KITSILANO** (known as "Kits"), a former low-rent haven for hippies that has been yuppified by baby boomers and young families, and the **WEST END**, home to Canada's most densely populated neighborhood and western Canada's largest gay and lesbian community. The West End is just south of Stanley Park; Kits is west across False Creek.

In **GASTOWN**, the city's oldest neighborhood, souvenir shops, galleries specializing in First Nations art, and avant-garde boutiques all have found homes in the restored brick buildings. **COMMERCIAL DRIVE**, on Vancouver's East Side, is an eclectic bohemian strip, where the multipierced and tattooed younger generation sips espresso alongside graying curmudgeons outside one of the many cafés.

The city's public transit system is an efficient way to get around town. **TRANS-LINK** (604/953-3333; www.translink.bc.ca) runs buses that travel throughout the metropolitan area; the SkyTrain that operates between downtown, the East Side, and the city's eastern suburbs; and the SeaBus that crosses the harbor between downtown and North Vancouver. A new rapid-transit line, currently under construction, is scheduled to connect the airport with downtown by 2009. More information is available from the **VANCOUVER TOURIST INFO CENTRE** (200 Burrard St; 604/683-2000; www.tourismvancouver.com). Or check the route planner on the Translink Web site for transit information and schedules.

MUSEUMS AND GALLERIES

Downtown's **VANCOUVER ART GALLERY** (750 Hornby St; 604/662-4719; www.vanartgallery.bc.ca) was once the elegant old courthouse designed by Francis Rattenbury. It now holds major exhibitions, and its permanent collection emphasizes regional artists, including more than 200 works by British Columbian Emily Carr. On the fourth Friday of each month, the gallery hosts FUSE, a popular performance art and music gathering, from 6 to 11pm.

If you're interested in Pacific Northwest art and culture, don't miss the **MUSEUM OF ANTHROPOLOGY** at the University of British Columbia (6393 NW Marine Dr; 604/822-3825; www.moa.ubc.ca). This stellar museum has an extensive collection of artifacts from coastal British Columbia Native cultures, including an impressive display of totem poles and a complex of Haida houses. Look for the sculpture *The Raven and the First Men* by noted Haida artist Bill Reid.

Part museum and part multimedia theatrical extravaganza, the **STORY-EUM** (142 Water St; 604/687-8142; www.storyeum.com), in Gastown, is a walk through British Columbia's history, with actors playing out scenes from early First Nations stories, British exploration and settlement, the gold rush, Chinese immigration, the construction of the transcontinental railroad, and British Columbia's role in the world wars. It's a bit Disney-esque and expensive, but for adults and older children—particularly those interested in history—it's entertaining.

Many of the city's commercial galleries are located across the water from downtown on the dozen blocks just south of the Granville Bridge, on and around Granville Street between 6th and 16th avenues. Art galleries here, including the **MONTE CLARK GALLERY** (2339 Granville St; 604/730-5000; www.monteclarkgallery.com) and the **BAU-XI GALLERY** (3045 Granville St;

VANCOUVER THREE-DAY TOUR

DAY ONE: Start your day at the **GRANVILLE ISLAND PUBLIC MARKET**, which opens at 9am; it's a good place to turn breakfast into a progressive meal: a chai at the **GRANVILLE ISLAND TEA COMPANY** (117-1689 Johnston St; 604/683-7491), apple focaccia from **TERRA BREADS**, candied salmon from **SEAFOOD CITY** (143-1689 Johnston St; 604/688-1818). After exploring the shops, studios, and galleries, hop on the SeaBus for a seaside lunch at sophisticated seafooder **C RESTAURANT** or the eclectic contemporary **NU**. Then continue on to Yaletown and check in to the oh-so-hip **OPUS HOTEL** or the budget-friendly **YWCA HOTEL**. Next stop: **CHINATOWN**, for a guided tour through the **DR. SUN YAT-SEN CLASSICAL CHINESE GARDEN**, before walking the frenzied streets looking for jade treasures or tasting steamed buns from one of the many bakeries. Return to your room and change for a run along the **STANLEY PARK SEAWALL** or a sunset stroll along **ENGLISH BAY BEACH** before heading to dinner at the **RAINCITY GRILL**, **CHAMBAR**, or **RARE**, which all showcase Vancouver's finest ingredients.

DAY TWO: Take a stroll to a nice café, perhaps **CHOCOATL** (1127 Mainland St; 604/676-9977) for Mexican-style hot chocolate, or fuel up at the **ELBOW ROOM** (560 Davie St; 604/685-3628), a quirky diner and local institution. Next, head to the University of British Columbia and the **MUSEUM OF ANTHROPOLOGY**

604/733-7011; www.bau-xi.com), represent internationally renowned painters and photographers.

Granville Island, site of the **EMILY CARR INSTITUTE OF ART AND DESIGN** (1399 Johnston St; 604/844-3800; www.eciad.bc.ca), has many pottery and craft studios. Work by local and regional artists is on display at the **GALLERY OF BC CERAMICS** (1359 Cartwright St; 604/669-3606; www.bcpotters.com) and at **CRAFTHOUSE** (1386 Cartwright St; 604/687-7270; www.cabc.net), run by the Crafts Association of British Columbia.

Vancouver's very small **CONTEMPORARY ART GALLERY** (555 Nelson St, at Richards; 604/681-2700; www.contemporaryartgallery.ca) downtown is worth a look if you're interested in avant-garde work. On a rough-around-the-edges block on the perimeter of Chinatown, check out a show at the emerging **CENTRE A** (2 W Hastings St; 604/683-8326; www.centrea.org), Vancouver's International Centre for Contemporary Asian Art.

Several Gastown galleries showcase First Nations artwork, including **INUIT GALLERY** (206 Cambie St; 604/688-7323; www.inuit.com) and **MARION SCOTT GALLERY** (308 Water St; 604/685-1934; www.marionscott gallery.com). In Yaletown, the **COASTAL PEOPLES FINE ARTS GALLERY**

to see impressive First Nations artifacts and the UBC **BOTANICAL GARDEN**, the oldest and one of the finest gardens in Canada. At lunch, stop for Malaysian food at **BANANA LEAF** or fiery Chinese fare at **GOLDEN SZECHUAN**. Then go back downtown to stroll **ROBSON STREET**, a trendy boulevard of prêt-à-porter boutiques and swank eateries, or head for up-and-coming **SOUTH MAIN STREET** to check out what the local designers are offering. If you'd like to take in a show, see what's available at the half-price booth at **TICKETS TONIGHT**; afterward, treat yourself to a late-night snack of "tapatizers" at **BIN 941 TAPAS PARLOUR**. Or skip the show in favor of a leisurely dinner featuring more local flavors at **BISHOP'S**, **AURORA BISTRO**, or **CRU** before returning to your hotel.

DAY THREE: Start the morning with a ride south to Richmond for dim sum at **SHIANG GARDEN**. Either browse the Asian malls nearby in Richmond, or go back toward downtown, stopping to take in the views at **QUEEN ELIZA-BETH PARK**. Spend a couple of hours at the **VANCOUVER ART GALLERY**, or if the weather is fine, cross over to the North Shore and do an easy hike in West Vancouver's **LIGHTHOUSE PARK** with its stunning city view. Back in **YALETOWN**, have chowder and a beer at **RODNEY'S OYSTER HOUSE** or sushi and sake at **BLUE WATER CAFÉ** before browsing the upscale boutiques. For dinner later, go all out with a four-star meal at **LUMIÈRE** or **WEST** before returning to your hotel.

(1024 Mainland St; 604/685-9298; www.coastalpeoples.com) has a particularly striking First Nations collection.

PARKS AND GARDENS

With its temperate climate, Vancouver is green throughout the year and especially pretty in spring and summer when flowers and trees are in bloom. Take a walk through the quiet rain forest in **STANLEY PARK** (west end of Beach and W Georgia sts to Lions Gate Bridge; 604/257-8400). This 1,000-acre/400-hectare park is within walking distance of downtown but feels worlds away. You can walk, jog, or bike along the **SEAWALL** that follows the park's perimeter; relax at **SECOND BEACH** or **THIRD BEACH** (on west side of park—especially nice as the sun is beginning to set); stroll in the formal rose gardens; take the kids to the **VANCOUVER AQUARIUM** (604/659-3474; www. vanaqua.org); stop in at one of several restaurants; ogle the totem poles; and hike numerous wilderness trails. Nearby, **ENGLISH BAY BEACH** (Beach Ave, at foot of Denman St) is a see-and-be-seen strip of sand that bustles even when the sky is gray.

At **QUEEN ELIZABETH PARK**, the highest point in Vancouver proper, dramatic winding paths, sunken gardens, and waterfalls skirt the **BLOEDEL**

CONSERVATORY (Cambie St and 33rd Ave; 604/257-8570), a domed structure that houses a variety of tropical flowers and birds; the brilliant floral displays will perk up a dreary winter's day. Near Queen Elizabeth Park, **VANDUSEN BOTANICAL GARDEN** (5251 Oak St; 604/878-9274; www.vandusengarden.org) stretches over 55 acres/22 hectares; check their online "bloom calendar" if you're interested in particular plants.

In Chinatown, the **DR. SUN YAT-SEN CLASSICAL CHINESE GARDEN** (578 Carrall St; 604/662-3207; www.vancouverchinesegarden.com) is a spectacular reconstruction of a Chinese scholar's garden, complete with pavilions and water walkways; it's worth taking a one-hour tour to learn about the garden's design.

The University of British Columbia boasts several superb gardens: the **BOTANICAL GARDEN** (UBC campus, 6804 SW Marine Dr; 604/822-9666; www.ubcbotanicalgarden.org), the Nitobe Memorial Garden (a serene Japanese garden), and the Physic Garden, which showcases traditional medicinal plants.

KITSILANO BEACH (Cornwall Ave and Arbutus St, bordering English Bay) is a year-round haven for joggers, dog walkers, and evening strollers, while farther west, **JERICHO BEACH** (off Point Grey Rd, at Wallace St, or off NW Marine Dr, at Discovery St), **LOCARNO BEACH** (NW Marine Dr), and **SPANISH BANKS BEACH** (NW Marine Dr) are local favorites for picnicking, strolling, and sunning.

SHOPPING

In **YALETOWN** (bordered by Pacific Blvd and Nelson, Cambie, and Seymour sts), former warehouse buildings house ultrahip clothing stores, including **BABE BELANGERE BOUTIQUE** (1092 Hamilton St; 604/806-4010), **GLOBAL ATOMIC DESIGNS** (1006 Mainland St; 604/806-6223; www.globalatomic.com), and **VASANJI** (1012 Mainland St; 604/669-0882).

Weekends are especially crowded along **ROBSON STREET** (between Beatty St and Stanley Park), when *tout le monde* strolls among its many boutiques and restaurants. There's a lot to see, from art books, jewelry, and gifts by local artists at the **GALLERY SHOP** in the Vancouver Art Gallery to a string of international chains to local clothing stores. The yogawear-turned-streetwear at **LULULEMON ATHLETICA** (1148 Robson St; 604/681-3118) is popular with everyone from teens to their parents, while the young and hip buy casual clothes at **ARITZIA** (1110 Robson St; 604/684-3251). Inside the main branch of the **VANCOUVER PUBLIC LIBRARY** (at Robson and Homer sts; 604/331-3603), designed by renowned architect Moshe Safdie, **BOOKMARK** (604/331-4040) has literary gifts.

PACIFIC CENTRE (700 W Georgia St to 777 Dunsmuir St; 604/688-7235; www.pacificcentre.ca), is downtown's biggest mall, with more than 140 outlets, including high-end department store **HOLT RENFREW** (604/681-3121; www.holtrenfrew.com). Also downtown is the **SINCLAIR CENTRE** (757 W Hastings St; 604/659-1009; www.sinclaircentre.com), a restored heritage building that houses the designer department store **LEONE** (604/683-1133; www.leone.ca) as well as upscale boutiques.

Emerging local designers have set up shop in **GASTOWN**, particularly along the 300 block of West Cordova Street and along the surrounding streets. Slip into **DREAM** (311 W Cordova St; 604/683-7326) or **OBAKKI** (332 Water St; 604/669-9727; www.obakki.com) for distinctive fashions.

Across False Creek from downtown, **SOUTH GRANVILLE**, along Granville Street from about 6th to 16th avenues, is home to art galleries, antique stores, and trendy designer clothing and housewares shops. Under the Granville Street Bridge on **GRANVILLE ISLAND** (604/666-5784), warehouses and factories have been transformed into a public market and craft shops. Some fine local designers are located in the Net Loft Building, and several intriguing studios are located along Railspur Alley, including **NORTHWEST BUNGALOW** (1333 Railspur Alley; 604/633-1351; www.nwbungalow.ca), a sliver of a shop where owner Fritz Muntean designs and builds beautiful Arts and Crafts–style furniture. At the **GRANVILLE ISLAND PUBLIC MARKET** (1689 Johnston St; 604/666-5784; www.granvilleisland.bc.ca), you can get everything from wild salmon to fresh produce to the best charcuterie in town—it's worth waiting in line for the high-quality pâtés and cured meats at **OYAMA SAUSAGE** (126-1689 Johnston St; 604/327-7407), which you can pair with a crusty baguette from **TERRA BREADS** (107-1689 Johnson St; 604/685-3102).

Foodies may want to detour just west of Granville Island to the city's best cheese shop, **LES AMIS DU FROMAGE** (1752 W 2nd Ave, near Burrard; 604/732-4218; www.buycheese.com), where the staff graciously offers advice about—and samples of—the 350 to 500 varieties in stock. On the same block, **BARBARA JO'S BOOKS TO COOKS** (1740 W 2nd Ave; 604/688-6755; www. bookstocooks.com) has a great selection of cookbooks, including many by Canadian chefs; check the Web site for a schedule of food-related events. There's also a smaller branch (604/684-6788) in the Net Loft Building on Granville Island.

In **KITSILANO**, there's good shopping in the boutiques along West 4th Avenue between Burrard and Vine streets. Look for **GRAVITY POPE** (2205 W 4th Ave; 604/731-7673; www.gravitypope.com) for designer shoes; **DUTHIE'S BOOKS** (2239 W 4th Ave; 604/732-5344; www.duthiebooks.com), a small but well-stocked independent bookstore; **MOULÉ** (1994 W 4th Ave; 604/732-4066) for distinctive crafts, gifts, and jewelry; and **KOOLHAUS** (2199 W 4th Ave; 604/875-9004; www.koolhausdesign.com) if you're in the market for funky, modern furniture.

SOUTH MAIN—or **SOMA**, as locals call the area around Main Street, from about 7th Avenue south to around 30th Avenue—has become Vancouver's hottest shopping district. If you're searching for one-of-a-kind clothing, head for the blocks between 20th and 23rd avenues. **EUGENE CHOO** (3683 Main St; 604/873-8874; www.eugenechoo.com) is the latest "it" boutique, and **TWIGG & HOTTIE** (3617 Main St; 604/879-8595; www.twiggandhottie. com) sells creations by local designers. If frilly and feminine is more your

style, visit the **BAREFOOT CONTESSA** (3715 Main St; 604/879-1137; www.
thebarefootcontessa.com).

The oldest and biggest of Vancouver's ethnic communities is **CHINATOWN**
(off Main St, on Pender and Keefer sts). During the summer, there's a weekend
open-air night market (6pm–midnight) at Main and Keefer streets. The fun
PEKING LOUNGE (83 E Pender St; 604/844-1559; www.pekinglounge.com)
isn't a bar but a furniture store, stocking antique armoires, tables, and textiles
from China. **MING WO** (23 E Pender St; 604/683-7268; www.mingwo.com)
sells dishes and kitchenware. Vancouver's large East Indian immigrant community has a shopping area called the **PUNJABI MARKET** (in south Vancouver
at 49th and Main sts), where you can bargain for a custom-fit *sari*, Rajastani
jewelry, or the latest Bollywood blockbuster on DVD.

PERFORMING ARTS

Theater/Dance

The **CENTRE IN VANCOUVER FOR PERFORMING ARTS** (777 Homer St;
604/602-0616; www.centreinvancouver.com), designed by Moshe Safdie
(who also designed Library Square), showcases touring megamusicals and the
occasional Chinese acrobatic troupe or dance company. The well-regarded
VANCOUVER PLAYHOUSE THEATRE COMPANY (Hamilton and Dunsmuir
sts; 604/873-3311; www.vancouverplayhouse.com) presents spectacular contemporary and classical productions.

The **ARTSCLUB THEATRE COMPANY** (604/687-1644; www.artsclub.com)
also performs a mix of works on two stages: the 650-seat art deco–style
STANLEY INDUSTRIAL ALLIANCE STAGE (2750 Granville St) and the 450-
seat **GRANVILLE ISLAND STAGE** (1585 Johnston St). Next door, the **REVUE
STAGE** (1585 Johnston St) is home to the improvisational **VANCOUVER THE-
ATRESPORTS LEAGUE** (604/687-1644; www.vtsl.com), which runs several
shows, including the NC-17-rated Extreme Improv weekends at 11:45pm.

Every summer, **BARD ON THE BEACH** (Kits Point at foot of Whyte Ave;
604/739-0559; www.bardonthebeach.org) performs Shakespeare's works in
tents at Vanier Park. Book in advance; they are popular.

For more avant-garde theater and dance, head to the East Side and the
VANCOUVER EAST CULTURAL CENTRE (1895 E Venables St, at Victoria
Dr; 604/251-1363; www.vecc.bc.ca), known the Cultch. They also offer a
popular kids' series that brings in world musicians, jugglers, and dancers on
several Saturdays.

BALLET BRITISH COLUMBIA (604/732-5003; www.balletbc.com), directed
by John Alleyne, performs striking contemporary dance at the elegant **QUEEN
ELIZABETH THEATRE** (Hamilton and W Georgia sts; 604/665-3050; www.
city.vancouver.bc.ca/theatres). Check with the **SCOTIABANK DANCE CENTRE**
(677 Davie St; 604/606-6400; www.thedancecentre.ca) for other events.

Music

Under the leadership of music director Bramwell Tovey, the 74-member **VANCOUVER SYMPHONY ORCHESTRA** (604/876-3434; www.vancouversymphony.ca) performs at several locations, including the 1927 **ORPHEUM THEATRE** (601 Smithe St) downtown. The **VANCOUVER OPERA** (Hamilton at W Georgia sts; 604/683-0222; www.vancouveropera.ca) presents four to five productions a year at the Queen Elizabeth Theatre.

On the UBC campus, international, national, and local musicians—from classical to world music—take the stage at the modern **CHAN CENTRE FOR THE PERFORMING ARTS** (6265 Crescent Rd; 604/822-9197; www.chancentre.com). Check the calendar at the **ROUNDHOUSE COMMUNITY ARTS & RECREATION CENTRE** (181 Roundhouse Mews, at Davie and Pacific sts; 604/713-1800; www.roundhouse.ca) in Yaletown, which presents an offbeat mix of music, dance, and literary offerings.

Big names play the **VANCOUVER INTERNATIONAL JAZZ FESTIVAL** (604/872-5200; www.jazzvancouver.com) each June, and the annual **VANCOUVER FOLK MUSIC FESTIVAL** (604/602-9798; www.thefestival.bc.ca) brings toe-tapping crowds to Jericho Beach in July. One of Vancouver's biggest summer events is the **HSBC CELEBRATION OF LIGHT** (www.celebration-of-light.com), a series of spectacular (and free) fireworks displays, with music simulcast on radio station 101.1 FM; it takes place on four nights in late July and early August. The center of the fireworks action is along the West End's English Bay beaches, but you can also see the show from Kitsilano Beach, Vanier Park, Jericho Beach, and many other spots around town.

TICKETMASTER (604/280-4444; www.ticketmaster.ca) has more information about events. **TICKETS TONIGHT** (200 Burrard St; 604/684-2787; www.ticketstonight.ca), in the Vancouver Tourist Information Centre, sells half-price day-of-show theater tickets.

FOOD AND WINE

As chefs bring multicultural influences to their craft and are committed to regional ingredients, Vancouver has become internationally renowned as a gastronomic destination. You'll also find wide-ranging wine lists, focusing on wines from British Columbia.

For two weeks in January and February, **DINE OUT VANCOUVER** showcases the city's best restaurants with three-course dinner menus offered at $15, $25, or $35; the top tables book fast, so make your reservations early. The Tourism Vancouver Web site (www.tourismvancouver.com) lists participating restaurants. The annual **VANCOUVER PLAYHOUSE INTERNATIONAL WINE FESTIVAL** (604/872-6622; www.playhousewinefest.com) attracts more than 20,000 people each spring to sample the wares of more than 175 wineries from at least 15 countries at tastings, dinners, and wine-related events.

To join a food-oriented tour of the Granville Island Public Market,

Chinatown, or Commercial Drive, or for other food events, contact **EDIBLE BRITISH COLUMBIA** (604/812-9660 or 888/812-9660; www.edible-british-columbia.com).

NIGHTLIFE

On an evening out, you can enjoy just about every clubbing experience imaginable, from an old-time rock 'n' roll bender to a no-holds-barred striptease show, to a till-dawn rave in a factory warehouse. Live pop, rock, and world music concerts lure aficionados to the **COMMODORE BALLROOM** (868 Granville St; 604/739-7469; www.hob.com), a 1929 downtown theater. For jazz, head to the **CELLAR JAZZ CLUB** (3611 W Broadway; 604/738-1959; www.cellarjazz.com) in Kitsilano.

Local bands play nightly at the unpretentious **RAILWAY CLUB** (579 Dunsmuir St; 604/681-1625; www.therailwayclub.com) downtown, while blues fans head for the long-standing **YALE HOTEL** (1300 Granville St; 604/681-9253; www.theyale.ca), particularly for the popular jam sessions on Saturday and Sunday afternoons. For Middle Eastern music, belly dancing, and a hookah lounge, check out **MONA'S** (see review) on Friday and Saturday nights. On the East Side, **RIME** (1130 Commercial Dr; 604/215-1130; www.rime.ca), a Turkish restaurant and music club, hosts a diverse mix of local performers.

A piano player serenades imbibers at the tony **BACCHUS** lounge (845 Hornby St, in Wedgewood Hotel; 604/608-5319) with everything from soft rock to old standards. Equally upscale, but as trendy as Bacchus is traditional, Yaletown's **OPUS BAR** (322 Davie St, in Opus Hotel; 604/642-0557) is a film-industry hangout.

Vancouverites like their microbrews, and several are brewed locally. Try the **YALETOWN BREWING COMPANY** (1111 Mainland St; 604/681-2739; www.drinkfreshbeer.com), **STEAMWORKS** (375 Water St; 604/689-2739; www.steamworks.com), or the waterfront patio at the **DOCKSIDE BREWING COMPANY** (1253 Johnston St, Granville Island; 604/685-7070; www.docksidebrewing.com).

To find out who's playing, check the alternative weekly *Georgia Straight* (www.straight.com), published on Thursday, and the Thursday entertainment section of the *Vancouver Sun* (www.vancouversun.com), the city's major daily newspaper.

SPORTS AND RECREATION

Cycling, running, hiking, and water sports are all popular in Vancouver. A good in-city route for runners or in-line skaters is along the 5.5-mile (8.85-km) **STANLEY PARK SEAWALL**. You can get cycling maps from the **CITY OF VANCOUVER** (www.city.vancouver.bc.ca/engsvcs/transport/cycling). **ECOMARINE** (888/425-2925; www.ecomarine.com) rents kayaks from three locations. The Granville Island shop (1668 Duranleau St; 604/689-7575) is open year-round; the Jericho Beach (1300 Discovery St, at Jericho Sailing Centre;

604/222-3565) and English Bay Beach (Beach Ave, at foot of Denman St; 604/68-KAYAK) locations are open from late April through September.

The NHL's **VANCOUVER CANUCKS** play at **GENERAL MOTORS PLACE** (800 Griffiths Way; 604/899-7400; www.canucks.com). The faithful stick with the team through good times and bad, which makes getting tickets a challenge. The Canadian Football League's **BC LIONS** play at **BC PLACE STADIUM** (777 Pacific Blvd; 604/589-7627; www.bclions.com).

The **VANCOUVER WHITECAPS** (www.whitecapsfc.com), professional men's and women's soccer teams, play at Burnaby's **SWANGARD STADIUM** (intersection of Boundary Rd and Kingsway; 604/899-9823). Their family-friendly games are popular with Vancouver's legions of soccer-playing youth and their parents.

Thoroughbreds race at **HASTINGS PARK** (Hastings and Renfrew sts; 604/254-1631; www.hastingspark.com; mid-Apr–Nov), at the Pacific National Exhibition grounds.

Tickets for most events are at the gates or **TICKETMASTER** (604/280-4444; www.ticketmaster.ca).

RESTAURANTS

Aurora Bistro / ★★★

2420 MAIN ST, VANCOUVER; 604/873-9944

In this minimalist modern storefront, an anchor in the redeveloping Main Street area, chef-owner Jeff Van Geest serves creative dishes emphasizing Pacific Northwest ingredients to a casually trendy crowd. On the always imaginative menu, you might find bison carpaccio, Fanny Bay oysters fried in a cornmeal crust, or sablefish in a miso-maple glaze, served with pickled sea asparagus. At brunch, locals line up for the five-spice donuts. *$$$; AE, MC, V; no checks; dinner Tues–Sun, brunch Sun; full bar; reservations recommended; www.aurorabistro.ca; at E 8th Ave.*

Bacchus Restaurant / ★★★

845 HORNBY ST (THE WEDGEWOOD HOTEL), VANCOUVER; 604/608-5319

This elegant retreat in one of the city's best hotels hums with local business-people by day. But in the evening—with its burgundy velvet benches, soft piano music, and servers who cater to your every whim—it lives up to its billing as the "most romantic restaurant in Vancouver." The changing menu might include salmon poached in extra-virgin olive oil, halibut with an artichoke fricasee, or roasted venison. *$$$$; AE, DC, MC, V; no checks; breakfast, lunch, dinner every day, brunch Sat–Sun; full bar; reservations required; www.wedgewoodhotel.com; between Robson and Smithe sts.* &

Banana Leaf / ★★

820 W BROADWAY, VANCOUVER; 604/731-6333
1096 DENMAN ST, VANCOUVER; 604/683-3333
3005 W BROADWAY, VANCOUVER; 604/734-3005
Like a tropical vacation, a meal in one of these three brightly decorated, laid-back Malaysian restaurants helps you escape the Northwest's sometimes dreary days. Settle under the colorful batik wall hangings and start with the *roti canai*, a fluffy crepe with a curry dipping sauce. Seafood is a specialty, so you might choose the chile-fried Dungeness crab or prawns in black peppercorn butter. Don't miss the piquant *sambal* green beans. The staff will consult with you about your spice tolerance, but there's a good range. Vegetarians, take note: Many dishes can be made meat-free. *$$; AE, MC, V; no checks; lunch, dinner every day; full bar; no reservations; www.bananaleaf-vancouver. com; between Laurel and Willow sts (820 W Broadway), between Pendrell and Comox sts (1096 Denman St), at Carnarvon St (3005 W Broadway).*

Bin 941 Tapas Parlour / ★★★
Bin 942 Tapas Parlour / ★★★

941 DAVIE ST, VANCOUVER; 604/683-1246
1521 W BROADWAY, VANCOUVER; 604/734-9421
Get to these tapas bars early: at these funky, shoebox-sized restaurants, lines can spill into the street. Order several "tapatizers" for two—perhaps flank steak with a maple-chipotle glaze and shoestring fries; mussels steamed with habaneros and kaffir lime leaf; or olive hummus paired with Navajo fry bread. Sit at the bar and watch the frenetic kitchen action. *$$; MC, V; no checks; dinner every day; beer, wine, and liqueurs; no reservations; www. bin941.com; between Burrard and Howe sts (Bin 941), between Fir and Granville sts (Bin 942).* &

Bishop's / ★★★★

2183 W 4TH AVE, VANCOUVER; 604/738-2025
One of Vancouver's first restaurant owners to support local, seasonal ingredients, John Bishop proudly states that his kitchen is almost 100 percent organic. A consummate host, Bishop warmly greets his guests and visits each table, serving, pouring, discussing. The dishes are light, with subtly complex flavors. Dungeness crab is matched with pear-cranberry chutney, and wild sockeye or spring salmon is perfectly grilled—while in season, of course. The smoked sablefish and any lamb dish are well worth ordering. *$$$$; AE, DC, MC, V; no checks; dinner every day (closed 2 weeks in Jan); full bar; reservations required; www.bishopsonline.com; between Yew and Arbutus sts.*

Bistro Pastis / ★★★

2153 W 4TH AVE, VANCOUVER; 604/731-5020
With hardwood floors, bold and bright banquettes, and mirrors reflecting well-dressed diners, this Kitsilano place is both stylish and affordable. You

could bring a business associate, a date, or your grandmother, and the staff would make them all feel equally at home. The kitchen turns out updated versions of French bistro classics, such as onion soup gratiné, bouillabaisse, cassoulet with duck confit and *merguez* sausage, or steak with *pommes frites* and your choice of béarnaise or peppercorn sauce. *$$$; AE, MC, V; no checks; lunch Tues–Fri, dinner Tues–Sun, brunch Sat–Sun; full bar; reservations recommended; www.bistropastis.com; just west of Arbutus St.*

Blue Water Café / ★★★☆

1095 HAMILTON ST, VANCOUVER; 604/688-8078
Spend an evening "bar-hopping" in this converted Yaletown warehouse turned posh seafood restaurant. First stop: the main bar, to slurp Cortes Island oysters and sip British Columbia's Blue Mountain Brut. Next stop: the raw bar, for elaborate sushi rolls with chilled sake. Finally, settle into a plush banquette for the formidable seafood tower, followed by the miso-crusted sablefish, Queen Charlotte Island halibut, or whole Dungeness crab. *$$$$; AE, DC, E, MC, V; no checks; dinner every day; full bar; reservations recommended; www.bluewatercafe.net; at Helmcken St.*

C Restaurant / ★★★☆

1600 HOWE ST, VANCOUVER; 604/681-1164
Chef Rob Clark is a seafood master. In this Zen-like room with a stellar view of False Creek and Granville Island, he sources the best sustainable seafood and creates cutting-edge dishes that are as dramatic on the palate as they are on the plate. Starters include Asian-flavored scallops or smoked Sechelt sturgeon. Among the main dishes, look for grilled rare albacore tuna with house-made bacon or dorado poached in olive oil. Try to nab a seat on the waterside patio, particularly around sunset. *$$$$; AE, DC, E, MC, V; no checks; lunch Mon–Fri (May–Sept only), dinner every day; full bar; reservations recommended; www.crestaurant.com; at Beach Ave.*

The Cannery Seafood House / ★★★

2205 COMMISSIONER ST, VANCOUVER; 604/254-9606
For fresh, straightforward seafood, it's worth the trek to this relatively remote east-end dockside location. Due to port security, access from downtown is via Clark Drive and through a security checkpoint. The restaurant itself looks modest, but the interior boasts expansive water and mountain views. Salmon Wellington has been a house specialty since 1971; it's still a winner, but so is the Alaskan black cod with British Columbia wild mushrooms in a chive-butter sauce. *$$$; AE, DC, MC, V; no checks; lunch Mon–Fri, dinner every day; full bar; reservations recommended; www.canneryseafood.com; off Clark Dr, north of E Hastings St.*

VANCOUVER'S BEST GOURMET MARKETS

These specialty food shops are the perfect places to stock up before hiking Grouse Mountain in North Vancouver or picnicking in Stanley Park. Just off the seawall in downtown's stylish Yaletown neighborhood, **URBAN FARE** (177 Davie St; 604/975-7550; www.urbanfare.com) offers upscale antipasto, custom mixed salads, imported cold cuts, sandwiches, breads, and pastries. The sidewalk tables boast some of the best people watching in the city.

MINERVA'S MEDITERRANEAN DELI in Kitsilano (3207 W Broadway; 604/733-3954) features an olive and feta bar with dozens of varieties of each, plus authentic Greek salad. All things organic can be found at **CAPERS COMMUNITY MARKETS** (2285 W 4th Ave; 604/739-6676), where bohemian values meet sophisticated taste. The custom-built sandwiches and homemade soups make great takeout, or eat in the café area that overlooks Kitsilano's bustling Fourth Avenue. Capers has other locations downtown (1675 Robson St; 604/687-5288) and on Cambie (3277 Cambie St; 604/909-2988).

The food hall at the **GRANVILLE ISLAND PUBLIC MARKET** (1689 Johnston

---

Century / UNRATED

432 RICHARDS ST, VANCOUVER; 604/633-2700

Mixing the elegance of a former bank—marble floors and soaring gilt-beam ceilings—with murals of cowboys and Cuban revolutionaries, this eclectic newcomer has one of the most distinctive spaces in the city. (You can even book a private party in the vault.) Not everything that comes out of the Nuevo Latino kitchen works as well as the offbeat decor, but the maple- and cinnamon-glazed pork bellies, barbecued octopus, and wild boar served on slightly sweet masa cakes are well worth sampling. The main plates come in full or half orders to encourage sharing nibbles over sangría or mojitos. *$$–$$$; AE, MC, V; no checks; lunch Mon–Fri, dinner every day; full bar; reservations recommended; www.centuryhouse.ca; between Dunsmuir and Pender sts.*

Chambar / ★★★

562 BEATTY ST, VANCOUVER; 604/879-7119

Chef-owner Nico Schuermans cooked at Michelin-starred restaurants in Belgium before he and his wife, Karri, opened this hot spot between the Queen Elizabeth Theatre and Chinatown. His cooking here is top quality, without a hint of stuffiness. Nico's Belgian background shows up in several incarnations of *moules frites* (mussels and french fries), but don't overlook his more eclectic creations. Try the cevichelike octopus Ecuadorian or North African–influenced lamb *tagine*. The long, lean space gets packed and loud; bring the

St; 604/666-6477; www.granvilleisland.ba.ca) features everything from farm-fresh local produce to specialty teas. Try the Stock Market for homemade soups and salad dressings. The city's best focaccia, baguettes, and specialty breads are at Terra Breads, while fine cheeses and charcuterie are at nearby Oyama Sausage Company. On the tony South Granville Rise, **MEINHARDT** (3002 Granville St; 604/732-4405; www.meinhardt.com) dishes up curry chicken-breast salad and roasted vegetables, plus old-fashioned favorites including berry trifle and huge chocolate-chip cookies. Next door is Picnic, Meinhardt's eat-in café that boasts one long marble community table.

Newcomer **QUINCE** (1780 W 3rd Ave; 604/731-4645; www.quince.ca) features gourmet vacuum-packed food to go, plus fare such as air-dried salami on country bread and shrimp and chervil salad. Then there's **CUPCAKES** (1116 Denman St; 604/974-1300; 2887 W Broadway; 604/974-1302; www.cupcakesonline.com), with its Mint Condition (chocolate cake topped with green butter cream) and Koo Koo (cream cheese frosting and shredded coconut slathered on coconut cake) confections that come in bite-size minis, too. *Definitely* grab a six-pack.

—Audrey D. Brashich

gang and savor some of the most entertaining food in town. *$$$; AE, MC, V; no checks; dinner every day; full bar; reservations recommended; www.chambar.com; between Dunsmuir and Pender sts.*

Chartwell / ★★★

791 W GEORGIA ST (THE FOUR SEASONS), VANCOUVER; 604/689-9333
Known for its distinctive personal service, this clubby white-tablecloth room in the opulent Four Seasons Hotel will pamper you. Start with a classic seafood cocktail or oysters on the half shell. The menu's main focus is the grill, a selection of steaks, chops, and seafood, with a mix-and-match list of sides and sauces. Try the juicy lamb chop with thick-cut fries or the grilled wild salmon with Parmesan gnocchi and roasted baby beets, and finish with a chocolate soufflé. *$$$$; AE, DC, DIS, JCB, MC, V; no checks; dinner every day; full bar; reservations recommended; www.fourseasons.com; at Howe St.* &

CinCin Ristorante & Bar / ★★★

1154 ROBSON ST, VANCOUVER; 604/688-7338
From the Mediterranean-inspired decor to the wood-fired open kitchen, this bustling room exudes warmth. The crowd-pleasing menu combines Italian influences with West Coast flavors. Be sure to order the antipasto platter, then, among the pastas, you might try squid-ink linguine with clams or *capellini di bottarga* (topped with mullet caviar). Other options include *panko*-crusted halibut with cauliflower purée, grilled Okanagan beef tenderloin with

a mushroom ragù, or a simple pizza topped with prosciutto and asparagus. Enjoy a cocktail at the bar, have a light meal in the lounge (till midnight), or dine on the heated terrace overlooking Robson Street. *$$$; AE, DC, MC, V; no checks; lunch Mon–Fri, dinner every day; full bar; reservations recommended; www.cincin.net; between Bute and Thurlow sts.*

Cioppino's Mediterranean Grill / ★★★☆
Cioppino's Enoteca / ★★★☆

1133 HAMILTON ST, VANCOUVER; 604/688-7466
The name is a pun on San Francisco's delicious seafood stew, cioppino, and that of talented chef-owner Pino Posteraro. Pino's Mediterranean creations— grilled calamari with mushrooms and black olives, linguine with lobster, and duck three ways—have earned him a loyal following in his side-by-side pair of Yaletown restaurants. For dessert, try chestnut cake with yogurt sauce, frangipane and pear tart, or *limoncello* cheesecake. Next door, the Enoteca is a low-key wine bar with a rotisserie. *$$$$; AE, DC, MC, V; no checks; lunch Mon–Fri, dinner Mon–Sat; full bar; reservations recommended; www. cioppinosyaletown.com; between Helmcken and Davie sts.*

Circolo / ★★★

1116 MAINLAND ST, VANCOUVER; 604/687-1116
Settle into a curvy banquette at Umberto Menghi's chic Tuscan eatery created for the *bella gente* ("beautiful people"). One of Canada's best-known restaurateurs, Menghi set out to capture the moods of his favorite cities, and in his Yaletown restaurant, you might imagine yourself at a bustling oyster bar in Manhattan, a romantic bistro in Paris, or a classic restaurant in Florence. Start by sharing some fresh oysters or the escargots. Then on to the *bistecca alla Fiorentina* for two: 32 ounces of grilled porterhouse, chased with a bottle of Tuscan Bambolo, and you'll feel rich and (contentedly) far from home. *$$$–$$$$; AE, DC, E, MC, V; no checks; dinner Mon–Sat; full bar; reservations recommended; www.umberto.com/circolo.htm; between Helmcken and Davie sts.* &

Cru / ★★★

1459 W BROADWAY, VANCOUVER; 604/677-4111
This inviting storefront restaurant, done in warm coffee and butterscotch hues, is designed for wine lovers. Each item on the imaginative menu is color-coded to match the wines (all sold by the glass). There's a three-course prix-fixe meal, but we recommend grazing through the small plates. The caesar salad is a signature dish, and Cru serves some of the best duck confit in town. Another good choice is the bruschetta trio: with fig and walnut tapenade; marinated peppers, fennel, and pine nuts; and white beans with sage. *$$; AE, MC, V; no checks; dinner every day; full bar; reservations recommended; www. cru.ca; between Granville and Hemlock sts.* &

Diva at the Met / ★★★

645 HOWE ST (METROPOLITAN HOTEL), VANCOUVER; 604/602-7788
Give your mouth a buzz with an appetizer of citrus-cured *hamachi*, paired with carbonated grapefruit. That's just one of the treats in this sleek, multi-tiered, contemporary dining room. There's a business buzz midday when financial types meet over lamb *panini* or crispy calamari; in the evenings, it's more sedate. Don't skip dessert; chocoholics go for pastry chef Thomas Haas's signature chocolate bar: a rich ganache with caramel crunch. *$$$–$$$$; AE, DC, JCB, MC, V; no checks; breakfast, lunch, dinner every day, brunch Sat–Sun; full bar; reservations recommended; www.metropolitan.com/diva; between Dunsmuir and W Georgia sts.* &

Feenie's / ★★★

2563 W BROADWAY, VANCOUVER; 604/739-7115
Celeb chef Rob Feenie's casually chic dining spot has been jammed since it opened next door to his high-end Lumière (see review)—perhaps because Feenie's is one of the city's best gourmet bargains. The sidewalk patio is laid-back, but inside, it's all slick high design. The menu is fun—from the "Feenie's Weenie" to the signature burger, with mushrooms, cheese, and bacon. There are updated classics, too, such as *poutine* or shepherd's pie with duck confit. Beware: Dress stylishly, or risk an upturned nose from the sometimes snooty staff. *$$–$$$; AE, DC, MC, V; no checks; lunch, dinner every day; full bar; reservations recommended; www.feenies.com; between Trafalgar and Larch Sts.* &

The Fish House at Stanley Park / ★★

8901 STANLEY PARK DR, VANCOUVER; 604/681-7275 OR 877-681-7275
Sure, it's touristy—but pull up a stool at the Oyster Bar, dine by the fireplace, or enjoy the gorgeous park surroundings from the patio, and you'll see why. They constantly re-invent the fresh sheet, with choices including wild salmon with a Parmesan-almond crust or pan-roasted sablefish in a soy-chile glaze. Try the seafood sampler, with house-smoked salmon pastrami, calamari marinated in smoked tomatoes, grilled prawns, and plump mussels. *$$$; AE, DC, DIS, JCB, MC, V; no checks; lunch Mon–Sat, dinner every day, afternoon tea every day, brunch Sun; full bar; www.fishhousestanleypark.com; at Lagoon Dr.* &

Go Fish / ★★

1505 W 1ST AVE, VANCOUVER; 604/730-5039
Gord Martin, chef-owner of Bin 941 and Bin 942 (see review), opened this fish shack on False Creek, a short stroll from Granville Island, and fish-and-chips has never been the same. The menu is simple: a few fresh fish dishes, paired with a tangy Asian-style slaw or fries. There are only a handful of tables, all outside, so you might have to take your meal to go. Primarily a lunch venue, closing times here vary; call to confirm. *$; MC, V; no checks; lunch Wed–Sun; no alcohol; no reservations; at False Creek Fisherman's Wharf.*

Golden Szechuan / ★★

1788 W BROADWAY, VANCOUVER; 604/738-3648
Authentic Szechuan fare is the draw at this no-frills West Side eatery that's popular with Asian families and groups of young people. Good choices include the rich and meaty double-cooked smoked pork, the hot and sour tofu, any of the dumplings, and whatever seasonal Chinese vegetable is available (ask for it garlic-fried). Spice hounds should request an off-the-menu special: fiery free-range whole chicken, poached and served cold. *$$; MC, V; no checks; lunch, dinner every day; full bar; no reservations; at Burrard St.*

Gotham Steakhouse & Cocktail Bar / ★★★

615 SEYMOUR ST, VANCOUVER; 604/605-8282
Meat is the main course in this downtown power dining room, where the steaks may be even more beautiful than the people. From the New York strip to the splendid 24-ounce porterhouse, it's a cattle drive for the taste buds. Vegetables are à la carte, so you can share mashed potatoes, creamed spinach, or crispy french fries. For the sheer entertainment value, take a seat at the bar and do some of the best people watching in Vancouver. Beware: This place prices under the assumption that everyone has a Swiss bank account. *$$$$; AE, DC, MC, V; no checks; dinner every day; full bar; reservations recommended; www.gothamsteakhouse.com; at Dunsmuir St.* ৬

Imperial Chinese Seafood Restaurant / ★★★☆

355 BURRARD ST, VANCOUVER; 604/688-8191
The opulent Imperial feels like a grand ballroom of eras past: a central staircase leads to the mezzanine, and windows look out onto Burrard Inlet and the North Shore mountains. The Chinese classics can be equally polished—lobster in black bean sauce with fresh egg noodles; sautéed spinach with minced pork and Chinese anchovies; a superb pan-smoked black cod; and the addictive beef sauté in chiles with honey walnuts. Dim sum is popular with local businesspeople, perhaps because service is courteous and informative. *$$$; DC, MC, V; no checks; lunch, dinner every day; full bar; reservations recommended; www.imperialrest.com; between Cordova and Hastings sts.*

Kitanoya Guu
Kitanoya Guu with Garlic
Kitanoya Guu with Otokomae / ★★

838 THURLOW ST, VANCOUVER; 604/685-8817
1698 ROBSON ST, VANCOUVER; 604/685-8678
105-375 WATER ST, VANCOUVER; 604/685-8682
Izakayas—casual Japanese pubs serving small plates—have sprouted up all over Vancouver, and at this friendly trio, you can sample this tapas-with-sake trend. The Thurlow Street location is handy for a lunchtime shopping break, while the Water Street branch "with Otokomae" (in a converted Gastown warehouse) is the most stylish. Locals flock to the tiny storefront "with Garlic" on Robson, though, for the best food. Don't miss the kimchi udon

(noodles with cod roe and cabbage), the kabocha *karokke* (an egg coated with pumpkin, then fried), or the grilled yellowtail cheeks. *$; AE, MC, V; no checks; lunch Mon–Sat, dinner every day (Kitanoya Guu), dinner every day (Guu with Garlic, Guu with Otokomae); beer and sake; reservations recommended; at Robson St (Kitanoya Guu), at Bidwell St (Guu with Garlic), at W Cordova St (Guu with Otokomae).*

Le Crocodile / ★★★★

100-909 BURRARD ST, VANCOUVER; 604/669-4298

Classic, elegant, and ever so francophone—that's French-born chef-owner Michel Jacob's graceful downtown restaurant. Everyone orders Jacob's savory onion tart and his Dover sole in a beurre blanc, but other classics, such as garlic-sautéed frogs' legs, double-cut veal chop, and sweetbreads with tarragon, all pay their respects to tradition. The professional service and European atmosphere make a meal at Le Crocodile an event. *$$$–$$$$; AE, DC, MC, V; no checks; lunch Mon–Fri, dinner Mon–Sat; full bar; reservations recommended; www.lecrocodilerestaurant.com; at Smithe St.* &

Lumière / ★★★★

2551 W BROADWAY, VANCOUVER; 604/739-8185

Rob Feenie's restless energy fuels the passion for perfection that is Lumière, creating arguably the city's best food. (Perhaps that same energy helped him win the Iron Chef America battle.) Choose from several seasonal tasting menus, including the 12-course "Signature" selection, designed to make you swoon, from lobster carpaccio with olive-oil sorbet to braised veal cheek with asparagus risotto and truffle foam, to spiced hot chocolate soup. If you're a foodie looking to celebrate, head for this contemporary Kitsilano dining room. *$$$$; AE, DC, MC, V; no checks; dinner Tues–Sun; full bar; reservations required; www.lumiere.ca; between Trafalgar and Larch sts.* &

Mistral / ★★⯪

2585 W BROADWAY, VANCOUVER; 604/733-0046

Take a bite of the pissaladière (a thin-crusted tart of onions, olives, and anchovies) at this sunny Kitsilano neighborhood bistro, and you may feel transported to the south of France. Chef-owner Jean-Yves Benoit prepares a menu of provençal classics, while his wife, Minna, adds her own sunshine to the small dining room. Duck lovers can share the platter of rillettes, pâté, and smoked duck breast, and the hearty cassoulet is comfort food, rain or shine. The dark chocolate mousse, the lemon tart, or the Brie with pears makes a suitably classic ending. *$$$; AE, MC, V; no checks; lunch Tues–Sat, dinner Mon–Sat; full bar; reservations recommended; www.mistralbistro.ca; at Trafalgar St.*

Mona's / ★★★

1328 HORNBY ST, VANCOUVER; 604/689-4050
A recent diner at Mona's said it was like "My Big Fat Lebanese Wedding."
It's kind of true. Chef-owner Mona Chaaban's grown kids, Ibrahim and Wassan, will greet and serve you, and husband Khalil is behind the scenes. (His paintings, though, are all over the walls.) The festive feeling is amped up on Saturday nights, when a live Arabic band gets everyone dancing. But it's the food that shines here. Mona's doesn't just turn out the traditional Middle Eastern plates you're used to, such as *baba ghanouj*, humous, and tabouleh. She makes authentic dishes served only in Lebanese homes, including baked *kafta*, eggplant casserole, and spinach stew. The downtown restaurant features a *nargila* ("hookah") room, a waterfall, an outside patio, and—our favorite—belly dancing. You'll feel as though you're part of a Lebanese family here. *$$–$$$; AE, V; no checks; dinner Tues–Sun; full bar; reservations recommended; www.lebanesecuisine.shawbiz.ca; between Drake and Pacific sts.* &

Montri's Thai Restaurant / ★★

3629 W BROADWAY, VANCOUVER; 604/738-9888
Located not far from the University of British Columbia, this pretty dining room that serves first-rate traditional Thai fare is always busy. The salads are excellent, particularly the *som tum* (a spicy mix of shredded green papaya, lime, and fish sauce) and the *larb gai* (ground chicken marinated with hot peppers, scallions, cilantro, and lime). Other favorites include the simple *lard nar* (fried rice noodles with broccoli in a soy gravy), the garlic pork, or the British Columbia salmon in a red curry sauce. Cool off with Thailand's Singha beer. *$$; MC, V; no checks; dinner Tues–Sun; full bar; reservations recommended; www.montri-thai.com; near Alma St.* &

Nat's New York Pizzeria / ★★

2684 W BROADWAY, VANCOUVER; 604/737-0707
1080 DENMAN ST, VANCOUVER; 604/642-0777
Nat and Franco Bastone learned how to create Naples-style pizza at their uncle's pie parlor in Yonkers and, along with their wise-cracking staff, now serve some of the best thin-crust pizza around. Pull up a chair under the Big Apple memorabilia and sink your teeth into a slice loaded with chorizo and mushrooms or artichokes and pesto. Kids and teens love it here; the West Broadway location gets jammed at noon with students from nearby Kitsilano High, where Nat himself went to school. *$; MC, V; no checks; lunch, dinner every day; no alcohol; no reservations; www.natspizza.com; between Stephens and Trafalgar sts (Broadway), at Helmcken St (Denman).*

Nu / ★★★

1661 GRANVILLE ST, VANCOUVER; 604/646-4668
Funky midcentury modern meets *The Jetsons* in this stylish space right on the water, with striking views over False Creek. After settling into your quirky bucket seat (which, unfortunately, won't win any prizes for comfort), graze

your way through wildly creative small plates, perhaps the duck and foie gras croquette or a salad of beets and hazelnut-crusted tuna. Then move on to the heartier caramelized lamb cheeks paired with a refreshing mix of radishes and mint or the crispy braised pork belly. Prices are surprisingly reasonable for the level of innovation in the kitchen. *$$–$$$; AE, MC, V; no checks; lunch, dinner every day, brunch Sat–Sun; full bar; reservations recommended; www. whatisnu.com; at Beach Ave, under Granville Bridge.* &

Ouzeri / ★★

3189 W BROADWAY, VANCOUVER; 604/739-9378

Vancouver has been gripped by small-plates fever, but this lively little Greek restaurant has been serving *mezethes*—dishes to share—long before the idea was trendy. Expect all the usual specialties, from stuffed grape leaves to moussaka to char-grilled lamb chops. Friendly, casual, and reasonably priced, it's especially pleasant in summer when it opens onto the sidewalk and small patio. Ouzeri is located in Kitsilano's Greektown area, where you can also pick up some tasty olives or baklava in the nearby markets and bakeries. *$$; AE, DC, MC, V; no checks; lunch Tues–Sat, dinner every day; full bar; no reservations; www.ouzeri.ca; at Trutch St.* &

Parkside / ★★★

1906 HARO ST, VANCOUVER; 604/683-6912

Whether you're entertaining a client or a special someone, this garden-level West End room, decorated in deep browns and creamy beiges, is a stylishly cozy choice. The food is a mix of innovation and comfort. On the three-course prix-fixe menu ($49), starters might include crisp asparagus wrapped in ham, or scallops paired with lentils and bacon. The Cornish game hen in an earthy wild-mushroom sauce is recommended, as is the roast lamb brightened with preserved lemon. *$$$; MC, V; no checks; dinner every day; full bar; reservations recommended; www.parksiderestaurant.ca; 2 blocks north of Denman St.*

Quattro on Fourth / ★★★☆

2611 W 4TH AVE, VANCOUVER; 604/734-4444

With its crimson walls and glowing wrought-iron chandeliers, this comfortable Italian trattoria radiates romance. You might start with grilled bocconcini wrapped in prosciutto and radicchio, or *ruccola balsamica*, a salad of arugula, duck confit, Asiago, and dried cranberries. Kudos for the grilled beef tenderloin in aged balsamic syrup, the grilled Cornish game hen, and the Spaghetti Quattro ("for Italians only"), a well-seasoned sauce of chicken, chiles, black beans, and plenty of garlic. The Corsi family, who own Quattro, also have restaurants in North Vancouver and Whistler. *$$$–$$$$; AE, DC, MC, V; no checks; dinner every day; full bar; reservations recommended; www. quattrorestaurants.com; at Trafalgar St.* &

Raincity Grill / ★★★

1193 DENMAN ST, VANCOUVER; 604/685-7337
This contemporary West End restaurant dazzles diners with views of English Bay and creative regional cuisine. Up-and-coming chef Andrea Carlson takes "all things local" seriously; she even introduced a "100-mile menu" with all ingredients sourced from within 100 miles. Start with the grilled chipotle-glazed quail or pasta with arugula–pumpkin seed pesto. The grilled duck breast might be paired with a crispy parsnip cake; trout might be marinated in tamari and fried. *$$$; AE, DC, MC, V; no checks; dinner every day, brunch Sat–Sun; full bar; reservations recommended; www.raincitygrill.com; at Davie St.* &

Rare / ★★★

1355 HORNBY ST, VANCOUVER; 604/669-1256
The chefs at this Vancouver newcomer aren't afraid to experiment, and the results, while not always perfect, range from admirable to breathtaking. A puff of truffle foam adds an ethereal yet earthy note to ravioli stuffed with hedgehog mushrooms; meaty boar bacon puts some oomph into a ratatouille that's served with tangy honey-glazed quail. Even the more conventional dishes—beef tenderloin, fresh halibut—are made with first-rate ingredients. *$$$–$$$$; AE, MC, V; no checks; dinner Tues–Sat; full bar; reservations recommended; www.rarevancouver.com; between Pacific and Drake sts.*

Rodney's Oyster House / ★★

1228 HAMILTON ST, VANCOUVER; 604/609-0080
All oysters, all the time—that's the reason to visit this unpretentious fish house and bar. While the slogan here is "The lemon, the oyster, and your lips are all that's required," you can choose one of several sauces instead of taking your oysters straight. Also offered are a choice of creamy chowders, steamed mussels and clams, and local Dungeness crab. There are a few tables upstairs, but the main-floor bar is where the action is. Prices are moderate, especially given its location in trendy Yaletown. *$$–$$$; AE, E, MC, V; no checks; lunch, dinner Mon–Sat; beer, wine, cider, Scotch, and Caesars (Canadian Bloody Marys); no reservations; between Davie and Drake sts.*

Stella's Tap and Tapas Bar / ★

1191 COMMERCIAL DR, VANCOUVER; 604/254-2437
Belgian beer on tap and funky small plates make this upbeat East Side newcomer a welcome addition to Commercial Drive. Like Vancouver itself, Stella's eclectic kitchen looks to Asia for inspiration, from the caramelized pork shoulder in a ginger-cilantro *jus* to the fried tofu glazed with *sambal* and soy, but it still remembers its European roots with caesar salad, *moules frites*, and, of course, its beer. It's the sort of place every neighborhood needs, where you can come by yourself or with the gang, wearing whatever you happen to

have on, to drink and graze. *$–$$; MC, V; no checks; lunch Mon–Fri, dinner every day, brunch Sat–Sun; full bar; no reservations; www.stellasbeer.com; at Napier St.*

Sun Sui Wah Seafood Restaurant / ★★★

3888 MAIN ST, VANCOUVER; 604/872-8822

Simon Chan brought the proven track record and signature dishes of this successful Hong Kong restaurant group to Vancouver, where fans have been savoring its Cantonese masterpieces since the mid-1980s. Recommended dishes include the crispy roasted squab; Alaskan king crab steamed with garlic; scallops on silky bean curd; chicken with broccoli, black mushrooms, and ham; and meaty geoduck clams. Or just ask the staff to suggest whatever seafood and vegetables are freshest. Traditional dim sum, with carts circling the bustling room, is deservedly popular. Sun Sui Wah has another branch in Richmond (4940 No 3 Rd; 604/273-8208). *$$; AE, DC, MC, V; no checks; lunch, dinner every day; full bar; reservations recommended; www.sunsuiwah. com; at E 23rd Ave.* ᵫ

Tojo's / ★★★★

202-777 W BROADWAY, VANCOUVER; 604/872-8050

Hidekazu Tojo is Vancouver's best-known sushi maestro. A loyal clientele fills his spacious upstairs restaurant; most want to sit at the 10-seat sushi bar, sip sake, and order *omakase*: "chef's choice." Tojo-san will create a parade of courses till you cry uncle. Although the *omakase* experience starts at $50 per person and goes up rapidly from there, it's worth putting yourself in Tojo-san's hands if your budget will bear it; he's endlessly innovative. He created the BC roll (barbecued salmon skin, green onions, cucumber, and daikon), now found in almost every Japanese restaurant in Vancouver. *$$$$; AE, DC, JCB, MC, V; no checks; dinner Mon–Sat; full bar; reservations recommended (required for omakase); www.tojos.com; between Heather and Willow sts.* ᵫ

Vij's / ★★★⯪

1480 W 11TH AVE, VANCOUVER; 604/736-6664

Gregarious owner Vikram Vij serves imaginative Indian fare that's as far from run-of-the-mill curries as Vancouver is from his native Mumbai. His signature dish is the lamb "popsicles"—dainty racks of charbroiled lamb in a creamy fenugreek-scented curry. Other items on the seasonally changing menu might include curried peppers and brussels sprouts, pork tenderloin with cauliflower, or a ginger-infused seafood stew. Arrive early, or be prepared to wait an hour or more. If you can't stomach the lines, or if you're dining midday, stop into Rangoli next door, which serves more casual versions of Vij's food for lunch, tea, and upscale takeout. *$$–$$$; AE, DC, MC, V; no checks; dinner every day; beer and wine; no reservations; www.vijs.ca; between Granville and Hemlock sts.* ᵫ

West / ★★★★

2881 GRANVILLE ST, VANCOUVER; 604/738-8938
West has won countless awards for chef David Hawksworth—no small task
in a town teeming with exceptional eateries. The beautifully designed room
with a cherry-wood-and-marble bar has a ceiling-high "wall of wine" with
special refrigeration. The menu might feature lobster salad with fresh hearts
of palm, wild salmon with Dungeness crab and leeks in a pine mushroom
velouté, or pancetta-wrapped rabbit with chorizo-squash ravioli. Go all out
and order one of the stellar tasting menus (there's a vegetarian version, too).
If you can dine before 6pm, the early prix-fixe meal is a great value. *$$$$; AE,
DC, E, MC, V; no checks; lunch Mon–Fri, dinner every day; full bar; reservations recommended; www.westrestaurant.com; at W 13th Ave.* &

Yoshi Japanese Restaurant / ★★

689 DENMAN ST, VANCOUVER; 604/738-8226
If you're craving authentic Japanese, head for this downtown dining room
with a considerate staff and an airy second-floor space near Stanley Park.
There's a huge selection of always-fresh sushi and sashimi, and any of the
grilled dishes from the *robata* are good choices. This is also the place for
classics such as tempura, teriyaki, and soba. If you dine on the pretty patio,
beware of the traffic noise from busy Georgia Street below. Solo diners will
feel welcome at the sushi bar. *$$–$$$; AE, DC, MC, V; no checks; lunch
Mon–Fri, dinner every day; full bar; reservations recommended; www.yoshi
japaneserestaurant.com; at W Georgia St.* &

LODGINGS

The Fairmont Hotel Vancouver / ★★★

**900 W GEORGIA ST, VANCOUVER;
604/684-3131 OR 800/441-1414**
One of the grand chateau-style hotels built by the Canadian Pacific Railway,
this stately hotel downtown dates back to 1887. The 556 spacious rooms
retain their elegance with dark-wood furnishings and comfortable seating
areas (ask for a room high above the street noise). There's a health club with
a lap pool beneath skylights, and on the lower level, the Absolute Spa pampers (try the chocolate body wrap or the rose facial). Unwind over drinks in
the 900 West Lounge, with live jazz every night. *$$$$; AE, DC, E, JCB, MC,
V; checks OK; www.fairmont.com; at Burrard St.* &

The Four Seasons / ★★★★

**791 W GEORGIA ST, VANCOUVER;
604/689-9333 OR 800/819-5053**
Guests are aswim in luxury at this sumptuous hotel in a modern tower connected to the Pacific Centre mall. Despite the city-center location, many
rooms offer appealing downtown views as well as peeks at the harbor. Relax
in the indoor-outdoor pool or the health club, or sip a martini in the soothing

VANCOUVER'S BEST SPAHHHS

Vancouverites love their outdoor activities, but they know how to kick back indoors, too. The **MIRAJ HAMMAM SPA** (1485 W 6th Ave; 604/733-5151; www. mirajhamman.com), an authentic Middle Eastern marble steam bath, features *gommage*, exfoliation performed with black olive soap and North African loofah mitts. The Arabic grooves, tiled fountains, and silk cushions give the spa an exotic, hedonistic feel. **SPA UTOPIA** (999 Canada Pl; 604/641-1351; www.spa utopia.ca), a no-expense-spared megafacility, offers the unique West Coast Seaweed Journey combo massage and wrap, which uses wild kelp to detoxify the skin.

Worth experiencing at the neighborhoody **RAINTREE DAY SPA** (13020 No 2 Rd, Richmond; 604/274-4426; www.raintreedayspa.com) is the Luk Pra Kob, a Thai massage that uses heated compresses filled with lemongrass and camphor to encourage deep muscle relaxation. For a healthy complexion and a shot of hip, head to **SKOAH** (1011 Hamilton St; 604/642-0200; www.skoah.com), a trendy, modern skin-care salon in Yaletown. The chill music and high-design space are in perfect sync with the luxurious-but-no-fuss treatments, such as the signature Facialiscious, a custom facial and hand-foot-neck massage.

For sleek manis, pedis, and waxing in an ultraclean, urban chic environment, head to **PURE NAIL BAR** (2137 W 4th Ave; 604/738-8990; www.purenailbar. com). Relax on the retro white leather couch and watch an episode of *Sex and the City* on the flat-screen TV.

—Audrey D. Brashich

Garden Terrace amid a lush array of ferns and flowers. Kids are welcomed not only with milk and cookies but also their own bathrobes and toys. *$$$$; AE, DC, JCB, MC, V; no checks; www.fourseasons.com; at Howe St.* ♿

Hotel le Soleil / ★★★

567 HORNBY ST, VANCOUVER; 604/632-3000 OR 877/632-3030

It's easy to walk right by the bland facade of this downtown boutique hotel. But inside, the lavish decor demands attention. The high-ceilinged lobby, a study in gilded opulence, features original oil paintings, a grand fireplace, and a cozy sitting area. The 112 guest suites are on the small side, but their layout is efficient, and they're decorated in regal reds and golds. If you grow weary of cocooning, you can use the state-of-the-art YWCA Fitness Centre next door. *$$$$; AE, DC, MC, V; no checks; www.lesoleilhotel.com; between Dunsmuir and Pender sts.*

"O Canada" House / ★★☆

1114 BARCLAY ST, VANCOUVER; 604/688-0555 OR 877/688-1114

This lavishly restored 1897 Victorian home in the West End is where the national anthem, "O Canada," was written in 1909. The front parlor with its welcoming fireplace and large, comfy chairs harkens back to gentler times; sherry is served here in the evenings. A wraparound porch looks out onto the English-style garden. The late-Victorian decor continues into the six guest rooms. The huge Penthouse Suite offers two gabled sitting areas, skylights, and a downtown view. A small separate guest cottage has a gas fireplace and private patio. *$$$; MC, V; no checks; www.ocanadahouse.com; at Thurlow St, 1½ blocks south of Robson St.*

Opus Hotel / ★★★☆

322 DAVIE ST, VANCOUVER; 604/642-6787 OR 866/642-6787

Fun-loving romantics won't want to leave this sexy boutique hotel in Yaletown. Each room is decorated in one of five bold design themes, from "Modern & Minimalist" to "Artful & Eclectic" to "Daring & Dramatic." All rooms feature spa bathrooms with oversize vanities, luxurious European toiletries, and Frette robes, while the penthouse suites boast double-sided fireplaces, plasma-screen TVs, and deep soaker tubs. If you're feeling voyeuristic, request a room overlooking the street; the bathroom has floor-to-ceiling windows and two sets of blinds—one allows you to see out but blocks the view in, and the other gives you complete privacy. *$$$; AE, DC, JCB, MC, V; no checks; www.opushotel.com; at Hamilton St.* &

Pacific Palisades Hotel / ★★

1277 ROBSON ST, VANCOUVER; 604/688-0461 OR 800/663-1815

If you want to be right in the heart of the downtown shopping district, look at this contemporary boutique hotel in two former apartment towers just off busy Robson Street. Not for everyone, the Miami-style rooms are done in eye-popping greens and yellows (except for the suites that mix cool teal with flaming orange). For the best views, request a room above the 10th floor. The large indoor pool and the nightly wine hour in the hotel art gallery are relaxing escapes. *$$$; AE, DC, MC, V; no checks; www.pacificpalisadeshotel. com; at Jervis St.* &

Pan Pacific Hotel / ★★★☆

**300-999 CANADA PL, VANCOUVER;
604/662-8111 OR 800/937-1515 (U.S.)**

No hotel in Vancouver has a more stunning location or architectural presence. The Pan Pacific's five famous giant white sails (which are actually the roof of the adjacent convention center) jut out into Vancouver's inner harbor. Many of the 506 rooms showcase spectacular water and mountain views; rooms are done in soft colors, with down duvets and marble bathrooms. Ask for a corner room (with views from your tub). Drink in the Cascades Lounge with its dramatic wall of windows, or claim a window table in the Five Sails restaurant (604/891-2892; dinner only) overlooking the harbor and North Shore mountains. *$$$$; AE, DC, E, JCB, MC, V; no checks; www.vancouver. panpacific.com; at foot of Burrard St.* ⓧ

The Sutton Place Hotel / ★★★★

845 BURRARD ST, VANCOUVER; 604/682-5511 OR 800/961-7555
When Hollywood stars show up in Vancouver, this residential-style hotel is often where they stay. With its plush interior, Sutton Place would rank as a top hotel in any European capital. Each of the 397 soundproof rooms and suites has all the amenities one could want. The beds are king-sized; the furnishings are quality reproductions of European antiques. The bellhops snap to attention when you arrive. The Fleuri restaurant (604/642-2900; breakfast, lunch, dinner) serves elegant meals, a civilized afternoon tea, and a decadent chocolate buffet. *$$$$; AE, DC, DIS, E, JCB, MC, V; no checks; www.suttonplace. com; between Robson and Smithe sts.* ⓧ

Sylvia Hotel / ★

1154 GILFORD ST, VANCOUVER; 604/681-9321
In such an ideal location opposite English Bay Beach, it may not matter that the 120 rooms in this ivy-covered brick landmark are simple and unadorned. You might feel as though you're staying with a favorite aunt in her slightly shabby but comfortable apartment house; in fact, it was built as an apartment building in 1912. If you don't need anything elaborate, it's reasonably priced, so book well in advance. Legend has it that Vancouver's first cocktail bar opened here in 1954, and you can still enjoy a predinner drink while watching the sun set. *$$; AE, DC, MC, V; checks OK; www.sylviahotel.com; at Beach Ave.*

Victorian Hotel / ★

514 HOMER ST, VANCOUVER; 604/681-6369 OR 877/681-6369
You get plenty of character for your money at this friendly 40-room inn in a restored 1898 building between downtown and Gastown. It's not fancy, but all the rooms have wood floors, puffy duvets, and high ceilings. The best are the "deluxe" rooms on the second floor, which are furnished with a brass or sleigh bed and a handful of antiques; rooms 205, 206, and 207 have peekaboo mountain views. Even the 20 inexpensive shared-bath rooms are comfortable (ask for one with a bay window). A continental breakfast is served in the small but graceful lobby. *$$; DIS, MC, V; no checks; www.victorianhotel. ca; between W Pender and Dunsmuir sts.*

The Wedgewood Hotel / ★★★

845 HORNBY ST, VANCOUVER; 604/689-7777 OR 800/663-0666
From its ideal downtown location just off Robson Street to its renowned Bacchus Restaurant (see review), this 80-room hotel is all that a small urban luxury hotel should be—and then some. The finely appointed rooms—surprisingly large and decorated with vibrant colors and English antiques—have

the feel of a grand home, full of old-world charm. Though views are lost to taller buildings in the neighborhood, this is the place to spend your honeymoon—and many do. *$$$; AE, DC, DIS, E, JCB, MC, V; no checks; www. wedgewoodhotel.com; between Robson and Smithe sts.* &

West End Guest House / ★★

1362 HARO ST, VANCOUVER; 604/681-2889 OR 888/546-3327
Don't be put off by the blazing-pink exterior of this 1906 Victorian home. Owner Evan Penner runs a fine eight-room B and B. Rooms are generally small but well furnished; all have feather beds; and there are antiques—as well as wireless Internet—throughout the house. Sherry or iced tea is offered on the deck overlooking the verdant garden or in the parlor, and breakfast is a three-course affair. Penner also rents a two-bedroom suite next door—a better choice for families with children than the main inn. *$$$; AE, DIS, MC, V; no checks; www.westendguesthouse.com; at Broughton St, 1 block off Robson St.*

YWCA Hotel / ★

733 BEATTY ST, VANCOUVER; 604/895-5830 OR 800/663-1424
If you expect the Y to be a dreary rooming house, think again. Vancouver's modern YWCA is a comfortable, family-friendly downtown hotel, close to the theaters, sports arenas, and library. The no-frills rooms, while small, are functional, with minifridges and sinks; baths are private, semiprivate, or down the hall. While there are few amenities (no tissues, clocks, or coffee makers here), there are kitchen and laundry facilities, and if your room feels cramped, you can stretch out in one of the communal lounges. Guests get free passes to the YWCA Fitness Centre, 10 blocks away (535 Hornby St). *$; AE, MC, V; checks OK only for deposit; www.ywcahotel.com; between Georgia and Robson sts.* &

Around Vancouver

Richmond

This Vancouver suburb south of the city, where the airport is located, is becoming known as "Asia West." Richmond has developed a food and shopping scene to cater to its significant Asian population, including many well-to-do immigrants from Hong Kong and Taiwan. The city houses an increasing number of outstanding Chinese restaurants as well as several postmodern shopping complexes where Asian pop culture meets the western strip mall. You'll find convincing iterations of life in Tokyo at **YAOHAN CENTRE** (3700 No 3 Rd; 604/231-0601), in Taipei at **PRESIDENT PLAZA** (3320-8181 Cambie Rd; 604/270-8677), or in Hong Kong at **ABERDEEN CENTRE** (4151 Hazelbridge Way; 604/273-1234) and at **PARKER PLACE MALL** (4380 No 3 Rd; 604/273-0276). From Taipei tank tops to calligraphy of Shanghai, to Hong Kong–style steamed buns, the wares of Asia are on sale. Bargain hunters could spend hours in the **DAISO** store (Aberdeen Centre; 604/295-6601), the North America flagship of a Japanese megachain, where every product sells for $2.

In the summer, join the crowds at the **RICHMOND NIGHT MARKET** (12631 Vulcan Way; 604/244-8448; www.richmondnightmarket.com; open Fri–Sat 7pm–midnight, Sun 7–11pm, mid-May–Sept), and you might think you've stumbled into a market in China. Its food stalls sell everything from fiery noodles to stinky tofu, and its vendors offer T-shirts, socks, acupressure massage, whiz-bang vacuum cleaners, and pretty much anything else you can imagine. Bargaining is de rigueur. To get here, take Bridgeport Road to Sweden Way, past the Home Depot.

The Richmond village of **STEVESTON** on the south edge of town showcases a different culture. This former fishing community is home to the **GULF OF GEORGIA CANNERY** (12138 4th Ave; 604/664-9009; www.pc.gc.ca/lhn-nhs/bc/georgia), a national historic site. You can explore the life of the cannery workers by trying your hand on the packing line and learn more about the area's fishing industry and marine life. Afterward, pick up fish-and-chips to go from one of the nearby shops and stroll along the riverfront boardwalk.

RESTAURANTS

Shiang Garden / ★★

2200-4540 NO 3 RD, RICHMOND; 604/273-8858
No visit to Richmond is complete without a stop for dim sum, and this Hong Kong–style seafood palace serves some of the best. It's unlikely you'd stumble on it, set back from No. 3 Road amid rows of strip malls, but it's worth seeking out. There are no carts of buns or dumplings in these ornate, high-ceilinged dining rooms; order off the menu (or point at whatever looks good at the neighboring tables), and the staff will whisk your selection from the kitchen piping hot. Although they serve commendable Cantonese fare in the evenings, dim sum is the star here. *$$; AE, MC, V; no checks; lunch, dinner every day; full bar; no reservations; at Leslie Rd.* &

LODGINGS

Fairmont Vancouver Airport / ★★★

3111 GRANT MCCONACHIE WAY, VANCOUVER INTERNATIONAL AIRPORT, RICHMOND; 604/207-5200 OR 800/676-8922
While most airport hotels simply cater to harried business travelers, this technologically advanced lodging is an oasis of tranquility. A lobby waterfall and soundproof glass on all floors eliminate outside noise. The room heat turns on when you check in; lights turn on when you insert your key and turn off when you leave; illuminating the "do not disturb" sign routes calls to voice mail. Even if you're not a guest, you can while away preboarding time by the large fireplaces, at the bar, or in the work-out facilities, or you can dine in the contemporary Globe@YVR (604/207-5200; breakfast, lunch, dinner), which emphasizes regional products. *$$$$; AE, DC, E, MC, V; checks OK; www. fairmont.com; on departure level of airport.*

North and West Vancouver

A trip to Vancouver isn't complete without a closer look at the natural setting that makes it such a beautiful city. As you head to North or West Vancouver, the ride across Lions Gate Bridge makes for picture-postcard views of the North Shore, Stanley Park, and Burrard Inlet.

In West Vancouver, **LIGHTHOUSE PARK** (Marine Dr; 604/925-7200) is a pleasant place for a rain-forest stroll and stellar city views. Skiers and 'boarders take to the slopes on **CYPRESS MOUNTAIN** (Cypress Bowl Rd, Cypress Provincial Park, exit 8 off Hwy 1; 604/926-5612; www.cypressmountain.com), the largest of the North Shore peaks. West Vancouver is also home to Canada's first shopping mall, the sprawling **PARK ROYAL** complex (Marine Dr at Taylor Way; 604/922-3211).

In North Vancouver, on the way up Capilano Road is Capilano Regional Park, home to a fish hatchery, the huge Cleveland Dam, and the 450-foot (137-m) **CAPILANO SUSPENSION BRIDGE** (3735 Capilano Rd; 604/985-7474; www.capbridge.com), a dizzying span across the most picturesque canyon inside any major city. Farther up the road, you can make the 3,600-foot (1,100-m) ascent of **GROUSE MOUNTAIN** aboard the Skyride gondola (604/984-0661; www.grousemountain.com) to ski, mountain bike, or simply take in the views. Another route to the top is the challenging 1.8-mile (2.9-km) **GROUSE GRIND** hiking trail that gains 2,880 feet (880 m) in elevation. Either way, at the top on a clear day you'll enjoy a superb vista of Vancouver and the Lower Mainland. You can have a meal or a drink in the casual **ALTITUDES BISTRO** (604/984-0661).

Back closer to sea level, the public market at **LONSDALE QUAY** (123 Carrie Cates Ct; 604/985-6261; www.lonsdalequay.com), adjacent to the SeaBus terminal, has two levels of shops and produce stands, selling everything from crafts to smoked salmon, chowder, and smoothies.

A large Iranian population has settled in North Vancouver, as the many **IRANIAN MARKETS**, bakeries, and restaurants attest. Inside the **YAAS BAZAAR** (1860 Lonsdale Ave, at 19th Ave; 604/990-9006), a small grocery selling nuts, spices, produce, and breads, a no-frills lunch counter serves excellent and inexpensive kebab plates. Walk down the street to the **GOLESTAN BAKERY** (1554 Lonsdale Ave; 604/990-7767) to pick up some bite-size baklava or other Persian pastries.

If you're still looking for something sweet, seek out the **THOMAS HAAS PÂTIS-SERIE** (128-998 Harbourside Dr; 604/924-1847), where this noted pastry chef (see Diva at the Met review) offers elegantly crafted chocolates, pastries, and cookies in a tiny shop adjacent to his factory. From Marine Drive, drive south on Fell Avenue and turn right onto Harbourside Drive into an industrial park. The patisserie is on the right at the end of the road.

RESTAURANTS

Gusto di Quattro / ★★☆

I LONSDALE AVE, NORTH VANCOUVER; 604/924-4444
A meal at Gusto makes a great excuse for a minicruise across the harbor on the SeaBus. At lunch, choices range from salads or grilled sandwiches to pan-seared salmon with caramelized onions. In the evening, start with the generous antipasto platter. Among the more intriguing pastas are *spaghetti neri al pesce*—black spaghetti with black cod and pea sprouts—and *fusilli anacapra*, with duck confit, olives, tomatoes, and goat cheese. The pistachio-crusted cod in a roasted-pepper sauce is recommended, as is the fresh halibut or the lamb chops. *$$–$$$; AE, DC, MC, V; no checks; lunch Mon–Fri, dinner every day; full bar; reservations recommended; www.quattrorestaurants.com; across from Lonsdale Quay Market.* &

La Régalade / ★★☆

2232 MARINE DR, WEST VANCOUVER; 604/921-2228
This bistro is as near to France as you can get—at least this side of the Lions Gate Bridge—from the rustic French cuisine to the homey decor, to the chalkboard menus. Not to be missed: the escargots, with plenty of garlic butter, and the *terrine maison*—thick slices of country-style pâté with cornichons. Slow-food aficionados will appreciate the beef bourguignon or other simmering stews that generally comprise several of the daily specials. Finish with the exceptional cheese selection or one of the classic desserts. *$$$; MC, V; no checks; lunch Tues–Fri, dinner Tues–Sat; full bar; reservations recommended; www.laregalade.com; at 22nd St.*

LODGINGS

Thistledown House / ★★★

3910 CAPILANO RD, NORTH VANCOUVER; 604/986-7173 OR 888/633-7173
Set amid a half acre of lush gardens, this white 1920 Craftsman-style home is a luxuriously furnished escape. In the six guest rooms, antiques and period pieces intermingle with eclectic international art. The romantic Under the Apple Tree has a two-person jetted tub and a private patio, while Pages, in the former library, would please more tailored tastes (and bibliophiles). The sumptuous multicourse breakfast might include homemade granola, breads and jams, nectarines in red wine, and a hearty dish such as pork on puff pastry. Genial owners Rex Davidson and Ruth Crameri also offer afternoon tea by the fireplace or on the porch. *$$$; AE, DC, E, MC, V; no checks; closed mid-Dec–Jan; www.thistle-down.com; north of Capilano Suspension Bridge.*

LOWER MAINLAND
BRITISH COLUMBIA

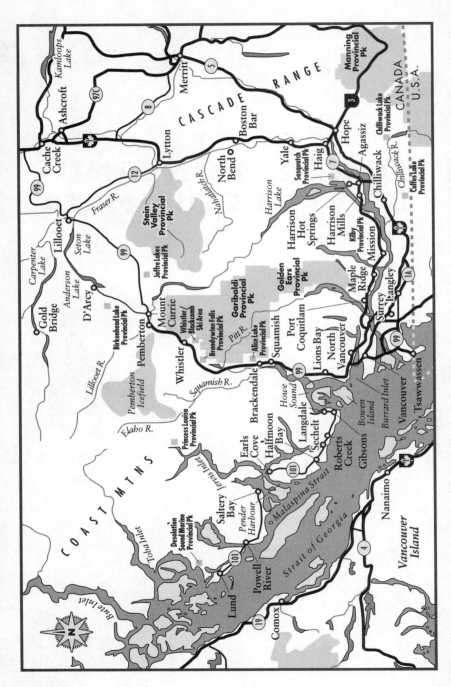

LOWER MAINLAND
BRITISH COLUMBIA

The entire Lower Mainland region has become a metropolitan area in which residents can, and do, live and work throughout, commuting to Vancouver from as far as Abbotsford, Bowen Island, and Squamish. Despite its transformation into a megalopolis, the Lower Mainland holds much for travelers, aside from the obvious appeal of Whistler. The eastern end of the lower Fraser Valley is an agricultural paradise. The Sunshine Coast offers a bevy of charming inns. Squamish has become a world-renowned recreation center. The entire Lower Mainland region has become a metropolitan area in which residents can, and do, live and work throughout, commuting to Vancouver from as far as Abbotsford, Bowen Island, and Squamish. Despite its transformation into a megalopolis, the Lower Mainland holds much for travelers, aside from the obvious appeal of Whistler. The eastern end of the lower Fraser Valley is an agricultural paradise. The Sunshine Coast offers a bevy of charming inns. Squamish has become a world-renowned recreation center.

ACCESS AND INFORMATION

Border crossings link Washington State and the Lower Mainland at four locations. The busiest are the crossings at Blaine, Washington, where Interstate 5 turns into Highway 99 at the Peace Arch, and at Douglas, linking with British Columbia's Highway 15. The others are located just south of Aldergrove and at Sumas just south of Abbotsford. (The latter is the "secret" crossing seasoned travelers use for access to interior British Columbia and much of the lower Fraser Valley.) The nearest major airport is **VANCOUVER INTERNATIONAL AIRPORT** (3211 Grant McConachie Way, Richmond; 604/207-7077; www.yvr.ca). Many Americans fly into Seattle-Tacoma International Airport and rent a car for the journey into British Columbia; it's about three hours from Sea-Tac to the U.S.-Canadian border.

HIGHWAY 1 (the Trans-Canada Highway) runs east-west and links the south Fraser Valley with Vancouver. **HIGHWAY 17** links **BC FERRIES** (www.bcferries.com) Tsawwassen terminal with **HIGHWAY 99**. The North Shore is reached by traveling west on Highway 1 across the Ironworkers Memorial Second Narrows Bridge, or via the Lions Gate Bridge from downtown Vancouver on Highway 99A. **HIGHWAY 1/99A** (or the Upper Levels Highway, as it is called on the North Shore) crosses North and West Vancouver to Horseshoe Bay, site of the BC Ferries terminal connecting the North Shore with Nanaimo on southern Vancouver Island, Langdale (and Highway 101) on the Sunshine Coast, and nearby Bowen Island. From Horseshoe Bay, Highway 99 (the Sea to Sky Highway) links the North Shore with Squamish, Whistler, Pemberton, and Lillooet. Travelers on Highway 99 should be aware that intensive upgrading of the road is readying it for the 2010 Winter Olympics—delays are common, and shutdowns occasionally take place.

WATCHING EAGLES SOAR

Even though bald eagles are the United States' national symbol, they are more common in British Columbia than anywhere else except Alaska; in both places the birds were never endangered as they were in the Lower 48 states. These majestic raptors are an iconic Pacific Northwest sight, soaring high in thermals over waters or forests. Each winter they migrate to congregate along lowland rivers that have late salmon runs, one of which is the Squamish River along the Sea-to-Sky Highway. (The other is the Skagit River in Washington State.)

Every year hundreds, and sometimes more than 1,000, eagles come to roost in the tall cottonwoods that line the Squamish in the Brackendale area. And as wildlife watching has grown, thousands of humans congregate in Brackendale to watch. The phenomenon led to creation of the **BRACKENDALE BALD EAGLE SANCTUARY** in 1996, which protects the habitat and imposes rules.

Peak viewing is December through February, when visitors can sometimes spot dozens of birds in the trees. Patient observation often rewards with the sight of a

The **VANCOUVER, COAST & MOUNTAINS TOURISM REGION** (250-1508 W 2nd Ave, Vancouver; 604/739-9011 or 888/430-3339; www.vcmbc.com) is a font of information.

Sea to Sky Highway (Highway 99)

The scenic Sea to Sky Highway crosses paths with two historic routes—the Pemberton Trail and the Gold Rush Trail—that linked the coast with the interior before there were cars.

Now vehicles can cover the entire 142-mile (236-km) Sea to Sky route between Horseshoe Bay and Lillooet in about five hours, making the transit from downtown Vancouver to Whistler in three hours.

Be alert to construction between Horseshoe Bay and Whistler as the region readies for the 2010 Winter Olympics, with frequent delays and occasional shutdowns (usually at night) on the Sea to Sky Highway.

ACCESS AND INFORMATION

GREYHOUND CANADA (604/482-8747 in Vancouver, 604/898-3914 in Squamish, 604/932-6236 in Whistler; www.greyhound.ca) offers frequent daily service between Vancouver, Squamish, Whistler, Pemberton, and Mount Currie. **WHISTLER AIR** (604/932-6615; www.whistlerair.ca; June–Sept) offers floatplane service between Vancouver and Whistler.

bird feasting on a spawned-out salmon that has washed up on a gravel bar. Best viewing is in early morning, before crowds gather, which often drives the birds to more distant trees.

The **BRACKENDALE ART GALLERY** (604-898-3333; www.brackendaleartgallery. com) has created a January festival and bird count to honor the phenomenon and offers guided walks to observe. **SUNWOLF OUTDOOR CENTRE** (www.sunwolf. net) and **CANADIAN OUTBACK ADVENTURES** (www.canadianoutback.com) offer guided float trips to watch. Bring warm waterproof clothing and binoculars—and please observe the eagle-protection code: Be quiet, don't try to get too near the birds, and don't ever land on a gravel bar where an eagle is feeding.

It's a wildlife spectacle rarely matched, an opportunity to experience the renewal of a timeless natural cycle. As the salmon give birth to a new generation and die, they enable the eagles to survive the rigors of winter and carry their kind on into generations beyond.

—Eric P. Lucas

Squamish

Squamish (population 14,250), or "Squish," as it is playfully known, is far smaller than Vancouver and much funkier than Whistler. Located between water and mountains, Squamish is a gateway to outdoor pursuits. It has so many things going for it—location, geography, wildlife, weather—that as the forest industry declines as the town's major employer, tourism and recreation have assumed almost equal importance. Not surprisingly, the town crowned itself the outdoor recreation capital of Canada in 2002.

Not all is 21st-century recreation here, though: right along Highway 99, 5 miles (8 km) south of Squamish proper, is the **BC MUSEUM OF MINING** (Hwy 99, Britannia Beach; 800-896-4044; www.bcmuseumofmining.com; May–Oct), which occupies what was once the world's largest copper mine. For area information, contact the **SQUAMISH CHAMBER OF COMMERCE AND VISITOR INFO CENTRE** (37950 Cleveland Ave, Squamish; 604/892-9244; www.squamish chamber.bc.ca).

RESTAURANTS

Red Heather Grill & Brew Pub / ★★

37801 CLEVELAND AVE (HOWE SOUND INN), SQUAMISH; 604/892-2603 OR 800/919-2537

Whether you put your feet up in the pub or spiff up for a meal in the Red Heather Grill (Squamish's most upscale dining room), the same creative kitchen comes up with the food for both. The grill's decor matches the indoor-outdoor feel of the inn, minus the sports on the pub's televisions. Pull up a chair to a wooden table, or settle in on a couch beside the fireplace. You can't go wrong with seafood specials such as skewers of sweet Thai ahi tuna. *$$; AE, MC, V; no checks; breakfast, lunch, dinner every day, brunch Sat–Sun; full bar; reservations recommended; www.howesound.com; downtown.* &

LODGINGS

Howe Sound Inn & Brewing Company / ★

37801 CLEVELAND AVE, SQUAMISH; 604/892-2603 OR 800/919-2537
This 20-room inn with a massive chimney (the exterior of which doubles as a climbing wall) is part pub, part restaurant, part hotel. Owner Dave Fenn fashioned his gathering place with outdoor enthusiasts in mind. Take in mountain views and stay in rooms 13 to 20, on the quiet side of the inn not above the pub. Rooms are compact. *$$; AE, MC, V; no checks; www.howe sound.com; downtown.* &

SunWolf Outdoor Centre / ★

70002 SQUAMISH VALLEY RD, BRACKENDALE;
604/898-1537 OR 877/806-8046
SunWolf's 10 cabins sit at the confluence of two rivers. The 5½-acre center makes an ideal base for exploring. Each of the cabins (some with kitchenettes) comes with a fireplace, fir floors, pine furnishings, and both a double and a single bed. Get light meals from the the café before white-water rafting and eagle-viewing float trips, two specialties here. *$$; MC, V; checks OK; www. sunwolf.net; 2½ miles (4 km) west of Hwy 99.*

Whistler

Oh, how things have changed in Whistler—and more change is to come as the town gears up for the 2010 Winter Olympics. What was once a quirky half-hippie, half-family ski area has transformed into one of the highest-profile resort towns on earth. Regularly ranked near the top in global popularity, Whistler draws the glitz-and-glamour crowd in droves, their members competing with hard-core boarders mindful of the mountain's extravagant statistics: 1 mile (1.6 km) of vertical, huge experts-only bowls and glaciers, and skiing well into summer.

The Resort Municipality of Whistler (population 8,900) nestles in a narrow valley below Blackcomb and Whistler mountains. No other valley in the Sea to Sky region enjoys such a wealth of small and medium-sized lakes. Remnants of the most recent ice age persist in glaciers on the highest peaks in **GARIBALDI PARK** (www.env.gov.bc.ca/bcparks), to the south of Whistler. Above all, no other **SKI AREA** offers quite what Whistler does: two massive gondola-served mountains (see below), reliable snow, and an almost-eternal season, with midsummer skiing on **BLACKCOMB GLACIER**. This resort, where the average house price now tops $1 million, is expensive, but you can generally count on outstanding value in return.

The town of Whistler consists of neighborhoods linked to the hotels and restaurants in the village core by roads and the pedestrian-friendly Valley Trail (see below). Hop on one of the Whistler and Valley Express—**WAVE** buses (604/932-4020; www.busonline.ca), which connect with all Whistler neighborhoods, from Function Junction to Emerald Estates, as well as the nearby towns of Pemberton and Mount Currie. WAVE operates a free village shuttle with stops at Whistler Village, Village North, Upper Village, and the Benchlands. All buses are equipped with racks for skis and snowboards in winter and bikes in summer.

WHISTLER MOUNTAIN, elevation 7,160 feet (2,182 m), and **BLACKCOMB MOUNTAIN**, elevation 7,494 feet (2,284 m), were rivals for two decades before merging under the Intrawest corporate umbrella in 1997, an event that fans of Whistler, the older mountain, viewed with some trepidation but have since accepted. You can just as easily explore one as the other; each offers a complementary perspective on its companion and has a loyal following. Whistler is usually considered the more family-friendly mountain; Blackcomb, the locale for experts, boarders, and serious skiers. Either is reached from the Whistler Village base—**GONDOLAS** that each depart just yards from each other—and Intrawest is proposing a mind-boggling peak-to-peak gondola that will link the upper areas of the two mountains.

Whistler and Blackcomb have developed trails covering more than 8,100 acres, and these trails have been shaped to hold snow in winter and provide downhill cycling in summer in **WHISTLER MOUNTAIN BIKE PARK**. For information, contact **WHISTLER-BLACKCOMB GUEST RELATIONS** (604/932-3434 or 800/766-0449; www.whistler-blackcomb.com).

Whistler Village's **LOST LAKE PARK** (604/905-0071; www.crosscountry connection.bc.ca) features a 20-mile (32-km) network of packed and tracked trails for **CROSS-COUNTRY SKIERS**, snowshoers, and, in summer, mountain bikers. Skiing around the lake takes 60–90 minutes. Trails are marked for beginners to experts; the 2-mile (4-km) **LOST LAKE LOOP TRAIL** is lit for night skiing. A designated cross-country ski trail in winter and a hiking, cycling, and in-line skating loop in summer, the 12-mile (20-km) **VALLEY TRAIL**'s access points include the Whistler Golf Course on Highway 99 in Whistler Village, the Meadow Park Sports Centre on Highway 99 in Alpine Meadows, and Rainbow Park on Alta Lake Road.

Snowmobiling is big at Whistler: **CANADIAN SNOWMOBILE ADVENTURES** (604/938-1616; www.canadiansnowmobile.com) and **COUGAR MOUNTAIN WILDERNESS ADVENTURES** (36-4314 Main St; 604/932-4086; www.cougarmountain.ca), which also offers dogsledding, horseback riding, snowshoeing, fishing, and mountain bike tours.

Heli-skiing or boarding at Whistler can be arranged with **WHISTLER HELI-SKIING** (3-4241 Village Stroll; 604/932-4105; www.whistlerheliskiing.com), **COAST RANGE HELISKIING** (604/894-1144 or 800/701-8744; www.coastrange-heliskiing.com), and **BLACKCOMB HELICOPTERS** (9990 Heliport; 604/938-1700; www.blackcombhelicopters.com).

WHISTLER THREE-DAY TOUR

DAY ONE: Check in to the **WESTIN WHISTLER**, just a three-minute walk from the gondola base in Whistler Village. Get a hearty breakfast at **CHEF BERNARD'S CIAO-THYME BISTRO**, then grab your gear from the ski valet and head to **WHISTLER-BLACKCOMB GUEST RELATIONS**, the all-encompassing ticket and information source for the two mountains; a three-day pass is the best bargain. Hop on the **WHISTLER VILLAGE GONDOLA** to ride to the top, warming up with a run or two down the slopes under the Emerald Express quad chair. Then hop the Peak Chair for its mind-boggling ride up over the cliffs of **WHISTLER MOUNTAIN** to the area's pinnacle at 7,160 feet (2,182 m). Stop to admire the view of the Coast Range, then glide down to the Saddle to ski through this gap that was blasted in the rock to open up the vast bowl for intermediate skiers. Head on down to the **CHIC PEA** for lunch, then all the way down to the bottom to get on the **EXCALIBUR GONDOLA** to whisk you up **BLACKCOMB MOUNTAIN**. Spend the afternoon exploring the vast intermediate terrain in 7th Heaven or the experts-only mecca on the **BLACKCOMB GLACIER**. After a rest in your room, walk five minutes to dinner at **BEARFOOT BISTRO**.

DAY TWO: Have breakfast and coffee at **MOGULS BAKERY** (4202 Village Square; 604/932-4845), then head back up to the top of **WHISTLER**

Some of the most inviting snowshoe trails in Whistler are those in the forest surrounding Olympic Station on Whistler Mountain. **OUTDOOR ADVENTURES AT WHISTLER** (4205 Village Square; 604/932-0647; www.adventureswhistler.com) offers rentals and guided tours, including evening outings on Blackcomb.

For summer visitors, golf choices include the scenic Arnold Palmer–designed **WHISTLER GOLF CLUB** (4001 Whistler Way; 604/932-3280) and the equally esteemed Robert Trent Jones Jr. **LINK COURSE** at Chateau Whistler (4599 Chateau Blvd; 604/938-2092). There is also **NICKLAUS NORTH** (8080 Nicklaus N Blvd; 604/938-9898), a Jack Nicklaus–designed course in the Green Lake area.

Tourism Whistler's **ACTIVITY AND INFORMATION CENTRE** (4010 Whistler Way; 604/932-2394) offers advice. With more than 2 million ski visits alone each winter, advance reservations are recommended for all lodging and restaurants. Many rooms in the area, as well as condos, are owned by individuals and investment companies but managed by rental combines or the hotel operator whose buildings they occupy. All may be reached through Tourism Whistler's **CENTRAL RESERVATIONS** (800/944-7853; www.tourismwhistler.com). For a complete listing of activities, consult **TOURISM WHISTLER** (4010 Whistler Way; 604/932-3928 in Whistler, 604/664-5625 in Vancouver, or 800/944-7853; www.mywhistler.com). The newly renovated **WHISTLER VISITOR INFO CENTRE** (2097 Lake Placid

MOUNTAIN to spend the morning skiing the wide expanses of the Flute Bowl. Head back down for lunch at **AUNTIE EM'S** (129 Lorimer Rd; 604/932-1163), a great soup-and-sandwich place. Then it's back over to the **EXCALIBUR GON-DOLA**, this time for a short ride up to the Tube Park. Spend a few hours with a gaggle of delirious parents and kids bombing down the tube runs—when the attendants at the top of the hill ask how fast you want to go, say "as fast as you can." Don't forget to ask them for a spin run. In the evening, put on your go-to-dinner clothes and reserve a table at **ARAXI RESTAURANT & BAR**, one of the best restaurants in British Columbia.

DAY THREE: Start with coffee and muffins at **HOT BUNS** (4324 Sunrise Alley; 604/932-6883), then hike over to **CROSS-COUNTRY CONNECTION** to pick up Nordic equipment for a 5-K jaunt along the **VALLEY TRAIL**. Then hop a shuttle to Green Lake for a few hours of skating on this 3-mile (4.8-km) "rink" where residents carve out hockey layouts. Back at Whistler Village, have a late lunch at **SUSHI VILLAGE**, then head back up the gondola for one last run from the peak. Afterward, for a change of pace, check in to the **ADARA HOTEL** and stroll through the village for window shopping. Have burgers-as-you-like at **SPLITZ GRILL**, then cap off your Whistler visit with homemade ice cream at **LA RÚA RESTAURANTE**. If you want to extend your ski vacation, add on two days in the pristine wilderness at **CALLAGHAN LODGE** in an alpine valley southwest of Whistler.

Rd, Whistler Conference Centre; 604/932-5528) is great. Three information kiosks are open in the summer: **VILLAGE BOOTH** (at Greyhound Bus Loop), the **VILLAGE KIOSK** (in Village Square), and the **NORTH KIOSK BY THE GAZEBO** (in Village North).

RESTAURANTS

Araxi Restaurant & Bar / ★★★★

4121 VILLAGE GREEN (LISTEL WHISTLER HOTEL), WHISTLER; 604/932-3433

Whistler's culinary cornerstone anchors the Village Square's patio scene. The restaurant's glittering ambience can be experienced either at the mahogany-topped bar or at one of the white-linen tables in the main dining room. With its emphasis on fresh, locally sourced fare prepared with French and Italian influences, Araxi's menu—just like its artwork—undergoes a complete make-over every six months. $$$; AE, DC, MC, V; no checks; lunch every day May–Dec, dinner every day; full bar; reservations required; www.araxi.com. &

Bearfoot Bistro / ★★★★

4314 MAIN ST (BEAR LODGE), WHISTLER; 604/932-4666
Though Bearfoot hews to the catalog of Pacific fish and hearty meat dishes that are so prevalent in Whistler, execution and imagination of these distinguish this fairly inconspicuous restaurant that some critics have called one of the best in the world—yes, the world. Diners select three courses for the nightly prix fixe of $90 or choose the chef's daily five-course menu. Add in the sommelier's five-course wine pairing, and you're looking at a $225 tab. Yes, those are breathtaking prices, but the result is worth it. Stuffed silly, many diners repair to Bearfoot's cigar bar after dinner, one of the few indoor smoking venues in the province. *$$$$; AE, DC, MC, V; no checks; lunch, dinner every day; full bar; reservations required; www.bearfootbistro.com; 1 block from Village Square.* &

Caramba! / ★★

4314 MAIN ST (EAGLE LODGE), WHISTLER; 604/938-1879
Caramba! proves dining out in Whistler doesn't have to break the bank. This fun, boisterous, Mediterranean-influenced restaurant holds down a corner of the Town Plaza on one of Village North's busiest walkways. High-energy service twins with big, soul-satisfying portions of pasta, pizza, and roasts. The open kitchen, zinc countertops, alder-fired pizza ovens, and sizzling rotisseries lend a warm, casual tone to the room. *$; AE, MC, V; no checks; lunch every day (in season), dinner every day; full bar; reservations recommended; www.caramba-restaurante.com; at Town Plaza Square.* &

Hoz's Pub / ★★
El Tipo's Mexican Grill / ★★

2129 LAKE PLACID RD, WHISTLER; 604/932-4424
Good, basic fare in a down-to-earth atmosphere can be elusive in Whistler, but this local favorite fits the bill. There's deluxe burgers, pasta, barbecued chicken, ribs, and big beef bones, plus cod or salmon fish-and-chips. Owner Ron "Hoz" Hosner, a fixture in the Creekside neighborhood, pursues his culinary passion in an adjacent room, the new 45-seat El Tipo's ("The Dude's") Mexican Grill. Hoz, sporting his trademark desperado mustache, surveys the crowd as he preps the Mexican dishes of his youth. *$; AE, DC, MC, V; no checks; breakfast, lunch, dinner every day; full bar; no reservations; www.hozspub.com; 1 block west of Hwy 99.*

La Rúa Restaurante / ★★★★

4557 BLACKCOMB WAY (LE CHAMOIS), WHISTLER; 604/932-5011
Longtime Whistler restaurateur Mario Enero's stylish restaurant is tucked away in Le Chamois hotel, one of Whistler's snazziest lodgings. Superb dishes created by R. D. Stewart, one of Whistler's top-ranked chefs, are served in portions that will satisfy the most ravenous. Though the menu has been simplified a bit, the basics remain the same: highly flavored presentations

of regional foods with a slight Mediterranean tinge. Start with a pyramid of bocconcini cheese or ravioli and scallops. No one prepares lamb better. *$$$; AE, DC, MC, V; no checks; dinner every day; full bar; reservations recommended; www.larua-restaurante.com; Upper Village, at Lorimer Rd.* &

Quattro at Whistler / ★★★

4319 MAIN ST (PINNACLE INTERNATIONAL HOTEL), WHISTLER; 604/905-4844

Quattro is upbeat, vibrant, and innovative. *La cucina leggera,* or "the healthy kitchen," is the motto here. Fungi fanciers love the carpaccio featuring sliced portobello mushrooms. Kudos also for the grilled scallops and prawns, served with a Dungeness crab risotto inside a phyllo roll. Pasta dishes are equally inspired. Portions are generous, and desserts are stunning. *$$$; MC, V; no checks; dinner every day (closed mid-Oct–mid-Nov); full bar; reservations recommended; www.quattrorestaurants.com; Village North, at Library Square.* &

Rim Rock Cafe and Oyster Bar / ★★★

2117 WHISTLER RD (HIGHLAND LODGE), WHISTLER; 604/932-5565 OR 877/932-5589

Manager Bob Dawson and chef Rolf Gunther dish out great food in their cozy, woody café with its centerpiece stone fireplace, and it's filled to the open rafters with locals (who consistently rate this Creekside cornerstone, little known to tourists, as their favorite). A daily fresh sheet features fish and game. Along with the café's reputation for superb seafood, the service here is ranked the best in town. *$$$; AE, MC, V; no checks; dinner every day (closed mid-Oct–mid-Nov); full bar; reservations recommended; www.rimrock whistler.com; 2 miles (3.5 km) south of Whistler Village.*

Splitz Grill / ★

4369 MAIN ST (ALPENGLOW), WHISTLER; 604/938-9300

It's been a long time since a hamburger has been this thick, juicy, and tantalizing. Small wonder Splitz tops the polls as Whistler's best burger joint. Burgers on crusty buns are elevated to new heights with your choice of umpteen toppings, such as lamb with *tzatziki.* A meal is less than $10, half that for kids, whose selections come with house-cut fries and a soft drink. Sweet temptations include a caramelized banana split. *$; V; no checks; lunch, dinner every day; beer and wine; no reservations; Village North, across from 7-Eleven.*

Sushi Village / ★★

4272 MOUNTAIN SQUARE (WESTBROOK HOTEL), WHISTLER; 604/932-3330

A mainstay for years in Whistler, Sushi Village is one of those popular local hangouts the parking valets will tell you about. Even though it's perched on the second floor of the Westbrook Hotel, people patiently wait in line. It's worth it. Extremely fresh sushi, sashimi, and *maki* platters, as well as combinations served in wooden sushi boats, are prepared by animated experts at the counter. Simple Japanese-style decor allows for privacy. *$$; AE, DC, MC, V; no checks; lunch Wed–Sun, dinner every day (Sat–Sun only, off-season); full bar; reservations recommended; www.sushivillage.com; Whistler Village, at Sundial Crescent.* &

Val d'Isère / ★★★

4314 MAIN ST (BEAR LODGE), WHISTLER; 604/932-4666
Val d'Isère offers a rare combination: fine dining, intimate ambience, and affordability. Glass chandeliers lend an art nouveau lamplight glow to chef Roland Pfaff's authentic brasserie. After 20 years as one of Whistler's pioneering chefs, Pfaff has his priorities straight. He skis like crazy in the mornings, then returns to conduct business in a French kitchen stamped with his French roots, as witnessed by Val d'Isère's signature dish: onion tart. *$$$; AE, DC, MC, V; no checks; lunch, dinner every day (closed mid-Oct–mid-Nov); full bar; reservations recommended; www.valdisere-restaurant.com; Village North, at Town Plaza Square.* &

LODGINGS

Adara Hotel / ★★★

4122 VILLAGE GREEN, WHISTLER; 604/905-4009 OR 866-502-3272
Deliberately designed to be the antithesis of the usual Whistler lodging, the Adara succeeds admirably at its mission—and at offering a splendid place to stay in the heart of the village. With candles and sculptures in the lobby and fake furs, molded plastic chairs, and zebra-wood furnishings in the rooms, it's hip. Exotic amenities range from bedside white-noise machines to personal oxygen devices in the bathrooms. *$$$$; AE, MC, V; www.adarahotel.com; Whistler Village.* &

Brew Creek Lodge / ★★★

1 BREW CREEK RD, WHISTLER; 604/932-7210
This sparkling hideaway sits at the foot of Brandywine Mountain south of Whistler. A sheltering forest buffers all sounds from the steady stream of nearby traffic on Highway 99. Brew Creek, the lodge's crowning feature, flows through the 12-acre property past a massive main lodge with six guest rooms. Nearby are two suites that share the Guest House; also on-site are the Trappers Cabin and the romantic Treehouse. No TVs or phones intrude on the calm, which is best appreciated from the creekside hot tub. *$$–$$$; AE, MC, V; no checks; www. brewcreek.com; 12 miles (16 km) south of Whistler.* &

Callaghan Lodge / ★★★

CALLAGHAN VALLEY, WHISTLER; 604/938-0616 OR 877/938-0616
It's hard to imagine a more sensational setting for a winter sports lodge. Perched on a small hill in the middle of an alpine valley at 6,000 feet, Callaghan Lodge overlooks a snowy wilderness. The lodge has comfy guest rooms, plus a two-level family suite. Packages include meals and access to

cross-country trails. The valley below the lodge will be the site for Nordic events in the 2010 Winter Olympics; for now, peace and quiet reign. Access is by snowmobile or snow cat only; the ride takes an hour from the Highway 99 pickup point. *$$$$; AE, MC, V; checks OK; www.callaghancountry.com.* &

Durlacher Hof Alpine Country Inn / ★★★

7055 NESTERS RD, WHISTLER; 604/932-1924 OR 877/932-1924
This farmhouse is a traditional country inn, right down to hut slippers that await guests' feet. Hand-carved furniture and fixtures adorn all eight guest rooms, plus the piano bar and cozy kitchen with its *kachenelofen*—an old-fashioned fireplace oven. For simple overnight stays, book one of the Sun-shine rooms with mountain views. Attention to detail is evident everywhere, such as in the cozy après-ski area where afternoon tea is served. *$$$$; MC, V; checks OK; www.durlacherhof.com; Nesters neighborhood.* &\

Fairmont Chateau Whistler Resort / ★★★★

4599 CHATEAU BLVD, WHISTLER; 604/938-8000 OR 800/606-8244
In keeping with the cachet its sister chateaus enjoy in Banff and Lake Lou-ise, the 12-story, 563-room Chateau Whistler is among Whistler's signa-ture accommodations. Anchoring the Upper Village neighborhood, it offers sweeping views of the mountains, an indoor-outdoor pool, and a spa. As at every upscale hotel, pampering is provided here. Given the grand impression of the foyer, however, standard rooms—particularly junior suites—are only adequately sized. The chateau's public areas are some of the most inviting in Whistler and deserve a look even if you're staying elsewhere. *$$$$; AE, DC, DIS, MC, V; checks OK; www.fairmont.com; at foot of Blackcomb.* &

Four Seasons / ★★★★

4591 BLACKCOMB WAY, WHISTLER; 604/935-3400 OR 800/819-5053
Canada's signature four-star hotel chain is ably represented in Whistler by this massive complex with 273 rooms, a separate building of 37 private residences, and a 15-room spa. The entry is quintessential Four Seasons: a sweeping driveway that leads to a discreetly elegant hallway with exquisite West Coast art and a hushed, professional atmosphere. The prevailing decor themes are earthy fabrics and woods in browns and tans. *$$$$; AE, DC, MC, V; no checks; www.fourseasons.com; at far eastern end of Upper Village.* &

Pan Pacific Village Centre / ★★★

4299 BLACKCOMB WAY, WHISTLER; 604/966-5501 OR 888/966-5575
Of the two Pan Pacific properties in Whistler, this is the newest, smallest, and nicest. With just 83 guest rooms (all of them suites), it offers an intimate atmosphere not possible at its bigger (121-room) sister property. The setting affords expansive views. The three penthouse suites are among the best-situated in Whistler, with sensational views of both mountains, if you're in the four-figures-per-night bracket. *$$$$; AE, DC, MC, V; no checks; www.pan pacific.com; off Blackcomb Way.* &

Westin Whistler / ★★★

4090 WHISTLER WY, WHISTLER; 604/905-5000 OR 888/634-5577
One of Whistler Village's largest new hotels is also one of its best. It's distinguished not by its guest rooms or its overall design, though these are great. It's the hotel's staff that shines—an obviously well-trained crew, friendly, knowledgeable, and remarkably competent, even in the face of the daunting crowds. Need help with a Rim Rock Cafe reservation? Not one, not two, but three workers staff the concierge desk. *$$$; AE, DC, MC, V; no checks; www. westinwhistler.com; off Blackcomb Way.* &

Pemberton and Mount Currie

In the decades before Highway 99 pushed through to Pemberton, this farming community that's evolving into a Whistler suburb existed in isolation from the rest of the Lower Mainland. Public transit now connects Pemberton and nearby Mount Currie, which is 3.7 miles (6 km) east of Pemberton, with Whistler 22 miles (35 km) to the south. For a schedule, contact **WAVE** (604/938-0388; www. busonline.ca).

Today, this valley is experiencing growth in both visitors and new residents, many of whom work in Whistler. To get the feel, attend the annual **CANADA DAY** celebration the last week in June. There won't be a potato in sight (Pemberton—or Spud Valley—is renowned for the quality of its seed potatoes), but you can try other specialties. By then there will be produce at **NORTH ARM FARMS** (1888 Sea to Sky Hwy, midway between Pemberton and Mount Currie; 604/894-6650).

This is also the territory of the Lil'wat people: Mount Currie and D'Arcy, 23½ miles (38 km) north of Mount Currie. Everyone is welcome at First Nation events, such as the **LILLOOET LAKE RODEO**, held each May in Mount Currie, and August's **D'ARCY SALMON FESTIVAL**.

The quaint **PEMBERTON PIONEER MUSEUM** (Camus and Prospect sts; 604/894-6135) offers a glimpse of pioneer life. **PEMBERTON BIKE COMPANY** (1392 Portage Rd; 604/894-6625) rents bikes. **PEMBERTON STABLES** (Pemberton Valley, north of town; 604/894-6615) sends guests out on pleasant rides.

In this area, small cafés such as **GRIMM'S GOURMET & DELI** (7433 Frontier Ave, Pemberton; 604/894-5303) are the standard for dining. **WICKED WHEEL PIZZA** (2021 Portage Rd, Mount Currie; 604/894-6622) is packed on all-you-can-eat nights.

PEMBERTON CHAMBER OF COMMERCE TOURISM INFORMATION (7400 Prospect St; 604/894-6175; www.pemberton.net) provides details, as does the **PEMBERTON VISITOR INFO CENTRE** (Hwy 99 and Portage Rd; May 15–Sept 1).

Lillooet

As the Sea to Sky Highway winds 62 miles (100 km) east and north from Mount Currie to Lillooet, it passes through an ever-changing landscape, some of the most picturesque and notably varied terrain of its entire length.

This steep-sided section of Highway 99 is also called the Duffey Lake Road. Cayoosh Creek runs east from Duffey Lake and accompanies the highway almost to Lillooet. Stop at one of the numerous pull-offs along the way and admire the snowcapped 10,000-foot peaks above you. Just before Lillooet, BC Hydro's recreation area at **SETON LAKE** offers a beach, salmon spawning channels, and a campground with an abandoned Chinese baking oven, a relic from the Cariboo Gold Rush era. In the late 1850s, Lillooet (population 2,740) was the staging ground for an estimated 50,000 stampeders as they headed north to Clinton and beyond (see Central and Northern British Columbia chapter).

Lillooet, where summer temperatures are among the hottest in Canada, is the gateway to the stunning **SOUTH CHILCOTINS BACKCOUNTRY**. While in town, check out the superb **LILLOOET BAKERY** (719 Main St; 250/256-4889). The **4 PINES MOTEL** (108 8th Ave; 250/256-4247 or 800/753-2576; www.4pinesmotel. com) is a good overnight option in town. The **LILLOOET INFO CENTRE** (790 Main St; 250/256-4308; May–Oct) is located in an A-frame former church, which it shares with the town museum.

RESTAURANTS

Dina's Place / ★

690 MAIN ST, LILLOOET; 250/256-4264

A whitewashed Greek restaurant suits Lillooet's summer days. Dina's patio is the place to be in early evening. Zesty panfried *saganaki* with goat cheese speaks to the Pulolos family's northern Greek roots. Twenty-six kinds of pizza keep one wood-fired oven busy; halibut steaks and calamari are must-try recommendations. *$$; MC, V; no checks; lunch Mon–Sat, dinner every day; full bar; no reservations; on east side of Main St.* &

LODGINGS

Tyax Mountain Lake Resort / ★★★

TYAUGHTON LAKE RD, GOLD BRIDGE; 250/238-2221

At 34,000 square feet (10,364 sq m), this is the largest log structure on the West Coast. The lodge sits beside Tyaughton Lake, with a huge park nearby. There's a sauna, an outdoor Jacuzzi, games and work-out rooms, a 100-seat restaurant, and a western lounge. Affable owner Gus Abel welcomes guests to explore the lake. The 34-unit lodge has floatplanes that take anglers and their kids up to the Trophy Lakes. In winter, the lodge is home base for TLH

Heli-skiing (www.tlhheliskiing.com), which flies guests into the snowfields of the south Chilcotin Mountains. *$$$; AE, MC, V; no checks; www.tyax.com; 56 miles (90 km) west of Lillooet on Hwy 40, then 3 miles (5 km) north on Tyaughton Lake Rd.* &

Fraser Valley

The wide, fertile Fraser Valley runs 93 miles (150 km) inland from the Pacific to the small town of Hope. The Fraser River—broad, deep, and muddy—flows down the middle of the valley. River crossings are limited, forcing road travelers to choose the north side (Highway 7) or the south side (Highway 1). Crossings are located at Abbotsford and Chilliwack, both south of the Fraser River and among the fastest growing in Canada, but this still rural valley supports a blend of farming and forestry, with outdoor recreation high on everyone's list. Another crossing is farther north at Hope.

Fort Langley

Several historic 19th-century forts in British Columbia serve as reminders of the West's original European settlers. In Fort Langley (population 2,600), on the south side of the Fraser off Highway 1, **FORT LANGLEY NATIONAL HISTORIC SITE** (23433 Mavis St; 604/513-4777) is a preserved and restored Hudson's Bay Company post. This is where British Columbia was proclaimed a crown colony in 1858, to fend off American designs after gold was discovered in the Cariboo. The **LANGLEY CENTENNIAL MUSEUM** (across from fort; 604/888-3922) houses a permanent collection of memorabilia. Glover Road, Fort Langley's **MAIN STREET**, features shops, cafés, and restaurants, many in heritage buildings; the large community hall has been lovingly preserved. Archival photographs from Fort Langley's past line the walls of the **FORT PUB** (9273 Glover Rd; 604/888-6166; www. fortpub.com).

Chilliwack

Odors in Chilliwack (population 62,930) are inescapably agricultural. Most travelers whizzing through on Highway 1 travel too fast to get more than a pungent whiff as they pass big-box stores interspersed with the occasional barn. They're missing the best corn in Canada—from early August through October, farm stands offer what longtime British Columbia residents all know just as "Chilliwack corn." To get beyond the facade of fast-food outlets, supply stores, and junkyards, follow historic Yale Road from exit 116 east into the hidden heart of Chilliwack, where the original city hall, built in 1912, now houses the excellent **CHILLIWACK MUSEUM** (45820 Spadina Ave; 604/795-5210; www.chilliwack. museum.bc.ca). Designed in Classic Revival style, the museum looks like the U.S. White House. Year-round information is available from the **CHILLIWACK**

INFO CENTRE (44150 Luckakuck Way; 604/858-8121 or 800/567-9535; www. tourismchilliwack.com).

Harrison Lake

All of 12 miles (18 km) long, the Harrison River, which drains south from Harrison Lake into the Fraser River, is among British Columbia's shortest yet most significant waterways. Throughout fall, major runs of spawning salmon make their way upstream into tributaries of the Harrison watershed. This quiet backwater is anchored by **KILBY PARK** (www.env.gov.bc.ca/bcparks) at the community of Harrison Mills on Highway 7, on the north side of the Fraser. **KILBY HISTORIC STORE** (adjacent to Kilby Park, Harrison Mills; 604/796-9576; May–Oct and Christmas) has a wonderful pioneer history.

Bigfoot (called Sasquatch locally) is said to frequent the southern end of Harrison Lake—perhaps itching for a soak in the renowned waters of **HARRISON HOT SPRINGS** (224 Esplanade Ave, Harrison Hot Springs; 604/796-2244). The indoor public bathing pool is one of the most inviting places in this lakefront town (population 1,345). Harrison Lake is too cold for most swimmers, but a constructed lagoon at the south end of the lake is rimmed by sand and a small, quiet row of low buildings. In summer, rent sailboats or bikes or hike nearby trails. Annual events include the long-running **HARRISON FESTIVAL OF THE ARTS** (June), the **WORLD CHAMPIONSHIP SAND SCULPTURE** competition (second weekend in Sept), and the **BALD EAGLE FESTIVAL** (Nov). Contact the **HARRISON HOT SPRINGS VISITOR INFO CENTRE** (499 Hot Springs Rd; 604/796-3425; www.harrison.ca) for details.

LODGINGS

Fenn Lodge Bed & Breakfast Retreat / ★★

**15500 MORRIS VALLEY RD, HARRISON MILLS;
604/796-9798 OR 888/990-3399**
Once home to a local lumber baron, this 1903 late-Victorian classic was lovingly restored in the mid-1990s. All classic touches were retained, and the decor is understated and bright. The owners are world travelers and art collectors, which shows in exotic touches they've added, such as the harem bed in the bridal suite and the Chinese artwork displayed. There's a heated spring-fed swimming pool, a meditation maze, and a playground. *$$–$$$; MC, V; no checks; www.fennlodge.com; 2 miles (4 km) northeast of Hwy 7.*

Harrison Beach Hotel / ★★

**160 ESPLANADE AVE, HARRISON HOT SPRINGS;
604/796-1111 OR 866/338-8111**
The newest accommodation in Harrison Hot Springs is a shiny four-story property facing the lake, with 42 spiffy guest rooms and suites and an excellent lakeside location. The suites are housekeeping units with spacious sitting areas and full kitchens. The earth-toned rooms all have balconies or patios,

443

and those on the north side of the building enjoy sensational views of Harrison Lake and its surrounding mountains. The town's hot-springs pool is just a block away, but the hotel itself has no mineral pool. *$$–$$$; AE, MC, V; checks OK (call for policy); www.harrisonbeachhotel.com; right in town.*

The Harrison Hot Springs Hotel / ★★

**100 ESPLANADE AVE, HARRISON HOT SPRINGS;
604/796-2244 OR 800/663-2266**
This legendary hotel on the south shore of Harrison Lake was built in 1926 to capitalize as much on its location as on the thermal springs nearby. The current establishment has 334 rooms and suites spread among the 100-room main building and two wings. Avoid the main building, where noise seeps between the walls. A maze of hot-springs pools is steps away from the newest wing, where each room has a view. The best rooms are the suites, which have been tastefully redone, replacing the old '60s and '70s chintz. The Copper Room is fun for big-band-style dancing. In 2003 the new hotel owners began a much-needed $16 million, five-year renovation. *$$–$$$; AE, DC, DIS, MC, V; checks OK; www.harrisonresort.com; west end of Esplanade Ave on lake.* &

Hope

Hope (population 6,185) is a pretty Fraser River town where the two main streets are lined with fast-food joints. Because it's an important highway junction, the heart of town is frequently overlooked. Spend a few minutes here, if for no other reason than to breathe the fresh air that characterizes Hope. Visit **HOPE MUSEUM** (south end of Water St) and **MANNING PROVINCIAL PARK** (16 miles/26 km east on Hwy 3; www.env.gov.bc.ca/bcparks), with the family-oriented **MANNING PARK LODGE** (Hwy 3, Manning Provincial Park; 250/840-8822 or 800/330-3321; www.manningparkresort.com; 37 miles/60 km east of Hope) and **PINEWOODS DINING ROOM** (250/840-8822). Check out the **HOPE VISITOR INFO CENTRE** (919 Water Ave; 604/869-2021; www.hopechamber.bc.ca).

The Sunshine Coast

The Sunshine Coast is aptly named: bright days outnumber gloomy ones by a wide margin. Even though the Sunshine Coast occupies a fairly narrow bench of land at the toe of the Coast Mountains, much of it is naturally hidden. Side roads with colorful names like Red Roof and Porpoise Bay lead to places that don't announce themselves until you stumble upon them, such as **SMUGGLER COVE MARINE PARK** near Sechelt and **PALM BEACH PARK** (a serene oasis, though there are no palms) south of the town of Powell River.

The region is split into two portions by Jervis Inlet. The southern half, between the ferry slips at Langdale and Earls Cove, consists of mainland British Columbia and the **SECHELT PENINSULA**; the northern half lies between the ferry slip at

Saltery Bay and the little port of Lund, the latter on the **MALASPINA PENINSULA**. The world's longest highway, the **PAN-AMERICAN**—Highways 1 and 101 in parts of the United States and Highways 99 and 101 in Canada—stretches 9,312 miles (15,020 km) from Chile to Lund on British Columbia's Sunshine Coast. The 87-mile (140-km) stretch of Highway 101 between Langdale and Lund leads to dozens of parks.

ACCESS AND INFORMATION

The Sunshine Coast is accessible from the rest of the Lower Mainland only by boat or floatplane. Travelers aboard **BC FERRIES** (604/669-121; www.bcferries.com) leave Horseshoe Bay in West Vancouver on one of eight daily sailings for a 45-minute ride to Langdale on the Sechelt Peninsula. During peak season, June–September, the extra investment ($17) in a reservation is well worth it. **HIGHWAY 101** links Langdale with Earls Cove, 50 miles (80 km) north. Another ferry crosses Jervis Inlet to Saltery Bay, a 60-minute ride. Highway 101 makes the second leg of its journey, extending 37 miles (60 km) north through the town of Powell River to Lund. BC Ferries also connects Powell River with Comox on the east side of central Vancouver Island.

One of the best parts about enjoying the Sunshine Coast in the off-season (Sept–May)—particularly midweek—is catching ferries without experiencing interminable lines. You'll still have to allow four hours to reach Powell River from Horseshoe Bay, but you can do it without hurrying. Ferry connections are scheduled to allow adequate time to make the drive from one dock to the next. Those traveling up the entire coast or returning via Vancouver Island should ask at the Horseshoe Bay terminal about special fares (saving up to 30 percent) for the circle tour of four ferry rides.

MALASPINA BUS LINE (604/885-2218 or 877/227-8287) runs daily scheduled service between Vancouver and Powell River, with stops on request anywhere in between. **PACIFIC COASTAL AIRLINES** (604/273-8666; www.pacific-coastal.com) flies daily between Vancouver and Powell River.

Get detailed **INFORMATION** (www.suncoastcentral.com) on the Sunshine Coast regarding current weather and transportation schedules before you go.

Gibsons

Gibsons (population 3,900), a colorfully low-key waterfront village 2½ miles (4 km) west of the BC Ferries dock in Langdale, is famous among Canadians as the setting of a long-popular, long-ago CBC-TV show, *The Beachcombers*. Make the **GIBSONS VISITOR INFO CENTRE** (1177 Stewart Rd; 604/886-2325; www.gibsonschamber.com) your first stop in the heart of town to stock up on maps and brochures. Then head to the nearby government wharf where there's often **FRESH SEAFOOD**. Take a walk along the harbor seawall that leads past homes and boat sheds with character. A cairn at **CHASTER REGIONAL PARK** (on Gower Point Rd; 604/886-2325) honors British Navy Captain George Vancouver, who camped here in June 1792.

RESTAURANTS

Chez Philippe / ★★

1532 OCEAN BEACH ESPLANADE (BONNIEBROOK LODGE)
GIBSONS; 604/886-2887 OR 877/290-9916

Parisian Philippe Lacoste trained in Normandy before coming to Vancouver, where he worked at the prestigious Le Crocodile and Le Gavroche restaurants. In the early 1990s, he and his wife, Karen, moved to Gibsons to start their own auberge. French-inspired, with Northwest influences, the menu features à la carte selections as well as a four-course fixed-price table d'hôte. Entrées include scallops in polenta shells, seafood ragù in Nantua sauce, chicken with wild mushrooms, rack of lamb, duck à l' orange, and a vegetarian platter. *$$$; AE, DC, MC, V; no checks; dinner every day (Fri–Sun, mid-Sept–Dec and Feb–mid-May; closed Jan); full bar; reservations recommended; www.bonniebrook.com; follow Gower Point Rd from downtown.*

LODGINGS

Bonniebrook Lodge / ★★

1532 OCEAN BEACH ESPLANADE, GIBSONS;
604/886-2887 OR 877/290-9916

This popular, stylishly renovated 1920s-era waterfront bed-and-breakfast features four self-contained suites spread between two upper floors. Two one-bedroom ocean-view suites occupy the yellow clapboard house's second floor, with two smaller penthouse suites with private decks above. The best values are the three "romance" suites set back in the forest. Explore the stretch of private beach that leads to nearby Chaster Park. Avid outdoor adventurers, the owners also rent kayaks and operate a shaded campground with RV sites. *$$; AE, MC, V; no checks; closed Jan; www.bonniebrook.com; follow Gower Point Rd from downtown.* &

Rosewood Country House Bed and Breakfast / ★★

575 PINE ST, GIBSONS; 604/886-4714

Frank and Susan Tonne built this Craftsman-style mansion with timber milled on the property and decorated it with fixtures from heritage homes like Victorian table lamps and glass cabinetry. The eclectic result harks back to the spacious elegance of earlier times, right down to the antique snooker table in the games room. The Victorian-theme Sunset Suite has its own private deck from which guests can watch as Alaska cruise ships parade past. The deluxe Garden Suite is decorated in Queen Anne style. Guests can request breakfast in bed, rolled in on a silver tea service. Romantic dinners are a specialty, served in a private dining room. Reserve several months in advance for weekends May–October. *$$$; V; checks OK; www.rosewoodcountryhouse.com; 4 miles (6.4 km) west of Gibsons.* &

Roberts Creek

The free-spirited community of Roberts Creek (population 2,250) lies 4 miles (7 km) north of Gibsons on Highway 10. Stop first at **MCFARLANE'S BEACH** at the south end of Roberts Creek Road. Early in the 19th century, Harry Roberts operated a freight shed here. On its side he painted "Sunshine Belt"—and visitors ever since have been referring to the area as the Sunshine Coast. From here, look north toward the beaches at **ROBERTS CREEK PARK** (Hwy 101, 9 miles/14 km north of Gibsons; www.env.gov.bc.ca/bcparks), popular for summer picnics. A reward for braving ferry traffic on **BC DAY** (604/886-2325; first weekend in Aug) is taking in the annual Gumboot parade and Mr. Roberts Creek contest.

RESTAURANTS

Georgia Strait / ★★

4349 SUNSHINE COAST HWY, WILSON CREEK;
604/885-1997 OR 800/893-6646
Housed in an old service station painted purple, this cheery bistro has brought gourmet dining to the Sechelt area, with an eclectic West Coast menu that ranges from the usual salmon, lamb, chicken, and crab to upscale deli items. The spacious interior is filled with light from large windows, and a southwest-facing deck basks in the sun. What distinguishes Georgia Strait above all else, though, is the best Reuben sandwich in British Columbia, perhaps the Northwest. *$$; MC, V; no checks; lunch, dinner every day; full bar; reservations recommended; 4 miles (6.4 km) north of Roberts Creek.*

Gumboot Garden Café

1057 ROBERTS CREEK RD, ROBERTS CREEK; 604/885-4216
As you drive down Roberts Creek's main drag, look for an old maroon house with a simple sign: café. Inside, a sun painted on the yellow wall radiates warmth, as do linoleum table mats. The menu shines with a Mexican influence. Try the Huevos Gumboot, a hearty breakfast dish available all day. Popular entrées include Thai salad and homemade veggie burgers. On Friday evenings, locals come to hang out and listen to music. In keeping with the community and clientele, service is relaxed. *$; MC, V; checks OK; breakfast, lunch every day, dinner Thurs–Sat; beer and wine; reservations recommended; www.thegumboot.com; junction with Lower Rd.* &

LODGINGS

Country Cottage B&B / ★★

1183 ROBERTS CREEK RD, ROBERTS CREEK; 604/885-7448
Philip and Loragene Gaulin's 2-acre sheep farm features the vintage Rose Cottage, tucked inside the front gate, and the more modern Cedar Lodge, set beside the pasture. The cozy one-room cottage has a fireplace, small kitchen, and quilt-covered bed. Farther back on the property, Cedar Lodge is a tree

447

house for grown-ups. Wood- and stonework set its tone, as do a loft bed and a chandelier fashioned from deer antlers. *$$–$$$; no credit cards; checks OK; www.countrycottagebb.com; 9 miles (14 km) from Langdale ferry, off Hwy 101.*

Sechelt

If it weren't for a small neck of land less than a half mile (0.8 km) wide, a large portion of the peninsula north of Sechelt would be an island. This wedge of sand backs ocean water, which flows in from the northwestern entrance to Sechelt Inlet near Egmont. Nestled on the wedge is Sechelt (population 7,775), one of the fastest-growing towns in Canada and home to the Sechelt First Nation, whose **HOUSE OF HEWHIWUS** (5555 Hwy 101; 604/885-8991)—"House of the Chiefs"— is both a cultural and an art center. Ask for a tour. The **SECHELT VISITOR INFO CENTRE** (5755 Cowrie St, Trail Bay Mall; 604/885-0662; www.secheltchamber. bc.ca) fills you in on the rest.

RESTAURANTS

Blue Heron Inn / ★★

5521 DELTA RD, SECHELT; 604/885-3847 OR 800/818-8977
The Blue Heron is one of the most consistently pleasant places to dine on the Sunshine Coast—partly for the waterfront views of Sechelt Inlet (complete with blue herons, of course). But the food is another draw: fresh clams, veal *limonie* with prawns, grilled wild salmon with fennel, smoked black cod with hollandaise, halibut fillet with red onion and strawberry salsa, creamy caesar salad, bouillabaisse. And the romantic atmosphere—fresh flowers, candle-light, local art, live music—is another plus. *$$; AE, MC, V; local checks only; dinner Wed–Sun; full bar; reservations recommended; west of Hwy 101 on Wharf St, right along Porpoise Bay Rd 1 mile (1.6 km), sign on left side.* &

Pender Harbour

At the north end of the Sechelt Peninsula, a puzzle-shaped piece of geography, it's hard to tell where freshwater lakes end and saltwater coves begin. Fingers of land separate the waters around Agamemnon Channel from a marvelous patch-work of small and medium-sized lakes. Three ocean-side communities—Madeira Park, Garden Bay, and Irvines Landing—lie tucked along the shoreline. Together they comprise Pender Harbour, which has decided to market itself as "Venice of the North." In summer, stop by the **PENDER HARBOUR TOURIST/VISITOR INFO BOOTH** (12895 Madeira Park Rd; 604/883-2561 or 877/873-6337; www. penderharbour.org). As you head north of Pender Harbour toward the BC Ferries terminal at Earls Cove, Highway 101 winds around Ruby Lake and climbs above it, allowing a view of the jewel-like setting.

LODGINGS

Rockwater Secret Cove Resort / ★★

5356 OLE'S COVE RD, HALFMOON BAY;
604/885-7038 OR 877/296-4593
New owner Kevin Toth is transforming a popular but aging property (formerly called Lord Jim's) into a distinctive resort. The main building still overlooks one of the largest swimming pools on the Sunshine Coast—which itself overlooks the Strait of Georgia. The lodge rooms and suites have been completely redone. The dining room, whose dinners feature good West Coast seafood, has a lavish Sunday brunch. The most spectacular feature, however, remains the waterfront bluffside location facing into the sunset. *$$$$; MC, V; no checks; closed Jan; www.lordjims.com; off Hwy 101, 1 mile past Secret Cove.*

Ruby Lake Resort / ★

RUBY LAKE, MADEIRA PARK; 604/883-2269 OR 800/717-6611
An engaging family from Milan—the Cogrossis—operate Ruby Lake Resort, with its 10 cedar cottages, each rustically decorated. Two B and B suites, with private entrances—and no TVs—are housed in the Dream Catcher cottage. The family's restaurant draws accolades for its Northern Italian cuisine and fresh seafood. Eagles drop by for their daily feeding at 6pm. In his spare time, chef Aldo Cogrossi builds birdhouses, more than 40 of which you'll see wherever you go. *$$; MC, V; no checks; closed Dec–Feb; www.rubylakeresort. com; 6 miles (10 km) south of Earls Cove.*

Sunshine Coast Resort / ★★

12695 SUNSHINE COAST HWY, MADEIRA PARK; 604/883-9177
Tucked demurely into a hillside overlooking one of Pender Harbour's innumerable tiny back bays, this small inn offers 14 splendid suites. The earth-tone decor is supplemented by warm Douglas-fir trim; full kitchens and soaker tubs are in most units. Rent the two-bedroom heritage house, with its own deck overlooking the bay. The resort's main deck has a large hot tub from which you can watch the harbor at night as it turns into a canvas of shoreline lights, bobbing boats, and starry sky. *$$; AE, MC, V; no checks; closed Dec–Feb; www.sunshinecoastresort.com; on Hwy 101, just past Madeira Park turnoff.*

Egmont

An impressive natural show occurs twice daily in **SKOOKUMCHUK NARROWS PARK** (Hwy 101; www.env.gov.bc.ca/bcparks) in the tiny district of Egmont, about 7 miles (12 km) north of Ruby Lake. One of the largest saltwater rapids on Canada's west coast boils as water forces through Skookumchuk Narrows at the north end of Sechelt Inlet. A gentle 2½-mile (4-km) walking-cycling trail leads to viewing sites at North Point and nearby Roland Point. At low tide, the bays around both points display astonishingly colorful and varied forms of marine life.

LODGINGS

West Coast Wilderness Lodge / ★★

MAPLE RD, EGMONT; 604/883-3667 OR 877/988-3838
Perched above island-specked Jervis Inlet, the 20-room West Coast Wilderness Lodge's name says it all. Opened in 1998 by Paul and Patti Hansen, the lodge's most endearing feature is a deck from which guests watch wildlife ranging from Pacific dolphins to swans. Inside, rattan chairs rescued from a Trader Vic's restaurant and comfy couches ring a fireplace that rises two floors above the inn's dining area and lounge. Guides work with guests to sharpen sea kayaking and paddling skills. When it's all over, head for the ocean-side sauna. *$$$; MC, V; checks OK; www.wcwl.com; 1 mile (1.6 km) north of Egmont harbor.* &

Powell River

Travelers looking to experience the pace of ferry sailings will enjoy the journey between Earls Cove and Saltery Bay on Jervis Inlet. Continuing north by car on Highway 101, Powell River (population 12,985) is a pleasant drive 19 miles (31 km) north of the ferry terminal at Saltery Bay. This mill town on Malaspina Strait is the jumping-off point to Texada and Vancouver islands, as well as the 12-lake Powell Forest canoe route, a full-on 35-mile (57-km) adventure. Powell River is also home to the **INTERNATIONAL CHORAL KATHAUMIXW FESTIVAL** (www. kathaumixw.org; early July). For information on Kathaumixw and the weeklong blackberry festival each August, contact the **POWELL RIVER VISITOR INFO CENTRE** (4690 Marine Ave; 604/485-4701 or 877/817-8669; www.discoverpowell river.com). Nearby is **ROCKY MOUNTAIN PIZZA & BAKERY** (4471 Marine Ave; 604/485-9111), where you can eat and people watch.

RESTAURANTS

jitterbug café / ★

4643 MARINE DR, POWELL RIVER; 604/485-7797
One of Powell River's most enduring eateries, the jitterbug café shares a stylishly renovated 1920s coastal home with the Wind Spirit Gallery. Art animates the walls of the brightly lit dining room. From a window table, take in sweeping views of islands. Better yet, enjoy a glass of sangria on the back deck. True to its name, the café features music on weekends. *$$; AE, MC, V; no checks; lunch, dinner Tues–Sat; full bar; reservations recommended; www. windspirit.com; downtown.* &

Lund

Little ports don't come better hidden than Lund, at the north end of the Sunshine Coast where the Malaspina Peninsula narrows to a thin finger of land wedged between Malaspina Strait and Okeover Arm. More boaters than vehicles make their way here. Lund retains much of the wilderness charm that drew settlers here from Finland. The historic 1918 **LUND HOTEL** (1436 Hwy 101; 604/414-0474 or 877/569-3999; www.lundhotel.com) has recently undergone a makeover. **FLO'S STARBOARD CAFÉ** (on Lund harbor) serves espresso in a little bistro. A red **WATER TAXI** (604/483-9749), the *Raggedy Anne*, ferries passengers to nearby Savary Island. **OKEOVER ARM PARK** (off Hwy 101, 3 miles/5 km east of Lund; www.env. gov.bc.ca/bcparks) is the kayakers' choice.

RESTAURANTS

The Laughing Oyster Restaurant / ★★

10052 MALASPINA RD, LUND; 604/483-9775
Though the view overlooking Okeover Arm is sensational—and tables on the deck are premium—the food remains the draw at Laughing Oyster. And while the menu is wide-ranging, seafood is the mainstay. There's nothing memorably inventive, but they make unfailingly excellent fish entrées that hew a bit toward old-fashioned chophouse standards; the popular "seafood harvest" platter for two is a great deal at $90. *$$$; AE, MC, V; no checks; lunch, dinner every day, brunch Sun (closed Mon–Tues Oct–Mar); full bar; reservations required; www.laughingoyster.ca; 20 minutes north of Powell River.* &

Nancy's Bakery / ★★

1431 HWY 101, LUND; 604/483-4180

Housed in an impressive new post-and-beam structure on the shoreline, Nancy's has certainly grown past its muffin-and-scones roots in a nearby shack. Today this is one of the best bakeries in British Columbia. Supplementing bakery items are soups, salads, pastas, and hearty sandwiches—get a pastrami sandwich, and you'll be enjoying meat smoked on the premises. Snag a table outside to scan the harbor while savoring your meal. *$; MC, V; no checks; breakfast, lunch every day; beer and wine; no reservations; end of Hwy 101.*

LODGINGS

Desolation Resort / ★★★

2694 DAWSON RD, LUND; 604/483-3592

The way the afternoon sun slants through the forest that embraces this resort's wood cabins makes the place seem like a movie set. Perched on 7 acres above quiet waters, and almost literally at the end of the road, the resort's 10 units offer splendid privacy, spaciousness, and comfort. The timber-frame fir and cedar interiors are warm, though not luxurious; two cottages (which the resort mysteriously calls chalets, though they're not) have their own hot tubs. Package deals include dinners at the Laughing Oyster Restaurant (see review) and guided kayak trips; rental canoes and kayaks are also available. *$$; AE, MC, V; no checks; www.desolationresort.com; 20 minutes north of Powell River.* &

VICTORIA AND VANCOUVER ISLAND

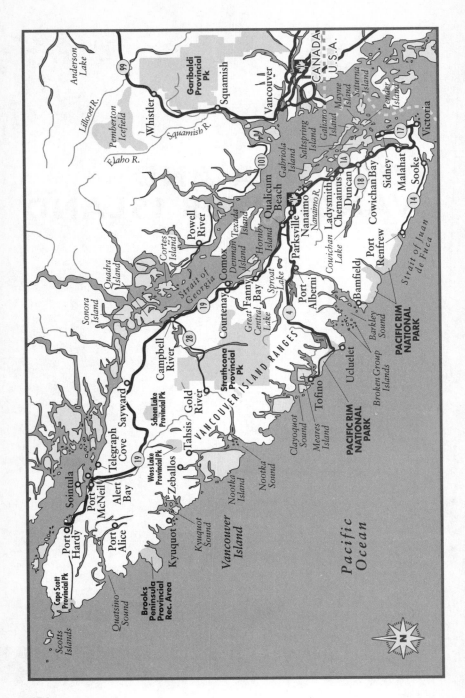

VICTORIA AND VANCOUVER ISLAND

Vancouver Island is famed worldwide as a place of extravagant beauty, sensational cuisine, memorable wilderness, and unexpected warmth.

The southern part of the island is a booming recreational and residential growth area, and the mountains and west coast are less inhabited than other parts of the Pacific Northwest, making this island a utopia for outdoor pursuits. Victoria, a city of gardens, was once known for subscribing to a whimsical character "more English than the English"; today it is a world culinary capital.

ACCESS AND INFORMATION

You get to the biggest island in North America by boat or by plane. From Western Washington, you have four options. From downtown Seattle, the **VICTORIA CLIPPER** (Pier 69; 206/448-5000 in Seattle, 250/382-8100 in Victoria, or 800/888-2535 elsewhere; www.victoriaclipper.com) zips to downtown Victoria in three hours via a high-speed passenger-only catamaran. You can also cruise to Victoria via the scenic San Juan Islands on **WASHINGTON STATE FERRIES** (two hours north of Seattle; 206/464-6400 or 888/808-7977; www.wsdot.wa.gov/ferries/); a two- to three-hour trip runs from Anacortes (follow prominent signage) to Sidney, British Columbia, 17 miles (27 km) north of Victoria by highway. **BLACK BALL TRANSPORT** (360/457-4491 in Port Angeles or 250/386-2202 in Victoria; www.cohoferry.com) operates the MV *Coho* car-and-passenger ferry from Port Angeles (follow signage in downtown Port Angeles) on the Olympic Peninsula to downtown Victoria, a 95-minute trip across the Strait of Juan de Fuca. Even though there are four daily sailings of the *Coho* in summer, reservations are essential. **VICTORIA SAN JUAN CRUISES** (360/738-8099 or 800/443-4552; www.whales.com; mid-May–early Oct) makes a three-hour passenger-only cruise—including whale-watching and a salmon dinner—between Bellingham and Victoria's Inner Harbour.

BC FERRIES (250/386-3431 or 888/223-3779; www.bcferries.com) runs car ferries from the British Columbia mainland (Tsawwassen terminal) into Swartz Bay, 20 miles (32 km) north of Victoria; from Horseshoe Bay north of Vancouver to Nanaimo; and from Departure Bay south of Nanaimo to Tsawwassen. Car reservations cost $15 in addition to the fare each way.

The fastest way to travel is straight to Victoria's Inner Harbour by air. **KENMORE AIR** (950 Westlake Ave N; 425/486-1257 or 800/543-9595; www.kenmoreair.com) makes regular daily flights from downtown Seattle. From Sea-Tac International Airport, **HORIZON AIR** (800/547-9308; www.horizonair.com) flies into **VICTORIA INTERNATIONAL AIRPORT** (250/953-7500), 15 miles (25 km) north of the city. From downtown Vancouver and Vancouver International Airport, **HELIJET INTERNATIONAL** (455 Waterfront Rd; 604/273-4688 or 800/665-4354; www.helijet.com) transports you to Victoria by helicopter. Seaplanes for **HARBOUR AIR** (1075 W Waterfront

Rd; 604/274-1277 or 800/665-0212; www.harbour-air.com) carry passengers from Vancouver. From Vancouver International Airport, fly with **AIR CANADA** (888/247-2262; www.aircanada.com).

In peak season—May through September and particularly July and August—crowds are greatest, prices are highest, and tourist services are best. Gardens and greenery are freshest in May and June; days are sunniest in July and August, except on the west coast, when fog is common. April and September are pleasant months for quieter, reduced-rate travel. Rates are often quite low November through April, except during holidays. **TOURISM VANCOUVER ISLAND** (250/754-3500; www.vancouverisland.travel) and **TOURISM VICTORIA** (250/953-2033 or 800/663-3883; www.tourismvictoria.com) have more information.

Victoria

Rudyard Kipling's hallowed turn-of-the-20th-century visit spurred Victoria to sell itself as a wee bit of Olde England. The fancy is an appealing one, conjuring red double-decker buses and high tea as keynote themes in the Garden City. Kilted bagpipers rub shoulders with Victoria's annual 3.65 million tourists, who come from America, Europe, Asia, and Latin America to walk along the waterside causeway, sit for caricature portraits, and marvel at jugglers. In the harbor, celebrity yachts rest within hailing distance of an antique three-masted sailing ship. But for sophisticated travelers, the city has grown far past its bucolic Brit persona.

The great thing about Victoria—rated among the world's top 10 cities by numerous upscale travel magazines—is that in the main central city, everything from the elegant Parliament buildings to old Chinatown is within walking distance. In recent years Victoria has seen an explosion of whale-watching tours, and outdoor enthusiasts can sea kayak or mountain bike from the city's doorsteps. Minutes from downtown, seaside **DALLAS ROAD** and **BEACH DRIVE** meander through the city's finest old residential districts, offering a view of the spectacular Olympic, Cascade, and Coast mountains south and east across the Straits of Juan de Fuca and Georgia.

ACCESS AND INFORMATION

A horse-drawn carriage ride with **VICTORIA CARRIAGE TOURS** (corner of Belleville and Menzies sts; 250/383-2207 or 877/663-2207) is a romantic favorite; the larger **TALLY-HO** carriages (corner of Belleville and Menzies sts; 250/383-5067 or 866/383-5067) offer rides at a family rate. The Inner Harbour is the locus of numerous popular maritime excursions; **VICTORIA HARBOUR FERRIES** (250/708-0201) offers tours of local waterways. Perched on the Inner Harbour across from the Empress Hotel, **TOURISM VICTORIA** (812 Wharf St; 250/953-2033; www.tourismvictoria.com) is helpful.

MAJOR ATTRACTIONS

Stroll through the main-floor hallways and shops of the venerable **FAIRMONT EMPRESS HOTEL** (721 Government St; 250/384-8111 or 800/441-1414; www.fairmont.com/empress), a postcard doyenne since 1908. The elegant Rattenbury-designed 1898 provincial **PARLIAMENT BUILDINGS** (501 Belleville St; 250/387-3046; www.legis.gov.bc.ca) can be seen via frequent tours. The **VICTORIA BUG ZOO** (631 Courtney St; 250/384-2847; www.bugzoo. bc.ca) fascinates children and adults alike, with features such as a surprisingly cute miniature apartment scaled to its cockroach denizens.

Opulent **CRAIGDARROCH CASTLE** (1050 Joan Crescent; 250/592-5323; www.craigdarrochcastle.com), once visited only by 19th-century socialites, is now open to the public to take in the parlors of Victoria's long-ago richest resident, coal baron Robert Dunsmuir. Heritage-home connoisseurs enjoy **POINT ELLICE HOUSE** (2616 Pleasant St; 250/380-6506; www.pointellice house.com), an early Victoria residence in tasteful Italianate style, and **EMILY CARR HOUSE** (207 Government St; 250/383-5843; www.emilycarr.com), the birth home of the legendary Canadian artist and writer.

MUSEUMS AND GALLERIES

Across the street from the Fairmont Empress Hotel, the **ROYAL BRITISH COLUMBIA MUSEUM** (675 Belleville St; 250/387-3014; www.royalbc museum.bc.ca) delights with its extensive collection of Canadian indigenous art and the Old Town display, a reconstructed 19th-century streetscape. Kids are drawn to the Open Oceans exhibit, a simulated submarine ride, and the IMAX theater. The **ART GALLERY OF GREATER VICTORIA** (1040 Moss St; 250/384-4101; aggv.bc.ca) is notable for its Asian art; the courtyard garden is home to North America's only Shinto shrine.

PARKS AND GARDENS

On the southern edge of downtown, the city's beloved **BEACON HILL PARK** (between Douglas and Cook sts; www.beaconhillpark.ca) boasts 184 acres of manicured gardens. The renowned **BUTCHART GARDENS** (800 Benvenuto Ave, Brentwood Bay; 250/652-5256 or 866/652-4422; www.butchart gardens.com) are 13 miles (21 km) north on the Saanich Peninsula. This 1904 estate masterpiece, laid into an old stone quarry, is crowded with blossoms in the manicured precincts of the Italian Garden, Rose Garden, and delicate Japanese Garden. If you're not driving, take city bus No. 75 Central Saanich; it stops in downtown Victoria on Douglas Street in front of Crystal Gardens.

SHOPPING

For those seeking English goods, **GOVERNMENT STREET** north to Yates Street offers the best selection of tweeds and china. For men's suits and casual wear, **BRITISH IMPORTERS** (1125 Government St; 250/386-1496) will please, as will upscale **W & J WILSON** (1221 Government St; 250/383-7177), featuring fine women's wear. Stop at **IRISH LINEN STORES** (1019 Government

VICTORIA THREE-DAY TOUR

DAY ONE: Breakfast at **LURE RESTAURANT**—try the eggs Benedict with candied salmon—at the **DELTA VICTORIA OCEAN POINTE RESORT AND SPA**, with seating overlooking the beautiful Inner Harbour. Then head out on a walking tour of downtown, strolling along **GOVERNMENT STREET** to **CHINATOWN**. Stop for dim sum for lunch at **DON MEE SEAFOOD RESTAURANT**. Return to the Inner Harbour promenade and flag down a **HORSE-DRAWN CARRIAGE** for a tour of **BEACON HILL PARK**. Ask the driver to wait a few minutes while you grab an ice cream at **BEACON DRIVE-IN RESTAURANT**, then visit the **EMILY CARR HOUSE** to learn about Victoria's most famous native daughter. Afterward, check in to the Windsor Suite at **PRIOR HOUSE BED & BREAKFAST INN**. Return to the Inner Harbour to catch a **VICTORIA HARBOUR FERRY** to **SONGHEES PARK** on Songhees Road, then meander five minutes along the waterfront to **SPINNAKERS BREWPUB**, where you sample Mount Tolmie Darks and relax into a pub-food dinner.

DAY TWO: After the lavish breakfast at Prior House, hop in your car to **MILE**

St; 250/383-6812) and **MURCHIE'S TEA & COFFEE** (1110 Government St; 250/383-3112) for well-known Fair Isle specialties.

Other obvious stops include **ROGER'S CHOCOLATES** (913 Government St; 250/384-7021), **CHOCOLATES BY BERNARD CALLEBAUT** (621 Broughton St; 250/380-1515), **OLD MORRIS TOBACCONISTS** (1116 Government St; 250/382-4811), and **MUNRO'S BOOKS** (1108 Government St; 250/382-2464). **SASQUATCH TRADING** (1233 Government St; 250/386-9033) and **COWICHAN TRADING** (1328 Government St; 250/383-0321) both offer Canadian and West Coast arts, crafts, and memorabilia. Buy a kite at **KABOO-DLES TOY STORE** (1320 Government St; 250/383-0931).

BEACON DRIVE-IN RESTAURANT (126 Douglas St; 250/385-7521) has the city's best soft ice cream. At **DEMITASSE CAFÉ** (1320 Blanshard St; 250/386-4442), breakfast is the thing. Heaping sandwiches feed office workers at **SAM'S DELI** (805 Government St; 250/382-8424). Outdoor seating is popular at **TORREFAZIONE ITALIA** (1234 Government St; 250/920-7203). The **CANOE BREWPUB** (450 Swift St; 250/361-1940), near Chinatown, is a good spot for a waterfront microbrew.

Johnson Street (between Government and Wharf sts) has quirky stores, highlighted by the enclosure of historic **MARKET SQUARE** (Johnson St, between Government and Store sts). Victoria's **CHINATOWN** (Fisgard St between Government and Store sts), the oldest in Canada, is worth visiting,

ZERO of the Trans-Canada Highway at Dallas Road and Douglas Street and take the scenic drive out **DALLAS ROAD** to **CLOVER POINT**. Fly your kite on the windy embankment, as residents do, or just take a stroll along the water. Then follow the Scenic Marine Drive signs along **BEACH DRIVE**, traversing the Uplands to gawk at million-dollar heritage homes, and travel north up Highway 17 to **SIDNEY** for lunch at **DOCK 503**. Afterward, head across the Saanich Peninsula to **BUTCHART GARDENS** to wander these world-famous, immaculately kept floral displays. Then head back to the city to check in to **FAIRHOLME MANOR**, resting a while before dinner at **PAPRIKA BISTRO**.

DAY THREE: After breakfast at the manor, stroll over to **CRAIGDARROCH CASTLE** to admire the opulent home of Victoria's first tycoon, coal magnate Robert Dunsmuir. Then walk down Fort Street's **ANTIQUE ROW** to poke your head in oddments shops, heading to Government Street for lunch at **SAM'S DELI**. Afterward, wander over to the Royal BC Museum to experience the marvelous collection of First Nations art, particularly masks. Follow up with afternoon tea at the **EMPRESS HOTEL**, then check in to a suite with a soaking tub (you'll need it) at **ABIGAIL'S HOTEL**. Return to Fort Street for dinner at **CAFÉ BRIO**.

especially to see narrow, shop-lined **FAN TAN ALLEY**. Outside Old Town, **ANTIQUE ROW** (Fort St east of downtown from Blanshard to Cook sts) beckons connoisseurs of 18th- to 20th-century goods.

PERFORMING ARTS

The **MCPHERSON PLAYHOUSE** (3 Centennial Square; 250/386-6121) is Victoria's leading live-theater venue. The **ROYAL THEATRE** (805 Broughton St; 250/386-6121) is home to a range of performances, from **PACIFIC OPERA VICTORIA** (1316B Government St; 250/385-0222) to the **VICTORIA SYMPHONY ORCHESTRA** (846 Broughton St; 250/385-6515). One of the most-anticipated public events is the sunset **SYMPHONY SPLASH**, an Inner Harbour concert held the first Sunday of August. The free weekly *Monday Magazine*, downtown in yellow boxes, has the best listings.

SPORTS AND RECREATION

For an ocean adventure in the Inner Harbour, you can rent a kayak at the **GORGE ROWING AND PADDLING CENTRE** (2940 Jutland Rd; 250/380-4668 or 877/380-4668); **OCEAN RIVER SPORTS** (1824 Store St; 250/381-4233 or 800/909-4233) rents kayaks and canoes and also runs guided paddles.

RESTAURANTS

Brasserie L'Ecole / ★★

1715 GOVERNMENT ST, VICTORIA; 250/475-6260
At this little brasserie, oddly located at the edge of Chinatown, eat simple French-country cooking. Rich pomegranate walls are decked out with fin de siecle bistro posters, and a long bar makes a welcoming snacking spot. The menu is classic, too: mussels and *frites*, steak *frites*, and warming onion soup; most of the meat and vegetables are organic, and the fish is wild-caught. Blackboards list the day's options for oysters, cheeses, and desserts. *$$–$$$; MC, V; no checks; dinner Tues–Sat; full bar; reservations recommended; www. lecole.ca; at Herald St.* &

Café Brio / ★★★

944 FORT ST, VICTORIA; 250/383-0009
This lively Antique Row restaurant glows warmth, from the recycled fir in the weathered floor and cozy booths to the movable feast of nudes and still lifes on the gold walls. The café serves contemporary regional cuisine with Italian leanings. Appetizers might include seared Alaskan scallops or confit of duck. Entrées range from red wine–braised beef short ribs to linguine with chanterelles, pancetta, cream, and fresh herbs. The 400-label wine list has one of the best selections of British Columbia wines in the province. *$$–$$$; AE, MC, V; no checks; dinner every day; full bar; reservations recommended; www. cafe-brio.com; at Vancouver St.* &

Don Mee Seafood Restaurant / ★★

538 FISGARD ST, VICTORIA; 250/383-1032
Though Don Mee serves an extensive and sophisticated Cantonese and classical Mandarin menu, dim sum is the draw. Its version of this lunchtime-only treat is among the most inventive in the Northwest, with particular emphasis on crab confections, such as the breaded and deep-fried crab claws. Reservations are a good idea during peak season, at lunch or dinner. *$–$$; AE, MC, V; no checks; lunch, dinner every day; beer and wine; www.donmee.com; in Chinatown between Government and Wharf sts.* &

Il Terrazzo Ristorante / ★★

555 JOHNSON ST, VICTORIA; 250/361-0028
You'll find a true taste of Italy in this beautiful restaurant tucked away on Waddington Alley. Surrounded by six outdoor fireplaces, plants, and flowers, Il Terrazzo offers a haven of privacy for alfresco dining in busy Old Town. Classic minestrone, char-grilled baby squid, wood-oven pizzas, pastas, and entrées such as osso buco attest to the menu's diversity. *$$$; AE, DC, MC, V; no checks; lunch Mon–Sat (Mon–Fri in winter), dinner every day; full bar; reservations recommended; www.ilterrazzo.com; near Market Square.* &

J & J Wonton Noodle House / ★

1012 FORT ST, VICTORIA; 250/383-0680
This busy, modest, spotlessly clean restaurant treats you to the flavors of Hong Kong, Sichuan, and northern China. A large kitchen window lets you watch chefs prepare wonton soup, Imperial Prawn with Spicy Garlic Wine Sauce, spicy ginger-fried chicken, or Sichuan braised-beef hot pot. Noodles are made fresh daily. Service is friendly, efficient, and knowledgeable. *$–$$; AE, MC, V; no checks; lunch, dinner Tues–Sat; beer and wine; reservations recommended; www.jjnoodlehouse.com; between Vancouver and Cook sts.* &

Paprika Bistro / ★★★

2524 ESTEVAN AVE, VICTORIA; 250/592-7424
The sheer savor and diversity of chef George Szasz's food belies (not intentionally) the whole fussy British Victoria ethos. This neighborhood bistro makes fresh sausage (pork *merguez*) daily, offers goulash almost every night, and is famed for its roast duck in cherry and ginger sauce. If you're lucky, they'll have roasted a whole spring lamb, and individual diners can order platters therefrom. *$$; MC, V; no checks; dinner Tues–Sat; beer and wine; reservations recommended; www.paprika-bistro.com; between Vancouver and Cook sts.* &

Re-Bar Modern Food / ★★

50 BASTION SQUARE, VICTORIA; 250/361-9223
Victoria's original vegetarian health-food restaurant is packed at lunch and dinner. Sip one of the refreshing fresh-fruit drinks, such as the Atomic Glow (apple, strawberry, and ginger juices) or the Cootie Bug (strawberry, pineapple, and orange juices) while perusing the menu. Delicious enchiladas, curries, and almond burgers are specialties, along with pastas and salads. Breads are all homemade. Friendly, helpful service exemplifies the Re-Bar's philosophy. *$–$$; AE, DC, MC, V; no checks; breakfast Mon–Fri, lunch every day, dinner Mon–Sat, brunch Sat–Sun; beer and wine; reservations recommended (brunch reservations not accepted); www.rebarmodernfood.com; at Langley St.*

Spinnakers Brewpub & Guesthouse / ★★

308 CATHERINE ST, VICTORIA; 250/386-2739 OR 877/838-2739
One of the first brew pubs in Canada, Spinnakers has been around since 1984. On the waterfront west of the Inner Harbour, it has one of the best views in Victoria. Traditional pub fare—fish-and-chips (lingcod, wild salmon, or Pacific halibut), burgers, pastas, and curries—is the order of the day. Try the Noggins chowder or one of the dinner specials, such as braised rockfish or ale-braised lamb shanks. Rooms and suites, all delightfully decorated with art and antiques, are available in three nearby houses. *$$; AE, DC, MC, V; no checks; breakfast, lunch, dinner every day; full bar; reservations recommended; www.spinnakers.com; across Johnson St Bridge from downtown.*

Temple / ★

525 FORT ST, VICTORIA; 250/383-2313
The slogan here evinces its philosophical bent: dinner is the start of the night, not the end of the day—to prove it, they're open until 11pm on weeknights, 1am on weekends. The look is cool and minimalist, but there's no hiding the enthusiasm of chef Sam Benedetto's devotion to organic cuisine. Most of the menu, from the wild coho salmon to the raw oysters, is Vancouver Island–caught or –raised; the style—light, with crisp, clean flavors and Asian touches—is also very West Coast. Feeling decadent? Book a table in the Moroccan Room, where you lounge on low cushions. *$$$; AE, MC, V; no checks; dinner Tues–Sun; full bar; reservations recommended; www.thetemple. ca; at Langley St.* &

LODGINGS

Abigail's Hotel / ★★★

906 MCCLURE ST, VICTORIA; 250/388-5363 OR 800/561-6565
The substantial, four-story Tudor facade of this elegant 23-room 1930 manor house promises grandeur, and the standard rooms, modernized and furnished with a mix of new and antique furniture, deliver. Top-floor suites, and those in the adjoining Coach House, display more elaborate furnishings and fixtures, such as wrought-iron bedsteads, vaulted ceilings, marble bathrooms, and double Jacuzzi tubs; some feature double-sided fireplaces, facing both the bedroom and the deep tub. Mornings bring a three-course breakfast. *$$$–$$$$; AE, MC, V; no checks; www.abigailshotel.com; at Quadra St, access from Vancouver St.*

Andersen House Bed & Breakfast / ★★★

301 KINGSTON ST, VICTORIA; 250/388-4565 OR 877/264-9988
An exceptionally ornate and well-preserved home built in 1891 for a sea captain, Andersen House has four rooms. Inside the Queen Anne–style structure, furnishings are a mix of antiques, Persian rugs, stained-glass windows, and contemporary art. The spacious Casablanca Room has a private balcony with steps to the garden. The even roomier two-bedroom Captain's Apartment can sleep five. Three rooms feature jetted tubs, and all offer robes and romantic touches such as champagne goblets. The dining room's 12-foot ceilings are rendered homey by a communal breakfast table. *$$$–$$$$; MC, V; checks OK; www.andersenhouse.com; at Pendray St.*

Beaconsfield Inn / ★★★

998 HUMBOLDT ST, VICTORIA; 250/384-4044
This nine-room Edwardian manor, built by businessman R. P. Rithet as a wedding gift for his daughter, is tastefully furnished in period antiques. In downstairs rooms, swirling art nouveau designs glimmer in rows of stained-glass windows. The Emily Carr and Duchess suites display understated, jewel-toned elegance. Most rooms have fireplaces, and many have whirlpool

tubs for two. The library, where full afternoon tea and sherry are served, harks back to the days of smoking jackets. Breakfast is served at intimate dining room tables or by the fountain in the conservatory. *$$$–$$$$; AE, JCB, MC, V; no checks; www.beaconsfieldinn.com; at Vancouver St.*

Delta Victoria Ocean Pointe Resort and Spa / ★★★

45 SONGHEES RD, VICTORIA; 250/360-2999 OR 800/667-4677
Dominating the Inner Harbour, along with the great monuments of the Empress and the Parliament Buildings, the modern Ocean Pointe has sweeping views. Standard rooms, done in a rich sage and burgundy, have tall windows and views from the water side of the hotel. For luxury, splurge on a suite. Family parking spots, kids' check-in packs, and story time with cookies and milk each evening make this one of Victoria's most family-friendly hotels. *$$$$; AE, DC, JCB, MC, V; no checks; www.deltahotels.com; across Johnson St Bridge.* &

Fairholme Manor / ★★★

683 ROCKLAND PL, VICTORIA; 250/598-3240 OR 877-511-3322
Perched on a hill above downtown in a neighborhood so exclusive the British royal family stays nearby, Fairholme is an Italianate mansion whose high-ceilinged suites are unsurpassed, even in the upper-crust B and B capital that is Victoria. With vast sitting areas, period furnishings, elegant but unfussy decor, fireplaces, soaking tubs, and bay windows overlooking the gardens, the five suites are sumptuous. Sylvia Main's European sensibilities color the discreet service and continental-style (including a hot entrée) breakfasts. *$$$–$$$$; AE, MC, V; no checks; www.fairholmemanor.com; in Rockland, at Charles St.*

Fairmont Empress Hotel / ★★★

721 GOVERNMENT ST, VICTORIA; 250/384-8111 OR 800/441-1414
This is one of the most famous hotels in the world—one of Canada's key landmarks. The hotel was built in 1908 in the style of a French chateau, and the rooms are furnished in Edwardian style. Though some of the rooms are compact, the draw is the location, harbor view, and overall atmosphere. In the public areas, tourists gather to sip afternoon tea; a separate lobby for guests assures privacy. All the high-end facilities are here, including an indoor pool, a fitness center, and a spa. The Empress Room is the most visually impressive dining room in Victoria. The grand space retains the original carved beams in the ceiling, the tapestried walls, and spacious tables. *$$$$; AE, DC, DIS, MC, V; no checks; www.fairmont.com/empress; between Humboldt and Belleville sts.* &

A Haterleigh Heritage Inn / ★★

243 KINGSTON ST, VICTORIA; 250/384-9995 OR 866/234-2244
This turn-of-the-20th-century heritage home, which architect Thomas Hooper built for himself in 1901, is decorated throughout with mint-condition

antiques under 12-foot ceilings. The original stained-glass windows are exceptional, and the rooms, all phone- and TV-free, are bright, roomy, and romantic: the main-floor Day Dreams Suite has a separate sitting area with a double-jetted tub, a bed with a satin-finish scrollwork headboard, and a trio of full-length windows topped with stained-glass panels. Beautiful as it is, the inn adopts an overly rigid service regime that often frustrates guests. *$$$–$$$$; MC, V; no checks; www.haterleigh.com; at Pendray St.*

Joan Brown's Bed & Breakfast / ★

729 PEMBERTON RD, VICTORIA; 250/592-5929

Joan Brown is a gregarious B and B proprietor, and she'll welcome you warmly into her 1883 mansion built for a former provincial lieutenant governor. The two sitting rooms are cheery with blue and yellow fabrics and contemporary art; the three rooms favor frills, pink, and Laura Ashley prints. Furnishings throughout are an eclectic (verging on eccentric) mix of antique and modern. Walk a block to the groomed gardens of the present lieutenant governor's mansion or three blocks to Craigdarroch Castle. *$$; no credit cards; checks OK; www.joanbrowns.com; off Fort St.*

Magnolia Hotel & Spa / ★★★

623 COURTNEY ST, VICTORIA; 250/381-0999 OR 877/624-6654

The 63-room Magnolia styles itself after European boutique hotels, with attentive service, tastefully luxurious rooms and suites, and a full-service spa. The lobby is paneled in rich mahogany, and underfoot are limestone tiles. Many rooms have fireplaces, such as our favored seventh-floor "diamond level" corner suite. Sumptuous bathrooms have marble counters, with deep soaker baths. Downstairs, Hugo's Grill and Brewhouse is all dark wood and artful metal trellising; if quiet is important to you, book a room several floors above the pub. *$$$$; AE, DC, DIS, E, JCB, MC, V; no checks; www. magnoliahotel.com; at Gordon St.* &

Prior House Bed & Breakfast Inn / ★★★

620 ST. CHARLES ST, VICTORIA; 250/592-8847 OR 877/924-3300

Truly a queen among B and Bs, this large 1912 manor has dramatic stonework on its lower levels and Tudor styling above. Gardens are visible from most of the six rooms; some have balconies. More-private, ground-level garden suites have separate entrances, patio space, and one or two bedrooms. An in-house chef creates the elaborate breakfasts and afternoon teas served daily. *$$$–$$$$; MC, V; checks OK; www.priorhouse.com; between Fairfield and Rockland sts.*

Sooke to Port Renfrew

Forty minutes west of Victoria on Highway 14, Sooke is a friendly little town set in idyllic surroundings. Beyond Sooke, the road continues past stellar beaches to Port Renfrew, southern trailhead for the famed West Coast Trail.

ROYAL ROADS UNIVERSITY (2005 Sooke Rd, Victoria; 250/391-2511 or 250/391-2600, ext. 4456; grounds open dawn–dusk every day), on the road to Sooke, is a grand former Dunsmuir family castle in medieval style; castle tours are available. In this area, the shallow, relatively warm waters of **WITTY'S LAGOON REGIONAL PARK** (west of Victoria via Hwy 14 and Metchosin Rd) are popular with local families. The swimming holes at **SOOKE POTHOLES PROVINCIAL PARK** (end of Sooke River Rd) are a treat on a hot day.

Locals pack the booths at the '50s-era **MOM'S CAFÉ** (2036 Shields Rd, Sooke; 250/642-3314) for hearty diner fare; traditional pub food warms travelers at the historic **17 MILE HOUSE** (5126 Sooke Rd, Sooke; 250/642-5942). Stop by the **SOOKE COUNTRY MARKET** (at Otter Point and West Coast rds, Sooke; 250/642-7528; Sat mid-May–Sept).

The entire coast between Sooke and Port Renfrew has parks with trails down to beaches; **CHINA BEACH** (23 miles/37 km west of Sooke) is the start of the rigorous **JUAN DE FUCA MARINE TRAIL**. **SOMBRIO BEACH** (34 miles/57 km west of Sooke) is popular with local surfers. **BOTANICAL BEACH** (follow signs at end of paved road just west of Port Renfrew) has miles of tide pools that expose sea life. The **SOOKE VISITOR INFORMATION CENTRE**, in the **SOOKE REGION MUSEUM** (2070 Phillips Rd, Sooke; 250/642-6351), has details. Hikers fuel up on mile-high cheesecakes and homemade pies at the **COUNTRY CUPBOARD CAFÉ**, 15 minutes west of Sooke (402 Sheringham Point Rd, Sooke; 250/646-2323).

RESTAURANTS

Markus' Wharfside Restaurant

1831 MAPLE AVE S, SOOKE; 250/642-3596

Markus Wieland's Mediterranean spot is housed in a former fisherman's cottage overlooking Sooke Harbour. Rare views of the water can be enjoyed from the two little antique-furnished dining rooms (one with a cozy fire) or from the patio. Risotto, Tuscan seafood soup, and baked goat cheese with roasted garlic are mainstays; the crab, when available, comes straight from the docks next door. *$$$; MC, V; no checks; lunch Mon–Sat, dinner every day, brunch Sun (check for winter closures); full bar; reservations recommended; www.markuswharfsiderestaurant.com; at foot of Maple Ave, off Hwy 14.* &

Point No Point Restaurant / ★★

1505 WEST COAST RD (POINT NO POINT RESORT), SOOKE; 250/646-2020

This little glass-enclosed restaurant, perched high on a bluff over the crashing waves, is widely known for more than its dramatic water and mountain views. At dinner, you can start with steamed local mussels with heirloom tomatoes or organic squash soup with lemon crème fraîche; entrées might include wild spring salmon with sweet corn and chanterelle mushrooms or braised halibut cheeks with tomato confit. *$$$; AE, MC, V; no checks; lunch, afternoon tea every day, dinner Wed–Sun (no dinner in Jan); beer and wine; reservations recommended; www.pointnopointresort.com; Hwy 14, 15 miles (24 km) west of Sooke.*

Sooke Harbour House / ★★★★

1528 WHIFFEN SPIT RD, SOOKE;
250/642-3421 OR 800/889-9688
More than two decades after they started setting Canadian cuisine on its ears, Frédérique and Sinclair Philip's globally famous restaurant remains ever-intriguing. Entrées range from sautéed rosethorn rockfish with a strawberry and begonia dressing to locally raised leg of lamb marinated in fenugreek, cumin, garlic, and golden rosemary. Thrill seekers can book ahead for the Gastronomic Adventure and enjoy seven to nine courses. The 600-label wine list, placed in the world's top 90 by *Wine Spectator* magazine, features excellent French vintages. The dining room, with its ocean views, fire, and roomy tables, is refreshingly informal. *$$$$; DC, E, JCB, MC, V; checks OK; dinner every day; full bar; reservations required; www.sookeharbourhouse.com; end of Whiffen Spit Rd, off Hwy 14.* &

LODGINGS

Hartmann House / ★★★

5262 SOOKE RD, SOOKE; 250/642-3761
This exquisite two-suite B and B is alive with blossoms: the bay-windowed exterior is draped with pink flowers in season; an old-fashioned porch with white wicker chairs overlooks an acre of cottage garden. Each of the two suites has a private entrance, a whirlpool tub, a fireplace, a kitchenette, and wide-plank fir floors. Expect to see herbs, fruits, and flowers in the breakfast cart delivered to your door. Two-night minimum. *$$$; V; no checks; www.hartmannhouse.bc.ca; 3½ miles (6 km) east of Sooke.*

Markham House / ★★★

1853 CONNIE RD, SOOKE; 250/642-7542 OR 888/256-6888
Guests choose Markham House for gentle pleasures: tea on the patio, country hospitality, feather beds, and fireside sherry before turning in. Immaculately groomed grounds include a hot tub in a gazebo, a small river, a trout pond, a putting green, and iris gardens. One of the three guest rooms has a double Jacuzzi overlooking the pond. The very private Honeysuckle Cottage makes an ideal romantic hideaway. *$$–$$$; AE, DC, DIS, E, JCB, MC, V; checks OK; www.markhamhouse.com; turn south off Hwy 14 east of Sooke.*

Point No Point Resort / ★★★

1505 WEST COAST RD, SOOKE; 250/646-2020
The Soderberg family owns a mile of beach and 40 acres of undeveloped coastline facing the Strait of Juan de Fuca. They rent 25 cabins among the trees near the cliff. Several newer, pricier cabins have hot tubs; in-room spa services are available. Wood is supplied, and each cabin has a fireplace and kitchen, though the restaurant (see review) serves excellent food. *$$$–$$$$; AE, MC, V; checks OK; www.pointnopointresort.com; Hwy 14, 15 miles (24 km) west of Sooke.* &

Richview House / ★★★

7031 RICHVIEW DR, SOOKE; 250/642-5520 OR 866/276-2480
Views of the Strait of Juan de Fuca and the Olympic Mountains from each room's private hot tub are just part of what keeps couples returning to this adult-oriented B and B on Sooke's waterfront. Each of the three rooms in François and Joan Gething's handcrafted, modern-with-a-touch-of-Tudor home has a private entrance, a deck or patio (with a hot tub), and a fireplace; the lower-floor room boasts a private steam room. Much of the lovely furniture and woodwork was crafted by François himself. *$$$; MC, V; no checks; www.bnbsooke.com; Whiffen Spit Rd off Hwy 14, turn right onto Richview Rd.*

Sooke Harbour House / ★★★★

1528 WHIFFEN SPIT RD, SOOKE; 250/642-3421 OR 800/889-9688
This bucolic waterside establishment is one of Canada's finest inns. Innkeepers Frédérique and Philip Sinclair's Northwest art collection—among the country's most extensive and intriguing—graces everything. The gardens, too, are works of art. Frédérique works with local craftspeople to create distinctive themes for each guest room. The Mermaid Room is lavished with mythic art; the Victor Newman Longhouse Room features museum-quality First Nations art. Most of the 28 rooms have water and mountain views, fireplaces, and Japanese-style deep soaking tubs on their balconies. The lavish complimentary breakfast—hazelnut–maple syrup waffles with loganberry purée, for example—is delivered to your room. *$$$$; DC, E, JCB, MC, V; checks OK; www.sookeharbourhouse.com; end of road, off Hwy 14.* &

Sidney and the Saanich Peninsula

This pretty rural area, although increasingly subject to urban development, holds bucolic corners, particularly off W Saanich Road. En route to the floral splendor of **BUTCHART GARDENS** (800 Benvenuto Ave, Brentwood Bay; 250/652-5256), stop at **VICTORIA ESTATE WINERY** (1445 Benvenuto Ave, Brentwood Bay; 250/652-2671) for a tasting or a meal on the wraparound veranda overlooking the vineyards. Bibliophiles like seaside **SIDNEY-BY-THE-SEA**, with 10 bookstores to browse through. While waiting in line for the ferry to Vancouver, duck into the nearby **STONEHOUSE PUB** (2215 Canoe Cove Rd, Sidney; 250/656-3498) for a snack or a beer.

RESTAURANTS

Deep Cove Chalet / ★★★

11190 CHALET RD, SIDNEY; 250/656-3541
Chef-owner Pierre Koffel brings European formality to this rural seaside setting. The large windows of this 1913 wooden lodge overlook lawns and a splendid view of Saanich Inlet. Guests can dine in the garden under a grape arbor on fine days. Lobster bisque, rack of lamb, coq au vin, and beef Wellington are among the continental classics. Book a suite upstairs for a private dinner or an overnight stay. *$$$$; AE, MC, V; local checks only; lunch Wed–Sun, dinner Tues–Sun; full bar; reservations recommended; www.deepcovechalet. com; northwest of Sidney, call for directions.* &

Dock 503 / ★★★

2320 HARBOUR RD, SIDNEY; 250/656-0828
Five hundred and two of the berths at Van Isle Marina are for visiting yachts; the 503rd is for dining. Blue-canvas blinds over marina-view windows create a low-key nautical air at this casual 55-seat spot, which is surrounded on three sides by water views. Although the ingredients are regional, the menu blends inspiration from Asia and Europe. Seafood is simplest and best— superb grilled oysters accompanied by yam fries make a satisfying meal. *$$$; AE, DC, MC, V; no checks; lunch Mon–Sat, dinner every day, brunch Sun; full bar; reservations recommended; www.dock503.vanislemarina.com; at marina north of Sidney.* &

The Latch Country Inn / ★★

2328 HARBOUR RD (SHOAL HARBOUR INN),
SIDNEY; 250/656-6622 OR 877/956-6622
This offbeat 1925 mansion was designed by noted Victoria architect Samuel Maclure as a summer home for the lieutenant governor of British Columbia. The exterior is rustic British Columbian; inside is all old-world elegance. West Coast fare with an Italian tinge might feature appetizers such as steamed mussels or a rabbit roulade with arugula, Belgian endive, and prosciutto. Entrées range from rack of lamb to Cowichan Bay duck breast or a vegetarian stuffed portobello mushroom. Six suites take advantage of antique wood paneling hewn from local Douglas fir; one has the original 1925 10-headed shower. *$$$; AE, DC, DIS, E, MC, V; no checks; dinner every day; full bar; reservations recommended; www.latchinn.ca; ½ mile (1 km) north of Sidney.*

LODGINGS

Brentwood Bay Lodge / ★★★

849 VERDIER AVE, BRENTWOOD BAY;
250/544-2079 OR 888/544-2079

Perched elegantly above its lovely namesake bay, this new post-and-beam lodge is the best accommodation in the vicinity of Butchart Gardens. (In fact, guests can paddle a canoe to Butchart's back entrance.) Decorated in subdued earth tones with clear fir trim, the 33 suites all have water views and feature fireside sitting areas, whirlpool tubs, and European linens. The swimming pool and spa are discreetly tucked into the garden level. The Arbutus Grille dining room, a dramatic space with 30-foot windows, takes a tapaslike approach to seafood. The charming Brentwood Bay–Mill Bay ferry, which docks next door, is one of British Columbia's best-kept secrets. *$$$$; DC, E, JCB, MC, V; www.brentwoodbaylodge.com.* &

Malahat

The Malahat is an ominous word among local drivers: it signals steep roads and winter fog and ice. But for leisurely drives, this section of the Trans-Canada Highway (Highway 1) from Victoria to Mill Bay is one of the prettiest drives on the island. Lush Douglas fir forests hug the narrow-laned highway, past beloved **GOLDSTREAM PROVINCIAL PARK** (3400 Trans-Canada Hwy/Hwy 1, 8 miles northwest of Victoria; 250/478-9414; www.goldstreampark.com), where hundreds of bald eagles gather to feed on salmon mid-December through February. At the summit, northbound pullouts offer breathtaking views over Saanich Inlet clasped by surrounding hills.

RESTAURANTS

The Dining Room at the Aerie Resort / ★★★
Bonelli / ★★★

600 EBEDORA LANE, MALAHAT; 250/743-7115 OR 800/518-1933

Perched high on Malahat Mountain, the Aerie Resort (see review) dining room is as spectacular and inspiring as its view. Chef Christophe Letard incorporates produce from nearby organic farms, local wild mushrooms, and other forest edibles into his multicourse tasting menus, creating such imaginative dishes as local prawn and chanterelle salad or roast of venison saddle with dark chocolate and venison sauce. Choose from a 7-course farmers market, seafood, or vegetarian menu or an 11-course discovery menu.

Bonelli (Italian for "eagle") is the Aerie's more casual dining option. The Mediterranean-themed à la carte menu for both lunch and dinner offers soups, salads, sandwiches, and straightforward main dishes such as lamb chops, beef strip loin, and free-range chicken breast with morel cream sauce—all from the same high-standard, made-from-scratch kitchen as the main dining room's. A plate of local artisan cheese or chocolate fondue for two are reason enough to linger. *$$$$ (Dining Room), $$$ (Bonelli); AE, DC, MC, V; no checks; dinner every day (Dining Room), lunch, dinner every day (Bonelli); full bar; reservations recommended; www.aerie.bc.ca; 30 minutes from downtown Victoria, take Spectacle Lake turnoff from Trans-Canada Hwy.* ♿ (Dining Room only)

Malahat Mountain Inn / ★★

265 TRANS-CANADA HWY, MALAHAT; 250/478-1944

Wrought-iron candelabras and local art punctuate the dramatic color scheme; booths offer intimacy; and a wide deck makes the most of the view over Finlayson Arm. The menu is big on seafood and pastas. At dinner, vegetarians dig into the spinach primavera penne; meatier fare includes lamb sirloin with merlot-Stilton cream sauce or veal osso buco. The Malahat Mountain Inn (250/478-1979 or 800/913-1944) operates 10 suites next door with soaker tubs, fireplaces, and, of course, views. *$$–$$$; AE, MC, V; no checks; breakfast, lunch, dinner every day; full bar; reservations recommended; www. malahatmountaininn.com; at top of Malahat Dr (Hwy 1).*

LODGINGS

The Aerie Resort / ★★★

600 EBEDORA LANE, MALAHAT; 250/743-7115 OR 800/518-1933

The Aerie is quite simply over the top—too much so for some tastes—but its faux-Mediterranean-Empire decadence draws celebrities seeking indulgence high atop Malahat. The 35 creamy white terraced units were designed as a modern take on Mediterranean villages. Set in 85 acres of woods and gardens, it achieves an idyllic Isle-of-Capri mood. Most guest rooms feature whirlpool tubs, fireplaces, private decks, and Persian and Chinese silk carpets. Romantics seeking ultimate privacy (and views) may opt for one of the six hilltop suites, several hundred feet up and away from the main building. *$$$$; AE, DC, MC, V; no checks; www.aerie.bc.ca; 30 minutes from downtown Victoria, take Spectacle Lake turnoff from Trans-Canada Hwy.*

The Gulf Islands

Dotting the azure Strait of Georgia are clusters of beautiful, bucolic islands, Canada's counterpart to the U.S. San Juans. Serene, remote, laid-back, artsy, and quirky, the Gulf Islands are divine places. Services can be sketchy on the smaller islands, so plan accordingly.

The Gulf Islands fall into three groups. The best known are the southern Gulf Islands; of these, Salt Spring, Galiano, Mayne, Saturna, and Pender are accessible via the BC Ferries terminal at Swartz Bay outside Victoria (or from Tsawwassen outside Vancouver), while Gabriola is reached from Nanaimo. Visited several times a day by ferry, the southern Gulf Islands—particularly Salt Spring and Galiano—offer the widest selection of services. Farther north, Denman and

Hornby islands, with trails beloved by mountain bikers, are a short hop from Buckley Bay, 12 miles (20 km) south of Courtenay. Quadra, Cortes, and Sonora make up the closely linked Discovery Islands—fishing and boating meccas east of Campbell River.

ACCESS AND INFORMATION

BC FERRIES (250/386-3431 or 888/223-3779; www.bcferries.com) offer many trips daily, but plan ahead in summer for car traffic; popular runs fill fast. Island hopping is possible, but schedules are complex and times do not always mesh. If you are planning to island hop, ask BC Ferries about their SailPass—it may save you some money. Advance reservations are possible between the British Columbia mainland and the southern Gulf Islands at no extra charge. Less stressful—and less expensive—is leaving the car at home; most inns and B and Bs offer ferry pickup. Bring your own bike or rent one; the islands (with the exception of busy Salt Spring) are wonderful—if hilly—for cycling. **TOURISM VANCOUVER ISLAND** (335 Wesley St, Ste 203, Nanaimo; 250/754-3500; www.vancouverisland.travel) has information on touring the Gulf Islands.

Salt Spring Island

Salt Spring is the largest and most populous of the southern Gulf Islands (with 10,000 residents) and has artisans' studios and pastoral farms. Non-Native settlement dates back to the mid-19th century, and early settlers included African Americans from San Francisco after the Civil War. The Kanakas, as the indigenous people of Hawaii were then called, also played a role in early settlement.

Today Salt Spring is a place where there are no fast-food chains (residents block proposals to build them) but dogs greet you everywhere. The landscape has a pioneer imprint of farms and forests, interspersed with lakes. From Victoria, ferries leave Swartz Bay and land 35 minutes later at Salt Spring's **FULFORD HARBOUR**, a small artists' village at the island's south end. Here you can fuel up for the 20-minute drive to Ganges at **TREEHOUSE SOUTH** (2921 Fulford-Ganges Rd, Salt Spring Island; 250/653-4833) or **MORNINGSIDE ORGANIC BAKERY AND CAFÉ** (107 Morningside Rd, Salt Spring Island; 250/653-4414).

MOUNT MAXWELL PROVINCIAL PARK (7 miles/11 km southwest of Ganges via Fulford-Ganges Rd and Cranberry Rd), on the west side of the island 2,000 feet (610 m) above sea level, has a rewarding view. For walk-in camping and seaside walks, head for **RUCKLE PROVINCIAL PARK** (10 minutes from Fulford Harbour ferry dock, take right onto Beaver Rd; 250/539-2115 or 877/559-2115; www.env. gov.bc.ca/bcparks) on the island's east side. **ST. MARY LAKE** and **CUSHEON LAKE** are good spots for a dip; the ocean waters are clean but chilly.

GARRY OAKS WINERY (1880 Fulford-Ganges Rd, Salt Spring Island; 250/653-4687; garryoakswine.com) and **SALT SPRING VINEYARDS** (151 Lee Rd off 1700 block of Fulford-Ganges Rd, Salt Spring Island; 250/653-9463; www. saltspringvineyards.com), which also has a B and B, is open for tastings May through October. Locals and tourists alike love the Salt Spring Island **SATURDAY MARKET**'s (Centennial Park, Ganges; 250/537-4448; www.saltspringmarket.com; Apr–Oct) cheeses, organic produce, pottery, hand-smoothed wooden bowls, and more. Similarly fine wares can be found at the **ARTCRAFT** sale (250/537-0899; June–mid-Sept) in Ganges's Mahon Hall. Dozens of arts and crafts studios throughout the island are open to the public. A Studio Tour map from the **SALT SPRING ISLAND VISITOR INFORMATION CENTRE** (121 Lower Ganges Rd, Ganges; 250/537-5252 or 866/216-2936; www.saltspringtoday.com) will show you the way.

The annual (since 1896) Salt Spring **FALL FAIR** (Farmer's Institute, 351 Rainbow Rd; Sept) is a family favorite, with sheep shearing, crafts, animals, games for kids, baked goods, and more. Enjoy a snack and organic coffee at the vegetarian bakery and café **BARB'S BUNS** (1-121 McPhillips Ave, Ganges; 250/537-4491); views, hearty meals, and microbrews at **MOBY'S MARINE PUB** (124 Upper Ganges Rd, Ganges; 250/537-5559); live music and wholesome, made-from-scratch meals at the **TREEHOUSE CAFÉ** (106 Purvis Lane, Ganges, 250/537-5379); and wood-fired pizzas at the **RAVEN STREET MARKET CAFÉ** (321 Fernwood Rd, north end of Salt Spring Island; 250/537-2273).

RESTAURANTS

Calvin's Bistro / ★

133 LOWER GANGES RD, GANGES; 250/538-5551
Calvin's harbor-view patio, fresh seafood, cozy booth seating, and local popularity have stood the test of time. The lunch menu features sandwiches, fish-and-chips, and a host of burgers: chicken, lamb, salmon, veggie, and—a nod to the owners' European roots—schnitzel. At dinner, fresh halibut, salmon, and prawns share the menu with lamb, pasta, and Thai specialties such as coconut prawns, pork spring rolls, and curried chicken. *$$–$$$; MC, V; no checks; breakfast, lunch, dinner Tues–Sat, brunch Sun; full bar; reservations recommended; www.calvinsbistro.com; on waterfront.*

Hastings House / ★★★

160 UPPER GANGES RD, GANGES; 250/537-2362 OR 800/661-9255
The dark-wood ambience of this well-known inn (see review) extends to its restaurant, where an enormous fireplace warms the foyer of a house built as a replica English country manor. The prix-fixe menu (choose from a three- or five-course option) changes daily, offering such appetizers as celeriac and prosciutto bisque or seared spring salmon with pattypan squash. Entrées run from peppered pheasant breast with orchard pears to saffron-steamed halibut with rosemary ratatouille. Local lamb is almost always available. *$$$$; AE, MC, V; no checks; lunch by arrangement, dinner every day (closed mid-Nov–mid-Mar); full bar; reservations required; www.hastingshouse.com; just north of Ganges.*

The Oystercatcher Seafood Bar & Grill / ★

1104 MANSON RD, GANGES; 250/537-5041
In summer, the tables at the casual Oystercatcher Seafood Bar & Grill spill out onto the terrace. This hip nautical spot, with its cozy booths, river-rock fireplace, and marina views, covers the ocean-based standards in the usual style, and does them well. Any of the five wild salmon options are a good bet. Steaks, burgers, pastas, and a kids' menu round out the offerings. Owner Barry Kazakoff has extended his domain downstairs with Shipstones, a one-room pub.*$$; MC, V; no checks; lunch, dinner every day; full bar; reservations recommended; oystercatcher@saltspring.com; at Mouat's Landing on waterfront.*

Restaurant House Piccolo / ★★★★

108 HEREFORD AVE, GANGES; 250/537-1844
Chef Piccolo Lyytikainen, a member of the prestigious Chaîne des Rôtisseurs, brings upscale European cuisine to this intimate Ganges restaurant, widely regarded as among the finest in the region. Set in a tiny heritage house, Piccolo's candlelit ambience is island-style informal. Main dishes range from charbroiled fillet of beef with Gorgonzola sauce to roasted Muscovy duck breast and local lamb. Enjoy the baked-to-order warm chocolate cake. *$$$$; AE, DC, E, MC, V; local checks only; dinner every day; full bar; reservations required; www.housepiccolo.com; downtown.*

LODGINGS

Anne's Oceanfront Hideaway / ★★

168 SIMSON RD, SALT SPRING ISLAND; 250/537-0851 OR 888/474-2663
Splendid views of Stuart Channel and Vancouver Island from this immaculate home invite its guests to contemplate the sunset from the wraparound veranda, and the aroma of morning baking invites them to anticipate breakfast. The inn's four guest rooms are decorated in country floral style. Wheelchair users praise accessibility here, and others applaud the hospitality of proprietors Rick and Ruth-Anne Broad. A four-course breakfast might include eggs in phyllo pastry with lamb patties and chutney. A hot tub, aromatherapy massage services, a canoe, and bikes help fill the time. *$$$; AE, MC, V; no checks; www.annesoceanfront.com; north of Vesuvius ferry terminal.* ♿

Bold Bluff Retreat / ★★

1 BOLD BLUFF, SALT SPRING ISLAND; 250/653-4377 OR 866/666-4377

This secluded retreat accessible only by private boat borders 2,600 acres of protected land. Salty's Cabin, which sleeps up to five, sits on a rocky outcropping where the tide rushes in and out right under the deck. The Garden Cottage, which sleeps up to six, is nestled in an old orchard. Singles and couples enjoy the single B and B room in the main house, a 1940 cedar lodge. The newest addition is a furnished tepee on the bluff's edge, with a deck, solar shower, and camp kitchen. Owner Tamar Griggs will gladly pick up guests for the 5-minute boat ride from Burgoyne Bay or the 10-minute jaunt from Maple Bay on Vancouver Island. One-week minimum in cabins July through August. *$–$$$; AE, MC, V; checks OK; Salty's Cabin closed Nov–Mar, B&B and tepee closed Oct–May; www.boldbluff.com; from Burgoyne Bay, 10 minutes northwest of Fulford Harbour, from Maple Bay on Vancouver Island.*

Hastings House / ★★★

160 UPPER GANGES RD, GANGES; 250/537-2362 OR 800/661-9255
The English-country ambience at this 25-acre seaside estate is as genuine as you can get outside the United Kingdom. The farm was founded by an immigrant British farmer in the 19th century. The Farmhouse has two spacious, two-level suites overlooking the water. In the Manor House, two upstairs suites feature the same lovely views. The Post is a compact cabin popular with honeymooners. Seven Hillside suites offer lofty ocean views in a modern board-and-batten building; these, however, get some road noise, lack the charm of the other units, and overlook the patio of the pub next door. *$$$$; AE, MC, V; no checks; closed mid-Nov–mid-Mar; www.hastingshouse.com; just north of Ganges.*

Sky Valley Inn / ★★

421 SKY VALLEY RD, SALT SPRING ISLAND; 250/537-9800
Imagine you've been invited to stay at a friend's villa in the south of France, where you can spend your days lounging by the pool or poking around in the garden. This B and B replicates just that kind of Mediterranean ease. Three rooms, in a pretty French-country style, have private entrances opening onto an ivy-draped courtyard, home to the heated outdoor pool. The light and airy Master Bedroom is the choicest, with a mix of French country and West Indies decor, as well as access to both the courtyard and a deck with far-reaching views. Breakfasts are lavish homemade affairs, and wine and hors d'oeuvres are served each evening. *$$$; MC, V; checks OK; closed Dec–Jan; www.sky valleyinn.com; 4 miles (6 km) south of Ganges.*

North and South Pender Islands

Pender "Island" is actually two islands united by a small bridge. Both are green and rural, though South Pender is the less developed of the two. The population here is decidedly residential, so don't expect many restaurants, lodgings, or shops. Beaches, however, abound: **MORTIMER SPIT** (western tip of South Pender) and **GOWLLAND POINT BEACH** (end of Gowlland Point Rd on South Pender) are among 30 public ocean-access points. Maps are available at the **PENDER ISLAND LIONS VISITOR INFORMATION CENTRE** (2332 Otter Bay Rd; 250/629-6541; www.penderisland.info; mid-May–Labor Day), near the Otter Bay ferry terminal on North Pender.

To take advantage of the fabled Gulf Island viewscape, the trails on **MOUNT NORMAN** (accessible from Ainslie Rd or Canal Rd on South Pender), part of the new **GULF ISLANDS NATIONAL PARK RESERVE**, are steep but rewarding. The gentle terrain of South Pender is particularly appealing for cyclists; rent bikes at **OTTER BAY MARINA** (2311 MacKinnon Rd, North Pender; 250/629-3579) and then head to South Pender. While waiting for the ferry at Otter Bay on North Pender, grab an excellent burger—try a venison, oyster, or ostrich variation—at the humble trailer called the **STAND** (Otter Bay ferry terminal, North Pender; 250/629-3292).

LODGINGS

Poets Cove Seaside Resort / ★★★

**9801 SPALDING RD, SOUTH PENDER ISLAND;
250/629-3212 OR 888/512-7638**
Known for years as Bedwell Harbour Resort, this new complex represents an almost complete revamp except for the sheltered cove and marina, backed by a wooded hillside, with stunning sunset views. The three-story lodge, with its stone detailing and pretty rounded gables, has 22 ocean-view, Arts and Crafts–style rooms with fireplaces and balconies. Cottages have kitchens, fireplaces, and balconies; most have views of the cove, and some have private hot tubs. A water-sports center offers lessons. Aurora Restaurant, located in the lodge, serves wild salmon, Pender Island lamb, and other treats. *$$$$; AE, MC, V; no checks; www.poetscove.com; from Vancouver Island, take resort's water taxi from Sidney or BC Ferries from Swartz Bay to Otter Bay.*

Saturna Island

The remotest of the southern Gulf Islands—it takes two ferries to get here—Saturna has a scant 300 residents, two general stores, a café, and a pub overlooking the Lyall Harbour ferry stop. No camping is available on the island, but hiking abounds on **MOUNT WARBURTON PIKE**, the second-highest peak in the southern Gulf Islands. **WINTER COVE PARK** (1 mile/1.6 km from ferry dock, off East Point Rd) is an inviting place to beachcomb or picnic above the Strait of Georgia. Or take the scenic ocean drive to the tidal pools and sculpted sandstone of remote **EAST POINT REGIONAL PARK** (eastern tip of island). **SATURNA ISLAND VINEYARDS** (8 Quarry Trail; 250/539-5139 or 877/918-3388; www.saturnavineyards. com) has merlot, semillon-chardonnay, and Gewürztraminer.

LODGINGS

Saturna Lodge and Restaurant / ★

130 PAYNE RD, SATURNA ISLAND; 250/539-2254 OR 888/539-8800
This lovely frame lodge sits high on a hill overlooking Boot Cove. Windows wrap around the dining room, and a fire beckons in the lower-floor lounge. Seven sunny rooms upstairs are contemporary in feel, with pleasant sitting

areas and ocean or garden views. Five have private baths; the honeymoon suite has a soaker tub and private balcony. The menu at the restaurant (serving breakfast to guests, dinner to the public; reservations required) offers lamb and organic produce; the wine cellar features Saturna's own wines. *$$–$$$; MC, V; no checks; closed mid-Oct–mid-May; www.saturna.ca; follow signs from ferry.*

Mayne Island

During the Cariboo Gold Rush of the mid-1800s, Mayne was the southern Gulf Islands' commercial and social hub, a way station between Victoria and Vancouver. Today, the pace of life is more serene. Rolling orchards and warm, rock-strewn beaches dominate this pocket-size island of 5 square miles (13 sq km). A complete bicycle tour of the island takes five hours; at **DINNER BAY PARK**, about a half mile (1 km) south of the ferry terminal at Village Bay, a traditional Japanese garden commemorates the many Japanese families who settled on the island before World War II.

RESTAURANTS

Oceanwood Country Inn / ★★★

630 DINNER BAY RD, MAYNE ISLAND; 250/539-5074
Exquisitely prepared four-course dinners in the dining room overlooking Navy Channel feature entrées such as nettle-and-almond-stuffed sole or boneless quail stuffed with mushrooms and hazelnuts. Appetizers are strikingly unique: smoked-sablefish and beet terrine with stinging-nettle juice, for example. At dessert, a goat-cheese cake with walnut sabayon and rosemary-caramel-roasted apples might make an appearance. *$$$$; MC, V; Canadian checks only; dinner every day (closed Nov–Mar); full bar; reservations required; www.oceanwood.com; right on Dalton Dr, right on Mariners St, immediate left onto Dinner Bay Rd, look for signs.*

LODGINGS

Oceanwood Country Inn / ★★★

630 DINNER BAY RD, MAYNE ISLAND; 250/539-5074
The split-level, high-ceilinged Wisteria Room, the largest of the Oceanwood's 12 guest rooms, has striking views over Navy Channel. Fireplaces, deep soaker tubs, and ocean views are features of many rooms. Some, like the Lilac Room, are done in a floral theme; others, like the blue-hued Heron Room, come in more masculine tones. After kayaking, bird-watching, or cycling (the inn has bikes on hand), eat in the excellent dining room (see review). *$$$–$$$$; MC, V; Canadian checks only; closed Nov–Mar; www.oceanwood. com; directions above.*

Galiano Island

Residents here dismiss bustling Salt Spring as "towny," as well they might from their undeveloped, secluded island. Dedicated locals protect the natural features along the island's narrow 19 miles (30 km): cliffs, bluffs, meadows, and harbors. Despite being the closest of the southern Gulf Islands to Tsawwassen (one hour), Galiano has just 1,000 residents and only a few services and shops, clustered at its south end at Sturdies Bay.

On **BODEGA RIDGE**, a clifftop walk rewards with views across the islands. From **BLUFFS PARK** and **MOUNT GALIANO** you can watch eagles, ferries, and sweeping tides on Active Pass. Most Galiano roads accommodate bicycles, but there's some steep going. Rent a bike at **GALIANO BICYCLE** (36 Burrill Rd; 250/539-9906). **MONTAGUE HARBOUR PROVINCIAL MARINE PARK** (5 miles/8 km west of ferry dock; 250/539-2115 or 877/559-2115, 800/689-9025 for camping reservations) is a sheltered bay with beaches and more. At **MONTAGUE HARBOUR MARINA**, just east of the park, go kayaking with **GULF ISLANDS KAYAKING** (250/539-2442), rent from **GALIANO MOPEDS & BOAT RENTALS** (250/539-3443), or stop for a barbecue on the deck of the **HARBOUR GRILL** (250/539-5733).

You'll find local color at the **HUMMINGBIRD PUB** (47 Sturdies Bay Rd; 250/539-5472), vegetarian-friendly lunches at **DAYSTAR MARKET CAFÉ** (George-son Bay Rd at Porlier Pass Rd; 250/539-2800), and, on weekends, four-course dinners at **LA BÉRENGERIE** (Montague Rd; 250/539-5392), a cozy house in the woods.

While away time in the Sturdies Bay ferry line at **TRINCOMALI BAKERY, DELI & BISTRO** (2540 Sturdies Bay Rd; 250/539-2004) or the funky, diner-style **GRAND CENTRAL EMPORIUM** (2470 Sturdies Bay Rd; 250/539-9885). The **GALIANO CHAMBER OF COMMERCE** (Sturdies Bay Village Center; 250/539-2233; www.galianoisland.com) runs a small information center in summer.

RESTAURANTS

Atrevida Restaurant at the Galiano Inn / ★★★

134 MADRONA DR, GALIANO ISLAND; 250/539-3388 OR 877/530-3939
Named for a Spanish ship that once explored these waters, Atrevida's charred-look wood floors and First Nations art combine Pacific Northwest and Spanish styles with grace. Entrées range from salmon to lamb. Under a lofty, open-beamed ceiling, every table in the curved atrium-style dining room has an expansive view of the seals, otters, and ferries plying Active Pass. *$$$; MC, V; no checks; lunch, dinner every day (no lunch Oct–Apr, except guests with packages); full bar; reservations required; www.galianoinn.com; uphill from ferry terminal, turn left on Madrona Dr.*

Woodstone Country Inn / ★★★

743 GEORGESON BAY RD, GALIANO ISLAND;
250/539-2022 OR 888/339-2022
The dining room at this inn (see review) ranks high: co-innkeeper and chef Gail Nielsen serves a fine four-course table d'hôte dinner that might include cioppino of fresh mussels, shrimp, and seafood; maple-baked salmon; rack of lamb; or vegetarian spinach and ricotta pie. Locals are fiercely loyal to the bread pudding with rum sauce. Enjoy a neoclassical room (think Italianate columns) overlooking a serene field. *$$$; AE, MC, V; local checks only; dinner every day (closed Dec–Jan); full bar; reservations recommended; www. woodstoneinn.com; bear left off Sturdies Bay Rd onto Georgeson Bay Rd.* &

LODGINGS

The Bellhouse Inn / ★★★

29 FARMHOUSE RD, GALIANO ISLAND;
250/539-5667 OR 800/970-7464
Andrea Porter and David Birchall are consummate gentlefolk farmers, conversing with guests and feeding sheep with equal aplomb. This historic farmhouse, painted cream and barn red, contains three lovely upstairs guest rooms. All have balconies, duvets made with wool from the farm's own sheep, and private bathrooms (though one is across the hall). The Kingfisher room is the largest, with a Jacuzzi plus picture windows allowing an expansive view of Bellhouse Bay from bed. *$$–$$$; MC, V; Canadian checks only; www. bellhouseinn.com; uphill from ferry terminal, left on Burrill Rd, left on Jack Rd, right on Farmhouse Rd.*

Galiano Inn / ★★★

134 MADRONA DR, GALIANO ISLAND;
250/539-3388 OR 877/530-3939
This new oceanfront inn, with its mix of Mediterranean and Northwest styles, has 20 spacious, ocean-view guest rooms, each with a private deck or patio, sitting area, and wood-burning fireplace. Some rooms have jetted tubs (with a separate shower), and all have luxurious touches. The rooms' creams, yellows, and blues are just right for winding down after a soak in the hot tub or a massage at the on-site Madrona del Mar Spa. A full breakfast and afternoon tea are included, and the Atrevida Restaurant (see review) serves Pacific Northwest fare. Two-night minimum on weekends. *$$$$; MC, V; no checks; www.galianoinn.com; uphill from ferry terminal, left on Madrona Dr.* &

Woodstone Country Inn / ★★★

743 GEORGESON BAY RD, GALIANO ISLAND;
250/539-2022 OR 888/339-2022
This modern, executive-style manor house overlooking field and forest is a choice stopover for cycling tours and business retreats. The best of the 12 guest rooms are on the lower level, with private patios. The refined decor

includes classic English-print fabrics; Persian and Chinese rugs warm the floors in some rooms; and antiques add country charm. All but two rooms have fireplaces, while one upper-end room has a double Jacuzzi. *$$–$$$; AE, MC, V; no checks; closed Dec–Jan; www.woodstoneinn.com; bear left off Sturdies Bay Rd onto Georgeson Bay Rd.* ⅙

The Cowichan Valley and Southeast Shore

The farmland and forest of the Cowichan Valley stretches from the town of Shawnigan Lake north to Duncan, then west to Cowichan Lake; the microclimate lends itself to grape growing, making it Vancouver Island's best-known vineyard region. Try a pinot noir at **BLUE GROUSE VINEYARDS** (4365 Blue Grouse Rd, off Lakeside Rd, Duncan; 250/743-3834; www.bluegrousevineyards.com); also visit **CHERRY POINT VINEYARDS** (840 Cherry Point Rd, Cobble Hill; 250/743-1272 or 866/395-5252; www.cherrypointvineyards.com) and **GLENTERRA VINEYARDS** (3897 Cobble Hill Rd, Cobble Hill; 250/743-2330). Time your lunch for a visit to **VIGNETI ZANATTA** (5039 Marshall Rd, Duncan; 250/748-2338; www.zanatta.com), which has a restaurant in a 1903 farmhouse.

Or head to **MERRIDALE CIDER WORKS** (1230 Merridale Rd, Cobble Hill; 250/743-4293 or 800/998-9908; www.merridalecider.com), where you can enjoy a meal in the new bistro. Merridale, one of the Northwest's few cideries, makes cider in the English tradition; the best time to visit is mid-September through mid-October, when apples are run through the presses. If you're traveling directly to the valley from the Sidney or Swartz Bay ferry terminal, taking the **BRENTWOOD BAY–MILL BAY FERRY** (250/386-3431 or 888/223-3779; www.bcferries.com) saves you a drive into Victoria.

Cowichan Bay

This charming little seaside village off Highway 1 is built on pilings over the water. Brightly painted stilt houses are home to restaurants and gift shops. The Wooden Boat Society displays and Native artisans' studio at the **COWICHAN BAY MARITIME CENTRE AND MUSEUM** (1761 Cowichan Bay Rd; 250/746-4955; www.classicboats.org) are worth a visit. The **ROCK COD CAFÉ** (1759 Cowichan Bay Rd; 250/746-1550) and the **UDDER GUYS ICE CREAM PARLOUR** (1759 Cowichan Bay Rd; 250/746-4300) can fulfill cravings for fish, chips, and ice cream.

RESTAURANTS

The Masthead Restaurant / ★
Chowder Café

1705 COWICHAN BAY RD, COWICHAN BAY; 250/748-3714

The Masthead, housed in the waterfront 1868 Columbia Hotel, hews to the overall island culinary bent: the salmon is wild, the vegetables come from local farms, and the cellar has the best selection of Vancouver Island wines anywhere. A favorite starter is the rich salmon and shrimp chowder. In summer the Masthead's seaside deck opens as the outdoor Chowder Café, serving a casual menu. *$$$ (Masthead), $ (Chowder Café); AE, MC, V; no checks; dinner every day (Masthead), lunch, dinner every day (Chowder Café; closed Oct–Apr); full bar (Masthead), beer and wine (Chowder Café); reservations recommended (Masthead), no reservations (Chowder Café); www.the mastheadrestaurant.com; at south end of village.*

LODGINGS

Dream Weaver Bed & Breakfast / ★

1682 BOTWOOD LANE, COWICHAN BAY;
250/748-7688 OR 888/748-7689

This modern wood-shake home is modeled on gabled, multistoried, Victorian-era construction. The large Magnolia Suite, nestled in the top-floor gables, is done in flower prints, with a double Jacuzzi tub. Downstairs, the Rosewood Suite is Victorian and floral, with wallpaper borders and a wrought-iron bedstead, while the Primrose Suite has a more masculine look, with deep plum and green hues and a Jacuzzi tub in the bedroom. Only the Magnolia has a view. *$$; MC, V; no checks; www.dreamweaverbedand breakfast.com; at south end of village.*

Duncan

Forty-five minutes north of Victoria on the Trans-Canada Highway (Highway 1), the City of Totems features modest totem poles sprinkled around the town's walkable core. Another claim to fame is the world's largest hockey stick, notably affixed to an arena. In the old downtown, a good lunch can be had at the popular **ISLAND BAGEL COMPANY & LIVINGSTONE'S GOURMET FOODS** (48 Station St; 250/748-1988) or at **GOSSIPS** (161 Kenneth St; 250/746-6466), which also serves Asian- and Mediterranean-inspired dinners and has a pretty patio. The **QUW'UTSUN' CULTURAL AND CONFERENCE CENTRE** (200 Cowichan Way; 250/746-8119 or 877/746-8119) on Duncan's southern edge is excellent. In summer, watch as the region's renowned Cowichan sweaters are made. The center also features an open-air carving shed, where carvers craft 12- to 20-foot totem poles.

RESTAURANTS

The Quamichan Inn / ★★

1478 MAPLE BAY RD, DUNCAN; 250/746-7028
Traditional fresh seafood dishes join inventions such as espresso-crusted rack of lamb at this turn-of-the-20th-century Tudor-style country manor. Outside, the garden is profuse with flowers. The proprietors gladly pick up yachties and drop them off after dinner. Accommodations consist of four guest rooms; rates include an English hunt breakfast: fruit, eggs, bacon, sausage, and fried tomato. *$$$; AE, MC, V; local checks only; dinner Wed–Sun; full bar; reservations recommended; www.thequamichaninn.com; just east of Duncan, follow signs to Maple Bay.*

LODGINGS

Fairburn Farm / ★★

3310 JACKSON RD, DUNCAN; 250/746-4637
This lovingly restored 1894 manor house overlooks a breathtaking 130-acre farm, where part of the charm is the chance to pitch in with chores. Anthea and Darrel Archer operate Canada's first water-buffalo dairy. Breakfasts include farm-raised products. The three guest rooms are simply decorated; tall windows offer views across the gardens, fields, and forest. Some rooms have fireplaces and whirlpool tubs, and all are phone- and TV-free. A two-bedroom cottage with a kitchen overlooks the fields. *$$; MC, V; checks OK; closed mid-Oct–Mar; www.fairburnfarm.bc.ca; 7 miles (11 km) southwest of Duncan (call for directions—no signs to farm).*

Chemainus

Heralded as "the little town that did," seaside Chemainus bounced back from the closure of its logging mill and turned to tourism with flair. Buildings are painted with murals depicting the town's colorful history, an idea since borrowed by other towns, notably Toppenish, Washington (see Southeast Washington chapter). The whole town has a theatrical feel, underlined by productions at the popular **CHEMAINUS THEATRE** (9737 Chemainus Rd; 250/246-9820 or 800/565-7738).

RESTAURANTS

The Waterford Restaurant / ★★

9875 MAPLE ST, CHEMAINUS; 250/246-1046
French cookery takes a West Coast bent at the Waterford, a cozy nine-table bistro with a greenery-draped veranda ensconced in an old-town heritage building. Lunch prices are surprisingly low for the upscale cuisine: paupiette of sole, mushroom or seafood crepes, or seafood marinara. Dinner is slightly pricier: Choices can include rack of lamb dijon, a traditional bouillabaisse, duck with blackberry port sauce, or local wild salmon. *$$; AE, MC, V; no*

checks; lunch, dinner Tues–Sat (Oct–Apr lunch Wed–Sat, dinner Thurs–Sat, call for hours in Jan); full bar; reservations recommended; waterfordrestaurant@ shaw.ca; a few blocks from downtown. &

LODGINGS

Bird Song Cottage / ★★

9909 MAPLE ST, CHEMAINUS; 250/246-9910 OR 866/246-9910
Bird Song Cottage is a treasure of imaginative Victoriana. The exterior of this lavender-and-white gingerbread cottage delights period purists. Inside, oil portraits, a baby grand piano, and a Celtic harp compete with a fancy hat collection. Songs of (caged) birds are also present. The Bluebird and Hummingbird rooms, all with private baths, overflow with lace and florals. The Nightingale is light and airy, with lace and sage green fabrics. *$$; AE, MC, V; no checks; www.vancouverislandaccommodation.bc.ca; a few blocks from downtown.*

Ladysmith

RESTAURANTS

Crow and Gate Neighbourhood Pub / ★★

2313 YELLOW POINT RD, LADYSMITH; 250/722-3731
The Crow and Gate was one of the first neighborhood pubs in British Columbia, and it retains pride of place as the nicest pub in this region. English fowl stroll the grounds, and quaint buildings give the feel of a gentleman's farm. Inside this popular watering hole, light from the flames of two substantial fires glints off diamond-pane windows; long plank tables invite conversation. Traditional English pub fare includes steak-and-kidney pie, ploughman's lunch, beef dip, and oysters. *$; AE, MC, V; no checks; lunch, dinner every day; full bar; no reservations; 8 miles (13 km) south of Nanaimo.*

LODGINGS

Yellow Point Lodge / ★★

3700 YELLOW POINT RD, LADYSMITH; 250/245-7422
This well-loved oceanfront lodge draws guests back every year, from honeymoon to anniversary—even in winter. The log-and-timber lodge has a big ocean-view lounge with a fireplace and simple but comfortable guest rooms. Cabins range from very rustic summer-only cabins to cozy one-bedroom cottages. The one-room White Beach cabins are closest to the water; each features a log bed with a view. Daily rates include most activities plus three meals and snacks served at group tables in the lodge: comfort foods such as prime rib and Yorkshire pudding or classic British Columbia salmon. *$$$; AE, MC, V; checks OK; www.yellowpointlodge.com; 9 miles (14.5 km) east of Ladysmith, take Cedar Rd exit off Hwy 1, south of Nanaimo.*

VANCOUVER ISLAND THREE-DAY TOUR

DAY ONE: From Victoria, get a healthful breakfast at **RE-BAR MODERN FOODS**, then head north and hop aboard one of the Swartz Bay ferries to **SALT SPRING ISLAND**. Browse the **SATURDAY MARKET** in the heart of Ganges. Have lunch at **MOBY'S MARINE PUB** and drive up Cranberry Road to the top of **MOUNT MAXWELL** for a panoramic view. Check in to the **SKY VALLEY INN** and eat dinner at **RESTAURANT HOUSE PICCOLO**.

DAY TWO: After breakfast at Sky Valley, zip out to Vesuvius Bay on the island's western side and catch the ferry to Crofton, on the mainland just south of Chemainus. From there, drive north on the Trans-Canada Highway (Highway 1). Just past **LADYSMITH**, take a side trip to Yellow Point to lunch at the **CROW AND GATE NEIGHBOURHOOD PUB**. At **NANAIMO**, continue north on the inland Highway 19 to **PARKSVILLE**, then take Highway 4A west to visit **COOMBS**; browse the **OLD COUNTRY MARKET**. Continue west, joining Highway 4, and pause on the road to Port Alberni to admire the trees of Cathedral Grove in **MACMILLAN PROVINCIAL PARK**. Keep on driving to the West Coast, then turn north to **TOFINO**. Check in to a room at the **MIDDLE BEACH LODGE** and dine by the surf at the **POINTE RESTAURANT** in the Wickaninnish Inn.

DAY THREE: After coffee and a muffin at Middle Beach Lodge, head out for a morning of whale-watching or kayaking. Pack your swimsuit and stop for a plunge at **HOT SPRINGS COVE** en route. Lunch at **SOBO** in the **TOFINO BOTANICAL GARDENS**, driving to the inimitable **LONG BEACH**. Spend the afternoon exploring the beach, then check in for the night at **TAUCA LEA RESORT AND SPA** in Ucluelet and dine at its **BOAT BASIN** restaurant.

Nanaimo

Nanaimo, once the island's coal capital, is more than the strip mall it appears to be from the highway—19 and 19A meet in Nanaimo. The **HUDSON'S BAY COMPANY BASTION** (at Bastion and Front sts; summer only), built in 1853, is one of the few forts of this type left in North America. It's part of the **NANAIMO DISTRICT MUSEUM** (100 Cameron Rd; 250/753-1821), which also has a replica of a Chinatown street.

In Nanaimo's old town, cafés mix with shops. At **DELICADO'S** (358 Wesley St; 250/753-6524) eat wraps, or go for Mexican at **GINA'S** (47 Skinner St; 250/753-5411), a popular restaurant. In summer, hop a ferry to the **DINGHY DOCK** (250/753-2373 for pub; 250/753-8244 for ferry information), a nautical floating pub. Nanaimo is best known as a transportation hub, with frequent sailings to Vancouver on **BC FERRIES** (250/386-3431 or 888/223-3779; www. bcferries.com).

The island's second-largest city is also a good place to launch a scuba-diving holiday. Thrill seekers head for the **BUNGY ZONE** (15 minutes south of Nanaimo; 250/753-5867 or 800/668-7771) to experience North America's only legal bungee-jumping bridge, over the Nanaimo River. Check out the **BATHTUB RACE** on the third weekend of July.

The spit at **PIPER'S LAGOON** (northeast of downtown), extending into the Strait of Georgia, is great for bird-watching. **NEWCASTLE ISLAND PROVINCIAL MARINE PARK** is an auto-free wilderness reached by ferry from Nanaimo's inner harbor.

Golf courses with views proliferate from Nanaimo northward. Most noteworthy is the **NANAIMO GOLF CLUB** (2800 Highland Blvd; 250/758-6332; www. nanaimogolfclub.ca), an 18-hole championship course 2 miles (3 km) north of the city. Others include **PRYDE VISTA GOLF COURSE** (155 Pryde Ave; 250/753-6188), 1 mile (2 km) northwest of Nanaimo, and **FAIRWINDS** (3730 Fairwinds Dr, Nanoose Bay; 250/468-7666 or 888/781-2777; www.fairwinds.bc.ca), at Nanoose Bay. **TOURISM NANAIMO** (2290 Bowen Rd; 250/756-0106; www. tourismnanaimo.com) has information.

RESTAURANTS

The Mahle House / ★★★

2104 HEMER RD, CEDAR; 250/722-3621
Find this cozy 1904 home-turned-restaurant in Cedar, just minutes southeast of Nanaimo, and sample the inventive cuisine of chef/co-owner Maureen Loucks. Begin with "porcupine" prawns, quickly deep-fried in shredded phyllo, then taste chicken stuffed with Dungeness crab and drizzled with preserved-lemon sauce. On Wednesdays, diners can sample numerous different dishes—all surprises selected by the chef. *$$$; AE, MC, V; no checks; dinner Wed–Sun; full bar; reservations recommended; www.mahlehouse.ca.* &

Parksville

Parksville and the surrounding area are renowned for sandy beaches, especially in lovely **RATHTREVOR BEACH PROVINCIAL PARK** (off Hwy 19A, 1 mile/2 km south of Parksville; 800/689-9025 for camping reservations; www.env.gov.bc.ca/ bcparks). Families love its lengthy shallows and relatively warm water, the camping, and August's annual sand-castle competition.

A little farther afield, picnic at thunderous **ENGLISHMAN RIVER FALLS PROVINCIAL PARK** (8 miles/12.8 km southwest of town; 800/689-9025 for camping reservations; www.env.gov.bc.ca/bcparks), then mosey along to shop in **COOMBS**, a tiny town on Highway 4A that hovers near kitsch with its overblown pioneer theme. Stop for a sandwich at the popular **OLD COUNTRY MARKET** (on Hwy 4 in

Coombs; 250/248-6272; Apr–Nov), where goats graze on the roof. **MACMILLAN PROVINCIAL PARK** (on Hwy 4, 20 miles/32 km west of Parksville; www.env.gov. bc.ca/bcparks) contains Cathedral Grove, an impressive old-growth forest.

LODGINGS

Tigh-Na-Mara Resort, Spa & Conference Centre / ★★

1095 E ISLAND HWY, PARKSVILLE; 250/248-2072 OR 800/663-7373

The grotto—a thermal mineral pool complete with waterfalls and cave effects—is the centerpiece of Tigh-Na-Mara's lavish three-story spa, which, combined with a wealth of supervised children's activities, makes this a great spot for parents in need of a little adult time. Log cottages, spread throughout 22 acres of wooded grounds, offer privacy, though the cottages are somewhat dark. Oceanfront condominiums are newer and spiffier, with log-beam details; some have jetted tubs and kitchens. The upscale Forest Studios and Woodland Suites surround the spa facility but are farthest from the beach. The Cedar Room restaurant has Pacific Northwest fare. $$–$$$; AE, DC, MC, V; local checks only; www.tigh-na-mara.com; 1¼ miles (2 km) south of Parksville on Hwy 19A.

Qualicum Beach

This little town 20 minutes north of Parksville on Highway 19A has a pleasant beach-front promenade and a growing shopping district. For its size, it boasts a good selection of cafés—a favorite is funky spot **MURPHY'S COFFEE & TEA COMPANY** (177 W 2nd Ave; 250/752-6693). For more retro character, drive 10 minutes north for a burger at the **COLA DINER** (6060 W Island Hwy; 250/757-2029), a joyful ode to the classic 1950s burger joint. At **MILNER GARDENS AND WOODLAND** (2179 W Island Hwy; 250/752-6153), you can stroll through 10 acres of gardens and stop for tea in a 1930s seaside manor.

RESTAURANTS

Lefty's / ★

710 MEMORIAL AVE, QUALICUM BEACH; 250/752-7530

The bright, funky ambience and art-filled walls here mirror the savor of baked-on-the-premises cheesecake and chocolate fudge cake. Specialties include flavorful chorizo pizza, cheddar corn pie, or wraps stuffed with fresh West Coast fusions like Cajun chicken. At dinner, Lefty's transitions to pastas, stir-fries, and steak and prawns. A Parksville location (101-280 E Island Hwy; 250/954-3886) offers the same menu. $$; MC, V; no checks; breakfast, lunch, dinner every day; full bar; reservations recommended; www.leftys.tv; at Fern St.

Old Dutch Inn / ★

2690 W ISLAND HWY, QUALICUM BEACH; 250/752-6914
Waitresses in triple-peaked, starched lace caps serve breakfast platters with
eggs Benedict or french-toast sandwiches. Have we wandered back in time?
The Dutch theme is taken seriously, with turned oak chairs and Delft tiles. At
lunch you can join retirees and tourists for a *uitsmijter*, an open-faced sandwich with Dutch smoked ham and cheese, or Indonesian-inspired *loempia*, a
10-spice spring roll with pork and roasted peanuts. Expansive windows look
out on Qualicum Bay. *$; AE, DC, DIS, MC, V; no checks; breakfast, lunch,
dinner every day; full bar; reservations recommended; www.olddutchinn.com;
on Hwy 19A.*

LODGINGS

Bahari / ★

5101 W ISLAND HWY, QUALICUM BEACH; 250/752-9278 OR 877/752-9278
The look here is 1980s West Coast with Asian touches, including a Japanese kimono hung in the two-story foyer. The two rooms and one suite all
open onto a deck, all have fireplaces, and two have ocean views (room 3 in
particular has an expansive view). Seven acres of lawn, gardens, and woods
include a trail down to a pebbly beach; a private hot tub in the woods over-
looks Georgia Strait and the northern Gulf Islands. *$$$–$$$$; AE, MC, V;
no checks; closed Dec–Feb; www.baharibandb.com; 10 minutes north of town
on Hwy 19A.*

Barkley Sound and Tofino

Most visitors pass through Port Alberni via Highway 4 to Tofino or take the scenic
boat trip on the **LADY ROSE** or **FRANCES BARKLEY** (250/723-8313 or 800/663-
7192) from Port Alberni to Bamfield, Ucluelet, or the Broken Group Islands. Boats
offer passenger day trips as well as freight service.

Port Alberni

Shops, galleries, and restaurants cluster at the Harbour Quay, where boats to Bar-
kley Sound dock in this industrial logging and fishing town. A favored nosh stop
is the **CLAM BUCKET** (4479 Victoria Quay; 250/723-1315).

Bamfield

This tiny fishing village of 500, home to a marine biology research station and
known for the big salmon pulled from nearby waters, is reached by boat (see Intro-
duction to this section) or via logging roads from Port Alberni or Lake Cowichan.
In Bamfield, the road extends only to the east side of the village. The west side,

across Bamfield Inlet, has no vehicle access; water taxis ($3 per trip) link the two. Bamfield bustles when the **WEST COAST TRAIL** summer season hits—it's the end of the line for the world-famous, five- to seven-day, mettle-testing wilderness trail that's so popular hikers have to make reservations. For information contact **HELLO BC** (250/387-1642 or 800/435-5622; www.hellobc.com). The **BAMFIELD CHAMBER OF COMMERCE** (250/728-3006; www.bamfieldchamber.com) also has information.

LODGINGS

Wood's End Landing / ★

380 LOMBARD ST, BAMFIELD; 250/728-3383 OR 877/828-3383
These four cute cedar-shake-and-driftwood cabins are on the peaceful, car-free west side of Bamfield. Proprietor Terry Giddens built them out of materials he beachcombed and recycled from tumbledown Bamfield buildings. The cabins and two additional suites, set among 50-year-old perennial gardens, overlook Bamfield Inlet. The hilltop Woodsman cabin and Angler suite have the best views. Cabins have two loft bedrooms. Canoes and rowboats are free for guests. *$$–$$$$; MC, V; no checks; www.woodsend.travel.bc.ca; across inlet from government dock via water taxi.*

Ucluelet

"Ukie" is still a little rough around the edges, as the economic staples of fishing and logging began to wane only a decade ago, but for many visitors, that's part of its charm. The town, with several fine B and Bs and lodges, aspires to tourism success like its sister town Tofino has enjoyed. A highlight is the **WILD PACIFIC TRAIL**, a two-part, 4-mile (6.5-km) path through the old growth and within sight of the pounding surf. It's the jump-off point for Barkley Sound kayak adventures.

Budget B and B accommodations line the road into town, offering easy access to **PACIFIC RIM NATIONAL PARK RESERVE** (250/726-4212); stop by the **VISITOR CENTRE** (at turnoff to Tofino on Hwy 4). The **BROKEN GROUP ISLANDS**, accessible only by boat, attract intrepid kayakers and scuba divers. Visitors to Ucluelet have come to enjoy the expanse of awe-inspiring **LONG BEACH**. The park's lone campground, **GREEN POINT** (at park's midway point, well marked by signs; 800/689-9025; www.pc.gc.ca), is often full during peak times and is closed in winter.

Six miles (10 km) north of Ucluelet, the **WICKANINNISH INTERPRETIVE CENTRE** (1 Wickaninnish Rd; 250/726-4701) has oceanic exhibits and an expansive view, shared by the on-site **WICKANINNISH RESTAURANT**—not to be confused with the Wickaninnish Inn (see review in Tofino section).

During March and April, 20,000 gray whales migrate along the West Coast on their way to the Bering Sea and can often be seen from shore; orcas and humpbacks cruise the waters much of the year. For close-up views, **WHALE-WATCHING**

TOURS leave from both Ucluelet and Tofino; tours are easy to arrange once you arrive. The **PACIFIC RIM WHALE FESTIVAL** (250/726-7742; mid-Mar–early Apr) hosts events here and in Tofino.

RESTAURANTS

The Boat Basin / ★★

1971 HARBOUR CREST (TAUCA LEA RESORT AND SPA), UCLUELET; 250/726-4625 OR 800/979-9303
The fresh wild seafood and great harbor views at Tauca Lea Resort's (see review) Boat Basin restaurant have significantly heightened dining in Ucluelet. The setting is airy and uncluttered; features include striking First Nations art and a deck overlooking the local fishing fleet. Start with diver scallops, tuna carpaccio, or a soba noodle soup with local shrimp. Your main course could be a fish pot of local seafood, five-pepper crusted albacore tuna, or whatever is fresh at the docks that day. *$$$; AE, DC, MC, V; no checks; dinner every day; full bar; reservations recommended; www.taucalearesort.com; from Hwy 4, turn left onto Seaplane Base Rd.*

Matterson House / ★★

1682 PENINSULA RD, UCLUELET; 250/726-2200
Tofino residents happily make the half-hour drive to Ucluelet for the generous helpings and reasonable prices at casual Matterson House. Breakfast standards such as eggs Benedict and huevos rancheros make way for lunch's Matterson Monster Burger, fully loaded with bacon, cheese, mushrooms, and more. Look for caesar salads, chicken burgers, and homemade bread—and nothing deep-fried. Dinner sees hungry hikers and residents dig into prime rib, salmon filo, or veggie lasagne. *$$; MC, V; local checks only; breakfast, lunch, dinner every day; full bar; reservations recommended; on Hwy 4 on way into town.*

LODGINGS

A Snug Harbour Inn / ★★

460 MARINE DR, UCLUELET; 250/726-2686 OR 888/936-5222
The million-dollar view here encompasses the rugged coast and islands where harbor seals, whales, and eagles play. All six rooms have private balconies and stunning views. Honeymooners prefer the tiered Atlantis Room, which has a spectacular view, and the Sawadee Room, with its fireplace and jetted tub. Others favor the split-level Lighthouse Room, with round brass ships' portholes and picture windows. *$$$–$$$$; MC, V; no checks; www.awesomeview.com; through village and right on Marine Dr.*

Eagle Nook Ocean Wilderness Resort / ★★★

VERNON BAY, BARKLEY SOUND; 250/723-1000 OR 800/760-2777
This wilderness lodge, reached only by boat or floatplane, caters to the out-doors lover. Visitors enjoy hiking the trails lacing the resort's 70 forested acres or joining cruises to see harbor seals, bald eagles, and possibly whales. Back at the resort, guests feast on beautifully prepared West Coast or continental meals from window seats before a fire. All 23 rooms have ocean views; two one-bedroom cabins have water views and sitting areas, fireplaces, and kitch-enettes. The resort's ocean-side deck features a hot tub and cedar-hut sauna. *$$$$; AE, MC, V; no checks; closed Oct–May; www.eaglenook.com; if driving to Vancouver Island, arrange to meet resort's water taxi in Ucluelet.*

Tauca Lea Resort & Spa / ★★★

1971 HARBOUR CREST, UCLUELET; 250/726-4625 OR 800/979-9303
Set on its own little peninsula on the edge of Ucluelet, Tauca Lea's one- and two-bedroom apartment-sized suites have kitchens and water views. The spa-cious, light-filled suites are decorated with leather armchairs and handcrafted furniture; a few higher-end units have hot tubs. The resort's Boat Basin res-taurant (see review) is one of the best places to eat in the area. *$$$–$$$$; AE, DC, MC, V; no checks; www.taucalearesort.com; from Hwy 4, turn left onto Seaplane Base Rd.*

Tofino

At the end of Highway 4 is the island's wild West Coast, drawing surfers, kayak-ers, storm watchers, and nature lovers from all over the world. Although it was once an area visited almost exclusively in summer, now winter storms draw hordes of visitors to watch the Pacific thrash the coast. A large number of international visitors has resulted in a greater number of excellent hotels, B and Bs, and restau-rants than one would expect from a town of fewer than 2,000 residents.

People arrive at Tofino primarily by car, via the winding mountainous route of Highway 4 (five hours from Victoria). **KENMORE AIR** (www.kenmoreair.com) flies from Seattle and **HARBOUR AIR** (www.harbour-air.com) from Vancouver—but you'll want a car here; try **BUDGET** (250/725-2060) for rentals.

You can explore the coast with one of numerous water-taxi or whale-watching companies, by floatplane, or by kayak. **TOFINO SEA KAYAKING COM-PANY** (320 Main; 250/725-4222 or 800/863-4664) offers kayak rentals or guided tours with experienced boaters and naturalists. **REMOTE PASSAGES** (71 Wharf St; 250/725-3330 or 800/666-9833) offers guided tours by kayak, Zodiac, or cov-ered whale-watching boat. The **PACIFIC RIM WHALE FESTIVAL** (250/726-7742; mid-Mar–early Apr) hosts events here and in Ucluelet. Retired Coast Guardsman Mike White of **BROWNING PASS CHARTERS** (250/725-3435; www.browning pass.com) offers knowledgeable and thoughtful, low-impact wildlife-watching tours in Clayoquot Sound.

A number of boat and floatplane companies, including **TOFINO AIR** (50 1st St; 250/725-4454 or 866/486-3247), offer day trips to the calming pools of **HOT SPRINGS COVE**; you can overnight at the six-room **HOT SPRINGS COVE LODGE** (250/670-1106 or 866/670-1106). The 12-acre **TOFINO BOTANICAL GARDENS** (1084 Pacific Rim Hwy; 250/725-1220) features indigenous plant life in a scenic waterfront setting.

Gift shops and galleries are sprinkled throughout town. The longhouse of the **EAGLE AERIE GALLERY** (350 Campbell St; 250/725-3235 or 800/663-0669) sells art by Coast Tsimshian artist Roy Henry Vickers. **HOUSE OF HIMWITSA** (300 Main St; 250/725-2017 or 800/899-1947) features First Nations masks, jewelry, and gifts. Get organic coffee, baked treats, and counterculture news at the **COMMON LOAF BAKE SHOP** (180 1st St; 250/725-3915), fresh sushi at the **INN AT TOUGH CITY** (350 Main St; 250/725-2021), or highly rated organic global takeout from **SOBO** (1184 Pacific Rim Hwy; 250/725-2341), a catering trailer and café at the botanical gardens. **CAFFE VINCENTE** (441 Campbell St; 250-725-2599) offers great coffee and sensational baked goods. The **TOFINO VISITORS INFO CENTRE** (1426 Pacific Rim Hwy; 250/725-3414; www.tofinobc.org) is on Highway 4, just south of town.

RESTAURANTS

The Pointe Restaurant / ★★★

OSPREY LANE AT CHESTERMAN BEACH (WICKANINNISH INN),
TOFINO; 250/725-3100 OR 800/333-4604

The Wick's restaurant is perched over a rocky headland; waves crash just outside the windows that have 240-degree panoramic views, adding drama to your meal. The distinctively West Coast–Canadian menu focuses on seafood ranging from oysters to seaweed and other produce. An à la carte menu features Long Beach Dungeness crab, grilled wild salmon, and good vegetarian selections, but many diners opt for one of the multicourse tasting menus. All is artfully presented. *$$$$; AE, DC, MC, V; no checks; breakfast, lunch, dinner every day; full bar; reservations required (dinner); www.wickinn.com; off Hwy 4, 3 miles (5 km) south of town.* &

RainCoast Café / ★★

120 4TH ST, TOFINO; 250/725-2215

Husband-and-wife team Lisa Henderson and Larry Nicolay operate one of the best restaurants in Tofino. The decor of their intimate room (with an outdoor patio) is sleek and modern—as is the menu, which focuses on seafood, often with an Asian twist. Starters range from Thai hot and sour seafood soup, chicken satay, and Samosa dragon rolls to fresh local oysters, clams, and mussels. Popular main dishes include halibut in Thai red curry sauce or trout stuffed with Dungeness crab and goat cheese. Dessert is a bit less cosmopolitan: chocolate–peanut butter pie. *$$$; AE, MC, V; local checks only; dinner every day; beer and wine; reservations recommended; www.raincoast cafe.com; near 4th St dock.* &

The Schooner on Second / ★

331 CAMPBELL ST, TOFINO; 250/725-3444

Every sea town needs a classic seafood house, and this historic central Tofino restaurant—part red clapboard building, part old schooner—dates back half a century, since long before Tofino got a rep. These days, the menu features seafood and plenty of hearty meat dishes. Try the Catface Bouillabaisse, a medley of finfish and shellfish in tomato-scented saffron broth. Breakfasts of huevos rancheros and eggs Benny with homemade hollandaise are popular. *$$; AE, MC, V; no checks; breakfast, lunch, dinner every day; full bar; reservations recommended; www.schoonerrestaurant.com; downtown, at corner of 2nd St.*

LODGINGS

Cable Cove Inn / ★

201 MAIN ST, TOFINO; 250/725-4236 OR 800/663-6449

Tucked at the edge of Tofino's town center, Cable Cove Inn has seven guest rooms that look out to the open sea. Rooms exude a distinguished air, with mahogany-toned furniture and green marble whirlpool tubs or private outdoor hot tubs. All have fireplaces and private, ocean-facing decks; one corner unit has a wraparound balcony. Steps lead to the sheltered cove below the inn. A cozy wood-burning stove in the upstairs lounge is surrounded by cushy leather couches. Two-night minimum in summer and on long weekends. *$$$; AE, MC, V; no checks; www.cablecoveinn.com; west end of Main St.*

Clayoquot Wilderness Resorts / ★★★

QUAIT BAY, CLAYOQUOT SOUND;
250/726-8235 OR 888/333-5405

Though this luxury resort's main lodge, which floats on a barge on the edge of Clayoquot Sound, helped inaugurate the wilderness lodge industry in British Columbia, it's now far better known for its safari-style tent camp at the inn's Wilderness Outpost on the banks of the Bedwell River. Both lodge and outpost are accessible only by boat or floatplane. Accommodations at the wildly popular Wilderness Outpost put a whole new spin on camping: guests sleep in roomy cabin tents outfitted with Oriental rugs, propane heaters, handmade furniture, and private decks; they dine on seafood and wine on china and crystal. Relax in the sauna or in one of the wood-fired hot tubs. Three-night minimum. *$$$$; AE, MC, V; no checks; lodge closed Nov–Feb, outpost closed Oct–Apr; www.wildretreat.com.*

InnChanter / ★★★

HOTSPRINGS COVE; 250/670-1149

This unique, luxuriously refitted 1920s boat is moored in Hotsprings Cove near the hot springs, one of the most popular (and overcrowded) attractions on Vancouver Island. The InnChanter is accessible only by floatplane, whale-watching tour, or water taxi from Tofino. The elegant floating B and B features five staterooms, a salon with a wood-burning fireplace, and a sundeck. Host Shaun Shelongosky is a brilliant and quirky conversationalist, as well as an excellent chef who attends to all meals (included in the room rate). He specializes in vegetarian fare but uses a lot of fresh seafood as well—look for a salmon barbecue on deck or halibut in Thai green coconut curry. *$$$; no credit cards; checks OK; www.innchanter.com; call inn for access details.*

Long Beach Lodge Resort / ★★★

1441 PACIFIC RIM HWY, TOFINO; 250/725-2442 OR 877/844-7873
This oceanfront lodge faces the booming surf of sandy Cox Bay—the town's most popular surfing beach. A welcoming great room, home to a bar, inviting sofas, and a massive granite fireplace, takes in the view through big picture windows. Choose from beach-front rooms with gas fireplaces and surf-view balconies, lower priced forest-view rooms, or a dozen two-bedroom cottages with kitchens and private baths. Lodge rooms have jetted or extra-large soaker tubs and separate showers; cottages have private hot tubs. *$$$–$$$$; AE, MC, V; no checks; www.longbeachlodgeresort.com; south of Tofino off Hwy 4.*

Middle Beach Lodge / ★★★

400 MACKENZIE BEACH RD, TOFINO;
250/725-2900 OR 866/725-2900
Decor is tasteful and homey at this oceanfront complex. Each of the two main lodges has a large lobby. The Lodge at the Beach is quiet with an adults-only policy. The newer, pricier Lodge at the Headlands welcomes kids over 12 and includes some suites with kitchens. Palatial, two-level oceanfront cabins have waterside balconies; some have private hot tubs; all have private baths. High season brings fresh-fish barbecues and nightly dinners in the restaurant (dinner Fri–Sat Nov–Feb). *$$–$$$$; AE, MC, V; no checks; www.middlebeach. com; south of Tofino off Hwy 4.*

Pacific Sands Resort / ★★★

COX BAY, TOFINO; 250/725-3322 OR 800/656-2322
The addition of snazzy new two-story villas has significantly upgraded this old-line family beach-front resort. The entire complex is geared to families, with all 77 units offering kitchenettes, but the new villas are attractive, with muted earth-tone fabrics that set off large pieces of fir furniture. The top-floor master bedrooms in the villas have private balconies, as well as soaker tubs that look out over the room and the ocean view. The kitchens are thoroughly equipped. The resort's property includes splendid beach access and a trail to Sunset Point. *$$–$$$$; AE, MC, V; no checks; www.pacificsands.com; south of Tofino off Hwy 4.*

Wickaninnish Inn / ★★★★

OSPREY LANE AT CHESTERMAN BEACH, TOFINO;
250/725-3100 OR 800/333-4604
My, what Charles McDiarmid started when he built his lavish, upscale inn in little Tofino and announced he would promote winter travel to watch storms crash ashore. Skeptics scoffed—but now the Wick, as it's known, reaches its highest occupancy in January. Set dramatically on the edge of its rocky headland, the inn includes architectural details by master carver Henry Nolla. The 75 rooms and suites feature ocean views, private balconies, and double soaker tubs. Ancient Cedars Spa offers pamperings. *$$$$; AE, DC, MC, V; no checks; www.wickinn.com; off Hwy 4, 3 miles (5 km) south of Tofino.* &

The Comox Valley

The Comox Valley, on the island's middle east coast, has skiing in winter, water sports in summer, and scenic access to Powell River on the mainland Sunshine Coast via **BC FERRIES** (250/386-3431 or 888/223-3779 in BC; www.bcferries.com). Skiers and, in summer, hikers and mountain bikers flock to **MOUNT WASHINGTON ALPINE RESORT** (13 miles west of Courtenay; 250/338-1386), where five chair lifts whisk alpine skiers and boarders to the top, and cross-country skiers enjoy 33 miles (55 km) of track leading into **STRATHCONA PROVINCIAL PARK**. The **CROWN ISLE RESORT & GOLF COMMUNITY** (399 Clubhouse Dr, Courtenay; 250/703-5050 or 888/338-8439) boasts the longest course on the island, an elaborate clubhouse, and chic condos.

Fanny Bay

Blink, and you'll miss this tiny hamlet. For a true roadhouse experience, stop at the **FANNY BAY INN** (7480 Island Hwy; 250/335-2323)—or the FBI, as it is more familiarly known. The mostly standard pub-fare menu features Fanny Bay oysters, panfried or in burgers. A couple miles north, the tiny **HARBOUR VIEW BISTRO** (5575 Hwy 19A, Union Bay; 250/335-3277) has a loyal following; diners book months ahead for weekend dinners of duck à l'orange or poached wild salmon.

LODGINGS

Ships Point Inn / ★★

7584 SHIPS POINT RD, FANNY BAY;
250/335-1004 OR 877/742-1004
At the end of a quiet country road, this white turn-of-the-20th-century waterfront home houses six lovely rooms, each with its own theme. The Bombay room is all Raj-era elegance, in rich reds and greens, with an elephant-patterned bed canopy, while the Bayview room has a West Indies colonial style

with a romantic canopy bed. Four-course breakfasts are served in the kitchen or on the wide deck with views. Gardens stretch down to a seaside walkway and a pebbly shore. *$$–$$$; AE, MC, V; local checks only; www.ships pointinn.com; exit 87 off Hwy 19, follow Ships Point Rd to its end.*

Courtenay and Comox

These adjacent towns are the hub of the valley. Courtenay's in-town browsing ranges from antiques, kitchenware, and retro clothing shops to the thought-of-everything **TRAVELLER'S TALE SHOP** (526 Cliffe Ave; 250/703-0168). Break for a delectable treat at **HOT CHOCOLATES** (238 5th St; 250/338-8211). Locals recommend the eclectic eats at **ATLAS CAFÉ** (250 6th St; 250/338-9838). Dinosaur fossils found in the Comox Valley are on display at the **COURTENAY AND DISTRICT MUSEUM AND PALAEONTOLOGY CENTRE** (207 4th St; 250/334-0686). The ferry to Denman Island leaves from Buckley Bay, about 10 minutes south of Courtenay.

RESTAURANTS

Kingfisher Dining Room / ★★★

4330 S ISLAND HWY, ROYSTON; 250/338-1323 OR 800/663-7929

Executive chef Ronald St. Pierre has applied a fertile imagination to seafood-based West Coast cuisine in this nautical-decor restaurant in its namesake resort (see review). It's hard to find something truly unique on a Vancouver Island menu these days, but raw Fanny Bay oysters with cilantro-carrot sorbet as a garnish will do, as will porcini mushroom raviolis with tomato-chipotle coulis. The once-a-month Grand Seafood Buffet offers more than 50 (yes, 50) items, ranging from salmon-shrimp terrine to pumpkin cheesecake. *$$$; AE, DC, DIS, JCB, MC, V; no checks; www.kingfisherspa.com; 5 miles (8 km) south of Courtenay off Hwy 19A.*

The Old House Restaurant / ★★

1760 RIVERSIDE LANE, COURTENAY; 250/338-5406

This carefully restored, rambling pioneer home rests amid flower gardens and trees. Four fireplaces beckon on cool days, while exposed beams and garden views create a country ambience. At this white-tablecloth establishment, start dinner with mushrooms stuffed with shrimp, crab, spinach, and cream cheese. Next, opt for a fresh salmon fillet baked on a cedar plank or panfried maple-rye pork medallions. *$$–$$$; AE, DC, MC, V; no checks; lunch, dinner every day; full bar; www.comoxvalleyrestaurants.ca; just before 17th St Bridge to Comox.* &

LODGINGS

Greystone Manor / ★

4014 HAAS RD, COURTENAY; 250/338-1422
Extensive English flower gardens are the jewel of this establishment; contemplate views of the Strait of Georgia and the Coast Mountains beyond. Three guest rooms with private baths (one is across the hall) give you all the basics, though some are fairly small. The parlor of this 1918 home has a cozy woodstove and original hardwood floors. *$$; MC, V; no checks; www.greystone manorbb.com; 2 miles (3 km) south of Courtenay off Hwy 19A.*

Kingfisher Oceanside Resort and Spa / ★★★

4330 S ISLAND HWY, ROYSTON; 250/338-1323 OR 800/663-7929
Though Kingfisher's up-to-date identity has been wrested from its previous incarnation as a seaside motel, the resort has been splendidly expanded, updated, and upgraded. The two dozen beach-front suites are the nicest accommodations. Ocean-view rooms, set back from the sea, are blander but a good value. The spa's centerpiece is the Pacific Mist Hydropath, where you spend an hour traveling through a grotto equipped with mineral pools and waterfall-like showers. A sauna, a steam room, a hot tub, tennis courts, and an outdoor swimming pool with a miniwaterfall add to the ethos. *$$$–$$$$; AE, DC, DIS, JCB, MC, V; no checks; www.kingfisherspa.com; 5 miles (8 km) south of Courtenay off Hwy 19A.*

Denman and Hornby Islands

Tranquil and pastoral, the sister islands of Denman and Hornby sit just off the east coast of central Vancouver Island. The larger, Denman—10 minutes by ferry from Buckley Bay, which is 12 miles (20 km) south of Courtenay—is known for farmlands and artisans. Most visitors skip right through to Hornby Island, but the beach at **FILLONGLEY PROVINCIAL PARK** (2 miles/3.2 km east of the ferry landing; 800/689-9025; www.env.gov.bc.ca/bcparks) is great; the island's flat landscape makes it a natural for cyclists. Stop at the **DENMAN BAKERY AND PIZZERIA** (3646 Denman Rd; 250/335-1310; Mon–Sat). On weekends, the **BISTRO** (at Denman Island Guesthouse, 3806 Denman Rd; 250/335-2688) serves organic meals; rooms in the farmhouse are available every day. Home-cooked meals are served every day at the **DENMAN CAFÉ** (in General Store, Northwest Rd and Denman Rd; 250/335-2999).

Ten minutes from Denman by ferry, Hornby is a dream for mountain bikers. The center of life on Hornby is at the island-owned **HORNBY CO-OP** (Central and Shields rds; 250/335-1121). Grab lunch at **JAN'S CAFÉ** (Ringside Market; 250/335-1487). Hornby's **HELLIWELL PROVINCIAL PARK** (southeast corner of the island; 800/689-9025; www.env.gov.bc.ca/bcparks) has seaside cliffs, while beach lovers go to **TRIBUNE BAY PROVINCIAL PARK** (Tribune Bay Rd; 800/689-9025; www.env.gov.bc.ca/bcparks).

LODGINGS

Outer Island R&R / ★★

4785 DEPAPE RD, HORNBY ISLAND; 250/335-2379 OR 800/364-1331
Karen Young's delightful farm (she calls her place an agri-villa) embraces 14
acres of pasture and orchard, with sheep, chickens, horses, and Dove, the
miniature donkey, to greet kids. Not all is rustic—there's a pool for summer
use. Stay in a lovely two-bedroom old farmhouse with eclectic country furnishings
and kitchenette looking out on the orchard, or in a larger, equally eclectic, wood-
trimmed rambler whose four bedrooms function as B and B rooms in summer.
$$$; MC, V; checks OK; www.outerisland.bc.ca; near Sandpiper Beach.

Sea Breeze Lodge / ★

5205 FOWLER RD, HORNBY ISLAND; 250/335-2321 OR 888/516-2321
Owned for decades by the Bishop family, Sea Breeze has evolved into a com-
fortable family retreat with a loyal following. Most of the 16 cottages are
along a bluff, with decks overlooking the water. Interiors are cheery, with
pine furniture and art. Romantics prefer the very rustic Nanoose Cabin,
which sits alone in a meadow. Rates include three home-cooked meals a
day June–mid-September. The restaurant, with its ocean-view wraparound
veranda, is also open to nonguests for dinner. *$$$–$$$$; MC, V; checks OK;
www.seabreezelodge.com; on Tralee Point.*

Campbell River
and North Vancouver Island

The north end of Vancouver Island has logging towns abutting wilderness and a
unique attraction: snorkeling Campbell River to watch spawning salmon. Camp-
bell River the town, home base of famed writer Roderick Haig-Brown and once
known almost solely as a fishing mecca, is developing a new identity as a retire-
ment center and recreation hub.

Seattle's **KENMORE AIR** (800/543-9595; www.kenmoreair.com) flies directly to
the area's fishing lodges. From Vancouver, **AIR CANADA** (888/247-2262; www.
aircanada.ca) and **PACIFIC COASTAL AIR** (800/663-2872; www.pacific-coastal.
com) serve Campbell River's airport.

The **MUSEUM AT CAMPBELL RIVER** (470 Island Hwy; 250/287-3103; www.
crmuseum.ca) is one of the island's best. The **CAMPBELL RIVER MARITIME
HERITAGE CENTRE** (621 Island Hwy; 250/286-3161) is home to BCP45, the
iconic fishing boat on the old Canadian five-dollar bill. For more art, the **WEI
WAI KUM HOUSE OF TREASURES** (1370 Island Hwy; 250/286-1440; www.
houseoftreasures.com) is set in a beautiful longhouse, incongruously tucked behind
a shopping mall. Locals like the fresh pastas at **FUSILLI GRILL** (220 Dogwood St;
250/830-0090).

STRATHCONA PROVINCIAL PARK (about 25 miles/40 km west of town on
Hwy 28; 800/689-9025) is a place of superlatives. It contains Canada's highest

waterfall as well as Vancouver Island's tallest mountain, 7,200-foot (2,195-m) Golden Hinde.

During August's **SALMON FESTIVAL**, this mall-rich town of 30,000 is abuzz with fisherfolk. The **VISITOR INFO CENTRE** (1235 Shoppers Row; 250/287-4636; visitorinfo.incampbellriver.com) has information.

RESTAURANTS

Koto Japanese Restaurant / ★★

80 10TH AVE, CAMPBELL RIVER; 250/286-1422
It makes sense: a very fresh sushi bar in the middle of fishing country. Chef Takeo (Tony) Maeda has single-handedly developed the locals' taste for nigiri-sushi. Teriyaki is a big seller too—beef, chicken, or salmon—but look for more-exotic food from the deep, such as freshwater eel, flying-fish roe, and local octopus. *$$; AE, DC, MC, V; no checks; lunch Tues–Fri, dinner Tues–Sat; full bar; reservations recommended; behind HSBC Bank bldg.*

LODGINGS

Painter's Lodge / ★★

1625 MCDONALD RD, CAMPBELL RIVER; 250/286-1102 OR 800/663-7090
Fishing is the raison d'être of this lodge run by the Oak Bay Marine Group of Victoria, but whale- and bear-watching tours, a pool, a hot tub, and tennis appeal to nonanglers, and the waterfront location is a plus. Strive to catch the big one here, and maybe your photo will join the row in the plush lobby. Fare in the Legends dining room is not especially inspired. A free 10-minute water taxi runs to April Point Lodge, Painter's sister resort on Quadra Island (see review in Discovery Islands section). *$$$–$$$$; AE, DC, MC, V; no checks; closed late Oct–Mar; www.obmg.com; 2½ miles (4 km) north of Campbell River.*

Strathcona Park Lodge and Outdoor Education Centre / ★★

**EDGE OF STRATHCONA PROVINCIAL PARK,
CAMPBELL RIVER; 250/286-3122**
Strathcona Provincial Park, one of the oldest in Canada, is a wilderness recreation paradise, and its namesake lakeside lodge is for those who enjoy active living. The instructors gently guide even the most timid city slickers through outdoor pursuits. The ropes course isn't as scary as it looks. The 50 varied units in the lodge and lakefront cabins are modest but attractive; some of the newer suites are quite chic, and everywhere are jaw-dropping views. *$$; MC, V; local checks only; limited facilities Dec–Feb; www.strathcona.bc.ca; 28 miles (45 km) west of Campbell River on Hwy 28.*

Discovery Islands

The closely linked Discovery Islands—fishing and boating meccas east of Campbell River—include **QUADRA**, **CORTES**, and **SONORA**. To visit the most accessible—Quadra and Cortes—take the 10-minute ferry ride from Campbell River to Quadra's Quathiaski Cove dock; from Heriot Bay on Quadra, another 45-minute ferry takes you to Cortes. Other islands in the chain are accessible only by private boat, water taxi from Campbell River, or floatplane.

LODGINGS

April Point Resort & Spa / ★★

**900 APRIL POINT RD, QUADRA ISLAND;
250/285-2222 OR 800/663-7090**
This island getaway, centered around a cedar lodge built on pilings over the water, draws serious fisherfolk from all over the world. April Point also offers activities such as bicycle, scooter, and kayak rentals; helicopter tours; and whale- and bear-watching trips. The 53 spacious units range from large houses to lodge rooms and comfortable cabins; some have jetted tubs, living rooms, and kitchens, and all have sundecks with water views. At the restaurant in the main lodge, seafood (including sushi) is the focus; wraparound windows and a sunny deck offer dramatic water views. *$$$; AE, DC, E, MC, V; no checks; www.aprilpoint.com; 10 minutes north of ferry dock, or accessible by free water taxi from Painter's Lodge in Campbell River.*

Hollyhock / ★★★

**MANSON'S LANDING, CORTES ISLAND;
250/285-2222 OR 800/663-7090**
Hollyhock is one of those institutions better known internationally than locally. Set into the woods at the southeast end of Cortes Island, this New Age center draws guests for retreats that focus on holistic health and human potential. Stay in comfortable accommodations that range from bunk beds to cozy cabins; all meals (vegetarian plus seafood) are included, and yoga, forest and beach walks, library reading, and hot tub soaking occupy the time. *$–$$; MC, V; no checks; www.hollyhock.ca; on Highfield Rd 11 miles (18 km) from the ferry dock.*

Sonora Resort / ★★★★

SONORA ISLAND; 604/233-0460 OR 888/576-6672
Fly-in lodges along British Columbia's wilderness central coast have sprung up everywhere lately, but this massive, ultradeluxe complex is the biggest and most lavish. Dozens of rooms and suites in 11 buildings are furnished in elegant furniture and wood trim. There are 25 hot tubs, a pool, a covered

tennis court, and a sensational water setting. Sonora's Eagle Rock Lodge, with four suites and a huge fireplace in the living room, is one of the most attractive accommodations in North America. *$$$$; AE, MC, V; checks OK; www.sonoraresort.com; boat or seaplane access only.*

Tsa-Kwa-Luten Lodge and RV Park / ★★

1 LIGHTHOUSE RD, QUADRA ISLAND; 250/285-2042 OR 800/665-7745
Built on an 1,100-acre forest preserve by the Laichwiltach First Nation, this handsome ocean-view lodge was inspired by traditional longhouse design. Native art is featured throughout. Stroll beaches to ponder ancient Native petroglyphs, visit the outstanding Kwagiulth Museum (45-minute walk; 250/285-3733), walk to nearby Cape Mudge Lighthouse, or opt for a massage. The lodge hosts First Nations cultural demonstrations and salmon barbecues monthly in summer. Stay in the main lodge's thirty varied rooms or five quiet waterfront cabins. In the Hamaelas dining room, seafood—sometimes including your own catch—and such First Nations dishes as cedar-baked salmon, venison, and clam fritters are the stars. *$$$; AE, DC, E, JCB, MC, V; no checks; closed mid-Oct–Apr; www.capemudgeresort.bc.ca; 15 minutes south of ferry dock.*

Port McNeill and Telegraph Cove

The major asset of the remote area near Vancouver Island's northeast end is its proximity to all things wild. The inspiring **U'MISTA CULTURAL CENTRE** (Front St, Alert Bay; 250/974-5403; www.umista.org) nearby is only a short ferry ride from the Port McNeill waterfront; learn about potlatch traditions of the local Kwakwaka'wakw people.

Whale-watching (June–Oct) is superior from Telegraph Cove, a village on stilts 13 miles (21 km) south of Port McNeill. **STUBBS ISLAND WHALE WATCHING** (24 Boardwalk, Telegraph Cove; 250/928-3185 or 800/665-3066) offers cruises to view orcas. Old homes in Telegraph Cove have been revived as lodgings at **TELEGRAPH COVE RESORT** (in Telegraph Cove; 250/928-3131 or 800/200-4665; www.telegraphcoveresort.com).

LODGINGS

Hidden Cove Lodge / ★★

HIDDEN COVE; 250/956-3916
Sandra and Dan Kirby's waterfront retreat on 8½ acres is interspersed with walking trails and offers back-to-basics relaxation 20 minutes south of Port McNeill. Eight guest rooms with private baths are furnished in pine, and rates include home-cooked breakfasts such as eggs Benedict or pancakes. In summer (mid-May–mid-Oct), Sandra and the lodge staff cook dinners of Dungeness crab, baby back spareribs, salmon, halibut, or other hearty favorites.

Two two-bedroom waterfront cottages with fireplaces and full kitchens allow families to cook on their own. $$–$$$$; MC, V; no checks; www.hidden covelodge.com; take Beaver Cove–Telegraph Cove cutoff from Hwy 19.

Port Hardy

A harbor-front promenade leavens your stay in this gritty town at the end of Highway 19 near Vancouver Island's far northeastern tip. Logging, fishing, and mining have provided most of the employment, though they're fading. Travelers stop to catch the acclaimed 15-hour **BC FERRIES** (250/386-3431 or 888/223-3779; reservations required) cruise north to Prince Rupert on the mainland or to Bella Coola and Bella Bella on the midcoast. Book summer well in advance: ferry passengers fill the hotels.

The famous Edward S. Curtis silent film *In the Land of the War Canoes* was filmed in nearby **FORT RUPERT** (off Hwy 19, 3 miles/5 km south of Port Hardy). The **COPPER MAKER GALLERY** (114 Copper Way, Fort Rupert; 250/949-8491) is nice.

Remote **CAPE SCOTT PROVINCIAL PARK** (37 miles/63 km west of Port Hardy; www.env.gov.bc.ca/bcparks) is among the most beautiful places on earth. A 1½-hour drive over gravel roads west of Port Hardy and a 45-minute walk take you to its spectacular **SAN JOSEF BAY**; camping is permitted. A more challenging hike leads to the island's northern tip; the **PORT HARDY VISITOR INFO CENTRE** (7250 Market St; 250/949-7622; www.ph-chamber.bc.ca) has information.

SOUTHERN INTERIOR AND THE KOOTENAYS

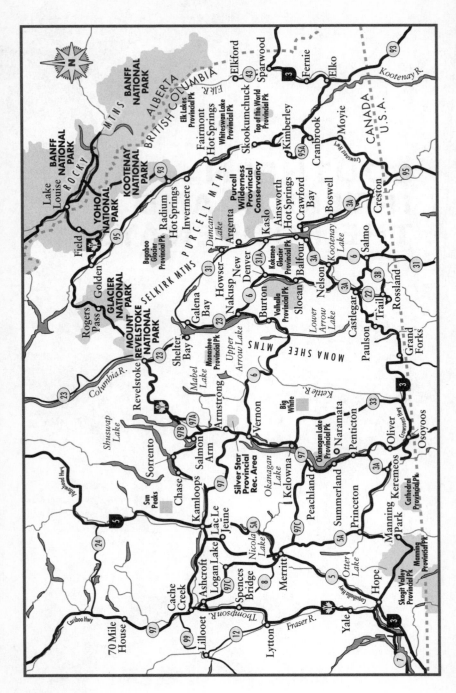

SOUTHERN INTERIOR
AND THE KOOTENAYS

British Columbia's southern interior, that vast territory that extends east and north past Hope in the Lower Mainland, is one of the most diverse, scenic, and sometimes challenging landscapes on earth. Innumerable mountain ranges crowd up beside each other: the Cascades, the Monashees, the Selkirks, the Purcells, the Bugaboos, and the mighty Rockies.

The West Kootenay lies in the central stretches of British Columbia's southern interior; to envision this area, imagine four mountain ranges furrowed together like an accordion.

ACCESS AND INFORMATION

Almost every main road or highway in southern British Columbia intersects the **TRANS-CANADA HIGHWAY** (Highway 1) at some point. In this region, **HIGHWAY 1** covers 372 miles (600 km) between Hope and Field on the B.C.-Alberta border. Other major highways here include **HIGHWAY 5** (the Yellowhead Highway), whose 130-mile (210-km) Coquihalla Highway portion (drivers must pay a $10 toll) provides the most direct route between Hope and Kamloops, 45 miles (73 km) shorter than Highway 1 between those two points; **HIGHWAY 97C**, linking Highway 1 at Cache Creek to Kelowna in the Okanagan; **HIGHWAY 97** through the Okanagan between Penticton and Kamloops; and **HIGHWAY 3** (the Crowsnest Highway), which parallels the U.S. border for 491 miles (792 km) between Hope and the B.C.-Alberta border east of Fernie.

KAMLOOPS is served by **AIR CANADA JAZZ** (888/247-2262; www.flyjazz. ca), **HORIZON AIR** (800-547-9308; www.horizonair.com), and **VIA RAIL** (888/842-7245; www.viarail.ca). **KELOWNA** is served by **AIR CANADA JAZZ**, **HORIZON AIR (800/547-9308; WWW.HORIZONAIR.COM), AND WESTJET (800/538-5696; WWW.WESTJET.COM). PENTICTON** is served by **AIR CANADA JAZZ. CRANBROOK** and **CASTLEGAR** are served by **AIR CANADA JAZZ** (800/663-3721); the latter two airports are notorious for cranky winter weather, with flights frequently canceled by fog. **GREYHOUND CANADA** (800/231-2222; www.greyhound.ca) offers daily service along the Trans-Canada Highway, through the Okanagan and the Kootenays.

The Thompson Plateau

As the Trans-Canada Highway (Highway 1) and the Coquihalla Highway (Highway 5) climb and wind their separate ways north from Hope (see Lower Mainland British Columbia chapter) before crossing paths again in Kamloops, they pass through a variety of climates, from the arid canyons carved by the Fraser, Nicola, and Thompson rivers to the gently rolling highlands of the Thompson Plateau.

SOUTHERN INTERIOR THREE-DAY TOUR

DAY ONE: Rise early for a walk along Kelowna's lakefront promenade, stopping to enjoy breakfast al fresco at the **GRAND OKANAGAN LAKEFRONT RESORT**. Drive over a unique floating bridge to **MISSION HILL FAMILY ESTATE** for a winery tour. Continue south along Lake Okanagan to **OSOYOOS**, stopping at one of the many roadside stalls to enjoy a picnic of your favorite variety of fruits and freshly squeezed juices. Walk off lunch along the interpretive boardwalk at the **DESERT CENTRE**, protecting Canada's only true desert. It's a three-hour drive through the wilderness of the Monashee Mountains to Rossland. Check in to your room at the **RAM'S HEAD INN** before descending to town, where you'll enjoy a casual dinner at the always-popular **SUNSHINE CAFÉ**. Spend the rest of the evening at the inn, curled up in front of a log fire with a good book.

DAY TWO: After breakfast at the Ram's Head, drive to Nelson for a self-guided walking tour of the historic downtown precinct. Grab lunch at the **RICE BOWL RESTAURANT** (301 Baker St; 250/354-4129). After lunch, drive north on Highways 3A and 31 to **AINSWORTH HOT SPRINGS**. Trade your clothes for a bathing suit and relax in the resort's public soaking pools. Drive the short distance

---

Merritt

The waters around Merritt (population 7,200) are famous for producing rainbow trout. Fly-casting is the style of choice. Close to 50 percent of British Columbia's total **FRESHWATER SPORT FISHING** occurs in the Thompson-Nicola region: The Thompson and Nicola rivers are historic salmon-spawning tributaries of the Fraser River, and the smaller feeder streams are also where rainbow trout, Dolly Varden char, and kokanee (freshwater salmon) spawn. The **MERRITT TOURIST/ VISITOR INFO BOOTH** (2185 Voght St; 250/378-5634 or 877/330-3377; www. merritt-chamber.bc.ca), conveniently beside Highway 5, is good. Every year in July, Merritt hosts a mammoth country music–themed event, the **MOUNTAIN MUSIC FESTIVAL** (www.mountainfest.com).

LODGINGS

Quilchena Hotel / ★★

HWY 5A, QUILCHENA; 250/378-2611
Visitors are forever parading into this heritage roadhouse's bar to inspect the bullet holes. That's interesting (so are the unproven stories about how they got there), but the hotel itself is a treasure. The 12 rooms and suites, some with private baths, are all different, high-ceilinged Edwardian marvels with period wallpaper and original furnishings that have been there since it

along Kootenay Lake to **KASLO**. Find a table on the patio at the **ROSEWOOD CAFÉ** for an early dinner, and revel in your newfound sense of well-being. Enjoy the scenic evening drive on Highway 31A between Kaslo and New Denver, and let your eyes do the work as you sightsee along Slocan and Upper Arrow lakes. Catch the ferry across Upper Arrow Lake from Galena Bay to Shelter Bay. It's only a short drive from Shelter Bay to **MULVEHILL CREEK WILDERNESS INN** south of Revelstoke.

DAY THREE: After a leisurely breakfast, head for the inn's beach on **UPPER ARROW LAKE**. When you're ready, drive into Revelstoke and stop at **THE 112** for a weekday lunch. Point your car's nose up the Meadows in the Sky Parkway in nearby **MOUNT REVELSTOKE NATIONAL PARK**. Have plenty of film ready to record the profusion of wildflowers. Look east toward Rogers Pass and the massive **ILLECILLEWAET GLACIER**. That's where you're headed once you return to the Trans-Canada Highway (Hwy 1). Pull over at the top of the pass for a visit to the uniquely shaped information center. Primed by your crash course in a century of mountaineering tradition in **GLACIER NATIONAL PARK**, enjoy the descent past the peaks to Golden. Drive on to **EMERALD LAKE LODGE** in **YOHO NATIONAL PARK** for dinner and the night.

opened in 1908. The dining room offers a savory blend of West Coast and ranch cuisine—ranch-raised steaks, rum-basted ribs, or grilled salmon—and the adjacent golf course is popular. *$$; MC, V; no checks; closed Nov–late Apr; www.quilchena.com; 12 miles (20 km) east of Merritt.* &

Cache Creek

Aside from a gas stop, quiet, dusty Cache Creek offers few other incentives to pause. The surrounding landscape, however, is one of the most striking in the province—wide-open views of sagebrush-covered mountainsides shaped by eons of weathering. Cache Creek is the junction of **HIGHWAY 97** (Cariboo Highway; see Northern Mainland British Columbia chapter) and **HIGHWAY 1**. From here, Highway 1/97 leads 52 miles (84 km) east to Kamloops.

Five miles north of Cache Creek, **HAT CREEK RANCH** (www.hatcreekranch. com) is one of the province's finest heritage attractions, an original Cariboo Road way station whose buildings have been lovingly restored. Stroll into the tack barn, and the atmosphere seems the same as it must have been a century ago. Visitors can ride horses, gallivant around in horse-drawn wagons, or stay the night in miner's tents, cabins, or a *kekuli*, the traditional First Nations lodge.

RESTAURANTS

Horstings Farm Market / ★★

HWY 97, CACHE CREEK; 250/457-6546
Jars of Horstings' brand pickles, beets, and other tasty treats line the walls of Ted and Donna Horsting's rambling fruit and vegetable store, café, and bakery. Best of all, nestled in the back is an eight-table restaurant in which soups, sandwiches, chili, bread, and pies comprise the modest menu. This is the best place north of the Okanagan to buy fresh fruit and vegetables. *$; MC, V; checks OK; lunch every day; no alcohol; no reservations; 1.2 miles (2 km) north of town on east side of hwy.* &

Sundance Ranch / ★★

KIRKLAND RANCH RD, ASHCROFT;
250/453-2422 OR 800/553-3533
Set in high, semidesert plateau country southeast of Cache Creek, surrounded by sagebrush and cottonwood, the guest ranch of the Rowe family offers sweeping views of the Thompson River. It's a ranch-resort hybrid with a heated outdoor pool and tennis courts. The real attraction here is the corral, where wranglers assemble 80 horses for daily rides. Immaculate guest rooms are divided between an adult and a kids' wing (though kids can bunk with their parents) and two separate sports lounges. Saturdays, there's a much-anticipated cowhand hoedown. *$$$; MC, V; no checks; closed Nov–Mar; www.sundance-ranch.com; 5 miles (8 km) south of Ashcroft.* &

Kamloops

Kamloops (population 77,280), the largest city on the Trans-Canada Highway between Vancouver and Calgary, Alberta, sprawls across the weathered benches above the Thompson River's north and south forks. The town's name is taken from this important geographical intersection; it translates from the local Secwepemc language as "where the rivers meet."

Nearby **SECWEPEMC NATIVE HERITAGE PARK** (E Shuswap Rd; 250/828-9801) features traditional pit-house dwellings and a huge wooden structure dubbed the "powwow arbor." Tall timbers thrust above the rounded arbor's square-shingled roof, which at its center opens to the sky. The **KAMLOOPS POW WOW**, held here on the third weekend in August, features more than a thousand performers and craftspeople.

Fly-in fishing lodges are on many of the area's 700 lakes, where anglers cast for Kamloops trout. The **KAMLOOPS VISITOR INFO CENTRE** (1290 W Trans-Canada Hwy; 250/374-3377 or 800/662-1994; www.tourismkamloops.com) offers more information.

RESTAURANTS

This Old Steak and Fish House / ★★

172 BATTLE ST, KAMLOOPS; 250/374-3227
New Mexican transplants Mickey and Betty Caldwell have been pampering guests with southwestern hospitality in this unique 1911 heritage home for a decade. Everything's fresh: seafood (wild salmon), lamb, ribs, and steaks, complemented by organic vegetables and authentic Southwest chili. The signature dish is an Asian sampler of seared ahi tuna, baby calamari, tiger prawns, and wonton-wrapped tiger rolls, served on a bed of shredded radish. *$$–$$$; AE, MC, V; no checks; lunch Mon–Fri, dinner every day; full bar; reservations recommended; www.steakhouse.kamloops.com; downtown.* &

LODGINGS

Riverland Motel / ★

1530 RIVER ST, KAMLOOPS; 250/374-1530 OR 800/663-1530
Centrally located, the Riverland offers quick access to major highways, and attractions are within walking distance. The motel's 58 standard rooms are spotless and pleasantly furnished, all with refrigerators. Though kitchen units are available, the adjacent Storms Restaurant features a full menu of creative pastas, seafood, ribs, and racks, best enjoyed on the sheltered patio overlooking the river. *$–$$; AE, MC, V; no checks; www.riverlandmotel.kamloops.com; exit 374 off Hwy 1, toward Jasper, then first left.* &

South Thompson Inn / ★★★

3438 SHUSWAP RD, KAMLOOPS; 250/573-3777 OR 800/797-7713
Poised on the north shore of the South Thompson 20 minutes outside Kamloops, this imposing inn looks like an overgrown cotton-plantation mansion, with white dormers, a long covered porch overlooking the river, and a broad lawn sweeping down to the water. "Kentucky style," the inn advertises itself, and life does seem more genteel here. All rooms offer vistas of the river or the mountains to the north; golf, swimming, and equestrian activities occupy guests here. *$–$$$; AE, MC, V; no checks; www.stigr.com; exit 390 (LaFarge) off Hwy 1, north across river, follow signs east along north shore 4 miles (6 km).* &

Sun Peaks Resort

Sun Peaks has outgrown the early buzz that declared it the "next Whistler," an identity it no longer wishes to assume. Today it is a family-oriented winter-sports resort, with three separate mountains to ski and a world of other activities. Eight slope-side hotels anchor a village of chalets, condos, town homes, and bed-and-breakfast inns. Most offer true ski-in, ski-out access to the lifts. In summer, a ski lift transports hikers and cyclists to high alpine meadows, while golfers stride the fairways of the golf course.

SKIING THE SOUTHERN INTERIOR

Since they spent their time mining Red Mountain, the northern Europeans who settled Rossland in the 1890s well knew how much snow fell on the mountain. So Olaus Jeldness, a Norwegian who'd prospected all over the West, organized a race, though he complained it was "far too steep and the snow conditions too extreme" for a satisfactory race. More than a century later, those exact characteristics have made the place, now called **RED RESORT**, a cult area for skiers who take their sport seriously. With two mountains now, and mountains of snow each winter to blanket them, Red Resort draws skiers from around the world.

And so does the rest of British Columbia's southern interior. Whistler has the top-of-the-heap international reputation, but with a dozen major areas elsewhere in the province, British Columbia is Canada's ski capital. The Okanagan and the Kootenays both offer destination resorts with excellent snow, large mountains, and fully developed base areas that offer complete visitor amenities. Skiers who think only of Whistler are missing a lot.

"In the past," says Olympic gold medalist Nancy Greene Raine of **SUN PEAKS RESORT** near Kamloops, "this was perceived as a place where a small group of rugged, wild, and woolly skiers went to enjoy some of the best powder skiing in the province." But Sun Peaks has transformed itself into a three-mountain, family-friendly resort with a lovely base village, exceptional intermediate skiing, and plenty of nonski activities, such as dogsledding, to keep the entire family occupied.

Located 30 miles (50 km) northeast of Kamloops on Highway 5 and Tod Mountain Road, Sun Peaks takes about 45 minutes to reach, much of it a pleasant drive beside the North Thompson River. Aside from the lodgings listed below, hundreds of condos and rental homes are available, all with excellent access to the slopes. Once you arrive at the resort, you won't need your car, though groceries are sparse. Contact **SUN PEAKS RESORT CORP** (3150 Creekside Wy, Ste 5; 250/578-7842 or 800/807-3257; www.sunpeaksresort.com).

LODGINGS

Father's Country Inn / ★★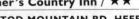

TOD MOUNTAIN RD, HEFFLEY CREEK;
250/578-7306 OR 866/578-7372
A stay at Father's Country Inn, a bed-and-breakfast hideaway 4 miles (7 km) west of Sun Peaks Resort, confirms that no matter how far you roam, you'll still find surprises. Proprietor David Conover Jr. markets not only his resort but also the images his father took of Marilyn Monroe, whom Conover Sr. befriended while he was on a photo shoot for the U.S. Army in Los Angeles

"We see ourselves as the second stop on a two-step holiday," says Greene Raine, who grew up and learned to ski at Red. "More visitors are coming to Canada on a two-week ski holiday. They spend a week at Whistler, then they want to come to a resort like ours where you can actually meet people."

Just as Sun Peaks has evolved into a world-class family resort, so have numerous others in the interior. **BIG WHITE** and **SILVER STAR** in the Okanagan both draw families for extended vacations; **APEX** near Penticton is a training mecca for serious skiers. **WHITEWATER** near Nelson is legendary for knee-deep light powder, and **KIMBERLEY ALPINE RESORT** has its own pseudo-Bavarian village.

In the Rockies, **FERNIE ALPINE RESORT** doubled its size in 1999, adding to the legendary appeal of its light powder snow. Nearby **PANORAMA**, at Invermere, is a very big (4,000-foot vertical) destination resort tucked into a valley in the Purcell Mountains with a charming village and amenities such as an outdoor hot-pools complex. **KICKING HORSE MOUNTAIN RESORT**, outside Golden, is another big area adding facilities, including a unique top-of-the-mountain guest suite whose occupants have an ironclad first-tracks guarantee when they wake up in the morning.

All of them are well suited for a week of skiing. Sure, you have to get that week at Whistler in first. Then go catch your breath at one of these smaller, more user-friendly spots.

—Eric P. Lucas and Andrew Hempstead

during World War II. The plain front of the inn masks the richness of its 6,000-square-foot interior, including an unheated swimming pool. *$; MC, V; checks OK; www.dconover.com; from Hwy 5, follow Tod Mountain Rd 14 miles (23 km) toward Sun Peaks Resort.*

Nancy Greene's Cahilty Lodge / ★★

220 VILLAGE WAY, SUN PEAKS RESORT;
250/578-7454 OR 800/244-8424

After perfecting their hotel skills at Whistler in the 1980s, Nancy Greene Raine and her husband, Al, migrated east in 1996 to Sun Peaks and opened the Cahilty Lodge, named for a local pioneer ranching family. This full-service condominium hotel's amenities range from rooms with modest cooking facilities to fully equipped suites that sleep eight. A hot tub and an exercise room, plus a ski and mountain-bike room, share the downstairs with Macker's Bistro (250/578-7894), one of the most consistent restaurants at Sun Peaks. Adjacent to the lodge is the resort's sports center with swimming pool and weight room, outdoor skating rink, and tennis courts. The lodge's centerpiece is Greene Raine's entrance-way trophy cabinet. Service here regularly out-performs guest expectations. *$$–$$$; AE, DC, JCB, MC, V; no checks; www. cahiltylodge.com; east on Creekside Way to Village Way.* &

Pinnacle Lodge / ★★★

2503 EAGLE CT, SUN PEAKS RESORT; 250/578-7850 OR 866/587-7850
Tucked into the base of Mount Morrissey, across the creek from the bustle of the main village, Pinnacle Lodge has the quiet elegance of a top-notch Euro-pean mountain inn. The timber-beam entrance opens into a stunning lounge and dining room whose 40-foot cathedral ceiling tops huge windows over-looking the mountain and golf course. The 21 rooms are spacious, furnished in warm wood. The lodge has its own compact ice rink. The Kla-Ora dining room, with a modest four-meal fresh sheet each night, is Sun Peaks' most elegant. *$$$; MC, V; no checks; www.pinnaclelodgesunpeaks.com; across from Sun Peaks Village.* &

The Okanagan Valley

Beloved for a mild, nurturing climate with more than 2,000 annual hours of sun-shine and an unparalleled landscape that ranges from desert to snowcapped peaks, the Okanagan has something for everyone: swimming, boating, golfing, biking, hiking, skiing and snowboarding, and innumerable orchards and vineyards. Medi-terranean-themed Osoyoos, at the valley's southern end, lays claim to the title of warmest resort area in Canada, with the warmest lake.

Highways 1 and 97 divide at Monte Creek, 19 miles (31 km) east of Kamloops. From there, Highway 97 runs south to the head of Okanagan Lake at Vernon in the North Okanagan, where it links with Highway 97A. (Highways 97A and 97B lead south from the Trans-Canada at Sicamous and Salmon Arm, respectively. Near Enderby, Highway 97B merges with 97A.) From Vernon, Highway 97 fol-lows the lake south to Penticton, then on to Osoyoos and Highway 3.

Orchards and vineyards testify to the presence of some of the best fruit- and vegetable-growing land in the world, while dozens of parks surround 79-mile (128-km) Okanagan Lake. As you pass through the lush South Okanagan and Similkameen regions, near the U.S.-Canadian border, remains of old mining settle-ments along Highway 97 have been replaced by innumerable fruit and produce stands. Travel information on the entire region is available from **THOMPSON OKANAGAN TOURISM** (800/567-2275; www.totabc.com). The region is painfully popular in July and August, when visitors must book coveted accommodations months or even a year ahead.

Vernon and Silver Star Mountain Resort

For decades, Vernon (population 33,500) was one of the largest fruit-producing towns in the British Empire, thanks to the abundance of freshwater for irrigation. One of many farms surrounding the city, **DAVISON ORCHARDS** (Bella Vista Rd; 250/549-3266) welcomes visitors with a self-guided walk, wagon tours, a petting zoo, a café, and fresh produce. Contact **VERNON TOURISM** (Hwy 97 S, Vernon; 250/542-3256 or 800/665-0795; www.vernontourism.com) for information.

High above Vernon, **SILVER STAR MOUNTAIN RESORT** (Silver Star Rd, 11 miles/17.5 km east of Hwy 97; 250/542-0224 or 800/663-4431; www.ski silverstar.com) is the outdoor hub of the North Okanagan, and it's usually called the area's best family resort (though critics carp, somewhat understandably, about its garish faux-Victorian architecture). Forested trails link the resort with adjacent **SOVEREIGN LAKE SKI AREA** in **SILVER STAR PROVINCIAL PARK** (www.env.gov. bc.ca/bcparks), where the Nordic lodge (250/558-3036; www.sovereignlake.com) sells tickets and has a café, wax room, and rental shop.

Once at Silver Star, whether you stay at a condo on Knoll Hill—where Victorian Gaslight–replica homes are decorated in four or five exterior hues and trimmed with cookie-cutter moldings—or in a hotel on Main Street with wrap-around verandas, everything is within walking (or skiing) distance. The **BUGA-BOOS BAKERY CAFÉ** (250/545-3208), and its new companion, Francuccino's, is noted for robust coffee, serious strudel, and ambrosial cinnamon buns made of croissant dough.

RESTAURANTS

Eclectic Med Restaurant / ★★

3117 32ND ST, VERNON; 250/558-4646

Andrew Fradley's Eclectic Med Restaurant has been winning the hearts (and palates) of epicureans in the North Okanagan since 1996. Fradley's culinary inclinations lean to Caribbean, Thai, and East Indian influences. Tuscan tuna, Moroccan lamb, Salmon Tropicana, and Calypso Pork top the extensive menu. Combinations hark back to North African–born Fradley's dozen years in Portugal. *$$; AE, MC, V; no checks; lunch Mon–Fri, dinner every day; full bar; reservations recommended; at 32nd Ave in central Vernon.* &

LODGINGS

Pinnacles Suite Hotel / ★

SILVER STAR MOUNTAIN RESORT; 250/542-4548 OR 800/551-7466

The Pinnacles Suite Hotel, poised on the open slopes above Silver Star's mountain village, has the best seat in town. Each of the 18 suites has a private entrance, spacious living area, full bath, kitchen, and ski locker. Relax in a rooftop hot tub after a day on the slopes. The adjacent Kickwillie Inn, Silver Star's original day lodge, is now renovated to hold seven suites. *$$; AE, MC, V; checks OK; www.pinnacles.com; 14 miles (22 km) northeast of Vernon.*

Kelowna

Sprawled alongside Okanagan Lake's hourglass waist, Kelowna ("grizzly bear" in the native Okanagan dialect) is the largest (population 105,000) and liveliest city in the valley and one of the fastest-growing in Canada. The new **CENTRE FOR THE ARTS AND KELOWNA ART GALLERY** (1315 Water St; 250/762-2226; www. galleries.bc.ca/kelowna) and 15,000-seat **SKYREACH PLACE** (1223 Water St; 250/979-0888; www.skyreachplace.com), home of the Western Hockey League's Kelowna Rockets, herald a renaissance fueled by an influx of young professionals, many of whom work for the 200 tech firms based here. Wineries also thrive.

In the heart of downtown, the Okanagan's oldest winery, **CALONA WINES** (1125 Richter St; 250/762-3332 or 888/246-4472; www.calonavineyards.ca), is a good starting point for a wine-country tour. **MISSION HILL FAMILY ESTATE** (1730 Mission Hill Rd, Westbank; 250/768-7611 or 888/999-1713; www.mission hillwinery.com), perched atop a ridge on the west side of Okanagan Lake, offers one of the best views. **SUMMERHILL** (4870 Chute Lake Rd; 250/764-8000 or 800-667-3538; www.summerhill.bc.ca), overlooking city and lake from a bench south of Kelowna, is a pioneer in organic wine-making, aging many of its wines in a massive pyramid. Its restaurant specializes in using Okanagan foodstuffs such as apples and other fruit, and summertime diners enjoy an unsurpassed vantage of the valley.

Kelowna is a jumping-off point for outdoor recreation, from cycling the **MISSION CREEK GREENWAY** or **KETTLE VALLEY TRAIL** to kiteboarding at a lakeside beach, to exploring the surrounding Monashee Mountains. **MONASHEE ADVENTURE TOURS** (470 Cawston Ave; 250/762-9253 or 888/762-9253; www. monasheeadventuretours.com) rents bikes and offers guided cycle tours. Kelowna also boasts 16 of the 39 **GOLF COURSES** (www.golfkelowna.com) between Vernon and Osoyoos, including some of Canada's highest-rated, such as Predator Ridge.

And the lake has its own version of the Loch Ness monster: Ogopogo. No one has yet claimed the $2 million reward for proof it exists, but its statue in downtown Kelowna is one of the most-photographed sights in the Okanagan. Contact the **KELOWNA VISITOR INFO CENTRE** (544 Harvey Ave; 250/861-1515 or 800/663-4345; www.tourismkelownacom).

RESTAURANTS

Doc Willoughby's Downtown Grill / ★

353 BERNARD AVE, KELOWNA; 250/868-8288

Darren Nicoll and Dave Willoughby (the restaurant is named for his grandfather) stripped this 1908 downtown landmark to the walls, then rebuilt with wood salvaged from a heritage site in Vancouver. Hardwood floors, maple tables, cozy booths, and a floor-to-ceiling bar provide atmosphere; upscale pub fare and regular live music define the flavor (so, too, does an unfortunate reputation for spotty service). $–$$; AE, MC, V; no checks; lunch Mon–Sat, dinner every day; full bar; no reservations; near Pandosy St. &

Fresco / ★★★★

1560 WATER ST, KELOWNA; 250/868-8805

Renowned chef Rod Butters and his wife, Audrey Surrao, arrived in 2001 via a string of notable British Columbia restaurants, including the Fairmont Chateau Whistler. The downtown heritage building was emptied to its frame and trimmed with light clear fir. The menu fuses Asian flavors, a dash of European flair for presentation, and a hint of Canadian wry humor—an amuse, for instance, of *auracana* egg froth with double-smoked prosciutto is called "green eggs and ham." Caesar salad has become so commonplace that Butters' sensational version, with sun-dried olives and double-smoked bacon, is a revelation. *$$; AE, DC, MC, V; no checks; dinner Tues–Sun; full bar; reservations recommended; www.frescorestaurant.net; 2 blocks from Harvey Ave.* &

LODGINGS

Casa Loma Resort / ★★★

2777 CASA LOMA RD, KELOWNA; 250/769-4630, 800/771-5253

Its location alone would make Casa Loma one of the most appealing accommodations in the Kelowna area. Not only is it right on the lakeshore, in a quiet corner across the water from the city's hubbub, but it also borders beautiful Kalamoir Park. The 20 cottages and villas are the best, with kitchens, living rooms, and decks, which are staggered to assure privacy. The 20 units in the main lodge are suites, too, but not as appealing. *$$$; AE, MC, V; no checks; casaloma.kelowna.com; 1 mile (1.6 km) south of Hwy 97C on east lakeshore.*

The Grand Okanagan Lakefront Resort / ★★★

1310 WATER ST, KELOWNA; 250/763-4500 OR 800/465-4651

The Grand's modernist design harkens back to Kelowna's Mission past and complements the city's burgeoning cultural and entertainment center. Rooms in the 10-story main tower have panoramic views. Standard rooms have full-length windows that open onto Romeo-and-Juliet balconies. For longer stays, two-bedroom condo suites are great. Amenities include a spa, hot tubs, saunas, and a pool. Three restaurants, two lounges, a pub, and the Mind Grind Internet Café share the main floor with the Lake City Casino (www.lakecitycasinos.com). *$$$$; AE, DC, DIS, MC, V; business checks only; www.grandokanagan.com; 5 blocks north of Hwy 97.* &

Hotel Eldorado / ★★

500 COOK RD, KELOWNA; 250/763-7500

In 1990, after a fire destroyed the original Eldorado Arms, owner Jim Nixon replicated the 1920s-era hotel. Each of the reasonably priced 19 original guest rooms features elegant touches; most have water views; one room includes a Jacuzzi. The brand-new 50-room addition lacks some of the inn's charm but is quieter. The Eldorado's waterfront location and private marina cement its popularity. *$$–$$$; AE, DC, MC, V; no checks; www.eldoradokelowna.com; 4 miles (6.5 km) south of downtown on Pandosy St and Lakeshore Rd.* ₺

Manteo Resort / ★★★

3766 LAKESHORE RD, KELOWNA; 250/860-1031 OR 800/445-5255
The brightly colored, four-story Manteo looks sunny even on cloudy days. Opened in 2000, the resort's 78 hotel rooms and 24 private villas are in an intimate setting on the shore of Okanagan Lake. Clean, quiet, and arty, the Tuscan-style lobby sets the right vacation tone. Thoughtful touches abound, such as fruit baskets. The resort is otherwise designed to keep every family member occupied. Their Wild Apple Grill features monthly specials inspired by fresh produce. Service throughout is superb. *$$–$$$$; AE, DC, MC, V; no checks; www.manteo.com; 4 miles (6.5 km) south of downtown at Pandosy St.* ₺

Big White Ski Resort

Less than an hour's drive southeast of Kelowna via Highway 33, on the perimeter of the Monashee Mountains, is **BIG WHITE SKI RESORT** (Big White Rd, 14 miles/23 km east of Hwy 33; 250/765-3101 or 800/663-2772; www.bigwhite. com). Set at the highest elevation of any winter resort in British Columbia (5,760 feet/1,755 m), Big White is one of the largest ski-in/ski-out resort villages in Canada.

The **HAPPY VALLEY ADVENTURE CENTRE** and theme park offers tubing, dogsledding, ice skating, and snowmobiling. Visitors can hop on a horse-drawn wagon as it trots by, then sit on a hay bale and let the team of Percherons do the rest. More than a dozen restaurants—**SNOWSHOE SAM'S** (250/765-5959), **COPPER KETTLE** (800/663-2772), and the **KETTLE VALLEY STEAKHOUSE** (250/491-0130) are best bets—dot the village. The Village Centre Lodge's wood-fired bakery has cinnamon buns with enough icing to rival the snow on the slopes.

LODGINGS

White Crystal Inn / ★★

BIG WHITE RD, KELOWNA; 800/663-2772
This classic four-story chalet has grown with the mountain and now offers 49 rooms spread between two wings. So successful was the original design that it was copied for Chateau Big White nearby. But they couldn't replicate the White Crystal's intimacy or its impeccable location next to the resort's gondola and Bullet Express quad chair. All rooms are outfitted in cedar and slate. On the lodge's main floor are the stylish Copper Kettle Restaurant and a more casual bistro. *$$; AE, MC, V; checks OK; www.bigwhite.com; on right as you enter resort, next to Village Centre.*

Penticton and Apex Mountain Resort

Penticton, the "Peach City" (population 30,985), might just as easily be called Festival City. There's always some serious fun going on in this town spread between Okanagan and Skaha lakes, including the **AUGUST PEACH FESTIVAL** (250/493-4055 or 800/663-5052), now in its sixth decade; **FEST-OF-ALE** in April; weeklong **WINE FESTIVALS** (250/861-6654; www.owfs.com) in May and October; the May **MEADOWLARK FESTIVAL** (250/492-5275 or 866/699-9453; www.meadowlark festival.bc.ca), which celebrates the environment; a campy Beach Blanket Film Festival in July; and a jazz festival in September.

Tons of ironmen and ironwomen turn out for the August swim-bike-run **TRI-ATHLON** every year. Some of the best **ROCK CLIMBING** in BC occurs at the **SKAHA BLUFFS** on the town's southeastern outskirts. **SKAHA ROCK ADVENTURES** (113-437 Martin St, Penticton; 250/493-1765; www.skaharockclimbing.com) guides climbers on many of the bluff's 120 cliffs.

Contact the **PENTICTON VISITOR INFO CENTRE** (888 Westminster Ave W, Penticton; 250/493-4055 or 800/663-5052; www.penticton.org) for details. For a wine tour, visit the **BC WINE INFORMATION CENTRE** at the same location (250/490-2006).

APEX MOUNTAIN RESORT (on Green Mountain Rd, Penticton; 250/292-8222 or 877/777-2739; www.apexresort.com) is 21 miles (33 km) west of town. Lift lines are virtually nonexistent, and the powder snow is dry and sparkling. On-hill accommodations are limited to two wonderfully cozy lodges: the **SADDLEBACK LODGE BED & BREAKFAST** (115 Clearview Crescent, Apex Mountain; 250/292-8118 or 800/863-1466; www.saddlebacklodge.com) and the **SHEEPROCK LODGE** (101 Clearview Crescent, Apex Mountain; 250/292-8558 or 877/677-1555; www.sheeprocklodge.com). Most visitors stay in Penticton, a half-hour drive away. A shuttle bus that makes the rounds of local hotels provides handy access to the slopes.

RESTAURANTS

Granny Bogner's Restaurant / ★★★

302 ECKHARDT AVE, PENTICTON; 250/493-2711
One of the Okanagan's oldest fine-dining restaurants is also one of the most consistent: great food, great location, and desserts that alone make the trip worthwhile. Diners relax in front of the rambling 1912 Arts and Crafts–style fireplace. A restaurant maxim states that the eyes eat first—nowhere more so than at Granny's, where chef Peter Hebel's entrées arrive garnished with an eye for color and shape. His bouillabaisse is a bargain and a meal in itself. *$$; AE, MC, V; no checks; dinner Tues–Sat; full bar; reservations recommended; www.grannybogners.com; 2 blocks south of Main St.* &

LODGINGS

God's Mountain Crest Chalet / ★★

4898 LAKESIDE RD, PENTICTON; 250/490-4800
It's difficult to adequately describe God's Mountain Crest Chalet, where Ulric Lejeune and his wife, Ghitta, have created the Club Med of B and Bs. The white Mediterranean-style mansion overlooks the Lejeune's vineyards, a lake, and the Okanagan Highlands. Inside is an eclectic blend of antiques and religious iconography. Quiet pervades, even at breakfast, when guests gather for sumptuous buffets. A large swimming pool and hot tub (perfect for late-night stargazing) are surrounded by gardens. *$$; MC, V; checks OK; www. godsmountain.com; 3 miles (5 km) south of Penticton.*

Naramata

North of Penticton off Hwy 97, the picturesque village of **NARAMATA** (250/496-5409; www.discovernaramata.com) is surrounded by wineries. Rugged Naramata Road leads north through slopes and headlands that jut out into the lake. You can easily spend a day and visit only half the wineries. Two that shouldn't be missed are **LANG VINEYARDS** (2493 Gammon Rd; 250/496-5987; www.langvineyards.com) and **RED ROOSTER WINERY** (910 Debeck Rd; 250/496-4041; www.redroosterwinery.com). Naramata (population 1,000) lies 10 miles (16 km) from downtown Penticton; turn east from Main Street (Highway 97) onto Jermyn Avenue and follow the signs.

LODGINGS

Naramata Heritage Inn / ★★★

3625 1ST ST, NARAMATA; 250/496-6808, 866/-617-1188
This 1908 landmark hotel, long vacant after midcentury life as a girl's school, has been lavishly restored into the Okanagan's most elegant heritage inn. The stucco exterior calls to mind Northern California inns of the period; the long porch pulls in morning sun while trees shade the grounds. Inside, clear fir floors and dark wood beams set off Mission-style furniture. The Rock Oven dining room offers a five-course dinner. *$$$; AE, MC, V; no checks; www. naramatainn.com; downtown.* &

Sandy Beach Lodge & Resort / ★★★

4275 MILL RD, NARAMATA; 250/496-5765
Sandy Beach's dozen log cabins are so popular that in July and August they are often completely booked two years in advance. That said, six B and B rooms in the restored 1940s main lodge—the real deal at this Okanagan Lake retreat—are usually still up for grabs. Each has its own covered veranda overlooking the lake. May and September are pleasant months to visit, when

competition is less fierce and the waters are almost as inviting as they are in summer. *$$–$$$$; MC, V; no checks; www.sandybeachresort.com; end of Mill Rd at Okanagan Lake.* ❧

Oliver and Osoyoos

The South Okanagan is a wondrous produce basket. Travelers on the 12-mile (20-km) stretch of Highway 97 between Oliver (population 4,225) and Osoyoos (population 4,295) pass the most bountiful agricultural land in the entire valley. Since the 1990s, this has become a prime region for growing classic European varietal grapes such as pinot noir and merlot, all of which thrive in the warm climate. The industry has grown to the point that Oliver has reconstituted itself as a "resort municipality," like Whistler, and small inns and bistros are planned throughout the area.

The **DESERT CENTRE** (west on 146th Ave off Hwy 97, Osoyoos; 250/495-2420 or 877/899-0897; www.desert.org) protects a "pocket desert," where less than 12 inches of precipitation fall annually and cacti, prickly pear, sagebrush, and rattlesnakes survive in the dry, sandy environment. Back roads on the east side of the valley lead past several award-winning wineries, including **BLUE MOUNTAIN** (by appointment only, 250/497-8244; www.bluemountainwinery.com), often cited by connoisseurs as the best of all British Columbia wineries.

From there, drivers and cyclists enjoy a unique perspective on the eroded west side of the valley. This is also the site of fledgling **SOUTH OKANAGAN NATIONAL PARK** (www.parkscanada.ca) as well as the new Okanagan Indian Band's **NK'MIP DESERT AND HERITAGE CENTRE** (1000 Ranch Creek Rd, Osoyoos; 250/495-7901 or 888/495-8555; www.nkmipdesert.com), a Native interpretive center adjacent to the new Spirit Ridge resort and winery. Contact the **OLIVER VISITOR INFO CENTRE** (36205 93rd Ave; 250/498-6321; www.oliverchamber.bc.ca) and the **OSOYOOS VISITOR INFO CENTRE** (Hwys 3 and 97; 250/495-3366 or 888/676-9667; www.destinationosoyoos.com) for details.

RESTAURANTS

Campo Marina Italian Restaurant / ★

5907 MAIN ST, OSOYOOS; 250/495-7650

Friendly and courteous service is the hallmark of the Campo Marina, where variety, great food, large servings, and moderate prices add up to good value at this self-defined "funky" eatery. They serve a blend of continental and Mediterranean flavors. Antiques and collectibles festoon the walls and tables, with an Okanagan vineyard ambience. *$$; MC, V; checks OK; dinner Tues–Sun; full bar; no reservations; www.sunnyosoyoos.com; across from Dairy Queen.*

Jacques Wine Country Inn / ★★

34646 HWY 97, OLIVER; 250/498-4418
For three decades, chef Jacques Guerin and his wife (and manager of the inn), Suzi, have been championing the region's natural abundance. Guerin's classical touch attests to his Parisian roots. Inspired entrées include pork or pan-seared pepper steak. The wine-cellar atmosphere is completed by a wood-beamed ceiling, built by Okanagan pioneer Charles Cranston. For privacy, request seating in the grotto. *$$; AE, MC, V; no checks; dinner Tues–Sun (closed Oct and Jan); full bar; reservations recommended; downtown at 346th St.*

Sonora Room at Burrowing Owl / ★★★

100 BURROWING OWL PL, OLIVER; 250/498-0620 OR 877/498-0620
After years of service with Pan Pacific hotels in Southeast Asia, British Columbia native Glenn Monk has returned home to lend a distinctly Asian air to the new bistro at one of the Okanagan's best wineries. Not surprisingly, some of his preparations evince Malaysian or Indonesian touches, such as the Balinese prawn satay or wild salmon poached in coconut broth. The balcony tables have a smashing view of a wetland. *$$$; AE, MC, V; no checks; lunch Mon–Sat, dinner every day; full bar; reservations recommended; www.bovwine.com; off Hwy 97, 7 miles (13 km) south of Oliver.* &

LODGINGS

Spirit Ridge Vineyard Resort / ★★

1200 RANCHER RD, OSOYOOS; 250/495-5445, 877/313-9463
Poised between vineyards and the desert beyond, this resort's stucco buildings house 30 bright suites and villas, all furnished in desert hues with views, all kitchenettes with patios. The Spirit Ridge winery is next door. Behind the resort, a short walk takes you to the biggest undeveloped stretch of desert in the south Okanagan. *$$$; AE, MC, V; no checks; www.spiritridge.ca; on east side of Osoyoos, 1 mile (1.6 km) north of Hwy 3.*

Vaseux Lake Lodge / ★★

9710 SUNDIAL RD, OLIVER; 250/498-0516
Vaseux Lake Lodge was built by Denise and Peter Axhorn in 1995. Sunlight floods through skylights and windows in the four units that overlook the private beach. Laquered pine furniture and down duvets provide warmth. No powerboats are allowed on the shallow lake, the center of a wildlife sanctuary. Bring your own beach toys and watercraft so you can paddle with turtles and beavers. *$$; MC, V; checks OK; www.vaseuxlakelodge.com; south end of Vaseux Lake, 1 block west of Hwy 97.*

The Kootenays

The Kootenays occupy the entire southeast portion of British Columbia. Winter sunlight barely brushes the valleys of the West Kootenay. Residents head to lively towns, such as Nelson, or to local ski areas. The majestic **COLUMBIA RIVER** winds through it all.

Transportation in the Kootenays is by road. Time zones shift between Pacific and Mountain from one town to the next. Some areas don't switch to daylight time. Get information (www.bcrockies.com) before visiting.

Rossland and Red Resort Ski Area

Rossland (population 3,645) is in the Monashee Mountains close to **RED RESORT SKI AREA** (3 miles/5 km northwest of Rossland on Hwy 3B; 250/362-7700, 250/362-7384, or 800/663-0105; www.redresort.com). In the 1890s, when Rossland was at the peak of its gold-mining boom, Red Mountain hosted the first Canadian ski racing championships. The mountain has since produced two of the best skiers to ever represent Canada. Today the resort is a cult favorite. Recently bought by Southern California tycoon Howard Katkov, the resort is undergoing significant expansion but intends not to go the Whistler route—it's focusing on condo accommodations rather than hotels, for instance. The **BLACK JACK CROSS-COUNTRY SKI CLUB** (Hwy 3B; 250/364-5445; www.skiblackjack.ca) lies at the base.

The heritage buildings that line many of Rossland's streets reflect the boom times of a century ago. Rossland's Winter Carnival, first held in 1897, is going strong the last weekend in January. The Rubberhead Mountain Bike Festival is held near Labor Day. Contact the **ROSSLAND VISITOR INFO CENTRE** (Columbia Ave and Hwy 3B, Rossland; 250/362-7722 or 888/448-7444; www.rossland.com; May–Sept) for details.

RESTAURANTS

Sunshine Café / ★

2116 COLUMBIA AVE, ROSSLAND; 250/362-5099
Everyone takes a shine to Rossland's favorite little café, where you can sit in the front of the restaurant to do some people watching or walk past the kitchen to the back room. The food doesn't try to be fancy, just good, and there's lots of it. Huevos rancheros is a breakfast favorite. Mealtimes are crowded. *$; MC, V; local checks only; breakfast, lunch, dinner every day; beer and wine; reservations recommended (ski season); just east of Queen St.*

LODGINGS

Angela's Bed & Breakfast and Guesthouse / ★★

1540 SPOKANE ST, ROSSLAND; 250/362-7790
Knowledgeable hosts make bed-and-breakfasts special. At Angela's, your host might offer to guide you through the tree runs at Red Resort: Angela Price has spent a lifetime pursuing her passion for powder skiing. Across the street, Price's newly renovated 1930s guesthouse has more suites, making a total of six bedrooms. Angela's annual oyster bash in February is worth timing your visit to enjoy. *$$; MC; checks OK; www.visitangela.com; 4 blocks downhill from Uplander Hotel.*

Ram's Head Inn / ★★★

RED MOUNTAIN RD, ROSSLAND; 250/362-9577 OR 877/267-4323
What sets the Ram's Head Inn apart is its cozy size—12 rooms, 34 guests maximum—and little touches, such as chalet slippers at the door. The inn's location at the foot of Red Resort doesn't hurt, either—it's the only traditional lodging at the area's base. Guests gather for a complimentary breakfast or relax on an overstuffed couch beside the granite fireplace; rooms are cozy affairs with warm wood decor. *$$–$$$; AE, DC, DIS, MC, V; checks OK; www.ramshead.bc.ca; off Hwy 3B at Red Mountain Rd.*

Nakusp

Nakusp (population 1,700) occupies a wide bench in a crook in the arm of Upper Arrow Lake, set squarely between the Monashee and Selkirk mountains. This is **HOT SPRING COUNTRY**. Along Highway 23 between Nakusp (at Highway 6) and Galena Bay at the northern end of Upper Arrow Lake (near Highway 1) are two commercial and four wilderness springs. You can't drive to the wilderness springs in winter (back roads aren't plowed); reach them on snowshoes or skis. Contact the **NAKUSP VISITOR INFO CENTRE** (92 6th Ave NW; 250/265-4234 or 800/909-8819; www.nakusphotsprings.com) for details.

LODGINGS

Halcyon Hot Springs Resort / ★

HWY 23, NAKUSP; 250/265-3554 OR 888/689-4699
In 1999, like the proverbial phoenix, Halcyon Hot Springs Resort rose from the ashes of its predecessor, which operated here on the shores of Upper Arrow Lake between the 1890s and 1950s. The 24 cabins and chalets sleep up to six. A restaurant is in the main building. Halcyon in Greek means "calm, serene," and that's how one feels after bathing in the two hottest pools, which share a vista of Arrow Lake with the main swimming pool. *$$; AE, MC, V; no checks; www.halcyon-hotsprings.com; 20 miles (32 km) north of Nakusp.* ♿

Kaslo

Kaslo, a former mining hub on **KOOTENAY LAKE**—almost 99 miles (160 km) long, one of British Columbia's largest freshwater lakes—retains the flavor of its heyday, much like the gloriously restored stern-wheeler **SS MOYIE** (324 Front St; 250/353-2525; 9:30am–4:30pm every day mid-May–mid-Sept). Kaslo, on Highway 31 between Highway 3 and Highway 1, remains the most appealing town on the lake. These days, it's best known for its jazz festival on the first weekend in August. Music lovers dig the tunes from dry land as the music flows from a stage anchored offshore. Contact **KASLO VISITOR INFO CENTRE** (324 Front St; 250/353-2525; www.kaslo.org; May–Oct) for details.

RESTAURANTS

Rosewood Café / ★★★

213 5TH ST, KASLO; 250/353-7673

The Rosewood has a loyal clientele from as far afield as Washington State. Reservations are a must in summer. The fact that chef Grant Mackenzie does much of his cooking outdoors on an 8-foot barbecue helps draw a crowd. About half the seats are on a spacious patio overlooking Kootenay Lake. You'll smell the chicken, pork, and beef ribs long before you reach the café's white picket fence. *$$; MC, V; local checks only; lunch, dinner every day, brunch Sun (closed Jan); full bar; reservations recommended; rosewood_cafe@ hotmail.com; at east end of 5th St.* &

LODGINGS

Wing Creek Cabins Resort / ★★

HWY 31, KASLO; 250/353-2475

Nestled in a clearing above the upper end of Kootenay Lake, Wing Creek Resort is a beautiful place to bask in the serenity of the area and the stunning view of the Purcell Wilderness across the lake. The five cozy timber-frame cabins all have fireplaces and face a large hillside with a meadow and orchards; a trail leads to the private beach. In winter, heli-skiers lift off from the meadow. *$$; AE, MC, V; no checks; www.wingcreekcabins.com; 4 miles (6 km) north of Kaslo.* &

Ainsworth Hot Springs

Ainsworth Hot Springs is a sleepy spot on Highway 31, about 12 miles (19 km) south of Kaslo and 30 miles (50 km) north of Nelson. It was a boomtown during the heyday of silver, zinc, and lead mining in the 1890s. Today, if it weren't for the hot springs, few travelers would slow down on their way through the small community perched above Kootenay Lake.

SOME LIKE IT HOT

Its position on the Pacific Rim "Ring of Fire" means British Columbia is geothermally very active, and the province has more than two dozen easily accessible hot springs (plus many more in wilderness locations known mostly to local residents). The area of greatest development of these natural spas is in the Kootenays, where hot mineral water burgeons out of mountainsides in numerous spots, several of which have been transformed into famous resorts.

AINSWORTH HOT SPRINGS is the most unusual of these. First used by Native inhabitants, then later by miners in the area, the 117-degree water is funneled first into an old horseshoe-shaped mine tunnel, which, after almost a century of mineral deposition, has become a cave. Bathers wade in through waist-deep waters to linger in nooks of the tunnel, which is in effect a steam bath. Committed enthusiasts can cool off in an icy plunge pool at the entrance to the tunnel; there is also an outdoor hot pool with sensational views across Kootenay Lake to the Purcell Mountains. The adjacent hotel offers lodging (see review) and a restaurant.

FAIRMONT HOT SPRINGS is a full-blown international resort with golf, skiing, tennis, horseback riding, hiking, and generally deluxe relaxation. A huge outdoor pool complex is open to the public; guests at the lodge (see review) have access to a smaller private pool. The resort drains the water each night, scrubs the pools, and then refills them, thus claiming its waters are "almost certainly the cleanest in North America." Hot-springs zealots won't be impressed by that, but the resort

LODGINGS

Ainsworth Hot Springs Resort / ★★

HWY 31, AINSWORTH HOT SPRINGS;
250/229-4212 OR 800/668-1171

Ainsworth Hot Springs Resort boasts a former mine shaft into which steamy mineral springs are vented. Hot water drips from the granite ceiling and flows through a tunnel into the resort's large outdoor pool. A hop into the icy plunge pool will restore your senses. Upgraded in 1999, but still unremarkable, the three-story resort's accommodations range from standard hotel rooms to suites with kitchenettes. The draw is the hot springs. *$$; AE, DC, MC, V; no checks; www.hotnaturally.com; 10 miles (16 km) north of Balfour on Hwy 31.* &

is a great place for a country club–style summer vacation.

Just up the road from Fairmont, **RADIUM HOT SPRINGS** is within Yoho National Park, tucked in a narrow creek canyon. The big bathing pool's 103-degree waters have a higher concentration of sulphate and other minerals than most hot springs—beware the water's effect on dye colors in your bathing suit. The adjacent lodge overlooks the pools.

NAKUSP HOT SPRINGS (8 miles/12 km east of Nakusp on Hot Springs Road; 250/265-4528; www.nakusphotsprings.com) is a complex operated by the village of Nakusp, along Arrow Lake. Its 130-degree source water is cooled to 108 and 100 degrees in the two bathing pools; a campground and rental chalets give the complex a more laid-back atmosphere than other hot-springs resorts.

Also in this area is **HALCYON HOT SPRINGS RESORT** (see review), an update of a colorful and historic resort that burned down in the 1950s—the complex was operated for 30 years by General Frederick Burnham, a doctor who banned bathing suits, smoking, and drinking. Halcyon developed an international reputation as a place of healing. Today's resort has a small lodge, several cabins, and bathing pools of varying temperatures overlooking the lake.

In the Nakusp area, hot water runs deep: Numerous undeveloped hot springs line the creek valleys in the region, to which residents might or might not offer directions if you ask nicely. Keep in mind the hot-springs code: no trash, no carousing, no pictures—and if you can't deal with nudity, don't go.

—Eric P. Lucas

Crawford Bay

The tiny community of Crawford Bay (population 200) across from Ainsworth Hot Springs on the east side of Kootenay Lake, accessible from Balfour on Highway 3A via the world's longest free ferry ride, is home to many artisans, including Canada's only **MANUFACTURER OF TRADITIONAL STRAW BROOMS** (www.kootenaylake.bc.ca/artisans). Crawford Bay is popular with golfers for the picturesque and challenging **KOKANEE SPRINGS GOLF COURSE** (16082 Woolgar Rd, Crawford Bay; 250/227-9226; www.kokaneesprings.com).

LODGINGS

Wedgwood Manor / ★★★

16002 CRAWFORD CREEK RD, CRAWFORD BAY; 250/227-9233 OR 800/862-0022

This lovely 1910 home, built on a 50-acre estate for the daughter of the renowned British china maker, is one of the finest lodgings in southeastern

British Columbia. The four upstairs rooms open onto a reading room; the lakeview Charles Darwin Room and the Commander's Room receive afternoon sun. The fully furnished Wildwood Cabin provides a cozy escape and, unlike the inn's rooms, is available year-round. *$$; MC, V; checks OK; closed mid-Oct–Mar; www.wedgwoodcountryinn.com; east of Nelson on Hwy 3A, take Balfour ferry to Kootenay Bay.* &

Nelson

Nestled on the shore of Kootenay Lake south of Balfour, Nelson (population 9,300) thrived during the silver and gold mining boom in the late 1890s and retains its late-Victorian character, luring filmmakers to use its downtown as a set. More than 350 heritage homes and buildings are designated heritage structures. Pick up a map, or join a free guided tour in summer, at the **NELSON VISITOR INFO CENTRE** (225 Hall St; 250/352-3433; www.discovernelson.com). Built on a hillside, Nelson's steep streets are best scaled in sturdy shoes. The best vantage on Nelson is from **GYRO PARK** (corner of Park and Morgan sts).

A pictorial exhibit is at the **NELSON MUSEUM** (402 Anderson St; 250/352-9813). In summer the town turns into an art gallery, with the work of some 100 artists exhibited in shops, restaurants, and galleries during the **NELSON ART-WALK** (250/352-2402; June–Aug). Art and crafts are displayed year-round at the **CRAFT CONNECTION** (441 Baker St; 250/352-3006). Outdoor enthusiasts shop at **SNOWPACK** (333 Baker St; 250/352-6411). The **KOOTENAY BAKER** (295 Baker St; 250/352-2274) stocks an excellent selection of healthy foods.

The Selkirk Mountains surrounding Nelson are a magnet for hikers and backcountry skiers; a popular destination is **KOKANEE GLACIER PARK** (18 miles/29 km northeast of Nelson off Hwy 3A; 250/825-4421; www.env.gov.bc.ca/bcparks). **BALDFACE SNOWCAT SKIING** (250/352-0006; www.baldface.net) offers cat-skiing.

WHITEWATER SKI & WINTER RESORT (12 miles/19 km south of Nelson on Hwy 6; 250/352-4944 or 800/666-9420; www.skiwhitewater.com) in the Selkirk Mountains is an old-school operation with four lifts. The high base elevation of 5,400 feet (1,640 m) ensures plentiful light, dry powder. The rustic resort is also home to the **WHITEWATER NORDIC CENTRE**.

RESTAURANTS

All Seasons Café / ★★★

620 HERRIDGE LANE, NELSON; 250/352-0101
This intimate café is great for a quick meal: you can sit near the bar, sip a microbrew, and enjoy an appetizer. Heavenly scented dishes emerge from the kitchen, and fresh sage-and-oregano bread arrives by the basket. To get in the full swing of All Seasons' "Left Coast Inland Cuisine," try the venison sausage in tomato sauce, followed by upside-down cake. *$$; MC, V; local checks only; dinner every day; full bar; reservations recommended; www.allseasonscafe. com; between Hall and Josephine sts.* &

Fiddler's Green / ★★

2710 LOWER SIX MILE RD, NELSON; 250/825-4466
Local opinion rates this estate home's three intimate dining rooms and one large formal area (plus summer patio) as the best atmosphere and garden dining in town. As the seasons change, menu offerings vary—such as a roasted winter vegetable and goat cheese tart. Vegetarian preferences are met with crisp artichoke and falafel. After savoring the salmon and prawn cakes, it's hard to find room for dessert. *$$; MC, V; local checks only; dinner Wed–Sun, brunch Sun; full bar; reservations recommended; www.fiddlersgreen.ca; north on Hwy 3A.*

LODGINGS

Inn the Garden B&B & Guest House / ★

408 VICTORIA ST, NELSON; 250/352-3226 OR 800/596-2337
This centrally located B and B is where many Nelson residents book their out-of-town guests. Lynda Stevens and Jerry Van Veen decorated their six-unit Victorian home, just a block from Main Street, in a garden theme. The best bargain is the three-bedroom bungalow. Stevens stocks its kitchen for breakfasts; B and B guests get a full hot breakfast. *$$; AE, MC, V; checks OK; www.innthegarden.com; 1 block south of Baker St.*

Willow Point Lodge / ★★

2211 TAYLOR DR, NELSON; 250/825-9411 OR 800/949-2211
Mel Reasoner and Ulli Huber's three-story 1920 Edwardian home just outside Nelson occupies 3½ acres. Of the six rooms, the Green Room sports a private covered balcony overlooking the lake and mountains. The garden has a gazebo, and a trail leads to three waterfalls. After a day at Whitewater Ski Resort, soak in Willow Point's large outdoor hot tub. The lodge fills quickly in summer. *$$; MC, V; local checks only; www.willowpointlodge.com; 2½ miles (4 km) north of Nelson.* ♿

Kimberley and Kimberley Alpine Resort

As with many foundering mining towns in the 1970s, Kimberley (population 6,900), on the west side of the broad Columbia Valley on Highway 93/95, looked to tourism and—like Leavenworth, Washington—chose a Bavarian theme to bolster its economy. Accordion music is played on loudspeakers at the center of the **BAVARIAN PLATZL**, the town's three-block pedestrian plaza. For a quarter, a yodeling puppet pops out of the upper window of Canada's largest cuckoo clock. If you're shopping for some goodies for your picnic lunch (or dinner at your condo), head for **KIMBERLEY SAUSAGE AND MEATS** (360 Wallinger Ave; 250/427-7766).

At 3,650 feet (1,113 m), Kimberley is the highest city in Canada. From this height, views of the snowcapped Rockies are stunning. The **HERITAGE**

MUSEUM (105 Spokane St; 250/427-7510) displays mining memorabilia. Gardeners shouldn't miss the **COMINCO GARDENS** (306 3rd Ave; 250/427-2293). A frenzy of expansion characterizes **KIMBERLEY ALPINE RESORT** (Gerry Sorenson Way; 250/427-4881 or 800/258-7669; www.skikimberley.com), where a Marriott anchors the resort.

RESTAURANTS

Old Bauernhaus / ★

280 NORTON AVE, KIMBERLEY; 250/427-5133
Tony and Ingrid Schwarzenberger, who built the House Alpenglow (see review), brought a 360-year-old farmhouse to Kimberley and reassembled it. As in the Alpenglow, wood is everywhere. The menu reflects the Schwarzenbergers' Swiss-German roots: goulash soup, wiener schnitzel, raclette. In summer, they set patio tables out in the garden. *$$; MC, V; local checks only; dinner every day (closed 2 weeks Nov and Apr); full bar; reservations recommended; www.kimberleybc.net/bauernhaus; left off Gerry Sorenson Way.* &

LODGINGS

House Alpenglow B&B / ★★

3 ALPENGLOW CT, KIMBERLEY; 250/427-0273 OR 877/257-3645
Merna Abel's three spacious and lovingly furnished rooms include the two-bedroom Sullivan suite with its private entrance to the outdoor hot tub and yard. After a complimentary plate of bratwurst and cheese on homemade bread, you may not need to eat again until supper. Kimberley Alpine Resort is several minutes uphill; the Old Bauernhaus across the road serves dinner (see review). *$; no credit cards; checks OK; www.kimberleybc.net/alpenglow; west side of Gerry Sorenson Way, near Trickle Creek Golf Resort.*

Fernie

An elegant stone courthouse anchors downtown Fernie (population 4,610), a mining and logging town on Highway 3, with historic buildings. The craggy cleft of the Lizard Range above **FERNIE ALPINE RESORT** (5339 Ski Area Rd; 250/423-4655 or 800/258-7669; www.skifernie.com) is likened to an open catcher's mitt. The resort, along with Whitewater and Red Mountain Resort, is a legendary stop on British Columbia's powder circuit. In the late 1990s, Fernie Alpine Resort began the largest expansion of any winter resort in North America, doubling its terrain with three new lifts. Seven new lodges have opened, but prime parking at the bottom of the slopes is still reserved for RVs from nearby small towns. With them in mind, Fernie provides a spiffy changing room, complete with showers.

The resort also offers sleigh rides (a handy way to get to the lifts from the parking lot), snowmobile tours, dogsledding, snowshoeing, as well as a twice-weekly torchlight ski run. In summer, the hills draw horseback riders, mountain bikers, hikers, and adventure racers. Winter Olympic alpine gold medalist Kerrin Lee-Gartner settled here in 1999 to construct **SNOW CREEK LODGE** (5258 Highline Dr; 250/423-7669 or 888/558-6878; www.fernieproperties.com). Her medals and memorabilia are displayed in the lodge's lobby. Visitors are as likely to cross paths with the downhiller and her young family at **OUR CAPPUCCINO CORNER** (501 2nd Ave) as they are on the slopes. A good source for outdoor equipment is the **GUIDES HUT** (671 2nd Ave; 250/423-3650). Contact the **FERNIE INFO CENTRE** (102 Commerce Rd; 250/423-6868; www.ferniechamber.com) for details or consult www.fernie.com.

LODGINGS

Griz Inn Sport Hotel / ★

5369 SKI AREA RD, FERNIE; 250/423-9221 OR 800/661-0118
When the Griz Inn opened in 1983, it signaled the beginning of a new era in tourism at Fernie Alpine Resort, which was primarily the preserve of locals. A sweeping list of new lodges and condos has joined in, but none supplants the Griz's prime location. Guests enjoy second-to-none views of the mountains and trails from private balconies. The largest suites sleep 16. The inn's Powderhorn Restaurant is a good bet. *$$; AE, MC, V; checks OK; closed briefly in late spring, early fall; www.grizzinn.com; off Hwy 3 west of Fernie.* &

Fairmont Hot Springs

Fairmont Hot Springs Resort, on Highway 93/95 north of Kimberley, has accommodated both soakers and skiers since the 1920s, with the biggest outdoor thermal pool and the only private (guests only) ski resort in western Canada. Don't miss the view from the switchback road above the resort: from the Columbia Valley to the Selkirk and Bugaboo mountains, including the headwaters of the Columbia River. Viewpoints in the East Kootenay don't come any better than this.

LODGINGS

Fairmont Hot Springs Resort / ★★★

FAIRMONT HOT SPRINGS; 250/345-6311 OR 800/663-4979
Fairmont Hot Springs Resort has odorless and sulfur-free thermal springs, a contrast to most. Many of its 140 units come with kitchens, and rooms have private balconies. The Olympic-sized hot-springs pool lies below, and lodge guests have their own pool. Rooms 492, 494, and 496 are the most private on the ground floor. The resort has a full-service dining room, coffee shop, and lounge. *$$$; AE, DC, DIS, MC, V; no checks; www.fairmonthotsprings.com; turn east off Hwy 93/95.* &

Invermere and Panorama Mountain Village

Set 2 miles (3 km) west of Highway 93/95 on Windermere Lake, Invermere (population 2,860) is the commercial hub, with a folksy main street, for the nearby towns of Radium Hot Springs and Fairmont Hot Springs. In summer, the beach at **JAMES CHABOT BEACH PARK** is the perfect place to swim and picnic, particularly if you've stopped at the **QUALITY BAKERY** (1305 7th Ave, Invermere; 250/342-9913). Look for an enormous pretzel poised above its roof. Espresso coffee and Swiss pastries are the feature attractions. For information, contact the **COLUMBIA VALLEY VISITOR INFO CENTRE** (Hwy 93/95, Invermere; 250/342-2844; www.adventurevalley.com).

PANORAMA MOUNTAIN VILLAGE (250/342-6941 or 800/663-2929; www.panoramaresort.com) lies at the end of a winding road 12 miles (20 km) west of Invermere. Self-contained at its remote location in the Purcell Mountains, Panorama is a destination resort with dining, shopping, and outdoor hot tubs, plus several other unique attractions, including a wolf sanctuary and a three-car gondola that ferries guests up and down the village. The ski area itself is a massive layout with a 4,000-foot vertical, deep powder snow, and several large bowls that serve both intermediate and expert skiers. Cross-country skiers are catered to at the village's **BECKIE SCOTT NORDIC CENTRE** (250/341-4100), named for the Olympic gold medal winner. In summer, the action switches to golf at the Greywolf Golf Course, tennis, horseback riding, hiking, fishing, and river rafting on Toby Creek.

Radium Hot Springs

Near the town of the same name, **RADIUM HOT SPRINGS** (Hwy 93, 2 miles/3 km from junction of Hwy 95; 250/347-9485; www.rhs.bc.ca) makes an ideal soaking stop at the base of the Kootenay Range. The hot springs, open to the public year-round and wheelchair accessible, are equipped with two pools: one heated, the other cooler for swimming.

Trans-Canada Highway and the National Parks, Field

You can't go much farther east than Field, the modest commercial hub, as it were, of Yoho National Park, and still be in British Columbia. With adjacent **BANFF, JASPER,** and **KOOTENAY NATIONAL PARKS,** Yoho is part of a vast Rocky Mountain wilderness designated by UNESCO as a World Heritage Site. The Trans-Canada Highway (Highway 1) parallels the Kicking Horse River from its headwaters as it winds down from the mountains through a valley. By the time it reaches the park's headquarters in Field, 18 miles (30 km) from its west gate, the tone of the landscape shifts to glaciated peaks. Extensive hiking is found along 190 miles (300 km) of trails in Yoho, a park characterized by rock walls and waterfalls. A highlight is the strenuous hike to the **BURGESS SHALE**, a world-famous site where mid-20th-century researchers unraveled the mysteries of a major stage of evolution. Access is permitted only with a registered guide from the **YOHO-BURGESS SHALE FOUNDATION** (800/343-3006; www.burgess-shale.bc.ca).

Contact the **FIELD VISITOR CENTRE** (250/343-6783; www.parkscanada.gc.ca/yoho). **NOTE:** A pass, available at the visitor center, is required for all visitors stopping in national parks. Permits are good in national parks throughout Canada.

LODGINGS

Emerald Lake Lodge / ★★★

YOHO NATIONAL PARK; 250/343-6321 OR 800/663-6336
When Emerald Lake Lodge opened in 1902, it was one of the Canadian Pacific Railway's crown jewels. After falling on hard times, the lodge was restored to elegance in 1986. Set on a 13-acre peninsula that overlooks the lake, the lodge has 85 spacious guest rooms spread among 24 chalet-style buildings. (Unfortunately, some cabins are less than soundproof.) Rooms feature twig furniture arranged around fireplaces. Private decks open onto the lake and Presidential Range peaks. In summer, stop for afternoon tea on the main lodge's veranda or enjoy casual fare at Cilantro, an airy bistro. *$$$$; AE, DC, MC, V; no checks; www.crmr.com; 6 miles (10 km) south of Hwy 1.* &

Golden and Kicking Horse Mountain Resort

Much like its neighbor, Revelstoke, on the west side of Rogers Pass, downtown Golden (population 4,020) lies hidden from those passing through on the Trans-Canada Highway. Not so for those exploring the Columbia Valley on Highway 95, which leads through Golden, at the confluence of the Columbia and Kicking Horse rivers. First came the railway, then logging. Now outdoor adventure draws people to Golden. Contact the **GOLDEN CHAMBER OF COMMERCE** (500 10th Ave N; 250/344-7125 or 800/622-4653; www.goldenchamber.bc.ca) for details.

KICKING HORSE MOUNTAIN RESORT (866/754-5425; www.kickinghorse resort.com), formerly called Whitetooth Ski Area, lies 7 miles (12 km) west of Golden. The resort's Golden Eagle Express gondola deposits you at 7,710 feet (2,350 m) elevation. The superb **EAGLE'S EYE RESTAURANT** demands a visit whether you intend to ski down or not, and the mountaintop lodge offers an accommodation unique in British Columbia: a deluxe suite in which guests can dine, stay overnight, and be absolutely guaranteed first tracks down in the morning.

LODGINGS

Hillside Lodge & Chalets / ★★

1740 SEWARD FRONTAGE RD, GOLDEN; 250/344-7281
A century ago, the Canadian Pacific Railway constructed several alpine-style chalets in Golden to house Swiss mountain guides. More recently, Hubert and Sonja Baier built similar cabins for guests in search of a tranquil retreat. Five

cabins and a main lodge are beside a river. Each is furnished with a fireplace and Bavarian furniture. Guests share the 60-acre property with wildlife and the Baiers' llamas. *$$; MC, V; no checks; www.hillsidechalets.com; 8 miles (13 km) west of Golden.*

Revelstoke

Revelstoke (population 7,500), nestled beside **MOUNT REVELSTOKE NATIONAL PARK** (250/837-7500; www.parkscanada.gc.ca/revelstoke), is a railway town beside the Columbia River, just the right size for a stroll; pick up a heritage tour brochure from the **REVELSTOKE VISITOR INFO CENTRE** (204 Campbell Ave; 250/837-5345 or 800/487-1493; www.revelstokecc.bc.ca). Steep-pitched metal roofs confirm the area's heavy snowfall, as does the **CANADIAN AVALANCHE CENTRE** (300 1st St W; 250/837-2435 or 800/667-1105; www.avalanche.ca) downtown. The 15-mile (25-km) **MEADOWS IN THE SKY PARKWAY** (open summer only) reaches the highest elevation of any public road in Canada, climaxing in a view of surrounding ice fields in Canada's Mount Revelstoke National Park.

RESTAURANTS

The 112 / ★★

112 1ST ST E, REVELSTOKE; 250/837-2107 OR 888/245-5523
Located in downtown Revelstoke's Regent Inn (built in 1931), the 112 is a unanimous favorite among locals. The dining room's cedar-paneled interior and historic ambience are great, but the food is its biggest draw. Chef Peter Mueller specializes in veal. On Sundays, when the 112 is closed, the Regent Inn's pub menu has solid fare with a neighborhood flavor. *$$; AE, MC, V; local checks only; lunch Mon–Fri, dinner Mon–Sat; full bar; reservations recommended; www.regentinn.com; beside Grizzly Plaza.* &

LODGINGS

Mulvehill Creek Wilderness Inn / ★★★

4200 HWY 23 S, REVELSTOKE; 250/837-8649 OR 877/837-8649
Cornelia and René Hueppi, a dynamic Swiss couple, have created a remarkable wilderness retreat south of Revelstoke. The inn, with a small tower room, is nestled in a tranquil, brightly lit clearing and holds eight suites, each with wildlife artwork and painted in soft shades. The Otter's Burrow is the largest, with private deck and Jacuzzi. A yard and garden contain a heated outdoor pool and hot tub. *$$; AE, MC, V; checks OK; www.mulvehillcreek. com; 12 miles (19 km) south of Revelstoke.*

CENTRAL BRITISH COLUMBIA

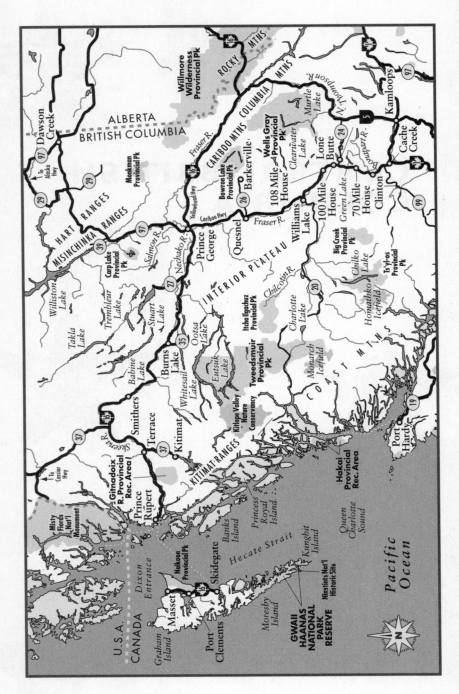

CENTRAL BRITISH COLUMBIA

Most of British Columbia north of the Okanagan is a vast, underpopulated wilderness—the size of California and Oregon combined—that stretches from the rain-forested West Coast to the northeastern Rockies and on into the Peace River country. Most of this territory is traversed by just a few roads. Legendary explorer Alexander Mackenzie walked this way in 1793, becoming the first European to cross North America by land, a decade before the Lewis and Clark expedition duplicated that feat.

At the heart of central British Columbia lies the Cariboo-Chilcotin region, which extends from Clinton to Prince George, a vast plateau bordered by imposing peaks and drained by wild, undammed rivers.

West of Prince George, the Pacific Coast of British Columbia encompasses a huge system of fjords and rivers, as well as Haida Gwaii—the Queen Charlotte Islands. Most of this remote area is visited by boat or air.

ACCESS AND INFORMATION

There are fewer highways in the province's central region than there are in southeastern British Columbia; Highways 5, 37, and 97 run roughly north-south through central and northern British Columbia; **HIGHWAY 16** is the main east-west route, extending from the Rockies at Jasper (and points east) to Prince Rupert on the coast.

HIGHWAY 97 is the main access road to the Cariboo-Chilcotin region from southern British Columbia (the highway is a continuation of US Highway 97 in Washington State's Okanogan). Many towns along Highway 97 between Clinton and Quesnel (pronounced "keh-NEL") are helpfully referred to by their distance from Lillooet (mile 0) north along the Gold Rush Trail, which preceded construction of the Cariboo Highway. Thus 70 Mile House, for example, marks the distance between Lillooet and this point, the original site of a pioneer roadhouse. Note, however, that Lillooet itself lies 45 miles (75 km) west of Highway 97 on Highway 99. (See the Lower Mainland British Columbia chapter.)

From Prince George, a bit north of Quesnel, Highway 97 winds northeast to Dawson Creek—mile 0 on the **ALASKA HIGHWAY**—and northwest to Watson Lake on the British Columbia–Yukon border, via Fort St. John and Fort Nelson, 737 miles (1,228 km) in all. Those venturing into this region should keep in mind that British Columbia is a vast province, and its interior highways are not suited for 70mph barreling-down-the-road travel. Plan itineraries accordingly.

HIGHWAY 5 runs between Highway 97 and the Rockies, connecting Kamloops with Highway 16 at Tete Jaune. **HIGHWAY 37** connects Kitimat and Stewart near the western end of Highway 16, between Prince George and Prince Rupert.

PRINCE GEORGE AIRPORT (4141 Airport Rd; 250/963-2400; www.pg airport.ca) is served by **WESTJET** (800/538-5696; www.westjet.com) and

AIR CANADA JAZZ (250/561-2905 or 888/247-2262; www.flyjazz.ca). Air Canada Jazz also flies from Vancouver to Sandspit on Moresby Island in Haida Gwaii (the Queen Charlotte Islands). **HARBOUR AIR** (800/689-4234; www.harbour-air.com) flies from Prince Rupert to Sandspit, Queen Charlotte City, and Masset in Haida Gwaii–Queen Charlotte Islands. Air Canada Jazz links southern British Columbia with Terrace and Smithers, on Highway 16 near Kitwanga in northwestern British Columbia.

VIA RAIL's *Skeena* (888/842-7245; www.viarail.com) provides east-west passenger rail service from Jasper, Alberta, to Prince George, Smithers, and Prince Rupert. **BC FERRIES** (250-386-3431 or 888-223-3779; www.bcferries.com) sail west from Prince Rupert to Skidegate Landing on Graham Island in Haida Gwaii–Queen Charlotte Islands and south to Port Hardy on Vancouver Island. In summer a popular ferry route takes a day to travel from Bella Coola to Port Hardy. The **ALASKA MARINE HIGHWAY** (800/642-0066; www.dot.state.ak.us/amhs/) links Prince Rupert with Skagway in Alaska to the north and Bellingham, Washington, to the south.

CARIBOO CHILCOTIN COAST TOURISM in Williams Lake (1148 Broadway S; 250/392-2226; www.landwithoutlimits.com) embraces most of central British Columbia. **NORTHERN BC TOURISM**, located in Prince George (1300 1st Ave; 800/663-8843; www.northernbctourism.com/), is a helpful source of information on the province north of the Cariboo-Chilcotin.

The Cariboo-Chilcotin Region

Clinton

Clinton (population 740) anchors mile 47 on the historic Gold Rush Trail. This frontier trading post's history is best seen in the **SOUTH CARIBOO HISTORICAL MUSEUM** (1419 Cariboo Hwy; 250/459-24420; June–Aug) housed in a former schoolhouse. Framed by wrought iron and pine, the **PIONEER MEMORIAL CEMETERY** (east side of Hwy 97) at the north end of town presents an apt gateway to central British Columbia's past. Catch the town's annual **MAY BALL RODEO** (250/459-2261), which kicks off with a dance that is the longest continually held event in British Columbia (more than 130 years). For more information on Clinton, contact the **MAYOR'S OFFICE** (306 Lebourdais Ave; 250/459-2261) or the **CLINTON AND DISTRICT CHAMBER OF COMMERCE** (1522 Cariboo Hwy; 250/459-2224; every day June–Sept).

LODGINGS

Big Bar Guest Ranch / ★

BOX 27, JESMOND; 250/459-2333
Big Bar Guest Ranch is not the oldest, snazziest, biggest, or most authentic guest ranch in the region, but it draws families back year after year to enjoy its splendid and economical combination of scenery and ranch flavor. Big

Bar offers plain but functional rooms in the Sagebrush Lodge, one-bedroom log cabins, the six-bedroom Coyote Lodge (for groups), plus tepees (summer only). *$$$; MC, V; checks OK; www.bigbarranch.com; 25 miles (40 km) west of Hwy 97 on Big Bar Rd.*

Echo Valley Ranch Resort / ★★★★

BOX 16, JESMOND; 250/459-2386 OR 800/253-8831

Echo Valley is one of the pioneers in the upscale guest-ranch industry. Retired tech tycoon Norm Dove and his wife, Nan, have an impressive collection of 21 peeled-spruce-log cabins and lodges, plus a Thai wellness center. Echo Valley offers gourmet meals, sensational scenery, and activities from yoga to field trips over to the legendary Gang Ranch, once the world's biggest. If the five-hour drive from Vancouver is undesirable, Norm will hop into his DeHavilland Beaver to pick you up and fly you back to the Cariboo. *$$$$; MC, V; no checks; www.evranch.com; on Big Bar Rd 30 miles (50 km) west of Hwy 97 at Clinton.* &

Interlakes District

Head east off Highway 97 at either 70 Mile or 93 Mile House, using the Green Lake Road or Hwy 24, and you'll be in the Interlakes District. **GREEN LAKE** is the first of hundreds of lakes, large and larger, strung between Highway 97 and Highway 5, which parallels the North Thompson River. For a quick sample, drive the **GREEN LAKE SCENIC LOOP** north from Green Lake to Lone Butte on Highway 24, which connects Highway 97 and Highway 5. Each lake boasts at least one guest ranch or fishing camp.

LODGINGS

Crystal Waters Guest Ranch / ★★

BOX 100 NORTH BONAPARTE RD, BRIDGE LAKE; 250/593-4252 OR 888/593-2252

At Crystal Waters, rodeo veteran Gary Cleveland and his wife, Marisa Peters, have distilled the appealing essence of a small guest ranch: intimacy and spontaneity. You can explore the 640-acre spread on one of the ranch's horses, then soak in the lakeshore hot tub. Fish for rainbow trout or paddle on Crystal Lake. Of the seven log cabins, the Loon's Nest is our favorite. *$$$$; MC, V; checks OK; closed Nov; www.crystalwatersranch.com; 3 miles (5 km) southwest of Hwy 24 at Bridge Lake.*&

Flying U Guest Ranch / ★

70 MILE HOUSE, HWY 97; 250/456-7717

Founded by rodeo star Jack Boyd in 1924, the Flying U is Canada's oldest guest ranch, its character embodied in the smoky whisky smell that emanates from the lodge's stone fireplace. Flying U has remote quirkiness—there's no

---

NORTHWEST COAST THREE-DAY TOUR

DAY ONE: Start your day in **PRINCE RUPERT** with a coffee and pastry at **COW-PUCCINO**, then a walk through downtown. Begin at the **MUSEUM OF NORTHERN BRITISH COLUMBIA** and a guided walking tour of **TOTEM POLES**. Tour the harbor and nearby Dodge Cove with the **PRINCE RUPERT WATER TAXI**. Have lunch at the **COW BAY CAFÉ** before heading to the **NORTH PACIFIC CANNERY VILLAGE NATIONAL HISTORIC SITE** in nearby Port Edward. After your explorations, check in to **EAGLE BLUFF BED AND BREAKFAST** and relax to the sound of the ocean. Then, off to dinner at nearby **SMILE'S SEAFOOD CAFÉ**.

DAY TWO: After breakfast at Eagle Bluff, head for the BC Ferries terminal for the all-day crossing to **HAIDA GWAII–QUEEN CHARLOTTE ISLANDS**. Grab lunch on the ferry, then when you arrive at **GRAHAM ISLAND**, visit the **HAIDA**

---

sign leading to the ranch gates. This is the only major guest ranch in the Northwest where clients can saddle their own horses, then ride out unescorted into the ranch's 25,000 acres. Vintage western movies, bonfires, hayrides, or square dancing often follow dinner. *$$$$; MC, V; checks OK; closed Nov–Mar; www.flyingu.com; 12 miles (20 km) east of 70 Mile House on N Green Lake Rd.*

100 Mile House

100 Mile House (population 1,740) is home to the annual 50-km "classic technique" **CARIBOO CROSS-COUNTRY SKI MARATHON** in February. Just to show how seriously locals take their sticks, the world's largest pair of skinny skis, accompanied by a 30-foot (9-m) pair of poles, points skyward in front of the **SOUTH CARIBOO VISITOR INFO CENTRE** (422 Cariboo Hwy 97 S, 100 Mile House; 877/511-5353). Arguably the best track-set cross-country skiing in British Columbia is found on the 120 miles (200 km) of trails between here and 108 Mile Ranch. For information, contact **GUNNER'S CYCLE AND X-COUNTRY SKI SHOP** (800/664-5414) in 108 Mile Ranch.

RESTAURANTS

Trails End Restaurant / ★★
1871 Lodge / ★★

HWY 97 (THE HILLS HEALTH AND GUEST RANCH), 108 MILE HOUSE; 250/791-5225 OR 800/668-2233

Trails End Restaurant sits in the main lodge of the Hills Health and Guest Ranch (see review). On weekends, 1871 Lodge is a more casual place to eat. The Trails End menu includes generously portioned Cariboo Country

GWAII MUSEUM before heading to either the COPPER BEECH HOUSE or the ALASKA VIEW LODGE for the night. Have dinner at TLELL RIVER HOUSE (Beitush Rd, Tlell; 250/557-4211), known for local seafood.

DAY THREE: Enjoy breakfast in your lodge with your hosts, then head 16 miles (26 km) north to MASSET to explore Rose Spit in NAIKOON PROVINCIAL PARK. Lunch at MARJ'S CAFÉ (1645 Man St, Masset; 250/626-9344) before following Highway 16 south to Tlell and have a sip from ST. MARY'S WELL, a roadside spring. They say if you taste its water, you'll be back. Return south to QUEEN CHARLOTTE CITY and eat dinner at OCEANIA CHINESE (3119 3rd Ave; 250/559-8683). Afterward, stroll the waterfront before heading to Skidegate Landing to catch the OVERNIGHT FERRY sailing back to the mainland at Prince Rupert.

selections and lighter spa fare. The emphasis is on meat, seafood, and vegetarian dishes, prepared by Anna Tanner, whose inspired touch can also be seen in the 1871 Lodge's dinner menu, which includes all-you-can-eat fondue and hot-rock steaks that diners cook themselves. *$$–$$$; AE, MC, V; checks OK; breakfast, lunch, dinner every day, brunch Sun; full bar; reservations recommended; www.spabc.com; east side of Hwy 97 just north of main intersection.* &

LODGINGS

The Hills Health and Guest Ranch / ★★★

HWY 97, 108 MILE HOUSE; 250/791-5225 OR 800/668-2233
Bankers refused to lend money to Pat and Juanita Corbett in 1983 when the couple pioneered a health-spa guest ranch. The Corbetts wanted to epitomize the area's essence: free-spirited and health-oriented. Three "International Specialty Spa of the Year" awards later, celebrities and others flock here. *$$$; AE, MC, V; checks OK; www.spabc.com; east side of Hwy 97 just north of main intersection.* &

The Wolf Den Country Inn / ★★

CANIM LAKE RD, FOREST GROVE;
250/397-2108 OR 877/397-2108
This country inn and outdoor adventure center is centered on a rambling log ranch house whose four rooms have floor-to-ceiling windows overlooking Bridge Creek. Evenings call guests to snuggle on the couches beside the fireplace in the private guest living room. Don't miss the outdoor hot tub and gourmet meals. *$–$$; MC, V; checks OK; www.wolfden-adventures.com; 19 miles (30 km) east of Hwy 97 at 100 Mile House.*

Williams Lake

The most exciting time to visit Williams Lake (population 11,150) is on the last weekend in June, when this lumber and cattle town hosts its annual **WILLIAMS LAKE STAMPEDE** (www.williamslakestampede.com)—second only to Calgary's within Canada. For information, contact the **WILLIAMS LAKE VISITOR INFO CENTRE** (1148 Broadway S; 250/392-5025; www.williamslakechamber.com).

Chilcotin Plateau and Bella Coola

From Highway 97 at Williams Lake, Highway 20 leads 274 miles (456 km) west across the Chilcotin Plateau and the Coast Mountains to Bella Coola on British Columbia's central coast. A small section of Highway 20 is unpaved, as are most smaller roads leading south into the heart of the plateau. Highway 20 takes you through a small section of Tweedsmuir Provincial Park, one of the province's oldest and biggest, home of countless bears, wolves, moose, and other wilderness icons.

Elkin Creek Ranch / ★★★★

SOUTH OF HWY 20, NEMAIAH VALLEY;
604/573-5008 OR 877-346-9378
Set in a beautiful, remote valley at the edge of the pristine Chilcotin Plateau, Elkin Creek Ranch is the ideal wilderness guest ranch. The seven elegantly furnished two-bedroom log cabins are in an aspen grove overlooking a pasture leading to the creek; guests dine in the nearby main lodge. The snowclad peaks of the nearby Coast Range overlook all. *$$$$; MC, V; checks OK; closed Nov–Apr; www.elkincreekranch.com; in Nemaiah Valley, 3 hours west of Hwy 97 at Williams Lake.*

Tweedsmuir Lodge / ★★

HWY 20, STUIE; 250/982-2404 OR 877-982-2402
Tucked into the far inland end of the Bella Coola valley, at the foot of Tweedsmuir Provincial Park, this heritage lodge occupies a blissful spot overlooking a broad meadow that leads down to a river. Choose from six chalets and four cabins. Linger on the veranda of the main lodge or your own porch and watch for grizzly bears. *$$; MC, V; no checks; closed Oct–Apr; www.tweedsmuirparklodge.com; 45 minutes from BC Ferries dock in Bella Coola.*

Prince George

Although Prince George, the largest city in the British Columbia interior (population 72,400), sits near the geographical center of the province—the exact center is Vanderhoof, 60 miles (100 km) northwest, on Highway 16—it's still thought of as deep in the northern half of the province. "P.G.," or the "City of Bridges," sits at a crossroads of rivers, railroads, and highways. The mighty Fraser and Nechako rivers blend near old **FORT GEORGE** (south end of 20th Ave), now a park; get information from the **FRASER–FORT GEORGE REGIONAL MUSEUM** (333 Becott Pl; 250/562-1612; www.theexplorationplace.com). Walk or bike the park's riverside pathways. From here, Highway 16 leads east to the Rockies and west to Prince Rupert; Highway 97 leads northeast to Dawson Creek and the Alaska Highway. A pool, an art gallery, and a park are downtown close to the **COAST INN OF THE NORTH** (770 Brunswick St; 250/563-0121 or 800/663-1144; www. coasthotels.com), the best bet if you're overnighting. For information, contact the **PRINCE GEORGE VISITOR INFO CENTRE** (1198 Victoria St; 250/562-3700 or 800/668-7646; www.tourismpg.com).

The Northwest Coast

Prince Rupert

Prince Rupert is home to one of the best displays of **TOTEM POLES** on the West Coast. In summer, the Museum of Northern British Columbia offers guided walking tours, or you can take a self-guided tour beginning at the **PRINCE RUPERT VISITOR INFO CENTRE** (215 Cow Bay Rd; 250/624-5637 or 800/667-1994; www.tourismprincerupert.com).

Just south of town is **PORT EDWARD**, 7 miles (11 km) southwest of Highway 16, where you'll find the **NORTH PACIFIC CANNERY VILLAGE NATIONAL HISTORIC SITE** (1889 Skeena Dr, Port Edward; 250/628-3538; May 15–Sept 15). Until the 1970s, it employed as many as 1,500 workers. Boardwalks link offices, stores, cafés, and homes with the West Coast's oldest standing cannery, perched at the mouth of the Skeena River.

RESTAURANTS

Cow Bay Café / ★★★

205 COW BAY RD, PRINCE RUPERT; 250/627-1212
Adrienne Johnston is reserved when you ask her what brought her from the British West Indies to this dockside site—but she makes the most of the seafood, incorporating the curry flavors of her heritage into the food. The result is the best, and most interesting, restaurant in Northern British Columbia. Where else are you ever going to try short-spined thorny-head? *$$; MC, V; no checks; breakfast, lunch, dinner every day (closed Jan); full bar; reservations recommended; in Cow Bay section of Prince Rupert.*

Smile's Seafood Café / ★

131 COW BAY RD, PRINCE RUPERT; 250/624-3072
The spirit of Prince Rupert's fish-plant heyday lives on at Smile's. Tucked demurely on the waterfront, Smile's offers up platters of typical seafood served in traditional ways. The quintessential dish here is the heaping platter

539

of fish and shellfish. *$$; MC, V; no checks; breakfast, lunch, dinner every day (closed Jan); full bar; no reservations; 2 blocks east of McBride St on 3rd Ave to Cow Bay Rd.*

LODGINGS

Eagle Bluff Bed & Breakfast / ★

201 COW BAY RD, PRINCE RUPERT;
250/627-4955 OR 800/833-1550
The waves of Cow Bay lap beneath Eagle Bluff's pilings on the waterfront, where the owners have restored five rustically elegant rooms in a former marine chandlery. Fireplaces in two of the rooms impart warmth, especially in stormy weather. A two-bedroom suite is ideal for families. *$–$$; MC, V; no checks; www.citytel.net/eaglebluff; on harbor, 1 block west of Hwy 16.* ♿

Haida Gwaii–Queen Charlotte Islands

These islands present one of the most evocative landscapes in the world. Sometimes called Canada's Galapagos, they are home to a distinctive ecosystem and people, the Haida First Nation. Dubbed the Queen Charlotte Islands by an 18th-century British sea captain, this place's older Haida name is Xhaaidlagha Gwaay-aai, or Haida Gwaii, "Islands at the Boundary of the World." The area is known by both names today.

Moresby and Graham are the largest of the 150 islands. Ferry traffic between Prince Rupert and Haida Gwaii docks at the BC Ferries' terminal at Skidegate Landing on **GRAHAM ISLAND**. Though the northeastern tip of Haida Gwaii lies just 60 miles (100 km) west of the British Columbia mainland, the overnight ferry crossing from Prince Rupert takes seven or eight hours. Just north of the ferry terminal is the **HAIDA GWAII MUSEUM** (at Qay'llnagaay, east of Hwy 16 at Second Beach; 250/559-4643), where whale spotting is almost guaranteed. **QUEEN CHARLOTTE CITY** (population 1,045), with a serene waterfront, lies 2½ miles (4 km) west of Skidegate on Highway 16.

For information on all aspects of a visit to the Queen Charlottes, contact the **VISITOR INFORMATION CENTRE** (3220 Wharf St, Queen Charlotte City; 250/559-8316; www.qcinfo.com); the interpretive center, located on Graham Island, is worth a visit. For tourism information, contact the **MASSET INFO CENTRE** (1455 Old Beach Rd, Masset; 888/352-9292; www.massetbc.com/), also on Graham.

Index

Best Places Northwest Report Form

Based on my personal experience, I wish to nominate the following restaurant, place of lodging, shop, nightclub, sight, or other as a "Best Place"; or confirm/correct/disagree with the current review.

_____

_____

_____

_____

(Please include address and telephone number of establishment, if convenient.)

REPORT

Please describe food, service, style, comfort, value, date of visit, and other aspects of your experience; continue on another piece of paper if necessary.

_____

_____

_____

_____

_____

_____

_____

I am not associated, directly or indirectly, with the management or ownership of this establishment.

_____

SIGNED

_____

ADDRESS

_____

_____

_____

PHONE   **DATE**

Please address to _Best Places Northwest_ and send to:
SASQUATCH BOOKS
119 SOUTH MAIN STREET, SUITE 400
SEATTLE, WA 98104
Feel free to email feedback as well: **CUSTSERV@SASQUATCHBOOKS.COM**

TRUST THE LOCALS!

"...travelers swear by the recommendations in the *Best Places*® guidebooks..."
—*Sunset* magazine

Best Places Seattle, 10th Edition
$18.95

Best Places Portland, 6th Edition
$19.95

Best Places Vancouver, 4th Edition
$18.95

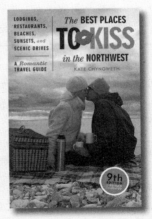

Best Places to Kiss in the Northwest,
9th Edition
$21.00

ALL **BEST PLACES**® GUIDEBOOKS ARE AVAILABLE AT BOOKSTORES EVERYWHERE

SASQUATCH BOOKS
www.sasquatchbooks.com